TAKING SIDES

Clashing Views on Controversial

Political Issues

FOURTEENTH EDITION

ports—websites; Practic

TAKING SIDES

Clashing Views on Controversial

Political Issues

FOURTEENTH EDITION

Selected, Edited, and with Introductions by

George McKenna
City College, City University of New York

and

Stanley Feingold
City College, City University of New York

McGraw-Hill/Dushkin
A Division of The McGraw-Hill Companies

*In memory of Hillman M. Bishop and Samuel
Hendel, masters of an art often neglected
by college teachers: teaching.*

Photo Acknowledgment
Cover image: Duncan Smith/Getty Images

Cover Art Acknowledgment
Charles Vitelli

Library of Congress Cataloging-in-Publication Data
Main entry under title:
Taking sides: clashing views on controversial political issues/selected, edited, and with
introductions by George McKenna and Stanley Feingold.—14th ed.
Includes bibliographical references and index.
1. United States—Politics and government—1945–. I. McKenna, George, *comp.*
II. Feingold, Stanley, *comp.*
320'.973
0-07-296888-5
ISSN: 1080-580X

Printed on Recycled Paper

Preface

Dialogue means two people talking to the same issue. This is not as easy as it sounds. Play back the next debate between the talking heads you see on television. Listen to them try to persuade each other—actually, the TV audience—of the truth of their own views and of the irrationality of their opponents' views.

What is likely to happen? At the outset, they will probably fail to define the issue with enough clarity and objectivity to make it clear exactly what it is that they are disputing. As the philosopher Alasdair MacIntyre has put it, the most passionate pro and con arguments are often "incommensurable"—they sail past each other because the two sides are talking about different things. As arguments proceed, both sides tend to employ vague, emotion-laden terms without spelling out the uses to which the terms are put. When the heat is on, they may resort to shouting epithets at one another, and the hoped-for meeting of minds will give way to the scoring of political points and the reinforcement of existing prejudices. For example, when the discussion of affirmative action comes down to both sides accusing the other of "racism," or when the controversy over abortion degenerates into taunts and name-calling, then no one really listens and learns from the other side.

It is our conviction that people *can* learn from the other side, no matter how sharply opposed it is to their own cherished viewpoint. Sometimes, after listening to others, we change our view entirely. But in most cases, we either incorporate some elements of the opposing view—thus making our own richer—or else learn how to answer the objections to our viewpoint. Either way, we gain from the experience. For these reasons we believe that encouraging dialogue between opposed positions is the most certain way of enhancing public understanding.

The purpose of this 14th edition of *Taking Sides* is to continue to work toward the revival of political dialogue in America. As we have done in the past 12 editions, we examine leading issues in American politics from the perspective of sharply opposed points of view. We have tried to select authors who argue their points vigorously but in such a way as to enhance our understanding of the issue.

We hope that the reader who confronts lively and thoughtful statements on vital issues will be stimulated to ask some of the critical questions about American politics. What are the highest-priority issues with which government must deal today? What positions should be taken on these issues? What should be the attitude of Americans toward their government? Our conviction is that a healthy, stable democracy requires a citizenry that considers these questions and participates, however indirectly, in answering them. The alternative is apathy, passivity, and, sooner or later, the rule of tyrants.

Plan of the book   Each issue has an issue *introduction,* which sets the stage for the debate as it is argued in the YES and NO selections. Each issue concludes with a *postscript* that makes some final observations and points the way to other questions related to the issue. In reading the issue and forming your own opinions you should not feel confined to adopt one or the other of the positions presented. There are positions in between the given views or totally outside them, and the *suggestions for further reading* that appear in each issue postscript should help you find resources to continue your study of the subject. We have also provided relevant Internet site addresses (URLs) on the *On the Internet* page that accompanies each part opener. At the back of the book is a listing of all the *contributors to this volume,* which will give you information on the political scientists and commentators whose views are debated here.

Changes to this edition   Over the past quarter century *Taking Sides* has undergone extensive changes and improvements, and we are particularly proud of this 14th edition. We have tied the record that we set in the last edition of adding seven new issues. This time the new issues are: *"Is There Too Much Democracy in the World?"* (Issue 1), *"Is the Filibuster of Judicial Nominees Justifiable"* (Issue 6), *"Should the President Be Allowed to Detain Citizens Indefinitely During Wartime?"* (Issue 10), *"Is "Middle Eastern" Profiling Ever Justified?"*(Issue 11), *"Should There Be a Constitutional Amendment Banning Gay Marriage?"* (Issue 13), *"Does the Patriot Act Abridge Essential Freedoms?"* (Issue 17), and *"Was the Invasion of Iraq Justified?"* (Issue 20). In addition, we have changed both of the selections in *"Must America Exercise World Leadership?"* (Issue 21) and *"Do the Media Have a Liberal Bias?"* (Issue 4) and one of the selections in each of these two issues: *"Are Tax Cuts Good for America?"* (Issue 15) and *"Is America Becoming More Unequal?"* (Issue 16). All told, 20 of the selections in this edition are new—about half the book.

　　We worked hard on what we hope will be a truly memorable 14th edition, and we think you will like the result. Let us know what you think by writing to us care of McGraw-Hill/Dushkin, 2460 Kerper Blrd., Dubuque, IA 52001 or e-mailing us at GMcK1320@aol.com or Stanleyfeingold@mindspring.com. Suggestions for further improvements are most welcome!

A word to the instructor   An *Instructor's Manual With Test Questions* (multiple-choice and essay) is available through the publisher for the instructor using *Taking Sides* in the classroom. A general guidebook, *Using Taking Sides in the Classroom,* which discusses methods and techniques for integrating the pro-con approach into any classroom setting, is also available. An online version of *Using Taking Sides in the Classroom* and a correspondence service for *Taking Sides* adopters can be found at http://www.dushkin.com/usingts/.

　　Taking Sides: Clashing Views on Controversial Political Issues is only one title in the Taking Sides series. If you are interested in seeing the table of contents for any of the other titles, please visit the Taking Sides Web site at http://www.dushkin.com/takingsides/.

Acknowledgments We are grateful to Laura McKenna for her help and suggestions in preparing this edition. Thanks also to the reference departments of City College's Morris Raphael Cohen Library and the public library of Tenafly, New Jersey—especially to Agnes Kolben.

We also appreciate the spontaneous letters from instructors and students who wrote to us with comments and observations. Many thanks to Larry Loeppke and Jill Peter for their able editorial assistance. Needless to say, the responsibility for any errors of fact or judgment rests with us.

George McKenna

Stanley Feingold

Contents In Brief

Contents

Former CBS reporter Bernard Goldberg argues that liberal bias is pervasive in news reporting, the result not from a conspiracy but of a mind-set among media elites acquired from the homogeneous social circles in which they live and work. Journalist Eric Alterman criticizes Goldberg's methodology and argues that there is a conservative bias in the media, citing as evidence the media's extensive corporate ties and what he regards as their favorable coverage of President Bush's presidency.

PART 2 THE INSTITUTIONS OF GOVERNMENT 105

Supreme Court chief justice William H. Rehnquist argues that Congress cannot regulate activities within a state that are not economic and do not substantially affect commerce among the states. Supreme Court justice Stephen G. Breyer upholds the right of Congress to regulate activities within a state if Congress has a rational basis for believing that it affects the exercise of congressional power.

Marcia Greenberger, co-president of the National Women's Law Center, contends the filibuster of judicial nominees serves the nation well by forcing the president to submit moderate, consensus nominees to the bench. Law professor John C. Eastman argues that the "dilatory" use of the filibuster flouts the will of the Senate, intrudes upon the president's power to nominate judges, and ultimately threatens the independence of the judiciary.

PART 3 SOCIAL CHANGE AND PUBLIC POLICY 139

Essayist Robert W. Lee argues that capital punishment is the only fair
way for society to respond to certain heinous crimes. Law professor Eric
M. Freedman contends that the death penalty does not reduce crime but
does reduce public safety and carries the risk of innocent people being
executed.

Issue 8.   Do We Need Tougher Gun Control Laws?   158

Writer Carl T. Bogus argues that even local gun control laws will reduce
the number of gun-related crimes. Social analyst John R. Lott, Jr.,
argues that giving law-abiding citizens the right to carry concealed
handguns deters street crime.

Issue 9.   Does Affirmative Action Advance Racial Equality?   180

Mary Frances Berry, chair of the U.S. Civil Rights Commission, contends
that affirmative action is needed because minorities have suffered so
much negative action throughout American history. Columnist Linda
Chavez argues that racial preferences create a surface appearance of
progress while destroying the substance of minority achievement.

Issue 10.   Should the President Be Allowed to Detain Citizens Indefinitely in Wartime?   198

Former federal prosecutor Andrew C. McCarthy believes citizens who are
terrorists should not enjoy the constitutional rights of common criminal
defendants, and they may be detained for the duration of hostilities.
Investigative reporter Lewis Z. Koch states that no American citizen has
ever been or ever should be indefinitely detained and deprived of the
right to counsel and trial on the assertion of the Attorney General.

Issue 11.   Is "Middle Eastern" Profiling Ever Justified?   214

Daniel Pipes, director of the Middle East Forum, argues that "heightened scrutiny" of Muslims and Middle Eastern–looking people is justified because, while not all Muslims are Islamic extremists, all Islamic extremists are Muslims. Law professor David A. Harris opposes profiling people of Middle Eastern appearance because, like racial profiling, it compromises civil liberties and actually damages our intelligence efforts.

Issue 12.   Should Hate Speech Be Punished?   230

Law professor Charles R. Lawrence III asserts that speech should be impermissible when, going beyond insult, it inflicts injury on its victims. Author Jonathan Rauch maintains that there can be no genuine freedom of expression unless it includes the freedom to offend those who oppose the expressed opinion.

Issue 13.   Should There Be a Constitutional Amendment Banning Gay Marriage?   246

Louisiana State University law professor Katherine Shaw Spaht argues that if a constitutional amendment banning same-sex marriage is not passed, the courts will take the issue away from the American people and abolish traditional marriage. University of Chicago law professor Cass Sunstein, recalling that amendments have almost always been reserved to ones expanding individual rights and correcting structural problems of the government, and observing the marriage amendment fit neither category, concludes that such an amendment is neither desirable nor necessary.

Issue 14.   Should Abortion Be Restricted?   262

Legal philosopher Robert P. George asserts that, since each of us was a human being from conception, abortion is a form of homicide and should be banned. Writer Mary Gordon maintains that having an abortion is a moral choice that women are capable of making for themselves, that aborting a fetus is not killing a person, and that antiabortionists fail to understand female sexuality.

to protect the United States against terrorists, contends that immigration gives America an economic edge, does not drain government finances, and is not remarkably high compared with past eras.

Introduction
Labels and Alignments in American Politics

George McKenna and Stanley Feingold

Like a giant tidal wave crashing ashore, the September 11, 2001, attacks on the United States seemed to wash away some of America's most recognizable political landmarks. Suddenly, America's competing political parties, interest groups, and ideologies—whose outlines had been prominent in congressional debates, political campaigns, and media talk shows—seemed irrelevant. In the face of these murderous attacks, who cared about petty political differences? In the most remarkable display of national unity since Pearl Harbor, Congress, with only one dissent, voted to authorize President George W. Bush to use "all necessary and appropriate force" against those he considered responsible for the attacks and even those nations harboring them. On September 20 some of Bush's harshest congressional critics were on their feet cheering his dramatic speech before a special joint session of Congress. As the Republican president left the chamber, he approached the Democratic Senate majority leader, Tom Daschle, and in a moment the two were locked in a fervent embrace. The act symbolized the embrace of all Americans at that moment. Democrats, Republicans, liberals, conservatives, moderates, radicals—none of these labels seemed to matter anymore: all Americans were in the trenches together.

But even the mightiest tidal wave must recede at some point. When it does, some of the features of the old landscape may start to reappear. Something like this happened in the American political landscape between the fall of 2001 and November 2004. It happened gradually, almost imperceptively, at first, but it rapidly accelerated as the 2004 presidential election year advanced. Some Democrats who had assured the president that he could count on their total support in the war on terror now began to wonder aloud whether some of the legal tools that they had given him to fight it, such as the Patriot Act, might not be going too far, endangering vital liberties. Then, in March 2003, when the war on terror began also to include the war in Iraq, many Democrats asked whether the President might not have jumped into this new theater of combat prematurely. The controversy subsided temporarily after coalition forces quickly subdued the enemy and rolled into the Iraqi capital of Baghdad, but flared up again the following year when unexpectedly stiff resistance began to emerge, especially in the so-called Sunni Triangle in central Iraq. By the summer of 2004, America was back on dry ground again: Democrats and Republicans were fighting it out even more bitterly than they did before 9/11, with leading Democrats charging that the Iraq war had been cooked up by "neoconservative" White House advisors even before Bush came into office, and Republicans charging that the voting record of the Democratic nominee, Senator John Kerry, showed his indifference to the nation's defense and his excessive liberalism in social-economic matters. Soon, everything got thrown into the mix. Democrats and Republicans squared off on issues as varied as the environment, race relations, gay marriage, homeland security, judicial appointments, capital punishment, and America's leadership in the world.

Some deplore this reemergence of "partisan wrangling." We regard it as the inevitable expression of political differences. Americans vote for different political parties because, however loosely, American parties help to give expression to competing ideologies embraced by Americans. In this introduction we shall attempt to explore these ideologies, put some labels on them—labels such as *liberal, conservative, moderate, extremist,* and *pluralist*—and see how they fit the issue positions presented in this book. We have sought to do our labeling gently and tentatively, not only because Americans generally shy away from political labels but also because, as we shall see, the meanings of some of these terms appear to have shifted over the past two and a half centuries.

Liberals Versus Conservatives: An Overview

Let us examine, very briefly, the historical evolution of the terms *liberalism* and *conservatism.* By examining the roots of these terms, we can see how these philosophies have adapted themselves to changing times. In that way, we can avoid using the terms rigidly, without reference to the particular contexts in which liberalism and conservatism have operated over the past two centuries.

Classical Liberalism

The classical root of the term *liberalism* is the Latin word *libertas,* meaning "liberty" or "freedom." In the early nineteenth century, liberals dedicated themselves to freeing individuals from all unnecessary and oppressive obligations to authority—whether the authority came from the church or the state. They opposed the licensing and censorship of the press, the punishment of heresy, the establishment of religion, and any attempt to dictate orthodoxy in matters of opinion. In economics, liberals opposed state monopolies and other constraints upon competition between private businesses. At this point in its development, liberalism defined freedom primarily in terms of freedom *from.* It appropriated the French term *laissez-faire,* which literally means "leave to be." Leave people alone! That was the spirit of liberalism in its early days. It wanted government to stay out of people's lives and to play a modest role in general. Thomas Jefferson summed up this concept when he said, "I am no friend of energetic government. It is always oppressive."

Despite their suspicion of government, classical liberals invested high hopes in the political process. By and large, they were great believers in democracy. They believed in widening suffrage to include every white male, and some of them were prepared to enfranchise women and blacks as well. Although liberals occasionally worried about "the tyranny of the majority," they were more prepared to trust the masses than to trust a permanent, entrenched elite. Liberal social policy was dedicated to fulfilling human potential and was based on the assumption that this often-hidden potential is enormous. Human beings, liberals argued, were basically good and reasonable. Evil and irrationality were believed to be caused by "outside" influences; they were the result of a bad social environment. A liberal commonwealth, therefore, was one that would remove the hindrances to the full flowering of the human personality.

The basic vision of liberalism has not changed since the nineteenth century. What has changed is the way it is applied to modern society. In that respect, liberalism has changed dramatically. Today, instead of regarding government with suspicion, liberals welcome government as an instrument to serve the people. The change in philosophy began in the latter years of the nineteenth century, when businesses—once small, independent operations—began to grow into giant structures that overwhelmed individuals and sometimes even overshadowed the state in power and wealth. At that time, liberals began reconsidering their commitment to the *laissez-faire* philosophy. If the state can be an oppressor, asked liberals, can't big business also oppress people? By then, many were convinced that commercial and industrial monopolies were crushing the souls and bodies of the working classes. The state, formerly the villain, now was viewed by liberals as a potential savior. The concept of freedom was transformed into something more than a negative freedom *from;* the term began to take on a positive meaning. It meant "realizing one's full potential." Toward this end, liberals believed, the state could prove to be a valuable instrument. It could educate children, protect the health and safety of workers, help people through hard times, promote a healthy economy, and—when necessary—force business to act more humanely and responsibly. Thus was born the movement that culminated in New Deal liberalism.

New Deal Liberalism

In the United States, the argument in favor of state intervention did not win an enduring majority constituency until after the Great Depression of the 1930s began to be felt deeply. The disastrous effects of a depression that left a quarter of the workforce unemployed opened the way to a new administration—and a promise. "I pledge you, I pledge myself," Franklin D. Roosevelt said when accepting the Democratic nomination in 1932, "to a new deal for the American people." Roosevelt's New Deal was an attempt to effect relief and recovery from the Depression; it employed a variety of means, including welfare programs, public works, and business regulation—most of which involved government intervention in the economy. The New Deal liberalism relied on government to liberate people from poverty, oppression, and economic exploitation. At the same time, the New Dealers claimed to be as zealous as the classical liberals in defending political and civil liberties.

The common element in *laissez-faire* liberalism and welfare-state liberalism is their dedication to the goal of realizing the full potential of each individual. Some still questioned whether this is best done by minimizing state involvement or whether it sometimes requires an activist state. The New Dealers took the latter view, though they prided themselves on begin pragmatic and experimental about their activism. During the heyday of the New Deal, a wide variety of programs were tried and—if found wanting—abandoned. All decent means should be tried, they believed, even if it meant dilution of ideological purity. The Roosevelt administration, for example, denounced bankers and businessmen in campaign rhetoric but worked very closely with them while trying to extricate the nation from the Depression. This set a pattern of pragmatism that New Dealers from Harry Truman to Lyndon Johnson emulated.

Progressive Liberalism

Progressive liberalism emerged in the late 1960s and early 1970s as a more militant and uncompromising movement than the New Deal had ever been. Its roots go back to the New Left student movement of the early 1960s. New Left students went to the South to participate in civil rights demonstrations, and many of them were bloodied in confrontations with southern police; by the mid-1960s they were confronting the authorities in the North over issues like poverty and the Vietnam War. By the end of the decade, the New Left had fragmented into a variety of factions and had lost much of its vitality, but a somewhat more respectable version of it appeared as the New Politics movement. Many New Politics crusaders were former New Leftists who had traded their jeans for coats and ties; they tried to work within the system instead of always confronting it. Even so, they retained some of the spirit of the New Left. The civil rights slogan "Freedom Now" expressed the mood of the New Politics. The young university graduates who filled its ranks had come from an environment where "nonnegotiable" demands were issued to college deans by leaders of sit-in protests. There was more than youthful arrogance in the New Politics movement, however; there was a pervasive belief that America had lost, had compromised away, much of its idealism. The New Politics liberals sought to recover some of that spirit by linking up with an older tradition of militant reform, which went back to the time of the Revolution. These new liberals saw themselves as the authentic heirs of Thomas Paine and Henry David Thoreau, of the abolitionists, the radical populists, the suffragettes, and the great progressive reformers of the early twentieth century.

While New Deal liberals concentrated almost exclusively on bread-and-butter issues such as unemployment and poverty, the New Politics liberals introduced what came to be known as social issues into the political arena. These included: the repeal of laws against abortion, the liberalization of laws against homosexuality and pornography, the establishment of affirmative action programs to ensure increased hiring of minorities and women, and the passage of the Equal Rights Amendment. In foreign policy, too, New Politics liberals departed from the New Deal agenda.

Because they had keener memories of the unpopular and (for them) unjustified war in Vietnam than of World War II, they became doves, in contrast to the general hawkishness of the New Dealers. They were skeptical of any claim that the United States must be the leader of the free world or, indeed, that it had any special mission in the world; some were convinced that America was already in decline and must learn to adjust accordingly. The real danger, they argued, came not from the Soviet Union but from the mad pace of America's arms race with the Soviets, which, as they saw it, could bankrupt the country, starve its social programs, and culminate in a nuclear Armageddon.

New Politics liberals were heavily represented at the 1972 Democratic national convention, which nominated South Dakota senator George McGovern for president. By the 1980s the New Politics movement was no longer new, and many of its adherents preferred to be called progressives. By this time their critics had another name for them: radicals. The critics saw their positions as inimical to the interests of the United States, destructive of the family, and fundamentally at odds with the views of most Americans. The adversaries of the progressives were not only conservatives but many New Deal liberals, who openly scorned the McGovernites.

This split still exists within the Democratic party, though it is now more skillfully managed by party leaders. In 1988 the Democrats paired Michael Dukakis, whose Massachusetts supporters were generally on the progressive side of the party, with New Dealer Lloyd Bentsen as the presidential and vice-presidential candidates, respectively. In 1992 the Democrats won the presidency with Arkansas governor Bill Clinton, whose record as governor seemed to put him in the moderate-to-conservative camp, and Tennessee senator Albert Gore, whose position on environmental issues could probably be considered quite liberal but whose general image was middle-of-the-road. Both candidates had moved toward liberal positions on the issues of gay rights and abortion. By 1994 Clinton was perceived by many Americans as being "too liberal," which some speculate may have been a factor in the defeat of Democrats in the congressional elections that year. Clinton immediately sought to shake off that perception, positioning himself as a "moderate" between extremes and casting the Republicans as an "extremist" party. (These two terms will be examined presently.)

Conservatism

Like liberalism, conservatism has undergone historical transformation in America. Just as early liberals (represented by Thomas Jefferson) espoused less government, early conservatives (whose earliest leaders were Alexander Hamilton and John Adams) urged government support of economic enterprise and government intervention on behalf of certain groups. But today, in reaction to the growth of the welfare state, conservatives argue strongly that more government means more unjustified interference in citizens' lives, more bureaucratic regulation of private conduct, more inhibiting control of economic enterprise, more material advantage for the less energetic and less able at the expense of those who are prepared to work harder and better, and, of course, more taxes—taxes that will be taken from those who have earned money and given to those who have not.

Contemporary conservatives are not always opposed to state intervention. They may support larger military expenditures in order to protect society against foreign enemies. They may also allow for some intrusion into private life in order to protect society against internal subversion and would pursue criminal prosecution zealously in order to protect society against domestic violence. The fact is that few conservatives, and perhaps fewer liberals, are absolute with respect to their views about the power of the state. Both are quite prepared to use the state in order to further *their* purposes. It is true that activist presidents such as Franklin Roosevelt and John Kennedy were likely to be classified as liberals. However, Richard Nixon was also an activist, and, although he does not easily fit any classification, he was far closer to conservatism than to liberalism. It is too easy to identify liberalism with statism and conservatism with antistatism: it is important to remember that it was liberal Jefferson who counseled against "energetic government" and conservative Alexander Hamilton who designed bold powers for the new central government and wrote, "Energy in the executive is a leading character in the definition of good government."

For a time, a movement calling itself *neoconservatism* occupied a kind of intermediate position between New Deal liberalism and conservatism. Composed for the most part of former New Deal Democrats and drawn largely from academic and publishing circles, neoconservatives supported most of the New Deal programs of federal assistance and regulation, but they felt that state intervention had gotten out of hand during the 1960s. In foreign policy, too, they worried about the directions in which the United States was going. In sharp disagreement with progressive liberals, they wanted a tougher stance toward the Soviet Union, fearing that the quest for detente was leading the nation to unilateral disarmament. After the disappearance of the Soviet Union, neoconcervatism itself disappeared—at least as a distinctive strain of conservatism—and most former neoconservatives either resisted all labels or considered themselves simply to be conservatives.

The Religious Right

A more enduring category within the conservative movement is what is often referred to as "the religious right." Termed "the new right" when it first appeared more than 20 years, ago, the religious right is composed of conservative Christians who are concerned not so much about high taxes and government spending as they are about the decline of traditional Judeo-Christian morality, a decline that they attribute in part to certain unwise government policies and judicial decisions. They oppose many of the recent judicial decisions on sociocultural issues such as abortion, school prayer, pornography, and gay rights, and they have been outspoken critics of the Clinton administration, citing everything from President Clinton's views on gays in the military to his sexual behavior while in the White House.

Spokesmen for progressive liberalism and the religious right stand as polar opposites: The former regard abortion as a woman's right; the latter see it as legalized murder. The former tend to regard homosexuality as a lifestyle that needs protection against discrimination; the latter are more likely to see it as a perversion. The former have made an issue of their support for the Equal Rights Amendment; the latter includes large numbers of women who fought against the amendment because they believed it threatened their role identity. The list of issues could go on. The religious right and the progressive liberals are like positive and negative photographs of America's moral landscape. Sociologist James Davison Hunter uses the term *culture wars* to characterize the struggles between these contrary visions of America. For all the differences between progressive liberalism and the religious right, however, their styles are very similar. They are heavily laced with moralistic prose; they tend to equate compromise with selling out; and they claim to represent the best, most authentic traditions of America. This is not to denigrate either movement, for the kinds of issues they address are indeed moral issues, which do not generally admit much compromise. These issues cannot simply be finessed or ignored, despite the efforts of conventional politicians to do so. They must be aired and fought over, which is why we include some of them, such as abortion (Issue 15), in this volume.

Neoconservatism

The term "neoconservatism" came into use in the early 1970s as a designation for former New Deal Democrats who had became alarmed by what they saw as the drift of their party's foreign policy toward appeasing Communists. When Senator George McGovern, the party's presidential nominee in 1972, stated that he would "crawl to Hanoi on my knees" to secure peace in Vietnam, he seemed to them to exemplify this new tendency. They were, then, "hawks" in foreign policy, which they insisted was the historic stance of their party; they regarded themselves as the true heirs of liberal presidents such as Truman and Kennedy and liberal Senators such as Henry ("Scoop") Jackson of Washington State. On domestic policy, they were still largely liberal, except for their reactions to three new liberal planks added by the "progressives": gay rights, which neoconservatives tended to regard as a distortion of civil rights; abortion, which to some degree or another went against the grain of their moral sensibilities; and affirmative action, which some compared to the "quota system" once used to keep down the number of Jews admitted to elite universities. In fact, a number of prominent neoconservatives were Jews, including Norman Podhoretz, Midge Decter, Gertrude Himmelfarb, and Irving Kristol (though others, such as Michael Novak and Daniel Patrick Moynihan, were Roman Catholics, and one, Richard John Neuhaus, was a Lutheran pastor who later converted to Catholicism and became a priest). The term "neoconservative" seemed headed for oblivion in the 1980s, when some leading neoconservatives dropped the "neo" part and classified themselves as conservatives, period. By the time the Soviet Union collapsed in 1991, it appeared that the term was no longer needed—the Cold War with "world Communism" was over. But the rise of Islamic terrorism in the 1990s, aimed at the West in general and the United States in particular, brought back alarms analogous to those of the Cold War period, with global terrorism now taking the place of world Communism. So, too, was the concern that liberal foreign policy might not be tough enough for the fight against these new, ruthless enemies of Western democracy. The concern was ratcheted up considerably after the events of 9/11, and now a new generation of neoconservatives was in the spotlight—some of its members literally the children of an earlier "neo" generation. They included Bill Kristol, John Podhoretz, Dauglas Feith, Paul Wolfowitz, Richard Perle, David Brooks, and (though he was old enough to overlap with the previous generation), Bill Bennett.

Radicals, Reactionaries, and Moderates

The label *reactionary* is almost an insult, and the label *radical* is worn with pride by only a few zealots on the banks of the political mainstream. A reactionary is not a conserver but a backward-mover, dedicated to turning the clock back to better times. Most people suspect that reactionaries would restore us to a time that never was, except in political myth. For many, the repeal of industrialism or universal education (or the entire twentieth century itself) is not a practical, let alone desirable, political program.

Radicalism (literally meaning "from the roots" or "going to the foundation") implies a fundamental reconstruction of the social order. Taken in that sense, it is possible to speak of right-wing radicalism as well as left-wing radicalism—radicalism that would restore or inaugurate a new hierarchical society as well as radicalism that calls for nothing less than an egalitarian society. The term is sometimes used in both of these senses, but most often the word *radicalism* is reserved to characterize more liberal change. While the liberal would effect change through conventional democratic processes, the radical is likely to be skeptical about the ability of the established machinery to bring about the needed change and might be prepared to sacrifice "a little" liberty to bring about a great deal more equality.

Moderate is a highly coveted label in America. Its meaning is not precise, but it carries the connotations of sensible, balanced, and practical. A moderate person is not without principles, but he or she does not allow principles to harden into dogma. The opposite of moderate is *extremist,* a label most American political leaders eschew. Yet there have been notable exceptions. When Arizona senator Barry Goldwater, a conservative Republican, was nominated for president in 1964, he declared, "Extremism in defense of liberty is no vice! . . . Moderation in the pursuit of justice is no virtue!" This open embrace of extremism did not help his electoral chances; Goldwater was overwhelmingly defeated. At about the same time, however, another American political leader also embraced a kind of extremism, and with better results. In a famous letter written from a jail cell in Birmingham, Alabama, the Reverend Martin Luther King, Jr., replied to the charge that he was an extremist not by denying it but by distinguishing between different kinds of extremists. The question, he wrote, "is not whether we will be extremist but what kind of extremist will we be. Will we be extremists for hate, or will we be extremists for love?" King aligned himself with the love extremists, in which category he also placed Jesus, St. Paul, and Thomas Jefferson, among others. It was an adroit use of a label that is usually anathema in America.

Pluralism

The principle of pluralism espouses diversity in a society containing many interest groups and in a government containing competing units of power. This implies the widest expression of competing ideas, and in this way, pluralism is in sympathy with an important element of liberalism. However, as James Madison and Alexander Hamilton pointed out when they analyzed the sources of pluralism in their *Federalist* commentaries on the Constitution, this philosophy springs from a profoundly pessimistic view of human nature, and in this respect it more closely resembles conservatism. Madison, possibly the single most influential member of the convention that wrote the Constitution, hoped that in a large and varied nation, no single interest group could control the government. Even if there were a majority interest, it would be unlikely to capture all of the national agencies of government—the House of Representatives, the Senate, the presidency, and the federal judiciary—each of which was chosen in a different way by a different constituency for a different term of office. Moreover, to make certain that no one branch exercised excessive power, each was equipped with "checks and balances" that enabled any agency of national government to curb the powers of the others. The clearest statement of Madison's, and the Constitution's, theory can be found in the 51st paper of the *Federalist:*

> It may be a reflection on human nature that such devices should be necessary to control the abuses of government. But what is government itself, but the greatest of all reflections on human nature? If men were angels, no government would be necessary.

This pluralist position may be analyzed from different perspectives. It is conservative insofar as it rejects simple majority rule; yet it is liberal insofar as it rejects rule by a single elite. It is conservative in its pessimistic appraisal of human nature; yet pluralism's pessimism is also a kind of egalitarianism, holding as it does that no one can be trusted with power and that majority interests no less than minority interests will use power for selfish ends. It is possible to suggest that in America pluralism represents an alternative to both liberalism and conservatism. Pluralism is antimajoritarian and antielitist and combines some elements of both.

Some Applications

Despite our effort to define the principal alignments in American politics, some policy decisions do not fit neatly into these categories. Readers will reach their own conclusions, but we may suggest some alignments to be found here in order to demonstrate the variety of viewpoints.

The conflicts between liberalism and conservatism are expressed in a number of the issues presented in this book. Issue 1 perhaps exemplifies the split between liberal and conservative sensibilities. Fareed Zakaria expresses a view voiced by American conservatives since the time of Alexander Hamilton and John Adams: there is too much democracy in the world; too much here, in America, with our voter initiatives in California and elsewhere, and too much there, in raw third-world countries, where newly minted democracies produce either chaos or majority tyranny (or both). Robert Kagan argues the classic Wilsonian position that democracy is good for us and just as good for the rest of the world. Another classic liberal-conservative split, this one revisits an argument famous during the New Deal era, concerns the reach of federal power. The Tenth Amendment states that all powers not delegated to the federal government nor denied to the states "are reserved to the States respectively, or to the people." Yet the federal government passes laws affecting many entities *within* states, from businesses to educational institutions. How can it do that? One of the main "hooks" for federal power within states is the constitutional clause authorizing Congress to regulate commerce "among the several states." The Supreme Court has interpreted the commerce clause to mean that any entity within a state that substantially "affects" interstate commerce can be regulated by the federal government. But how close should the "effect" be? Conservatives insist that the effects on interstate commerce must be quite direct and tangible, while liberals would give Congress more leeway in regulating "intrastate" activities. This liberal/conservative dichotomy is crisply illustrated in the majority opinion versus one of the dissents in the Supreme Court case of *United States v. Lopez* (1995), both of which we present in Issue 5. The immediate question is whether or not the federal government has the authority to ban handguns from the vicinity of public schools, but the larger issue is whether or not the federal government can regulate activities within a state that do not directly and tangibly affect interstate commerce. Liberals say yes, conservatives say no.

The death penalty is another issue dividing liberals and conservatives. Robert Lee's defense of the death penalty (Issue 7) is a classic conservative argument. Like other conservatives, Lee is skeptical of the possibilities of human perfection, and he therefore regards retribution—giving a murderer what he or she "deserves" instead of attempting some sort of "rehabilitation"—as a legitimate goal of punishment. Issue 16, on whether or not the gap between the rich and the poor is increasing, points up another disagreement between liberals and conservatives. Most liberals would agree with Jeff Madrick that socioeconomic inequality is increasing and that this undermines the basic tenets of American democracy. Christopher DeMuth, representing the conservative view-point, maintains that Americans are becoming more equal and that virtually all people benefit from increased prosperity because it takes place in a free market. Then there is the battle over taxes, the hardiest perennial of all the issues that divide liberals and conservatives. Issue 15 features Amity Shlaes, who advances the conservative argument that "the greedy hand" of government is taking too much from taxpayers, versus Paul Krugman, who reject the idea that the pretax money was "theirs," in any meaningful sense, in the first place.

Filibusters have been used by both liberals and conservatives at various times. Conservative, actually segregationist, Southern Senators used them very successfully from the late 1940s to nearly the mid-1960s to defeat civil rights legislation. Now they are being used, again quite successfully, by liberals to keep conservative judges off federal courts. In Issue 6 we feature a liberal conservative debate on the filibustering of judicial nominees.

In Issue 18, "Should America Restrict Immigration?" Patrick Buchanan worries about the effect of "newcomers" on the U.S. economy and culture, which is not a surprising view for someone who is deeply committed to stability and continuity of culture, as conservatives are Daniel Griswold argues that America thrives on the energies brought to its shores by immigrants.

In foreign and defense policy, since the Vietnam war, liberals are usually chary about the use of American military force, at least without the sanction of some sort of international organization. Neoconservatives, on the other hand, make a point of challenging just this tenet of liberalism. They think that the post-Vietnam reluctance to use force and to exercise hegemony have emboldened the enemies of democracy, such as Al Qaeda, to sow chaos in the developing world and inflict terrible blows on the West. The opposition between liberalism and neoconservatism can be seen in Issue 20, where Robert Kagan and William Kristol debate Michael Ignatieff on the war in Iraq, and Issue 21, where Charles Krauthammer and Niall Ferguson debate one another over the question of whether America should exercise world leadership.

Affirmative action (Issue 9) has become a litmus test of the newer brand of progressive liberalism. The progressives say that it is not enough for the laws of society to be color-blind or gender-blind; they must now reach out to remedy the ills caused by racism and sexism. New Deal liberals, along with conservatives and libertarians, generally oppose affirmative action. One major dispute between liberals and conservatives concerns liberalism itself: whether or not it pervades news coverage in the media. In Issue 4, Bernard Goldberg, a former CBS reporter, takes a position often held by conservatives when he argues that it does. Eric Alterman, a journalist himself, argues that, on the contrary, the major media are dominated by conservative viewpoints.

This book contains a few arguments that are not easy to categorize. The issue on hate speech (Issue 12) is one. Liberals traditionally have opposed any curbs on free speech, but Charles Lawrence, who would certainly not call himself a conservative, contends that curbs on speech that abuses minorities may be necessary. Opposing him is Jonathan Rauch, who takes the traditional liberal view that we must protect the speech even of those whose ideas we hate. Issue 14, on whether or not abortion should be restricted, also eludes easy classification. The pro-choice position, as argued by Mary Gordon, is not a traditional liberal position. Less than a generation ago legalized abortion was opposed by liberals such as Senator Edward Kennedy (D-Massachusetts) and the Reverend Jesse Jackson, and even recently some liberals, such as the late Pennsylvania governor Robert Casey and columnist Nat Hentoff, have opposed it. Nevertheless, most liberals now adopt some version of Gordon's pro-choice views. Opposing Gordon is Robert George, whose argument here might be endorsed by liberals like Hentoff. The debate over whether there should be a constitutional amendment banning gay marriage (Issue 13) is also difficult to fit into a liberal/conservative dichotomy, This may not be apparent at first glance. After all, gay marriage is abhorrent to conservatives, while liberals are likely to include it within the ambit "equal rights." But the picture is more cloudy when it comes to the idea of putting a new amendment into the Constitution. Conservatives by nature resist sudden changes in our structure of government, and constitutional amendment does involve structural change; this one in particular would p1ace an explicit limitation on the judicial systems of all fifty states. It is possible, then, for a conservative to strenuously oppose gay marriage, yet also oppose amending the constitution.

Obviously one's position on the issues in this book will be directed by circumstances. However, we would like to think that the essays in this book are durable enough to last through several seasons of events and controversies. We can be certain that the issues will survive. The search for coherence and consistency in the use of political labels underlines the options open to us and reveals their consequences. The result must be more mature judgments about what is best for America. That, of course, is the ultimate aim of public debate and decision making, and it transcends all labels and categories.

On the Internet . . .

In addition to the Internet sites listed below, type in key words, such as "democracy," "political campaigns," and "media bias," to find other listings.

The Federal Web Locator

Use this handy site as a launching pad for the Web sites of U.S. federal agencies, departments, and organizations. It is well organized and easy to use for informational and research purposes.

http://www.infoctr.edu/fwl/

The Library of Congress

Examine this Web site to learn about the extensive resource tools, library services/resources, exhibitions, and databases available through the Library of Congress in many different subfields of government studies.

http://www.loc.gov

U.S. Founding Documents

Through this Emory University site you can view scanned originals of the Declaration of Independence, the Constitution, and the Bill of Rights. The transcribed texts are also available, as are the *Federalist Papers*.

http://www.law.emory.edu/FEDERAL/

Hoover Institution Public Policy Inquiry: Campaign Finance

Use this Stanford University site to explore the history of campaign finance as well as the current reforms and proposals for future change.

http://www.campaignfinancesite.org

Poynter.org

This research site of the Poynter Institute, a school for journalists, provides extensive links to information and resources about the media, including media ethics and reportage techniques. Many bibliographies and Web sites are included.

http://www.poynter.org/research/index.htm

The Gallup Organization

Open this Gallup Organization page for links to an extensive archive of public-opinion poll results and special reports on a huge variety of topics related to American society, politics, and government.

http://www.gallup.com

PART 1

Democracy and the American Political Process

*D*emocracy *is derived from two Greek words,* demos *and* kratia, *and means "people's rule." The prerequisites for the people's rule include free speech and other liberties, a well-informed citizenry, a free presentation of differing points of view, and an equal counting of votes. Do these conditions exist, or can they be created everywhere? Or are there circumstances under which the goal of democracy is futile? At home, Americans must deal with issues concerning their own democracy. Does the campaign process really clarify issues, or does it confuse them? Are voters informed and inspired to make the most rational choices among candidates? Are Americans hearing all points of view before they vote, or are news and opinion in the mass media slanted in some direction? In this section, we address these and related issues.*

- Is There Too Much Democracy in the World?

- Do Political Campaigns Promote Good Government?

- Is There an Emerging Democratic Majority?

- Do the Media Have a Liberal Bias?

ISSUE 1

Is There Too Much Democracy in the World?

YES: Fareed Zakaria, from *The Future of Freedom* (W. W. Norton & Company, 2003)

NO: Robert Kagan, from "The Ungreat Washed," *The New Republic* (July 7 & 14, 2001)

ISSUE SUMMARY

YES: *Newsweek* writer Fareed Zakaria argues that unrestrained democracy threatens vital liberties and concludes that "what we need in politics today is not more democracy but less."

NO: Robert Kagan, senior associate at the Carnegie Endowment for International Peace, contends that in today's world, democracy is the only practical means of protecting vital liberties.

The Greek philosopher Plato characterized democracy as "an agreeable form of anarchy with plenty of variety and an equality of a peculiar kind for equals and unequals alike." Plato was contemptuous of Greek democracy because it gave equal power to citizens regardless of their intelligence, knowledge, or moral character. Until relatively recent times—in considering the merits of democracy—political thinkers have largely echoed the founder of Western philosophy. Medieval thinkers, though wary of unchecked rule by secular elites, were at least as opposed to direct rule by the people, and even during the Enlightenment Period of the eighteenth century, most major political thinkers were decidedly cool to democracy. In *The Federalist #10*, on the best kind of government for countering the dangers of a majority "faction," James Madison briefly considered what he called "pure democracy"—government by direct vote of the people. Such a governing system, he wrote, would be the worst means of controlling a majority faction because "there is nothing to check the inducements to sacrifice the weaker party or an obnoxious individual."

These concerns were still being voiced in America in the early years of the nineteenth century. But with the broadening of the suffrage, the term "democracy" acquired a more positive connotation, and by the time of Andrew Jackson's election in 1828 it was surrounded with a romantic aura. Still, there were voices of caution. Alexis de Tocqueville, the famous French visitor to America in the 1830s, worried about the dangers of a coming "democratic despotism" that could crush America's vaunted liberties and stifle people's initiative.

By the close of the nineteenth century hardly anyone of importance in America questioned the ideal of democracy. If the predominant sentiment pointed anywhere, it was toward extending and deepening its influence through reforms in voting, bringing elite economic "trusts" to heel, and curtailing the excessive power of the so-called rubber barons who owned large corporations. In 1912 newly elected president Woodrow Wilson, declared his intention "to break up the little coterie that has determined what the government of the nation should do."

President Wilson had been in office for little more than a year when World War I broke out, and during the next three years his attention was diverted from domestic reform to preparing the nation for major war. Even so, the ideal of democracy was not forgotten. In asking Congress to declare war against Germany in 1917, Wilson insisted that his purpose was to fight "for the ultimate peace of the world and for the liberation of its peoples, the German peoples included." Then, memorably, he added: "The world must be made safe for democracy."

Within twenty years, a large portion of the world was under the control of dictators. Nevertheless, the ideal of democracy never lost its attractiveness. During the second half of the century, some actual developments even lent credibility to the claim that democracy was a universal human aspiration. World War II brought democracy to Germany and Japan. The apartheid regime in South Africa was ended peacefully by a multiracial coalition that established a constitutional democracy. The dictatorial empire of the Soviet Union collapsed, bringing varying degrees of democracy to its former satellites, some of its member states, and even to Russia itself.

In this new century, then, there are grounds for hope that Plato was fundamentally wrong to equate democracy with anarchy and stupidity. Yet there are also reminders that democracy is a delicate plant, difficult to root and easily washed away. At this point, attempts to install or encourage democracies in the Middle East, Afghanistan, and Iraq have not been notably successful. Russian democracy, such as it was, seems to be degenerating into illiberal presidential rule. Even American democracy has been severely strained by cultural clashes, bitter partisanship, and disputed elections.

Fareed Zakaria suggests, the problem lies with democracy itself, or at least with unrestrained democracy. Distinguishing between democracy, on the one hand, and "liberalism" (by which he means the protection of rights and liberties) on the other, he argues that the former often destroys the latter. What we need today, he contends, "is not more democracy but less." Robert Kagan, sharply disputes this view, arguing that in today's world, democracy is the only practical means of protecting people's liberty.

Fareed Zakaria  **YES**

The Democratic Age

We live in a democratic age. Over the last century the world has been shaped by one trend above all others—the rise of democracy. In 1900 not a single country had what we would today consider a democracy: a government created by elections in which every adult citizen could vote. Today 119 do, comprising 62 percent of all countries in the world. What was once a peculiar practice of a handful of states around the North Atlantic has become the standard form of government for humankind. Monarchies are antique, fascism and communism utterly discredited. Even Islamic theocracy appeals only to a fanatical few. For the vast majority of the world, democracy is the sole surviving source of political legitimacy. Dictators such as Egypt's Hosni Mubarak and Zimbabwe's Robert Mugabe go to great effort and expense to organize national elections—which, of course, they win handily. When the enemies of democracy mouth its rhetoric and ape its rituals, you know it has won the war.

We live in a democratic age in an even broader sense. From its Greek root, "democracy" means "the rule of the people." And everywhere we are witnessing the shift of power downward. I call this "democratization," even though it goes far beyond politics, because the process is similar: hierarchies are breaking down, closed systems are opening up, and pressures from the masses are now the primary engine of social change. Democracy has gone from being a form of government to a way of life.

Consider the economic realm. What is truly distinctive and new about today's capitalism is not that it is global or information-rich or technologically driven—all that has been true at earlier points in history—but rather that it is *democratic*. Over the last half-century economic growth has enriched hundreds of millions in the industrial world, turning consumption, saving, and investing into a mass phenomenon. This has forced the social structures of societies to adapt. Economic power, which was for centuries held by small groups of businessmen, bankers, and bureaucrats has, as a result, been shifting downward. Today most companies—indeed most countries—woo not the handful that are rich but the many that are middle class. And rightly so, for the assets of the most exclusive investment group are dwarfed by those of a fund of workers' pensions.

From THE FUTURE OF FREEDOM, July 4 & 14, 2001, pp. 13–15, 18–23, 105–106, 109, 114–117, 248–251, 254–256. Copyright © 2001 by W.W. Norton. Reprinted with permission.

Culture has also been democratized. What was once called "high culture" continues to flourish, of course, but as a niche product for the elderly set, no longer at the center of society's cultural life, which is now defined and dominated by popular music, blockbuster movies, and prime-time television. Those three make up the canon of the modern age, the set of cultural references with which everyone in society is familiar. The democratic revolution coursing through society has changed our very definition of culture. The key to the reputation of, say, a singer in an old order would have been *who* liked her. The key to fame today is *how many* like her. And by that yardstick Madonna will always trump Jessye Norman. Quantity has become quality.

What has produced this dramatic shift? As with any large-scale social phenomenon, many forces have helped produce the democratic wave—a technological revolution, growing middle-class wealth, and the collapse of alternative systems and ideologies that organized society. To these grand systemic causes add another: America. The rise and dominance of America—a country whose politics and culture are deeply democratic—has made democratization seem inevitable. Whatever its causes, the democratic wave is having predictable effects in every area. It is breaking down hierarchies, empowering individuals, and transforming societies well beyond their politics. Indeed much of what is distinctive about the world we live in is a consequence of the democratic idea. . . .

In a world that is increasingly democratic, regimes that resist the trend produce dysfunctional societies—as in the Arab world. Their people sense the deprivation of liberty more strongly than ever before because they know the alternatives; they can see them on CNN, BBC, and Al-Jazeera. But yet, newly democratic countries too often become sham democracies, which produces disenchantment, disarray, violence, and new forms of tyranny. Look at Iran and Venezuela. This is not a reason to stop holding elections, of course, but surely it should make us ask, What is at the root of this troubling development? Why do so many developing countries have so much difficulty creating stable, genuinely democratic societies? Were we to embark on the vast challenge of building democracy in Iraq, bow would we make sure that we succeed?

First, let's be clear what we mean by political democracy. From the time of Herodotus it has been defined, first and foremost, as the rule of the people. This definition of democracy as a process of selecting governments is now widely used by scholars. In *The Third Wave*, the eminent political scientist Samuel P. Huntington explains why:

> Elections, open, free and fair, are the essence of democracy, the inescapable sine qua non. Governments produced by elections may be inefficient, corrupt, shortsighted, irresponsible, dominated by special interests, and incapable of adopting policies demanded by the public good. These qualities make such governments undesirable but they do not make them undemocratic. Democracy is one public virtue, not the only one, and the relation of democracy to other public virtues and vices can only be understood if democracy is clearly distinguished from the other characteristics of political systems.

This definition also accords with the commonsense view of the term. If a country holds competitive, multiparty elections, we call it "democratic." When public participation in a country's politics is increased—for example, through the enfranchisement of women—that country is seen as having become more democratic. Of course elections must be open and fair, and this requires some protections for the freedom of speech and assembly. But to go beyond this minimal requirement and label a country democratic only if it guarantees a particular catalog of social, political, economic, and religious rights—which will vary with every observer—makes the word "democracy" meaningless. After all, Sweden has an economic system that many argue curtails individual property rights, France until recently had a state monopoly on television, and Britain has a state religion. But they are all clearly and identifiably democracies. To have "democracy" mean, subjectively, "a good government" makes it analytically useless.

Constitutional liberalism, on the other hand, is not about the procedures for selecting government but, rather, government's goals. It refers to the tradition, deep in Western history, that seeks to protect an individual's autonomy and dignity against coercion, whatever the source—state, church, or society. The term marries two closely connected ideas. It is liberal[1] because it draws on the philosophical strain, beginning with the Greeks and Romans, that emphasizes individual liberty. It is constitutional because it places the rule of law at the center of politics. Constitutional liberalism developed in Western Europe and the United States as a defense of an individual's right to life and property and the freedoms of religion and speech. To secure these rights, it emphasized checks on the power of government, equality under the law, impartial courts and tribunals, and the separation of church and state. In almost all of its variants, constitutional liberalism argues that human beings have certain natural (or "inalienable") rights and that governments must accept a basic law, limiting its own powers, to secure them. Thus in 1215 at Runnymede, England's barons forced the king to limit his own authority. In the American colonies these customs were made explicit, and in 1638 the town of Hartford adopted the first written constitution in modern history. In 1789 the American Constitution created a formal framework for the new nation. In 1975 Western nations set standards of behavior even for nondemocratic regimes. Magna Carta, the Fundamental Orders of Connecticut, the American Constitution, and the Helsinki Final Act are all expressions of constitutional liberalism.

Since 1945 Western governments have, for the most part, embodied both democracy and constitutional liberalism. Thus it is difficult to imagine the two apart, in the form of either illiberal democracy or liberal autocracy. In fact both have existed in the past and persist in the present. Until the twentieth century, most countries in western Europe were liberal autocracies or, at best, semidemocracies. The franchise was tightly restricted, and elected legislatures had limited power. In 1830 Great Britain, one of the most democratic European countries, allowed barely 2 percent of its population to vote for one house of Parliament. Only in the late 1940s did most Western countries become full-fledged democracies, with universal adult suffrage. But one hundred years earlier, by the late 1840s, most of them had adopted important aspects of constitutional liberalism—the rule of law, private property rights, and increasingly, separated powers and free speech and assembly. For much of modern history, what characterized governments in Europe and North America, and differentiated them from those around the world, was not democracy but constitutional liberalism. The "Western model of government" is best symbolized not by the mass plebiscite but the impartial judge.

For decades the tiny island of Hong Kong was a small but revealing illustration that liberty did not depend on democracy. It had one of the highest levels of constitutional liberalism in the world but was in no way a democracy. In fact in the 1990s, as the Chinese takeover of Hong Kong drew near, many Western newspapers and magazines fretted about the dangers of this shift to Hong Kong's democracy. But of course Hong Kong had no democracy to speak of. The threat was to its tradition of liberty and law. We continue to confuse these two concepts. American and Israeli politicians have often chided the Palestinian Authority for its lack of democracy. But in fact Yasser Arafat is the only leader in the entire Arab world who has been chosen through reasonably free elections. The Palestinian Authority's problem lies not in its democracy—which while deeply flawed is at least half-functioning—but in its constitutional liberalism, or lack thereof.

Americans in particular have trouble seeing any tension between democracy and liberty because it is not a dominant theme in our own history—with one huge exception. Slavery and segregation were entrenched in the American South through the democratic system. From the founding of the republic, those who abhorred slavery faced the problem that the majority of southern voters defended it passionately. In the end, slavery died not because it was lost in a vote but because the forces of the North crushed the South. Eventually the Jim Crow system that succeeded slavery in the South was destroyed during the 1950s and 1960s not by democracy but despite it. Although the final act of emancipation, the Civil Rights Act of 1964, was passed by Congress, all previous progress took place through the executive branch's fiat—as with the desegregation of the armed forces—or the Supreme Court's writ—as with school desegregation. In America's greatest tragedy, liberty and democracy were often at odds.

The American Model

During the 1990s, an American scholar traveled to Kazakhstan on a U.S. government-sponsored mission to help the country's new parliament draft its electoral laws. His counterpart, a senior member of the Kazak parliament, brushed aside the many options the American expert was outlining, saying emphatically, "We want our parliament to be just like your Congress." The American was horrified, recalling, "I tried to say something other than the three words that had immediately come screaming into my mind: 'No you don't!'" This view is not unusual. Americans in the democracy business tend to see their own system as an unwieldy contraption that no other country should put up with. In fact, the philosophy behind the U.S. Constitution, a fear of accumulated power, is as relevant today as it was in 1789. Kazakhstan, as it happens, would be particularly well served by a strong parliament—like the American Congress—to check the insatiable appetite of its president.

It is odd that the United States is so often the advocate of unrestrained democracy abroad. What is distinctive about the American system is not how democratic it is but rather how undemocratic it is, placing as it does multiple constraints on electoral majorities. The Bill of Rights, after all, is a list of things that the government may not do, regardless of the wishes of the majority. Of America's three branches of government, the Supreme Court—arguably the paramount branch—is headed by nine unelected men and women with life tenure. The U.S. Senate is the most unrepresentative upper house in the world, with the lone exception of the House of Lords, which is powerless and in any event on the verge of transformation. Each American state sends two senators to Washington, D.C., regardless of its population. Thus California's 30 million people have as many votes in the Senate as Arizona's 3.7 million—hardly one man, one vote.[2] In state and local legislatures all over the United States, what is striking is not the power of the majority party but the protections accorded to the minority party, often to an individual legislator. Private businesses and other nongovernmental groups—what Alexis de Tocqueville called "intermediate associations"—make up yet another crucial stratum within society. This rich fabric of civil society has been instrumental in shaping the character of American democracy.

But it is wearing thin, producing America's own version of illiberal democracy. America's problems are different from—and much smaller than—those that face Third World countries. But they are related. In America, laws and rights are firmly established. The less-formal constraints, however, that are the inner stuffing of liberal democracy are disappearing. Many of these social and political institutions—political parties, professions, clubs, and associations—are undemocratic in their structure. They are all threatened by a democratic ideology that judges the value of every idea and institution by one simple test: Is power as widely dispersed as it can be? Are they, in other words, as democratic as they can be? Thus the U.S. Congress, although by definition democratic, used to function in a hierarchical and closed manner, at some distance from public pressures. Now it is a transparent body, utterly open to its constituents' views and pressures. Congress has become a more responsive, more democratic, and more dysfunctional body. . . .

Tyranny of the Majority

If the first source of abuse in a democratic system comes from elected autocrats, the second comes from the people themselves. James Madison explained in the Federalist Papers that "the danger of oppression" in a democracy came from "the majority of the community." Tocqueville warned of the "tyranny of the majority," writing, "The very essence of democratic government consists in the absolute sovereignty of the majority." This problem, alive and urgent to Madison and Tocqueville, may seem less important in the West today because elaborate protections for individual and minority rights exist here. But in many developing countries, the experience of democracy over the past few decades has been one in which majorities have—often quietly, sometimes noisily—eroded separations of power, undermined human rights, and corrupted long-standing traditions of tolerance and fairness.

Let me illustrate this point with some reflections on India, the country in which I grew up. India has a hallowed place in discussions of democracy. Despite being desperately poor it has had a functioning democracy since 1947. Whenever someone wants to prove that you do not need to develop economically to become democratic they use as their one example—India. Much of this praise is warranted. India is a genuinely free and freewheeling society. But looking under the covers of Indian democracy one sees a more complex and troubling reality. In recent decades, India has become something quite different from the picture in the hearts of its admirers. Not that it is less democratic: in important ways it has become more democratic. But it has become less tolerant, less secular, less law-abiding, less liberal. And these two trends—democratization and illiberalism—are directly related. . . .

Religious intolerance is only the first glimpse of the new face of Indian democracy. Massive corruption and a disregard for the rule of law have transformed Indian politics. Consider Uttar Pradesh (UP), India's largest state, the political base of Nehru and the other titans of the Congress Party. UP is now dominated by the BJP and two lower-caste parties. The political system there can only be described as "bandit democracy." Every year elections are rigged, ballot boxes are stuffed. The winning party packs the bureaucracy—sometimes even the courts—with its cronies and bribes opposition legislators to defect to its ranks. The tragedy for the millions of new lower-caste voters is that their representatives, for whom they dutifully vote en masse, have looted the public coffers and become immensely rich and powerful while mouthing slogans about the oppression of their people. . . .

Ethnic conflict is as old as recorded history, and dictatorships are hardly innocent in fomenting it. But newly democratizing societies display a disturbingly common tendency toward it. The reason is simple: as society opens up and politicians scramble for power, they appeal to the public for votes using what ends up being the most direct, effective language, that of group solidarity in opposition to some other group. Often this stokes the fires of ethnic or religious conflict. Sometimes the conflict turns into a full-scale war. . . .

Elections require that politicians compete for people's votes. In societies without strong traditions of multiethnic groups or assimilation, it is easiest to organize support along racial, ethnic, or religious lines. Once an ethnic group is in power, it tends to exclude other ethnic groups. Compromise seems impossible; one can bargain on material issues such as housing, hospitals, and handouts, but how does one split the difference on a national religion? Political competition that is so divisive can rapidly degenerate into violence. Opposition movements, armed rebellions, and coups in Africa have often been directed against ethnically based regimes, many of which came to power through elections. Surveying the breakdown of African and Asian democracies in the 1960s, two scholars concluded that democracy "is simply not viable in an environment of intense ethnic preferences." Recent studies, particularly of Africa and Central Asia, have confirmed this pessimism. A distinguished expert on ethnic conflict, Donald Horowitz, concluded, "In the face of this rather dismal account . . . of the concrete failures of democracy in divided societies . . . one is tempted to throw up one's hands. What is the point of holding elections if all they do in the end is to substitute a Bemba-dominated regime for a Nyanja regime in Zambia, the two equally narrow, or a southern regime for a northern one in Benin, neither incorporating the other half of the state?"

Over the past decade, one of the most spirited debates among scholars of international relations concerns the "democratic peace"—the assertion that no two modern democracies have gone to war against each other. The debate raises interesting substantive questions (Does the American Civil War count? Do nuclear weapons better explain the peace?), and even the statistical findings have raised interesting dissents. (As the scholar David Spiro has pointed out, given the small number of both democracies and wars over the last two hundred years, sheer chance might explain the absence of war between democracies. No member of his family has ever won the lottery, yet few offer explanations for this impressive correlation.) But even if the statistics are correct, what explains them?

Immanuel Kant, the original proponent of the democratic peace, contended that in democracies, those who pay for wars—that is, the public—make the decisions, so they are understandably cautious. But that claim suggests that democracies are more pacific than other states, when in fact, they are more warlike, going to war more often and with greater intensity than most other states. . . .

The distinction between liberal and illiberal democracies sheds light on another striking statistical correlation. Political scientists Jack Snyder and Edward Mansfield contend, using an impressive data set, that over the past 200 years democratizing states went to war significantly more often than either stable autocracies or liberal democracies. In countries not grounded in constitutional liberalism, the rise of democracy often brings with it hypernationalism and war-mongering. When the political system is opened up, diverse groups with incompatible interests gain access to power and press their demands. Political and military leaders, who are often embattled remnants of the old authoritarian order, realize that to succeed they must rally the masses behind a national cause. The result is invariably aggressive rhetoric and policies, which often drag countries into confrontation and war. Noteworthy examples range from

Napoleon III's France, Wilhelmine Germany, and Taisho Japan to the more recent Armenia and Azerbaijan and the former Yugoslavia. The democratic peace is real, but it turns out to have little to do with democracy. . . .

Less Is More

What we need in politics today is not more democracy but less. By this I do not mean we should embrace strongmen and dictators but rather that we should ask why certain institutions within our society—such as the Federal Reserve and the Supreme Court—function so well and why others—such as legislatures—function poorly. As it happens, Alan Blinder, a Princeton professor, pondered just this question in a fascinating essay in *Foreign Affairs* magazine in 1997. Blinder had completed two stints in government, first at the White House on the Council of Economic Advisers and then at the Federal Reserve, where he served as vice chairman. He noted in his essay that policy-making at the White House was dominated by short-term political and electoral considerations, whereas policy-making at the Federal Reserve was concerned largely with a policy's social, economic, and legal merits. This difference in large part accounted for the consistently high quality of decision-making at the Fed.

Blinder argued that Federal Reserve decision-making was insulated from politics for three good reasons. First, interest rates are a technical subject that specialists are better equipped to handle than amateurs. Second, monetary policy takes a long time to work and so requires patience and a steady hand. Finally, the pain of fighting inflation (higher unemployment) comes well before the benefits (permanently lower costs of goods, lower interest rates, etc.). As a result, good interest-rate policy cannot be made in an atmosphere dominated by short-term considerations. But then Blinder admitted that "a nasty little thought kept creeping through my head: the argument for the Fed's independence applies just as forcefully to many other areas of government. Many policy decisions require complex technical judgments and have consequences that stretch into the distant future." He cited health care, environmental policy, and tax policy as just such cases.

Consider the U.S. federal income tax. In its first incarnation in 1914, the entire tax code was 14 pages long, and individuals' tax returns fit on a single page. Today the tax code runs over 2,000 pages, with 6,000 pages of regulations and tens of thousands of pages of rulings and interpretations. The Internal Revenue Service publishes 480 tax forms and 280 forms to explain them. It is unclear exactly how much it costs Americans to comply with these Byzantine rules; estimates go as high as $600 billion per year, but most scholars place the number at about $100 billion, or about 15 percent of income-tax revenue (about $375 to $450 per person per year). Dale Jorgenson, chairman of the Economics Department at Harvard, calculates that moving to a flat-rate tax on consumption would raise as much revenue as the current income-tax system while increasing economic growth by more than $200 billion a year.

The tax code has become time-consuming, complex, and expensive for a simple reason: democratic politics. It presents a golden opportunity for politicians to fund their favorite programs, groups, and companies without attracting much attention. An outright grant would be noticed; a small change in tax law will not. Corporations with very similar balance sheets can pay widely differing taxes, depending on whether they have effective lobbyists who can bully Congress into rewriting the code to their benefit. Often a new law is so narrowly written as to be in effect a subsidy to one particular company. Although each tax break might seem small, the overall cost is staggering, totaling more than $550 billion in forgone revenue for the federal government in 2001. Some of these "tax expenditures" are designed to support programs with broad public approval, but others—such as narrowly targeted tax breaks for industry—can only be described as corporate welfare.

Americans of all political stripes agree that the tax code is unwieldy, inefficient, and unfair. Yet no one believes it will ever be reformed, because it is embedded in democratic politics. Blinder points out that the three reasons that the Federal Reserve is independent all apply particularly strongly to tax policy. He proposes the creation of an independent federal tax authority, much like the Federal Reserve. Congress would give it broad directions and guidelines, and on this basis it would prepare tax legislation. Congress would then vote on the bill but no amendments would be allowed. Although hardly flawless, such a system would undoubtedly produce a better tax code than the one we have now.

The United States government already experiments will this kind of delegation in some areas. The president is usually given the authority to negotiate trade agreements, which are then presented to Congress as a complete package. Congress votes on the bill as a whole with no amendments allowed. Congress used a similar procedure in the early 1990s, when it needed to close dozens of military bases as the country demobilized after the Cold War. Faced with a crisis, legislators realized that the only way to arrive at a fair outcome was to take politics out of the process. Otherwise members of Congress would all be strongly in favor of closing bases, just not the ones in their districts. They delegated the task of determining which bases should be closed to a nonpartisan commission. The final list was presented to Congress for a single vote, up or down, with no changes permitted. These processes have all worked well, combing effective government with democratic control.

Delegation is the modern-day equivalent of the strategy that Homer's wandering hero, Ulysses, used as he sailed passed the Sirens, whose singing made men cast themselves into the sea. Ulysses had his sailors fill their ears with wax so that they could not hear the Sirens' calls. For his part, he wanted to hear the music, so he had himself bound tightly to the mast of his ship and told his men that no matter what he said, they were not to untie him. As they passed the treacherous waters, Ulysses was seduced by the music and begged to be released. But the system worked. His men held to his initial orders and kept him bound. As a result, the boat and its sailors emerged safely from their trial. Politicians today should bind themselves more often to the ship of state as they pass through turbulent political waters.

The Highest Stakes

In developing countries the need for delegation is even greater because the stakes are often higher. Governments must demonstrate deep commitment and discipline in their policies or else markets quickly lose faith in them. They must focus on the long-term with regard to urban development, education, and health care, or their societies will slowly descend into stagnation or even anarchy. Far-sighted policies pay huge dividends; short-term patronage politics have immense costs.

In general dictators have not done better at these policies than democrats—far from it. Most dictators have ravaged their countries for personal gain. Scholars have asked whether democracy helps or hurts the economic growth of poor countries and, despite many surveys, have come to no conclusive answer. But over the past fifty years almost every success story in the developing world has taken place under a liberal authoritarian regime. . . .

Onward and Downward

. . . The institutions and attitudes that have preserved liberal democratic capitalism in the West were built over centuries. They are being destroyed in decades. Once torn down they will not be so easy to repair. We watch this destruction without really being able to stop it—that would be undemocratic. But it will leave its mark on our politics, economics, and culture, all of which will increasingly be dominated by short-term interests and enthusiasms. Edmund Burke once described society as a partnership between the dead, the living, and the yet unborn. It is difficult to see in the evolving system who will speak for the yet unborn, for the future.

Meanwhile, public dissatisfaction with the effects of all these changes will continue to grow. If these problems build, eventually people will define democracy by what it has become: a system, open and accessible in theory, but ruled in reality by organized or rich or fanatical minorities, protecting themselves for the present and sacrificing the future. This is a very different vision from that of the enthusiasts of direct democracy, who say that the liberating new world we will live in will harken back to the city-states of ancient Greece. I leave it to the reader to judge whether Californian politics today resembles Athenian democracy in its prime. In any event, it is worth remembering that direct democracy was tried only in a few small cities in ancient Greece where a few thousand men were allowed to vote. It is also worth remembering that within a hundred years all those democracies collapsed into tyranny or chaos—frequently both.

Such gloom may seem far-fetched, but if current trends continue, democracy will undoubtedly face a crisis of legitimacy, which could prove crippling. Legitimacy is the elixir of political power. "The strongest is never strong enough to be the master," Jean-Jacques Rousseau observed, "unless he translates strength into right and obedience into duty." Only democracy has that authority in the world today. But it can lose its hold on our loyalties. The greatest danger of unfettered and dysfunctional democracy is that it will discredit democracy itself, casting all popular governance into a shadowy light. This would not be unprecedented. Every wave of democracy has been followed by setbacks in which the system is seen as inadequate and new alternatives have been proposed by ambitious leaders and welcomed by frustrated people. The last such period of disenchantment, in Europe during the interwar years, was seized upon by demagogues, many of whom capitalized on the public's disenchantment with democracy. It is worth remembering that the embrace of communism and fascism in the 1930s did not seem as crazy at the time as it does now. While the democracies were mired in depression and gloom, authoritarian states had mobilized their societies and were on the march.

Modern democracies will face difficult new challenges—fighting terrorism, adjusting to globalization, adapting to an aging society—and they will have to make their system work much better than it currently does. That means making democratic decision-making effective, reintegrating constitutional liberalism into the practice of democracy, rebuilding broken political institutions and civic associations. Perhaps most difficult of all, it requires that those with immense power in our societies embrace their responsibilities, lead, and set standards that are not only legal, but moral. Without this inner stuffing, democracy will become an empty shell, not simply inadequate but potentially dangerous, bringing with it the erosion of liberty, the manipulation of freedom, and the decay of a common life.

This would be a tragedy because democracy, with all its flaws, represents the "last best hope" for people around the world. But it needs to be secured and strengthened for our times. Eighty year ago, Woodrow Wilson took America into the twentieth century with a challenge to make the world safe for democracy. As we enter the twenty-first century, our task is to make democracy safe for the world.

Notes

1. I use the term "liberal" in the nineteenth-century sense, meaning concerned with individual economic, political, and religious liberty, which is sometimes called "classical liberalism," not in the modern, American sense, which associates it with the welfare state, affirmative action, and other policies.

2. This particular aspect of American democracy has had mostly terrible effects, giving small states with tiny populations huge political influence and massive subsidies. Still, American democracy benefits greatly from most of its "undemocratic" features.

The Ungreat Washed: Why Democracy Must Remain America's Goal Abroad

Midway through Fareed Zakaria's attack on democracy, one realizes that his animus toward popular government is not only theoretical but also personal, and in some ways it is even quite understandable. The unique perils of democracy upon which Tocqueville long ago speculated—the "tyranny of the majority," the debasement of the culture, the tearing down of elites—are not abstractions for Zakaria, but phenomena that he experienced first-hand as an Indian Muslim growing up in Bombay in the 1960s and 1970s. . . .

Democratization in India, in Zakaria's view, proved disastrous for the nation, and especially for its large Muslim minority. The most potent new challenger to the Congress Party was the Hindu fundamentalist Bharatiya Janata Party (BJP). In its years in opposition, Zakaria recounts, the BJP employed an anti-Muslim and anti-Christian "rhetoric of hatred" to fire up its voters. Since coming to power, the BJP—although mellowed somewhat by the need for political compromise—has still been leading a Hindu nationalist revival. The consequences, Zakaria insists, have ranged from the horrific to the absurd. In Gujarat in 2002, the local BJP government was complicit in "India's first state-assisted pogrom," in which thousands of innocent Muslim men, women, and children were massacred. (For some reason. Zakaria does not mention the massacre of fifty-eight Hindus that preceded the anti-Muslim violence.) India's largest state, Uttar Pradesh, dominated by the BJP and "two lower-caste parties," has become a sea of corruption, a "bandit democracy." The Indian justice system has become, according to Zakaria, "a corrupt handmaiden of political power." Zakaria's hometown of Bombay, "a city built by its great minority communities," once "vibrant, meritocratic, and tolerant," has been destroyed by this officially sponsored Hindu revival in service to what Zakaria considers a ludicrous Hindu nationalist mythology. "The renaming of Bombay as Mumbai in 1996," he remarks, "illustrates the invented quality of much of Hindu nationalism."

From THE FUTURE OF FREEDOM, July 4 & 14, 2001, pp. 23–37. Copyright © 2001 by W.W. Norton. Reprinted with permission.

"This is the reality of democracy in India," Zakaria declares in the most intensely personal passage of his new book. And yet, he complains, "no one in the West wishes to look at it too closely. We prefer to speak romantically about the beauty of Indians voting and the joys of the world's largest democracy." "Thoughtful Indians," Zakaria explains, "do not quite see it this way."

Zakaria himself is not romantic about democracy and democratization. He holds democracy responsible for many of the modern world's evils, from ethnic violence to poverty, repression, and war, and even for international terrorism, which he calls the "democratization of violence." About one-third of his book derives from an essay that he published in *Foreign Affairs* in 1997, called "The Rise of Illiberal Democracy," in which he argued that democracy was not the necessary, appropriate, or even desirable form of government for many if not most countries around the world. In describing what he thinks is the new phenomenon of "illiberal democracy," Zakaria argued—and he repeats the argument in his book—that "democratically elected regimes" are row "routinely ignoring constitutional limits on their power and depriving their citizens of basic rights and freedoms." Citing examples from Russia and Belarus to the Philippines, Kazakhstan, Venezuela, and Argentina, Zakaria claims that "in many developing countries, the experience of democracy over the past few decades has been one in which majorities have—often quietly, sometimes noisily—eroded separations of power, undermined human rights, and corrupted long-standing traditions of tolerance and fairness." Curiously, Zakaria does not mention India, although it seems by his own description to be the quintessential example of a democracy gone "illiberal"—"less tolerant, less secular, less law-abiding, less liberal."

The sins of democracy go beyond the trampling of rights to include economic malfeasance and the impoverishment of peoples (in Russia, for instance, and post-Suharto Indonesia), the unleashing of religious fanaticism (notably in the Muslim world), the stoking of ethnic hatreds (in the Balkans, Africa, Central Asia, and the subcontinent). Drawing on the work of the political scientists Edward Mansfield and Jack Snyder, Zakaria even asserts that, contrary to conventional wisdom about the "democratic peace," democracies are more prone to militarism and war. When political systems are "opened up," he claims, new groups of enfranchised voters make incompatible demands on leaders, who in turn try to "rally the masses" behind aggressive nationalist crusades.

And what of the biggest and oldest democracy of them all? In his essay, Zakaria made a distinction between the "illiberal" democracies proliferating around the developing world and the liberal democracy enjoyed by the United States. But the subtitle of his new book is "Illiberal Democracy at Home and Abroad," and Zakaria devotes almost half the book to cataloguing the catastrophic effects of "illiberal" democracy in the United States. "The troubles of American democracy," he argues, "are similar to those being experienced by countries across the globe." Most Americans are disgusted with their democratic system; "they are repulsed by it." They "have lost faith in their democracy." They are experiencing a "crisis of faith" in democratic governance. And with good reason, Zakaria insists, because "something has gone seriously wrong with American democracy."

The problem with democracy in America, Zakaria maintains, is that there is simply too much of it. The old powerful elites that used to dominate every segment of American society have been pulled down and replaced by "a simple-minded populism," with disastrous consequences. In the realm of politics, "the quality of political leadership has declined." Fifty years ago the nation had Dwight D. Eisenhower; today it has George W. Bush—thus Zakaria quotes an unnamed "scholar in his eighties." ("We were having lunch in the paneled dining room of one of New York City's grand clubs.") Meanwhile, direct democracy in the form of initiatives and referenda has taken governance out of the hands of political elites and placed it in the hands of an irresponsible and shortsighted citizenry. Proposition 13, the famous California tax-cutting measure of 1978 so celebrated by Reaganera conservatives, was a terrible precedent, in Zakaria's view, because it led to an explosion of such citizen movements. As a result of this democratization, especially within the American party system, for three decades Americans have had "their leaders bow and scrape before them."

And the unfortunate impact of democracy extends well beyond politics. It has also had pernicious effects on business, law, medicine, religion, journalism, and culture. There, too, the nation has suffered from "the eclipse of the class of elites who ran these institutions" and has been harmed by "the opening up of many American industries and professions to outsiders." Zakaria traces the undoing of the American financial system, for instance, in part to Chase Manhattan Bank's shift in the 1990s toward a strategy of "catering to the great unwashed." There was a time, Zakaria argues, when American bankers such as J. P Morgan awarded credit to men with good "character"; but his successors failed in "a financial world dominated by mass rather than class." Today's stock market is "geared toward everyday investors . . . everyone, king and commoner alike, has become a capitalist"—a partial fulfillment, Zakaria complains, of the Southern populist Huey Long's rallying cry, "Every man a king!" If the "symbol of the old order was a Wall Street club where a handful of power brokers lunched, the symbol of the new was CNBC, where CEOs vied for airtime to speak to a mass audience." The once elite legal profession has destroyed itself by permitting lawyers to advertise to the common man. And doctors, too, have "lost their privileged perch" in society and become like everybody else.

Catering to the "great unwashed" has also destroyed the media. In television. Zakaria complains, the days are gone when Don Hewitt, producer of the "now-legendary" *60 Minutes,* could be told by his network bosses simply to "make us proud." Yes, Zakaria concedes, there may still be some "serious news programs . . . [that] were started decades ago and built their audience gradually over those years" (he may be referring to ABC's *This Week,* on which he appears), but ever since ABC and the two other "traditional networks" lost their monopoly, television news has been engaged in a "race to the bottom." And the same goes for print journalism. While there still remain, for Zakaria, a few serious publications whose owners "are willing to subsidize excellence," such as *The New Yorker* (where he also appears), and while there is at least one mass-circulation magazine that "still covers the news seriously and in depth," such as "*Newsweek,* where I work," these quality publications are becoming fewer and fewer.

The problem extends even to think tanks. Venerable institutions such as the Council on Foreign Relations, where Zakaria also worked, are "worthy and dutiful" for having created a "foreign-policy discussion for the country that was civil and not permeated with partisanship." But Zakaria's own think tank and the equally venerable Brookings Institution (also "designed to serve the country beyond partisanship and party politics") are exceptional in this respect, for "almost every institute and think tank created in the past thirty years is deeply ideological." In Zakaria's view, this is principally because the new think tanks were founded by conservatives seeking to erect a "counter-establishment" to challenge the old elites. But instead of creating "independent institutions" for "free-thinking intellectuals," the conservative think tanks have blindly "pushed their own partisan line." The scholars at these conservative institutions, Zakaria writes, are "chosen for their views, not their expertise." As a result, they produce "lots of predictable polemics and little serious analysis."

Finally, there is the debasement of the culture by its democratization. There was a time, Zakaria recalls, when the nation's tastes were set by men who "had a feel" for what Zakaria calls "cultural content"—men such as Harold Ross, the "legendary" editor of *The New Yorker.* But no longer. There was a time when Americans looked for guidance to Philippe de Montebello, the "legendary" director of the Metropolitan Museum of Art, but now museum directors pander to the masses.

Zakaria's answer to this rampant excess of democracy in America is to "resurrect, in some form, the institutions and elites" that dominated America in the past, and to return to them the authority that they have lost. Specifically, he has in mind the sweeping delegation of economic, political, social, and cultural power away from average Americans to an elite corps of experts. Zakaria's model for American government is the American corporation. "Delegation is, after all, how modern business is run. Shareholders own companies but hand over their management to people who can devote time and energy to it and who have expertise in the field. Shareholders retain ultimate control but recognize that they cannot run the companies themselves." Zakaria argues that it is ridiculous to believe that "any amateur" should determine the policies of the nation. Americans somehow think that "although we cannot file our tax forms, write our wills, or configure our computers, we can pass laws ourselves." He insists that it is time for Americans to "admit that, without guidance or reference to authority, people can make bad choices." What the United States needs, in short, "is not more democracy but less."

In making his case against American-style democracy, Zakaria points admiringly to the European Union as an example of how "undemocratic policy-making" can be preferable to democratic policy-making. While many in the United States and Great Britain complain about the EU's so-called "democracy deficit" and the bloated, imperious bureaucracy of Brussels, Zakaria finds much to admire in the EU bureaucracy. It is effective, he argues, "precisely because it is insulated from political pressures." Zakaria asserts that economic reforms made in Europe over the last decade were possible only because of the "pressure" and "power" of Brussels.

The United States can learn from the example of the European Union, Zakaria believes. Above all, American policymakers must learn to ignore public opinion. Zakaria begins his book by recounting the story of Odysseus ordering his men to tie him to the ship's mast so that he would not follow the Sirens' call and wreck his vessel on the rocks toward which their sweet singing beckoned. In Zakaria's analogy the Sirens are the American people—the "great unwashed"—who are destroying their nation because their political leaders cannot resist their alluring call. The power now held by the American masses must be transferred to the elites; and America's elites need to grasp that power. They must recover their nerve and recapture their old ethos of responsibility. Noblesse oblige: for Zakaria, this must be the American ideal. He sees it perfectly epitomized in the slogans of Groton Academy, whose motto, "to serve is to reign," aimed to produce "men who played hard but fair, followed a moral code, and believed in public service as a responsibility that came with power."

The Future of Freedom offers, in the words of Niall Ferguson, a "classical defense of aristocratic rule" as a superior alternative to American democracy. And perhaps, as Ferguson suggests, it is a brave thing for Zakaria to make such a case for conservative counter-revolution. For Americans have traditionally looked askance at aristocracy and taken a dim view of the idea that non-elected elites, insulated from politics, should assume much greater authority to run the nation's affairs. To be sure, American elites have always been more enthusiastic about such ideas, and it is notable, if not surprising, to find *The New Yorker's* Nicholas Lemann, ABC's Peter Jennings, and would-be Secretary of State Richard Holbrooke among those adorning the dust jacket of Zakaria's book with praise of its anti-democratic thesis. But Zakaria, who remarked in that *New York* magazine piece that "my friends all say I am going to be secretary of state," has nonetheless taken the risk, as he puts it, of speaking out about the "dark sides" of democracy. Meanwhile others hide in the shadows, "silenced by fears of being branded 'anti-democratic'" and "out of sync with the times."

Although Zakaria is courageous enough to cast his harsh spotlight on the evils of democracy, he claims oddly that he is not anti-democratic, that he wants only to protect democracy from its worst tendencies and thereby to strengthen it. But it is difficult to read his book, or the essay from which it derives, and conclude that Zakaria has much fondness for governance by the "great unwashed." The whole thrust of Zakaria's argument and analysis is, by any reasonable understanding of the word, anti-democratic. His critique of democracy "at home and abroad" is a sweeping, no-holds-barred indictment, clearly intended to be damning. That he very occasionally utters some praise of democracy—"overwhelmingly it has had wonderful consequences"—is not at all convincing, especially when each tidbit of praise is followed by the inevitable "but. . . ." Nor is it clear why Zakaria should shy away from the "anti-democratic" label. Zakaria's prescriptions for government both "at home and abroad" are so overtly and objectively "anti-democratic" in intent that it belittles his argument for him to pretend otherwise.

For Zakaria's "classical defense of aristocratic rule" for the United States is matched by an equally classical defense of authoritarian rule for most of the rest of the world. "The need for delegation" in the developing world, Zakaria argues delicately, "is even higher." Most countries, he believes, are unready for democratic government. They would be better off under some form of dictatorship, or what he calls "liberal autocracy." According to Zakaria, "almost every success story in the developing world has taken place under a liberal authoritarian regime." By "liberal," Zakaria means chiefly economic liberalization; and by "success" he means chiefly economic success. Citing Singapore, Indonesia, Taiwan, Thailand, and China, Zakaria argues that only autocratic governments "were able to make shrewd choices for the long term" that allowed the country to prosper and to modernize economically. Meanwhile, "it is difficult to think of a Third World democracy that has achieved sustained growth rates."

Although many readers may be encountering this argument for the first time, the bulk of Zakaria's analysis of the developing world is a simplified recycling of what three decades ago used to be called "modernization theory." The central hypotheses of modernization theory were, first, that authoritarian governments are better than democracies at promoting economic growth and, second, that economic growth and industrialization are prerequisites for the emergence and success of democracy. In the late 1950s and 1960s, many leading political scientists concluded that democracies were an obstacle to economic growth because popular pressures forced governments away from the most efficient economic decisions. Popular government led to inflation, budget deficits, and chronic low growth. The obvious answer was less democracy and more dictatorship. As Samuel Huntington and Joan Nelson put it back then, "Political participation must be held down, at least temporarily, to promote economic development." Once a period of stable authoritarianism created sufficient national wealth, then a transition to democracy became possible, and perhaps even inevitable.

As the political scientist Adam Przeworski describes the presumption of modernization theory, there was a "benign line" running from "economically successful dictatorships to democracy. . . . Dictatorships would generate development, and development would create democracy as a by-product." Of course, as Przeworski also points out, this assumption "justified supporting dictatorships and letting modernization do the rest." The effect of the Cold War on the thinking of that era is evident in retrospect, as it was to many at the time: the "modernization thesis" fit nicely with the occasional American propensity during the Cold War to support "friendly" dictators as a bulwark against possible Communist revolution.

For Zakaria, not much has changed. The alleged correlation between economic success and democracy is a central pillar in his argument for dictatorship as the preferred mode of government for most of the developing world. More even than many of the modernization theorists upon whom his work relies, Zakaria's argument approaches economic determinism. As he puts it, "Karl Marx understood that when a country modernizes its economy, embraces capitalism, and creates a bourgeoisie, the political system will change to reflect that transformation. Changes in the 'base,' in Marxist lingo, always produce changes in the 'superstructure,'" National wealth, as measured by per capita gross domestic product, is the surest indicator of a nation's readiness to sustain democratic government. . . .

When democracy is adopted in countries that are not ready for it, then democracy itself becomes pernicious, and not only for the people of the nation in which it is unwisely planted. The product of premature democratization is Zakaria's "illiberal democracy," repressive, intolerant, violent, prone to war. Indeed, the proliferation of these "illiberal democracies," Zakaria insists, is the greatest threat that the world faces today—greater even than the world's tyrannies. In a recent *Newsweek* column, Zakaria excoriated those who for many years "had a tendency to vastly exaggerate the threat posed by tyrannical regimes," specifically the Soviet Union during the Cold War and more recently Saddam Hussein's Iraq. Woodrow Wilson had once sought to make the world safe for democracy, but Zakaria insists that it is necessary to "make democracy safe for the world." This is to be accomplished by sharply limiting its spread to those very few places where its pernicious excesses can be contained.

This neologism "illiberal democracy . . . is his principal contribution to the present discussion of political development. . . . It is also central to Zakaria's purpose, for only by demonstrating the reality and significance of "illiberal democracy" as a phenomenon in the modern world can Zakaria make his case that the world suffers not from too little democracy but from too much.

For there have indeed been setbacks in democracies, and perhaps permanent failures to promote democracy in many parts of the world. Political scientists . . . and democracy experts such as Thomas Carothers have long catalogued and ruminated over these failures. But they, like almost everyone else, have asked why democracy has failed. Zakaria's perspective is different. In his view, the problem in many countries is not that democracy fails, but that it succeeds. The evils that we see in the world, he insists, represent the product of democratization, not the failure of democratization. This is not just a question of semantics. Declaring a democracy failed and declaring it an illiberal democracy lead to entirely different prescriptions. If a democracy fails, then democracy itself is not implicated in the disasters that follow, and the remedy might be more democracy. But if the disasters are the product of the success of democracy, then the remedy is, as Zakaria insists, more dictatorship.

⋅⊙⋅

So how real and significant is the phenomenon of "illiberal democracy"? Zakaria claims that it is rampant. But perusing the list of countries he describes as suffering from "illiberal democracy," one discovers that the term, as he deploys it, is rather elastic and inclusive. Indeed, at the heart of Zakaria's analysis is what political scientists like to call a methodological problem.

Consider the example of Belarus. Zakaria labels Belarus an "illiberal democracy," presumably because its ruler, Alexander Lukashenko, won the presidency in a free election in 1994. Immediately after winning, however, Lukashenko began ruling as an authoritarian dictator. In 1996 he extended his term of office by means of a rigged "referendum," and he was "re-elected" in 2001 in another rigged election marked, according to the State Department, by "sweeping human rights violations and nondemocratic practices throughout the election period, including massive vote-counting fraud." The survey of world nations conducted annually by Freedom House, which Zakaria himself cites, correctly places Belarus in the non-democratic camp. In short, Belarus is not an "illiberal democracy," or a democracy of any kind. It is a dictatorship.

Nor is Lukashenko's method of hijacking a democracy and turning it into a tyranny exactly a new phenomenon. The history books are filled with democratically elected leaders entrenching themselves in power by undemocratic means. If Belarus is an "illiberal democracy," then so was Nicaragua under three generations of the Somoza dynasty. The Somozas held repeated elections and referenda, too, and they won them all.

One would have thought that to qualify as an "illiberal democracy," a country would first have to meet the minimal standards necessary to qualify as a democracy. Zakaria himself defines the requirements of democracy as "competitive, multiparty elections"; the elections themselves "must be open and fair," which in turn "requires some protections for the freedom of speech and assembly." This is a fairly narrow definition. Huntington more appropriately defines modern democracy as a system in which "the most powerful collective decision makers are selected through fair, honest, *and periodic* elections in which candidates freely compete for votes and in which virtually all the adult population is eligible to vote [emphasis added]." Most political scientists would agree that a nation cannot be called a democracy after only one election. Huntington adds that democracy "also implies the existence of those civil and political freedoms to speak, publish, assemble, and organize that are necessary to political debate and the conduct of electoral campaigns."

So let us return to Belarus. Lukashenko's government does not meet even Zakaria's narrower requirements for a democracy, much less the more generally accepted requirements spelled out by Huntington and others. Why, then, does Zakaria list it as an "illiberal democracy"? He also lists Kazakhstan as an "illiberal democracy"—a nation whose president, Nursultan Nazarbayev, has been in office for a dozen years. Freedom House categorizes Kazakhstan as non-democratic, and Zakaria himself describes it as a "near-tyranny." Zakaria states that "many illiberal democracies," especially in Central Asia, "have quickly and firmly turned into dictatorships." Indeed many have, and so quickly and firmly that no reasonable observer would designate them as having ever been democracies at all. . . .

Zakaria also employs other means of smearing democracy. Often he blames democracies for problems for which they bear no responsibility. In order to demonstrate that democracies are incompetent at stimulating economic growth, he cites the case of Indonesia. "Since it embraced democracy." Zakaria observes, "Indonesia's gross domestic product has contracted by almost 50 percent, wiping out a generation of economic progress and pushing more than 20 million people below the poverty line." This is a rather appalling distortion. Indonesia's economy collapsed not after Indonesia "embraced" democracy but before, during the last two years of the Suharto dictatorship and as a result of the Asian financial crisis of 1997–1998. Per capita GDP dropped from $1,100 in 1997 to $487 in 1998, the year Suharto fell. Indonesia's first parliamentary elections were held a year later, in June 1999, by which time the economy had already collapsed and the 50 percent contraction to which Zakaria refers had already taken place.

This tendency to blame democracy for problems for which it cannot justly be blamed permeates Zakaria's book. He blames democratization for the ethnic warfare in Yugoslavia as it broke up in the early 1990s, arguing that "the introduction of democracy" there "actually fomented nationalism, ethnic conflict and even war," and that this proves his general point, which is that "democratizing societies display a disturbingly common tendency toward" violent behavior. But does Zakaria believe that ethnic conflict would have been avoided after the breakup of Yugoslavia had Serbia been in the hands of an unelected dictator? No, he shies away from making such an absurd claim. He admits that dictatorships are "hardly innocent" of fomenting ethnic conflict. Indeed they are not. Nor does the history of the Balkans, filled as it is with ethnic violence over the centuries, lend support to Zakaria's assertion that somehow it was "the introduction of democracy" that was responsible for sparking ethnic warfare in the 1990s. Nor would any sensible person hold democratization responsible for ethnic conflict in parts of Africa, where tribal warfare has thrived in all political climates.

Zakaria also blames democracy for unleashing Islamic radicalism and religious conflicts that, he claims, had been kept under control by "liberal autocrats." He cites Indonesia as one such case. Suharto's "strongman" rule was "far more tolerant and secular" than the democracy that followed his overthrow in 1998, and whose "newly open political system has . . . thrown up Islamic fundamentalists." This is another historical distortion. It is true that in the first decades after independence, secularism was part of the Indonesian social compact. But as Jacques Bertrand, the prominent expert on Indonesia, explained in a recent article in *Pacific Affairs,* the roots of religious conflict in Indonesia can be traced back to the 1980s and 1990s, when Suharto, worried about his increasingly precarious control of the country, deliberately "shifted to Islamic groups for political support." Zakaria himself notes that in Pakistan it was the military dictator Zia ul-Haq who embarked on an "Islamization" program that fostered the militant fundamentalism we know today, and with the funding provided by another dictatorship, the Saudi Arabian monarchy.

In an offhanded remark Zakaria even claims that democracy was responsible for the perpetuation of slavery in the United States. "Slavery and segregation were entrenched in the American South through the democratic system," he argues, because "the majority of southern voters defended it passionately." This is a marvelous inversion of history. Slavery, in fact, was perpetuated not by democracy—slaveholders and their supporters in the South represented a minority of voters in the nation—but precisely by all the undemocratic elements of the American system of government that Zakaria now celebrates and wishes to recover: by one undemocratic clause in the Constitution that counted a non-voting slave as three-fifths of a voter so as to give Southern states a disproportionate influence in Congress, and by another clause in the Constitution that gave each state two senators regardless of their population, which was also partly designed to give disproportionate weight to the slaveholding South; by an undemocratic Supreme Court that consistently upheld the "liberal" principle that the slaveholders' human "property" could not be taken away by the government, even in non-slave states; and by a Senate, already weighted undemocratically in the South's favor, in which the slave states were capable of thwarting the will of the non-slave-state majority by means of the filibuster and other undemocratic practices. Southern Senators employed those same practices to block civil rights legislation during the century that followed the Civil War.

⋅◦◉◦⋅

Zakaria's proclivity to expose the "dark sides" of democracy, including many that do not exist, is matched by his propensity to mythologize the virtues of what he calls "liberal autocracies" and to turn a blind eye to their vices. Although he spends comparatively little of his time describing the nature of the dictatorship that he would like to impose on most of the developing world in place of democracy, and although he cannot name more than one "liberal autocracy" in today's world—it is, of course, the tiny city-state of Singapore, which he admires—Zakaria does find much to praise in the dictatorships of the past: the governments that ruled South Korea and Taiwan from the 1950s through the late 1980s, Augusto Pinochet's Chile, Suharto's Indonesia, the onetime dictatorships of Malaysia and Thailand, the late one-party dictatorship of Mexico.

All of these dictatorships Zakaria lumps together under the benign narrative of the "modernization" paradigm. In his version of history, these dictatorships "liberalized, people's lives improved, [and] economic reforms took place, followed by democratic openings." The dictators made "shrewd choices" that created "economic growth." They "liberalized the economy, the legal system, and rights of worship and travel, and then, decades later, held free elections," The "liberalizing autocracies" thus "laid the groundwork for stable liberal democracies"; democracies would not have been possible without the work done by the dictatorships that preceded them. In the end, of course, the autocrats were overthrown by an angry populace, despite their benevolent rule. But this was in the nature of things, the inevitable course of modernization theory's "benign line."

Zakaria likens these dictators to Moses: "The role of the modernizing autocrat is biblical; like Moses, he can lead his country forward, but he rarely makes it to the promised land himself." This analogy may be the most revealing clue about Zakaria's whole way of thinking about dictatorship and democracy. For it implies not only that dictatorships objectively create the conditions for democracy, but also that such is their intent. But the reader may be left with a question: if democracies followed dictatorships in these countries, was it because of the dictators or in spite of them?

Take the case of Suharto's Indonesia. Zakaria praises Suharto for having "achieved order, secularism, economic liberalization," and tolerance in that difficult country. In Zakaria's telling, Indonesia under the Suharto dictatorship followed the classic modernization narrative. Suharto was one of those "liberal autocrats" who made "shrewd choices" about the nation's economy. Suharto's Indonesia "liberalized its economy," which grew at 7 percent per year for almost three decades. And then, Zakaria notes, Indonesia "embraced democracy."

The remarkable thing about this story is that Zakaria himself contradicts it elsewhere in his book, albeit when he is trying to make a different point about Indonesia. In addition to wanting to praise the dictator Suharto, Zakaria also wants to argue that Indonesian democracy is a failure because democracy came to Indonesia prematurely. When making this particular argument, Zakaria points out that Suharto had not prepared Indonesia for a democratic transition after all. It was "bereft of political institutions, since Suharto ran the country through a small group of courtiers, paying little attention to the task of institution-building." Nor had Suharto alleviated Indonesia's dependence on natural resources as its main source of wealth. Nor, according to Zakaria, had Suharto managed to lift Indonesia's per capita GDP to the magical "zone of transition." "Strike three," Zakaria declares in condemning the struggling democracy of Indonesia to likely failure. But if anyone struck out, it was Suharto, not Indonesian democracy. And one might add a fourth strike, since Suharto's "shrewd" economic decisions—including the shrewd decision to plunder the Indonesian economy for his own and his courtiers' personal enrichment—helped to plunge the nation into the abyss in 1997 and 1998. . . .

Zakaria's sympathy for the dictator, his tendency to attribute to tyrants a decisive role in preparing the ground for democracy, is related to his rather contemptuous view of the "great unwashed" over whom they ruled. Not only does Zakaria presume that the people, left to themselves, could never have reached the promised land without their tyrannical Moses. In Zakaria's view, the dictators saved their countries, and the world, from the inherent, dangerous illiberalism of the masses.

Today Zakaria hopes that other dictators will do the same. He praises many dictators in this book, but he singles one out for special acclaim. Some readers may be surprised to learn that Zakaria's paragon is Pervez Musharraf, the current dictator of Pakistan. According to Zakaria, this "liberal autocrat" has "boldly, decisively, and effectively" pursued a "path of radical political, social, educational, and economic reform." And Zakaria insists that "if genuine liberalization and even democracy come to Pakistan it will come not because of its history of illiberal democracy but because it stumbled on a liberal autocrat."

Again one puzzles over Zakaria's categories, since Musharraf, like Lukashenko, not so long ago held a "referendum" extending his term as president by another five years (he claimed to have won 97.5 percent of the vote), and there have been elections for Pakistan's parliament. But whatever designation one gives to Pakistan's form of government under Musharraf, it would not include the word "liberal." The State Department, with no incentive to criticize this essential "partner" in the war on terrorism, describes Musharraf's human rights record as "poor." Freedom House places Pakistan squarely in the "Not Free" category, neither democratic nor liberal. And as Zakaria's own book went to press, he found it necessary to admit that "as of this writing, Musharraf seems somewhat more autocratic and somewhat less liberal than he seemed at first flush [sic]." Yes, that happens. But this late realization has not affected Zakaria's unbounded admiration for Musharraf. Perhaps one may be forgiven for concluding, therefore, that Zakaria likes Musharraf not because he is a "liberal autocrat" but simply because he is an autocrat and "because he did not have to run for office." . . .

At its core Zakaria's argument is not really about "illiberal democracy" versus "liberal autocracy." All his disclaimers to the contrary notwithstanding, it becomes painfully clear reading his book that Zakaria simply has a preference for aristocratic government over democratic government at home, and for autocratic government over democratic government abroad.

This is a respectable point of view, although it was perhaps a bit more respectable a quarter of a millennium ago than it is today. Zakaria is in this respect the most literal kind of conservative, which is rare in the United States. He is nostalgic for a time when there was indeed "less democracy" in the world. He yearns for the restoration of an earlier age when in places such as England (though perhaps only in England) monarchy and autocracy, as well as aristocracy, were compatible with a developing liberalism.

That combination never really existed in the United States, where democracy and liberalism co-existed from the beginning. And it is almost impossible to imagine re-creating it in the modern world. Which people today are ready to accept the return of divine-right monarchy? Which tyrants today can be counted on to protect the liberties of the individuals over whom they wield absolute power? How would Zakaria or anyone else presume to know which dictator could be entrusted with the well-being of his or her people? And most important of all, does Zakaria or anyone else really believe that we know how to create a liberal society without democracy? The truth is that, as many experts are now beginning to admit, we have not had so much success in promoting "the rule of law" and "all that stuff."

Indeed, for the United States and other democratic nations to support the promotion of democracy abroad is not a sign of arrogance. It is a sign of humility. We do not really know how to build a liberal society, any more than we know how to build a human body. But we do know a free and fair election when we see one. And we know what we believe: that the rights enumerated in the Declaration of Independence belong to all humankind, and therefore that liberalism in the modern world can only be genuine when the people have the right to choose—and to dismiss—their rulers. When democracies fail, we should try again to help them succeed. And when democracies falter, the answer is, yes, more democracy.

POSTSCRIPT

Is There Too Much Democracy in the World?

Fareed Zakaria's distinction between democracy and liberalism is one that is frequently blurred in common usage, at least in America. For most Americans, "democratic" can be anything from making decisions by the arithmetical majority to protecting religious freedom. For Zakaria, only the first of these fit the category of "democracy" and thus one can imagine democracies that are hostile to religious freedom. Yet it may not be verbal carelessness but a wise instinct that causes Americans to equate democracy with liberalism. It is at least questionable whether democracy even in the arithmetical sense could exist for very long without the oxygen of freedom.

In the same vein as Zakaria, Robert D. Kaplan has argued ("Was Democracy Just a Moment," *Atlantic Monthly,* December 1997) that not all nations have the conditions that allow democracy to thrive, and that some are better off without it. For an opposing view, see Michael McFaul, "The Liberty Doctrine," *Policy Review* (April, 2002). Donald N. Wood, in *Post-Intellectualism and the Decline of Democracy* (Praeger, 1997) worries that the rise of global corporations and worldwide communications will homogenize culture and thus destroy the pluralist nerve of democracy in the world. Within the space of a few years, political scientists Samuel P. Huntington changed his position from a positive view of the spread of democracy in *The Third Wave: Democratization in the Late Twentieth Century* (University of Oklahoma Press, 1991) to a negative outlook in *The Clash of Civilizations and the Remaking of the World Order* (Simon & Schuster, 1996). In his more recent *The Challenges to America's National Identity* (Simon & Schuster, 2004), Huntington focuses on America and worries that "denationalized elites" may be causing a deep fissure in the national consensus. In *Wealth and Democracy: A Political History of the American Rich* (Broadway, 2003) Kevin Phillips traces the intersection of democracy, class, and economic growth in the United States, comparing it with similar intersections in Spain, the Netherlands, and the United Kingdom. Theda Skocpol, in *Diminished Democracy: From Membership to Management in American Civic Life* (University of Arizona Press, 2004) traces the decline in actual participation in voluntary groups throughout the nation, showing how they deepened Americans' commitment to democracy in the nineteenth century.

The central question raised by Zakaria is whether democracy deserves to be encouraged and augmented, especially if it ends up reversing economic progress, oppressing minorities, and pulling apart the fabric of national consensus. But if not democracy, then what? Zakaria rests his hope on "liberal autocracies," which he thinks can prepare the soil for the eventual emergence of democracy. Robert Kagan doubts whether such benign autocracies really exist. Yet there is also reason to doubt whether democracy is always the answer, or whether it can be transplanted into regions that have never experienced it. Still, we are reassured by Kagan that "when democracies falter, the answer is, yes, more democracy." There is boldness, even courage, in this declaration, whatever its logical difficulties.

ISSUE 2

Do Political Campaigns Promote Good Government?

YES: Samuel L. Popkin, from *The Reasoning Voter: Communication and Persuasion in Presidential Campaigns* (University of Chicago Press, 1991)

NO: Anthony King, from "Running Scared," *The Atlantic Monthly* (January 1997)

ISSUE SUMMARY

YES: Professor of political science Samuel L. Popkin argues that presidential election campaigns perform a unique and essential service in informing and unifying the American people.

NO: Political scientist Anthony King contends that American office-holders spend too much time and effort running for office, which detracts from their responsibility to provide good government.

Americans have the opportunity to vote more often to elect more office-holders than the citizens of any other democracy. Many elected officials serve two-year terms (members of the House of Representatives and many local and state officials), some serve four-year terms (the president, vice president, and other state and local officials), and only a few serve as long as six years (members of the Senate). In addition, voters may participate in primary elections to choose the candidates of the major parties for each of these offices. In the case of the presidential nominee, voters may select national convention delegates, whose election will determine who the party's nominee will be.

As a consequence, Americans are engaged in an almost ceaseless political campaign. No sooner is one congressional election over than another one begins. Given the long period required for organization and delegate-seeking prior to a presidential nomination, those who would be their party's nominee are off and running almost as soon as the last election has been decided.

Does this virtually nonstop campaigning serve the interests of American democracy? It surely makes for the most sustained appeal for public support by would-be candidates and those who finally win their party's support. During the height of the campaign season, lavish amounts of television time are bought for candidates' commercials, speeches, and sound bites on evening news broadcasts. Voters who want to learn more about the candidates and their positions can expose themselves to more information than they can absorb in daily newspapers, the news weeklies, talk radio, and C-SPAN. Less-interested adults cannot entirely escape political campaigns by switching their televisions to sitcoms and dramas, because they will be inundated with 30- and 60-second commercials for the candidates.

Yet despite this surfeit of information and advertisement, a smaller proportion of the eligible American electorate votes in presidential elections than did a century ago, and this proportion is smaller than those of other major democracies throughout the world. Only approximately one-half of the eligible electorate voted for president in recent elections. An even smaller percentage votes in congressional, state, and local elections.

Declining voter turnout may derive in part from the reduced role of political parties, which once organized community rallies and door-to-door voter solicitation. In other democracies, party committees choose candidates; in the United States, candidates for national, state, and local office seek nomination by voters in primary elections. This diminishes the influence of parties and increases the amount and cost of campaigning. In presidential campaigns, the national party convention used to be an exciting affair in which the delegates actually chose from among competing candidates. As a result of changes in the method of delegate selection, the winning nominee is now known long before the formal decision, and the convention has been reduced to a carefully scripted show. As a result, the television networks have cut back their coverage, and viewer interest has diminished.

Critics argue that television has not only supplanted traditional campaigning but has placed candidates in contrived settings and reduced issues to slogans. Furthermore, long campaigns become negative and candidates attempt to show their opponents in as bad a light as possible. Examples from recent campaigns abound, including mudslinging, character bashing, and the blatant misrepresentation of opponents' records.

Many supporters of the American electoral system believe that more campaigning is needed in order to educate potential voters and to inspire their participation. The campaign serves the invaluable function of illuminating the common interests of varied economic, social, ethnic, and racial groups in America's heterogeneous society. As for low voter turnout, some maintain that this represents satisfaction with the workings of American democracy. That is, if the two major parties do not represent diametrically opposed positions on the gravest issues, it is precisely because most Americans approve of moderate policies and few would be attracted to extreme views.

A classic text that provides an overview of presidential campaigns is Nelson W. Polsby and Aaron Wildavsky, *Presidential Elections: Strategies and Structures of American Politics,* 10th ed. (Chatham House, 2000). Recent presidential elections have produced a spate of books providing insightful analysis and insider revelations regarding the conduct of the campaign.

Samuel L. Popkin  **YES**

The Reasoning Voter

I believe that voter turnout has declined because campaign stimulation, from the media and from personal interaction, is also low and declining, and there is less interaction between the media and the grass-roots, person-to-person aspects of voter mobilization. The lack of campaign stimulation, I suggest, is also responsible for the large turnout gap in this country between educated and uneducated voters.

The social science research shows clear relations between the turnout and social stimulation. Married people of all ages vote more than people of the same age who live alone. And much of the increase in turnout seen over one's life cycle is due to increases in church attendance and community involvement. I believe that in this age of electronic communities, when more people are living alone and fewer people are involved in churches, PTA's, and other local groups, interpersonal social stimulation must be increased if turnout is to increase. . . .

Political parties used to spend a large portion of their resources bringing people to rallies. By promoting the use of political ideas to bridge the gap between the individual "I" and the party "we," they encouraged people to believe that they were "links in the chain" and that the election outcome would depend on what people like themselves chose to do. Today, less money and fewer resources are available for rallies as a part of national campaigns. And parties cannot compensate for this loss with more door-to-door canvassing; in the neighborhoods where it would be safe to walk door-to-door, no one would be home.

Some of the social stimulation that campaigns used to provide in rallies and door-to-door canvassing can still be provided by extensive canvassing. This is still done in Iowa and New Hampshire. These are the first primary states, and candidates have the time and resources to do extensive personal campaigning, and to use campaign organizations to telephone people and discuss the campaigns. In research reported elsewhere, I have analyzed the effect of the social stimulation that occurs in these states. People contacted by one political candidate pay more attention to all the candidates and to the campaign events reported on television and in the papers. As they watch the campaign they become more aware of differences between the candidates. And as they become more aware of the differences, they become more likely to vote.

From Samuel L. Popkin, *The Reasoning Voter: Communication and Persuasion in Presidential Campaigns* (University of Chicago Press, 1991). Copyright © 1991 by Samuel L. Popkin. Reprinted by permission of University of Chicago Press. Notes omitted.

This suggests a surprising conclusion: The best single way to compensate for the declining use of the party as a cue to voting, and for the declining social stimulation to vote at all, might be to increase our spending on campaign activities that stimulate voter involvement. There are daily complaints about the cost of American elections, and certainly the corrosive effects of corporate fund-raising cannot be denied; but it is not true that American elections are costly by comparison with those in other countries. Comparisons are difficult, especially since most countries have parliamentary systems, but it is worth noting that reelection campaigns to the Japanese Diet—the equivalent of the U.S. House of Representatives—cost over $1.5 million per seat. That would be equivalent to $3.5 million per congressional reelection campaign, instead of the current U.S. average of about $400,000 (given the fact that Japan has one-half the U.S. population and 512 legislators instead of 435). Although the differences in election systems and rules limit the value of such comparisons, it is food for thought that a country with a self-image so different from America's spends so much more on campaigning.

I believe that voters should be given more to "read" from campaigns and television, and that they need more interpersonal reinforcement of what they "read." Considering the good evidence that campaigns work, I believe that the main trouble lies not with American politicians but in the fact that American campaigns are not effective enough to overcome the increasing lack of social stimulation we find in a country of electronic as well as residential communities. This confronts us with some troubling questions. What kinds of electronic and/or social stimulation are possible today? To what extent can newspaper and television coverage provide the kinds of information citizens need to connect their own concerns with the basic party differences that campaigns try to make paramount? Is there a limit to what electronic and print stimulation can accomplish, so that parties must find a way to restore canvassing and rallies, or can electronic rallies suffice? Does watching a rally on television have the same effect as attending a rally? Could a return to bumper stickers and buttons, which have become far less prominent since campaigns began pouring their limited resources into the media, make a difference by reinforcing commitments and encouraging political discussions?

The problem may also be not simply a *lack* of social stimulation, but the growing *diversity* of social stimulation, and a resulting decline in reinforcement. In 1948, Columbia sociologists collected data about the social milieu of each voter and related the effects of the mass media on the voter to the political influences of family, friends, church, etc. They found that a voter's strength of conviction was related to the political homogeneity of the voter's associates. At that time, most voters belonged to politically homogeneous social groups; the social gulf between the parties was so wide that most voters had no close friends or associates voting differently from them. A decline in the political homogeneity of primary groups would lead to less social reinforcement; since the political cleavage patterns which exist today cut more across social groups, voters are in less homogeneous family, church, and work settings and are getting less uniform reinforcement. Whether there is less overall social stimulation today, or whether there is simply less uniformity of social stimulation, the demands on campaigns to pull segments together and create coalitions are vastly greater today than in the past.

What Television Gives Us

Television is giving us less and less direct communication from our leaders and their political campaigns, Daniel Hallin, examining changes in network news coverage of presidents from 1968 to 1988, has found that the average length of the actual quote from a president on the news has gone from forty-five seconds in 1968 to nine seconds today. Instead of a short introduction from a reporter and a long look at the president, we are given a short introduction from the president and a long look at the reporter.

In the opinion of Peggy Noonan, one of the most distinguished speechwriters of recent years, who wrote many of President Reagan's and President Bush's best speeches, the change from long quotes to sound bites has taken much of the content out of campaigning: "it's a media problem. The young people who do speeches for major politicians, they've heard the whole buzz about sound bites. And now instead of writing . . . a serious text with serious arguments, they just write sound bite after sound bite." With less serious argument in the news, there is less material for secondary elites and analysts to digest, and less need for candidates to think through their policies.

We also receive less background information about the campaign and less coverage of the day-to-day pageantry—the stump speeches, rallies, and crowds. Moreover, as Paul Weaver has shown, the reporter's analysis concentrates on the horse-race aspect of the campaign and thus downplays the policy stakes involved. To a network reporter, "politics is essentially a game played by individual politicians for personal advancement . . . the game takes place against a backdrop of governmental institutions, public problems, policy debates, and the like, but these are noteworthy only insofar as they affect, or are used by, players in pursuit of the game's rewards.

As a result of this supposedly critical stance, people are losing the kinds of signals they have always used to read politicians. We see fewer of the kinds of personalized political interactions, including the fun and the pageantry, that help people decide whose side they are on and that help potential leaders assemble coalitions for governing.

Gerald Ford went to a fiesta in San Antonio because he wanted Hispanic voters to see his willingness to visit them on their own ground, and to demonstrate that some of their leaders supported him. He also wanted to remind them of his willingness to deal respectfully with the sovereignty issues raised by the Panama Canal question. But when he bit into an unshucked tamale, these concerns were buried in an avalanche of trivial commentary. Reporters joked that the president was going after the "klutz" vote and talked about "Bozo the Clown." From that moment on, Ford was pictured in the media as laughably uncoordinated. Reporters brought up Lyndon Johnson's contemptuous jibe that Ford "was so dumb he couldn't walk and chew gum at the same time." Jokes circulated that he had played too much football without his helmet. For the rest of the campaign, his every slip was noted on the evening news. Yet the news photos supposedly documenting the president's clumsiness reveal a man of remarkably good balance and body control, given the physical circumstances—not surprising for a man who had been an all-American football player in college and was still, in his sixties, an active downhill skier.

Similarly, during the 1980 campaign, Ronald Reagan visited Dallas and said, in response to a question, that there were "great flaws" in the theory of evolution and that it might be a good idea if the schools taught "creationism" as well. This statement was characterized in the media as the sort at verbal pratfall to be expected from Reagan, and much of the coverage related such gaffes *entirely* to questions about his intellectual capacity, not to the meaning of his appearance or the implications of the appearance for the coalition he was building.

What difference would it have made if press and television reporters had considered these actions by Ford and Reagan as clear and open avowals of sympathy for political causes dear to their hearts? What if Ford's political record on issues dear to Hispanics had been discussed, or if the guest list for the fiesta had been discussed to see which prominent Hispanics were, in fact, endorsing him? The nature of the gathering Reagan attended was noted at the time, but it was never referred to again. It was not until 1984 that Americans uninvolved in religious fundamentalism understood enough about what the Moral Majority stood for to read anything from a politician's embrace of Jerry Falwell, its president, or a religious roundtable such as the one Reagan attended in 1980. By 1988, as more people on the other side of the fundamentalism debates learned what the Moral Majority stood for, the group was disbanded as a political liability.

Television, in other words, is not giving people enough to read about the substance of political coalition building because it ignores many important campaign signals. That rallies and other campaign events are "staged" does not diminish their importance and the legitimate information they can convey to voters. When Richard Nixon met Mao Tse Tung in 1972, the meeting was no less important because it was staged. And when Jesse Jackson praised Lloyd Bentsen by noting the speed with which he could go from biscuits to tacos to caviar, he was acknowledging another fact of great importance: in building coalitions, a candidate must consider the trade-off between offering symbols and making promises.

If politicians cannot show familiarity with people's concerns by properly husking tamales or eating knishes in the right place with the right people, they will have to promise them something. As Jackson noted, the tamales may be better than promises, because promises made to one segment of voters, or one-issue public, will offend other groups and therefore tie the politician's hands in the future policy-making process.

Is it more meaningful when a governor of Georgia hangs a picture of Martin Luther King Jr. in the statehouse, or when a senator or congressman votes for a bill promising full employment? Is it better for a politician to eat a kosher hot dog or to promise never to compromise Israel's borders? When voters are deprived of one shortcut—obvious symbols, for example—obvious promises, for example—instead of turning to more subtle and complicated forms of Information.

How good a substitute are electronic tamales for the real thing? Does watching a fiesta provide any of the stimulation to identification and turnout that attendance at a fiesta provides? How long does it take to bring us together, at least in recognizable coalitions? We need not have answers to these questions to see that they speak to the central issue of stimulating turnout and participation in elections in an age of electronic communities. The media *could* provide more of the kinds of information people use to assess candidates and parties. However, I do not know if electronic tamales provide the social stimulation of interacting with others, or the reinforcement of acting with others who agree, and I do not know how much more potent are ideas brought clearly to mind through using them with others. The demands placed on television are greater than the demands ever placed on radio or newspapers because the world is more diverse today and there are more segments which need to be reunited in campaigns.

Objections and Answers

Two notable objections can be made to my suggestions for increasing campaigning and campaign spending. The first is the "spinmaster" objection: contemporary political campaigns are beyond redemption because campaign strategists have become so adept at manipulation that voters can no longer learn what the candidates really stand for or really intend to do. Significantly, this conclusion is supported by two opposing arguments about voter behavior. One objection is that voters are staying home because they have been turned off by fatuous claims and irrelevant advertising. A variant of this is that voters are being manipulated with great success by unscrupulous campaign advertising, so that their votes reflect more concern with Willie Horton[1] or school prayer or flag burning than with widespread poverty, the banking crisis, or global warming. The second objection is that popular concern with candidates and with government in general has been trivialized, so that candidates fiddle while America burns. In the various versions of this hypothesis, voter turnout is down because today's political contests are waged over small differences on trivial issues. While Eastern Europe plans a future of freedom under eloquent spokesmen like Vaclav Havel, and while Mikhail Gorbachev declares an end to the cold war, releases Eastern Europe from Soviet control, and tries to free his countrymen from the yoke of doctrinaire communism, in America Tweedledum and Tweedledee argue about who loves the flag more while Japan buys Rockefeller Center, banks collapse, and the deficit grows.

Both of these critiques of the contemporary system argue that campaigns themselves are trivial and irrelevant, that campaign advertising and even the candidates' speeches are nothing but self-serving puffery and distortion. This general argument has an aesthetic appeal, especially to better-educated voters and the power elite; campaign commercials remind no one of the Lincoln-Douglas debates, and today's bumper stickers and posters have none of the resonance of the Goddess of Democracy in Tiananmen Square. But elite aesthetics is not the test of this argument; the test is what voters learn from campaigns.

There is ample evidence that voters *do* learn from campaigns. Of course, each campaign tries hard to make its side look better and the other side worse. Despite that, voter perceptions about the candidates and their positions are more accurate. Furthermore, . . . there is no evidence that people learn less from campaigns today than they did in past years. This is a finding to keep in mind at all times, for many of the criticisms of campaigns simplistically assume that because politicians and campaign strategists have manipulative intentions, campaigns necessarily mislead the voter. This assumption is not borne out by the evidence; voters know how to read the media and the politicians better than most media critics acknowledge.

. . . Voters remember past campaigns and presidents, and past failures of performance to match promises. They have a sense of who is with them and who is against them; they make judgments about unfavorable new editorials and advertisements from hostile sources, ignoring some of what is favorable to those they oppose and some of what is unfavorable to those they support. In managing their personal affairs and making decisions about their work, they collect information that they can use as a reality test for campaign claims and media stories, They notice the difference between behavior that has real consequences, on one hand, and mere talk, on the other.

. . . The ability of television news to manipulate voters has been vastly overstated, as one extended example will suggest. In television reporting—but not in the academic literature—it was always assumed before 1984 that winning debates and gaining votes are virtually one and the same. But on Sunday, October 7, 1984, in the first debate between Walter Mondale and Ronald Reagan, this assumption was shown to be flawed. Mondale, generally a dry speaker, was unexpectedly relaxed and articulate, and Reagan, known for his genial and relaxed style, was unexpectedly tense and hesitant. Mondale even threw Reagan off guard by using "There you go again," the jibe Reagan had made famous in his 1980 debate with Jimmy Carter. Immediately after the debate, the CBS News/*New York Times* pollsters phoned a sample of registered voters they had interviewed before the debate, to ask which candidate they were going to vote for and which they thought had done a better job in the debate. Mondale was considered to have "done the best job" by 42 percent to 36 percent, and had gained 3 points in the polls. As a result of similar polls in the next twenty-four hours by other networks and news organizations, the media's main story the rest of the week was of Mondale's upset victory over the president in the debate. Two days later, when another CBS News/*New York Times* poll asked voters about the debate and about their intended vote, Mondale was considered to have "done the best job" not by 42 percent to 36 percent margin of Sunday, but by 65 percent to 17 percent. Media reports, then, claimed that millions of voters had changed their minds about what they themselves had just seen days earlier. Yet in the three days during which millions changed their minds about who had won the debate, the same poll reported, few if any changed their minds about how they would vote.

This example emphasizes just how complex the effects of television can be. Voters now have opinions about opinions. When asked who won the debate, they may say not what they think personally, but what they have heard that the majority of Americans think. It is easier to change their opinions about what their neighbors think than to change their own opinions. And most important of all, it is clear that they understand the difference between a debater and a president, and that they don't easily change their political views about who they want to run the country simply on the basis of debating skills.

Critics of campaign spinmasters and of television in general are fond of noting that campaigners and politicians intend to manipulate and deceive, but they wrongly credit them with more success than they deserve. As Michael Schudson has noted, in the television age, whenever a president's popularity has been high, it has been attributed to unusual talents for using television to sell his image. He notes, for example, that in 1977 the television critic of the *New York Times* called President Carter "a master of controlled images," and that during the 1976 primaries David Halberstam wrote that Carter "more than any other candidate this year has sensed and adapted to modern communications and national mood. . . . Watching him again and again on television I was impressed by his sense of pacing, his sense of control, very low key, soft." A few years later this master of images still had the same soft, low-key voice, but now it was interpreted as indicating not quiet strength but weakness and indecision. Gerald Rafshoon, the media man for this "master of television," concluded after the 1980 campaign that all the television time bought for Carter wasn't as useful as three more helicopters (and a successful desert rescue) would have been.

As these examples suggest, media critics are generally guilty of using one of the laziest and easiest information shortcuts of all. Assuming that a popular politician is a good manipulator of the media or that a winner won because of his media style is not different from what voters do when they evaluate presidents by reasoning backward from known results. The media need reform, but so do the media critics. One cannot infer, without astonishing hubris, that the American people have been successfully deceived simply because a politician wanted them to believe his or her version of events. But the media critics who analyze political texts without any reference to the actual impact of the messages do just that.

Negativism and Triviality

Campaigns are often condemned as trivial—as sideshows in which voters amuse themselves by learning about irrelevant differences between candidates who fiddle over minor issues while the country stagnates and inner cities burn—and many assume that the negativism and pettiness of the attacks that candidates make on each other encourage an "a pox on all your houses" attitude. This suggests a plausible hypothesis, which can be given a clean test in a simple experiment. This experiment can be thought of as a "stop and think" experiment because it is a test of what happens if people stop and think about what they know of the candidates and issues in an election and tell someone what they know. First, take a random sample of people across the country and interview them. Ask the people selected what they consider to be the most important issues facing the country, and then ask them where the various candidates stand on these issues. Then ask them to state their likes and dis-likes about the candidates' personal qualities and issue stands, and about the state of the country. Second, after the election, find out whether these interviewees were more or less likely to vote than people who were not asked to talk about the campaign. If the people interviewed voted less often than people not interviewed, then there is clear support for the charge that triviality, negativism, and irrelevancy are turning off the American people and suppressing turnout.

In fact, the National Election Studies done by the University of Michigan's Survey Research Center, now the Center for Political Studies, are exactly such an experiment. In every election since 1952, people have been asked what they care about, what the candidates care about, and what they know about the campaign. After the election people have been reinterviewed and asked whether they voted; then the actual voting records have been checked to see whether the respondents did indeed vote.

The results convincingly demolish the triviality and negativism hypothesis. In every election, people who have been interviewed are more likely to vote than other Americans. Indeed, the reason the expensive and difficult procedure of verifying turnout against the voting records was begun in the first place was that the scholars were suspicious because the turnout reported by respondents was so much higher than either the actual turnout of all Americans or the turnout in surveys conducted after the election. So respondents in the national election studies, after seventy minutes of thinking about the candidates, the issues, and the campaign, were both more likely than other people to vote and more likely to try to hide the fact that they did not vote! Further, if people are reinterviewed in later elections, their turnout continues to rise. Still further, while an interview cuts nonvoting in a presidential election by up to 20 percent, an interview in a local primary may cut nonvoting by as much as half.

The rise in no-shows on voting day and the rise of negative campaigning both follow from the rise of candidate-centered elections. When voters do not have information about future policies they extrapolate, or project, from the information they have. As campaigns become more centered on candidates, there is more projection, and hence more negative campaigning. Negative campaigning is designed to provide information that causes voters to stop projecting and to change their beliefs about a candidate's stand on the issues. "Willie Horton . . . was a legitimate issue because it speaks to styles and ways of governance. In that case Dukakis's."

As Noonan has also noted of the 1988 campaign, "There should have been more name-calling, mud slinging and fun. It should have been rock-'em-sock-'em the way great campaigns have been in the past. It was tedious." Campaigns cannot deal with anything substantive if they cannot get the electorate's attention and interest people in listening to their music. Campaigns need to make noise. The tradition of genteel populism in America, and the predictable use of sanitary metaphors to condemn politicians and their modes of communication, says more about the distaste of the people who use the sanitary metaphors for American society than it does about the failing politicians.

The challenge to the future of American campaigns, and hence to American democracy, is how to bring back the excitement and the music in an age of electronic campaigning. Today's campaigns have more to do because an educated, media-centered society is a broadened and segmented electorate which is harder to rally, while today's campaigns have less money and troops with which to fight their battles.

·◄◉►·

When I first began to work in presidential campaigns I had very different ideas about how to change campaigns and their coverage than I have today. Coverage of rallies and fiestas, I used to think, belonged in the back of the paper along with stories about parties, celebrity fund-raisers, and fad diets. Let the society editor cover banquets and rubber chickens, I thought; the reporters in Washington could analyze the speeches and discuss the policy implications of competing proposals.

I still wish that candidates' proposals and speeches were actually analyzed for their content and implications for our future. I still wish that television told us more about how elites evaluate presidential initiatives than what my neighbors said about them in the next day's polls. However, I now appreciate the intimate relationships between the rallies and governance which escaped me in the past. I now appreciate how hard it is to bring a country together, to gather all the many concerns and interests into a single coalition and hold it together in order to govern.

Campaigns are essential in any society, particularly in a society that is culturally, economically, and socially diverse. If voters look for information about candidates under streetlights, then that is where candidates must campaign, and the only way to improve elections is to add streetlights. Reforms can only make sense if they are consistent with the gut rationality of voters. Ask not for more sobriety and piety from citizens, for they are voters, not judges; offer them instead cues and signals which connect their world with the world of politics.

Note

1. [Willie Horton, a convicted murderer, escaped a prison furlough approved by then-governor of Massachusetts Michael Dukakis and committed a violent crime. George Bush exploited the incident in his campaign against Dukakis during the 1988 presidential race.—Eds.]

NO

Anthony King

Running Scared

To an extent that astonishes a foreigner, modern America is *about* the holding of elections. Americans do not merely have elections on the first Tuesday after the first Monday of November in every year divisible by four. They have elections on the first Tuesday after the first Monday of November in every year divisible by two. In addition, five states have elections in odd-numbered years. Indeed, there is no year in the United States—ever—when a major statewide election is not being held somewhere. To this catalogue of general elections has of course to be added an equally long catalogue of primary elections (for example, forty-three presidential primaries [in 1996]). Moreover, not only do elections occur very frequently in the United States but the number of jobs legally required to be filled by them is enormous—from the presidency of the United States to the post of local consumer advocate in New York. It has been estimated that no fewer than half a million elective offices are filled or waiting to be filled in the United States today.

Americans take the existence of their never-ending election campaign for granted. Some like it, some dislike it, and most are simply bored by it. But they are all conscious of it, in the same way that they are conscious of Mobil, McDonald's, *Larry King Live,* Oprah Winfrey, the Dallas Cowboys, the Ford Motor Company, and all the other symbols and institutions that make up the rich tapestry of American life.

To a visitor to America's shores, however, the never-ending campaign presents a largely unfamiliar spectacle. In other countries election campaigns have both beginnings and ends, and there are even periods, often prolonged periods, when no campaigns take place at all. Other features of American elections are also unfamiliar. In few countries do elections and campaigns cost as much as they do in the United States. In no other country is the role of organized political parties so limited.

America's permanent election campaign, together with other aspects of American electoral politics, has one crucial consequence, little noticed but vitally important for the functioning of American democracy. Quite simply, the American electoral system places politicians in a highly vulnerable position. Individually and collectively they are more vulnerable, more of the time, to the vicissitudes of electoral politics than are the politicians of any other democratic country. Because they are more vulnerable, they devote more of their time to electioneering, and their conduct in office is more continuously governed by electoral considerations. I will argue that American politicians' constant and unremitting electoral preoccupations have deleterious consequences for the functioning of the American system. They consume time and scarce resources. Worse, they make it harder than it would otherwise be for the system as a whole to deal with some of America's most pressing problems. Americans often complain that their system is not sufficiently democratic. I will argue that, on the contrary, there is a sense in which the system is too democratic and ought to be made less so. . . .

Fear and Trembling

Politics and government in the United States are marked by the fact that U.S. elected officials in many cases have very short terms of office *and* face the prospect of being defeated in primary elections *and* have to run for office more as individuals than as standard-bearers for their party *and* have continually to raise large sums of money in order to finance their own election campaigns. Some of these factors operate in other countries. There is no other country, however, in which all of them operate, and operate simultaneously. The cumulative consequences, as we shall see, are both pervasive and profound.

The U.S. Constitution sets out in one of its very first sentences that "the House of Representatives shall be composed of members chosen every second year by the people of the several states." When the Founding Fathers decided on such a short term of office for House members, they were setting a precedent that has been followed by no other major democratic country. In Great Britain, France, Italy, and Canada the constitutional or legal maximum for the duration of the lower house of the national legislature is five years. In Germany and Japan the equivalent term is four years. Only in Australia and New Zealand, whose institutions are in some limited respects modeled on those of the United States, are the legal maximums as short as three years. In having two-year terms the United States stands alone.

Members of the Senate are, of course, in a quite different position. Their constitutionally prescribed term of office, six-years, is long by anyone's standards. But senators' six-year terms are not all they seem. In the first place, so pervasive is the electioneering atmosphere that even newly elected senators begin almost at once to lay plans for their re-election campaigns. Senator Daniel Patrick Moynihan, of New York, recalls that when he first came to the Senate, in 1977, his colleagues when they met over lunch or a drink usually talked about politics and policy. Now they talk about almost nothing but the latest opinion polls. In the second place, the fact that under the Constitution the terms of a third of the Senate end every two years means that even if individual senators do not feel themselves to be under continuing electoral pressure, the Senate as a whole does. Despite the Founders' intentions, the Senate's collective electoral sensibilities increasingly resemble those of the House.

Most Americans seem unaware of the fact, but the direct primary—a government-organized popular election to nominate candidates for public office—is, for better or worse, an institution peculiar to the United States. Neither primary elections nor their functional equivalents exist anywhere else in the democratic world. It goes without saying that their effect is to add a further dimension of uncertainty and unpredictability to the world of American elective politicians.

In most other countries the individual holder of public office, so long as he or she is reasonably conscientious and does not gratuitously offend local or regional party opinion, has no real need to worry about renomination. To be sure, cases of parties refusing to renominate incumbent legislators are not unknown in countries such as France, Germany, and Canada, but they are relatively rare and tend to occur under unusual circumstances. The victims are for the most part old, idle, or alcoholic.

The contrast between the rest of the world and the United States could hardly be more striking. In 1979 no fewer than 104 of the 382 incumbent members of the House of Representatives who sought re-election faced primary opposition. In the following three elections the figures were ninety-three out of 398 (1980), ninety-eight out of 393 (1982), and 130 out of 409 (1984). More recently, in 1994, nearly a third of all House incumbents seeking re-election, 121 out of 386, had to face primary opposition, and in the Senate the proportion was even higher: eleven out of twenty-six. Even those incumbents who did not face opposition could seldom be certain in advance that they were not going to. The influence—and the possibility—of primaries is pervasive. As we shall see, the fact that incumbents usually win is neither here nor there.

To frequent elections and primary elections must be added another factor that contributes powerfully to increasing the electoral vulnerability of U.S. politicians: the relative lack of what we might call "party cover." In most democratic countries the fate of most politicians depends not primarily on their own endeavors but on the fate—locally, regionally, or nationally—of their party. If their party does well in an election, so do they. If not, not. The individual politician's interests and those of his party are bound together.

In contrast, America's elective politicians are on their own—not only in relation to politicians in most other countries but also in absolute terms. Party is still a factor in U.S. electoral politics, but it is less so than anywhere else in the democratic world. As a result, American legislators seeking re-election are forced to raise their own profiles, to make their own records, and to fight their own re-election campaigns.

If politicians are so vulnerable electorally, it may be protested, why aren't more of them defeated? In particular, why aren't more incumbent congressmen and senators defeated? The analysis here would seem to imply a very high rate of turnover in Congress, but in fact the rate—at least among incumbents seeking re-election—is notoriously low. How can this argument and the facts of congressional incumbents' electoral success be reconciled?

This objection has to be taken seriously, because the facts on which it is based are substantially correct. The number of incumbent congressmen and senators defeated in either primary or general elections *is* low. But to say that because incumbent members of Congress are seldom defeated, they are not really vulnerable electorally is to miss two crucial points. The first is that precisely because they are vulnerable, they go to prodigious lengths to protect themselves. Like workers in nuclear-power stations, they take the most extreme safety precautions, and the fact that the precautions are almost entirely successful does not make them any less necessary.

Second, congressmen and senators go to inordinate lengths to secure re-election because, although they may objectively be safe (in the view of journalists and academic political scientists), they do not *know* they are safe—and even if they think they are, the price of being wrong is enormous. The probability that anything will go seriously wrong with a nuclear-power station may approach zero, but the stations tend nevertheless to be built away from the centers of large cities. A congressman or a senator may believe that he is reasonably safe, but if he wants to be re-elected, he would be a fool to act on that belief.

How They Came to Be Vulnerable

American politicians run scared—and are right to do so. And they run more scared than the politicians of any other democratic country—again rightly. How did this come to be so?

The short answer is that the American people like it that way. They are, and have been for a very long time, the Western world's hyperdemocrats. They are keener on democracy than almost anyone else and are more determined that democratic norms and practices should pervade every aspect of national life. To explore the implications of this central fact about the United States, and to see how it came to be, we need to examine two different interpretations of the term "democracy." Both have been discussed from time to time by political philosophers, but they have never been codified and they certainly cannot be found written down in a constitution or any other formal statement of political principles. Nevertheless, one or the other underpins the political practice of every democratic country—even if, inevitably, the abstract conception and the day-to-day practice are never perfectly matched.

One of these interpretations might be labeled "division of labor." In this view, there are in any democracy two classes of people—the governors and the governed. The function of the governors is to take decisions on the basis of what they believe to be in the country's best interests and to act on those decisions. If public opinion broadly supports the decisions, that is a welcome bonus. If not, too bad. The views of the people at large are merely one datum among a large number of data that need to be considered. They are not accorded any special status. Politicians in countries that operate within this view can frequently be heard using phrases like "the need for strong leadership" and "the need to take tough decisions." They often take a certain pride in doing what they believe to be right even if the opinion of the majority is opposed to it.

The function of the governed in such a system, if it is a genuine democracy, is very important but strictly limited. It is not to determine public policy or to decide what is the right thing to do. Rather, it is to go to the polls from time to time to choose those who will determine public policy and decide what the right thing is: namely, the governors. The deciding of issues by the electorate is secondary to the election of the individuals who are to do the deciding. The analogy is with choosing a doctor. The patient certainly chooses which doctor to see but does not normally decide (or even try to decide) on the detailed course of treatment. The division of labor is informal but clearly understood.

It is probably fair to say that most of the world's major democracies— Great Britain, France, Germany, Japan—operate on this basis. The voters go to the polls every few years, and in between times it is up to the government of the day to get on with governing. Electing a government and governing are two different businesses. Electioneering is, if anything, to be deplored if it gets in the way of governing.

This is a simplified picture, of course. Democratically elected politicians are ultimately dependent on the electorate, and if at the end of the day the electorate does not like what they are doing, they are dead. Nevertheless, the central point remains. The existing division of labor is broadly accepted.

The other interpretation of democracy, the one dominant in America, might be called the "agency" view, and it is wholly different. According to this view, those who govern a country should function as no more than the agents of the people. The job of the governors is not to act independently and to take whatever decisions they believe to be in the national interest but, rather, to reflect in all their actions the views of the majority of the people, whatever those views may be. Governors are not really governors at all; they are representatives, in the very narrow sense of being in office solely to represent the views of those who sent them there.

In the agency view, representative government of the kind common throughout the democratic world can only be second-best. The ideal system would be one in which there were no politicians or middlemen of any kind and the people governed themselves directly; the political system would take the form of more or less continuous town meetings or referenda, perhaps conducted by means of interactive television. Most Americans, at bottom, would still like to see their country governed by a town meeting.

Why Their Vulnerability Matters

In this political ethos, finding themselves inhabiting a turbulent and torrid electoral environment, most American elective officials respond as might be expected: in an almost Darwinian way. They adapt their behavior—their roll-call votes, their introduction of bills, their committee assignments, their phone calls, their direct-mail letters, their speeches, their press releases, their sound bites, whom they see, how they spend their time, their trips abroad, their trips back home, and frequently their private and families' lives—to their environment: that is, to their primary and overriding need for electoral survival. The effects are felt not only in the lives of individual officeholders and their staffs but also in America's political institutions as a whole and the shape and content of U.S. public policy.

It all begins with officeholders' immediate physical environment: with bricks, mortar, leather, and wood paneling. The number of congressional buildings and the size of congressional staffs have ballooned in recent decades. At the start of the 1960s most members of the House of Representatives contented themselves with a small inner office and an outer office; senators' office suites were not significantly larger. Apart from the Capitol itself, Congress was reasonably comfortably housed in four buildings, known to Washington taxi drivers as the Old and New House and Senate Office Buildings. The designations Old and New cannot be used any longer, however, because there are now so many even newer congressional buildings.

Congressional staffs have grown at roughly the same rate, the new buildings having been built mainly to house the staffs. In 1957 the total number of people employed by members of the House and Senate as personal staff was 3,556. By 1991 the figure had grown to 11,572—a more than threefold increase within the political lifetime of many long-serving members. [In 1996] the total number of people employed by Congress in all capacities; including committee staffs and the staffs of support agencies like the Congressional Research Service, was 32,820, making Congress by far the most heavily staffed legislative branch in the world.

Much of the growth of staff in recent decades has been in response to the growth of national government, to Congress's insistence on strengthening its policymaking role in the aftermath of Vietnam and Watergate, and to decentralization within Congress, which has led subcommittee chairmen and the subcommittees themselves to acquire their own staffs. But there is no doubt that the increase is also in response to congressional incumbents' ever-increasing electoral exposure. Congress itself has become an integral part of America's veritable "elections industry."

One useful measure of the changes that have taken place—and also an important consequence of the changes—is the increased proportion of staff and staff time devoted to constituent service. As recently as 1972 only 1,189 House employees—22.5 percent of House members' personal staffs—were based in home-district offices. By 1992 the number had more than doubled, to 3,128, and the proportion had nearly doubled, to 42.1 percent. On the Senate side there were only 303 state-based staffers in 1972, making up 12.5 percent of senators' personal staffs, but the number had more than quadrupled by 1992 to 1,368, for fully 31.6 percent of the total. Since a significant proportion of the time of Washington-based congressional staffs is also devoted to constituent service, it is a fair guess that more than half of the time of all congressional staffs is now given over to nursing the district or state rather than to legislation and policymaking.

Much constituent service is undoubtedly altruistic, inspired by politicians' sense of duty (and constituents' understandable frustration with an unresponsive bureaucracy); but at the same time nobody doubts that a large proportion of it is aimed at securing re-election. The statistics on the outgoing mail of members of Congress and their use of the franking privilege point in that direction too. Congressional mailings grew enormously in volume from some 100 million pieces a year in the early 1960s to more than 900 million in 1984—nearly five pieces of congressional mail for every adult American. New restrictions on franking introduced in the 1990s have made substantial inroads into that figure, but not surprisingly the volume of mail emanating from both houses of Congress is still invariably higher in election years.

The monetary costs of these increases in voter-oriented congressional activities are high: in addition to being the most heavily staffed legislative branch in the world, Congress is also the most expensive. But there is another, non-monetary cost: the staffs themselves become one of the congressman's or senator's constituencies, requiring management, taking up time, and always being tempted to go into business for themselves. American scholars who have studied the burgeoning of congressional staffs express concern about their cumulative impact on Congress as a deliberative body in which face-to-face communication between members, and between members and their constituents, facilitates both mutual understanding and an understanding of the issues. Largely in response to the requirements of electioneering, more and more congressional business is conducted through dense networks of staffers.

One familiar effect of American politicians' vulnerability is the power it accords to lobbyists and special-interest groups, especially those that can muster large numbers of votes or have large amounts of money to spend on campaigns. Members of Congress walk the electoral world alone. They can be picked off one by one, they know it, and they adjust their behavior accordingly. The power of the American Association of Retired Persons, the National Rifle Association, the banking industry, and the various veterans' lobbies is well known. It derives partly from their routine contributions to campaign funds and the quality of their lobbying activities in Washington, but far more from the votes that the organizations may be able to deliver and from congressmen's and senators' calculations of how the positions they take in the present may affect their chances of re-election in the future—a future that rarely is distant. Might a future challenger be able to use that speech against me? Might I be targeted for defeat by one of the powerful lobbying groups?

A second effect is that American politicians are even more likely than those in other countries to engage in symbolic politics: to use words masquerading as deeds, to take actions that purport to be instrumental but are in fact purely rhetorical. A problem exists; the people demand that it be solved; the politicians cannot solve it and know so; they engage in an elaborate pretense of trying to solve it nevertheless, often at great expense to the taxpayers and almost invariably at a high cost in terms of both the truth and the politicians' own reputations for integrity and effectiveness. The politicians lie in most cases not because they are liars or approve of lying but because the potential electoral costs of not lying are too great.

At one extreme, symbolic politics consists of speechmaking and public position-taking in the absence of any real action or any intention of taking action; casting the right vote is more important than achieving the right outcome. At the other extreme, symbolic politics consists of whole government programs that are ostensibly designed to achieve one set of objectives but are actually designed to achieve other objectives (in some cases simply the re-election of the politicians who can claim credit for them).

Take as an example the crime bills passed by Congress in the 1980s and 1990s, with their mandatory-minimum sentences, their three-strikes-and-you're-out provisions, and their extension of the federal death penalty to fifty new crimes. The anti-drug and anti-crime legislation, by the testimony of judges and legal scholars, has been at best useless and at worst wholly pernicious in its effects, in that it has filled prison cells not with violent criminals but with drug users and low-level drug pushers. As for the death penalty, a simple measure of its sheer irrelevance to the federal government's war on crime is easily provided. The last federal offender to be put to death, Victor H. Feguer, a convicted kidnapper, was hanged in March of 1963. By the end of 1995 no federal offender had been executed for more than thirty years, and hardly any offenders were awaiting execution on death row. The ferocious-seeming federal statutes were almost entirely for show.

The way in which the wars on drugs and crime were fought cannot be understood without taking into account the incessant pressure that elected officeholders felt they were under from the electorate. As one former congressman puts it, "Voters were afraid of criminals, and politicians were afraid of voters." This fear reached panic proportions in election years. Seven of the years from 1981 to 1994 were election years nationwide; seven were not. During those fourteen years Congress passed no fewer than seven major crime bills. Of those seven, six were passed in election years (usually late in the year). That is, there was only one election year in which a major crime bill was *not* passed, and only one nonelection year in which a major crime bill *was* passed.

Another effect of the extreme vulnerability of American politicians is that it is even harder for them than for democratically elected politicians in other countries to take tough decisions: to court unpopularity, to ask for sacrifices, to impose losses, to fly in the face of conventional wisdom—in short, to act in what they believe to be their constituents' interest and the national interest rather than in their own interest. Timothy J. Penny, a Democrat who left the House of Representatives in 1994, put the point starkly, perhaps even too harshly, in *Common Cents* (1995).

> Voters routinely punish lawmakers who try to do unpopular things, who challenge them to face unpleasant truths about the budget, crime, Social Security, or tax policy. Similarly, voters reward politicians for giving them what they want—more spending for popular programs—even if it means wounding the nation in the long run by creating more debt. . . .

What, if Anything, Might Be Done?

Precisely because American politicians are so exposed electorally, they probably have to display—and do display—more political courage more often than the politicians of any other democratic country. The number of political saints and martyrs in the United States is unusually large.

There is, however, no special virtue in a political system that requires large numbers of politicians to run the risk of martyrdom in order to ensure that tough decisions can be taken in a timely manner in the national interest. The number of such decisions that need to be taken is always likely to be large; human nature being what it is, the supply of would-be martyrs is always likely to be small. On balance it would seem better not to try to eliminate the electoral risks (it can never be done in a democracy) but to reduce somewhat their scale and intensity. There is no reason why the risks run by American politicians should be so much greater than the risks run by elective politicians in other democratic countries.

How, then, might the risks be reduced? What can be done? A number of reforms to the existing system suggest themselves. It may be that none of them is politically feasible—Americans hold tight to the idea of agency democracy—but in principle there should be no bar to any of them. One of the simplest would also be the most radical: to lengthen the terms of members of the House of Representatives from two years to four. The proposal is by no means a new one: at least 123 resolutions bearing on the subject were introduced in Congress in the eighty years from 1885 to 1965, and President Lyndon B. Johnson advocated the change in his State of the Union address in January of 1966.

A congressman participating in a Brookings Institution round table held at about the time of Johnson's message supported the change, saying, "I think that the four years would help you to be a braver congressman, and I think what you need is bravery. I think you need courage." Another congressman on the same occasion cited the example of another bill that he believed had the support of a majority in the House. "That bill is not going to come up this year. You know why it is not coming up? . . . Because four hundred and thirty-five of us have to face election. . . . If we had a four-year term, I am as confident as I can be the bill would have come to the floor and passed."

A similar case could be made for extending the term of senators to eight years, with half the Senate retiring or running for re-election every four years. If the terms of members of both houses were thus extended and made to coincide, the effect in reducing America's never-ending election campaign would be dramatic.

There is much to be said, too, for all the reasons mentioned so far, for scaling down the number of primary elections. They absorb extravagant amounts of time, energy, and money; they serve little democratic purpose; few people bother to vote in them; and they place additional and unnecessary pressure on incumbent officeholders. Since the main disadvantage of primaries is the adverse effect they have on incumbents, any reforms probably ought to be concerned with protecting incumbents' interests.

At the moment, the primary laws make no distinction between situations in which a seat in the House or the Senate is already occupied and situations in which the incumbent is, for whatever reason, standing down. The current laws provide for a primary to be held in either case. An incumbent is therefore treated as though the seat in question were open and he or she were merely one of the candidates for it. A relatively simple reform would be to distinguish between the two situations. If a seat was open, primaries would be held in both parties, as now; but if the incumbent announced that he or she intended to run for re-election, then a primary in his or her party would be held only if large numbers of party supporters were determined to have one—that is, were determined that the incumbent should be ousted. The obvious way to ascertain whether such determination existed would be by means of a petition supervised by the relevant state government and requiring a considerable number of signatures. The possibility of a primary would thus be left open, but those who wanted one would have to show that they were both numerous and serious. A primary would not be held simply because an ambitious, possibly demented, possibly wealthy individual decided to throw his or her hat into the ring.

Any steps to strengthen the parties as institutions would be desirable on the same grounds. Lack of party cover in the United States means that elective officeholders find it hard to take tough decisions partly because they lack safety in numbers. They can seldom, if ever, say to an aggrieved constituent or a political-action committee out for revenge, "I had to vote that way because my party told me to," or even "I had to vote that way because we in my party all agreed that we would." Lack of party cohesion, together with American voters' disposition to vote for the individual rather than the party, means that congressmen and senators are always in danger of being picked off one by one.

Ballot Fatigue

What might be done to give both parties more backbone? Clearly, the parties would be strengthened—and elective officeholders would not need to raise so much money for their own campaigns—if each party organization became a major source of campaign funding. In the unlikely event (against the background of chronic budget deficits) that Congress ever gets around to authorizing the federal funding of congressional election campaigns, a strong case could be made for channeling as much of the money as possible through the parties, and setting aside some of it to cover their administrative and other ongoing costs.

The party organizations and the nexus between parties and their candidates would also be strengthened if it were made easier for ordinary citizens to give money to the parties and for the parties to give money to their candidates. Until 1986, when the program was abolished, tax credits were available for taxpayers who contributed small sums to the political parties. These credits could be restored. Larry J. Sabato, a political scientist at the University of Virginia, has similarly suggested that citizens entitled to a tax refund could be allowed to divert a small part of their refund to the party of their choice. Such measures would not, however, reduce candidates' dependence on donations from wealthy individuals and PACS [political action committees] unless they were accompanied by measures enabling the parties to contribute more generously to their candidates' campaigns. At the moment there are strict legal limits on the amount of money that national or state party organizations can contribute to the campaigns of individual candidates. The limits should be raised (and indexed to inflation). There is even a case for abolishing them altogether.

All that said, there is an even more straightforward way of reducing incumbents' dependence on campaign contributions. At present incumbents have to spend so much time raising funds because the campaigns themselves are so expensive. They could be made cheaper. This, of course, would be one of the effects of making U.S. elections less numerous and less frequent than they are now. Another way to lower the cost of elections would be to provide candidates and parties with free air time on television and radio.

POSTSCRIPT

Do Political Campaigns Promote Good Government?

The right of people to choose their governors is the essence of democracy. In that spirit Popkin argues that Americans need more democracy—that is, more participation by the people, inspired by more campaigning and political education. Roderick P. Hart, in *Campaign Talk: Why Elections Are Good for Us* (Princeton University Press, 2000), endorses the view that campaigns inform us, explain the concerns of others, and encourage voting, or at least a heightened sense of the political world. King vigorously dissents, asserting that America has an excess of democracy and that the burden imposed by so many and so frequent elections is too great and leads to disillusion and nonvoting.

Catherine Shaw, a three-term mayor of Ashland, Oregon, has written an illuminating how-to book on political campaigning entitled *The Campaign Manager: Running and Winning Local Elections*, 2d ed. (Westview Press, 2000). Shaw's book provides some support for those who value campaigns for the information and understanding that they provide for voters as well as for those who bemoan the time and effort it takes to run for office.

In order to stimulate greater voter participation, beginning in 1972 radical reforms were adopted to ensure that the presidential nominees of the two major parties would be those favored by the largest proportion of party members participating in the primaries and caucuses in which the national convention delegates were chosen. The local party organization plays a greatly reduced role because it no longer hand-picks the delegates. The national convention plays a greatly reduced role because it no longer engages in any real deliberation regarding the choice of nominee. For better or worse, the electorate gets the presidential candidate endorsed by the largest number of delegates.

More directly, the people vote in primaries in order to designate candidates for all other elective offices. This means that voters are exposed to more and longer campaigns; they should therefore be motivated and informed both in the long primary campaign before the party choices are made and in the months leading up to the election before the officeholders are chosen.

A classic text that provides an overview of presidential campaigns is Nelson W. Polsby and Aaron Wildavsky, *Presidential Elections: Strategies and Structures of American Politics*, 10th ed. (Chatham House, 2000). Ever since Theodore White began his distinguished series of vivid accounts with *The Making of the President 1960* (Atheneum, 1961), each presidential election has produced a spate of books providing insightful analysis and insider revelations regarding the conduct of the campaign. One of the best is Richard Ben Cramer, *What It Takes: The Way to the White House* (Random House, 1992). In the tradition of White's intimate journalism is Bob Woodward's account of the 1996 presidential campaigns of President Bill Clinton and Senator Bob Dole, *The Choice: How Clinton Won* (Simon & Schuster, 1997).

ISSUE 3

Is There an Emerging Democratic Majority?

YES: John B. Judis and Ruy Teixeira, from *The Emerging Democratic Majority* (Scribner, 2002)

NO: Daniel Casse, from "An Emerging Republican Majority?" *Commentary* (January 2003)

ISSUE SUMMARY

YES: Social analysts John B. Judis and Ruy Teixeira argue that on key issues the Democratic Party is more in line with the values of modern, postindustrial America than the Republican Party is.

NO: Public communications director Daniel Casse contends that the Republicans occupy the middle ground on domestic issues, driving the Democrats to adopt less popular, extreme positions.

Since the election of Abraham Lincoln in 1860, there have been two—and only two—major political parties in the United States: the Republican Party and the Democratic Party. Throughout the nation's history, the major parties have played indispensable roles: presenting candidates, serving as convenient labels for differing views, getting out the vote, and providing "a place at the table" for previously disfranchised or neglected populations, such as the Irish in the late nineteenth century and African Americans in the twentieth.

For many decades after the Civil War the two major parties differed on major issues, but only in degree, so that one party could be characterized as more conservative or liberal on a particular issue. This was seen as desirable in order for the parties to make the broadest possible appeal to the largest number of voters. An example of this may be seen in the Democratic Party from the 1930s to the 1960s, which contained both the strongest supporters of federal civil rights, liberals and African Americans, and the strongest opponents, the southerners who had been the backbone of the party since the Civil War and who usually occupied key leadership positions in Congress.

Curiously, the most significant sign of the realignment of the parties occurred when each nominated a candidate who was identified as clearly ideological but who was perceived by many voters as out of the mainstream.

This occurred when the Republicans nominated Senator Barry Goldwater, who unabashedly called himself a conservative, but was defeated in a landslide by President Lyndon Johnson in 1964. This was almost the political mirror image of what happened just eight years later, in 1972, when the Democrats nominated Senator George McGovern, who proudly defended his liberal principles and who was roundly defeated by President Richard Nixon.

Goldwater and McGovern were harbingers of a movement toward more ideologically polarized parties. That began to happen with the election of conservative Republican Ronald Reagan to the presidency in 1980 and culminated with the Republican capture of congressional majorities in 1994. The once "solid South" for Democrats became increasingly Republican, suburbs that were once safely Republican became more competitive, and the political map became more ideological. Voters can, by and large, expect Democrats to favor the right to abortion and Republicans to oppose it. Similarly, voters can expect most Republicans to support cutting taxes and most Democrats to spend more tax money on social programs such as Medicare and prescription drug coverage.

In 1969 political commentator Kevin Phillips wrote the book *The Emerging Republican Majority,* urging that Republicans adopt a "Southern strategy" that would require an increasing appeal to white conservatives and an abandonment of any effective appeal to the Northeast liberal establishment or African American voters. This is what happened, and race along with the issues that voters identify with race (including civil rights, affirmative action, and the rights of accused persons) became a dominant, if often unspoken, theme of American politics. Because of this strategy, no Democratic presidential candidate since Johnson has received a majority of the votes cast by white voters, not even in the three elections of Jimmy Carter and Bill Clinton. This is not to say that either party has not reached out to interests that have not been closely allied with it. Nevertheless, there has been a conspicuous ideological, racial, sectional, and economic class realignment of the parties.

As the prominence of a particular issue rises and falls, so do the fortunes of the major parties. Since 1995 Republicans have controlled the House for ten consecutive years and the Senate for only two years less (because of the defection of a Republican senator). Does this mean that an era marked by a Republican majority has begun? Or is it just an aberration? In the first decade of the twenty-first century, the prospect of either party controlling the presidency, the two houses of Congress, and over a period of time the federal judiciary depends on the movement of American politics in a more conservative (Republican) or a more liberal (Democratic) direction.

In the following selections, John B. Judis and Ruy Teixeira contend that the pendulum is swinging back to the Democrats and a greater role for government in dealing with the economic and social issues of a postindustrial economy. Daniel Casse argues that this viewpoint is contradicted by the election results in 2002 and the more favorable image that voters have of Republicans and of its more moderate image.

John B. Judis and
Ruy Teixeira

 **YES**

The Progressive Center

These are turbulent and unusual times. In the 1990s, America saw its longest peacetime economic expansion, including a half decade of spectacular economic performance, led by computer automation and the Internet. Although superficially identified with twenty-something millionaires making a killing on dotcom stocks, the period presaged a postindustrial society in which advanced electronic technology would progressively liberate human beings from repetitive drudgery and toil; in which knowledge and intelligence would displace brute physical power as the engine of economic growth; and in which citizens could increasingly devote their lives to the pursuit of knowledge and happiness. The boom of the nineties was followed, of course, by a recession and by the onset of a war against radical Islamic terrorists who, if successful in their jihad, would have undermined the promise of postindustrial society and plunged the world back into the dark uncertainty and otherworldly fanaticism of the Middle Ages.

In the midst of these tumultuous times, the United States has been undergoing a significant political transition from a conservative Republican majority, which dominated American politics during the 1980s and maintains a weak grip on national power, to a new Democratic majority, which began to emerge during the Clinton presidencies of the 1990s. This new majority is intimately bound up with the changes that America began to go through in the last part of the twentieth century: from an industrial to a postindustrial society, from a white Protestant to a multiethnic, religiously diverse society in which men and women play roughly equal roles at home and at work, and from a society of geographically distinct city, suburb, and country to one of large, sweeping postindustrial metropolises.

The conservative Republican realignment of the 1980s was in large part a reaction to the turmoil of the sixties and seventies. It sought to contain or roll back the demands of civil rights protesters, feminists, environmentalists, welfare rights organizers, and consumer activists. It was also a reaction to the changes wrought in family structure, work, neighborhood, and ethnic composition by the transition to postindustrial capitalism. And it was a protest against government programs that cost too much and accomplished too little in the midst of a stagnating economy.

Much of that political reaction was inevitable and understandable. Some government programs did waste resources and did little to promote better citizens and a better society. Welfare, as originally devised, did encourage family breakup; much public housing fostered ghetto crime. And the intersection of war and social protest gave the movements of the sixties an apocalyptic edge. The civil rights movement degenerated into ghetto riots and gun-toting militants; feminists ended up challenging the utility of the family and of marriage; consumer activists looked down upon the tastes and habits of average Americans; the counterculture championed drugs and mocked traditional religion in favor of fads and cults; and community organizers encouraged the poor to depend on government handouts.

But the conservative reaction has ranged to extremes of its own. It exploited white Southern resistance to racial desegregation; it denigrated single mothers and working women while stigmatizing homosexuals; it rejected any government intervention into the market and called for abolishing whole sections of the federal government; and it sought to impose the strictures of sectarian religion on education and scientific research. The emerging Democratic majority is a corrective to this Republican counterrevolution—an attempt to come to terms with what was positive and enduring in the movements of the sixties and in the transition to postindustrial capitalism. It does not represent a radical or aggressively left-wing response to conservatism, but a moderate accommodation with what were once radical movements. Like the Republican realignment of 1896, it seeks to ratify and consolidate progressive views that increasingly dominate the center of American politics.

Security, Stability, and Free Markets

In the early twentieth century, Republican progressives pioneered the idea of a regulatory capitalism that stood between laissez-faire capitalism and socialism. This kind of public intervention through government attempted to reduce the inequities and instability created by private growth without eliminating the dynamism of markets. It preserved private ownership of farms, factories, and offices, but subjected them to regulation on behalf of the public interest. Franklin Roosevelt's New Deal expanded the scope of government regulation and intervention, creating a system that worked well for many decades. By the 1970s, however, the system was breaking down and became mired in a crippling stagflation that government seemed helpless to correct. Many liberal Democrats came to believe that measures like nationalization of the energy industry, the control of wages, prices, and even investments, and publicly guaranteed full employment were necessary to get the system back on track.

At that point, Republican conservatism provided a useful corrective, a reassertion of the importance of markets and entrepreneurial risk to economic growth. But the Republican support for markets became hardened into a laissez-faire dogma. By the midnineties, the economy was booming, aided by technology-driven productivity growth, but it was also generating new kinds of inequity, instability, corruption, and insecurity—problems that would become even more apparent during the downturn that began in late 2000. Yet Republican conservatives continued to argue for reducing regulations and for cutting taxes for corporations and the wealthy even further.

They were motivated partly by laissez-faire ideology, but also by alliances with business lobbies in Washington that heavily funded their campaigns.

By the nineties, the Republican approach put them at odds not only with public opinion, but with the demands that the new postindustrial economy was putting on Americans. For one thing, Republicans seemed oblivious to Americans' concern about their quality of life. Air pollution continued to pose a risk to public health and, through global warming, to the planet's future. But after winning the Congress in 1994, Republicans tried to virtually close down the EPA [Environmental Protection Agency]. When Democrats tried to toughen air standards in 1997, Republicans and their business allies blocked the new rules through a court suit. A decade before, Democrats had used the same legal tactics to block Republican attempts to weaken regulations. What was a sign of political weakness in the Democrats of the eighties was equally a sign of political weakness and desperation in the Republicans of the nineties.

When George W. Bush became president, he undid Clinton administration environmental regulations and pulled the United States out of negotiations for a global-warming treaty. Bush equally ignored popular concern about product quality and safety, appointing regulatory foes to head the Federal Trade Commission and the Consumer Product Safety Commission. Bush's moves were so controversial that he eventually had to back off on some of them, including the reduction of clean water standards. Mindful of potential public opposition, the administration resorted to eliminating regulations by quietly negotiating them away in response to industry suits that were brought against them.

Republicans also ignored public concerns with the corruption of the campaign finance system. In the aftermath of 1996 campaign finance scandals, Democrats and a few moderate Republicans, including John McCain, backed a modest measure—well short of public financing of elections—that would have eliminated unlimited "soft money" contributions by corporations, unions, and wealthy individuals to candidates. But conservative Republicans, led by Kentucky senator Mitch McConnell, blocked the legislation. After George W. Bush took office, a campaign finance bill passed the Senate over Bush's objection, but conservative Republicans were able to stop it in the House. Finally, in the wake of the Enron scandal, moderate Republicans in the House banded together with Democrats to pass the campaign bill and Bush, facing a public revolt, finally signed it, though with a conspicuous lack of enthusiasm.

Republicans seemed equally oblivious to the insecurities created by the postindustrial economy. In the older industrial economy, a blue-collar worker at an automobile or steel factory could expect to hold his job until he retired and to enjoy health insurance and a pension. So could a white-collar worker at a bank or insurance company. In the postindustrial economy of global competition and automation, these kinds of jobs declined in number and could also suddenly disappear as companies moved overseas or reorganized or automated at home. Many of the newer jobs in low-wage services and professions were without the kind of fringe benefits that American workers of the 1950s had enjoyed. From 1979 to 1998, the percentage of private sector workers with employer-provided health insurance went down 7.3 percent. The drop was the sharpest among the lowest-paid workers. Of those in the bottom fifth of wage earners, coverage went down by 11.1 percent. Americans also lacked the kind of job protections they had enjoyed earlier. Their sense of insecurity rose, even during a period of recovery. In 1978, 29 percent of workers believed they were in some danger of losing their job; by 1996, the percentage had risen 10.7 percent to 39.7 percent. During the recession, these figures rose still further. In 2001 alone, 1.2 million Americans lost their health insurance.

Democrats sought to respond to this new insecurity through a national health insurance program, but when the public balked at that level of government intervention, they began considering a series of incremental measures. These included extending medicare downward to Americans fifty-five years and older and to children under eighteen; providing prescription drug coverage as part of medicare; eliminating abuses by health maintenance organizations; making health insurance and pensions portable; and providing universally available retirement accounts that workers can use to increase their old-age pensions. By contrast, Republicans have insisted that Americans would be best off in the hands of private markets and with government removed entirely from the economy. "We do have an economic game plan," the House Republicans declared in *Restoring the Dream*, "and its central theme is to get bureaucratic government off of America's back and out of the way." They advocated turning medicare into a voucher system and partially replacing social security with private investment accounts. Only in the face of widespread public support for the Democratic programs did they sponsor their own version of a patients' bill of rights or medicare prescription drug coverage—and in both cases, their proposed alternatives were intentionally so full of loopholes as to be virtually ineffective.

The rise of postindustrial capitalism and the increase of global competition has also put a premium on educated workers. Over the last three decades, only workers with a four-year college degree or more have seen their real wages increase, while workers with less than a college degree have seen their real earnings actually decline. Workers with a high school degree, for instance, made $13.34 an hour in 1973 and $11.83 an hour in 1999 (in 1999 dollars). In the same period, workers with advanced degrees saw their income rise from $23.53 an hour to $26.44 an hour. The clear message to workers was to acquire more education. That message was reinforced by changes in the global economy in which manufacturing work—the most remunerative of noncollege occupations—increasingly shifted from the United States to less developed capitalist countries.

Democrats have advocated more money for job retraining and early childhood education and to allow every high school graduate to attend a two-year college. They have also called for more money for school buildings, science and computer equipment, and teacher salaries. By contrast, Republicans, after taking control of Congress in 1994, tried unsuccessfully to shut down the Department of Education. In many states, Republicans, led by the

religious right, have promoted home schooling or exotic theories of education. Nationally, Republicans have made a special priority of vouchers—a
program with particular appeal to some white Catholic and evangelical
Protestant voters, but remarkably unpopular with much of the electorate.
Republicans have deservedly criticized some Democratic efforts as merely
"throwing money at problems" and correctly emphasized the need for high
standards, but they have used these deficiencies in the Democrats' approach
as an excuse to neglect needed spending. Even in a recession, the Bush
administration cut funds for worker training—a key component of any
education program—in the fiscal year 2002 budget.

Democrats, reflecting their New Deal heritage, have also tried to use
government policy to reduce the income inequality created by the new
postindustrial economy. In 1993, the Clinton administration dramatically
raised the earned income tax credit (EITC) for low-wage workers, while
raising the top rate for upper-income Americans. According to the Harvard
political scientist Jeffrey B. Liebman, the increase in the EITC worked
wonders for low-income workers: "As recently as 1993, a single-parent family
with two children and a full-time minimum-wage workers made $12,131 (in
today's dollars) with the EITC. . . . Because of the expansions of the EITC
during the 1990s, that family now makes $14,188—a 17 percent boost above
the poverty line. The Census Bureau estimates that the EITC lifts 4.3 million
people out of poverty, including 2.3 million children."

By contrast, the Republican efforts of Reagan, the Republican Congresses
of the 1990s, and the George W. Bush administration have widened income
inequality by bestowing tax breaks disproportionately on the most wealthy
and on corporations. In the Bush plan that Congress passed in August 2001,
the tax cuts, phased in over ten years, will primarily benefit the top 10 percent
of income earners. After 2001, they will receive 70.7 percent of the tax
benefits, while the bottom 60 percent will get 6.5 percent of the benefits.

These broad differences between the parties became even more apparent after the September 11 terrorist attacks. With the economy slumping,
Democrats wanted to give the bulk of money in a stimulus package to unemployed workers who would spend it immediately, with some extra money
thrown in to help the newly jobless buy health insurance. By contrast,
Republicans in the House, with the Bush administration's support, passed a
bill that would primarily have provided tax benefits to corporations and
wealthy individuals. Under the bill, almost three-quarters of the tax benefits
would have gone to the top 10 percent of income earners, and incredibly, no
benefits whatsoever would have gone to a typical family of four with an
income of $50,000. In addition, *Fortune* 500 companies would have gotten a
$25-billion windfall through the retroactive elimination of the corporate
"alternative minimum tax." Almost all of the tax measures in the Republican
bill would have taken effect too late to help the economy.

Democrats blocked the Republican stimulus package in the Senate, but
in its 2002 budget, the Bush administration was back at redistributing the
country's wealth to the wealthy. With deficits rising, the administration
actually proposed accelerating when the ten-year tax cuts that Congress had

passed would take effect. The administration also proposed making them permanent after ten years rather than subject to congressional review.

Race and Realignment

Republicans were the original party of racial equality. In the 1950s and early 1960s, leaders from both parties attempted to come to terms with the new Southern civil rights movement. But after 1964, the Democrats embraced, and the Republicans rejected, the cause of civil rights. The new conservative movement took root in opposition to the federal civil rights acts of 1964 and 1965. It gained a wider following and credibility in the 1970s and 1980s— attracting many whites without any animus toward black civil rights— because of the extremes to which some black militants, such as New York's Reverend Al Sharpton, the author of the infamous Tawana Brawley hoax, went and because of the corruption and venality of some black Democratic officials, such as Washington, D.C.'s Marion Barry. The backlash was also sustained by white voters' frustrations with 1970s stagflation and by the utter inadequacy of many of the civil rights remedies proposed by liberal Democrats. School busing, for instance, often had the effect of encouraging white flight rather than integrating schools. Some public housing programs put the entire onus of integration on working-class white neighborhoods. But Republicans used the corruption of the black officials and the inadequacy of these programs to stigmatize the Democrats and to avoid offering any constructive remedies of their own.

Republicans, particularly in the South, sought to build a new majority by wooing the white who had backed segregationist George Wallace in 1964 and 1968. South Carolina Republican Hastings Wyman, a former aide to Strom Thurmond, recalled the tactics by which Republicans built this new majority in the South: "I was there, and I remember denouncing the 'block vote'; opposing busing so long and so loud that rural voters thought we were going to do away with school buses; the lurid leaflet exposing 'the integrationist ties' of our Democratic opponents—leaflets we mailed in plain white envelopes to all the white voters in the precincts that George Wallace had carried. . . . Racism, often purposely inflamed by many Southern Republicans, either because we believed it, or because we thought it would win votes, was a major tool in the building of the new Republican Party in the South."

In 1980, when the realignment finally occurred, it was based to some extent on disenchantment with Democratic economics and foreign policy. But opposition to the civil rights movement and to a cluster of race-based or race-identified policies was particularly important in the South and in the ethnic suburbs of the Midwest and Northeast. In many of those areas, the two parties became identified with their different racial compositions—the Republicans as the "white party" and the Democrats as the "black party." Such an identification was inimical to the cause of racial reconciliation. It created a dynamic by which the Republicans, to maintain their majority, sought to divide whites from blacks. It also created an incentive for Republicans to ignore black economic inequality in their policy proposals and legislation.

Some Republican politicians, such as former congressman Jack Kemp, tried to develop a multiracial Republican Party and strategy, but they were ignored. (Kemp was popular among Republicans because of his outspoken advocacy of tax cuts, not because of his support for racial equality.) Most Republican politicians were swept away by the racial logic underlying the Republican majority. Faced with the prospect of defeat at the hands of a Democratic opponent, Republicans from Jesse Helms to the elder George Bush used racial wedge issues to win over erstwhile white Democrats. And while Bush's son avoided these sorts of tactics in his own run for president, as recently as fall 2001 two other Republicans—both of whom, interestingly, had reputations for racial reconciliation—pulled out the race card once they found themselves trailing in the polls.

Early on in his run for the governorship of Virginia, Republican attorney general Mark Early had boasted of his membership in the NAACP and vowed that he would not ignore the black vote. But by the summer's end, Early was trailing Democrat Mark Warner by 11 percent in the polls. Warner was even ahead in Southside Virginia, where small-town white voters had deserted the Democrats for Wallace in 1968 and had subsequently backed Republican presidential candidates. To win back Southside whites, who were drawn to Warner's message of encouraging high-tech growth, Early and the Virginia Republican Party ran radio ads and passed out leaflets in the area accusing Warner and the Democratic candidates for lieutenant governor and attorney general of supporting gun control, same-sex marriage, and the abolition of capital punishment. The charges were false, and without foundation. And they grouped together the candidates in spite of the fact that they had been nominated separately, disagreed on a range of issues, and were running entirely separate campaigns. What was most striking about the leaflets, however, was not what they said about the candidates' positions, but what they showed; a photograph of Warner with that of attorney general candidate Donald McEachin. Warner is white and McEachin is African-American. Such a technique, pioneered by Helms's political machine in North Carolina, was designed to demonstrate to these white Southside voters, who had a history of racial voting, that Warner was the candidate of the "black party."

In New Jersey, Republican Bret Schundler had captured the mayor's office in Jersey City twice, winning substantial black votes each time. But, as he fell far behind Democrat Jim McGreevey in the race for governor, Schundler increasingly resorted to issues with a strong racial component. In New Jersey, these issues pivot around the differences between the primarily black cities and primarily white suburbs. In his first debate with McGreevey, Schundler, without any prompting, raised his opposition to the New Jersey Supreme Court's Mount Laurel decision. This 1975 decision forced developers in affluent suburbs to devote a "fair share" of their new properties to affordable housing. Schundler said he wanted to "get rid of" the decision because it increased "suburban sprawl." Although people tend to worry about suburban sprawl because they're concerned about pollution or want to ease congestion on the roads, the link to the Mount Laurel decision made it obvious that Schundler had something other than the environment or traffic in mind: Schundler was proposing to curb the movement by the poor—overwhelmingly black and Hispanic—into more affluent, mostly white suburbs.

In the closing months of his campaign, Schundler also highlighted his plan to provide vouchers. Some conservatives have advocated vouchers so that ghetto children could afford to go to private schools as an alternative to failing public schools. But in his campaign, Schundler brazenly appealed to Catholic and religious right parents who already send their children to private schools. He attacked spending on public education as a subsidy to urban— that is, minority—schools and presented vouchers as a way of rewarding suburban parents who send their children to private schools. Schundler charged that McGreevey, who opposes vouchers, "wants to just throw more money into urban school districts and cut money for suburban and rural school districts." McGreevey, in Schundler's coded words, was guilty of favoring primarily black cities over primarily white suburban and rural school districts.

Early and Schundler, like the elder Bush, showed no sign of personally being racist. But as Republicans, they inherited a coalition and a strategy that divided the parties along racial lines and that encouraged Republicans, when in trouble, to stress their opposition to race-based or race-identified programs. In the seventies and early eighties, these tactics frequently worked. But as Democrats abandoned programs like busing, and as a new generation of black leaders, including Washington, D.C., mayor Anthony Williams and Detroit mayor Dennis Archer, replaced the old, race-baiting began to backfire on Republicans, particularly among professionals and women voters who were raised in the sixties ethos of racial tolerance. In Virginia's 1989 gubernatorial race, African-American candidate Douglas Wilder's standing in the Washington, D.C., affluent suburbs shot up after a Virginia Republican attempted to paint Wilder as a black militant. And in the 2001 Virginia and New Jersey races, Republicans had no success whatsoever using these kinds of tactics.

Stem Cells, Gay Rights, and the Religious Right

In 1980, when Ronald Reagan called on Americans to affirm the values of "family, work, and neighborhood," he was drawing a distinction between these values and those that the extremes of the sixties counter-culture had embraced. Republicans became the party opposed to the drug culture, bra burning, sexual promiscuity, teenage pregnancy, and the New Age denigration of religion. And they won elections on this basis. But in the 1980s, as Republicans embraced the religious right of Falwell and Robertson, they went well beyond repudiating the most extreme movements of the sixties. They rejected the new values and social structure that postindustrial capitalism is creating and nourishing.

Most important among these are women's equality at home and at work. The transition to postindustrial capitalism has profoundly altered family structure and the role of women, as the public sector and private industry have increasingly absorbed tasks at home that women traditionally performed. The imperative to have large families has disappeared. Women, no longer consigned to the home, have entered the workforce and many have taken up professional careers. The numbers of divorced women and single mothers have risen; so has the number of college-educated women professionals. *Father Knows Best* has given way to *An Unmarried Woman*. Modern feminism arose in response to these changes. Like other political movements, it included apocalyptic and utopian extremes, but at its core, it represented an attempt to remove the contradiction between an older patriarchal ideology and the growing potential for equality between men and women.

The Republicans, prodded by the religious right and by conservatives who sought its support, rejected the Equal Rights Amendment and the right of women to have an abortion. They balked at federal money for child care and held up the older ideal of the family. (Pat Robertson stated the case in 1992: "I know this is painful for the ladies to hear, but if you get married, you have accepted the headship of a man, your husband. Christ is the head of the household and the husband is the head of the wife, and that's the way it is, period.") Republicans highlighted the most extreme aspects of the women's movement in order to reject the whole. By contrast, Democrats absorbed the mainstream of the new feminist movement, exemplified by the abortion rights organizations and the National Organization for Women. Democrats also advanced proposals for child care and paid family leave to accommodate the reality that so many others were not working outside the home.

Democrats and Republicans have similarly parted ways on encouraging sexual education among teenagers and on preventing discrimination against homosexuals in housing or employment. Like the controversies about prohibition in the 1920s, these seem peripheral to the heart of politics, but in fact arise directly from the transition from one way of life to another. Prohibition was the cause of the small town against city, the ordered life of the farmer and craftsman against the chaos and squalor of the factory city, and of Anglo-Saxon Protestants against ethnic immigrants. Similarly, the Republicans, goaded by the religious right, have become the defenders of the mores of Middletown against those of the postindustrial metropolis.

Republicans, as the party of the religious right, have upheld the older ideal of sexual abstinence and of family life as not merely the norm, but as a moral imperative. They have opposed sexual education, if not sex itself, for teenagers. In December 1994, congressional Republicans forced the Clinton administration's surgeon general, Jocelyn Elders, to resign because she responded favorably to an off-the-cuff question at a press conference about the advisability of discussing masturbation as part of sexual education. Republicans have also adopted the religious right's attitude toward homosexuals as purposeful sinners who represent a threat to public morals. They opposed not only Clinton's unpopular proposal to allow gays to serve openly in the military, but also began to mount initiative campaigns to deny gays protection from discrimination in housing and employment. In Congress, Senate Republicans even refused to confirm a Clinton administration choice for ambassador to Luxembourg because he was a homosexual. They have also indicted homosexuals for causing the AIDS epidemic. In Virginia's 2001 contest for lieutenant governor, the Republican candidate, Jay Katzen, declared that AIDs "is the product, sadly, in most cases of a choice that people have made. . . . We recognize that homosexuality is a choice. It's a lifestyle with public health consequences."

These Republican attitudes were common, of course, fifty and a hundred years ago, but they have lost ground in postindustrial America. Americans today see sex not simply as a means to procreation, but as a source of pleasure and enjoyment. Many still cringe at the sight or prospect of homosexuality but recognize it as a possibly inherited form of sexual expression that, if denied and closeted, could prevent a person's pursuit of happiness. They may not want gays to be honest about their sexual preference in the military, but they see conservative attempts to punish and stigmatize gays as bigotry and intolerance.

Conservative Republicans and Democrats also part ways on the relationship of religion to science. Here, there was little provocation by the Democratic left or even from the counterculture, unless the arch-Victorian Charles Darwin is seen as representative of the left-wing counterculture. In search of votes, the conservative Republicans of the 1980s made a devil's pact with religious fundamentalists that entailed their indulgence of crackpot religious notions. While Democrats have opposed the imposition of sectarian religious standards on science and public education, the Republicans have tried to make science and science education conform to Protestant fundamentalism. Throughout the South and the Midwest, Republicans have promoted teaching creationism instead of or in competition with the theory of evolution. Creationists hold that the Bible is the literal truth and that the world began several thousand rather than billions of years ago. One leading creationist, for instance, holds that dinosaurs roamed the earth in the twentieth century.

Prominent Republican politicians and intellectuals, including Irving Kristol, William Bennett, and Robert Bork, have refused to repudiate these notions. Instead, they have sanctioned the idea that creationism and Darwinian evolution are merely two competing theories. In the 2000 presidential campaign, George W. Bush endorsed this view: "I believe children ought to be exposed to different theories about how the world started." Later Bush's official spokeswoman said, "He believes both creationism and evolution ought to be taught. He believes it is a question for states and local school boards to decide but he believes both ought to be taught."

The Republican rejection of modern science reached an apogee during Bush's first year in office when he became embroiled in a controversy over whether the government should fund stem-cell research. Stem cells were finally isolated and reproduced for research purposes in 1998 by a University of Wisconsin scientist. These cells could provide the basis for a new "regenerative medicine" that would aid, and even cure, victims of Parkinson's, Alzheimer's, heart disease, stroke, diabetes, and some forms of cancer by replacing or regenerating cells. Stem cells have been garnered from embryos at fertility clinics. Some one hundred thousand embryos are currently frozen and, if not used, will eventually be discarded. Scientists want to use them for scientific research, and the Clinton administration agreed to fund research on new stem cells.

But Republicans sided with the religious right who argued that these embryos are living beings that cannot be "murdered" for the sake of scientific research.[1] This notion of life prompted journalist Michael Kinsley to ask in *Time* magazine, "Are we really going to start basing social policy on the assumption that a few embryonic cells equal a human being?" But Bush, after claiming to spend months pondering the issue of life in a petri dish, finally announced in a nationwide address that researchers could only use stem cells that had already been created from embryos. They could not use new embryos. Such a decision bore out the degree to which conservative Republicans had become hostage to the religious right's campaign against modernity and postindustrial America.

On many of these economic and social issues, conservative Republicans initially won support by standing resolutely against excesses of the sixties and of post—New Deal liberal Democrats. But clearly they have gone to extremes of their own. They are putting forth remedies for problems that no longer exist and ignoring problems that do. They are fighting the future on behalf of the past. In the meantime, Democrats, chastened by defeat during the eighties, have repudiated their own extremes and moved to the political center, which itself has gravitated in a broadly progressive direction. Ironically, the party that the Democrats most clearly resemble is the one that Bush and Rove claim for themselves—the progressive Republicans of the early twentieth century. Like the progressive Republicans, today's Democrats stand between the extremes of right and left and at the gateway at the end of one era of capitalism and the beginning of another. They are the new party of progressive centrism.

Today's Americans, whose attitudes have been nurtured by the transition to postindustrial capitalism, increasingly endorse the politics of this progressive centrism. They want government to play an active and responsible role in American life, guaranteeing a reasonable level of economic security to Americans rather than leaving them at the mercy of the market and the business cycle. They want to preserve and strengthen social security and medicare, rather than privatize them. They want to modernize and upgrade public education, not abandon it. They want to exploit new biotechnologies and computer technologies to improve the quality of life. They do not want science held hostage to a religious or ideological agenda. And they want the social gains of the sixties consolidated, not rolled back; the wounds of race healed, not inflamed. That's why the Democrats are likely to become the majority party of the early twenty-first century.

Note

1. Bush also solicited the views of the pope and other Catholic leaders on whether to fund stem-cell research. Bush was not similarly concerned about Catholic views on capital punishment or on government aid to the poor. His interest in Catholic views seemed to flow from the interest of his political adviser Karl Rove in winning votes for 2004.

NO

Daniel Casse

An Emerging Republican Majority?

By the time Al Gore conceded the presidency to George W. Bush in December 2000, there was widespread agreement that the razor-close election they had just fought, and the fractious litigation that followed it, had exposed a disturbingly deep fissure in our national politics. In newspapers and magazines and on television, brightly colored maps showed a country divided almost exactly in half into red (Republican) and blue (Democratic) voting patterns. "There are now two distinct Americas," proclaimed *Business Week* in a typical cover story, "split along geographic, social, religious, and racial lines." So disparate were the tastes and attitudes of the people inhabiting those two different Americas, the story continued, as to "demand entirely different things from government."

Not only was the country said to be fractured, it was also said to be, on that account, ungovernable—and certainly ungovernable by George W. Bush. Wherever the new President turned, averred the political scientist Walter Dean Burnham, he was bound to find himself crippled by severely "limited opportunities" to forge a consensus behind his policies.

It was in this very circumstance, indeed, that some in the still-smarting Democratic party saw a sign of hope. Although the Democrats had lost not only the presidency but, as it then seemed, both houses of Congress, opportunity lurked in Bush's irreparable weaknesses. The new President, after all, was woefully inexperienced, especially in foreign affairs. The Republican coalition that had supported him—an unlikely mix of business groups, social conservatives, and libertarians—remained as fragile as ever. Only through the tie-breaking vote of the Vice President could the GOP expect to hold its majority in the Senate. And, as if these difficulties were not enough, the new administration was facing the first serious downturn in the national economy after eight years of remarkable prosperity presided over by a Democratic executive.

As the 2000 results were further digested, Democratic strategists took particular comfort in their reading of the red-blue map. The blue metropolitan clusters that had gone for Al Gore were composed disproportionately of educated professionals, women, and minorities—groups that were projected to grow more quickly than the rural and suburban voters who had pulled the lever for Bush. These demographic trends, along with the swooning stock market and other economic woes, suggested that Democrats might be well positioned to mount a fresh challenge to the GOP as early as the mid-term election of 2002. The party's prospects brightened further when, in June 2001, Senator James Jeffords announced that he was bolting the GOP and would henceforth vote as an independent—thus giving Democrats a majority in the Senate. In July, for the first rime since Bush's inauguration, a Zogby poll showed a majority of Americans disapproving of his performance. Around Washington, "Re-Elect Gore" bumper stickers began to appear.

But then came September 11, followed by the war in Afghanistan and the budding confrontation with Saddam Hussein—events whose political importance served to boost George W. Bush's popularity to once-unimaginable levels and make the Gore defeat fade into memory. [The 2002] mid-term campaign, on which the Democrats had pinned so much hope, became instead a months-long exercise in frustration; by November 5, the actual results left in tatters the party's dream of a public backlash against an "accidental" President and of its own quick reemergence in American politics. In fact, its fortunes today are lower than they were in November 2000. Two years after the country seemed split down the middle, it is George W. Bush's Republicans who look to be on the verge of creating a new and wholly unexpected political majority.

⋞◈⋟

To get a sense of the magnitude of the Democratic defeat, it helps to bear in mind that only twice since 1862 has the party not holding the White House failed to gain seats in the House of Representatives in a mid-term election, and seldom has it failed to gain in the Senate. As November 5 approached, however, candid Democratic leaders were already admitting they had little hope of winning the House (though none foresaw the loss of fully seven Democratic seats). As for the Senate, eleven races were still deemed to be toss-ups through the final weekend before the balloting. Stunningly, the Republicans went on to win all but one of them. At the end of the balloting, the President enjoyed larger majorities in both houses of Congress than on the day he took office.

The morning after the voting, the line from the Democratic National Committee (DNC) was that the party's losses in Congress were offset by significant gains in gubernatorial races, including in such former Republican strongholds as Michigan, Pennsylvania, Wisconsin, Kansas, and Arizona. But this was spin. Not a single elected Republican governor lost on November 5. Most of the Democratic victories occurred in states where Republicans had held the governor's mansion for twelve years or more, making it relatively easy for Democratic candidates to call for a change. Moreover, many of the victorious Democrats had campaigned on explicitly conservative platforms, and in Tennessee, Kansas, and Arizona they had vigorously opposed tax increases. The one notable exception was Mark Fernald in New Hampshire, who advocated an increase in state taxes and lost to the Republican candidate by 21 points.

Democratic gubernatorial victories also have to be seen against even more surprising wins by the GOP. Sonny Perdue became the first Republican governor to be elected in Georgia since Reconstruction. Robert Ehrlich, a graduate of Newt Gingrich's congressional class of 1994, defeated Kathleen

Kennedy Townsend in Maryland, a state widely viewed as the most Democratic in the nation. And Jeb Bush, the President's brother, resoundingly upset the prediction of DNC chairman Jerry McAuliffe that he would soon be "gone," defeating his challenger by thirteen points.

There were other significant reverses at the state level as well, where Democrats lost control of seven legislatures. Republicans now control 21 state capitols nationwide, compared with only seventeen still in the hands of Democrats. (Another eleven are split.) This marks the first time since 1952 that Republicans have enjoyed such a majority. In Texas, the state House of Representatives is ruled by Republicans for the first time since 1870; in Missouri, for the first time since 1955.

⎯⎯

From one perspective, of course, the results of the November election were not so astonishing. Ever since September 11, President Bush's approval rating had stood at historically high levels, and in most polls a majority of Americans were saying that the country was on the right track. In the new era of patriotism and national unity, the deep political chasms that separated Bush voters and Gore voters had become less meaningful.

The mid-term election reflected this changed mood in more ways than one. Although many Senate races were closely contested, and there were many tight gubernatorial races, none was a pitched ideological battle. In no contest did abortion, the death penalty, gun control, race, or class warfare play a major role. With the exception of the late Paul Wellstone, no candidate for the U.S. Senate actively argued against disarming Saddam Hussein or removing his regime from power. Even on the economy, which remains worrisome to most voters, the campaigns produced no clear party-line disagreements that might have tipped the balance one way or another in the hundreds of local races.

If the country was no longer so bitterly torn, however, Democratic activists failed to notice it—or so their campaign strategy would suggest. Many in the party's leadership appeared to believe that Bush's post-September 11 popularity was ephemeral, and that the lingering wounds of the "stolen" election of 2000 would be enough in themselves to excite the Democratic base. "We must never, ever forget what happened" in 2000, intoned Ralph Neas, president of People for the American Way. Donna Brazile, Gore's former campaign manager, advised activists to "go out and say, 'Remember what happened in Florida.'"

It may well have been this mistaken assumption of a generalized desire for payback that lay behind the failure of the party's elites to present a genuine challenge to Bush's Republicans. That failure, at any rate, was the burden of much post-election analysis. The Democrats, lamented Peter Beinart, the editor of the *New Republic,* had "fought this election from the meek and cynical center." Two former Clinton advisers, Tom Freedman and Bill Knapp, sounded a similar note in the *New York Times,* complaining that the Democrats had "ended up arguing over seemingly esoteric differences [and] let bigger national trends, like the war on terrorism, dominate."

But what all such Monday-morning criticisms ignore is that, from the very start of the election year, Democrats in Congress had in fact tried to seize upon every possible issue by which to create a clear distinction between their own priorities and those of the White House. In every instance, however, they found themselves outmaneuvered by a President who seemed determined not to let them get the upper hand on any contentious matter.

Thus, early in 2002, Democrats proposed a reconsideration of the Bush tax cut, only to be waylaid by a White House gleefully reminding reporters of the many Democrats who had initially supported the cut. When, soon thereafter, congressional Democrats joined Senator John McCain's call to rid election campaigns of soft money, they found the President suddenly willing to sign a campaign-finance bill even if it was patently defective and constitutionally suspect. Democrats hoping to tie a cascade of corporate scandals to Republicans and their business donors came up against a White House that welcomed bipartisan legislation to contain corporate fraud. On government-financed prescription-drug benefits—a winning Democratic issue according to every poll—the GOP produced a plan that to the casual eye was indistinguishable from the Democrats'. And so it went.

In short, the Democratic problem in 2002 was not just the failure to win a fight but the inability even to pick one. Politically, the war on terror was off-limits—even John Ashcroft, Bush's attorney general and the Democrats' nemesis, was given a relatively free hand to implement his controversial measures for detaining and investigating suspected terrorists. And in the meantime, again and again, domestic issues that had once seemed the exclusive preserve of the Democratic party were being quietly co-opted by a President riding a crest of popularity and a White House enjoying a unique moment of immunity to complaints from the Right that it was pandering to liberals or selling out its own political base.

❧

So what has happened to the red and blue map, with its supposedly hard-line divisions between Democratic and Republican voters? Few analysts of American politics could have been more confounded by the electoral transformation wrought by Bush than John Judis and Ruy Teixeira. Ever since the 2000 election, these two authors had been arguing tirelessly that the demographic facts signified by that famous map augured well for the Democratic party. In a book bearing the now-embarrassing title *The Emerging Democratic Majority*— a play on Kevin Phillips's prescient book of 1969, *The Emerging Republican Majority*—Judis and Teixeira drew a profile of the new, winning coalition. Its members are the educated professionals, working women, minorities, and middle-class Americans who live in large metropolitan areas—"ideopolises," in the authors' coinage—and are affiliated with the technology sector, universities, social-service organizations, and government.

Today it still seems indisputable that these urban clusters will be increasingly important in national elections—and also that, as Judis and Teixeira demonstrate, they are growing faster than the older suburbs and rural areas in the South and West where Republicans have dominated. But the core of the Judis-Teixeira argument rests less on shared demographics than on shared ideas. What has drawn this particular group of voters together, they contend, is a new kind of politics, or rather a new combination of political attitudes, to which they give the collective name "progressive centrism."

If the name sounds somewhat oxymoronic, that is for a reason. On the one hand, the authors write, these voters

> do not subscribe to the [Republican] gospel of deregulation and privatization. They want to supplement the market's invisible hand with the visible hand of government. . . . They want to strengthen social-insurance programs . . . [and they] reflect the outlook of the social movements that first arose during the 60's. . . . They oppose government interference in people's private lives . . . [and] support targeted programs to help minorities that trail the rest of the population in education and income.

But, on the other hand, this is not your father's brand of progressivism. Although these voters may indeed "flavor government intervention," they do not, "except in very special circumstances," favor

> the government's supplanting and replacing the operation of the market. . . . They want incremental, careful reforms that will substantially increase health-care coverage. . . . They want aid to minorities, but they oppose the large-scale imposition of quotas or the enactment of racial reparations.

And so forth, Judis and Teixeira are quite deliberate in defining what is to their mind this winning combination of fiery Democratic populism with the tempered incrementalism of "New Democrat" politics a la Bill Clinton. This "new synthesis," they believe, accurately reflects the transformation of America into a post-industrial society characterized by large, diverse metropolitan centers; it speaks to the interests and preferences not only of the blue (Democratic) states but of most denizens of "ideopolises" who are hungering for a new political brew. And it is the natural property of the Democratic party, its two components having been clearly if separately at work in, respectively, Clinton's 1992 centrist appeal and Gore's populist defiance of corporate power in 2000. The successful amalgam of these two strategies is what, in their view, will help usher in the new era of Democratic dominance.

After the divisive election of 2000, it was surely not unreasonable to suggest that a new brand of politics would emerge. But Judis and Teixeira's analysis, shaped by hopes as much as by facts, was out of date even as they were writing it, and is at odds with the current disposition of both political parties.

❦

Concerning the Republicans, Judis and Teixeira are stuck in the year 1994, the year of Newt Gingrich's Contract with America. Their straw man is a GOP supposedly rife with racial hatred, disdainful of single mothers and homo-sexuals, hostile to all government programs, and eager to infiltrate religious orthodoxy into every nook and cranny of American fife. This overheated car-icature prevents them from recognizing a lesson that in retrospect can be seen emerging out of their own reading of the 2000 election data. Two years later, not only had major parts of the agenda of "progressive centrism" been seized by a Republican President, but the party he led was no longer, if it ever had been, the party of their imagining.

Judis and Teixeira are hardly the only observers who thought the Republicans were heading for the precipice in the mid-1990's. As Christopher Caldwell wrote in the *Atlantic Monthly* in 1998, the party had allowed itself to be captured by a Southern voting bloc that socially and culturally was far to the Right of the rest of the country, and as a result it had lost the confidence of the electorate. But if voters once told pollsters that they trusted Democrats more on everything from education to the economy to crime and taxes, that is surely not the case today.

In a Gallup survey conducted a few days after November's mid-term elections, respondents consistently held a much more positive image of Republicans than of Democrats, and regarded them as better equipped to lead the country by a margin of 57 to 47 percent. To be sure, those findings reflected the afterglow of a Republican electoral triumph, and would undergo revision in later surveys. But the fact remains that, thanks largely to Bush, Republicans have become more palatable to a majority of Americans, and they have done so by moving away from some of the defining themes of late-20th-century Republicanism.

I have already mentioned a number of signposts from last year, but the shift really goes back to the fall of 2001. It was then, in the weeks immediately following the attacks of September 11, that Bush sent a signal of things to come by adroitly acquiescing in Democratic demands to federalize airport security workers. The shift could be seen again last spring when he announced the imposition of tariffs on imported steel, a stunning retreat from the free-trade principles he himself had advocated during his campaign for the pre-sidency. Since then, he has signed a massive expansion of farm subsidies, reversing a market-driven policy instituted just a few years earlier; agreed to a corporate-accounting law that includes a high level of new regulation and a considerable expansion of federal intrusiveness; and created a $37-billion Department of Homeland Security that may augment and consolidate federal power to a breathtaking degree.

One can defend each of these initiatives on its merits, or at least try to explain why it has been politically necessary. But that is beside the point. Nowhere in this list can one find the themes—limited government, reduced spending, local empowerment—that preoccupied Republican leaders only a few election cycles ago.

As those themes have faded, so, too, have the cultural hot buttons that gave the GOP such strength among social and religious conservatives. As the columnist John Podhoretz has pointed out, it was only three years ago that prominent conservative spokesmen, notably including Lynne Cheney, appeared before Congress to condemn the violence purveyed in rap lyrics by stars like Eminem. But when Eminem's semi-autobiographical movie *8 Mile* opened to large crowds recently, not a syllable of conservative criticism was to be heard. Of course, rap singers in general and Eminem in particular have somewhat moderated the raw brutality of their message in recent months; but it is also true that, in the age of terrorism, the battle against the liberal culture has faded as a key component of Republican politics.

If once high-profile conservative causes are losing their punch, the same can be said of certain high-profile conservative spokesmen. Jerry Falwell may have permanently lost his place in acceptable conservative circles when, on the heels of the September 11 attacks, he appeared to plate the blame on America's "tolerant" culture. More recently, the Bush White House has distanced itself from both Falwell and his fellow Christian broadcaster Pat Robertson for antagonistic: remarks about the Muslim religion.

Nor are conservative Christian activists the only ones out of favor with the White House. In the lead-up to the mid-term elections, it was widely reported that Karl Rove, the President's top political strategist, was discouraging openly ideological candidacies. In California's GOP primaries, Richard Riordan, the former mayor of Los Angeles, known as a moderate, was said to be favored by the White House over the conservative activist Bill Simon. In Minnesota, the majority leader of the state House of Representatives was reportedly dissuaded by Vice President Richard Cheney from challenging Democrat-turned-Republican Norm Coleman in the primary. Both stories, if true, reflect an effort to shape the public face of GOP challengers, and in retrospect the political judgment involved is hard to fault: Coleman's victory in Minnesota relied in part on his ability to attract Democratic voters, while Bill Simon, who won the Republican primary in California, went on to be trounced by the incumbent Gray Davis in a race that many thought Riordan would have won.

⌘

This is hardly to say that George W. Bush is out to create a Republican party in the mold of a James Jeffords or even a John McCain. After all, he pressed for and signed the largest tax-cut package in more than a decade and is now seeking to make those cues permanent. He has consistently selected bona-fide conservatives as his nominees to the federal bench. He fought, successfully, to keep the new Homeland Security Department exempt from federal-employee union rules. He is a strong opponent of human cloning, and has severely restricted the use of stem cells in federal medical research. His administration has proposed privatizing thousands of government jobs. In his personal style, and in his religious faith, he appears genuinely conservative. And this is not even to mention his vigorous stance in foreign policy, clearly reminiscent of Ronald Reagan and clearly distinct from the typical Democrat of today.

But there is also no mistaking the fact that Bush is prepared to offer voters something different from Reaganism and Gingrichism, something that goes beyond even the "compassionate conservatism" he introduced in his campaign for the presidency. What he and his advisers—and his party—appear to have grasped is that mustering the kind of bipartisan support required by a wartime Republican President depends on the ability to stand in or near the Center, and so turn to advantage the same demographic and cultural trends that, a mere two years ago, seemed so threatening to the GOP's future. The question is whether the palpable successes of Bush and the new GOP as measured in the mid-term elections are an artifact of the moment, or whether they can be molded into something more permanent, and more meaningful.

That will depend in large measure on the Democrats, and on how they play the hand they have now been dealt. So far—and here again is where Judis and Teixeira go wrong—there are abundant signs that they will play it not by sticking to "progressive centrism" but by moving Left. For all the alleged changes that the Democratic party underwent during the Clinton years, it now appears that its congressional wing is retreating to a familiar form of interest-group populism. Despite all the attempts to create a coalition of the Center, the party as a whole remains hostage to public-employee unions, trial lawyers, and organized lobbyists of every kind.

The choice of the unreconstructed liberal Nancy Pelosi to lead the minority caucus in the House, together with the emergence of Senator Hillary Rodham Clinton in a leadership role in the Senate, is a clear indication of the Left's determination to claim for its own the shreds of the party's fortunes. . . .

If this pattern continues, one can safely predict that on the road to the next presidential campaign, even as Republicans continue to downplay their "wedge" issues, Democrats will be more and more likely to emphasize theirs—especially in such areas as environmental protection and guaranteed health insurance, already emerging as favored themes. So far, faced with challenges on these or similar issues—the Patient's Bill of Rights, protection of the domestic steel industry—Bush Republicans have tended to respond with their now-standard "me, too." But a more left-wing, populist Democratic party may render this strategy, unworkable by robbing Bush of any chance of compromise.

That will be a testing moment for the GOP—and, conceivably, an opportunity to define itself for the foreseeable future. If it is to hold on to its edge, the party may be driven to articulate a more consistent and more truly conservative approach to issues of policy, if not to evolve a true conservative philosophy of governance. This does not mean veering sharply Right in a move mirroring the Democrats' turn to the Left. It does mean, in the broadest terms, developing a constantly reiterated commitment to the virtues of limited government over expanded entitlements, to market incentives over command-and-control regulation, to competition in place of entrenched bureaucratic monopolies, to economic growth over austerity, to conservation over radical environmentalism.

Such an exercise has much to recommend it, and not just in order to reassure doubting conservatives that Republican politics is about more than winning elections from Democrats. There is, in fact, a real danger in the strategy being pursued by the White House. In the hands of a less gifted, or less convincing, politician than Bush, and in circumstances other than wartime, it may represent less a blueprint for future political dominance than a reversion to an older and thoroughly failed Republican role. I am thinking, of course, of the long decades after the New Deal when the GOP was defined primarily by its efforts to slow the inexorable march of liberal ideas—not by substituting better ones but by accommodating them and sanding down their sharper edges. This is essentially a defensive form of politics, and it is a losing proposition. By contrast, making the case for limited government in a consistent and serious and positive manner could actually increase the appeal of the GOP in the eyes of many centrist and/or traditional Democratic voters wire have been drawn to it in the months since September 11.

Over the last three decades, the GOP has gone through a number of minor revolutions in an effort to reinvent itself. Kevin Phillips chronicled the start of the process in *The Emerging Republican Majority,* where he forecast a GOP majority based in the new entrepreneurial communities of the South and West rather than in the old WASP business elites. Ronald Reagan transformed the political face of the party, combining supplyside economics and anti-big-government themes at home with internationalism abroad. Fifteen years later, Gingrich shook up the party once again, demanding the reform of Congress and a shifting of power from Washington to state governments.

Today, Bush's mix of aggressive foreign policy, expanded government in the interest of domestic security, and a willingness to find a middle ground on domestic issues long owned by the Democrats has given him strengths that have defied almost every prediction of how his presidency would evolve. To be sure, he is a beneficiary of extraordinary circumstances. Nor do we yet know whether the brand of politics he has practiced is ultimately driven by expediency or by principle. But it is certain to set the terms of political debate for the balance of his first term, inform his reelection bid two years hence, and just possibly determine whether his party will emerge unexpectedly as a new political majority.

POSTSCRIPT

Is There an Emerging Democratic Majority?

Judis and Teixeira concede that on some issues, such as welfare and civil rights, the Democrats once went too far and provoked a majority backlash, while Casse is willing to admit that some of the old Republican positions on "hot button" issues no longer appeal to the majority. But both sides insist that their parties have learned from their past mistakes and now occupy the true "center." This suggests that a reputation for centrism is highly valued by the leaders of America's major parties, a preoccupation that distinguishes them from many parties in other countries.

An understanding of the changing fortunes of America's political parties can be gained from studies of electoral behavior over the past quarter century. The title of Ronald Radosh's book *Divided They Fell: The Demise of the Democratic Party, 1964–1996* (Free Press, 1996) reflects the author's view that the Democrats have been badly hurt (but not destroyed) by racial and rights issues, coercive and redistributive government tax policies, and Vietnam and antiwar protests. *The Rise of Southern Republicans* by Earl Black and Merle Black (Belknap Press, 2002) is an analysis of how southern politics has been transformed from the solidly Democratic South from the 1930s through the 1970s to a highly competitive area in which the Republicans have enjoyed a clear majority. A different southern perspective is offered in Alexander P. Lamis, ed., *Southern Politics in the 1990s* (Louisiana State University Press, 1999), which describes the movement of so-called New Democrats to oppose the welfare system and to favor the death penalty. Stanley Greenberg and Theda Skocpol, eds., *The New Majority* (Yale University Press, 1997) contains essays that examine strategies that the Democrats might follow in order to achieve future success. In *They Only Look Dead* (Simon & Schuster, 1996), E. J. Dionne supports a resurgence of Democratic Party power. Dan Balz and Ronald Brownstein, in *Storming the Gates: Protest Politics and the Republican Revival* (Little, Brown, 1996), contend that the parties have become so polarized that they have alienated moderate voters.

Evaluating the arguments in the preceding essays is controversial at this time because events are moving quickly and their outcomes are uncertain. A Republican majority could emerge from success in the struggle against terrorism, establishment of a stable and democratic Iraq, and economic recovery in the United States. Failure to achieve these goals could set the stage for a Democratic majority. The reader will be in a better position to judge than the authors in these essays.

Perhaps it is premature at this time to predict a long term majority for either party. The Republican majority of the first three decades of the twentieth century was ended by the Great Depression and the four elections of President Franklin D. Roosevelt. After a fifth Democratic victory by President Harry Truman, Republican candidates won seven of the next ten presidential elections, although the Democratic Party was the majority party in the House of Representatives for sixty of the sixty-four years between the elections of 1930 and 1994 and the majority party in the Senate for all but twelve. The Republicans won back both houses for six of Clinton's eight years in the presidency.

Far from having a clear majority party, at least one house of Congress has not had a majority of the president's party for 32 of the 48 years (two-thirds of the time) between 1954 and the election of 2000. The closeness of the 2000 presidential election is a reminder of how closely divided the country is, and how difficult it is to predict which party, if either, will be the next majority party. But be sure that both will be trying to be the one.

ISSUE 4

Do the Media Have a Liberal Bias?

YES: Bernard Goldberg, from *Arrogance: Rescuing America from the Media Elite* (Warner Books, 2003)

NO: Eric Alterman, from *What Liberal Media? The Truth About Bias and the News* (Basic Books, 2003)

ISSUE SUMMARY

YES: Former CBS reporter Bernard Goldberg argues that liberal bias is pervasive in news reporting, the result not from a conspiracy but of a mind-set among media elites acquired from the homogeneous social circles in which they live and work.

NO: Journalist Eric Alterman criticizes Goldberg's methodology and argues that there is a conservative bias in the media, citing as evidence the media's extensive corporate ties and what he regards as their favorable coverage of President Bush's presidency.

$\mathbf{A}$s demonstrated in the introduction to this book, it is not easy to define *liberal* and *conservative*. Not only have the meanings changed over the years, but even in our own time we encounter different kinds of liberalism and conservativism. There are *economic* liberals ("New Deal liberals"), whose emphasis is on the need for government action in regulating business and providing social welfare; and there are *social* liberals, who favor the liberalization of American social mores. A social liberal would likely favor the abolition of laws against homosexuality, oppose restrictions on abortion, and believe that there should be a wall of separation between church and state. On the conservative side, the picture reverses itself: economic conservatives (sometimes called "fiscal conservatives") want low taxes and small government, while social conservatives favor restrictions on abortion, oppose same-sex marriage, and want to see a greater public role for religion. There is, of course, considerable overlap between these two ideological sets, and even a kind of mix-and-match quality about them. Many economic liberals are also social liberals, but many are not, and the same can be said of conservatives. A person could be a liberal on abortion, for example, but conservative on taxes and government spending, or vice-versa.

For decades, conservatives of both varieties have been complaining that American journalists put a liberal spin on the news. The complaint reached high decibels during the Nixon administration, when Vice President Spiro Agnew charged that network TV was controlled by "a small group of men" who foist their liberal opinions on viewers. Agnew, other Nixon operatives, and Nixon himself returned to the theme a number of times, using terms like "elite snobs" and "nattering nabobs of negativism" to describe the journalistic community.

The Nixon administration was brought down by the Watergate scandal (Agnew himself was forced to resign in a separate bribery scandal), but the complaint lived on and, if anything, took on new life as the media began covering some of the new, divisive issues of the 1970s and 1980s. The charge of bias continues today, and conservatives are not the only ones who offer it. Some on the left believe that corporate ownership of the media, which is becoming increasingly concentrated, has made news divisions afraid to expose the questionable practices of the far-flung empires that sponsor their programs.

With few exceptions, journalists reject the charge of bias. They insist that they cover the news with professional neutrality and that the impression of bias is simply "in the eye of the beholder." Who is right? A debate can hardly get under way without agreement on what media are being considered: news and opinion media or "hard" news media only? If opinion is included, then mentioning programs such as Rush Limbaugh's three-hour radio talk show, which inject a good deal of conservatism into the mix, cannot be avoided. But Limbaugh and others like him are openly labeled "conservative," so the word *bias* seems to lose its force. What conservative media critics argue is that those who *claim* to be delivering hard news are actually coloring it with their own liberal views. But is this true? Polls suggest that journalists' views on social issues such as abortion, homosexuality, and school prayer are well to the left of those of most Americans, yet their opinions on such issues as the legitimacy of American capitalism are about the same as or slightly more conservative than the views of most other Americans. But the real question is not whether journalists have liberal or conservative biases but whether or not they carry their biases into their reporting. The claim that they are professionals, that they leave their political opinions at the newsroom door, can perhaps be critically examined. Yet most attempts to do so have been conducted by organizations heavily freighted with their own left or right ideologies. Some studies by political scientists with no apparent ax to grind have followed media coverage of a few presidential elections. Their conclusion is that, while the media have sometimes come down hard on one candidate or another, the bias has not been the result of ideology but a variety of other factors, such as the desire to keep the horse race interesting by slowing down the front-runner. But presidential elections are not ideal for studying the issue of ideological bias in the media, since news directors, reporters, and editors know that they are being watched closely and jealously by political partisans on both sides. The question, then, remains unresolved.

Bernard Goldberg  **YES**

Arrogance: Rescuing America from the Media Elite

Introduction

So I'm sitting in a very nice conference room in the very nice Time & Life Building, high above bustling West Fiftieth Street in Manhattan, for my first meeting on this book. There are about ten big shots from Warner Books sitting around a very nice long table waiting to hear what I have in mind, which basically is to use my earlier book *Bias* as a jumping-off point to examine the powerful behind-the-scenes forces that have turned too many American newsrooms into bastions of political correctness; to examine those forces and see why they generate bias in the news and how they sustain it; and to tell the media elites, who are too arrogant to see for themselves, the ways they'd better change if they want to stay relevant. Because if they don't, they'll cease to be serious players in the national conversation and become the journalistic equivalent of the leisure suit—harmless enough but hopelessly out of date.

But as I'm sitting there I'm not thinking about any of that. To be perfectly honest, what I am thinking is, before *Bias* caught on with so many Americans, before it became such a hit, no one in the liberal, highbrow book business would have thrown water on me if I were on fire. None of them would have dirtied their hands on a book that would have dismayed their smart, sensitive liberal friends. Before *Bias* I would have been the skunk at their garden party. *But now they can't wait to hear what I think?*

But about fourteen seconds in, I am brought back to earth when one of the participants informs me that a friend of his thinks the whole idea of liberal bias is bogus.

I smile the kind of insincere smile I detest in others and look at the guy, wondering if I'm also looking at his "friend." I'm also wondering if everyone else in the room also thinks that bias in the news is just the stuff of right-wing paranoia. I am in Manhattan, after all, the belly of the beast.

And besides, Manhattan is one of those trendy places where the new hot media chic thing is not only to dismiss the notion of liberal bias in the news, but actually to say, with a straight face, that the real problem is . . . *conservative bias!*

This is so jaw-droppingly bizarre you almost don't know how to respond. It reminds me of a movie I saw way back in the sixties called

A Guide for the Married Man. In one scene, Joey Bishop plays a guy caught by his wife red-handed in bed with a beautiful woman. As the wife goes nuts, demanding to know what the hell is going on, Joey and the woman get out of bed and calmly put on their clothes. He then casually straightens up the bed and quietly responds to his wife, who by now has smoke coming out of her ears, "What bed? What girl?" After the woman leaves, Joey settles in his lounge chair and reads the paper, pausing long enough to ask his wife if she shouldn't be in the kitchen preparing dinner!

Joey's mantra in such situations is simple: Deny! Deny! Deny! And in this scene his denials are so matter-of-fact and so nonchalant that by the time the other woman leaves the bedroom, leaving just Joey and his wife, her head is spinning and she's so bamboozled that she's seriously beginning to doubt what she just saw with her own two eyes. She's actually beginning to believe him when he says there was no other woman in the room!

Just think of Joey Bishop as the media elite and think of his wife as *you*—the American news-consuming public.

You have caught them red-handed over and over again with their biases exposed, and all they do is Deny! Deny! Deny! Only now the media have become even more brazen. Simply denying isn't good enough anymore. Now they're not content looking you in the eye and calmly saying, "What bias?" Now they're just as calmly turning truth on its head, saying the real problem is *conservative bias.*

What's next? They look up from their paper and ask why you're not in the kitchen preparing dinner?

⚜

Having been on the inside for as long as I have, twenty-eight years as a CBS News correspondent, I should have known it would be just a matter of time before they would stop playing defense and go on the offensive. Given their arrogance, I should have known that sooner or later they would say, "*We* don't have a bias problem—and if you think we do, then that proves that *you're* the one with the bias problem." Never mind that millions of Americans scream about liberal bias in the media; all the journalists can say is "You're the one with the bias!" The emperors of alleged objectivity have been naked for quite some time now, and sadly, they're the only ones who haven't noticed. Or as Andrew Sullivan, the very perceptive observer of all things American, so elegantly puts it, "Only those elite armies of condescension keep marching on, their privates swinging in the breeze."

But to deny liberal bias, the elites not only have had to brush off their own viewers, they also have had to paint their critics as wild-eyed ideologues—and then completely misrepresent what they say. For example, on March 4, 2003, this is how Nicholas Kristoff began his column in the *New York Times:* "Claims that the news media form a vast liberal conspiracy strike me as utterly unconvincing." Well, they strike *me* as utterly unconvincing, too. Exactly who, Nick, is making those "claims"? Got any names? Because I travel all over the country and speak about bias in the media, and I haven't met one serious conservative—not one—who believes that a "vast liberal conspiracy" controls the news. And for what it's worth, I write on page four of the introduction to *Bias* that "It is important to know, too, that there isn't a well-orchestrated, vast left-wing conspiracy in America's newsrooms." What I and many others do believe, and what I think is fairly obvious, is that the majority of journalists in big newsrooms slant leftward in their personal politics, especially on issues like abortion, affirmative action, gay rights, and gun control; and so in their professional role they tend to assume those positions are reasonable and morally correct. Bias in the news stems from *that*—not from some straw man conspiracy concocted by liberals in the supposedly objective, mainstream media.

Yet the idea that socially liberal reporters might actually take a liberal tack in their reporting is a proposition too many journalists on the Left refuse even to consider. Better to cast conservatives as a bunch of loonies who see conspiracies under every bed, around every corner, behind every tree and, most important of all, in every newsroom.

In fact, right on the heels of the Kristoff column, the conspiracy thing pops up again in—surprise, surprise—the *New York Times*. This time in a book review: "The notion that a vast left-wing conspiracy controls America's airwaves and newsprint [is] . . . routinely promoted as gospel on the right."

Wrong again! But they are right about one thing: There is plenty of paranoid talk about a "vast left-wing conspiracy" in the newsroom. The problem is, the paranoids dreaming it up aren't conservatives—*they're liberals!*

And the uncomfortable truth—uncomfortable for ideologues on the Left, anyway—is that there now exists "a huge body of literature—including at least 100 books and research monographs—documenting a widespread left-wing bias in the news," according to Ted Smith III of Virginia Commonwealth University, who has done extensive research into the subject. And much of the evidence comes *not* from conservatives with axes to grind but straight from the journalists themselves, who in survey after survey have identified themselves as liberal on all the big, important social issues of our time.

Despite the overwhelming evidence, despite all the examples of bias that were documented in my book and others, despite the surveys that show that large numbers of Americans consider the elite media too liberal, *despite all of that*, the elites remain in denial. Why? Well, for starters, as I say, a lot them truly don't understand what the fuss is all about, since they honestly believe that their views on all sorts of divisive issues are not really controversial—or even liberal. After all, their liberal friends in Manhattan and Georgetown share those same views, which practically by definition make them moderate and mainstream. So, the thinking goes, it is all those Middle Americans who take the opposing view on, say, guns or gay marriage who are out of the mainstream, the ones who are "fringe." Journalists don't usually use the word—not in public anyway—but those supposedly not-too-sophisticated "fringe" Americans are smart enough to pick up on the condescension. . . .

Deny! Deny! Deny! By now it's not only their mantra, it's practically official newsroom policy. In one way or another Dan Rather, Peter Jennings, and Tom Brokaw have all dismissed the very idea of liberal bias in the news. Rather has called it a "myth" and a "canard" and has actually said that "Most reporters don't know whether they're Republican or Democrat." Jennings thinks that "It's just essential to make the point that we are largely in the center, without particular axes to grind, without ideologies which are represented in our daily coverage." Ditto Brokaw, Couric, Lauer, Stahl, Wallace, and Bradley. The list, as they say, goes on and on.

But as strategies go, this new wrinkle—*"There is no liberal bias in the news, but there is a conservative bias"*—is far better. This is what you say if you're a media liberal who is not only tired of playing defense but wants to put his critics on the defensive for a change. This is what you say if you're trapped in a corner, and you don't know what else to do and you think you're fighting for your life. . . .

⚜

This seems like a good place to state the obvious: Yes, Republicans do indeed have friends in some conservative places like talk radio, Fox News, and the *Washington Times,* whom I'm sure they use to get their talking points out. But what Al Gore and his pals in the media forget to mention is that Democrats also have friends, in some very powerful *liberal* places, and the Democrats use them to get *their* talking points out. Places like major newspapers in every big city in the country, big-circulation mainstream news magazines, television networks with their millions and millions of viewers— all very large platforms that journalists use, intentionally or not, to frame the national debate on all sorts of big important issues, in the process creating "conventional" and "mainstream" points of view. *That* is what media power is really about.

The fact is, Rush Limbaugh, Fox News, and the *Washington Times* might not even exist if weren't for the routine (and the generally *unconscious*) liberal tilt of the mainstream media. Liberal journalists may indeed try to keep their biases in check (as they keep telling us), but—mainly because they don't even recognize that their liberal views are liberal—they often don't succeed. As I once told Bill O'Reilly, he should send a case of champagne to Rather, Brokaw, and Jennings with a nice little note that reads, "Thanks a lot, guys, for sending over all those viewers." . . .

⚜

"Well, what about all those media outlets with right-wing point of view?" the guy in the conference room wants to know, repeating what his friend (who doesn't think there's a liberal bias in the news) told him. "There's Bill O'Reilly; there's talk radio; there are a bunch of conservative syndicated columnists . . ."

I'm not sure if he or anyone else in the room notices that my eyes are rolling around my head in lazy circles. I have heard this one about 40 million times.

I find it both tiresome and disingenuous when liberals say, "Stop your whining about liberal bias; you've got plenty of conservatives in the media." Of course there's a conservative media. There's Rush Limbaugh and Sean Hannity and George Will and Robert Novak and Cal Thomas and Fred Barnes and Bill Buckley. But let's not forget that just about every editorial writer and columnist at the big powerful mainstream news outlets like the *New York Times, Los Angeles Times, Washington Post,* and *Boston Globe* are *liberals!* So conservatives have clout in the world of opinion and liberals have clout in the world of opinion. Wonderful! But, fundamentally, that's not the point. The point is that opinion is one thing and news is another. So telling me that there are all those conservative commentators out there and that I should stop my whining doesn't make me feel even the slightest bit better about the liberal bias of supposedly objective *news* reporters. News reporters are supposed to play it straight. It's that simple!

But even beyond that, in the media world, power and influence come from numbers. So consider these: The evening newscasts on ABC, CBS, NBC, and PBS total about 35 million viewers a night compared to *Special Report* with Brit Hume—Fox's evening newscast—which (right before the war in Iraq) was averaging about 1.3 million viewers. (Over an entire twenty-four-hour news cycle, Fox averaged about 1.058 million viewers; again, that's just before the war began.) Yes, it's true that Brit Hume brings certain conservative sensibilities to his newscast, but then Dan Rather brings certain liberal sensibilities to his. So, let's review: 35 million for the supposedly mainstream, nonliberal, nonbiased media, and just over a million for conservative Fox News. I repeat my earlier question: And we're supposed to fret about *conservative* influence on the news?

Of course, part of what *really* bothers so many liberals—though you can bet very few have actually thought about it this way—is that there even exists a more conservative alternative to the mainstream news outlets. Liberals, you see, had the playing field to themselves for so many years, controlling the rules of the game, that to them it had come to seem the natural order of things. It's ironic, isn't it, that liberals, who are always telling us that they're for change, that they're against the status quo, that *that* is what largely defines liberalism and (of course) makes liberals better, don't really mean it when the change doesn't quite suit them, when it means they will have a little competition—irreverent, edgy competition at that—to contend with. That's when they embrace the status quo with everything they've got and pine for the good old days, the days before those annoying *outsiders* got into the act, when the Big Three networks had to compete only with themselves. So while many Americans are encouraged that there's now some genuine diversity out there, many liberals regard this news as distressing—even *disorienting,* especially since ratings at the old news networks have been dropping for years while the upstart

Fox News has been coming on strong, picking up new viewers just about every month since it went on the air in October 1996.

❧❦❧

"Then what about the mainstream media's treatment of Clinton? You can't possibly think they went easy on him, can you?" is what liberals always ask.

It's a fair question. And the answer is, no, they didn't go easy on Clinton. The truth is, reporters will go after any politician—liberal or conservative— if the story is big enough and the politician is powerful enough. Still, all things being equal, there's no question the media elites salivate more when they're going after Republicans and conservatives—even the elites would admit to that, I think, after a few drinks.

But the entire premise of the question is wrong, because party politics is not primarily what liberal bias is about. What media bias is mainly about are the fundamental assumptions and beliefs and values that are the stuff of everyday life. The reason so many Americans who are pro-life or anti-affirmative action or who support gun rights detest the mainstream media is that day after day they fail to see in the media any respect for their views. What they see is a mainstream media seeming to legitimize one side (the one media elites agree with) as valid and moral, while seeking to cast the other side as narrow, small-minded, and bigoted. Even the editor of the liberal *Los Angeles Times* noticed that. On May 22, 2003, John Carroll wrote a scathing memo to his staff about political bias in the paper, singling out what he considered a liberally biased page-one story on abortion. "I'm concerned about the perception," he wrote, "and the occasional reality that the *Times* is a liberal, 'politically correct' newspaper. Generally speaking, this is an inaccurate view, but occasionally we prove our critics right. . . . The reason I'm sending this note to all section editors is that I want everyone to understand how serious I am about purging all political bias from our coverage. We may happen to live in a political atmosphere that is suffused with liberal values (and is unreflective of the nation as a whole), but we are not going to push a liberal agenda in the news pages of the *Times*."

Three cheers for John Carroll of the *Los Angeles Times!* The only part I'd take issue with is where he says, "generally speaking, [it] is an inaccurate view" to think the *Los Angeles Times* is a "liberal, 'politically correct' newspaper." No, generally speaking, it's quite an accurate view to believe the *Times* "is a liberal, 'politically correct' newspaper." And then there's the only "*occasionally* we prove our critics right." I don't think so. But I don't want to quibble. And besides, I understand he's got to live with these people. . . .

❧❦❧

Even the good guys give you reason to despair. In early 2003, David Shaw of the *Los Angeles Times,* who is one of the top media writers in the country, came up with an earth-shaking theory. There is no significant liberal bias in the news, he told us, but there *is* another kind of bias, one that is far more dangerous. "We're biased in favor of bad news, rather than good news. We're biased in favor of conflict rather than harmony. Increasingly we're biased in favor of sensationalism, scandal, celebrities and violence as opposed to serious, insightful coverage of important issues of the day."

There's a scoop, huh? Anyone who has tuned into *48 Hours, 20/20,* or *Dateline* for two or three seconds knows all of that. But now we're being told that just because there's a bias toward crap in the news—which there most certainly is—we need to worry far more about that than "about any ideological infiltration" in the news, as David Shaw puts it. Sorry, David, I can walk and chew gum at the same time. And I can worry about two kinds of bias at the same time, too, because, despite what you seem to think, *both* exist.

But I don't want to make this point, or any of the others, simply to people who already know it. Which is why one of the things I'm hoping this book will do is reach beyond the traditional conservative "ghetto" to reasonable and well-intentioned people across the political spectrum—to people with an open mind, no matter what their politics. To be sure, in today's highly polarized world, that will not be easy. Too often we talk right past each other in our culture—and no one, liberal or conservative, has clean hands on this one. Still, it seems to me that liberals—the very people who take such pride in seeing themselves as civil and open-minded—have, in a sad kind of way, become precisely what they accuse conservatives of: being close-minded and nasty. Many liberals these days—and ironically, especially the elites who think of themselves as worldly and sophisticated— are even narrower and more provincial than they imagine the rest of America to be. How can this be? It's easy when you live in a bubble, surrounded by others who think the same way about almost everything.

Yes, it's true that many conservatives also spend too much time in their own bubble, surrounded by like-minded souls who are always agreeing with one another. But here's the difference: Liberal culture in America is pervasive. You get it in movies and you hear it in music and you read it in magazines and you watch it on TV, in sitcoms and dramas as well as on the news. In America, unless you live in a cave, it's nearly impossible *not* to be exposed to liberal attitudes and assumptions on all sorts of issues ranging from guns to gay rights. Liberals, on the other hand, if they avoid just a couple of spots on the radio and TV dial—and especially if they live in liberal ghettoes like Beverly Hills or the Upper West Side of Manhattan— can pretty much stay clear of conservative attitudes and assumptions *and even conservative people,* secure in the knowledge that they're not really missing anything worth knowing.

Examples of this are not hard to come by, but some, like the following, are just amazingly telling. On February 6, 2003, while America was deeply divided on whether we should go to war with Iraq, veteran *Washington Post* columnist Mary McGrory wrote these remarkable words: "Among people I know, nobody was for the war." Imagine that. What a single-minded little world she must live in where, among all the people she knows, nobody— absolutely *nobody*—thought that invading Iraq was a good idea.

They live in a world, these bubble people, that is reassuringly uncomplicated and blissfully unchallenged by new ideas. As far as many liberals are concerned, all that's necessary to know is that different ideas can be dangerous ideas, embraced by the narrow-minded and intolerant, a threat to everything that good and decent people (like themselves) believe in.

In fact, the only reason so many smart liberals are convinced there is no liberal bias in the news in the first place is that this is what they keep hearing from the mainstream media they rely on for so much of their information. Since almost no one in these liberal circles ever risks exposure to another point of view, they truly don't understand why so many Middle Americans are so upset with Big Media. Yet what I have often found is that when liberals, for whatever reason, actually do come face-to-face with some of these scary ideas, they surprise themselves by how much they agree with them. . . .

A Final Word

George Orwell, the British essayist and author of *Animal Farm* and *1984*, once wrote about how societies censor themselves. "At any given moment there is a sort of all-pervading orthodoxy, a general tacit agreement not to discuss large and uncomfortable facts." He might just as well have been talking about the orthodoxies and the agreements that pervade America's most elite newsrooms.

Fair-minded reporters see and hear things all the time that they know just aren't right, large and uncomfortable facts they tacitly agree not to discuss. It doesn't take a genius to understand that certain issues aren't covered with equal respect for all points of view. The American people know that powerful assumptions about right and wrong, good guys and bad guys, influence and often distort the way certain stories are handled.

One of the most telling examples is how the media cover the abortion story. Every poll shows that Americans are sharply divided on the issue, regarding it as deeply troubling ethically and morally, and that while a majority support the right to legal abortion in the first trimester, large segments of the population favor important restrictions on the procedure.

But in many newsrooms—including the most powerful news organizations—such doubts are almost never heard. Those on the pro-life side are assumed to be fanatics, religious and otherwise. They are anti-women. They are the enemy.

And while it is almost never expressed explicitly, a rare revealing slip was Dan Rather's question to a U.S. senator, wondering if he thought Supreme Court Justice David Souter's views were "antiabortion or anti–women's rights, whichever way you want to put it," as if the two were one and the same. But even when it's not so blatant, those on the other side can read between the lines, and they are justly offended. As *New York Times* science writer Gina Kolata told an interviewer, "Anybody who reads the *New York Times* who doesn't think the *New York Times* is pro-choice, they are out of their minds. . . . We send messages all the time about what we think."

But the fact is, there are many, many journalists more troubled by the prevailing atmosphere than they let on. Some actually differ with newsroom sentiment on the most controversial issues of the day; others just recognize the crucial importance of a lively ongoing debate. But either way, they are more silent about their feelings than they should be.

That is the nature of peer pressure. Everyone understands that it's good for your career if you're a team player. No one wants to be seen as a troublemaker—or worse, as a right-wing crazy.

That has to change. Reporters need to start standing up to newsroom orthodoxies, not merely because it's right, but also because it's good policy. An ongoing civil conversation in the newsroom about contentious issues, challenging pat assumptions and unexamined beliefs, by its very nature will start to open minds. Inevitably it will make for fuller, fairer coverage of the news.

The next time a *Washington Post* reporter writes that the pope at times "speaks with the voice of a conservative crank" because he won't budge on issues like abortion and birth control, someone in the newsroom needs to say that using language like that is not just wrong—it's also deeply offensive.

When an ABC News reporter offers the view that while, since September 11, *terrorist* has come to mean *Islamic and foreign,* "many believe we have as much to fear from a homegrown group of antiabortion crusaders," someone in the newsroom needs to stand up and say, "Really? You *really* believe many Americans think antiabortion crusaders pose as big a threat to Americans as Osama bin Laden?"

And if Dan Rather repeats that the Republican Congressional agenda will "demolish or damage government programs, many of them designed to help children and the poor," someone needs to stand up and say, "You know, Dan, that kind of language is way over the top and offends a lot of people who aren't even Republicans."

I'm not saying there will never be consequences. Some of the biggest names in journalism are also some of the biggest bullies. They confuse even mild dissent with disloyalty. But reporters like to pride themselves on their guts. Ask a reporter to name his or her favorite movie, and the chances are good you'll hear *High Noon* or *To Kill a Mockingbird*—movies built around brave figures risking everything on principle. That's why they're so quick to condemn cops who won't speak up against other cops who step out of line, and doctors who won't speak out against other doctors; and priests who overlook wrongdoing in their ranks.

They're right—principle matters. Fairness matters. Standing up for those things is how character is defined.

Many journalists, of course, have shown remarkable courage covering wars and insurrections. It's now time for many more to be brave enough to stand up in their own newsrooms and say, "I think this is wrong. Let's talk about it." . . .

NO

Eric Alterman

Introduction: Bias, Slander, and BS

. . . Social scientists talk about "useful myths," stories we all know are not necessarily true, but that we choose to believe anyway because they seem to offer confirmation of what we already know (which raises the question, if we already know it, why the story?). Think of the wholly fictitious but illustrative story about little George Washington and his inability to lie about that cherry tree. For conservatives, and even more many journalists, the "liberal media" is just that: a myth, to be certain, but a useful one. If only it were true, we might have a more humane, open-minded, and ultimately effective public debate on the issues facing the nation. Alas, if pigs could fly. . . .

Republicans of all stripes have done quite well for themselves during the last five decades fulminating about the liberal cabal/progressive thought-police who spin, supplant, and sometimes suppress the news we all consume. Indeed, it's not only conservatives who find this whipping boy to be an irresistible target. Dwight David Eisenhower received one of the biggest ovations of his life when, at the 1952 Republican convention, he derided the "sensation-seeking columnists and commentators" who sought to undermine the Republican Party's efforts to improve the nation. The most colorful example of this art form, however, is probably a toss-up between two quips penned by William Safire when he was a White House speech-writer for Vice President Spiro Agnew, who denounced both the "nattering nabobs of negativism" and the "effete corps of impudent snobs" seeking to sink the nation's morale. His boss, Richard Nixon (who had been Ike's VP), usually held his tongue in public, but complained obsessively in private to the evangelist Billy Graham of "a terrible liberal Jewish clique" that "totally dominates the media" and "erodes our confidence, our strength. "Just about everyone wants to get in on the fun. Even Bill Clinton whined to *Rolling Stone* that he did not get "one damn bit of credit from the knee-jerk liberal press." The presidency's current occupant, George W. Bush, continues this tradition, complaining that the media "are biased against conservative thought." On a trip to Maine in January 2001, he quite conspicuously carried a copy of the best-selling book, *Bias*, by Bernard Goldberg, as if to the give the so-called "liberal media"—hereafter SCLM—a presidential thumb in the eye. . . .

Bias proved a smashing success. The *New York Times*'s publishing columnist, Martin Arnold, termed its sales to be "the most astonishing publishing event in the last 12 months." Indeed, with its publisher claiming more than 440,000 copies in print, the book's sales figures alone are taken by many to be evidence of the truth of its argument. In many ways, the conservative side was hardly better served in its arguments by Goldberg than by Coulter. To those who do not already share Goldberg's biases, his many undocumented, exaggerated assertions have the flavor of self-parody rather than reasoned argument. Among these are such statements as: "Everybody to the right of Lenin is a 'right-winger' as far as media elites are concerned." Opposition to the flat tax, he claims, comes from the same "dark region that produces envy and the seemingly unquenchable liberal need to wage class warfare." Roughly 72 of the 232 pages of *Bias* are devoted to attacks or score-settling with Dan Rather, whom Goldberg believes to have ruined his career. "If CBS News were a prison instead of a journalistic enterprise, three-quarters of the producers and 100 percent of the vice-presidents would be Dan's bitches," Goldberg says. Much of the rest of *Bias* consists of blasts at unnamed liberals who are accused of exaggerating data and manipulating the truth for their own purposes. How strange, therefore, that Goldberg seeks to make his case with statements about: "America's ten-trillion-page tax code," tuition fees that are "about the same as the cost of the space shuttle," and Laurence Tribe's "ten million" appearances on CBS News during the 1980s.

Taking the conservative ideology of wealthy white male victimization to hitherto-unimagined heights, Goldberg employs an extended Mafia metaphor to describe his departure from CBS. He speaks of having broken his pledge of "omerta" by writing an op-ed in the *Wall Street Journal* attacking his colleagues. "So what happened?" he writes. "Well, as Tony Soprano might put it to his old pal Pussy Bompensiero in the Bada Bing! Lounge: Bernie G. opened his big mouth to the wrong people—and he got whacked." You believe this heartbreaking tale until you discover that CBS had every right to fire him for violating the terms of his contract by attacking the network news program in a public forum. Instead, his superiors found him a comfortable job where he was allowed him to quietly qualify for a higher pension. (On *The Sopranos,* and indeed, in most Mafia lore, the term "to whack" carries rather different connotations, as evidenced by Big Pussy's undisturbed slumber with "the fishes.")

During the course of over 220 pages of complaining, Goldberg never bothers to systematically prove the existence of liberal bias in the news, or even define what he means by the term. About as close as we get is: "I said out loud what millions of TV news viewers all over America know and have been complaining about for years: that too often, Dan and Peter and Tom and a lot of their foot soldiers don't deliver the news straight, that they have a liberal bias, and that no matter how often the network stars deny it, it is true." A few of his examples, such as those involving corporate self-censorship in the event that a certain segment might offend the audience or advertisers, or the preference for interviewees with blond hair and blue eyes over people of color, actually serve to make the opposite case. With a keen eye to his likely audience of conservative talk-show hosts and book-buyers, the author simply assumes the existence of a liberal bias in the media to be an undisputable fact.

This same undocumented assumption characterized the conservative celebration of the book. The editors of the *Wall Street Journal* thundered: "There are certain facts of life so long obvious they would seem beyond dispute. One of these—that there is a liberal tilt in the media. . . ." *U.S. News and World Report* columnist John Leo added, in praise of *Bias,* that "the reluctance of the news business to hold seminars and conduct investigations of news bias is almost legendary." Glenn Garvin, television critic of the *Miami Herald,* added, "That newsrooms are mostly staffed by political liberals is pretty much beyond dispute, although a few keep trying to argue the point." That newspaper's executive editor, Tom Fielder, was said to be so impressed by *Bias* that he invited Goldberg to lunch with top members of his staff. He told Garvin, "I hate to say there's a political correctness that guides us, but I think there is. We tend to give more credibility to groups on the liberal side of the spectrum than on the conservative side."

If, in an alternative universe, all of Goldberg's claims somehow turned out to be justified, the crux of his argument would nevertheless constitute a remarkably narrow indictment. Goldberg did not set out to prove a liberal bias across the entire media, nor even across all television news. He concerned himself only with the evening news broadcasts, and not even with politics, but with social issues. Moreover, he appears to have done little research beyond recounting his own experiences and parroting the complaints of a conservative newsletter published by Brent Bozell's Media Research Center. It is hard to see what so excited conservative readers about the book. The broadcasts in question represent a declining share of viewers' attention, and, increasingly, an old and, at least from advertisers' standpoint, undesirable audience. It is possible that these particular news programs—if not their very format—will not survive the retirement ages of the current generation of anchors.

Goldberg appears to consider this fact. However, he attributes the relative decline in viewership of the network nightly news to viewer unhappiness with the widespread liberal bias he clams to have uncovered. "It's as if the Berlin Wall had come down," he explains. "But instead of voting with their feet, Americans began voting with their remote control devices. They haven't abandoned the news. Just the news people they no longer trust." "How else can we account for Bill O'Reilly and *The O'Reilly Factor* on The Fox News Channel? . . . As far as I'm concerned, the three people Bill owes so much of his success to are Tom Brokaw, Peter Jennings, and Dan Rather.

The logic of the above argument is genuinely difficult to fathom. Goldberg is correct to note that all three networks have seen a significant decline in their ratings for their news programs. But so has just about everything on network programming, due, quite obviously, to the enormous rise in viewer choice—the result of the replacement of a three-network television universe with one that features hundreds of choices on cable and satellite TV and the Internet. Viewership for all four networks—ABC, CBS, NBC, and Fox—during the ratings period September 24, 2001, to March 3, 2002, for instance, made up only 43 percent of TV watchers, compared with more than twice that percentage for just three networks two decades earlier. Still the network news programs' numbers remained impressive. The combined audience of the three network news programs is well over thirty million Americans, and better than fifteen times the number tuning into Mr. O'Reilly. It is also more than ten times the combined total prime-time audience for Fox News Channel, CNN, and MSNBC. These ratios render Goldberg's logic entirely nonsensical. Had he, or anyone related to the book, had enough respect for his readers to bother with even ten minutes of research, this claim would have never made it into print.

Not all of Goldberg's arguments are quite as easy to disprove, but most are no less false or misleading. One of the claims that many critics and television interviewers have considered the strongest in the book was the one the author credited with having inspired his initial interest in the topic:

> not because of my conservative views but because what I saw happening violated my liberal sense of fair play. Why, I kept wondering, do we so often identify conservatives in our stories, yet rarely identify liberals? Over the years, I began to realize that this need to identify one side but not the other is a central component of liberal bias. There are right-wing Republicans and right-wing Christians and right-wing radio talk show hosts. The only time we journalists use the term "left-wing" is if we're talking about a part on an airplane.

Goldberg illustrates his point with an example taken from the Clinton impeachment proceedings, during which, he claims, Peter Jennings identified senators as they came to sign their names in the oath book. According to Goldberg, Jennings described Mitch McConnell of Kentucky as a "very determined conservative," Rick Santorum of Pennsylvania as "one of the younger members of the Senate, Republican, very determined conservative," and Bob Smith of New Hampshire as "another very, very conservative Republican" but did not describe liberals accordingly. Goldberg also complained that CBS identifies the radical feminist Catharine MacKinnon as a "noted law professor" while Phyllis Schlafly is a "conservative spokeswoman." Rush Limbaugh, says Goldberg, is the "conservative radio talk show host" but Rosie O'Donnell is not described as the liberal TV talk show host. "Robert Bork is the 'conservative' judge. But liberal Laurence Tribe, who must have been on *CBS Evening News* ten million times in the 1980s," is identified simply as a "Harvard law professor."

Well, it would be interesting if true. And many of even the sharpest SCLM critics of Goldberg's book assumed it to be true, perhaps out of the mistaken belief that he must have done at least this much research. Both Howard Kurtz and Jeff Greenfield failed to challenge it on CNN. Jonathan Chait accepted it in his extremely critical cover story on the book in the

New Republic but then went on to explain why, aside from liberal bias, it might be the case. And the then-dean of the Columbia School of Journalism, Tom Goldstein, writing in the *Columbia Journalism Review,* mocked Goldberg's ad hominem claims but nevertheless credited Goldberg for "get[ting] down to specifics . . . [that] have the ring of truth" on this point.

In fact, all were overly generous. Goldberg presents no testable evidence and his arguments bear little relationship to the truth. At a 2002 bookstore appearance broadcast on C-Span, a political science professor asked Goldberg something almost no television interviewer had bothered to inquire: Did he have any systematic data to back up this point? The author scoffed at the very idea of evidence. "I didn't want this to be written from a social scientist point of view," Goldberg explained. "I have total confidence that the point here is accurate."

Another audience member then challenged him on this point and here, Goldberg got a bit testy:

> Let me say this. And I want to say this as clearly as I can. You are dead wrong. Dead wrong. Not even close about Teddy Kennedy. You have not, almost every time they mention his name, heard "liberal." I will say this—you have heard the word "liberal" almost never mentioned when they say his name, on the evening newscasts. They just don't. That part—I mean you gave me an easy one, and I appreciate that. It doesn't happen.

Goldberg seems to think that such statements become true by emphatic repetition. In fact, they are testable and it is Bernard Goldberg who is "dead wrong." On the small, almost insignificant point of whom Peter Jennings identified with what label on a single broadcast, Goldberg's point is a partial, and deliberately misleading, half-truth. As the liberal Daily Howler Web site pointed out, "the incident occurred on January 7, 1999, and Jennings did not identify 'every conservative' as the senators signed the oath book." He identified only three of them as such, failing to offer the label of conservative to such stalwarts as Senators Gramm, Hatch, Helms, Lott, Mack, Thurmond, Lugar, Stevens, Thompson, and Warner. Most of the labels had nothing to do with politics and were peppered with personal asides about a given senator's age, interests, or personality. On the larger point regarding a liberal bias in the labeling of conservatives, but not liberals, Goldberg could hardly be more wrong, even using the very examples he proposes. For instance, Ted Kennedy does not appear on the news with much frequency, but during the first six months of 2001, when he did, it was almost always accompanied by the word "liberal." As for the "million" respectful references to Laurence Tribe that appeared without the appendage "liberal," the indefatigable Howler checked those as well. According to Lexis, Howler found, Tribe has appeared on the *CBS Evening News* just nine times since 1993, almost always identified with a liberal label. On one occasion, May 14, 1994, CBS News even used Tribe and Robert Bork together, described as "legal scholars from both ends of the political spectrum." . . .

You're Only as Liberal as the Man Who Owns You

"Repeat something often enough and people will believe it" goes the adage, and this is nowhere truer than in American political journalism. As four scholars writing in the *Journal of Communication* observed in a study of the past three elections, "claiming the media are liberally biased perhaps has become a core rhetorical strategy by conservative elites in recent years." As a result, these unsupported claims have become a "necessary mechanism for moving (or keeping) analytical coverage in line with their interests." Another way of saying this is that conservatives have successfully cowed journalists into repeating their baseless accusations of liberal bias by virtue of their willingness to repeat them . . . endlessly. . . .

Examine, for a moment, the corporate structure of the industry for which the average top-level journalist labors. Ben Bagdikian, former dean of the journalism school at the University of California at Berkeley, has been chronicling the concentration of media ownership in five separate editions of his book, *The Media Monopoly*, which was first published in 1983 when the number of companies that controlled the information flow to the rest of us—the potential employment pool for journalists—was fifty. Today we are down to six.

Consider the following: When AOL took over TimeWarner, it also took over: Warner Brothers Pictures, Morgan Creek, New Regency, Warner Brothers Animation, a partial stake in Savoy Pictures, Little Brown & Co., Bullfinch, Back Bay, Time-Life Books, Oxmoor House, Sunset Books, Warner Books, the Book-of-the-Month Club, Warner/Chappell Music, Atlantic Records, Warner Audio Books, Elektra, Warner Brothers Records, Time-Life Music, Columbia House, a 40 percent stake in Seattle's Sub-Pop records, *Time* magazine, *Fortune, Life, Sports Illustrated, Vibe, People, Entertainment Weekly, Money, In Style, Martha Stewart Living, Sunset, Asia Week, Parenting,* Weight Watchers, *Cooking Light,* DC Comics, 49 percent of the Six Flags theme parks, Movie World and Warner Brothers parks, HBO, Cinemax, Warner Brothers Television, partial ownership of Comedy Central, El, Black Entertainment Television, Court TV, the Sega channel, the Home Shopping Network, Turner Broadcasting, the Atlanta Braves and Atlanta Hawks, World Championship Wrestling, Hanna-Barbera Cartoons, New Line Cinema, Fine Line Cinema, Turner Classic Movies, Turner Pictures, Castle Rock productions, CNN, CNN Headline News, CNN International, CNN/SI, CNN Airport Network, CNNfi, CNN radio, TNT, WTBS, and the Cartoon Network. The situation is not substantially different at Disney, Viacom, General Electric, the News Corporation, or Bertelsmann.

The point of the above is to illustrate the degree of potential conflict of interest for a journalist who seeks to tell the truth, according to the old *New York Times* slogan, "without fear or favor," about not only any one of the companies its parent corporation may own, but also those with whom one of the companies may compete, or perhaps a public official or regulatory body that one of them may lobby, or even an employee at one of them with whom one of his superiors may be sleeping, or divorcing, or remarrying, or one of *their* competitors, or competitors' lovers, ex-lovers, and so on. While the consumer is generally unaware of these conflicts, the possibilities are almost endless—unless one is going to restrict one's journalism to nothing but preachy pabulum and celebrity gossip. The natural fear for journalists in this context is direct censorship on behalf of the parent's corporate interests. The number of incidents of even remotely documented corporate censorship is actually pretty rare. But focusing on examples of direct censorship in the U.S. media misses the point. Rarely does some story that is likely to arouse concern ever go far enough to actually need to be censored at the corporate level. The reporter, the editor, the producer, and the executive producer all understand implicitly that their jobs depend in part on keeping their corporate parents happy.

Television viewers received a rare education on the corporate attitude toward even the slightest hint of criticism of the big cheese when, on the morning after Disney look over ABC, *Good Morning America* host Charles Gibson interviewed Thomas S. Murphy, chairman of Capital Cities/ABC, and Disney's Michael D. Eisner. "Where's the little guy in the business anymore?" Gibson asked. "Is this just a giant that forces everybody else out?" Murphy, now Gibson's boss, replied, "Charlie, let me ask you a question. Wouldn't you be proud to be associated with Disney? . . . I'm quite serious about this."

While some editors and producers profess to be able to offer the same scrutiny to properties associated with their own companies that they offer to the rest of the world, in most cases, it taxes one's credulity to believe them. Journalists, myself included, are usually inclined to give their friends a break. If you work for a company that owns a lot of other companies, then you automatically have many such friends in journalism, in business, and in government. Michael Kinsley, the founding editor of Slate.com, which is funded entirely by the Microsoft Corporation, did the world a favor when he admitted, "Slate will never give Microsoft the skeptical scrutiny it requires as a powerful institution in American society—any more than *Time* will sufficiently scrutinize Time Warner. No institution can reasonably be expected to audit itself. . . . The standard to insist on is that the sins be of omission, not distortion. There will be no major investigations of Microsoft in Slate." Eisner said much the same thing, perhaps inadvertently, when he admitted (or one might say, "instructed"), "I would prefer ABC not to cover Disney. . . . I think it's inappropriate."

Media magnates have always sought to reign in their reporters, albeit with mixed success. In 1905, Standard Oil baron John D. Rockefeller predicted of the New York *World*, in 1905, "The owner of the *World* is also a large owner of property, and I presume that, in common with other newspaper owners who are possessed of wealth, his eyes are beginning to be opened to the fact that he is like Samson, taking the initiative to pull the building down upon his head." Similarly, advertisers have always attempted to exert pressure on the news and occasionally succeeded. What has changed is the scale of these pressures, given the size and the

scope of the new media conglomerates, and the willingness of news executives to interfere with the news-gathering process up and down the line.
One-third of the local TV news directors surveyed by the Pew Project for
Excellence in Journalism in 2000 indicated that they had been pressured
to avoid negative stories about advertisers, or to do positive ones. Again,
by the time you get to actual pressure on an editor or writer, a great many
steps have already been taken. A 2000 Pew Research Center study found
that more than 40 percent of journalists felt a need to self-censor their
work, either by avoiding certain stories or softening the ones they wrote,
to benefit the interests of the organizations for which they work. As the
editors of the *Columbia Journalism Review* put it: "The truth about self-
censorship is that it is widespread, as common in newsrooms as deadline
pressure, a virus that eats away at the journalistic mission." And it doesn't
leave much room for liberalism. . . .

⋅⟨❀⟩⋅

Like most lucky people, George W. Bush helped make his own luck, particularly with regard to charming the media. Consider the coverage of the brief
China "crisis" of spring 2001: A U.S. spy plane collided with a Chinese
fighter, killing its pilot. I dwell a bit on this now-forgotten incident to
demonstrate that Bush, the unelected conservative Republican, received
extremely indulgent coverage from the so-called "liberal media" long before
September 11. In fact, Bush's behavior was often examined with little
more critical distance than I employ when critiquing the art projects of
my four-year-old daughter.

Recall that the Chinese held twenty-four U.S. soldiers and demanded
an apology. Even the hint of such an admission would have likely crippled
the Clinton administration among punditocracy hawks, who dominate all
discourse in times of perceived military threat. But the Bush administration managed to say "sorry" to the Commies and paid almost no political
price whatever. Moreover it succeeded in manipulating the media to the
point where its incompetence was portrayed as heroism, despite the
amazingly thin gruel it offered up in support of this case. The *Washington
Post,* for instance, presented readers with a twenty-six-paragraph, front-page
analysis of Bush's talks, replete with inside anecdotes designed to make the
president appear somehow simultaneously in charge and comfortable
with delegation of details.

Never mind that no *Post* reporters were present during the events
they so breathlessly reported as fact. To question the official version of
events handed out by the president's propaganda machine is apparently
no longer part of the job description. As Josh Marshall pointed out of this
incident, "Sadly enough, such articles are too often the result of an unspoken, almost Faustian arrangement. Official sources provide the essential
inside details and reporters then regurgitate the official line, giving up
their independence and skepticism for a quotation from the boss that he
might or might not actually have said."

Bush actually screwed up quite a few times during this crisis, but you'd be hard-pressed to learn this from the press coverage. For no apparent reason, and perhaps without even knowing what he was doing, the president appeared on ABC's *Good Morning America* to announce that the United States would do "whatever it took" to defend Taiwan if China attacked. This pledge, long desired by the Taiwanese, had been specifically avoided by every U.S. president since the beginning of the nation's "two-China" policy in 1979, owing to the concern that it might embolden Taiwan's rulers to start a war. Various administration spokespeople tried to pretend that that U.S. policy remained unchanged, but nobody really knew for certain whether Bush was trying to change it or even if he understood it in the first place. But the Chinese surely noted it in *their* buildings. "This shows that the United States is drifting further down a dangerous road," averred Foreign Ministry spokeswoman Zhang Qiyue. "It will . . . harm peace and stability across the Taiwan Strait, and further damage U.S.-China relations." Even so, Bush enjoyed oceans of SCLM slack. As an April 13 *Los Angeles Times* news analysis put it, "Bush Gets High Marks for Low-Key Approach." Just about the only vocal criticism to be found in the media during this period came from the right. Writing in the *Weekly Standard,* for instance, Robert Kagan and William Kristol thundered about "the profound national humiliation that President Bush has brought upon the United States." With his hemming and hawing, they complained, "President Bush has revealed weakness. And he has revealed fear. . . . The American capitulation will also embolden others around the world who have watched this crisis carefully to see the new administration's mettle tested." (To read these words in hindsight would be to see an implication that perhaps Mr. bin Laden was among those "emboldened" by the administration's "capitulation." And we can imagine that exactly such an accusation might have been leveled by these very authors—if it had been President Clinton "capitulating.") . . .

That the elite media—much less the SCLM—chose to celebrate the performance of an unelected president who apparently lacked the intellectual curiosity to learn the finer points of his job may inspire a bit of cognitive dissonance on the part of those seeking to make sense of American politics, but there it is. And it would prove the rule, rather than the exception, of Bush's pre-September 11 presidency. Frank Bruni, whose issueless *New York Times* coverage of Bush's campaign had proven so indulgent that it inspired Bush to frequently tell Bruni that he "loved" him, continued the kind of reporting on Bush's presidency that would earn any politician's affection. On a trip to Mexico where Bush met with that nation's new president, Vincente Fox, Bruni professed to spy Bush's boots "peek[ing] out mischievously" from beneath his trousers. He did not elaborate as to what variety of mischief said boots might have in mind. On a later trip to Europe, Bruni seemed to find absolutely everything Bush said or did to be unspeakably fabulous. The reporter noted that upon meeting Tony Blair, Bush "broke into a smile, indulged a mischievous impulse and offered him a greeting less formal than the ones the

British leader usually hears. 'Hello, Landslide!' Mr. Bush shouted out. It was a reference—an irreverent, towel-snapping one at that—to Mr. Blair's recent re-election, and it recalled the playful dynamic . . . when he cracked during a news conference that he and Mr. Blair liked the same brand of toothpaste." It was odd to say the least. Past *New York Times* coverage of presidential missions abroad have not, by and large, celebrated "irreverent towel-snapping" comments to leaders of other nations. The "playful dynamic" of the toothpaste "crack" might just as easily have been termed a "doltish" or "obnoxious frat-boy" crack. And, since Tony Blair actually did win his job in a landslide, it's hard to see just what is so "irreverent" about pointing it out. (Now if the Prime Minister had greeted the unelected/court-appointed Bush as "Landslide," I might have laughed.) . . .

ఇం

The attacks of 9/11 initially appeared to cause a tectonic shift in virtually every aspect of American politics and the media that covered it. Anchor people started sprouting American flags on their lapels, and in their station's new logos. Behind the scenes, network and newspaper executives agreed to a variety of administration requests to withhold information from the public, and Fox's Roger Ailes sent secret strategic advice to the President.

As is natural in times of war or quasi-war, political dissent and even truthful reporting on those in power became a luxury that many believed to be unaffordable, and so the right seized on its political opening. Ari Fleischer seemed eager to shut down all criticism of the U.S. government when the ABC comedian, Bill Maher, called American pilots cowards for "lobbing cruise missiles from 2,000 miles away." The comment was actually a critique of the Clinton Administration's policies, not of Bush's, and a transparently foolish one at that. (How many missions had the millionaire comedian flown?) But Fleischer used the opportunity to warn against all forms of criticism of any U.S. government action. Americans, Fleischer said, "need to watch what they say, watch what they do." This ominous warning was echoed by Attorney General John Ashcroft, who insisted at a congressional hearing a few days later that any criticism of the administration—be it on grounds of the protection of civil liberties, pragmatic considerations, or anything else—would "only aide terrorists— for they erode our national unity and diminish our resolve. They give ammunition to America's enemies, and pause to America's friends."

Many conservatives took up the cause, seeking to silence anyone and everyone who was ever heard to utter a critical word about the United States of America under the guise of the need for wartime unity. CNN's Robert Novak ruled out the very possibility of patriotic dissent. In a response to the e-mail of a viewer, who wrote, "It is patriotic to debate foreign policy, especially when we have troops on the ground whose lives depend on our making sound policy," Novak replied, his history askew, "It was people like you who undermined our forces in the Vietnam War and brought Communist tyranny to a country that doesn't deserve it." . . .

Dan Rather, formerly conservative public enemy number one, announced to viewers of the David Letterman program that the reason the terrorists and their supporters viewed America with such unbridled hostility was simple: It was "because they're evil," and "they're jealous of us." Even Bernard Goldberg, author of *Bias*, praised the post-9/11 media to the sky, writing:

> On September 11, 2001, America's royalty, the TV news anchors got it right. They gave us the news straight, which they don't always do. They told us what was going on without the cynicism and without the attitude. For that, they deserve our thanks and admiration.

Judging by conservatives' reaction to 9/11, their critique that the media was too liberal to report the news objectively has been thrown out the window. What conservatives wanted, apparently, was a mainstream media that reported and discussed the news from their own conservative perspective. In the aftermath of 9/11, that is what they got. . . .

꧁◉꧂

By far the most significant beneficiary of September 11 from a media/political standpoint was President Bush. Even in "normal" times, Peter Wolson, a former president of the Los Angeles Institute and Society for Psychoanalytic Studies, has explained, "The public has a need for an idealized hero. The public wants the president to succeed, even though there may be envy and lots of other conflicted feelings. There's a wish that the president will be a strong, powerful father figure." In the case of a trauma such as 9/11, this kind of nascent hero worship might be applied directly to the media, temporarily transforming George W. Bush from the military's commander-in-chief to the media's as well. Rather even appeared on David Letterman's program and announced, "George Bush is the president, he makes the decisions, and, you know, as just one American, if he wants me to line up, just tell me where." As David Carr observed at the time, "There's been a collective decision to re-imagine the president, and the media is fully cooperating. Journalists are very anxious to help him construct a wartime presidency, because we may be at war and he's the only president we have."

Made nervous by never-ending conservative attacks on their values and patriotism, the media reacted to the events of September 11 as if accused of a crime of which they secretly believed themselves to be guilty. The evidence of this "crime" could be seen in their overcompensation, orchestrated to demonstrate their patriotism like a community of new immigrants for an enemy nation, all to the benefit of Bush and his administration. CNN, for instance, ever defensive about its alleged anti-American agenda, could not get enough of the president, no matter what he was doing or where. According to one study, beginning January 1, 2002, CNN carried 157 live events featuring administration officials. Over the same time, the network carried only seven events featuring elected leaders of the

Democratic Party. This was a clear break from previous administrations. For the first fifteen months of the Bush administration, for instance, CNN cut into regular programming approximately 150 times to feature Bush speaking live. Most of these features showed the president addressing extremely partisan audiences, pushing the Republican domestic agenda. In comparison, during the final fifteen months of Bill Clinton's presidency, the network did so just eighteen times. Of the 150 cut-ins, a mere 44 turned out to be primarily related to the war. (Note that even before September 11, CNN had already broadcast sixty-five of Bush's speeches live.)

Moreover, the tone of the coverage of Bush's presidency after September 11 could hardly have been kinder if it had been vetted by his mother. On a relatively trivial level, as Maureen Dowd noted, "Garry Trudeau has pulled his featherweight-Bush cartoons. Barbra Streisand has taken anti-Bush diatribes off her Web site. David Letterman has been as diplomatic as Colin Powell. 'Saturday Night Live' will tone down its scorching Bush satires." But the seminal organs of the media stood as if at attention to their newly anointed commander in chief. A typical post-9/11 *New York Times* headline read "To Reassure World, Bush Flies Confidently and Forcefully Without a Net." A typical *New York Times* editorial found the president to be "a different man from the one who was just barely elected president last year, or even the man who led the country a month ago. He seemed more confident, determined, and sure of his purpose and was in full command of the complex array of political and military challenges that he faces in the wake of the terrible terrorist attacks of Sept. 11." A typical punditocracy exchange found Tucker Carlson accusing Paul Begala of making "a treasonous statement" on *Crossfire* when the latter stated his opinion that Tony Blair was "the finest leader in the free world."

In the aftermath of 9/11, even Bush's weaknesses became virtues. Making a virtue of necessity, Frank Bruni found that the president's effect "wasn't that of the ignorant or aloof" but came from someone bolstered by his religious faith, a "keen sense of destiny," and a "ready acceptance of fate." "An unthreatening, easygoing man for unthreatening, easygoing times," Bush was transformed by the terrorist attacks, in Bruni's decidedly straining-for-praise formulation, "into one of the most interesting presidents in decades."

Believe it or not, the Bush people even got the members of the media to go along, however briefly, with the notion that Bush had somehow morphed into a Daniel Patrick Moynihan–type politician/intellectual, though why they thought this was a good idea was never clear. Nevertheless, when Bush offered up the commencement address at Ohio State in the spring of 2002, a *Washington Post* reporter announced, "The president who spoke here today was not the same president who spoke in New Haven a year ago." The reason? "Bush aide John Bridgeland told reporters this morning that the president's speech, serious and grave, was inspired by the writings of Alexis de Tocqueville, Adam Smith, George Eliot, Emily Dickinson, William Wordsworth, Pope John Paul II, Aristotle, Benjamin Rush, Thomas Jefferson, George Washington, Abraham Lincoln and Cicero."

Bridgeland also said that he had discussed Nicomachean ethics in the Oval Office with the president, as well as the Patrick Henry–James Madison debate." Beyond Bridgeland's claims, however, the newspaper failed to present any evidence of these soaring claims about the awakening of Bush's intellectual capacities, as the president did not mention any of these in his speech. Nor was this new respect for scholarly learning consistent with the actions of the man who publicly, just a few weeks earlier, had responded to a U.S. reporter's questioning the president of France in French—as is proper, after all; foreign reporters do not question Bush in Czech or Romanian—"Very good, the guy memorizes four words, and he plays like he's intercontinental. I'm impressed." . . .

* * *

Done well, journalism can be a noble, even heroic calling. Compared to professions such as law, medicine, or investment banking, it offers relatively meager pay and social status. In the greatest but most pitiless book ever written about the profession. Honore de Balzac's *Illusions Perdues,* the author terms journalism "a hell, a sink of iniquity, lies and betrayals that no one can pass through, or emerge from uncorrupted. . . ." Honest journalists are rarely appreciated by the citizens they serve, even less so by those on whom they report. In recent years, good journalism has become increasingly devalued by the very people who are supposed to support it: the media companies who own the various newspapers, magazines, television, radio stations, and Internet sites where it is produced. In journalism, as in life, virtue is increasingly deemed to be its own reward. . . .

Many conservatives who attack the media for its alleged liberalism do so because the constant drumbeat of groundless accusation has proven an effective weapon in weakening journalism's watchdog function. Conservatives like William Kristol of the *Weekly Standard* are well aware, as he put it, that "The press isn't quite as biased and liberal. They're actually conservative sometimes." But conservatives also know that if the press is effectively intimidated, either by the accusation of liberal bias or by a reporter's own mistaken belief in the charge's validity, the institutions that conservatives revere—the military, corporate America, organized religion, and the powerful conservative groups themselves—will be able to escape scrutiny and increase their influence. Working the refs works, as I hope I have demonstrated in the previous pages.

Powerful people and institutions have strong, self-interested reasons to resist the media's inspection, and the public accountability it can inspire. But the net effect of their efforts is to weaken the democratic bond between the powerful and powerless that can, alone, prevent the emergence of unchecked corruption where it matters most. These irresponsible attacks come at the cost of the kind of information citizens require to understand the political, social, and economic context of their lives. The decades-long conservative ideological offensive constitutes yet another significant threat to journalism's ability to help us protect our families and ensure our freedoms. Tough-minded reporting, as the legendary *Washington Post* editor

Ben Bradlee explained, "is not for everybody." It is not "for those who feel that all's right with the world, not for those whose cows are sacred, and surely not for those who fear the violent contradictions of our time." But it is surely necessary for those of us who wish to answer to the historically honorable title of "democrat," "republican," or even that wonderfully old-fashioned title, "citizen." Knowledge is power, goes the saying. Here's hoping this helps.

POSTSCRIPT

Do the Media Have a Liberal Bias?

Both Bernard Goldberg and Eric Alterman seem ambivalent about the continuing influence of broadcast news. Goldberg makes the point that its viewership is declining, which he attributes to Americans' perception of its liberal bias and their opportunity to go elsewhere for news. But if that is true, why worry about its bias? But he also makes the point that its viewership is many times greater than that of the more conservative Fox News. Alterman, for his part, concedes that broadcast TV news is losing viewers, but attributes the loss not to liberal bias but to "the enormous rise in viewer choice" due to cable TV. This still leaves open the question of why viewers of the news have decided to *exercise* their choice, deserting mainstream programs as soon as they are offered the opportunity. Without answering that question, he then goes on—as Goldberg does—to note that their viewership is still much larger than that of Bill O'Reilly's more conservative news/commentary program. On this question, then, the arguments of both Goldberg and Alterman are hard to follow.

The selection from Goldberg excerpted in this issue is from a sequel to an earlier book by him entitled *Bias: A CBS Insider Exposes How the Media Distort the News* (Regnery, 2002), which, as Alterman notes, President Bush was once seen conspicuously carrying to his helicopter. Jim Hightower, a liberal talk show host, shares Alterman's view that there is actually a conservative bias in the media. See his *There's Nothing in the Middle of the Road but Yellow Stripes and Dead Armadillos: A Work of Political Subversion* (HarperPerennial, 1997). William McGowan, in *Coloring the News* (Encounter Books, 2001), argues that liberalism in the media has resulted from well-meaning attempts to "diversify" newsrooms with sprinklings of college-educated blacks, Latinos, gays, and women—groups composed disproportionately of liberals.

Some observers have suggested that the popularity of such programs as *The O'Reilly Factor* and other Fox News offerings proves that there is a hunger among segments of the American public for a conservative alternative to regular network news. Is there at least as much hunger for undisguisedly liberal perspectives on the news? Perhaps that question will be tested in the coming years. Air America, a liberal radio network, was launched in the spring of 2004, with shows hosted by comedian Al Franken, actress Janeane Garofalo, and other well-known personalities on the left. The show got off to a rocky start, with only four stations, and by the summer some had already begun to drop the program, yet there were hopes that after this shakedown it would enter a period of slow but steady growth. Stay tuned.

In addition to the Internet sites listed below, type in key words, such as "American federalism," "commerce power," "presidential appointments," and "government regulation," to find other listings.

U.S. House of Representatives

This page of the U.S. House of Representatives will lead you to information about current and past House members and agendas, the legislative process, and so on. You can learn about events on the House floor as they happen.

http://www.house.gov

The United States Senate

This page of the U.S. Senate will lead you to information about current and past Senate members and agendas, legislative activities, committees, and so on.

http://www.senate.gov

The White House

Visit the White House page for direct access to information about commonly requested federal services, the White House Briefing Room, and the presidents and vice presidents. The Virtual Library allows you to search White House documents, listen to speeches, and view photos.

http://www.whitehouse.gov/index.html

Supreme Court Collection

Open this Legal Information Institute (LII) site for current and historical information about the Supreme Court. The LII archive contains many opinions issued since May 1990 as well as a collection of nearly 600 of the most historic decisions of the Court.

http://supct.law.cornell.edu/supct/index.html

International Information Programs

This wide-ranging page of the U.S. Department of State provides definitions, related documentation, and a discussion of topics of concern to students of American government. It addresses today's hot topics as well as ongoing issues that form the foundation of the field. Many Web links are provided.

http://usinfo.state.gov

PART 2

The Institutions of Government

*T*he Constitution creates a division of power between the national government and the states, and within the national government power is further divided between three branches: Congress, the President, and the federal courts, each of which can exercise checks upon the others. What are the limits to national power? To what extent can any branch of government inhibit the exercise of power by the other branches? Does government itself have any limits? These issues have existed since the beginning of the nation, and they are likely to survive.

- Is Congress Barred from Regulating Commerce Within a State?

- Is the Filibuster of Judicial Nominees Justifiable?

ISSUE 5

Is Congress Barred from Regulating Commerce Within a State?

YES: William H. Rehnquist, from Majority Opinion, *United States v. Lopez*, U.S. Supreme Court (April 26, 1995)

NO: Stephen G. Breyer, from Dissenting Opinion, *United States v. Lopez*, U.S. Supreme Court (April 26, 1995)

ISSUE SUMMARY

YES: Supreme Court chief justice William H. Rehnquist argues that Congress cannot regulate activities within a state that are not economic and do not substantially affect commerce among the states.

NO: Supreme Court justice Stephen G. Breyer upholds the right of Congress to regulate activities within a state if Congress has a rational basis for believing that it affects the exercise of congressional power.

Federalism—the division of power between the national government and the states—is a central principle of American government. It is evident in the country's name, the United States of America.

The 13 founding states, long separated as British colonies and later cherishing their hard-earned independence, found it necessary to join together for economic stability and military security, but they would not surrender all of their powers to an unknown and untested national government. Many expressed fear of centralized tyranny as well as the loss of state sovereignty.

To reduce those fears, the Framers of the Constitution sought to limit the action of the new government to defined powers. Article 1, Section 8, of the Constitution enumerates the powers granted to Congress, implicitly denying any other. The grants of national power were stated in very general terms to enable the new government to act in unforeseen circumstances. Recognizing that they could not anticipate how powers would be exercised, the Framers added that the national government could make all laws that were "necessary and proper" to execute its constitutional powers.

Even after the Constitution was ratified, the surviving fear of the proposed Constitution's critics that a too-powerful national government might undermine the powers of the states led to incorporation of the Tenth Amendment into the Bill of Rights. It states that powers not enumerated in the Constitution as belonging to the national government belong to the states and the people.

In the first important test of federalism, *McCulloch v. Maryland* (1819), Chief Justice John Marshall wrote, "If any one proposition could command the universal assent of mankind, we might expect it to be this—that the government of the Union, though limited in its powers, is supreme within its sphere of action." Forthright as that sounds, precisely what that sphere of action is has never been definitively decided.

For more than two centuries, the constitutional debate between the two levels of government has focused principally on Congress's powers to regulate commerce among the states and to tax and spend for the general welfare. The greatest challenges to states' rights developed when the national government, in the administrations of Presidents Woodrow Wilson and Franklin D. Roosevelt, began to regulate activities once thought to be wholly within the power of the states. The U.S. Supreme Court declared unconstitutional laws that they thought exceeded the bounds of national power.

The Supreme Court did an about-face in 1941 when it unanimously upheld a federal minimum wage law and reduced the Tenth Amendment to "a truism that all is retained which has not been surrendered." For more than 50 years, it appeared that the Supreme Court would sanction no limits on national power except those explicitly stated in the Constitution, as in the Bill of Rights.

In recent years a more conservative Court has reestablished some limits. In the 1990s it ruled that Congress cannot compel the states to enact and enforce legislation carrying out the will of Congress. More far-reaching is the Supreme Court's 1995 decision in *United States v. Lopez*. In 1990 Congress had outlawed the possession of guns in or near a school. In a five-to-four decision, the Supreme Court concluded that Congress cannot regulate within a state without demonstrating the substantial effect of the regulated activities on commerce among the states. In 2000 the same narrow majority declared unconstitutional a federal law that permitted victims of rape, domestic violence, and other crimes "motivated by gender" to seek remedies in federal courts. Chief Justice William H. Rehnquist declared that "the Constitution requires a distinction between what is truly national and what is truly local." In 2002 the same five-member majority again upheld the claims of a state against the federal government. The Eleventh Amendment forbids private parties to sue states in federal court, but the majority has now extended state "sovereign immunity" to cover proceedings before federal regulatory agencies.

In the following selections from *United States v. Lopez*, Chief Justice Rehnquist, in his majority opinion, concludes that the law barring guns within the vicinity of a school was too far removed from Congress's commerce power or any other valid national power. Associate Justice Stephen G. Breyer, dissenting with three other justices, argues that reducing the risk of violence in education is a valid exercise of congressional power.

William H. Rehnquist  **YES**

Majority Opinion

United States *v.* Lopez

Chief Justice Rehnquist delivered the opinion of the Court.

In the Gun-Free School Zones Act of 1990, Congress made it a federal offense "for any individual knowingly to possess a firearm at a place that the individual knows, or has reasonable cause to believe, is a school zone." The Act neither regulates a commercial activity nor contains a requirement that the possession be connected in any way to interstate commerce. We hold that the Act exceeds the authority of Congress "[t]o regulate Commerce . . . among the several States. . . ." U.S. Const., Art. I, § 8, cl. 3.

On March 10, 1992, respondent, who was then a 12th-grade student, arrived at Edison High School in San Antonio, Texas, carrying a concealed .38-caliber handgun and five bullets. Acting upon an anonymous tip, school authorities confronted respondent, who admitted that he was carrying the weapon. He was arrested and charged under Texas law with firearm possession on school premises. The next day, the state charges were dismissed after federal agents charged respondent by complaint with violating the Gun-Free School Zones Act of 1990. 18 U.S.C. § 922(q)(1)(A) (1988 ed., Supp. V).[1]

A federal grand jury indicted respondent on one count of knowing possession of a firearm at a school zone, in violation of § 922(q). Respondent moved to dismiss his federal indictment on the ground that § 922(q) "is unconstitutional as it is beyond the power of Congress to legislate control over our public schools." The District Court denied the motion, concluding that § 922(q) "is a constitutional exercise of Congress' well-defined power to regulate activities in and affecting commerce, and the 'business' of elementary, middle and high schools . . . affects interstate commerce." Respondent waived his right to a jury trial. The District Court conducted a bench trial, found him guilty of violating § 922(q), and sentenced him to six months' imprisonment and two years' supervised release.

On appeal, respondent challenged his conviction based on his claim that § 922(q) exceeded Congress' power to legislate under the Commerce Clause. The Court of Appeals for the Fifth Circuit agreed and reversed respondent's conviction. It held that, in light of what it characterized as insufficient congressional findings and legislative history, "section § 922(q), in the full reach of its terms, is invalid as beyond the power of Congress under the

From *United States v. Lopez,* 514 U.S. 549 (1995). Some notes, references, and case citations omitted.

Commerce Clause." Because of the importance of the issue, we granted certiorari, 511 U.S. 1029 (1994), and we now affirm.

We start with first principles. The Constitution creates a Federal Government of enumerated powers. See Art. I, § 8. As James Madison wrote, "The powers delegated by the proposed Constitution to the federal government are few and defined. Those which are to remain in the State governments are numerous and indefinite." The Federalist No. 45. . . .

The Constitution delegates to Congress the power "[t]o regulate Commerce with foreign Nations, and among the several States, and with the Indian Tribes." Art. I, § 8, cl. 3. The Court, through Chief Justice Marshall, first defined the nature of Congress' commerce power in *Gibbons v. Ogden,* 9 Wheat. 1, 189–190 (1824):

> "Commerce, undoubtedly, is traffic, but it is something more: it is intercourse. It describes the commercial intercourse between nations, and parts of nations, in all its branches, and is regulated by prescribing rules for carrying on that intercourse."

The commerce power "is the power to regulate; that is, to prescribe the rule by which commerce is to be governed. This power, like all others vested in Congress, is complete in itself, may be exercised to its utmost extent, and acknowledges no limitations, other than are prescribed in the constitution." *Id.,* at 196. The *Gibbons* Court, however, acknowledged that limitations on the commerce power are inherent in the very language of the Commerce Clause.

> "It is not intended to say that these words comprehend that commerce, which is completely internal, which is carried on between man and man in a State, or between different parts of the same State, and which does not extend to or affect other States. Such a power would be inconvenient, and is certainly unnecessary.
>
> "Comprehensive as the word 'among' is, it may very properly be restricted to that commerce which concerns more States than one. . . . The enumeration presupposes something not enumerated; and that something, if we regard the language, or the subject of the sentence, must be the exclusively internal commerce of a State." *Id.,* at 194–195.

For nearly a century thereafter, the Court's Commerce Clause decisions dealt but rarely with the extent of Congress' power, and almost entirely with the Commerce Clause as a limit on state legislation that discriminated against interstate commerce. Under this line of precedent, the Court held that certain categories of activity such as "production," "manufacturing," and "mining" were within the province of state governments, and thus were beyond the power of Congress under the Commerce Clause.

In 1887, Congress enacted the Interstate Commerce Act, and in 1890, Congress enacted the Sherman Antitrust Act. These laws ushered in a new era of federal regulation under the commerce power. When cases involving these laws first reached this Court, we imported from our negative Commerce Clause cases the approach that Congress could not regulate activities such as "production," "manufacturing," and "mining." Simultaneously, however, the Court held that, where the interstate and intrastate aspects of commerce were so mingled together that full regulation of interstate commerce required incidental regulation of intrastate commerce, the Commerce Clause authorized such regulation.

In *A. L. A. Schecter Poultry Corp. v. United States*, 295 U.S. 495, 550 (1935), the Court struck down regulations that fixed the hours and wages of individuals employed by an intrastate business because the activity being regulated related to interstate commerce only indirectly. In doing so, the Court characterized the distinction between direct and indirect effects of intrastate transactions upon interstate commerce as "a fundamental one, essential to the maintenance of our constitutional system." Activities that affected interstate commerce directly were within Congress' power; activities that affected interstate commerce indirectly were beyond Congress' reach. The justification for this formal distinction was rooted in the fear that otherwise "there would be virtually no limit to the federal power and for all practical purposes we should have a completely centralized government."

Two years later, in the watershed case of *NLRB v. Jones & Laughlin Steel Corp.*, 301 U.S. 1 (1937), the Court upheld the National Labor Relations Act against a Commerce Clause challenge, and in the process, departed from the distinction between "direct" and "indirect" effects on interstate commerce. The Court held that intrastate activities that "have such a close and substantial relation to interstate commerce that their control is essential or appropriate to protect that commerce from burdens and obstructions" are within Congress' power to regulate.

In *United States v. Darby*, 312 U.S. 100 (1941), the Court upheld the Fair Labor Standards Act, stating:

> "The power of Congress over interstate commerce is not confined to the regulation of commerce among the states. It extends to those activities intrastate which so affect interstate commerce or the exercise of the power of Congress over it as to make regulation of them appropriate means to the attainment of a legitimate end, the exercise of the granted power of Congress to regulate interstate commerce."

In *Wickard v. Filburn*, the Court upheld the application of amendments to the Agricultural Adjustment Act of 1938 to the production and consumption of home-grown wheat. 317 U.S., at 128–129. The *Wickard* Court explicitly rejected earlier distinctions between direct and indirect effects on interstate commerce, stating:

> "[E]ven if appellee's activity be local and though it may not be regarded as commerce, it may still, whatever its nature, be reached by Congress if it exerts a substantial economic effect on interstate commerce, and this irrespective of whether such effect is what might at some earlier time have been defined as 'direct' or 'indirect.'" *Id.*, at 125.

The *Wickard* Court emphasized that although Filburn's own contribution to the demand for wheat may have been trivial by itself, that was not "enough to remove him from the scope of federal regulation where, as here, his contribution, taken together with that of many others similarly situated, is far from trivial."

Jones & Laughlin Steel, Darby, and *Wickard* ushered in an era of Commerce Clause jurisprudence that greatly expanded the previously defined authority of Congress under that Clause. In part, this was a recognition of the great changes that had occurred in the way business was carried on in this country. Enterprises that had once been local or at most regional in nature had become national in scope. But the doctrinal change also reflected a view that earlier Commerce Clause cases artificially had constrained the authority of Congress to regulate interstate commerce.

But even these modern-era precedents which have expanded congressional power under the Commerce Clause confirm that this power is subject to outer limits. In *Jones & Laughlin Steel,* the Court warned that the scope of the interstate commerce power "must be considered in the light of our dual system of government and may not be extended so as to embrace effects upon interstate commerce so indirect and remote that to embrace them, in view of our complex society, would effectually obliterate the distinction between what is national and what is local and create a completely centralized government." Since that time, the Court has heeded that warning and undertaken to decide whether a rational basis existed for concluding that a regulated activity sufficiently affected interstate commerce.

Similarly, in *Maryland v. Wirtz,* 392 U.S. 183 (1968), the Court reaffirmed that "the power to regulate commerce, though broad indeed, has limits" that "[t]he Court has ample power" to enforce. In response to the dissent's warnings that the Court was powerless to enforce the limitations on Congress' commerce powers because "[a]ll activities affecting commerce, even in the minutest degree, may be regulated and controlled by Congress," the *Wirtz* Court replied that the dissent had misread precedent as "[n]either here nor in *Wickard* has the Court declared that Congress may use a relatively trivial impact on commerce as an excuse for broad general regulation of state or private activities." Rather, "[t]he Court has said only that where *a general regulatory statute bears a substantial relation to commerce,* the *de minimis* character of individual instances arising under that statute is of no consequence." (emphasis added).

Consistent with this structure, we have identified three broad categories of activity that Congress may regulate under its commerce power. First, Congress may regulate the use of the channels of interstate commerce. Second, Congress is empowered to regulate and protect the instrumentalities of interstate commerce, or persons or things in interstate commerce, even though the threat may come only from intrastate activities. Finally, Congress' commerce authority includes the power to regulate those activities having a substantial relation to interstate commerce, *Jones & Laughlin Steel,* 301 U.S., at 37, i.e., those activities that substantially affect interstate commerce.

Within this final category, admittedly, our case law has not been clear whether an activity must "affect" or "substantially affect" interstate commerce in order to be within Congress' power to regulate it under the Commerce

Clause. We conclude, consistent with the great weight of our case law, that the proper test requires an analysis of whether the regulated activity "substantially affects" interstate commerce.

We now turn to consider the power of Congress, in the light of this framework, to enact § 922(q). The first two categories of authority may be quickly disposed of: § 922(q) is not a regulation of the use of the channels of interstate commerce, nor is it an attempt to prohibit the interstate transportation of a commodity through the channels of commerce; nor can § 922(q) be justified as a regulation by which Congress has sought to protect an instrumentality of interstate commerce or a thing in interstate commerce. Thus, if § 922(q) is to be sustained, it must be under the third category as a regulation of an activity that substantially affects interstate commerce.

First, we have upheld a wide variety of congressional Acts regulating intrastate economic activity where we have concluded that the activity substantially affected interstate commerce. Examples include the regulation of intrastate coal mining, intrastate extortionate credit transactions, restaurants utilizing substantial interstate supplies, inns and hotels catering to interstate guests, and production and consumption of home-grown wheat. These examples are by no means exhaustive, but the pattern is clear. Where economic activity substantially affects interstate commerce, legislation regulating that activity will be sustained.

Even *Wickard,* which is perhaps the most far reaching example of Commerce Clause authority over intrastate activity, involved economic activity in a way that the possession of a gun in a school zone does not. Roscoe Filburn operated a small farm in Ohio, on which, in the year involved, he raised 23 acres of wheat. It was his practice to sow winter wheat in the fall, and after harvesting it in July to sell a portion of the crop, to feed part of it to poultry and livestock on the farm, to use some in making flour for home consumption, and to keep the remainder for seeding future crops. The Secretary of Agriculture assessed a penalty against him under the Agricultural Adjustment Act of 1938 because he harvested about 12 acres more wheat than his allotment under the Act permitted. The Act was designed to regulate the volume of wheat moving in interstate and foreign commerce in order to avoid surpluses and shortages, and concomitant fluctuation in wheat prices, which had previously obtained. . . .

Section § 922(q) is a criminal statute that by its terms has nothing to do with "commerce" or any sort of economic enterprise, however broadly one might define those terms. Section § 922(q) is not an essential part of a larger regulation of economic activity, in which the regulatory scheme could be undercut unless the intrastate activity were regulated. It cannot, therefore, be sustained under our cases upholding regulations of activities that arise out of or are connected with a commercial transaction, which viewed in the aggregate, substantially affects interstate commerce.

. . . The Government argues that possession of a firearm in a school zone may result in violent crime and that violent crime can be expected to affect the functioning of the national economy in two ways. First, the costs of violent crime are substantial, and, through the mechanism of insurance, those costs are spread throughout the population. Second, violent crime reduces the willingness of individuals to travel to areas within the country that are perceived to be unsafe. The Government also argues that the presence of guns in schools poses a substantial threat to the educational process by threatening the learning environment. A handicapped educational process, in turn, will result in a less productive citizenry. That, in turn, would have an adverse effect on the Nation's economic well-being. As a result, the Government argues that Congress could rationally have concluded that § 922(q) substantially affects interstate commerce.

We pause to consider the implications of the Government's arguments. The Government admits, under its "costs of crime" reasoning, that Congress could regulate not only all violent crime, but all activities that might lead to violent crime, regardless of how tenuously they relate to interstate commerce. Similarly, under the Government's "national productivity" reasoning, Congress could regulate any activity that it found was related to the economic productivity of individual citizens: family law (including marriage, divorce, and child custody), for example. Under the theories that the Government presents in support of § 922(q), it is difficult to perceive any limitation on federal power, even in areas such as criminal law enforcement or education where States historically have been sovereign. Thus, if we were to accept the Government's arguments, we are hard-pressed to posit any activity by an individual that Congress is without power to regulate.

Although Justice Breyer argues that acceptance of the Government's rationales would not authorize a general federal police power, he is unable to identify any activity that the States may regulate but Congress may not. Justice Breyer posits that there might be some limitations on Congress' commerce power, such as family law or certain aspects of education. These suggested limitations, when viewed in light of the dissent's expansive analysis, are devoid of substance.

Justice Breyer focuses, for the most part, on the threat that firearm possession in and near schools poses to the educational process and the potential economic consequences flowing from that threat. Specifically, the dissent reasons that (1) gun-related violence is a serious problem; (2) that problem, in turn, has an adverse effect on classroom learning; and (3) that adverse effect on classroom learning, in turn, represents a substantial threat to trade and commerce. This analysis would be equally applicable, if not more so, to subjects such as family law and direct regulation of education.

For instance, if Congress can, pursuant to its Commerce Clause power, regulate activities that adversely affect the learning environment, then, *a fortiori*, it also can regulate the educational process directly. Congress could determine that a school's curriculum has a "significant" effect on the extent of classroom learning. As a result, Congress could mandate a federal curriculum for local elementary and secondary schools because what is taught in local schools has a significant "effect on classroom learning," and that, in turn, has a substantial effect on interstate commerce.

Justice Breyer rejects our reading of precedent and argues that "Congress . . . could rationally conclude that schools fall on the commercial side of the line." Justice Breyer's rationale lacks any real limits because, depending on the level of generality, any activity can be looked upon as commercial. Under the dissent's rationale, Congress could just as easily look at child rearing as "fall[ing] on the commercial side of the line" because it provides a "valuable service—namely, to equip [children] with the skills they need to survive in life and, more specifically, in the workplace." . . .

The possession of a gun in a local school zone is in no sense an economic activity that might, through repetition elsewhere, substantially affect any sort of interstate commerce. Respondent was a local student at a local school; there is no indication that he had recently moved in interstate commerce, and there is no requirement that his possession of the firearm have any concrete tie to interstate commerce.

To uphold the Government's contentions here, we would have to pile inference upon inference in a manner that would bid fair to convert congressional authority under the Commerce Clause to a general police power of the sort retained by the States. Admittedly, some of our prior cases have taken long steps down that road, giving great deference to congressional action. The broad language in these opinions has suggested the possibility of additional expansion, but we decline here to proceed any further. To do so would require us to conclude that the Constitution's enumeration of powers does not presuppose something not enumerated, and that there never will be a distinction between what is truly national and what is truly local. This we are unwilling to do.

Note

1. The term "school zone" is defined as "in, or on the grounds of, a public, parochial or private school" or "within a distance of 1,000 feet from the grounds of a public, parochial or private school." § 921(a)(25).

NO

Stephen G. Breyer

Dissenting Opinion of Stephen G. Breyer

J ustice Breyer, with whom Justice Stevens, Justice Souter, and Justice Ginsburg join, dissenting.

The issue in this case is whether the Commerce Clause authorizes Congress to enact a statute that makes it a crime to possess a gun in, or near, a school. 18 U.S.C. § 922(q)(1)(A) (1988 ed., Supp. V). In my view, the statute falls well within the scope of the commerce power as this Court has understood that power over the last half century.

I

In reaching this conclusion, I apply three basic principles of Commerce Clause interpretation. First, the power to "regulate Commerce . . . among the several States," U.S. Const., Art. I, § 8, cl. 3, encompasses the power to regulate local activities insofar as they significantly affect interstate commerce. As the majority points out, the Court, in describing how much of an effect the Clause requires, sometimes has used the word "substantial" and sometimes has not. . . . And, as the majority also recognizes . . . the question of degree (how *much* effect) requires an estimate of the "size" of the effect that no verbal formulation can capture with precision. I use the word "significant" because the word "substantial" implies a somewhat narrower power than recent precedent suggests. But to speak of "substantial effect" rather than "significant effect" would make no difference in this case.

Second, in determining whether a local activity will likely have a significant effect upon interstate commerce, a court must consider, not the effect of an individual act (a single instance of gun possession), but rather the cumulative effect of all similar instances (*i.e.*, the effect of all guns possessed in or near schools). As this Court put the matter almost 50 years ago:

> "[I]t is enough that the individual activity when multiplied into a general practice . . . contains a threat to the interstate economy that requires preventative regulation."

Third, the Constitution requires us to judge the connection between a regulated activity and interstate commerce, not directly, but at one remove.

From *United States v. Lopez*, 514 U.S. 549 (1995). Some references and case citations omitted.

Courts must give Congress a degree of leeway in determining the existence of a significant factual connection between the regulated activity and interstate commerce—both because the Constitution delegates the commerce power directly to Congress and because the determination requires an empirical judgment of a kind that a legislature is more likely than a court to make with accuracy. The traditional words "rational basis" capture this leeway. Thus, the specific question before us, as the Court recognizes, is not whether the "regulated activity sufficiently affected interstate commerce," but, rather, whether Congress could have had "*a rational basis*" for so concluding.

I recognize that we must judge this matter independently. "[S]imply because Congress may conclude that a particular activity substantially affects interstate commerce does not necessarily make it so." And, I also recognize that Congress did not write specific "interstate commerce" findings into the law under which Lopez was convicted. Nonetheless, as I have already noted, the matter that we review independently (*i.e.*, whether there is a "rational basis") already has considerable leeway built into it. And, the absence of findings, at most, deprives a statute of the benefit of some *extra* leeway. This extra deference, in principle, might change the result in a close case, though, in practice, it has not made a critical legal difference. It would seem particularly unfortunate to make the validity of the statute at hand turn on the presence or absence of findings. Because Congress did make findings (though not until after Lopez was prosecuted), doing so would appear to elevate form over substance. . . .

II

Applying these principles to the case at hand, we must ask whether Congress could have had a *rational basis* for finding a significant (or substantial) connection between gun-related school violence and interstate commerce. Or, to put the question in the language of the *explicit* finding that Congress made when it amended this law in 1994: Could Congress rationally have found that "violent crime in school zones," through its effect on the "quality of education," significantly (or substantially) affects "interstate" or "foreign commerce"? As long as one views the commerce connection, not as a "technical legal conception," but as "a practical one," the answer to this question must be yes. Numerous reports and studies—generated both inside and outside government—make clear that Congress could reasonably have found the empirical connection that its law, implicitly or explicitly, asserts.

For one thing, reports, hearings, and other readily available literature make clear that the problem of guns in and around schools is widespread and extremely serious. These materials report, for example, that four percent of American high school students (and six percent of inner-city high school students) carry a gun to school at least occasionally; that 12 percent of urban high school students have had guns fired at them; that 20 percent of those students have been threatened with guns; and that, in any 6-month period, several hundred thousand schoolchildren are victims of violent crimes in or near their schools. And, they report that this widespread violence in schools throughout the Nation significantly interferes with the quality of education in those schools. Based on reports such as these, Congress obviously could have thought that guns and learning are mutually exclusive. Congress could therefore have found a substantial educational problem—teachers unable to teach, students unable to learn—and concluded that guns near schools contribute substantially to the size and scope of that problem.

Having found that guns in schools significantly undermine the quality of education in our Nation's classrooms, Congress could also have found, given the effect of education upon interstate and foreign commerce, that gun-related violence in and around schools is a commercial, as well as a human, problem. Education, although far more than a matter of economics, has long been inextricably intertwined with the Nation's economy. When this Nation began, most workers received their education in the workplace, typically (like Benjamin Franklin) as apprentices. As late as the 1920's, many workers still received general education directly from their employers—from large corporations, such as General Electric, Ford, and Goodyear, which created schools within their firms to help both the worker and the firm. As public school enrollment grew in the early 20th century, the need for industry to teach basic educational skills diminished. But, the direct economic link between basic education and industrial productivity remained. Scholars estimate that nearly a quarter of America's economic growth in the early years of this century is traceable directly to increased schooling; that investment in "human capital" (through spending on education) exceeded investment in "physical capital" by a ratio of almost two to one); and that the economic returns to this investment in education exceeded the returns to conventional capital investment.

In recent years the link between secondary education and business has strengthened, becoming both more direct and more important. Scholars on the subject report that technological changes and innovations in management techniques have altered the nature of the workplace so that more jobs now demand greater educational skills. . . .

Increasing global competition also has made primary and secondary education economically more important. The portion of the American economy attributable to international trade nearly tripled between 1950 and 1980, and more than 70 percent of American-made goods now compete with imports. Yet, lagging worker productivity has contributed to negative trade balances and to real hourly compensation that has fallen below wages in 10 other industrialized nations. At least some significant part of this serious productivity problem is attributable to students who emerge from classrooms without the reading or mathematical skills necessary to compete with their European or Asian counterparts. . . .

Finally, there is evidence that, today more than ever, many firms base their location decisions upon the presence, or absence, of a work force with a basic education. . . . In light of this increased importance of education to individual firms, it is no surprise that half of the Nation's manufacturers have become involved with setting standards and shaping curricula for local schools, that 88 percent think this kind of involvement is important, that more than 20 States have recently passed educational reforms to attract new business, and that business magazines have begun to rank cities according to the quality of their schools.

The economic links I have just sketched seem fairly obvious. Why then is it not equally obvious, in light of those links, that a widespread, serious, and substantial physical threat to teaching and learning *also* substantially threatens the commerce to which that teaching and learning is inextricably tied? That is to say, guns in the hands of six percent of inner-city high school students and gun-related violence throughout a city's schools must threaten the trade and commerce that those schools support. The only question, then, is whether the latter threat is (to use the majority's terminology) "substantial." The evidence of (1) the *extent* of the gun-related violence problem, (2) the *extent* of the resulting negative effect on classroom learning, and (3) the *extent* of the consequent negative commercial effects, when taken together, indicate a threat to trade and commerce that is "substantial." At the very least, Congress could rationally have concluded that the links are "substantial." . . .

To hold this statute constitutional is not to "obliterate" the "distinction between what is national and what is local," nor is it to hold that the Commerce Clause permits the Federal Government to "regulate any activity that it found was related to the economic productivity of individual citizens," to regulate "marriage, divorce, and child custody," or to regulate any and all aspects of education. First, this statute is aimed at curbing a particularly acute threat to the educational process—the possession (and use) of life-threatening firearms in, or near, the classroom. The empirical evidence that I have discussed above unmistakably documents the special way in which guns and education are incompatible. This Court has previously recognized the singularly disruptive potential on interstate commerce that acts of violence may have. Second, the immediacy of the connection between education and the national economic well-being is documented by scholars and accepted by society at large in a way and to a degree that may not hold true for other social institutions. It must surely be the rare case, then, that a statute strikes at conduct that (when considered in the abstract) seems to removed from commerce, but which (practically speaking) has so significant an impact upon commerce.

In sum, a holding that the particular statute before us falls within the commerce power would not expand the scope of that Clause. Rather, it simply would apply pre-existing law to changing economic circumstances. It would recognize that, in today's economic world, gun-related violence near the classroom makes a significant difference to our economic, as well as our social, well-being. In accordance with well-accepted precedent, such a holding would permit Congress "to act in terms of economic . . . realities," would interpret the commerce power as "an affirmative power commensurate with the national needs," and would acknowledge that the "commerce clause does not operate so as to render the nation powerless to defend itself against economic forces that Congress decrees inimical or destructive of the national economy." . . .

IV

In sum, to find this legislation within the scope of the Commerce Clause would permit "Congress . . . to act in terms of economic . . . realities." It would interpret the Clause as this Court has traditionally interpreted it, with the exception of one wrong turn subsequently corrected. Upholding this legislation would do no more than simply recognize that Congress had a "rational basis" for finding a significant connection between guns in or near schools and (through their effect on education) the interstate and foreign commerce they threaten. For these reasons, I would reverse the judgment of the Court of Appeals. Respectfully, I dissent.

POSTSCRIPT

Is Congress Barred from Regulating Commerce Within a State?

The difference of views on today's divided Supreme Court may be defined (concededly too simply and neatly) in terms of whether the powers of the states are *reserved,* that is, secure against encroachment or abridgement by Congress or the president, or whether state powers are *residual,* that is, the powers that are left after upholding valid claims of national power.

On the one hand, the historical evidence leaves no doubt that the Constitution was designed to create a national government powerful enough to deal with areas that the states believed required unified action (such as commerce, coinage, and national defense) but not so powerful as to diminish the authority of the states in all other areas. The Constitution's authors went to some pains to define and confine the powers of the new central government.

States' rights theory is founded on a historical proposition: that the states were originally sovereign and that, in the act of forming a Union, they did not surrender their sovereignty. The states formed the nation, acting as states. Delegates to the Convention were chosen by existing states; none were selected by a popular process. They sat in convention as delegates of the states, voting as states, and always aware that the document they were composing would be referred back to the states for their approval. In fact, the Constitution was sent to the states for action by state conventions called by the state legislatures. The approval of nine states was necessary for the Constitution to go into effect, and it could not be made binding on states that had not given their approval. The opening words of the Preamble, "We the people," is a literary substitution for the enumeration of the states, because it would have been impossible and improper to anticipate which states would join the Union.

On the other hand, Chief Justice John Marshall has stated the logic of delegated national power: "Let the end be legitimate, let it be within the scope of the Constitution, and all means which are appropriate, which are plainly adapted to that end, which are not prohibited, but consistent with the letter and spirit of the Constitution, are constitutional." If Congress's exercise of power is valid, no matter how far it extends, the power of the states is reduced by that much.

The constitutional justification for a liberal interpretation of national power can be derived from the critical clauses that, first, allow breadth—the implied powers clause—and then give primacy—the supremacy clause—to the acts of the national government. The Framers deliberately designed a constitutional system in which national power would be explicitly set forth, partly to insure that the requisite power would exist and could be exercised, partly to guard against the assumption of power that was intended to remain within the authority of the states. Without regard to which was greater and which lesser, which more numerous and which less, federal power precedes state power, not in the history of the nation, but in the logic of the Constitution.

The impressive arguments on both sides have been echoed in numerous decisions of the Supreme Court, congressional hearings on proposed national legislation, and works of political scholarship. In *The Delicate Balance: Federalism, Interstate Commerce and Economic Freedom in the Technological Age* (Heritage Foundation, 1998), Adam D. Thierer seeks to redefine and defend federalism in the modern world. Edward B. McLean and other scholars deplore what they call *Derailing the Constitution: The Undermining of American Federalism* (Doubleday, 1997). In *Disunited States* (Basic Books, 1997), John D. Donahue expresses skepticism of the judicial movement toward reducing the exercise of national power.

Despite the learned constitutional and historical arguments, one may harbor the suspicion that where one stands on the balance of power in American federalism often depends less on abstract theory than on practical considerations of public policy. Perhaps there is a more than a coincidental correspondence between positions on civil rights or national welfare legislation and the defense of either the principle of national supremacy or that of states' rights. As long as political differences exist as to whether we should have "more" or "less" national government, the constitutional debate will continue.

ISSUE 6

Is the Filibuster of Judicial Nominees Justifiable?

YES: Marcia Greenberger, from Testimony, *Senate Judiciary Committee* (May 6, 2003)

NO: John C. Eastman, from Testimony, *Senate Judicial Committee* (May 6, 2003)

ISSUE SUMMARY

YES: Marcia Greenberger, co-president of the National Women's Law Center, contends the filibuster of judicial nominees serves the nation well by forcing the president to submit moderate, consensus nominees to the bench.

NO: Law professor John C. Eastman argues that the "dilatory" use of the filibuster flouts the will of the Senate, intrudes upon the president's power to nominate judges, and ultimately threatens the independence of the judiciary.

T he House of Representatives permits its leadership routinely to set strict limits on the amount of time each member can speak on the floor. The Senate has no such limits, so Senators can speak as long as they like. On some occasions, they use this privilege as a means of preventing a vote. "Filibuster" is the term commonly used for this kind of prolonged speechmaking.

The term comes from the Dutch *vrijbuiter*, via the French *flibustier*, which the Spanish rendered *filibustero*. It means "pirate" or "military adventurer" (the English "freebooter" comes from the same root) and was first applied to buccaneers who preyed on South American coasts in the seventeenth century. It was introduced into American English in the nineteenth century when it was applied to adventurers who led illegal military expeditions into South American countries. Over the years, it has come to mean "obstruction of legislation in the Senate by the prolonged speechmaking of a few," after a disgusted congressman in the nineteenth century described one such prolonged speech as "filibustering against the United States."

The filibuster has a long history in the Senate, and Senators from all parties and viewpoints have used it. In 1841, when the Democratic minority used it to block a bank bill of majority leader Henry Clay, Clay threatened to change Senate rules to allow the majority to close debate, and was promptly rebuked by another Senator for stifling the Senate's hallowed rule of unlimited debate. In 1917 it was the Democrats' turn to chafe under this same rule, when Republicans filibustered President Wilson's proposal to arm America merchant ships. In retaliation, Wilson got the Senate to adopt Rule 22, which allowed the Senate to end debate by a two-thirds vote. This is called "cloture," and in 1975 it was modified to a three-fifths vote of the entire Senate, which means 60 votes.

While individual Senators with leather lungs and steel bladders have held the floor for marathon performances, the most effective filibusters have been organized affairs, the *filibusteros* spelling each other off until the majority either gives up or somehow manages to get a supermajority to end debate. The longest group filibuster was staged by a band of Southern Democrats in 1964 who occupied the Senate for fifty-seven working days, including six Saturdays, in an attempt to prevent passage of the 1964 Civil Rights bill. Democratic whip Hubert Humphrey was able to impose cloture after rounding up the sixty-seven votes required at the time.

Today's filibusters are not the spectacles they used to be. The Senate rules do not require Senators actually to hold the floor in order to stage a filibuster. Today they simply inform Senate leaders that they have 41 Senators who are prepared to support a filibuster, and that is usually enough to deter the leaders from bringing the matter to the floor; whatever it was that was going to be voted on is scuttled while the rest of the business of the Senate goes on as usual.

By now, both parties have such a long history of filibustering legislation that there seems to be an implicit bipartisan understanding: controversial bills are fair game for it. What causes real bitterness is the filibustering of presidential appointments. Here we must distinguish between appointments to cabinet or administrative posts and appointments of judges. The former, it is generally agreed, are "the president's men" (or women), and every president is entitled to leeway in choosing the people who will serve the administration. The latter, however, are not supposed to be servants of any administration but nonpartisan judges; they will be deciding matter of great national importance long after the president has left office. Everyone agrees on these facts, but there are sharp differences about what the facts imply. For some, the obvious implication is that judicial appointments are indeed fair game for filibusters once it appears that the president is attempting to fill the federal bench with appointees who will be translating the president's ideology into federal law decades after he has left office. For others, what the facts add up to is that requiring a supermajority of 60 Senators to give consent to a presidential judicial appointment, instead of the 51 stipulated in the Constitution, violates both the letter and spirit of our nation's charter.

In the following selections, Marcia Greenberg inclines to the first view, arguing that the filibuster of judicial nominees forces the president to submit moderate, consensus nominees to the bench, while John C. Eastman claims that the filibuster of judicial nominees intrudes upon the president's power to nominate judges and threatens the independence of the judiciary.

 **YES**

Testimony

Introduction and Overview

The Constitution confers on the U.S. Senate a role in determining the composition of the federal courts that is co-equal to the role of the President: the President nominates appointments to the federal bench, but his nominees may serve if and only if the Senate gives its "advice and consent." It is clear why the framers of the Constitution concluded that an independent Senate role is appropriate: the judiciary is independent from the executive and legislative branches (and indeed is sometimes called upon to resolve disputes between the two), and federal judges sit on the bench not just for the term of the President who names them, but for life. So while it may be appropriate for Senators generally to give deference to a President's choices of Cabinet officers or other high-level executive branch officials to join his Administration and implement his policies, similar deference is not appropriate when it comes to the President's selection of judicial nominations.

In exercising their Constitutional responsibility to give or withhold consent to the President's judicial nominations, Senators necessarily operate within the rules of the Senate. In accordance with these rules, most nominations are decided by a confirmation vote on the Senate floor and approved if a simple majority of Senators vote in favor. Many nominations, however, are resolved in other ways; in some cases, for example, Senate leaders decide not to schedule a floor vote on a nomination (e.g., due to a "hold" placed on the nomination by even just one Senator), or the Judiciary Committee rejects the nomination or fails to take any action on it. And some nominations are decided only after a cloture vote is taken pursuant to Senate Rule 22—that is, after 60 Senators (three-fifths of the Senators in office) vote to invoke cloture and the nomination is allowed to go forward, or the cloture vote fails and it is not.

In fact, as shown below, cloture votes on judicial nominations have ample precedent in contemporary U.S. history, and there are a number of bases on which Senators may reasonably conclude that the use of this

From testimony before the Senate Judiciary Committee, May 6, 2003.

Senate procedure on judicial nominations is appropriate in some circumstances. Cloture votes are routine in the Senate today, and have occurred on judicial nominations in numerous instances in the past few decades—on judicial nominations submitted to the Senate by Presidents of both parties, including nominations to the Supreme Court as well as lower federal courts. They have been based at least in part on concerns about the ideology or judicial philosophy of the nominee, or objections to the nomination process, or both. As further shown below, requiring cloture on some judicial nominations is particularly appropriate at this juncture in our history. At present, the stakes are particularly high: one party controls two branches of government; the remaining branch, the judiciary, is tilted to the right; the balance that normally occurs over time as Administrations change has not occurred because of the obstruction of the last Administration's nominations; and the President is explicitly seeking to move the judiciary further to the right and, without consultation with the Senate, is selecting nominees with extreme, out-of-the-mainstream views on critical legal issues. . . .

The cloture vote is the mechanism for ending debate on the Senate floor, which otherwise may continue without limit under the Senate's rules. Until recent decades, cloture was generally used to try to bring to a close old-fashioned filibusters, in which Senators opposing a legislative measure (or nomination) engaged in a non-stop debate, for days and nights on end, in an effort to talk the measure to death. In the contemporary Senate, however, cloture votes are not reserved for actual filibusters, which are rare; rather, they are often prompted simply when even a single Senator signals strong opposition to a measure—e.g., by placing a "hold" on the matter. As a result, according to the Congressional Research Service (CRS), cloture votes have become increasingly common. While there were only 23 cloture votes in the entire period of 1919 through 1960 (and in at least 24 of those years, there were no cloture votes at all), in just one recent Congress (1997-98), the Senate voted on 53 cloture motions and invoked cloture 18 times. Indeed, as summarized in one scholarly analysis, "[I]t is now commonly said that sixty votes in the Senate, rather than a simple majority, are necessary to pass legislation and confirm nominations."

While used most often in the context of legislation, cloture votes on nominations are also increasingly frequent. CRS reports that from 1949 (when cloture on nominations was first permitted under the rules) through 2002, cloture was sought on 35 nominations. Of these, 17 were cloture votes on judicial nominations, including 14 Court of Appeals or District Court nominations since 1980. They include cloture votes on nominations submitted to the Senate by Democratic and Republican Presidents alike. The opposition to the nomination in every case was based at least in part on objections to the ideology or judicial philosophy of the nominee, or on procedural grounds such as concerns that the Judiciary Committee had inadequately examined the nominee's record, or both.

According to CRS, cloture motions were filed on the following judicial nominations:

- In 1968, President Lyndon Johnson nominated Associate Justice Abe Fortas to replace Earl Warren as Chief Justice of the Supreme Court when Warren announced his intention to retire. The Judiciary Committee approved the Fortas nomination by a vote of 11 to 6, but conservative Senators, led by Senator Strom Thurmond and others, mounted a filibuster on the floor on the motion to proceed to the nomination. Their objections to Fortas were based, among other things, on concerns that his opinions as a member of the Warren Court were too liberal in the areas of civil liberties and the rights of the accused as well as concerns about Justice Fortas' refusal to respond to some allegations leveled against him. Fortas' supporters failed to invoke cloture, forcing the president to withdraw the nomination.
- When William Rehnquist was nominated to serve on the Supreme Court by President Nixon in 1971, the nomination was opposed by civil rights groups based, among other things, on his past opposition to Arizona civil rights legislation and a school desegregation plan and allegations that he had been involved in the harassment of minority voters. Senate opponents of the nomination cited the need for extended debate, and two cloture motions were filed. Although supporters failed to invoke cloture, opponents subsequently permitted a vote to occur. Rehnquist was confirmed to the Court in December 1971.
- When Justice Rehnquist was nominated by President Reagan to serve as Chief Justice in 1986, he was again criticized for his civil rights record, which by then also included his lone dissent in the Bob Jones University case, in which the Court held that tax-exempt status may be denied to a university with racially discriminatory policies. In addition, some Senators sought an additional hearing to examine a discrepancy between Justice Rehnquist's testimony before the Committee and other evidence that had come to light. After Senator Kennedy refused to consent to a time agreement to limit debate, a cloture motion was filed. Cloture was invoked and Rehnquist was confirmed as Chief Justice.
- In December 1980, a floor vote on the nomination of Stephen Breyer (now a Supreme Court Justice) to the First Circuit was blocked by Senators protesting what they considered overly expedited treatment of the nomination during a lame duck session and trying to keep judicial seats open until incoming President Ronald Reagan could fill them. In addition, Senator Humphrey of New Hampshire (one of the states in the First Circuit) complained that he had not received the "usual" senatorial courtesies. A cloture motion was filed, cloture was invoked, and the nomination was confirmed.
- Democrats mounted vigorous opposition to several nominees of Presidents Reagan and George H.W. Bush to the Courts of Appeals—and one District Court nominee—in the 1980's and early 1990's, forcing cloture votes on them. . . .

- Strong Republican opposition to several of President Clinton's nominees for Courts of Appeals, and the use of extreme delaying tactics against them, prompted cloture votes during the 1990's. . . .

In short, history supplies ample precedents for subjecting controversial judicial nominations to cloture votes. . . .

It is hardly surprising that opponents of controversial judicial nominations sometimes force cloture votes, given what is at stake. Federal judges comprise a powerful branch of the U.S. government, and they sit with lifetime tenure. Once confirmed by the Senate, there is no means of holding them accountable for their actions, short of the extreme (and extremely rare) remedy of impeachment. Indeed, although cloture votes occur more often in connection with executive branch nominees than judicial nominees, and far more often on legislation, the stakes are higher for judicial confirmations: after all, legislation can always be amended or repealed, and executive branch appointments last only for finite terms or at the pleasure of the President, not for life. Moreover, the decisions that judges on federal courts render last through the ages and determine the scope and application of the most fundamental rights and liberties of American citizens. The Supreme Court, by interpreting the Constitution and federal statutes, establishes legal principles that reach every aspect of American life. And although the rulings of the Courts of Appeals are subject to Supreme Court review and the lower courts are required to abide by the high court's precedents, in reality the Courts of Appeals sit as the courts of last resort for the vast majority of litigants (since the Supreme Court decides fewer than 100 cases per year, while the Courts of Appeal decide over 28,000 per year) and they have tremendous latitude to interpret and apply the broad principles laid down by the Supreme Court.

At this juncture in U.S. history, moreover, even more is at stake than is normally the case. One party holds power in two of the three branches of government—the White House and both houses of the U.S. Congress—and its leaders seek to impose their philosophy on the judicial branch as well. At the same time, Justices who share the President's conservative philosophy already dominate the Supreme Court, and judges nominated by the President's party currently dominate the majority of the Courts of Appeals around the country. The "tilt" to the right on the lower courts is partly due to the use of obstructionist tactics that blocked an inordinately large number of Clinton Administration nominees—over one-third of President Clinton's nominations to the Courts of Appeals—which meant that the balancing process that normally takes place over time, as administrations change, did not occur. We are now on the brink of a wholesale transformation of the federal judiciary as this Administration seeks to tip the scales of justice even further toward the right. The filibuster, in some cases, is the last line of defense against this ideological shift.

Requiring 60 votes to invoke cloture has sometimes been criticized as "anti-majoritarian," usually by proponents of the measure being blocked. However, cloture is far from the only way in which matters are decided in the Senate without a vote of a simple majority of Senators, and without specific Constitutional language specifying a supermajority requirement (as there is, for example, with impeachment verdicts, veto overrides, treaty approval, and constitutional amendments). Legislative measures and nominations often die quiet deaths when committee chairs fail to schedule them for committee action, or the committee rejects them, or the leadership declines to call them up for a vote—due to a hold placed by a Senator, sometimes anonymously, or for some other reason. Indeed, from 1995 to 2001, many highly qualified judicial nominees received no hearing at all, including two Hispanic nominees to the Fifth Circuit (Jorge Rangel and Enrique Moreno) and others received a hearing but no Judiciary Committee action. In these situations, there is no Senate debate at all, much less votes on the floor for which all Senators can be held accountable. These practices, which could hardly be said to reflect the will of a majority of the Senate and are not even visible to the public, could be considered far less democratic than filibusters and cloture votes.

It has been argued, moreover, that by forcing a supermajority cloture vote to cut off debate, the filibuster provides necessary protection for the rights of the minority and is an important feature of a democracy. Senator [Orrin] Hatch [D., Utah] is one of those who has defended the filibuster. When other Senators were filibustering a Clinton Administration nomination to the Third Circuit in 1994, he called the filibuster "one of the few tools that the minority has to protect itself and those the minority represents." Similarly, when he participated in a filibuster against labor legislation in 1978, he said, "The filibuster rule is the only way the majority of the people, who are represented by a minority in the Senate, can be heard." Former Senate Majority Leader Howard Baker (R-TN) also has defended the filibuster as a protection for the rights of the minority and the deliberative process of the Senate itself. And conservative commentator George Will argued, when he opposed Clinton Administration legislation that was being filibustered in the Senate:

[T]he Senate is not obligated to jettison one of its defining characteristics, permissiveness regarding extended debate, in order to pander to the perception that the presidency is the sun around which all else in American government—even American life—orbits. . . . Democracy is trivialized when reduced to simple majoritarianism—government by adding machine. A mature, nuanced democracy makes provision for respecting not mere numbers but also intensity of feeling."

In light of all that is at stake in the confirmation of federal judges, especially at this time, those Senators with an "intensity of feeling" about the importance of a judiciary committed to civil rights and civil liberties should be expected to require cloture votes before troublesome nominations can move forward. . . .

There is ample precedent supporting the decision to mount strong opposition to controversial judicial nominations, such that cloture is needed. And just as the failure to invoke cloture on legislation—or the mere threat of a cloture vote and the need for a 60-vote majority—often forces proponents of a measure to agree to compromises in order to gain passage, the failure to invoke cloture on judicial nominations—or the prospect of needing 60 votes for a nomination to move forward—could lead the current Administration to consult with potential Senate opponents and agree to submit moderate, consensus nominees who are confirmable, as occurred during the Clinton administration. If this occurs now, the nation's interests will be well served.

John C. Eastman

 **NO**

Hijacking the Confirmation Process: The Filibuster Returns to Its Brigand Roots

We are here today to address a Senate procedural tactic—the filibuster—that dates back at least to Senator John C. Calhoun's efforts to protect slavery in the old South and that, until now, was used most extensively by southern Democrats to block civil rights legislation in the 1960s. In its modern embodiment, the tactic has been termed the "stealth filibuster." Unlike the famous "Mr. Smith Goes to Washington" movie image of Jimmy Stewart passionately defending his position until, collapsing, he persuades (or shames) his opponents to change their position, the modern practitioners of the brigand art of the filibuster have been able to ply their craft largely outside the public eye (and hence without the political accountability that is the hallmark of representative government). I am thus truly pleased to be here today, to help you and this committee in your efforts to "ping" the filibuster and make it not only less stealthy but perhaps restore to it some nobility of purpose.

Let me first note that I am not opposed to the filibuster per se, either as a matter of policy or of constitutional law. I think the Senate is, within certain structural limits, authorized to enact procedural mechanisms such as the filibuster, pursuant to its power under Article I, Section 5 of the Constitution to "determine the Rules of its Proceedings." And I think that, by encouraging extensive debate, the filibuster has in no small measure contributed to this body's reputation as history's greatest deliberative body. But I think it extremely important to distinguish between the *use* of the filibuster to enhance debate and the *abuse* of the filibuster to thwart the will of the people, as expressed through a majority of their elected representatives. The use of the filibuster for dilatory purposes is particularly troubling in the context of the judicial confirmation process, for it thwarts not just the majority in the Senate and the people who elected that majority—as any filibuster of ordinary legislation does—but it intrudes upon the President's power to nominate judges, and threatens the very independence of the Judiciary itself. . . .

From testimony before the Senate Judiciary Committee, May 6, 2003.

First, it is important to realize that the use of the filibuster in the judicial confirmation context raises structural constitutional concerns not present in the filibuster of ordinary legislation. Second, these constitutional concerns are so significant that this body should consider modifying Senate Rule XXII so as to preclude the use of the filibuster against judicial nominees. Third, any attempt to filibuster a proposal to change the rules would itself be unconstitutional. And finally, I believe that if this body does not act to abolish the supermajority requirement for ending debate on judicial nominees, it could be forced to do so as the result of litigation initiated by a pending nominee, by a member of this body, or even by the President himself. . . .

Article II of the Constitution provides that the President "shall nominate, and *by and with the Advice and Consent of the Senate,* shall appoint, . . . Judges of the Supreme Court" and of such inferior courts as Congress has ordained and established. This is one of the fundamental components of the separation of powers mechanism devised by our nation's founders to protect against governmental tyranny. By it, the Senate provides an important check on the power of the President, but it is only a check; recent claims that the advice and consent clause gives to the Senate a co-equal role in the appointment of federal judges simply are not grounded either in the Constitution's text or in the history and theory of the appointment's process. Necessarily, the claim that such power exists in less than a majority of the Senate is even more problematic. . . .

The President Alone Has the Power to *Nominate*

Article II of the Constitution provides that *the President "shall nominate, and* by and with the Advice and Consent of the Senate, *shall appoint . . .* Judges of the Supreme Court [and such inferior courts as the Congress may from time to time ordain and establish]." As the text of the provision makes explicitly clear, the power to choose nominees—to "nominate"—is vested solely in the President, and the President also has the primary role to "appoint," albeit with the advice and consent of the entire Senate. The text of the clause itself thus demonstrates that the role envisioned for the Senate was a much more limited one that is currently being claimed by some, and it was, in any event, a role assigned to the entire Senate, not to a minority faction. . . .

The convention delegates were primarily concerned about improper influence in the appointments process, and most of the debate centered on whether assigning the appointment power to the President or to the Senate would serve as a better check on that influence. Those who, like Madison, argued that the President should have the sole power of appointment believed that this procedure would best prevent such political bargaining. As Edmund Randolph noted, "[a]ppointments by the Legislatures have generally resulted from cabal, from personal regard, or some other consideration than a title derived from the proper qualifications."

In the end, the Convention agreed that the President would make the nominations, and the Senate—the entire Senate—would have a limited power to withhold confirmation as a check against political patronage or nepotism. Governeur Morris put the decision succinctly: "as the President was to nominate, there would be responsibility, and as the Senate was to concur, there would be security." As the Supreme Court subsequently recognized, "the Framers anticipated that the President would be less vulnerable to interest-group pressure and personal favoritism than would a collective body."

Madison, for instance, arguing in defense of his suggested compromise—that a 2/3 vote of the Senate could disqualify a judicial nomination, but otherwise giving the President a free hand—noted that

> The Executive Magistrate w^d be considered as a national officer, acting for and equally sympathizing with every part of the U. States. If the 2^d branch alone should have this power, the Judges might be appointed by a minority of the people, tho' by a majority, of the States, which could not be justified on any principle as their proceedings were to relate to the people, rather than to the States. . . .

Note that in Madison's proposal, a supermajority would have been required *to reject* a President's nominee, demonstrating just how preeminent was the role Madison envisioned for the President. Although the convention ultimately settled on a majority vote requirement, by assigning the sole power to nominate (and the primary power to appoint) judges to the President, the Convention specifically rejected a more expansive Senate role; such would undermine the President's responsibility, and far from providing security against improper appointments, would actually lead to the very kind of cabal-like behavior that the Convention delegates feared. These concerns are significantly exacerbated when, through use of the filibuster, a minority faction can thwart confirmation of a presidential nominee who enjoys majority support. . . .

The Framers Envisioned a Narrow Role for the Senate in the Confirmation Process

Of course, there is more to the appointment power than the power to nominate, and the Senate unquestionably has a role to play in the *confirmation* phase of the appointment process. But the role envisioned by the framers was as a check on improper appointments by the President, one that would not undermine the President's ultimate responsibility for the appointments he made. As James Iredell—later a Justice of the Supreme Court himself—noted during the North Carolina Ratification Convention, "[a]s to offices, the Senate has no other influence but a restraint on improper appointments. . . . This, in effect, is but a restriction on the President." Here, as elsewhere during the debates, the "restraint" on presidential appointments was to be exercised by the Senate as a body, acting pursuant to majority rule, not at the hands of a minority faction.

The degree to which the founders viewed the power of appointment as being vested solely in the President can be gauged by the fact that John Adams objected even to the Senate's limited confirmation role, contending that it "lessens the responsibility of the president." To Adams, the President should be *solely* responsible for his choices, and should alone pay the price for choosing unfit nominees. Under the current system, Adams complained, "Who can censure [the President] without censuring the senate . . .?" The appointment power is, Adams wrote, an "executive matter[]," which should be left entirely to "the management of the executive." James Wilson echoed this view: "The person who nominates or makes appointments to offices, should be known. His own office, his own character, his own fortune, should be responsible. He should be alike unfettered and unsheltered by counsellors." . . .

The Senate's confirmation power therefore acts only as a relatively minor check on the President's authority—it exists only to prevent the President from selecting a nominee who "does not possess due qualifications for office." Essentially, it exists to prevent the President from being swayed by nepotism or mere political opportunism. Assessing a candidate's "qualifications for office" arguably did not give the entire Senate grounds for imposing an ideological litmus on the President's nominees, at least where the questioned ideology did not prevent a judge from fulfilling his oath of office. It necessarily did not give such a power to a small faction of the Senate, as has become the practice through the use of ideologically-grounded holds or filibusters. . . .

The advice and consent role envisioned by the Constitution's text is one conferred on the Senate as a body, acting pursuant to the ordinary principal of majority rule. As . . . Michael Gerhardt has argued, "the Framers required a simple majority for confirmations to balance the demands of relatively efficient staffing of the government with the need to check abusive exercised of the president's discretion." Yale Law School Professor Bruce Ackerman apparently agrees, as his 1998 recommendation to adopt a supermajority vote for confirmation of Supreme Court justices was made by way of a proposed constitutional amendment rather than Senate rules. As Professor Gerhardt has rightly pointed out, "it is hard to reconcile [a supermajority requirement] with the Founders' reasons for requiring such a vote for removals and treaty ratifications but not for confirmations." Instead, the Constitution embodies a presumption of judicial confirmation, because it requires [only] a majority for approval" and not the two thirds vote required for treaty ratification or removals.

Professor Ackerman's proposal for a constitutional amendment requiring a supermajority vote for judicial confirmations has not garnered much support, of course, but the unprecedented use of the filibuster to block circuit court nominees who enjoy majority support is having the same effect even absent the constitutional amendment. Whether the filibuster is an unconstitutional restriction on a majority of the Senate in ordinary legislation has been much debated, but its use in the judicial confirmation process is particularly troubling. Again referring to Professor Gerhardt's work:

> [J]udicial nominations trigger separation-of-powers concerns not present in many of the other areas in which the Senate does not take final action on matters committed to its discretion. The fate of the third branch is conceivably at risk, because individual senators and committees might be able to impede filling enough judicial vacancies to reach the tipping point at which the quality of justice administered by the federal courts has been seriously compromised or sacrificed.

When President Clinton and Chief Justice Rehnquist make similar appeals to this body, as they did in 1997 and 1998, to curtail the use of "holds" by individual Senators because of the increasing number of vacancies on courts in "judicial emergency" status, I think it fair to conclude that the tipping point is at hand, quite apart from any ideological considerations. And the vacancy crisis has only grown worse since those warnings were made.

Some, such as Senator Dennis DeConcini and Law Professor Yvette Barksdale, have gone so far as to argue that the text of the advice and consent clause requires an up or down vote on every nominee—suggesting that individual holds and even the filibuster itself is an unconstitutional infringement on the President's appointment power. Others, including several sitting Senators now participating in the filibuster against Miguel Estrada, have contended that the use of the filibuster to block judicial nominees is an unconstitutional restriction on the power of the Senate majority. On January 4, 1995, for example, Senator [Joseph] Lieberman [D., Conn.] stated on the floor of the Senate that "there is no constitutional basis for [the filibuster] . . . [I]t is, in its way, inconsistent with the Constitution, one might almost say an amendment of the Constitution by rule of the U.S. Senate." Senator [Thomas] Daschle [D., South Dakota] noted on the Senate Floor on January 30, 1995, that "the Constitution is straightforward about the few instances in which more than a majority of the Congress must vote: A veto override, a treaty, and a finding of guilt in an impeachment proceeding. Every other action by the Congress is taken by majority vote. The Founders debated the idea of requiring more than a majority. . . . They concluded that putting such immense power into the hands of a minority ran squarely against the democratic principle. Democracy means majority rule, not minority gridlock." And on March 1, 1994, Senator [Thomas] Harkin [D., Ia.] said on the Senate Floor: "I really believe that the filibuster rules are unconstitutional. I believe the Constitution sets out five times when you need majority or supermajority votes in the Senate for treaties, impeachment." . . .

A filibuster rule designed to encourage necessary debate is certainly within the scope of this constitutional provision, but a filibuster designed not to encourage debate but to thwart the will of the majority long after the debate has run its course runs afoul of other constitutional norms, such as the requirement for majority rule in the absence of a specific constitutional provision to the contrary.

As I said, the anti-majoritarian nature of the filibuster is troubling even in ordinary legislation, but it is particularly troubling in the context of judicial confirmations. The judiciary is itself designed to be a counter-majoritarian institution, but that means the institutional checks on it must be given special heed. One check is the possibility of impeachment merely for lack of "good behavior" rather than "high crimes and misdemeanors" standard applicable to other officers of the government—a check that has been largely meaningless since the ill-fated impeachment of Justice Samual Chase during the Presidency of Thomas Jefferson. The other principal check—the only one that is still viable—is the ability of the electorate, through the choice of a President (or succession of Presidents) to have an impact, over time, on the judiciary through the President's appointment power. Individual members of the Senate are simply not accountable to the entire nation in the way that the President is.

To be sure, the President is not without other countervailing powers, powers that can be used to counter an abusive use of the Senate's rules to thwart the majority will. Article II, Section 2 gives the President the power to make recess appointments, but in the context of the judiciary, these appointments are not without their own separation of powers issues. Recess appointments are temporary, lasting only until the end of the next session of Congress. Those appointed necessarily lack the independence that comes with life tenure, one of the key institutional protections afforded to the judiciary. While nothing in the text of the Recess Appointments Clause forbids such appointments—President Clinton used the recess appointment power to name Roger Gregory to a seat on the Fourth Circuit Court of Appeals, for example—such structural concerns counsel for its use only as a last resort, when a rump faction of the Senate has persisted in blocking judicial nominees who command majority support. . . .

There are three principal ways to address the filibuster problem. First, and most drastically, the filibuster could be abolished altogether, not just in judicial confirmations but for ordinary legislation as well. Such a move would seem compelled by the absolutist position taken by Senators Lieberman, Daschle, and Harkin, described above, that would not permit anything but a majority vote to be dispositive except in the specific instances where the Constitution proscribes a supermajority requirement. Whatever the merits of such a proposal, it is beyond the scope of my presentation today.

A second alternative is to amend Senate Rule XXII so as to preclude the use of the filibuster in judicial confirmations. While this alternative is certainly within the Senate's prerogative, pursuant to the Article I, Section 5 power to establish its own rules, I think it fails to give sufficient play to the valuable role that a limited filibuster can play in fostering the deliberative process.

A third alternative would be to amend Senate Rule XXII to allow for a limited use of the filibuster to guarantee a reasonable time for debate without ultimately giving to a minority faction a veto power over a Senate majority. This alternative would distinguish between the *use* of the filibuster for deliberative ends, a use that I believe is constitutional, and the *abuse* of the filibuster for obstructionist, undemocratic ends, a use that I believe may well be unconstitutional. . . .

Conclusion

In sum, there is good reason that the filibuster has only rarely been used in the context of judicial confirmations, and never before against a circuit court judge. The use of the filibuster thwarts the will of the majority, and is therefore not only undemocratic but very likely unconstitutional. Moreover, should the Senate decide on its own initiative to repeal the offending use of the filibuster rule, any attempt to use the filibuster to entrench the filibuster would itself be unconstitutional, and would provide grounds for court intervention either by nominees, by individual Senators, or perhaps by the President himself, to insure that the constitutional norm of majority rule is given effect.

POSTSCRIPT

Is the Filibuster of Judicial Nominees Justifiable?

One rhetorical device used by both Marcia Greenberger and John C. Eastman is to quote people on the *other* side of controversy who at one time or another supported *their* side. Greenberg, for example, quotes Senator Orrin Hatch, who harshly criticized the Democrats' filibuster, when he defended a Republican filibuster during the Clinton administration. Eastman, for his part, quotes Senator Thomas Daschle and other Democrats condemning the filibuster during that same period. It is difficult not to suspect that there are no purely "principled" positions on the filibuster. Perhaps, as one Supreme Court justice said of another "principled" argument, "it all depends on whose ox is being gored."

Greenberger's and Eastman's remarks were among the testimonies presented to the Senate Judiciary Committee in May 2003. Others included those of Professor Michael Gerhardt of William & Mary Law School, who argued the legitimacy of filibustering judicial nominees, and Professor Steven Calabresi of Northwestern University Law School, who took the opposing view. Both of these can be found on the Web at http://judiciary.senate .gov/testimony.cfm?id=744&wit_id/. Jack Newfield credits Robert Caro's book, *Master of the Senate* (Vintaage Books, 2003) with emboldening Senate Minority Leader Tom Daschle to stick to his filibuster of President Bush's court nominees. The first two chapters of Caro's book lionize Senators Paul Douglas, Herbert Lehman, and Hubert Humphrey as role models "in the fight for social justice." See Newfield, "The Judiciary Wars," *The Nation* (June 2, 2003, pp. 6–7). In "Let's Get Ideological," *Commonweal* (April 11, 2003, pp. 11–12). Mark A. Sargent argues that Presidents have a perfect right to appoint judges on the basis of their political ideology and Senators have a similar right to filibuster their nominations because they oppose their ideology. This, he says, would cut out much of the "baloney" that now surrounds these ideological battles: "the expression of phony 'concerns' about qualifications, experience, or judicial temperament."

During the bitter fight over the filibuster of President Bush's Appeals Court appointees, some of the more zealous Republicans urged Senate Majority Leader Bill Frist to resort to what they called "the nuclear option"—changing Senate rules to prohibit filibusters of judicial appointees. Whether such a motion would itself be "filibuster-able" can be debated by lawyers and parliamentarians, but it was never attempted. Cooler heads among the Republicans reasoned that, with a changeover of parties in the White House and Senate, they themselves might need the filibuster.

In addition to the Internet sites listed below, type in key words, such as "capital punishment," "gun control," and "affirmative action," to find other listings.

New American Studies Web

This eclectic site provides links to a wealth of Internet resources for research in American studies, including agriculture and rural development, government, and race and ethnicity.

http://www.georgetown.edu/crossroads/asw/

Public Agenda Online

Public Agenda, a nonpartisan, nonprofit public opinion research and citizen education organization, provides links to policy options for issues ranging from abortion to Social Security.

http://www.publicagenda.org

NCPA Idea House

Through this site of the National Center for Policy Analysis, access discussions on an array of topics that are of major interest in the study of American government, from regulatory policy and privatization to economy and income.

http://www.ncpa.org/iss/

RAND

RAND is a nonprofit institution that works to improve public policy through research and analysis. Links offered on this home page provide for keyword searches of certain topics and descriptions of RAND activities and major research areas.

http://www.rand.org

Policy Library

This site provides a collection of documents on social and policy issues submitted by different research organizations all over the world.

http://www.policylibrary.com/US/index.html

PART 3

Social Change and Public Policy

*E*conomic and moral issues divide Americans. Americans appear to increasingly line up on one side or the other on issues as diverse as economic equality and opportunity, capital punishment and gun control laws, affirmative action and racial distinctions, abortion and gay marriage. Disagreement has spilled out of Congress and the state legislatures into the courts. These controversial issues generate intense emotions because they ask us to clarify our values and understand the consequences of the public policies America adopts in each of these areas.

- Is Capital Punishment Justified?

- Do We Need Tougher Gun Control Laws?

- Does Affirmative Action Advance Racial Equality?

- Should the President Be Allowed to Detain Citizens Indefinitely in Wartime?

- Is "Middle Eastern" Profiling Ever Justified?"

- Should Hate Speech Be Punished?

- Should There Be a Constitutional Amendment Banning Gay Marriage?

- Should Abortion Be Restricted?

- Are Tax Cuts Good for America?

- Is America Becoming More Unequal?

- Does the Patriot Act Abridge Essential Freedoms?

- Should America Restrict Immigration?

ISSUE 7

Is Capital Punishment Justified?

YES: Robert W. Lee, from "Deserving to Die," *The New American* (August 13, 1990)

NO: Eric M. Freedman, from "The Case Against the Death Penalty," *USA Today Magazine* (March 1997)

ISSUE SUMMARY

YES: Essayist Robert W. Lee argues that capital punishment is the only fair way for society to respond to certain heinous crimes.

NO: Law professor Eric M. Freedman contends that the death penalty does not reduce crime but does reduce public safety and carries the risk of innocent people being executed.

From 1995 through 1999, 373 inmates were executed in the United States, and at the beginning of 2000, 3,652 more were on death row. The numbers are small relative to the murder rate during those years, but the issue of capital punishment remains bitterly divisive.

Polls have shown that somewhat more than half of all Americans approve of capital punishment. If a shift in opinion is taking place, it is in response to the concern that innocent people may be executed in error. In 2000 Illinois governor George Ryan, who supports the death penalty, announced a moratorium on executions because he believed that the state's criminal justice system, in which 13 death row inmates had been exonerated since 1987, was "fraught with error." In Texas, where one-third of the executions in America have taken place in recent years (127 from 1995 through 1999), Governor George W. Bush expressed confidence that every person executed in that state was guilty.

Capital punishment is an ancient penalty, but both the definition of a capital crime and the methods used to put convicted persons to death have changed dramatically. In eighteenth-century Massachusetts, for example, capital crimes included blasphemy and the worship of false gods. Slave states often imposed the death penalty upon blacks for crimes that were punished by only two or three years' imprisonment when committed by whites. It has been estimated that in the twentieth century approximately 10 percent of all legal executions have been for the crime of rape, 1 percent for all other crimes except murder (robbery, burglary, attempted murder, etc.), and nearly 90 percent for the commission of murder.

Long before the Supreme Court severely limited the use of the death penalty, executions in the United States were becoming increasingly rare. In the 1930s there were 1,667; the total for the 1950s was 717. In the 1960s the numbers fell even more dramatically. For example, seven persons were executed in 1965, one in 1966, and two in 1967.

Then came the Supreme Court case *Furman v. Georgia* (1972), which many thought—mistakenly—"abolished" capital punishment in America. Actually, only two members of the *Furman* majority thought that capital punishment *per se* violates the Eighth Amendment's injunction against "cruel and unusual punishment." The other three members of the majority took the view that capital punishment is unconstitutional only when applied in an arbitrary or racially discriminatory manner, as they believed it was in this case. The four dissenters in the *Furman* case were prepared to uphold capital punishment both in general and in this particular instance. Not surprisingly, then, with a slight change of Court personnel—and with a different case before the Court—a few years later, the majority vote went the other way.

In the latter case, *Gregg v. Georgia* (1976), the majority upheld capital punishment under certain circumstances. In his majority opinion in the case, Justice Potter Stewart noted that the law in question (a new Georgia capital punishment statute) went to some lengths to avoid arbitrary procedures in capital cases. For example, Georgia courts were not given complete discretion in handing out death sentences to convicted murderers but had to consult a series of guidelines spelling out "aggravating circumstances," such as if the murder had been committed by someone already convicted of murder, if the murder endangered the lives of bystanders, and if the murder was committed in the course of a major felony. These guidelines, Stewart said, together with other safeguards against arbitrariness included in the new statute, preserved it against Eighth Amendment challenges.

Although the Court has upheld the constitutionality of the death penalty, it can always be abolished by state legislatures. However, that seems unlikely to happen in many states. If anything, the opposite is occurring. Almost immediately after the *Furman* decision of 1972, state legislatures began enacting new death penalty statutes designed to meet the objections raised in the case. By the time of the *Gregg* decision, 35 new death penalty statutes had been enacted.

In response to the public mood, Congress has put its own death penalty provisions into federal legislation. In 1988 Congress sanctioned the death penalty for drug kingpins convicted of intentionally killing or ordering anyone's death. More recently, in the 1994 crime bill, Congress authorized the death penalty for dozens of existing or new federal crimes, such as treason or the murder of a federal law enforcement agent.

In the following selections, Robert W. Lee argues that capital punishment is an appropriate form of retribution for certain types of heinous offenses, while Eric M. Freedman asserts that the practice of capital punishment fails every practical and moral test that may be applied to it.

Robert W. Lee  **YES**

Deserving to Die

A key issue in the debate over capital punishment is whether or not it is an effective deterrent to violent crime. In at least one important respect, it unquestionably is: It simply cannot be contested that a killer, once executed, is forever deterred from killing again. The deterrent effect on others, however, depends largely on how swiftly and surely the penalty is applied. Since capital punishment has not been used with any consistency over the years, it is virtually impossible to evaluate its deterrent effect accurately. Abolitionists claim that a lack of significant difference between the murder rates for states with and without capital punishment proves that the death penalty does not deter. But the states with the death penalty on their books have used it so little over the years as to preclude any meaningful comparison between states. Through July 18, 1990 there had been 134 executions since 1976. Only 14 states (less than 40 percent of those that authorize the death penalty) were involved. Any punishment, including death, will cease to be an effective deterrent if it is recognized as mostly bluff. Due to costly delays and endless appeals, the death penalty has been largely turned into a paper tiger by the same crowd that calls for its abolition on the grounds that it is not an effective deterrent!

To allege that capital punishment, if imposed consistently and without undue delay, would not be a deterrent to crime is, in essence, to say that people are not afraid of dying. If so, as columnist Jenkin Lloyd Jones once observed, then warning signs reading "Slow Down," "Bridge Out," and "Danger—40,000 Volts" are futile relics of an age gone by when men feared death. To be sure, the death penalty could never become a 100-percent deterrent to heinous crime, because the fear of death varies among individuals. Some race automobiles, climb mountains, parachute jump, walk circus high-wires, ride Brahma bulls in rodeos, and otherwise engage in endeavors that are more than normally hazardous. But, as author Bernard Cohen notes in his book *Law and Order*, "there are even more people who refrain from participating in these activities mainly because risking their lives is not to their taste."

Merit System

On occasion, circumstances *have* led to meaningful statistical evaluations of the death penalty's deterrent effect. In Utah, for instance, there have been three executions since the Supreme Court's 1976 ruling:

- Gary Gilmore faced a firing squad at the Utah State Prison on January 17, 1977. There had been 55 murders in the Beehive State during 1976 (4.5 per 100,000 population). During 1977, in the wake of the Gilmore execution, there were 44 murders (3.5 per 100,000), a 20 percent decrease.
- More than a decade later, on August 28, 1987, Pierre Dale Selby (one of the two infamous "hi-fi killers" who in 1974 forced five persons in an Ogden hi-fi shop to drink liquid drain cleaner, kicked a ballpoint pen into the ear of one, then killed three) was executed. During all of 1987, there were 54 murders (3.2 per 100,000). The count for January through August was 38 (a monthly average of 4.75). For September–December (in the aftermath of the Selby execution) there were 16 (4.0 per month, a nearly 16 percent decrease). For July and August there were six and seven murders, respectively. In September (the first month following Selby's demise) there were three.
- Arthur Gary Bishop, who sodomized and killed a number of young boys, was executed on June 10, 1988. For all of 1988 there were 47 murders (2.7 per 100,000, the fewest since 1977). During January–June, there were 26; for July–December (after the Bishop execution) the tally was 21 (a 19 percent difference).

In the wake of all three Utah executions, there have been notable decreases in both the number and the rate of murders within the state. To be sure, there are other variables that could have influenced the results, but the figures are there and abolitionists to date have tended simply to ignore them.

Deterrence should never be considered the *primary* reason for administering the death penalty. It would be both immoral and unjust to punish one man merely as an example to others. The basic consideration should be: Is the punishment deserved? If not, it should not be administered regardless of what its deterrent impact might be. After all, once deterrence supersedes justice as the basis for a criminal sanction, the guilt or innocence of the accused becomes largely irrelevant. Deterrence can be achieved as effectively by executing an innocent person as a guilty one (something that communists and other totalitarians discovered long ago). If a punishment administered to one person deters someone else from committing a crime, fine. But that result should be viewed as a bonus of justice properly applied, not as a reason for the punishment. The decisive consideration should be: Has the accused *earned* the penalty?

The Cost of Execution

The exorbitant financial expense of death penalty cases is regularly cited by abolitionists as a reason for abolishing capital punishment altogether. They prefer to ignore, however, the extent to which they themselves are responsible for the interminable legal maneuvers that run up the costs. . . .

As presently pursued, death-penalty prosecutions *are* outrageously expensive. But, again, the cost is primarily due to redundant appeals, time-consuming delays, bizarre court rulings, and legal histrionics by defense attorneys:

> Willie Darden, who had already survived three death warrants, was scheduled to die in Florida's electric chair on September 4, 1985 for a murder he had committed in 1973. Darden's lawyer made a last-minute emergency appeal to the Supreme Court, which voted against postponing the execution until a formal appeal could be filed. So the attorney (in what he later described as "last-minute ingenuity") then requested that the emergency appeal be technically transformed into a formal appeal. Four Justices agreed (enough to force the full court to review the appeal) and the execution was stayed. After additional years of delay and expense, Darden was eventually put out of our misery on March 15, 1988.
>
> Ronald Gene Simmons killed 14 members of his family during Christmas week in 1987. He was sentenced to death, said he was willing to die, and refused to appeal. But his scheduled March 16, 1989 execution was delayed when a fellow inmate, also on death row, persuaded the Supreme Court to block it (while Simmons was having what he expected to be his last meal) on the grounds that the execution could have repercussions for other death-row inmates. It took the Court until April 24th of [1990] to reject that challenge. Simmons was executed on June 25th.
>
> Robert Alton Harris was convicted in California of the 1978 murders of two San Diego teenagers whose car he wanted for a bank robbery. Following a seemingly interminable series of appeals, he was at last sentenced to die on April 3rd of [1990]. Four days earlier, a 9th U.S. Circuit Court of Appeals judge stayed the execution, largely on the claim that Harris was brain-damaged and therefore may possibly have been unable to "premeditate" the murders (as required under California law for the death penalty). On April 10th, the *Washington Times* reported that the series of tests used to evaluate Harris's condition had been described by some experts as inaccurate and "a hoax."
>
> The psychiatric game is being played for all it is worth. On May 14th, Harris's attorneys argued before the 9th Circuit Court that he should be spared the death penalty because he received "inadequate" psychiatric advice during his original trial. In 1985, the Supreme Court had ruled that a defendant has a constitutional right to "a competent psychiatrist who will conduct an appropriate examination." Harris had access to a licensed psychiatrist, but now argues that—since the recent (highly questionable) evaluations indicated brain damage and other alleged disorders that the original psychiatrist failed to detect (and which may have influenced the jury not to impose the death sentence)—a new trial (or at least a re-sentencing) is in order. If the courts buy this argument, hundreds (perhaps thousands) of cases could be reopened for psychiatric challenge.
>
> On April 2, 1974 William Neal Moore shot and killed a man in Georgia. Following his arrest, he pleaded guilty to armed robbery and

murder and was convicted and sentenced to death. On July 20, 1975 the Georgia Supreme Court denied his petition for review. On July 16, 1976 the U.S. Supreme Court denied his petition for review. On May 13, 1977 the Jefferson County Superior Court turned down a petition for a new sentencing hearing (the state Supreme Court affirmed the denial, and the U.S. Supreme Court again denied a review). On March 30, 1978 a Tattnall County Superior Court judge held a hearing on a petition alleging sundry grounds for a writ of *habeas corpus,* but declined on July 13, 1978 to issue a writ. On October 17, 1978 the state Supreme Court declined to review that ruling. Moore petitioned the U.S. District Court for southern Georgia. After a delay of more than two years, a U.S. District Court judge granted the writ on April 29, 1981. After another two-year delay, the 11th U.S. Circuit Court of Appeals upheld the writ on June 23, 1983. On September 30, 1983 the Circuit Court reversed itself and ruled that the writ should be denied. On March 5, 1984 the Supreme Court rejected the case for the third time.

Moore's execution was set for May 24, 1984. On May 11, 1984 his attorneys filed a petition in Butts County Superior Court, but a writ was denied. The same petition was filed in the U.S. District Court for Georgia's Southern District on May 18th, but both a writ and a stay of execution were denied. Then, on May 23rd (the day before the scheduled execution) the 11th Circuit Court of Appeals granted a stay. On June 4, 1984 a three-judge panel of the Circuit Court voted to deny a writ. After another delay of more than three years, the Circuit Court voted 7 to 4 to override its three-judge panel and rule in Moore's favor. On April 18, 1988, the Supreme Court accepted the case. On April 17, 1989 it sent the case back to the 11th Circuit Court for review in light of new restrictions that the High Court had placed on *habeas corpus.* On September 28, 1989 the Circuit Court ruled 6 to 5 that Moore had abused the writ process. On December 18, 1989 Moore's attorneys again appealed to the Supreme Court.

Moore's case was described in detail in *Insight* magazine for February 12, 1990. By the end of [1989] his case had gone through 20 separate court reviews, involving some 118 state and federal judges. It had been to the Supreme Court and back four times. There had been a substantial turnover of his attorneys, creating an excuse for one team of lawyers to file a petition claiming that all of the prior attorneys had given ineffective representation. No wonder capital cases cost so much!

Meanwhile, the American Bar Association proposes to make matters even worse by requiring states (as summarized by *Insight*) "to appoint two lawyers for every stage of the proceeding, require them to have past death penalty experience and pay them at 'reasonable' rates to be set by the court."

During an address to the American Law Institute on May 16, 1990, Chief Justice Rehnquist asserted that the "system at present verges on the chaotic" and "cries out for reform." The time expended between sentencing and execution, he declared, "is consumed not by structured review . . . but in fits of frantic action followed by periods of inaction." He urged that death row inmates be given one chance to challenge their sentences in state courts, and one challenge in federal courts, period.

Lifetime to Escape

Is life imprisonment an adequate substitute for the death penalty? Presently, according to the polls, approximately three-fourths of the American people favor capital punishment. But abolitionists try to discount that figure by claiming that support for the death penalty weakens when life imprisonment without the possibility of parole is offered as an alternative. (At other times, abolitionists argue that parole is imperative to give "lifers" some hope for the future and deter their violent acts in prison.)

Life imprisonment is a flawed alternative to the death penalty, if for no other reason than that so many "lifers" escape. Many innocent persons have died at the hands of men previously convicted and imprisoned for murder, supposedly for "life." The ways in which flaws in our Justice system, combined with criminal ingenuity, have worked to allow "lifers" to escape include these recent examples:

- On June 10, 1977, James Earl Ray, who was serving a 99-year term for killing Dr. Martin Luther King Jr., escaped with six other inmates from the Brushy Mountain State Prison in Tennessee (he was captured three days later).
- Brothers Linwood and James Briley were executed in Virginia on October 12, 1984 and April 18, 1985, respectively. Linwood had murdered a disc jockey in 1979 during a crime spree. During the same spree, James raped and killed a woman (who was eight months pregnant) and killed her five-year-old son. On May 31, 1984, the Briley brothers organized and led an escape of five death-row inmates (the largest death-row breakout in U.S. history). They were at large for 19 days.
- On August 1, 1984 convicted murderers Wesley Allen Tuttle and Walter Wood, along with another inmate, escaped from the Utah State Prison. All were eventually apprehended. Wood subsequently sued the state for $2 million for violating his rights by allowing him to escape. In his complaint, he charged that, by allowing him to escape, prison officials had subjected him to several life-threatening situations: "Because of extreme fear of being shot to death, I was forced to swim several irrigation canals, attempt to swim a 'raging' Jordan River and expose myself to innumerable bites by many insects. At one point I heard a volley of shotgun blasts and this completed my anxiety."
- On April 3, 1988 three murderers serving life sentences without the chance of parole escaped from the maximum-security West Virginia Penitentiary. One, Bobby Stacy, had killed a Huntington police officer in 1981. At the time, he had been free on bail after having been arrested for shooting an Ohio patrolman.
- On November 21, 1988 Gonzalo Marrero, who had been convicted of two murders and sentenced to two life terms, escaped from New Jersey's Trenton state prison by burrowing through a three-foot-thick cell wall, then scaling a 20-foot outer wall with a makeshift ladder.
- In August 1989 Arthur Carroll, a self-proclaimed enforcer for an East Oakland street gang, was convicted of murdering a man. On

September 28th, he was sentenced to serve 27-years-to-life in prison. On October 10th he was transferred to San Quentin prison. On October 25th he was set free after a paperwork snafu led officials to believe that he had served enough time. An all-points bulletin was promptly issued.

- On February 11, 1990 six convicts, including three murderers, escaped from their segregation cells in the maximum security Joliet Correctional Center in Illinois by cutting through bars on their cells, breaking a window, and crossing a fence. In what may be the understatement of the year, a prison spokesman told reporters: "Obviously, this is a breach of security."

Clearly, life sentences do not adequately protect society, whereas the death penalty properly applied does so with certainty.

Equal Opportunity Execution

Abolitionists often cite statistics indicating that capital punishment has been administered in a discriminatory manner, so that the poor, the black, the friendless, etc., have suffered a disproportionate share of executions. Even if true, such discrimination would not be a valid reason for abandoning the death penalty unless it could be shown that it was responsible for the execution of *innocent* persons (which it has not been, to date). Most attempts to pin the "discrimination" label on capital convictions are similar to one conducted at Stanford University a few years ago, which found that murderers of white people (whether white or black) are more likely to be punished with death than are killers of black people (whether white or black). But the study also concluded that blacks who murdered whites were somewhat *less* likely to receive death sentences than were whites who killed whites.

Using such data, the ACLU attempted to halt the execution of Chester Lee Wicker in Texas on August 26, 1986. Wicker, who was white, had killed a white person. The ACLU contended that Texas unfairly imposes the death penalty because a white is more likely than a black to be sentenced to death for killing a white. The Supreme Court rejected the argument. On the other hand, the execution of Willie Darden in Florida attracted worldwide pleas for amnesty from sundry abolitionists who, ignoring the Stanford study, claimed that Darden had been "railroaded" because he was black and his victim was white.

All criminal laws—in all countries, throughout all human history—have tended to be administered in an imperfect and uneven manner. As a result, some elements in society have been able to evade justice more consistently than others. But why should the imperfect administration of justice persuade us to abandon any attempt to attain it?

The most flagrant example of discrimination in the administration of the death penalty does not involve race, income, or social status, but gender. Women commit around 13 percent of the murders in America, yet, from 1930 to June 30, 1990, only 33 of the 3991 executions (less than 1 percent) involved women. Only one of the 134 persons executed since 1976 (through July 18th [1990]) has been a woman (Velma Barfield in North Carolina on November 2, 1984). One state governor commuted the death sentence of a woman because "humanity does not apply to women the inexorable law that it does to men."

According to L. Kay Gillespie, professor of sociology at Weber State College in Utah, evidence indicates that women who cried during their trials had a better chance of getting away with murder and avoiding the death penalty. Perhaps the National Organization for Women can do something about this glaring example of sexist "inequality" and "injustice." In the meantime, we shall continue to support the death penalty despite the disproportionate number of men who have been required to pay a just penalty for their heinous crimes.

Forgive and Forget?

Another aspect of the death penalty debate is the extent to which justice should be tempered by mercy in the case of killers. After all, abolitionists argue, is it not the duty of Christians to forgive those who trespass against them? In Biblical terms, the most responsible sources to extend mercy and forgiveness are (1) God and (2) the victim of the injustice. In the case of murder, so far as *this* world is concerned, the victim is no longer here to extend mercy and forgiveness. Does the state or any other earthly party have the right or authority to intervene and tender mercy on behalf of a murder victim? In the anthology *Essays on the Death Penalty,* the Reverend E. L. H. Taylor clarifies the answer this way: "Now it is quite natural and proper for a man to forgive something you do to *him*. Thus if somebody cheats me out of $20.00 it is quite possible and reasonable for me to say, 'Well, I forgive him, we will say no more about it.' But what would you say if somebody had done you out of $20.00 and I said, 'That's all right. I forgive him on your behalf'?"

The point is simply that there is no way, in *this* life, for a murderer to be reconciled to his victim, and secure the victim's forgiveness. This leaves the civil authority with no other responsible alternative but to adopt *justice* as the standard for assigning punishment in such cases.

Author Bernard Cohen raises an interesting point: ". . . if it is allowable to deprive a would-be murderer of his life, in order to forestall his attack, why is it wrong to take away his life after he has successfully carried out his dastardly business?" Does anyone question the right of an individual to kill an assailant should it be necessary to preserve his or her life or that of a loved one?

Happily, however, both scripture and our legal system uphold the morality and legality of taking the life of an assailant, if necessary, *before* he kills us. How, then, can it be deemed immoral for civil authority to take his life *after* he kills us?

Intolerant Victims?

Sometimes those who defend the death penalty are portrayed as being "intolerant." But isn't one of our real problems today that Americans are *too tolerant* of evil? Are we not accepting acts of violence, cruelty, lying, and immorality with all too little righteous indignation? Such indignation is not, as some would have us believe, a form of "hatred." In *Reflections on the Psalms,* C. S. Lewis discussed the supposed spirit of "hatred" that some critics claimed to see in parts of the Psalms: "Such hatreds are the kind of thing that cruelty and injustice, by a sort of natural law, produce. . . . Not to perceive it at all—not even to be tempted to resentment—to accept it as the most ordinary thing in the world—argues a terrifying insensibility. Thus the absence of anger, especially that sort of anger which we call indignation, can, in my opinion, be a most alarming symptom."

When mass murderer Ted Bundy was executed in Florida on January 24, 1989, a crowd of some 2000 spectators gathered across from the prison to cheer and celebrate. Many liberal commentators were appalled. Some contended that it was a spectacle on a par with Bundy's own callous disrespect for human life. One headline read: "Exhibition witnessed outside prison was more revolting than execution." What nonsense! As C. S. Lewis observed in his commentary on the Psalms: "If the Jews cursed more bitterly than the Pagans this was, I think, at least in part because they took right and wrong more seriously." It is long past time for us all to being taking right and wrong more seriously. . . .

Seeds of Anarchy

As we have seen, most discussions of the death penalty tend to focus on whether it should exist for murder or be abolished altogether. The issue should be reframed so that the question instead becomes whether or not it should be imposed for certain terrible crimes in addition to murder (such as habitual law-breaking, clearly proven cases of rape, and monstrous child abuse).

In 1953 the renowned British jurist Lord Denning asserted: "Punishment is the way in which society expresses its denunciation of wrongdoing; and in order to maintain respect of law, it is essential that the punishment for grave crimes shall adequately reflect the revulsion felt by a great majority of citizens for them." Nineteen years later, U.S. Supreme Court Justice Potter Stewart noted (while nevertheless concurring in the Court's 1972 opinion that temporarily banned capital punishment) that the "instinct for retribution is part of the nature of man and channeling that instinct in the administration of criminal justice serves an important purpose in promoting the stability of a society governed by law. When people begin to believe that organized society is unwilling or unable to impose upon criminal offenders the punishment they 'deserve,' then there are sown the seeds of anarchy—of self-help, vigilante justice, and lynch law."

To protect the innocent and transfer the fear and burden of crime to the criminal element where it belongs, we must demand that capital punishment be imposed when justified and expanded to cover terrible crimes in addition to murder.

Eric M. Freedman

 **NO**

The Case Against the Death Penalty

On Sept. 1, 1995, New York rejoined the ranks of states imposing capital punishment. Although the first death sentence has yet to be imposed, an overwhelming factual record from around the country makes the consequence of this action easily predictable: New Yorkers will get less crime control than they had before.

Anyone whose public policy goals are to provide a criminal justice system that delivers swift, accurate, and evenhanded results—and to reduce the number of crimes that actually threaten most people in their daily lives—should be a death penalty opponent. The reason is simple: The death penalty not only is useless in itself, but counterproductive to achieving those goals. It wastes enormous resources—fiscal and moral—on a tiny handful of cases, to the detriment of measures that might have a significant impact in improving public safety.

Those who believe the death penalty somehow is an emotionally satisfying response to horrific crimes should ask themselves whether they wish to adhere to that initial reaction in light of the well-documented facts:

Fact: The death penalty does not reduce crime.

Capital punishment proponents sometimes assert that it simply is logical to think that the death penalty is a deterrent. Whether or not the idea is logical, it is not true, an example of the reality that many intuitively obvious propositions—*e.g.,* that a heavy ball will fall faster if dropped from the Leaning Tower of Pisa than a light one—are factually false.

People who commit capital murders generally do not engage in probability analysis concerning the likelihood of getting the death penalty if they are caught. They may be severely mentally disturbed people like Ted Bundy, who chose Florida for his final crimes *because* it had a death penalty.

Whether one chooses to obtain data from scholarly studies, the evidence of long-term experience, or accounts of knowledgeable individuals, he or she will search in vain for empirical support for the proposition that imposing the death penalty cuts the crime rate. Instead, that person will find:

- The question of the supposed deterrent effect of capital punishment is perhaps the single most studied issue in the social sciences. The results are as unanimous as scholarly studies can be in finding the death penalty not to be a deterrent.
- Eighteen of the 20 states with the highest murder rates have and use the death penalty. Of the nation's 20 big cities with the highest murder rates, 17 are in death penalty jurisdictions. Between 1975 and 1985, almost twice as many law enforcement officers were killed in death penalty states as in non-death penalty states. Over nearly two decades, the neighboring states of Michigan, with no death penalty, and Indiana, which regularly imposes death sentences and carries out executions, have had virtually indistinguishable homicide rates.
- Myron Love, the presiding judge in Harris County, Tex. (which includes Houston), the county responsible for 10% of all executions in the entire country since 1976, admits that "We are not getting what I think we should be wanting and that is to deter crime. . . . In fact, the result is the opposite. We're having more violence, more crime."

Fact: The death penalty is extraordinarily expensive.

Contrary to popular intuition, a system with a death penalty is vastly more expensive than one where the maximum penalty is keeping murderers in prison for life. A 1982 New York study estimated the death penalty cost conservatively at three times that of life imprisonment, the ratio that Texas (with a system that is on the brink of collapse due to underfunding) has experienced. In Florida, each execution runs the state $3,200,000—six times the expense of life imprisonment. California has succeeded in executing just two defendants (one a volunteer) since 1976, but could save about $90,000,000 *per year* by abolishing the death penalty and re-sentencing all of its Death Row inmates to life.

In response, it often is proposed to reduce the costs by eliminating "all those endless appeals in death penalty cases." This is not a new idea. In recent years, numerous efforts have been made on the state and Federal levels to do precisely that. Their failure reflects some simple truths:

- Most of the extra costs of the death penalty are incurred prior to and at trial, not in postconviction, proceedings. Trials are far more likely under a death penalty system (since there is so little incentive to plea-bargain). They have two separate phases (unlike other trials) and typically are preceded by special motions and extra jury selection questioning—steps that, if not taken before trial, most likely will result in the eventual reversal of the conviction.
- Much more investigation usually is done in capital cases, particularly by the prosecution. In New York, for instance, the office of the State Attorney General (which generally does not participate in

local criminal prosecutions) is creating a new multi-lawyer unit to provide support to county district attorneys in capital cases.

• These expenses are incurred even though the outcome of most such trials is a sentence other than death and even though up to 50% of the death verdicts that are returned are reversed on the constitutionally required first appeal. Thus, the taxpayers foot the bill for all the extra costs of capital pretrial and trial proceedings and then must pay either for incarcerating the prisoner for life or the expenses of a retrial, which itself often leads to a life sentence. In short, even if all post-conviction proceedings following the first appeal were abolished, the death penalty system still would be more expensive than the alternative.

In fact, the concept of making such an extreme change in the justice system enjoys virtually no support in any political quarter. The writ of *habeas corpus* to protect against illegal imprisonment is available to every defendant in any criminal case, whether he or she is charged with being a petty thief or looting an S&L. It justly is considered a cornerstone of the American system of civil liberties. To eliminate all those "endless appeals" either would require weakening the system for everyone or differentially with respect to death penalty cases.

Giving less due process in capital cases is the opposite of what common sense and elementary justice call for and eventually could lead to innocent people being executed. Since the rate of constitutional violations is far greater in capital cases than in others—capital defendants seeking Federal *habeas corpus* relief succeed some 40% of the time, compared to a success rate of less than five percent for non-capital defendants—the idea of providing less searching review in death penalty cases is perverse.

Considering that the vast majority of post-conviction death penalty appeals arise from the inadequacies of appointed trial counsel, the most cost-effective and just way of decreasing the number of years devoted to capital proceedings, other than the best way—not enacting the death penalty—would be to provide adequate funding to the defense at the beginning of the process. Such a system, although more expensive than one without capital punishment, at least would result in some predictability. The innocent would be acquitted speedily; the less culpable would be sentenced promptly to lesser punishments; and the results of the trials of those defendants convicted and sentenced to death ordinarily would be final.

Instead, as matters now stand, there is roughly a 70% chance that a defendant sentenced to death eventually will succeed in getting the outcome set aside. The fault for this situation—which is unacceptable to the defense and prosecution bars alike—lies squarely with the states. It is they that have created the endless appeals by attempting to avoid the ineluctable monetary costs of death penalty systems and to run them on the cheap by refusing to provide adequate funding for defense counsel.

Fact: The death penalty actually reduces public safety.

The costs of the death penalty go far beyond the tens of millions of dollars wasted in the pursuit of a chimera. The reality is that, in a time of fixed or declining budgets, those dollars are taken away from a range of programs that would be beneficial. For example:

- New York State, due to financial constraints, can not provide bullet-proof vests for every peace officer—a project that, unlike the death penalty, certainly would save law enforcement lives.
- According to FBI statistics, the rate at which murders are solved has dropped to an all-time low. Yet, empirical studies consistently demonstrate that, as with other crimes, the murder rate decreases as the probability of detection increases. Putting money into investigative resources, rather than wasting it on the death penalty, could have a significant effect on crime.
- Despite the large percentage of ordinary street crimes that are narcotics-related, the states lack the funding to permit drug treatment on demand. The result is that people who are motivated to cure their own addictions are relegated to supporting themselves through crime, while the money that could fund treatment programs is poured down the death penalty drain.

Fact: The death penalty is arbitrary in operation.

Any reasonably conscientious supporter of the death penalty surely would agree with the proposition that, before someone is executed by the state, he or she first should receive the benefits of a judicial process that is as fair as humanly possible.

However, the one thing that is clear about the death penalty system that actually exists—as opposed to the idealized one some capital punishment proponents assume to exist—is that it does not provide a level of fairness which comes even close to equaling the gravity of the irreversible sanction being imposed. This failure of the system to function even reasonably well when it should be performing excellently breeds public cynicism as to how satisfactorily the system runs in ordinary, non-capital cases.

That reaction, although destructive, is understandable, because the factors that are significant in determining whether or not a particular defendant receives a death sentence have nothing at all to do with the seriousness of his or her crime. The key variables, rather, are:

- Racial discrimination in death-sentencing, which has been documented repeatedly. For instance, in the five-year period following their re-institution of the death penalty, the sentencing patterns in Georgia and Florida were as follows: when black kills white—Georgia, 20.1% (32 of 159 cases) and Florida, 13.7% (34 of 249); white kills white—Georgia, 5.7% (35 of 614) and Florida, 5.2% (80 of 1,547); white kills black—Georgia, 2.9% (one of 34) and Florida, 4.3% (three of 69); black kills black—Georgia, 0.8% (11 of 1,310) and Florida, 0.7% (three of 69).
  A fair objection may be that these statistics are too stark because they fail to take into account other neutral variables—*e.g.,* the

brutality of the crime and the number and age of the victims. Nevertheless, many subsequent studies, whose validity has been confirmed in a
major analysis for Congress by the General Accounting Office, have
addressed these issues. They uniformly have found that, even when all
other factors are held constant, the races of the victim and defendant
are critical variables in determining who is sentenced to death.

Thus, black citizens are the victim of double discrimination.
From initial charging decisions to plea bargaining to jury sentencing,
they are treated more harshly when they are defendants, but their
lives are given less value when they are victims. Moreover, all-white
or virtually all-white juries still are commonplace in many places.

One common reaction to this evidence is not to deny it, but
to attempt to evade the facts by taking refuge in the assertion that
any effective system for guarding against racial discrimination
would mean the end of the death penalty. Such a statement is a
powerful admission that governments are incapable of running
racially neutral capital punishment systems. The response of any
fair-minded person should be that, if such is the case, governments
should not be running capital punishment systems.

- Income discrimination. Most capital defendants can not afford an
  attorney, so the court must appoint counsel. Every major study of
  this issue, including those of the Powell Commission appointed by
  Chief Justice William Rehnquist, the American Bar Association,
  the Association of the Bar of the City of New York, and innumerable scholarly journals, has found that the quality of defense representation in capital murder trials generally is far lower than in
  felony cases.

  The field is a highly specialized one, and since the states have
  failed to pay the amounts necessary to attract competent counsel,
  there is an overwhelming record of poor people being subjected to
  convictions and death sentences that equally or more culpable—
  but more affluent—defendants would not have suffered.

- Mental disability. Jurors are more likely to sentence to death people who seem different from themselves than individuals who
  seem similar to themselves. That is the reality underlying the stark
  fact that those with mental disabilities are sentenced to death at a
  rate far higher than can be justified by any neutral explanation.
  This reflects prejudice, pure and simple.

Fact: Capital punishment inevitably will be inflicted on the innocent.

It is ironic that, just as New York was reinstating the death penalty, it
was in the midst of a convulsive scandal involving the widespread fabrication
of evidence by the New York State Police that had led to scores of people—
including some innocent ones—being convicted and sentenced to prison
terms. Miscarriages of justice unquestionably will occur in any human system, but the death penalty presents two special problems in this regard:

- The arbitrary factors discussed above have an enormous negative
  impact on accuracy. In combination with the emotional atmosphere generally surrounding capital cases, they lead to a situation

where the truth-finding process in capital cases is *less* reliable than in others. Indeed, a 1993 House of Representatives subcommittee report found 48 instances over the previous two decades in which innocent people had been sentenced to death.

- The stark reality is that death is final. A mistake can not be corrected if the defendant has been executed.

How often innocent people have been executed is difficult to quantify; once a defendant has been executed, few resources generally are devoted to the continued investigation of the case. Nonetheless, within the past few years, independent investigations by major news organizations have uncovered three cases, two in Florida and one in Mississippi, where people were put to death for crimes they did not commit. Over time, others doubtless will come to light (while still others will remain undiscovered), but it will be too late.

The fact that the system sometimes works—for those who are lucky enough to obtain somehow the legal and investigative resources or media attention necessary to vindicate their claims of innocence—does not mean that most innocent people on Death Row are equally fortunate. Moreover, many Death Row inmates who have been exonerated would have been executed if the legal system had moved more quickly, as would occur if, as those now in power in Congress have proposed, Federal *habeas corpus* is eviscerated.

The death penalty is not just useless—it is positively harmful and diverts resources from genuine crime control measures. Arbitrarily selecting out for execution not the worst criminals, but a racially determined handful of the poorest, most badly represented, least mentally healthy, and unluckiest defendants—some of whom are innocent—breeds cynicism about the entire criminal justice system.

Thus, the Criminal Justice Section of the New York State Bar Association—which includes prosecutors, judges, and defense attorneys—opposed reinstitution of the death penalty because of "the enormous cost associated with such a measure, and the serious negative impact on the delivery of prosecution and defense services throughout the state that will result." Meanwhile, Chief Justice Dixon of the Louisiana Supreme Court put it starkly: "Capital punishment is destroying the system."

POSTSCRIPT

Is Capital Punishment Justified?

In their arguments, Lee and Freedman cite some of the same facts and figures but draw opposite conclusions. Both, for example, note how expensive it is to keep prisoners on death row for so many years while appeals continue. Lee, however, draws from this the conclusion that appeals should be limited, while Freedman uses it to show that it costs taxpayers less to keep a felon in prison for life than to try to kill him.

Note that Lee does not rest his case for capital punishment on deterrence. He calls deterrence a "bonus" but not a primary justification. What really counts, he says, is whether or not the accused has "earned" the death penalty. For a similar argument developed at greater length, see Walter Berns, *For Capital Punishment: Crime and the Morality of the Death Penalty* (Basic Books, 1979). Directly opposed to the contention that capital punishment is moral is the view of the late judge Lois G. Forer: "Killing human beings when carried out by government as a matter of policy is, I believe, no less abhorrent than any other homicide." Forer's case against capital punishment is presented in her book *A Rage to Punish: The Unintended Consequences of Mandatory Sentencing* (W. W. Norton, 1994). For a moving account of how one condemned man was put into the electric chair *twice* (the first time the jolt was not enough to kill him) after losing a Supreme Court appeal based on "double jeopardy" and "cruel and unusual punishment," see chapter 10 of Fred W. Friendly and Martha Elliott, *The Constitution: That Delicate Balance* (Random House, 1984). *Dead Man Walking: An Eyewitness Account of the Death Penalty in the United States* by Helen Prejean (Vintage Books, 1994) is an impassioned account by a Catholic nun of her friendship with two death row inmates and her pleas for the abolition of capital punishment. Prejean makes all the expected arguments against capital punishment, but the book's power lies in her account of executions. (This story has been made into a motion picture of the same name.)

How often are innocent people convicted of crimes punishable by death? How often are these innocent people executed? In *In Spite of Innocence: Erroneous Convictions in Capital Cases* (Northeastern University Press, 1992), Michael L. Radelet, Hugo Adam Bedau, and Constance E. Putnam describe more than 400 incidents in which they contend that wrongful convictions in capital cases occurred as a result of confused eyewitness testimony, perjury, coerced confessions, or police conspiracy. In *The Death Penalty: An American History* (Harvard University Press, 2002), Stuart Banner provides an overview of American attitudes toward capital punishment from the seventeenth century to the present.

The United States and Japan are the only two industrial democracies which allow the death penalty. It was outlawed in Western Europe, for the most part between the 1940s and the '80s, although the Netherlands banned it as early as 1870. Most of the countries permitting it are either in Africa or the Middle East, though countries as varied as North Korea and South Korea, Cuba and Mongolia still use it. Whether the U.S. will ever ban it remains highly doubtful, since the Supreme Court has refused to consider it a "cruel and unusual punishment" under the Eighth Amendment and neither of our political parties is prepared to support a movement to take it off the books.

ISSUE 8

Do We Need Tougher Gun Control Laws?

YES: Carl T. Bogus, from "The Strong Case for Gun Control," *The American Prospect* (Summer 1992)

NO: John R. Lott, Jr., from *More Guns, Less Crime: Understanding Crime and Gun-Control Laws* (University of Chicago Press, 1998)

ISSUE SUMMARY

YES: Writer Carl T. Bogus argues that even local gun control laws will reduce the number of gun-related crimes.

NO: Social analyst John R. Lott, Jr., argues that giving law-abiding citizens the right to carry concealed handguns deters street crime.

$\mathbf{A}$ slow but significant decline in the murder rate and violent crime in the United States generally began in 1992. By 1998 the murder rate had declined to its lowest level in three decades. But the country was in for a shocking series of gun murders by young people directed primarily at other young people in schools.

In 1998 alone, two boys, aged 11 and 13, shot at classmates and teachers from the woods in Arkansas, killing 4 students and 1 teacher and wounding 10 others during a false fire alarm; a 14-year-old boy killed a teacher and wounded 2 students at a dance at a Pennsylvania middle school; an 18-year-old killed his ex-girlfriend's new boyfriend in the parking lot of a Tennessee high school; and 15-year-old Kip Kinkel killed 2 students and wounded 22 others in an Oregon high school cafeteria. A day before the shooting, Kinkel had been arrested and released to his parents after it was discovered that he had a gun at school. His parents were later found dead in their home. The nation's deadliest school shooting took place the following year at a Colorado high school, when two students, aged 17 and 18, killed 12 students and a teacher and wounded 23 before they killed themselves.

These tragic events brought to public attention the shocking fact that in a single year more than 4,000 children are killed by guns in the United States. In May 2000 the Million Mom March brought several hundred thousand mothers and others to the Washington Mall to advocate more gun control. The demonstrators urged licensing, safety checks, and limiting purchases to one handgun per month.

What has been done? What can be done? Can gun control make a difference, or are the causes of gun violence and its reduction to be found elsewhere?

In November 1993, after seven years of wrangling, Congress finally passed the Brady Bill. For several years, James Brady, a press secretary to President Ronald Reagan who was partially paralyzed by a bullet intended for Reagan in 1981, had been heading a campaign to regulate handguns. The National Rifle Association (NRA) and other opponents of gun control had fought hard against any such legislation, and Republican presidents had largely agreed with the NRA position that the best way to curb gun violence is not to ban guns but to stiffen penalties against those who use them illegally. But President Bill Clinton threw his support behind the Brady Bill, and it was enacted by Congress.

The Brady Act, requiring a background check on potential gun purchasers, has resulted in the rejection of 100,000 prospective gun buyers, but criminals can buy weapons on the black market or abroad, obtain them in informal transactions, and steal them.

The year following passage of the Brady Act, Congress confirmed the fears of those who argued that it would be the opening wedge for more gun control. The 1994 crime act included a ban on assault weapons. An assault weapon has a magazine capable of holding many rounds that can be fired each time the trigger is pulled. The 1994 law placed a 10-year ban on the manufacture and sale of 19 types of assault weapons as well as copycat models and certain other guns with features similar to assault weapons.

Is it too late to curb gun possession in the United States? There are at least 200 million guns in private hands in the United States, and approximately one-half of all American households contain at least one gun. This has not changed much over the past 40 years, which means that most people who buy guns already own guns. In some rural areas, it is unusual for a household not to have a gun.

Advocates and opponents differ in their assessments of the consequences of gun control laws. Those supporting gun control point to Great Britain and Japan, which have very tough firearm laws and very low murder rates. Opponents respond that low murder rates in these countries result from their cultures. They point to countries like Switzerland, New Zealand, and Israel, where firearms are prevalent and murder rates are very low. Opponents also echo the National Rifle Association's argument that "guns do not kill people; people do." Supporters of gun control point out that it is harder to kill (especially large numbers of) people without guns.

In the following selections, Carl T. Bogus and John R. Lott, Jr., focus on the consequences of gun control and reach opposed conclusions. Bogus presents evidence suggesting that, even with other demographic factors held nearly constant, there is less gun-related crime in areas that have gun control. Lott's research indicates that depriving law-abiding citizens of the right to own and carry handguns takes away a powerful deterrent to crime.

Carl T. Bogus  **YES**

The Strong Case for Gun Control

While abhorring violence, Americans generally believe that gun control cannot do much to reduce it. A majority of Americans questioned in a 1992 CBS–*New York Times* poll responded that banning handguns would only keep them away from law-abiding citizens rather than reduce the amount of violent crime. Many serious scholars have accepted the argument that the huge number of guns already in circulation would make any gun control laws ineffective. Until recently, it has been difficult to answer these objections. But in the past few years, new research has demonstrated that some gun control laws do work, dramatically reducing murder rates.

Gun violence is a plague of such major proportions that its destructive power is rivaled only by wars and epidemics. During the Vietnam War, more than twice as many Americans were shot to death in the United States as died in combat in Vietnam. Besides the 34,000 Americans killed by guns each year, more than 60,000 are injured—many seriously—and about a quarter of a million Americans are held up at gunpoint.

Measures that demonstrably reduce gun violence would gain wide public support. But that has been exactly the problem: A public that approves of gun control by wide margins also is skeptical about its effectiveness and even its constitutionality. Both of these sources of doubt can now be put to rest.

A Tale of Two Cities

Perhaps the most dramatic findings about the efficacy of gun control laws come from a study comparing two cities that have followed different policies for regulating handguns: Seattle, Washington and Vancouver, British Columbia.[1] Only 140 miles apart, the two cities are remarkably alike despite being located on opposite sides of an international border. They have populations nearly identical in size and, during the study period (1980–86), had similar socioeconomic profiles. Seattle, for example, had a 5.8 percent unemployment rate while Vancouver's was 6.0 percent. The median household income in Seattle was $16,254; in Vancouver, adjusted in U.S. dollars, it was $16,681. In racial and ethnic makeup, the two cities are also similar. Whites represent 79 percent of Seattle's inhabitants and 76 percent of Vancouver's. The principal racial difference is that Asians make up a larger

Figure 1

Aggravated Assaults per 100,000 People, 1980 1983, by Weapon

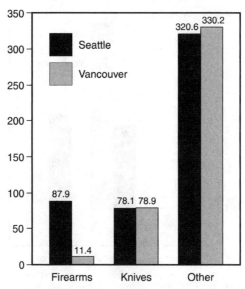

Source: John Henry Sloan, et al., "Handgun Regulations, Crime, Assaults, and Homicide," *The New England Journal of Medicine,* Nov. 10, 1988, pp. 1256–62. Reprinted by permission.

share of Vancouver's population (22 percent versus 7 percent). The two cities share not only a common frontier history but a current culture as well. Most of the top ten television shows in one city, for example, also rank among the top ten in the other.

As one might expect from twin cities, burglary rates in Seattle and Vancouver were nearly identical. The aggravated assault rate was, however, slightly higher in Seattle. On examining the data more closely, the Sloan study found "a striking pattern." There were almost identical rates of assaults with knives, clubs and fists, but there was a far greater rate of assault with firearms in Seattle. Indeed, the firearm assault rate in Seattle was nearly eight times higher than in Vancouver [see Figure 1].

The homicide rate was also markedly different in the two cities. During the seven years of the study, there were 204 homicides in Vancouver and 388 in Seattle—an enormous difference for two cities with comparable populations. Further analysis led to a startling finding: the entire difference was due to gun-related homicides. The murder rates with knives—and all other weapons excluding firearms—were virtually identical, but the rate of murders involving guns was five times greater in Seattle [see Figure 2]. That alone accounted for Seattle having nearly twice as many homicides as Vancouver.

People in Seattle may purchase a handgun for any reason after a five-day waiting period; 41 percent of all households have handguns. Vancouver on the other hand, requires a permit for handgun purchases and issues them

Figure 2

Murders per 100,000 People, 1980–1986, by Weapon

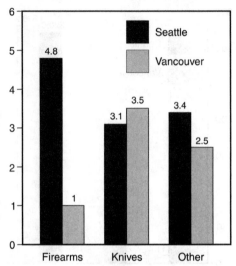

Source: John Henry Sloan, et al., "Handgun Regulations, Crime, Assaults, and Homicide," *The New England Journal of Medicine,* Nov. 10, 1988, pp. 1256–62. Reprinted by permission.

only to applicants who have a lawful reason to own a handgun and who, after a careful investigation, are found to have no criminal record and to be sane. Self-defense is not a valid reason to own a handgun, and recreational uses of handguns are strictly regulated. The penalty for illegal possession is severe—two years' imprisonment. Handguns are present in only 12 percent of Vancouver's homes.

The Seattle-Vancouver study provides strong evidence for the efficacy of gun control. Sloan and his colleagues concluded that the wider proliferation of handguns in Seattle was the sole cause of the higher rate of murders and assaults. The study answered other important questions as well.

- *Do handguns deter crime?* If handguns deter burglary, the burglary rate in Seattle—where so many more homes have handguns— should have been lower than the burglary rate in Vancouver. But it was not.
- *How often are handguns used for self-defense?* Less than 4 percent of the homicides in both cities resulted from acts of self-defense.
- Perhaps most important: *If handguns are unavailable, will people merely use other weapons instead?* The answer must be "no." Otherwise, the cities would have had similar total murder rates and Vancouver would have had higher rates of homicide with other weapons.

A more recent study measured gun control legislation more directly.[2] In 1976 the District of Columbia enacted a new gun control law. Residents who lawfully owned firearms had sixty days to reregister them. After the sixty-day period, newly acquired handguns became illegal. Residents could continue to register rifles and shotguns, provided they purchased them from licensed dealers and complied with other regulations.

The researchers compared gun-related violence in the nine years prior to the law's enactment with the following nine years. They also compared the experience within the District with that of the immediately surrounding metropolitan area. The law was, of course, only in force within the boundaries of the District itself and not in contiguous areas of Maryland and Virginia that belong to the same metropolitan area, as the Census Bureau defines it.

The results of the study were surprising even to the most ardent gun control advocates. Within the District, gun-related homicides fell by more than 25 percent and gun-related suicides declined by 23 percent. Meanwhile, there was no statistically significant change in either gun-related homicides or suicides in the adjacent areas. Here again the data demonstrated that people did not switch to other weapons: within the District there was no statistically significant change in either homicides or suicides with other weapons.

Perhaps most surprising of all was the suddenness of the change. Any decline in murders and suicides was expected to be gradual, as the number of weapons in the district slowly shrank. Yet homicides and suicides abruptly declined when the law went into effect. The D.C. law, therefore, had a significant and virtually immediate benefit.

The D.C. study demonstrates that gun control can work in the United States. Despite the similarities between Seattle and Vancouver, some critics of the Sloan study have suggested that Canada and the United States are sufficiently different to make extrapolations questionable. The D.C. study shows that even local gun control laws can be effective in the U.S. Previously, the prevailing opinion was that only national legislation could be effective. Critics said that if local laws blocked handgun purchases, buyers would simply import one from a nearby area. Many people probably do just that, and there is little doubt that national legislation would be far more effective.

Washington D.C.'s gun control law has not transformed the city into a utopia. It has remained a violent city and—along with many other large cities—its murder rate rose sharply in the last few years of the study (1986–88), when the use of "crack" cocaine was increasing. Yet the fact remains that for the full nine-year period after the gun control law was enacted, the mean D.C. murder rate was more than 25 percent lower and its mean suicide rate was 23 percent lower than in the preceding nine years. The effect of the law was not only immediate but sustained as well.

Why Gun Control Works

The gun lobby is fond of saying, "If guns are outlawed, only outlaws will have guns." What's wrong with this picture?

The National Rifle Association (NRA) slogan leads us to envision two groups—solid citizens and hardened criminals—but the real world cannot be neatly divided into good guys and bad guys. Many people are law-abiding citizens until they become inflamed in a domestic dispute, a drunken argument in a bar, even a fender-bender on the highway. Murder is usually an act of rage; it is more often impulsive than premeditated. In fact, 80 percent of all murders occur during altercations and 71 percent involve acquaintances, including lovers, family members, and neighbors. Only 29 percent of those arrested for murder are previously convicted felons.

Rage can pass quickly, but if there is a gun available, even a few seconds may not be soon enough. Of course, enraged lovers and brawlers use other weapons, but it is better to be attacked with anything other than a gun. Guns are, by far, the most lethal weapons. The second deadliest is the knife, but knife attacks result in death only one-fifth as often as those with guns.

For the same reason that it is better to face a knife than a gun in a lover's quarrel, it is better to be robbed at knife point rather than gunpoint. There are good reasons to believe that reducing the number of guns in the general population will reduce them in the hands of muggers and robbers. Prison inmates report that they acquired one-third of their guns by stealing them, typically in home burglaries. There are also people at the margin—not yet career criminals but drifting in that direction—who are more inclined to have guns if they are cheap and readily available. And since handguns are lawful almost everywhere, these people do not even have to cross a psychological Rubicon to get a gun.

⁎⟨❦⟩⁎

Many of the people at the margin are youngsters. Nearly 70 percent of all serious crimes are committed by boys and young men, ages fourteen to twenty-four. Many of them are not yet career criminals. They are the children of despair, kids from dysfunctional families and impoverished communities who thirst for a feeling of importance. They are angry, immature, and unstable. In the 1950s, they carried switchblades, but since the early 1960s they have increasingly been carrying handguns. Packing a gun makes them feel like men, and it just takes a little alcohol or drugs, a buddy's dare, or a moment of bravado to propel them into their first mugging or holdup of a convenience store. Many juvenile robbers say that they did not intend to commit a robbery when they went out. The nation will be a less dangerous place if these kids go out without guns.

There is a frightening increase in the number of youngsters carrying guns. The National Adolescent Student Health Survey discovered that by 1987, nearly 2 percent of all eighth and tenth graders across the nation said that they carried a gun to school within the past year. A third of those said they took a gun to school with them every day, which translates into more than 100,000 students packing a pistol all the time. In just the first two months of 1992, more than a hundred firearms were confiscated in New York City schools.

And kids are not just carrying guns, they are using them. New York City was shaken earlier this year when, moments before Mayor David Dinkins was to give a speech to the students at Brooklyn's Thomas Jefferson High School, a fifteen-year-old pulled out a Smith & Wesson .38 and killed two other students. Had it not been for the mayor's presence at the school, the shootings might not have been front-page news.

It is somewhat disingenuous to be shocked about youths with handguns. Kids emulate adults. They live in a society that has not attached a sense of gravity to owning handguns. In half of the fifty states, handguns are completely unregulated; anyone may walk into a gun shop and buy a handgun just as easily as a quart of milk at a grocery. Most of the other states have only modest handgun regulations; four states, for example, have forty-eight hour waiting periods. Except in a very few locales, automobiles are regulated far more rigorously than handguns.

There are 35 million handguns in the United States; a quarter of all homes have at least one handgun in them. We can tell a teenage boy that he is really safer if he does not pack a gun. But why should he believe adults who keep handguns in their nightstand drawers, even though they have been told that a gun in the home is six times more likely to be used to shoot a family member than an intruder?

For more than a decade some observers, such as Charles Silberman, have noted a rising tide of savagery. Today, for example, my morning newspaper carries a report about a robbery at a local McDonald's restaurant. A man with a pistol demanded the restaurant's cash, which the manager immediately gave him. The robber then told the manager and two other employees to lie down, and proceeded to shoot two to death while one of the three ran away. Not long ago it would have been extraordinarily rare for a robber—with the money in his hand—to kill his victims gratuitously; now it seems commonplace. We may wonder what impels someone to top off a robbery with a double murder, but whatever the motive, the handgun makes that act possible.

◆

We are also witnessing a bewildering escalation in suicides. In 1960 there were about 19,000 suicides in the United States; now there are more than 30,000 each year. (This represents a rise in the suicide rate from 10.6 per 100,000 in 1960 to 12.4 per 100,000 in 1988.) Nearly two-thirds of all suicides in the United States are committed with firearms, more than 80 percent of those with handguns. The rising number of suicides is due almost completely to firearm suicides. While the number of suicides with other weapons has remained relatively stable (even slightly declining over the past two decades), the number of firearm suicides has more than doubled since 1960.

Why should that be so? If someone really wants to kill himself, is he not going to find a way to do so regardless of whether a handgun is available?

This is something of a trick question. The rabbit in the hat is the phrase "really wants to kill himself" because suicide, like murder, is often an impulsive act, particularly among the 2,000 to 3,000 American teenagers who commit suicide each year. If an individual contemplating suicide can get through the moment of dark despair, he may reconsider. And if a gun is not available, many potential suicides will resort to a less lethal method, survive, and never attempt suicide again. Nothing is as quick and certain as a gun. The desire to die need only last as long as it takes to pull a trigger, and the decision is irrevocable.

In the Seattle-Vancouver study, the researchers found a 40-percent higher suicide rate among the fifteen- to twenty-five-year-olds in Seattle, a difference they discovered was due to a firearm suicide rate that is ten times higher among Seattle adolescents. Other research reveals that a potentially suicidal adolescent is *seventy-five times* as likely to kill himself when there is a gun in the house.[3]

This is the one area, however, where the type of gun may not matter. While more than 80 percent of all gun-related suicides are with handguns, research suggests that when handguns are not available, people attempting suicide may just as readily use long guns. But many homes only have a handgun, and reducing the number of homes with handguns will therefore reduce the number of suicides.

What Kind of Gun Control Works?

No one suggests that gun control legislation will be a panacea. Nevertheless, the strong evidence is that the right kind of gun control legislation can reduce murders, suicides, and accidents substantially in the United States.

First and foremost, gun control means controlling handguns. Handguns account for only about one-third of all firearms in general circulation, but they are used in more than 75 percent of all gun-related homicides and more than 80 percent of all gun-related robberies. No other weapon is used nearly so often to murder: While handguns are used in half of all murders in America, knives are used in 18 percent, shotguns in 6 percent, rifles in 4 percent.

Two basic approaches are available to regulate handguns. One is to allow anyone to have a handgun, except for individuals in certain prohibited categories such as convicted felons, the mentally ill, drunkards, and the like. This approach is fatally flawed. The vast majority of people who end up abusing handguns to not have records that place them in a high-risk category. Whenever someone commits a murder, we can in retrospect always say that the murderer was mentally unstable, but it is not easy to check potential handgun purchasers for signs of instability or smoldering rage. There is no test to give. Many mentally unstable individuals have no record of psychiatric treatment and, even if they do, their records are confidential. Because we want to encourage people who need psychological help to seek treatment, legislation that would open psychiatric records to the government or place them in some national data bank would be counterproductive. Moreover, even someone who clearly falls into a prohibited category, such as a convicted felon, can easily circumvent this system by sending a surrogate to purchase a handgun for him.

～●～

The second approach, known as a need-based or a restrictive permitting system, allows only people who fall within certain categories to own handguns. Handgun permits are, of course, issued to law enforcement personnel, but among the general population someone who wants a handgun permit must demonstrate a special need. Simply wanting a handgun for self-defense is not enough, but someone who can provide a sufficiently concrete reason to fear attack would be granted a handgun permit. Sportsmen can obtain special permits, but their handguns must be kept under lock and key at a gun club. It may inconvenience them, but when public safety is balanced against recreation, public safety must win out.

Many states have similar systems for permits to carry a concealed weapon in public, but in the United States only New Jersey and a few cities have true need-base permitting systems for handgun possession. Canada adopted this system nationally in 1978. . . .

Handgun registration should be part of a restrictive permitting system. Owners should be required to register their handguns, and a permanent identification number should be engraved on every handgun. All transfers should be recorded. Everyone who has a driver's license or owns a car understands such a system, and even 78 percent of gun owners in America favor the registration of handguns, according to a 1991 Gallup poll.

～●～

With one exception, long guns do not present the same kind of threat to public safety as handguns. The exception, of course, is assault weapons. We remember how Patrick Purdy fired his AK-47 into a schoolyard in Stockton, California. In less than two minutes, he fired 106 rounds at children and teachers, killing five and wounding twenty-nine.

The NRA argues that it is impossible to differentiate an assault weapon from a standard hunting rifle—and to some extent it is right. Both hunting rifles and the assault weapons that are sold to the general public are semi-automatic. With a semi-automatic, firing repeat rounds requires pulling the trigger back for each one; with an automatic weapon, one must only pull the trigger back once and keep it depressed. This, however, is an inconsequential difference. A thirty-round magazine can be emptied in two seconds with a fully automatic weapon and in five seconds with a semi-automatic.

The way to regulate long guns, therefore, is to limit the size of magazines. Civilians should not be permitted to have magazines that hold more than five rounds. This simply means that after firing five rounds one must stop, remove the empty magazine and either reload it or insert another full magazine. No hunter worth his salt blasts away at a deer as if he were storming the beach at Guadalcanal, and therefore this is no real inconvenience for hunters. But as Patrick Purdy demonstrated with his seventy-five-round magazine in Stockton, large-capacity magazines pose an unreasonable danger to public safety and should not be available to civilians.

The gun lobby urges that instead of regulating handguns (or assault weapons), severe and mandatory penalties should be imposed on persons who violate firearm laws. The weight of the evidence, however, suggests that these laws are not as effective. In 1987, for example, Detroit enacted an ordinance that imposed mandatory jail sentences on persons convicted of unlawfully concealing a handgun or carrying a firearm within the city. The strategy was to allow the general population to keep guns in their homes and offices but to reduce the number of people carrying guns on the streets. After evaluating the law, researchers concluded that, at best, "the ordinance had a relatively small preventive effect on the incidence of homicides in Detroit."[4] The researchers were, in fact, dubious that there was any effect. An analysis of the case histories of more than a thousand persons charged under the ordinance revealed that only 3 percent spent time in prison. With overcrowded jails, judges choose instead to incarcerate people convicted of more serious crimes. This is consistent with other studies of mandatory sentencing laws.[5] . . .

❧◈❧

Blame for the failure of gun control is generally laid at the feet of the NRA, but the problem is not so much a zealous minority as it is a quiescent majority. There has not been a sufficiently clear understanding of why the majority of Americans want gun control but do not want it enough to make it a priority in the voting booth. Much effort has been wasted describing the magnitude and horror of gun violence in America. The gun lobby has taken one broadside after another—from television network specials and newsweekly cover stories—all to no avail.

In talking about the horror of gun violence, however, the news media are preaching to the converted. Americans are aware of the level of gun violence, and they detest it. But news specials decrying gun violence may unwittingly have the same effect as the entertainment media's glorification of gun violence. They only reinforce a sense of hopelessness. If things could be different, Americans think, they would be. Otherwise, the carnage would not be tolerated. The media portrayals may also have a numbing effect. Research shows that if people are frightened but believe there is no way to escape or to improve conditions, the fear becomes debilitating.

Majority passivity is rooted in the belief that the status quo is immutable. It is this attitude that gun control advocates must try to change, by communicating the evidence that gun control laws do work. Americans know how bad gun violence is; they must now hear the evidence that reducing the violence is possible.

Notes

1. John Henry Sloan, et al., "Handgun Regulations, Crime, Assaults, and Homicide," *The New England Journal of Medicine,* Nov. 10, 1988, pp. 1256–62.

2. Colin Liftin, et al., "Effects of Restrictive Licensing of Handguns on Homicide and Suicide in the District of Columbia," *The New England Journal of Medicine,* Dec. 5, 1991, pp. 1615–1649.

3. David A. Brent, et al., "The Presence and Accessibility of Firearms in the Homes of Adolescent Suicides," *Journal of the American Medical Association,* Dec. 4, 1991, pp. 2989–93.

4. Patrick W. O'Carroll, "Preventing Homicide: An Evaluation of the Efficacy of a Detroit Gun Ordinance," *American Journal of Public Health,* May 1991, pp. 576–81.

5. Alan Lizotte and Marjorie A. Zatz, "The Use and Abuse of Sentence Enhancement for Firearms Offenses in California," *Law and Contemporary Problems* (1986), pp. 199–221.

John R. Lott, Jr.  **NO**

More Guns, Less Crime

American culture is a gun culture—not merely in the sense that 75 to 86 million people own a total of about 200 to 240 million guns, but in the broader sense that guns pervade our debates on crime and are constantly present in movies and the news. How many times have we read about shootings, or how many times have we heard about tragic accidental gun deaths— bad guys shooting innocent victims, bad guys shooting each other in drug wars, shots fired in self-defense, police shootings of criminals, let alone shooting in wars? We are inundated by images through the television and the press. Our kids are fascinated by computer war games and toy guns.

So we're obsessed with guns. But the big question is: What do we really know? How many times have most of us actually used a gun or seen a gun being used? How many of us have ever seen somebody in real life threatening somebody else with a gun, witnessed a shooting, or seen people defend themselves by displaying or firing guns?

The truth is that most of us have very little firsthand experience with using guns as weapons. Even the vast majority of police officers have never exchanged shots with a suspect. Most of us receive our images of guns and their use through television, film, and newspapers.

Unfortunately, the images from the screen and the newspapers are often unrepresentative or biased because of the sensationalism and exaggeration typically employed to sell news and entertainment. A couple of instances of news reporting are especially instructive in illustrating this bias. In a highly publicized incident, a Dallas man recently became the first Texas resident charged with using a permitted concealed weapon in a fatal shooting. Only long after the initial wave of publicity did the press report that the person had been savagely beaten and in fear for his life before firing the gun. In another case a Japanese student was shot on his way to a Halloween party in Louisiana in 1992. It made international headlines and showed how defensive gun use can go tragically wrong. However, this incident was a rare event: in the entire United States during a year, only about 30 people are accidentally killed by private citizens who mistakenly believe the victim to be an intruder. By comparison, police accidentally kill as many as 330 innocent individuals annually. In neither the Louisiana case nor the Texas case did the courts find the shooting to be criminal.

While news stories sometimes chronicle the defensive uses of guns, such discussions are rare compared to those depicting violent crime committed with guns. Since in many defensive cases a handgun is simply brandished, and no one is harmed, many defensive uses are never even reported to the police. I believe that this underreporting of defensive gun use is large, and this belief has been conformed by the many stories I received from people across the country after the publicity broke on my original study. On the roughly one hundred radio talk shows on which I discussed that study, many people called in to say that they believed having a gun to defend themselves with had saved their lives. For instance, on a Philadelphia radio station, a New Jersey woman told how two men simultaneously had tried to open both front doors of the car she was in. When she brandished her gun and yelled, the men backed away and fled. Given the stringent gun-control laws in New Jersey, the woman said she never thought seriously of reporting the attempted attack to the police. . . .

Criminals are motivated by self-preservation, and handguns can therefore be a deterrent. The potential defensive nature of guns is further evidenced by the different rates of so-called "hot burglaries," where a resident is at home when a criminal strikes. In Canada and Britain, both with tough gun-control laws, almost half of all burglaries are "hot burglaries." In contrast, the United States, with fewer restrictions, has a "hot burglary" rate of only 13 percent. Criminals are not just behaving differently by accident. Convicted American felons reveal in surveys that they are much more worried about armed victims than about running into the police. The fear of potentially armed victims causes American burglars to spend more time than their foreign counterparts "casing" a house to ensure that nobody is home. Felons frequently comment in these interviews that they avoid late-night burglaries because "that's the way to get shot."

To an economist such as myself, the notion of deterrence—which causes criminals to avoid cab drivers, "dope boys," or homes where the residents are in—is not too surprising. We see the same basic relationships in all other areas of life: when the price of apples rises relative to that of oranges, people buy fewer apples and more oranges. To the non-economist, it may appear cold to make this comparison, but just as grocery shoppers switch to cheaper types of produce, criminals switch to attacking more vulnerable prey. Economists call this, appropriately enough, "the substitution effect."

Deterrence matters not only to those who actively take defensive actions. People who defend themselves may indirectly benefit other citizens. . . . [C]ab drivers and drug dealers who carry guns produce a benefit for cab drivers and drug dealers without guns. In . . . "hot burglaries," homeowners who defend themselves make burglars generally wary of breaking into homes. These spillover effects are frequently referred to as "third-party effects" or "external benefits." In both cases criminals cannot know in advance who is armed.

The case for allowing concealed handguns—as opposed to openly carried handguns—relies on this argument. When guns are concealed, criminals are unable to tell whether the victim is armed before striking, which raises the risk to criminals of committing many types of crimes. On the other hand, with "open-carry" handgun laws, a potential victim's defensive ability is readily identified, which makes it easier for criminals to choose the more vulnerable prey. In interviews with felony prisoners in ten state correctional systems, 56 percent claimed that they would not attack a potential victim who was known to be armed. Indeed, the criminals in states with high civilian gun ownership were the most worried about encountering armed victims. . . .

The Numbers Debate and Crime

Unfortunately, the debate over crime involves many commonly accepted "facts" that simply are not true. For example, take the claim that individuals are frequently killed by people they know. . . . According to the FBI's *Uniform Crime Reports,* 58 percent of the country's murders were committed either by family members (18 percent) or by those who "knew" the victims (40 percent). Although the victim's relationship to their attackers could not be determined in 30 percent of the cases, 13 percent of all murders were committed by complete strangers.

Surely the impression created by these numbers has been that most victims are murdered by close acquaintances. Yet this is far from the truth. In interpreting the numbers, one must understand how these classifications are made. In this case, "murderers who know their victims" is a very broad category. A huge but not clearly determined portion of this category includes rival gang members who know each other. In larger urban areas, where most murders occur, the majority of murders are due to gang-related turf wars over drugs.

The Chicago Police Department, which keeps unusually detailed numbers on these crimes, finds that just 5 percent of all murders in the city from 1990 to 1995 were committed by nonfamily friends, neighbors, or roommates. This is clearly important in understanding crime. The list of nonfriend acquaintance murderers is filled with cases in which the relationships would not be regarded by most people as particularly close: for example, relationships between drug pushers and buyers, gang members, prostitutes and their clients, bar customers, gamblers, and cabdrivers killed by their customers.

While I do not wish to downplay domestic violence, most people do not envision gang members or drug buyers and pushers killing each other when they hear that 58 percent of murder victims were either relatives or acquaintances of their murderers. If family members are included, 17 percent of all murders in Chicago for 1990–95 involved family members, friends, neighbors, or roommates. While the total number of murders in Chicago grew from 395 in 1965 to 814 in 1995, the number involving family members, friends, neighbors, or roommates remained virtually unchanged. What has grown is the number of murders by nonfriend acquaintances, strangers, identified gangs, and persons unknown. . . .

The news media also play an important role in shaping what we perceive as the greatest threats to our safety. Because we live in such a national news market, we learn very quickly about tragedies in other parts of the country. As a result, some events appear to be much more common than they actually are. For instance, children are much less likely to be accidentally killed by guns (particularly handguns) than most people think. Consider the following numbers: in 1995 there were a total of 1,400 accidental firearm deaths in the entire country. A relatively small portion of these involved children: 30 deaths involved children up to four years of age and 170 more deaths involved fire- to fourteen- year-olds. In comparison, 2,900 children died in motor-vehicle crashes, 950 children lost their lives from drowning, and over 1,000 children were killed by fire and burns. More children die in bicycle accidents each year than die from all types of firearm accidents.

Of course, any child's death is tragic, and it offers little consolation to point out that common fixtures in life from pools to heaters result in even more deaths. Yet the very rules that seek to save lives can result in more deaths. For example, banning swimming pools would help prevent drowning, and banning bicycles would eliminate bicycling accidents, but if fewer people exercise, life spans will be shortened. Heaters may start fires, but they also keep people from getting sick and from freezing to death. So whether we want to allow pools or space heaters depends not only on whether some people may be harmed by them, but also on whether more people are helped than hurt.

Similar trade-offs exist for gun-control issues, such as gun locks. As President [Bill] Clinton has argued many times, "We protect aspirin bottles in this country better than we protect guns from accidents by children." Yet gun locks require that guns be unloaded, and a locked, unloaded gun does not offer ready protection from intruders. The debate is not simply over whether one wants to save lives or not; it involves the question of how many of these two hundred accidental gun deaths would have been avoided under different rules versus the extent to which such rules would reduce people's ability to defend themselves. . . .

The survey evidence of defensive gun use weighs importantly in this debate. At the lowest end of these estimate, . . . according to Phillip Cook, the U.S. Department of Justice's National Crime Victimization Survey reports that each year there are "only" 80,000 to 82,000 defensive uses of guns during assaults, robberies, and household burglaries. Other national polls weight regions by population and thus have the advantage, unlike the National Crime Victimization Survey, of not replying too heavily on data from urban areas. These national polls should also produce more honest answers, since a law-enforcement agency is not asking the questions. They imply much higher defensive use rates. Fifteen national polls, including those by organizations such as the *Lose Angeles Times,* Gallup, and Peter Hart Research Associates, imply that there are 760,000 to 3.6 million defensive uses of guns per years. Yet even if these estimates are wrong by a very large factor, they still suggest that defensive gun use is extremely common.

Some evidence on whether concealed-handgun laws will lead to increased crimes is readily available. Between October 1, 1987, when Florida's "concealed-carry" law took effect, and the end of 1996, over 380,000 licenses had been issued, and only 72 had been revoked because of crimes committed by license holders (most of which did not involve the permitted gun). A statewide break down on the nature of those crimes is not available, but Dade County records indicate that for crimes involving a permitted handgun took place there between September 1987 and August 1992, and none of those cases resulted in injury. Similarly, Multnomah County, Oregon, issued 11,140 permits over the period from January 1990 to October 1994; only five permit holders were involved in shootings, three of which were considered justified by grand juries. Of the other two cases, one involved a shooting in a domestic dispute, and the other involved an accident that occurred while a gun was being unloaded; neither resulted in a fatality. . . .

During state legislative hearings on concealed-handgun laws, the most commonly raised concerns involved fears that armed citizens would attack each other in the heat of the moment following car accidents or accidentally shoot a police officer. The evidence shows that such fears are unfounded: although thirty-one states have so-called nondiscretionary concealed-handgun laws, some of them decades old, there exists only one recorded incident of a permitted, concealed handgun being used in a shooting following a traffic accident, and that involved self-defense. No permit holder has ever shot a police officer, and there have been cases where permit holders have used their guns to save officers' lives.

Let us return to the fundamental issue of self-protection. For many people, the ultimate concerns boils down to protection from violence. Unfortunately, our legal system cannot provide people with all the protection that they desire, and yet individuals are often prevented from defending themselves. A particularly tragic event occurred recently in Baltimore:

> Less than a year ago, James Edward Scott shot and wounded an intruder in the back yard of his West Baltimore home, and according to neighbors, authorities took away his gun.
>
> Tuesday night, someone apparently broke into his three-story row house again. But this time the 83-year-old Scott didn't have his .22-caliber rifle, and police said he was strangled when he confronted the burglar.
>
> "If he would have had the gun, he would be OK," said one neighbor who declined to give his name, fearing retribution from the attacker, who had not been arrested as of yesterday. . . .
>
> Neighbors said burglars repeatedly broke into Scott's home. Ruses [a neighbor] said Scott often talked about "the people who would harass him because he worked out back by himself."

Others find themselves in a position in which either they no longer report attacks to the police when they have used a gun to defend themselves, or they no longer carry guns for self-defense. Josie Cash learned this lesson the hard way, though charges against her were ultimately dropped. "The Rockford [Illinois] woman used her gun to scare off muggers who tried to take her pizza delivery money. But when she reported the incident to police, they filed felony charges against her for carrying a concealed weapon."

A well-known story involved Alan Berg, a liberal Denver talk-show host who took great delight in provoking and insulting those with whom he disagreed. Berg attempted to obtain a permit after receiving death threats from white supremacists, but the police first attempted to talk him out of applying and then ultimately rejected his request. Shortly after he was denied, Berg was murdered by members of the Aryan Nations. . . .

Overall, my conclusion is that criminals as a group tend to behave rationally—when crime becomes more difficult, less crime is committed. Higher arrest and conviction rates dramatically reduce crime. Criminals also move out of jurisdictions in which criminal deterrence increases. Yet criminals respond to more than just the actions taken by the police and the courts. Citizens can take private actions that also deter crime. Allowing citizens to carry concealed handguns reduces violent crimes, and the reductions coincide very closely with the number of concealed-handgun permits issued. Mass shootings in public places are reduced when law-abiding citizens are allowed to carry concealed handguns.

Not all crime categories showed reductions, however. Allowing concealed handguns might cause small increases in larceny and auto theft. When potential victims are able to arm themselves, some criminals turn away from crimes like robbery that require direct attacks and turn instead to such crimes as auto theft, where the probability of direct contact with victims is small.

There were other surprises as well. While the support for the strictest gun-control laws is usually strongest in large cities, the largest drops in violent crime from legalized concealed handguns occurred in the most urban counties with the greatest populations and the highest crime rates. Given the limited resources available to law enforcement and our desire to spend those resources wisely to reduce crime, the results of my studies have implications for where police should concentrate their efforts. For example, I found that increasing arrest rates in the most crime-prone areas led to the greatest reductions in crime. Comparisons can also be made across different methods of fighting crime. Of all the methods studied so far by economists, the carrying of concealed handguns appears to be the most cost-effective method for reducing crime. Accident and suicide rates were unaltered by the presence of concealed handguns.

Guns also appear to be the great equalizer among the sexes. Murder rates decline when either more women or more men carry concealed handguns, but the effect is especially pronounced for women. One additional woman carrying a concealed handgun reduces the murder rate for women by about 3–4 times more than one additional man carrying a concealed handgun reduces the murder rate for men. This occurs because allowing a woman to defend herself with a concealed handgun produces a much larger change in her ability to defend herself than the change created by providing a man with a handgun.

While some evidence indicates that increased penalties for using a gun in the commission of a crime reduce crime, the effect is small. Furthermore, I find no crime-reduction benefits from state-mandated waiting periods and background checks before people are allowed to purchase guns. At the federal level, the Brady law [the violence prevention act named for former White House press secretary James Brady, who was wounded in a 1981 assassination attempt on President Ronald Reagan] has proven to be no more effective. Surprisingly, there is also little benefit from training requirements or age restrictions for concealed-handgun permits. . . .

Many factors influence crime, with arrest and convictions rates being the most important. However, nondiscretionary concealed-handgun laws are also important, and they are the most cost-effective means of reducing crime. The cost of hiring more police in order to change arrest and conviction rates is much higher, and the net benefits per dollar spent are only at most a quarter as large as the benefits from concealed-handgun laws. Even private, medium-security prisons cost state governments about $34 a day per prisoner ($12,267 per year). For concealed handguns, the permit fees are usually the largest costs borne by private citizens. The durability of guns allows owners to recoup their investments over many years. Using my yearly cost estimate of $43 per concealed handgun for Pennsylvanians, concealed handguns pay for themselves if they have only 1/285 of the deterrent impact of an additional year in prison. This calculation even ignores the other costs of the legal system, such as prosecution and defense costs—criminals will expend greater effort to fight longer prison sentences in court. No other government policy appears to have anywhere near the same cost-benefit ratio as concealed-handgun laws.

Allowing citizens without criminal records or histories of significant mental illness to carry concealed handguns deters violent crimes and appears to produce an extremely small and statistically insignificant change in accidental deaths. If the rest of the country had adopted right-to-carry concealed-handgun provisions in 1992, about 1,500 murders and 4,000 rapes would have been avoided. On the other hand, consistent with the notion that criminals respond to incentives, county-level data provide some evidence that concealed-handgun laws are associated with increases in property crimes involving stealth and in crimes that involve minimal probability of contact between the criminal and the victim. Even though both the state-level data and the estimates that attempt to explain why the law and the arrest rates change indicate that crime in all the categories declines, the deterrent effect of nondiscretionary handgun laws is largest for violent crimes. Counties with the largest populations, where the deterrence of violent crimes is the greatest, are also the counties where the substitution of property crimes for violent crimes by criminals is the highest. The estimated annual gain in 1992 from allowing concealed handguns was over $5.74 billion.

Many commonly accepted notions are challenged by these findings. Urban areas tend to have the most restrictive gun-control rules and have fought the hardest against nondiscretionary concealed-handgun laws, yet they are the very places that benefit the most from nondiscretionary concealed-handgun laws. Not only do urban areas tend to gain in their fight against crime, but reductions in crime rates are greatest precisely in those urban areas that have the highest crime rates, largest and most dense populations, and greatest concentrations of minorities. To some this might not be too surprising. After all, law-abiding citizens in these areas must depend on themselves to a great extent for protection. Even if self-protection were accepted, concerns would still arise over whether these law-abiding citizens would use guns properly. This study provides a very strong answer: a few people do and will use permitted concealed handguns improperly, but the gains completely overwhelm these concerns.

Another surprise involves women and blacks. Both tend to be the strongest supporters of gun control, yet both obtain the largest benefits from nondiscretionary concealed-handgun laws in terms of reduced rates of murder and other crimes. Concealed handguns also appear to be the great equalizer among the sexes. Murder rates decline when either more women or more men carry concealed handguns, but the effect is especially pronounced for women. An additional woman carrying a concealed handgun reduces the murder rate for women by about three to four times more than an additional man carrying a concealed handgun reduces the murder rate for men. Providing a woman with a concealed handgun represents a much larger change in her ability to defend herself than it does for a man.

The benefits of concealed handguns are not limited to those who use them in self-defense. Because the guns may be concealed, criminals are unable to tell whether potential victims are carrying guns until they attack, thus making it less attractive for criminals to commit crimes that involve direct contact with victims. Citizens who have no intention of ever carrying concealed handguns in a sense get a "free ride" from the crime-fighting efforts of their fellow citizens. However, the "halo" effect created by these laws is apparently not limited to people who share the characteristics of those who carry the guns. The most obvious example is the drop in murders of children following the adopting of nondescretionary laws. Arming older people not only may provide direct protection to these children, but also causes criminals to leave the area.

Nor is the "halo" effect limited to those who live in areas where people are allowed to carry guns. The violent-crime reduction from one's own state's adopting the law is in fact greatest when neighboring states also allow law-abiding citizens to carry concealed handguns. The evidence also indicates that the states with the most guns have the lowest crime rates. Urban areas may experience the most violent crime, but they also have the smallest number of guns. Blacks may be the racial group most vulnerable to violent crime, but they are also much less likely than whites to own guns. . . .

Preventing law-abiding citizens from carrying handguns does not end violence; it merely makes victims more vulnerable to attack. While people have strong views on either side of this debate, and one study is unlikely to end this discussion, the size and strength of my deterrence results and the lack of evidence that holders of permits for concealed handguns commit crimes should at least give pause to those who oppose concealed handguns. In the final analysis, one concern unites us all: Will allowing law-abiding citizens to carry concealed handguns save lives? The answer is yes, it will.

POSTSCRIPT

Do We Need Tougher Gun Control Laws?

What does the Second Amendment mean? In its entirety it reads, "A well regulated Militia, being necessary to the security of a free State, the right of the people to keep and bear Arms, shall not be infringed." Does this confer an unqualified right to bear arms? Or is it a right conditioned by the clause preceding the statement of right? Does the militia refer to the people generally, or does it specifically relate to the organized ("well regulated") military bodies of state and national guards and the armed forces?

Wayne LaPierre, chief executive officer and spokesman for the National Rifle Association (NRA), has written *Guns, Crime, and Freedom* (Regnery, 1994), which may be the most authoritative defense of the NRA's unqualified opposition to gun control. Gary Wills, in "To Keep and Bear Arms," *New York Review of Books* (September 21, 1995), argues that the constitutional right to bear arms is limited to its military usage.

As far back as 1976, Barry Bruce-Briggs anticipated some of the arguments made by Lott. See "The Great American Gun War," *The Public Interest* (Fall 1976). For a similar view, see Don B. Kates, Jr., *Restricting Handguns: The Liberal Skeptics Speak Out* (North River Press, 1979). Neal Bernards, *Gun Control* (Lucent Books, 1991) and David E. Newton, *Gun Control: An Issue for the Nineties* (Enslow, 1992) are both attempts to summarize fairly the chief arguments for and against gun control. To put the issue of guns in a larger historical perspective, readers may wish to examine the impact of the American frontier, with its gun-slinging heroes and villains, on modern American culture. Richard Slotkin's *Gunfighter Nation* (Atheneum, 1992) is an illuminating study of this enduring American myth.

In the second edition of *More Guns, Less Crime: Understanding Crime and Gun Control Laws* (University of Chicago Press, 2000), Lott rebuts some criticisms of his thesis and provides up-to-date statistics to support it. A related defense of gun ownership is examined in the editorial "Gun Availability and Violent Death," *American Journal of Public Health* (June 1997). In a 1993 survey gun owners indicated that in an incident during the previous year, someone "almost certainly would have" died if a gun had not been used for protection. In contrast, 38,000 people died in that year because of injuries due to firearms. The result would appear to be that guns took far fewer lives than they saved. But how exaggerated are the estimates of certain death? How many of the deaths by firearms might have taken place by other means if guns had not been available?

It may well be that permission to carry firearms could deter crime in some areas and in others result in tragedy. In rural areas, where people hunt for sport and are familiar with firearms, a thug might well be deterred from a crime because he has reason to fear that his intended victim is "packing something." But the thought of large numbers of people in urban areas going around with firearms is sobering, if not frightening. An honest citizen with a gun in a crowded subway may intend to confront a would-be mugger but in the end may wound or kill other honest citizens who happened to be in the line of fire. The "right to bear arms" is a right which needs to be qualified—as do all our other rights—in the light of particular situations.

ISSUE 9

Does Affirmative Action Advance Racial Equality?

YES: Mary Frances Berry, from "Affirmative Action: Why We Need It, Why It Is Under Attack," in George E. Curry, ed., *The Affirmative Action Debate* (Perseus, 1996)

NO: Linda Chavez, from "Promoting Racial Harmony," in George E. Curry, ed., *The Affirmative Action Debate* (Perseus, 1996)

ISSUE SUMMARY

YES: Mary Frances Berry, chair of the U.S. Civil Rights Commission, contends that affirmative action is needed because minorities have suffered so much negative action throughout American history.

NO: Columnist Linda Chavez argues that racial preferences create a surface appearance of progress while destroying the substance of minority achievement.

We didn't land on Plymouth Rock, my brothers and sisters—Plymouth Rock landed on *us!*" Malcolm X's observation is borne out by the facts of American history. Snatched from their native land, transported thousands of miles—in a nightmare of disease and death—and sold into slavery, blacks were reduced to the legal status of farm animals. Even after emancipation, blacks were segregated from whites—in some states by law, and by social practice almost everywhere. American apartheid continued for another century.

In 1954 the Supreme Court declared state-compelled segregation in schools unconstitutional, and it followed up that decision with others that struck down many forms of official segregation. Still, discrimination survived, and in most southern states blacks were either discouraged or prohibited from exercising their right to vote. Not until the 1960s was compulsory segregation finally and effectively challenged. Between 1964 and 1968 Congress passed the most sweeping civil rights legislation since the end of the Civil War. It banned discrimination in employment, public accommodations (hotels, motels, restaurants, etc.), and housing; it also guaranteed voting rights for blacks and even authorized federal officials to take over the job of voter registration in areas suspected of disenfranchising blacks. Today, several agencies in the federal government exercise sweeping powers to enforce these civil rights measures.

But is that enough? Equality of condition between blacks and whites seems as elusive as ever. The black unemployment rate is double that of whites, and the percentage of black families living in poverty is nearly four times that of whites. Only a small percentage of blacks ever make it into medical school or law school.

Advocates of affirmative action have focused upon these *de facto* differences to bolster their argument that it is no longer enough just to stop discrimination. The damage done by three centuries of racism now has to be remedied, they argue, and effective remediation requires a policy of "affirmative action." At the heart of affirmative action is the use of "numerical goals." Opponents call them "racial quotas." Whatever the name, what they imply is the setting aside of a certain number of jobs or positions for blacks or other historically oppressed groups. Opponents charge that affirmative action penalizes innocent people simply because they are white, that it often results in unqualified appointments, and that it ends up harming instead of helping blacks.

Affirmative action has had an uneven history in U.S. federal courts. In *Regents of the University of California v. Allan Bakke* (1978), which marked the first time the Supreme Court directly dealt with the merits of affirmative action, a 5–4 majority ruled that a white applicant to a medical school had been wrongly excluded due to the school's affirmative action policy; yet the majority also agreed that "race-conscious" policies may be used in admitting candidates—as long as they do not amount to fixed quotas. Since *Bakke,* Supreme Court decisions have gone one way or the other depending on the precise circumstances of the case. In recent years, however, most of the Court's decisions seem to have run against affirmative action programs. For example, the Court has ruled against federal "set-aside" programs, which offer fixed percentages of federal contracts to minority-owned firms, although in the past it has permitted them. A more direct legal challenge to affirmative action was handed down by a federal appeals court in 1996 when it struck down the affirmative action policy of the University of Texas law school on grounds that it discriminated against whites, Asians, and other groups. The university appealed the case, but the Supreme Court declined to review it.

The most radical popular challenge to affirmative action was the ballot initiative endorsed by California voters in 1996. Proposition 209 banned any state program based upon racial or gender "preferences." Among the effects of this ban was a sharp decline in the numbers of non-Asian minorities admitted to the elite campuses of the state's university system, especially Berkeley and UCLA. (Asian admissions to the elite campuses either stayed the same or increased, and non-Asian minority admissions to some of the less-prestigious branches increased.)

In the following selections, Mary Frances Berry contends that affirmative action is needed because minorities have suffered so much negative action throughout American history, while Linda Chavez argues that racial preferences create only the appearance of progress, all the while destroying the substance of minority achievement.

Mary Frances Berry

 **YES**

Affirmative Action: Why We Need It, Why It Is Under Attack

Those now calling for an end to affirmative action—including Republican leaders on Capitol Hill and some black conservatives—ignore one fundamental fact: the reason we need affirmative action is because we minorities have suffered so much negative action throughout American history. Those negative actions began with slavery and have continued, with African-Americans being treated at best as second-class citizens for more than two centuries.

Contrary to the recent headlines, the battle over affirmative action is not new. For its entire history, affirmative action has been subject to attack. Political opponents such as Senator Jesse Helms, former attorney general Edwin Meese, and former assistant attorney general William Bradford Reynolds repeatedly tried to overturn it in the past fifteen years. Their efforts have drawn support from African-American writers such as Shelby Steele, Stephen Carter, and Thomas Sowell. Each time they have been defeated by civil rights groups, rank-and-file Americans, business leaders, and Republicans and Democrats both in Congress and across the nation. . . .

The History Behind Today's Affirmative Action

Since the end of slavery, African-Americans have struggled for economic justice, an equal opportunity to enter the workplace and to have access to higher education. Generations of African-Americans swept the floors in factories while being denied the opportunity to become higher-paid operatives on the machines. In grocery and department stores, clerks were white and janitors and elevator operators were black. College-educated African-Americans worked as bellboys, porters, and domestics if they could not get the scarce teaching positions in local all-black schools, which were usually the only alternative to preaching or perhaps working in the post office. Some progress in job opportunities for African-Americans was made during the labor shortages of World War II and beyond, but it was limited. By the 1960s African-Americans were still segregated for the most part in low-wage jobs.

The pre-affirmative action racial reality also included thousands of towns and cities in which police and fire departments remained entirely white and male. Women and African-Americans were even forbidden to apply. There were no merit standards for employing the white men who occupied the best jobs, because merit would have required accepting applications from all corners and picking the best people. Men with the benefit of white skin, whether their granddaddies ever owned slaves or not, whether they themselves or their remote ancestors were immigrants, had the good-job pie all to themselves.

In higher education, most African-Americans attended predominantly black colleges, many established by states as segregated institutions. Most concentrated on teacher training, to the exclusion of professional education. A few African-Americans went to largely white institutions; in 1954, that figure was about 1% of entering freshmen.

The history of corrective measures dates to the 1930s, when federal labor legislation required employers to use affirmative action to remedy unfair labor practices. In the civil rights context, affirmative action derives from presidential executive orders to end discrimination in employment. In 1941, President Franklin Roosevelt issued an order in response to a threat by A. Philip Randolph, the president of the Brotherhood of Sleeping Car Porters, to march on Washington to protest racial discrimination by defense contractors. Roosevelt's order established the first Fair Employment Practices Committee. But little progress resulted for African-Americans. The federal compliance programs were routinely understaffed and underfunded, and they lacked enforcement authority.

The ten million workers on the payrolls of the one hundred largest defense contractors included few blacks in 1960. The $7.5 billion in federal grants-in-aid to the states and cities for highway, airport, and school construction went almost exclusively to white businesses. The number of skilled black workers on public housing and slum clearance projects was minuscule. The U.S. Employment Service, which provided funds for state-operated employment bureaus, encouraged skilled blacks to register for unskilled jobs, accepted requests from lily-white employers, and made no effort to get employers to hire African-American workers. Black businesses had expanded and diversified since the days of slavery, but they were still excluded from competing on contracts offered by state and local governments. Essentially, using taxes paid in part by African-Americans, the government was directly subsidizing discrimination.

As a result of the civil rights movement, President John F. Kennedy's executive order on contract compliance created the Committee on Equal Employment Opportunity. In 1965 President Lyndon Johnson issued Executive Order 11246, which required federal contractors to take affirmative action to ensure equality of employment opportunity. It said, in part, "the contractor will, in all solicitations or advertisements for employees placed by or on behalf of the contractor, state that all qualified applicants will receive consideration for employment without regard to race, creed, color or national origin. . . ."

Under the prodding of the U.S. Civil Rights Commission and Arthur Fletcher, a black Republican assistant secretary of labor, the Nixon administration issued specific requirements for enforcing contract compliance which established the general outlines of the program as it exists today. The employer self-analyzes the employment of minorities and women in all job categories; assesses the level of utilization compared with those in the workforce; and develops goals and timetables for each job group in which minorities and women are underrepresented. Compliance officers are supposed to review the results. The goals are not inflexible targets; all that is required is a good-faith effort, and no employer is required to hire unqualified applicants.

Title VII of the Civil Rights Act of 1964 and its amendments were enacted to end discrimination by large private employers, whether or not they had government contracts. The Equal Employment Opportunity Commission, which was established by the act, was to resolve complaints. The act aims to compensate employees for illegal discrimination and to encourage employers to end discrimination. It calls for voluntary action. A valid affirmative action plan includes a systematic, comprehensive, and reviewable effort to dismantle discrimination processes. Measures that implicitly take race, sex, national origin, or religion into account may also be implemented apart from an affirmative action plan. Affirmative action may involve simply remaining aware of the need to broaden the search for qualified people unlike those already in the workforce. The 1971 Supreme Court decision in *Griggs v. Duke Power* further reinforced the policy, directing that employment qualifications must be related to the job in question and not designed simply to perpetuate racial exclusion.

Affirmative action has also been important in alleviating discrimination in higher education for women as well as African-Americans and other people of color. After the enactment of Title VI of the Civil Rights Act of 1964 and Title IX of the educational amendments of 1972 and through voluntary affirmative action efforts, women and racial minorities have taken advantage of increased opportunities in higher education. The enrollment of women in higher education has risen steadily. Women now make up more than 50% of undergraduate students and 50% or more of the students in law and medicine and other graduate and professional schools. Through the availability of student aid programs and aggressive recruitment and retention programs, the college-going rate for blacks and whites who graduated from high school was about equal by 1977. . . .

The Backlash Is Based on Distortions

In [the] latest assault on affirmative action, opponents have armed themselves with old and new arguments. Opponents of affirmative action distort the meaning of the principle, rewrite history, and ignore present realities in their eagerness to prevail. They claim that the test of whether affirmative action is needed is whether it alleviates poverty. Affirmative action was never intended to substitute for jobs, nutritional aid for poor families, and other social programs. But it has lifted many out of poverty by providing enhanced job and entrepreneurial opportunities, and their success sends out a ray of hope to the poor that if they make the effort, they will be able to better themselves.

Opponents also argue that affirmative action requires a lowering of standards, pointing to standardized test scores as the measure of who is worthy for a job or seat in a college or professional school. Of course, they cannot be serious, because neither African-Americans nor non-Jewish whites are the leaders in test score performance. If opportunity were awarded only on the basis of test scores, Asian- and Jewish Americans would hold the best jobs everywhere and almost entirely fill the best colleges and universities, since they uniformly make the highest scores on standardized tests. In any case, experts agree that using standardized test scores alone is probably the worst way to determine admissions or who is hired for a job.

To be sure, our economic system creates certain dilemmas. When there is not enough economic opportunity for everyone, keeping blacks out of jobs or seats in our universities allows whites to continue to dominate both the workplace and our educational system. If the rationale for excluding African-Americans can be based on lack of qualifications or inability to perform, then so much the better. We African-Americans may even believe that we *should* be excluded and confined to the lowest ranks. The conundrum is that when we have been included, we have usually performed.

Critics also ask why we do not replace affirmative action based on race and sex with affirmative action based entirely on poverty or economic disadvantage. The answer is that race and sex discrimination are one thing and poverty is another. There is no reason not to support targeted efforts to relieve poverty, but that does not preclude relieving discrimination based on race or sex, which may or may not accompanied by poverty. For example, affirmative action can help middle-class African-American employees to break through the glass ceiling when they seek promotions in the workplace.

Opponents also argue that targeting remedies by race or gender is contrary to the American belief in individualism. However, an African-American is discriminated against not because his name is James or John but because he is an African-American. A woman is discriminated against not because her name is Nancy or Jane but because she is a woman. Those who want to eradicate group remedies should first eradicate group discrimination.

Enemies of affirmative action cloak their views with rhetoric about the ideal of color blindness, which requires the removal of the affirmative action blot from our understanding of the Constitution. We must never forget that as appealing as the idea may appear on the surface, our society has never been color-blind. From the beginning the Constitution permitted discrimination on the basis of color and sex. Congress knowingly perpetuated slavery and the subjugation of African-Americans, as reflected in its pro-slavery compromises. American society remained color conscious despite the Civil War, Emancipation, and the enactment of the Thirteenth, Fourteenth, and Fifteenth Amendments.

Societal and constitutional color consciousness made race-conscious remedies necessary. The brief submitted by the NAACP Legal Defense and Educational Fund in the 1978 *Bakke* case describes how color-conscious remedies were enacted by the same Congress that wrote the Fourteenth Amendment. That Congress enacted a series of social welfare laws expressly delineating the racial groups entitled to participate in or benefit from each program. It did so over the objections of critics who opposed targeting particular groups.

The Fourteenth Amendment appeared to provide legal equality for all Americans. However, while corporations used it successfully for protection against stage regulation, both federal and state governments helped to maintain the subordination of African-Americans. Indeed, in the 1896 *Plessy v. Ferguson* decision the Court majority affirmed racial discrimination, which is why Justice Harlan had to *dissent* in order to insist that the Constitution is color-blind. Not until *Brown v. Board of Education* in 1954 did the Court reverse "separate but equal" as legal doctrine. Nevertheless, race-conscious discrimination continues to plague African-Americans today and requires race-conscious remedies.

In a report several years ago, the Federal Reserve Board, drawing on the records of more than nine thousand lending institutions, found that not only were African-Americans more likely to experience discrimination, but the rejection rate for blacks in the highest income bracket was identical to the denial rates of the poorest whites. Housing and Urban Development secretary Henry Cisneros concluded that the report "tells us that discrimination is still alive and well in America." Hugh Price, president of the National Urban League, observed in a speech to the Commonwealth Club in San Francisco, "It is not yet time for impatient whites and successful blacks to hoist the gangplank behind them." African-Americans who object to affirmative action apparently have a different view. Some, perhaps, do not understand how they got where they are. Some may be in denial or refuse to believe the policy is needed. Some may really believe African-Americans are inferior or that there is something called pure "merit" and that white people have more of it, which is just about as rational as believing their ice is colder.

Affirmative Action Remains Constitutional

The courts, aware of the perpetuation of invidious discrimination, have routinely upheld race- and gender-conscious affirmative action. Unlike opponents of affirmative action, who keep speaking of discrimination as something that used to happen, they are aware that discrimination exists here and now. The Supreme Court has upheld ordering unions to hire numerically to make up for excluding nonwhites from membership. In the 1987 case *United States v. Paradise*, the Court also upheld a remedial order requiring one black promotion for every white one for state troopers in the Alabama Department of Public Safety. The department had refused to promote African-Americans after it finally began permitting them to become troopers, though by the 1980s blacks made up about 25% of the force. The Court ordered one-to-one promotions until the share of officers was about the same as in the ranks. The order was temporary and could be waived. No one who did not meet the requirements had to be promoted.

Even in the 1989 case *Richmond v. J. A. Croson Co.*, in which the Court invalidated a set-aside program for African-American businesses, the justices did not rule out race-conscious relief. The Court upheld the rule that race-conscious relief is permitted, but specified that it must be narrowly tailored. However, those who challenged the set-aside achieved their objective, to reduce the possibility that blacks, who had received less than 1% of municipal contracts before the set-aside program, could gain a larger share of Richmond's construction business.

The Supreme Court has also ruled in favor of voluntary affirmative action plans. In *United Steelworkers of America v. Brian Weber* (1979), the Court upheld a voluntary plan reserving half of the places in a training program for blacks as remedial and not unnecessarily trammeling the rights of white men. The plan was designed to eliminate conspicuous racial imbalance in Kaiser Steel's almost exclusively white craft workforce by reserving for black employees half of the openings in plant training programs, until the number of black craftworkers was commensurate with the size of the workforce. At the time, only 1.8% of skilled workers at Kaiser were black. The Court held that the law did not intend to constrain management, and that Kaiser could lawfully break down patterns of racial segregation and hierarchy.

In *Johnson v. Transportation Agency* (1987), the Court upheld a voluntary affirmative action plan under which a government agency alleviated the underrepresentation of women in certain job categories by using sex as one factor in evaluating otherwise qualified candidates. There had never been a female road dispatcher in the agency. The plan was challenged by a man who was passed over for promotion to a position in favor of a qualified white woman. The Court determined that it was not unreasonable to take sex into account as one factor under the circumstances.

In the education arena, the 1978 *Bakke* case is still the major precedent. The case grew out of the reservation of sixteen out of one hundred available places in the University of California Medical School at Davis for qualified minorities. The Supreme Court essentially decided that, in the absence of proof of past discrimination, setting aside a specific number of places was illegal but that minority status could be used in admissions as a factor in an applicant's favor. The desire to obtain a "diverse" student body was a permissible goal.

In 1995 the Supreme Court decided a major case that tested its support of the principle of affirmative action. In the *Adarand Constructors, Inc. v. Pena,* the Court considered whether to further restrict the use of set-asides for minority contractors. A white contractor who submitted the low bid for a government-funded highway project claimed that a Hispanic company received the contract because race was used as a plus factor. The Court in a five-to-four decision decided that the *Croson* standards apply to federal government minority contracting programs. It remains to be seen how many federal contractors are able to meet the standards.

The Ongoing Battle for Advantage

The irony is that even though whites still receive the lion's share of contracts, scholarships, or well-paying jobs, many white Americans will make any argument and go to any lengths to fight to withdraw any portion that might be awarded to African-Americans. President Clinton has finally come down on the side of "mending" but not ending affirmative action. However, his voice is only one among many in the contention for state and national political advantage.

Although the social conditions that occasioned affirmative action have improved for some African-Americans, victory is far from won. For more than a generation, American law has prohibited race, national origin, and gender discrimination. However, government reports as well as television documentaries show that African-Americans, whether middle-class, upper-class, or no class, suffer discrimination in obtaining jobs or promotions, borrowing money to buy houses or start businesses, renting apartments, or getting served in restaurants. You can be a government official, Oprah Winfrey, or Johnnie or Susie No-Name—it sometimes makes no difference.

This brings to mind a story told by one vigorous opponent of affirmative action in the 1980s, Clarence Pendleton, Jr., then chairman of the U.S. Commission on Civil Rights. He was pleased to be invited to a major White House dinner soon after his first media forays on behalf of the Reagan administration's policy and was enjoying himself enormously. As he walked from his table to greet some acquaintances on the other side of the room, one of the white guests collared him to say that his table needed more wine. Pendleton recalled, "It was obvious the bastard thought I was a waiter." . . .

When civil rights concerns were in vogue, the African-American protest tradition at its most vibrant, and enforcement likely, affirmative action worked to increase opportunity for blacks. That evidence means we need more affirmative action, however we label it—promoting "diversity" or "banana" or something else. African-Americans are only slowly mobilizing to repel a very real threat, which is part of the across-the-board war on the poor in general and African-Americans in particular.

When I despair, my mother always says, "God is my president and also the Speaker of my House," But the Lord helps those who help themselves. If we do not see to our own interests and consolidate our allies, the Congress and the states are likely to repeal affirmative action, along with anything else characterized as benefiting African-Americans. The political signaling that has already had a chilling effect in the workplace in recent years will further constrain the opportunities of qualified African-Americans. The anger and alienation of young African-Americans, many of whom are separatists or black nationalists and have already written off the system, are likely to increase. . . . The problem of the twenty-first century, like that of the twentieth, will remain that W. E. B. Du Bois called the problem of the color line.

NO

Linda Chavez

Promoting Racial Harmony

Senator Hubert Humphrey took the floor of the Senate in 1964 to defend the landmark Civil Rights Act. Humphrey, the bill's chief sponsor, had to respond to conservatives who said that the bill would violate individual rights. He declared that the Civil Rights Act would make it a crime to classify human beings into racial groups and give preference to some groups but not others. He denied assertions that the bill would force employers to hire less qualified people because of their race. The goal, he said, was to ensure race-neutral treatment for all individuals. "Title VII [of the bill]," he noted, "does not require an employer to achieve any sort of racial balance in his work force by giving preferential treatment to any individual or group." Sure of his principles, Humphrey promised to eat the pages of the Civil Rights Act if it ever came to require racial preferences.

Today, of course, the Civil Rights Act of 1964 is interpreted by many civil rights advocates as requiring all sorts of racial preference programs. Assistant attorney general for civil rights Deval Patrick cited that law in court to defend race-based layoffs being used in a New Jersey school district to maintain racial balance. A law that was intended to replace racial rights with individual rights is being used to install a new system of racial rights.

The very words "affirmative action" have also been bent to new purposes. Originally, that phrase referred only to outreach and training programs to help minorities compete equally with whites. Today it designates programs that exclude whites from participation altogether (such as minority scholarships and government contract "set-asides") or enforce artificially low standards for minorities.

Playing the Game by the Rules

My recent exchange with William Raspberry shows the difference. At a National Press Club panel discussion and in his syndicated *Washington Post* column, Mr. Raspberry drew an analogy he thought would put the issue in focus. Suppose, he said, that during halftime at a basketball game it is discovered that the referees cheated during the first half of the game. The crooked referees allowed one team to rack up sixteen undeserved points. The referees are expelled from the game, but that doesn't fix the score. What to do?

My response to Mr. Raspberry was simple: Compensate the victims of discrimination. Give sixteen points to the team that was discriminated against. Wherever we can, in basketball or in society, we should apply specific remedies to specific victims of discrimination. The antidiscrimination laws of this country already allow us to do just that. Courts are empowered to force employers to hire or promote victims of discrimination and award the back pay and seniority those employees would have had. Similar tools are available to redress discrimination in housing, schools, and contracting. It's not even necessary for every person who is discriminated against to file a complaint; courts routinely provide relief to whole groups of people when they find that an individual or company has discriminated against more than one person.

Let's return to the basketball analogy. If a particular team in a particular game has been unfairly deprived of sixteen points, it would certainly be foolish and unfair to award sixteen extra points to that team in every game it plays from that time forward. It would be even more perverse to extend this preferential treatment to the children of the players on that team, awarding them extra points in their playground games because their parents suffered. Yet government-sponsored racial preference programs, which disregard individual cases of discrimination, are considered by some to be the only reasonable solution to discrimination.

Now, the analogy between a basketball game and American society may not be perfect, but it certainly is instructive. In sports, all participants are treated in a race-neutral manner. Team colors, not skin colors, are the basis of group affiliation. It may be true that the rules are often broken, but specific remedies and punishments for specific violations are available when this happens. Everybody is expected to play by the same rules—in fact, fans are never angrier than when they think the referees favor one team. Isn't that the model we should strive toward in our society?

The alternative to that model is to continue classifying our citizens by race, attaching an official government label "black," "white," "Asian," "Hispanic," and so on to each individual. Then the all-wise federal bureaucracy can decide how much special privilege each group deserves and spoon out benefits based on the labels: five portions to this group, three to that one, seven and a half to the next.

The Race Box Problem

Any attempt to systematically classify human beings according to race will fail, because race is an arbitrary concept. There will always be people—lots of them—who disagree with the way the labels are dispensed. An ugly power struggle among racial groups competing to establish their claims to victimhood is the inevitable result.

Native Hawaiians, for example, are currently classified as Native Americans. But many of them want their own racial classification. . . . The National Congress of American Indians, however, insists that Native Hawaiians are really just Native Americans. The classification of 250,000 Native Hawaiians is at stake, and being able to claim a quarter-million people in your racial group makes a big difference when it's time to dole out federal benefits.

Other groups make similar claims. Many Americans of eastern European ancestry complain about being lumped into the "white" box. Five different Asian groups have petitioned for sub-boxes. The U.S. Department of Housing and Urban Development has gone so far as to establish preference for "Hasidic Jewish Americans." Before he changed his mind about racial preferences, California governor Pete Wilson approved a law that gives special protections to Portuguese-Americans.

For years, the government of Puerto Rico has forbidden the Census Bureau from asking any question about race on forms distributed on the island, so vexing is the issue among Puerto Ricans. Now the national council of La Raza demands that "Hispanics," currently an ethnic group, be declared a separate race. When the Census Bureau created a special racial category for Mexicans in the 1930 census, the government of Mexico lodged an official protest that the move was racist. The bureau quickly abandoned the practice. My, how times change.

Black leaders who demand "race-conscious" remedies are discovering that race consciousness cuts both ways. A proposal to add a "multiracial" box to census forms brought outrage from those leaders. The most recent study, done in 1980, found that 70% of multiracial Americans check "black" on the census—meaning that a multiracial box would reduce the number of people defined as black, and hence the power base of black leaders, because a significant number of people who now check "black" would check "multiracial" instead. Roderick Harrison, head of the Census Bureau's Racial Statistics division, estimated that a multiracial box would reduce the "black" population by 10%.

Aware of this possibility, Billy Tidwell of the National Urban League complained in a hearing before the House Census Subcommittee in June 1993 that a multiracial box would "turn the clock back on the well-being" of African-Americans because it would be divisive, splitting light-skinned blacks from dark-skinned ones. Perhaps it has not occurred to him that any kind of racial classification is arbitrarily divisive in the same way—splitting light-skinned Americans from dark-skinned ones and, to the extent that they are treated differently, turning them against each other. Is it divisive for the government to group black people and treat them differently on the basis of their skin color, but acceptable—even necessary—for it to group other Americans and treat them differently on the basis of skin color?

Racial categories are never permanent anyway. Earlier this century, "whites" were not considered a single race. Nativists like Madison Grant, writing in his book *The Passing of the Great Race,* worried about the dilution of "Nordic" bloodlines by immigrants from eastern and southern Europe. Alarmists cried out that within fifty years "Nordic" Americans, a false category if there ever was one, would sink into the minority. By the time that actually occurred, nobody noticed. Nobody cared about the purity of "Nordic" blood anymore. The definition of race had changed.

Today, alarmists cry out that within fifty years whites will be in the minority in the United States. But today's young people, raised in a society where racism is no longer acceptable, marry between races at record rates. Half of all Mexican-Americans in California now marry non-Hispanic spouses. Half of Japanese-Americans now marry non-Japanese spouses, and similarly high rates prevail among other Asian groups. More and more children defy racial classification. In fifty years, our racial categories will no longer exist as such. Should we write those categories into our laws today, and count on the government to update them constantly to reflect the changing population? Better we should acknowledge the simple fact that categorizing people by race is not just divisive and degrading. It is impossible.

Who Really Needs Help?

Just as it's impossible to classify people by race, it's impossible to say that one race or ethnic group is clearly lagging behind whites socially and economically. Minorities are not clearly lagging behind anybody.

Hispanics, as I have said for years, are doing quite well. The category of "Hispanics" seems to trail others because it includes a large number of immigrants—nearly half of the adult Hispanic population is foreign-born. These immigrants often come to this country with practically nothing and therefore skew the economic numbers downward. Unfortunately, most statistics do not distinguish between native-born and foreign-born Hispanics. Those that do, however, indicate that native-born Hispanics earn wages commensurate to their educational level. Mexican-American men with thirteen years of education, for example, earn 93% of the earnings of non-Hispanic whites with comparable education. Other statistics indicate that even immigrants do just find if they work hard and learn English. Despite all this, people who claim to represent the interests of Hispanics continue to deny their record of success, painting them as a failed underclass in order to persuade government bureaucrats to give them special treatment. Rather than treat them as a downtrodden minority, we should see Hispanics for what they are—an upwardly mobile immigrant group.

Asian-Americans are also doing well. By many measures, they are doing better than whites. In fact, they are doing so well that racial preference programs sometimes discriminate against them in order to make room for other races. For years, the University of California has, as a matter of official policy, denied bright young Asian-American students admission to college, law school, medical school, and the rest of the university system because they are Asian-American. They have "too many" qualified Asian-American applicants, so discrimination against them is necessary to uphold the system of racial rights.

According to Michael Lynch of the Pacific Research Institute, Asian-American applicants to the University of California [UC] qualify for admission based on merit at more than six times the rate of blacks and Hispanics, and more than two and a half times the rate of whites. "These inconvenient facts create problems for UC administrators seeking ethnic proportionality," says Lynch. "Without bending the rules for some groups, there is no hope of achieving proportionality." According to a report released by the UC,

Asian-American admissions would increase by 15 to 25% if the university based its decisions on academics and socioeconomic status but not race. That means countless Asian-Americans have been shut out of UC by racial preferences.

In a very recent case, two grade-schoolers in Montgomery County, Maryland, were initially denied permission to transfer to a new school in order to participate in a French language immersion program. The two girls are half Asian-American, and country bureaucrats decided that their departure would disrupt the delicate racial balance of the school they are currently attending. The school system denied these students an extraordinary educational opportunity solely because they are of the wrong race. If they were white, county policy would have favored them. The *Washington Post,* hardly a right-wing newspaper, denounced this discrimination in an editorial titled "Asians Need Not Apply." Under public pressure, the girls were allowed to transfer.

Blacks, too, are moving up in society. There is a healthy, thriving black middle class in America. There are blacks at the top levels of society. A recent *New York Times* story, for example, reported that 18% of working, non-Hispanic blacks in New York City between the ages of twenty-five and sixty-five held managerial or professional jobs, and that another 28% held technical, sales, and administrative support positions. Furthermore, 30% were living in households with incomes of $50,000 or more. Statistics that seem to show lingering effects of racism often hide other explanations. For example, household income among blacks is lower than household income among whites, but to a large extent this is caused by the fact that black households are much more likely than white households to include only one adult, usually a single woman, and therefore only one income.

I am the first to say that some minorities are wrestling with enormous problems, racial discrimination among them. Significant groups of minorities, especially blacks, are living in poverty. The condition of our inner cities is a disgrace, and that is a special problem that deserves special attention. But we have to ask: Do all minorities face these problems?

Clearly, the answer to the first part of that question is no. People from ethnic minorities have been successful in climbing into the middle class. If we are going to help minorities who are still struggling, we have to find programs that target those minorities and not the broad spectrum of blacks, Hispanics, and other minorities in the middle class. But racial preferences are irrelevant to minorities who are truly in need. Richard Rodriguez writes in the *Baltimore Sun:* "I was talking to a roomful of black teen-agers, most of them street kids or kids from the projects. Only one of them in a room of 13 had ever heard of anything called affirmative action." Racial preferences, he says, don't reach the people who need help because they depend on a trickle-down effect that never actually occurs. "Many leftists today have [a] domino theory," he writes. "They insist that by creating a female or a non-white leadership class at Harvard or Citibank, people at the bottom will be changed."

The time is past when every member of a racial minority is truly "disadvantaged." It is illogical, even cynical, to cite statistics about minority inner-city poverty in defense of preferences for minority bankers, CEOs, contractors, and investors, but this is what happens all the time. The federal government has nineteen separate regulations giving preferential treatment to rich, but "economically disadvantaged," bank owners. It has innumerable "minority set-asides" for its public contracts, which go to corporations owned by minorities who are rich enough to own corporations. It allows rich minorities to buy broadcasting licenses and facilities far below market values—in one famous case, the then mayor of Charlotte, North Carolina, Harvey Gantt, who is black, and his partners made $3 million by buying a TV station under minority-preference rules and then selling it to whites four months later at full price. This didn't advance the status of blacks in society, but it did boost Gantt's bank account. Ironically, anyone who is already in a position to benefit from racial preference programs in these fields does not need special help in the first place.

The same can be said of racial preference policies at universities. Contrary to what many big universities say, racial preference programs in university admissions generally help people who don't really need the help. The vast majority of minority applicants to top universities come from comfortable, middle-class homes. Some of them come from affluent families. The University of California at Berkeley says that the average Hispanic student admitted through its racial preference program comes from a middle-class family; many, if not most, attended integrated schools, often in the suburbs. In fact, 17% of Hispanic entering freshmen in 1989, along with 14% of black freshmen, were truly well off, coming from families with incomes over $75,000. That's about twice the median family income in the United States. Yet these comfortable middle- and upper middle-class students were admitted under reduced standards because of their race. Why should a university lower its expectations of affluent students who are minorities?

Racial Preferences Don't Help Minorities

The answer to the further question of whether racial preferences are effective in solving the problems some minorities face is also no. Not only do racial preference programs generally help people who don't need help, but more important, racial preferences create a surface appearance of progress while destroying the substance of minority achievement. Holding people to lower standards or giving them special help will make them look as if they are succeeding, but it can't make them succeed. B students who are admitted to top universities because of their race are still B students.

The Pacific Research Institute's Michael Lynch cites graduation rates at UCLA of 50% for blacks and 62% for Hispanics. By comparison, whites and Asians graduate at rates of 80% and 77%, respectively. UCLA admits blacks and Hispanics based on drastically lower standards. Forty-one percent of Hispanic students and over half of black students at UCLA gained admission on a special "minority track," where the standards are significantly lower than they are for other students. These students could have gone to any of California's less competitive colleges and received their degrees, but instead they were placed in California's most rigorous colleges by racial preference programs.

Companies that aren't efficient enough to survive in the marketplace but which get government contracts anyway because they are owned by minorities are still inefficient businesses. "The prospect of getting government contracts as a result of belonging to a protected group is sometimes a false inducement for people to go into business without being adequately prepared," wrote successful black businessman and University of California regent Ward Connerly in *Policy Review.* "They often are undercapitalized and lack the business acumen to remain in business without government contracts." Ultimately, success depends on ability. No preference program can protect minorities from that fact forever. In the meantime, the beneficiaries of such programs *are* protected from having to learn the skills and habits they need to become truly successful.

Furthermore, racial preferences rob minorities of the credit they deserve. How many times have people assumed that a particular member of a minority got a job, a promotion, a college admission, a scholarship, or any other achievement because of racial preferences? The hard work of minority executives, employees, and students can easily be brushed off if there is even a small chance that their honors and accolades were awarded because of their skin color. "It is time for America to acknowledge that affirmative action doesn't work," writes black businessman Daniel Colimon, head of a litigation support firm with over two hundred clients, in *Policy Review.* "Affirmative-action programs have established an extremely damaging stereotype that places African-Americans and other racial minorities in a very precarious position. We are now perceived as a group of people who regardless of how hard we work, how educated we become, or what we achieve, would not be where we are without the preferential treatment afforded by affirmative-action programs."

Remember Rutgers president Francis Lawrence? A strong supporter of racial preferences throughout his career, he let the cat out of the bag [recently] when he told a faculty group that minorities need admissions preferences because they are a "disadvantaged population that doesn't have the genetic hereditary background" to do as well as whites on the SAT. Racial preferences encourage that kind of belief, and they will continue to do so as long as they exist.

Along with that is the racial antagonism caused by racial preferences. More and more whites are getting angry and resentful about perceived reverse discrimination. No doubt many whites exaggerate the extent to which they have been discriminated against, but that's beside the point. Any time groups are treated differently because of their race, the group that is treated worse has a legitimate complaint. This makes it all the more difficult to get whites to feel sympathy across racial lines. "If anything, the white 'backlash' to affirmative action has perpetuated the polarization of America's various ethnic groups," writes Colimon. When whites complain about racial preference programs, many minority supporters of these programs become all the more antagonistic toward whites. It's a vicious circle that can't be broken as long as racial preferences programs are in force.

Racial preferences may not cause whites to hate minorities when they would not otherwise do so, but they undeniably stir up negative feelings.

Paul Sniderman, a political science professor at Stanford University, and Thomas Piazza, a survey researcher at the University of California at Berkeley, authors of the 1993 book *The Scar of Race,* found that "merely asking whites to respond to the issue of affirmative action increases significantly the likelihood that they will perceive blacks as irresponsible and lazy." In a poll, they asked one group of whites to evaluate certain images of black people in general. They asked another group of whites the same questions, but this group was first asked to give an opinion on a racial preference program in a nearby state. Forty-three percent of whites who were first asked about racial preferences said that blacks in general were "irresponsible," compared with 26% of whites who were not asked about racial preferences. "No effort was made to whip up feelings about affirmative action," wrote the authors. But one neutral question about racial preferences "was sufficient to excite a statistically significant response, demonstrating that dislike of particular racial policies can provoke dislike of blacks, as well as the other way around."

That is why racial preferences cannot be justified by the desire for "diversity." Some say employers and college administrators should seek to promote diversity by hiring more minorities than they otherwise would. But racial harmony and integration are much more important goals than diversity—the purpose of seeking diversity is to promote racial harmony and the integration of different races into one society. Racial preferences produce a diversity of skin colors but a division of sentiments. They put people of many different races together in a way that makes each racial group see other racial groups as competitors for arbitrary advantage. That's not the way to produce an integrated, harmonious society.

Racial preferences have divided us for too long. We are all for equal opportunity. We all agree that antidiscrimination laws should be vigorously enforced. We have the legal tools and the consensus we need to go after people who discriminate against minorities. We should be getting on with that job instead of arguing over how much privilege the government should dispense to which racial groups. Nobody should be entitled to something just for being born with a certain color of skin.

POSTSCRIPT

Does Affirmative Action Advance Racial Equality?

Much of the argument between Berry and Chavez turns on the question of "color blindness." To what extent should our laws be color-blind? During the 1950s and early 1960s, civil rights leaders were virtually unanimous on this point. Martin Luther King, Jr., in a speech given at a civil rights march on Washington, said, "I have a dream that my four little children will one day live in a nation where they will not be judged by the color of their skin but by the content of their character." This was the consensus view in 1963, but today it may need to be qualified: In order to *bring about* color blindness, it may be necessary to become temporarily color-conscious. But for how long? And is there a danger that this temporary color consciousness may become a permanent policy?

Chavez recounts the evolution of her own thinking on matters of race relations in *An Unlikely Conservative: The Transformation of a Renegade Democrat* (HarperCollins, 2001). Girardeau A. Spann's *The Law of Affirmative Action: Twenty-Five Years of Supreme Court Decisions on Race and Remedies* (New York University Press, 2000) is a comprehensive chronicle of the Supreme Court's involvement with the affirmative action issue from *DeFunis v. Odegaard* in 1974 through the cases decided in the Court's 1998–1999 term. Clint Bolick, in *The Affirmative Action Fraud: Can We Restore the Civil Rights Vision?* (Cato Institute, 1996), argues that racial and gender preferences deepen racial hostilities and undermine individual freedom without doing minorities much good. Columnist Jim Sleeper's *Liberal Racism* (Viking, 1997) is critical of affirmative action and other race-based programs, as is a book by *ABC News* reporter Bob Zelnick, *Backfire: A Reporter's Look at Affirmative Action* (Regnery, 1996). Barbara Bergmann supports affirmative action in *In Defense of Affirmative Action* (Basic Books, 1996), while Stephan Thernstrom and Abigail Thernstrom, in their comprehensive survey of racial progress in America entitled *America in Black and White: One Nation, Indivisible* (Simon & Schuster, 1997), argue that it is counterproductive. In *Collision Course: The Strange Convergence of Affirmative Action and Immigration Policy in America* (Oxford University Press, 2002), Hugh David Graham maintains that affirmative action is now at loggerheads with America's expanded immigration policies, in that employers use affirmative action to hire new immigrants at the expense of American blacks.

Affirmative action is one of those issues, like abortion, in which the opposing sides seem utterly intransigent. But there may be a large middle sector of opinion that is simply weary of the whole controversy and may be willing to support any expedient solution worked out by pragmatists in the executive and legislative branches of the government.

ISSUE 10

Should the President Be Allowed to Detain Citizens Indefinitely in Wartime?

YES: Andrew C. McCarthy, from "Comforting the Enemy," *National Review Online* (December 19, 2003)

NO: Lewis Z. Koch, from "Dirty Bomber? Dirty Justice," *Bulletin of the Atomic Scientists* (January/February 2004)

ISSUE SUMMARY

YES: Former federal prosecutor Andrew C. McCarthy believes citizens who are terrorists should not enjoy the constitutional rights of common criminal defendants, and they may be detained for the duration of hostilities.

NO: Investigative reporter Lewis Z. Koch states that no American citizen has ever been or ever should be indefinitely detained and deprived of the right to counsel and trial on the assertion of the Attorney General.

Imagine that there was probable cause for the American government to believe that terrorists had secretly placed a powerful explosive device set to go off at a predetermined time with the likely consequence that it would kill thousands of innocent people—unless it could be discovered and defused. An American citizen has been apprehended who may be part of the subversive enterprise that planned this attack. He fails to cooperate. Perhaps he has nothing important to tell, but perhaps he does, and thousands of lives may be saved if he can be compelled to reveal what the government thinks that he may know. Should he have the benefit of specific charges, legal counsel, and a court hearing, and the likelihood that he will not reveal whatever he may know? Or should the government be empowered to employ unlimited detention in order to extract the vital information that it believes the prisoner may possess or to prevent him from playing a role in what it believes to be a terrorist plot?

Dramatic as this hypothetical threat may appear, it corresponds to real circumstances in a world where the greatest dangers American national security confronts come from terrorists who wear no uniforms and whose tactics do not conform to conventional forms of warfare. The response of the U.S. government has been that such persons are "unlawful combatants" who do not deserve and should not be given the benefit of the constitutional guarantee of habeas corpus, a court order to bring a body before a judge or court, implying a right to counsel, the placing of charges against the defendants, and a trial to determine guilt or innocence.

President Lincoln suspended the writ of habeas corpus in 1861, but after the Civil War the Supreme Court rejected the operation of military courts in states where the federal courts were open and operating. When the United States entered the Second World War, President Roosevelt ordered the internment of all West Coast residents of Japanese descent, including American citizens, because the government feared the prospect of a Japanese invasion. A divided Supreme Court upheld this action, but decades later the government expressed its regret. An American citizen was among eight Nazi spies who secretly landed in the United States from submarines in order to commit sabotage. They were tried and convicted by a military court, and six were executed.

Critics point to the U.S. Constitution's Sixth Amendment as protection against indefinite detention. That amendment states: "In all criminal proceedings, the accused shall enjoy the right to a speedy and public trial by an impartial jury of the state and district wherein the crime shall have been committed . . . and to be informed of the nature and cause of the accusation, to be confronted with the witnesses against him; to have compulsory process for obtaining witnesses in his favor, and to have the assistance of counsel for his defense."

Congress and the courts have recognized exceptional circumstances in which persons may be indefinitely detained. The Bail Reform Act of 1984 allows the preventive detention of defendants who pose a prospective danger to the community. In upholding this law in 1987, the Supreme Court concluded: "In times of war or insurrection, when society's interest is at its peak, the Government may detain individuals whom the Government believes to be dangerous. Even outside the exigencies of war, we found that sufficiently compelling governmental interests can justify detention of dangerous persons." The issue has been raised more recently in the cases of sex offenders who have already served their sentence for the crimes for which they were convicted.

At least two American citizens have been among the several thousand persons held in indefinite detainment since 9/11 at Guantanamo Bay, an American naval base in Cuba. When their appeal from detention was argued before the U.S. Supreme Court in April 2004, Deputy Solicitor General Paul Clement argued that "you have to trust the executive to make the kind of quintessential military judgments that are involved." Defense attorney Frank Dunham responded that "we didn't trust the executive branch when we founded this government."

Andrew C. McCarthy concludes that to fight terrorists with legal procedures is suicidal, and that Congress has authorized the president to use all necessary and appropriate force in opposing terrorism. Lewis Z. Koch warns that a movement into martial law has the probable consequence of destroying all constitutional guarantees.

Andrew C. McCarthy  **YES**

Comforting the Enemy

If you were under the impression that the 9/11 atrocities marked the long-overdue end of a suicidal government philosophy that terrorists and bombs should be fought with indictments and trials instead of missiles in the air and boots on the ground, guess again. A number of our esteemed federal judges did not get the memo. And having been such a ringing success at running prisons, schools, and housing developments, they've now decided to give micromanaging the prosecution of war a try.

Such is the unmistakable message . . . by a divided panel of the U.S. Court of Appeals for the Second Circuit in New York in the case of Jose Padilla (a.k.a. "Abdullah al Muhajir"), alleged to be an al Qaeda–trained dirty bomber. Despite the existence of very active military hostilities against an international terror network that has already executed domestic mass murder, the two-judge majority held that the president, the commander in chief responsible for conducting the war, is without authority to detain as an unlawful combatant an operative he found to have been dispatched by the terror network to carry out further slaughter, including the detonation of a radiological weapon of mass destruction. Padilla must instead, according to Circuit Judges Rosemary S. Pooler and Barrington D. Parker Jr., be charged and tried in a civilian court, where he would be entitled to the panoply of rights accorded criminal defendants—including, of course, massive amounts of discovery regarding what we know about his al Qaeda activities and how we know it.

Padilla, an American citizen and multiple prior felon with a juvenile murder conviction on his résumé, moved to Egypt and adopted militant Islam after being released from prison following a 1991 Florida weapons conviction. According to information proffered by the government to the federal district court, he traveled through the Middle East, eventually teaming up with al Qaeda in Afghanistan. In 2001—long after bin Laden had already declared war against the United States, simultaneously bombed our embassies in Kenya and Tanzania (killing well over 200), and attacked the U.S.S. *Cole* in Yemen (killing 17 of our military personnel)—Padilla is said to have proposed to one of bin Laden's most intimate aides, the infamous Abu Zubaydeh, a plan to steal radioactive material within the United States in order to build a dirty bomb (or "radiological dispersal device"). Al Qaeda made available a safe house in Lahore, Pakistan, for research on the project, provided Padilla with the necessary training for this and other terror operations, and then dispatched him to the United States to make mayhem.

Fortunately, the government managed to develop enough evidence to detain him on a material-witness arrest warrant once he landed in Chicago, from Pakistan, on May 8, 2002. Then, as now, Americans were engaged in robust fighting against al Qaeda in Afghanistan and elsewhere; then as now, al Qaeda was promising new attacks against the United States and its allies. And while, thanks to the president's steely determination to take a military war to a military enemy, the terror network has not succeeded in reprising September 11 here at home, it has continued to conduct murderous bombing operations in Tunisia, Kenya, Indonesia, Morocco, Saudi Arabia, Turkey, and Iraq.

There being a war against al Qaeda, and Padilla being an al Qaeda operative sent here to conduct attacks, the president made the eminently sensible decision to declare Padilla an enemy combatant and to have the Defense Department detain him. The authority under the laws of war to detain enemy combatants for the duration of hostilities has a rich pedigree. The logic, as explicitly recognized by the Geneva Conventions in 1949, is "to prevent military personnel from taking up arms once again against the captive state."

Under the Hague Convention of 1910, enemy combatants may be lawful or unlawful, based on whether they are subject to a formal chain of command, wear uniforms, carry their weapons openly, and conduct their operations in accordance with the laws and customs of war. Obviously, those who serve al Qaeda, a non-sovereign, multinational terrorist organization that clandestinely designs and executes indiscriminate mass homicide, are unlawful combatants.

While lawful combatants generally must be released at the cessation of hostilities unless some egregious conduct has rendered them triable as war criminals, unlawful combatants have no such right. It was once common for them to be executed summarily, although as Chief U.S. District Judge Michael B. Mukasey observed earlier in the litigation, "such Draconian measures have not prevailed in modern times in what some still refer to without embarrassment as the civilized world." Instead, it has long been established, as the Supreme Court recognized in its 1942 decision in *Ex Parte Quirin*, that unlawful combatants may be tried by military tribunals—even when civilian courts are available.

Faithful to these principles, District Judge Mukasey, deservedly among the most well-respected jurists in America and nonpareil in matters of national security, upheld President Bush's decision in a thoughtful, painstaking 102-page opinion. The dissenting third member of the Second Circuit's *Padilla* panel, Judge Richard C. Wesley, would have adopted the district court's ruling in all respects. Nevertheless, the panel majority reversed in a nettlesome opinion that both turns its back on settled law and displays a startling insouciance about the reality on the ground.

To arrive at their conclusion, Judges Pooler and Parker first had to tiptoe around about 150 years of jurisprudence, beginning with the Prize Cases of 1862 (arising out of President Lincoln's Civil War blockade of secessionist states), which holds that the president is not merely fully vested by Article II of the Constitution, but in fact obligated, to resist by all appropriate measures, including the use of force, a forcible attack against the United States. Similarly, the majority needed to end-around the commonsense separation of powers doctrine that it is for the president, not federal judges, to determine what measures are necessary to protect the country in time of war.

The majority paid lip service to these principles, but undermined them nonetheless by a demonstrably specious distinction: *viz.*, whether the president's responsive measures are employed against "the outside world" or "turned inward" to United States territory. This notion the majority augmented with a loopy "zone of combat" theory—hypothesizing that even if the president can turn his powers war inward, he can only do so in a zone of active combat. The majority did not explain what "zone of combat" is, and who gets to decide whether there is one; they simply insisted that, wherever it was, Padilla was not in it.

Leaving aside al Qaeda's palpable success in fighting the war right in the heart of New York City—indeed, the chasm that was once the World Trade Center can be seen from the windows of the courthouse where the Second Circuit sits—the majority found this alleged distinction by mining language from a concurring opinion in the steel-seizure case (in which the Supreme Court undid President Truman's appropriation of American steel mills during the Korean War). Of course, that case had nothing to do with enemy combatants or an entity in hostilities with—and directing military operations inside—the United States.

A case that did deal directly with that situation was the aforementioned *Quirin*. There, Nazi operatives, including one who claimed to be an American citizen, stole into the United States by ship, shed their uniforms upon hitting the shore, and spread out to conduct sabotage operations against war industries and facilities. They, like Padilla (an American citizen), were captured before they could execute their designs. Importantly unlike Padilla, who at the moment is merely being detained, they were both detained and subjected to military tribunals. When they challenged that treatment, the Supreme Court ruled that, regardless of citizenship, persons who aligned themselves with an enemy and sought covertly to harm the United States in our territory while hostilities were ongoing could be declared unlawful combatants and subjected to military tribunals.

Recognizing that the Supreme Court's decisions are binding on lower federal courts, Judge Mukasey logically reasoned that if the Supreme Court had found prosecution by military tribunal (which could carry the death penalty) permissible, then mere detention must *a fortiori* be authorized for Padilla. The Second Circuit majority, however, contorted itself to draw a contrary conclusion.

First, the panel majority misleadingly suggested that *Quirin* was distinguishable because in World War II Congress had expressly authorized military tribunals. But Padilla's case is about *detention,* not military tribunals (at least not yet); and, more to the point, the *Quirin* Court expressly relied not only on the congressional grant of authority but also the president's independent constitutional authority as commander in chief under Article II. Second, the majority noted that the *Quirin* defendants had acknowledged their status as Nazi agents while Padilla "from all indications, intends to dispute his designation as an enemy combatant"—a bizarre point since it would hinge the propriety of presidential action to protect a nation at war on the subjective assertions of terrorists regarding whether they were really unlawful combatants. (One could strongly disagree with, but understand, a court saying that *it*, rather than the president, had the final word on who could be considered an enemy combatant; the thought of leaving the matter up to the terrorists themselves, however, is breathtaking.)

Third, and most plausibly, the majority noted that when *Quirin* was decided, an important statute, Section 4001(a) of Title 18, United States Code, had not yet been enacted. Section 4001(a) states that "[n]o citizen shall be imprisoned or otherwise detained by the United States except pursuant to an Act of Congress." This provision clearly spells trouble for the argument—advanced by the government—that the president still retains plenary constitutional authority to detain unlawful combatants. Such a contention would call for either holding Section 4001(a) unconstitutional (as an improper legislative infringement on the president's Article II authority as commander-in-chief)—something courts should do only as a last, unavoidable resort—or for finding a fairly straightforward statute somehow ambiguous and inapplicable.

Nonetheless, as the district court had wisely found, there was no need in Padilla's case to go down either of these unsavory paths because an Act of Congress authorizing Padilla's detention was ready to hand. Specifically, one week after the September 11 attacks, Congress passed a joint resolution, broadly authorizing the president to "use all necessary and appropriate force against those nations, organizations, or persons he determines planned, authorized, committed or aided the terrorist attacks that occurred on September 11, 2001, or harbored such organizations or persons, in order to prevent any future acts of international terrorism against the United States by such nations, organizations or persons."

District Judge Mukasey had found that Padilla easily fell within the ambit of the joint resolution. Palpably, al Qaeda carried out the September 11 attacks, Padilla is alleged to be an al Qaeda operative who trained with the organization, and he was sent here precisely to commit "future acts of international terrorism against the United States." Remarkably, however, the Second Circuit majority quibbled that the resolution permitting "all necessary and appropriate *force*" (emphasis added)—which obviously includes killing enemy operatives—"contains no language authorizing detention." That should be interesting to try to apply in the field: You can shoot 'em but make sure you don't hold 'em.

The majority airily puttered that it was required under the circumstances to carve out for Padilla a lacuna in the sweep of the joint resolution because the Constitution enshrines civil rights just as it does the enumerated powers of government. Forgetting for the moment that we are in a war with soldiers and civilians being murdered, and even ignoring the dispositive rationale of *Quirin* that withers such high-minded ephemera, the majority's reasoning here cannot even withstand the steel seizure opinion it purports to regard as its analytical guide. There, as Judge Wesley pointedly noted in his *Padilla* dissent, the Supreme Court asserted: "When the President acts pursuant to an express or implied authorization of Congress, his authority is at its maximum, for it includes all that he possesses in his own right plus all that Congress can delegate." In such instances—as here, where President Bush prosecutes a war with the unambiguous and sweeping support of a legislative enactment—the civil rights of would-be dirty-bombers must take a back seat.

Concerns about detention of enemy combatants are not persuasive, but neither are they frivolous. There is no end in sight for the war on terror, which means there is in theory no set end date for release of al Qaeda fighters from detention—just as the American people have no set end date when their anxiety over the possibility of another September 11 might ebb. But there is no justification at this point to inflate the dimensions of Padilla's plight. We are not in a mere technical state of war; we are in a real, live shooting war. There is no rational fear here that the president is rounding up political enemies or suspect ethnic classes under the cover of phony hostilities; there are exceedingly few persons being held as unlawful combatants, and there is a reasoned basis for each of those detentions—indeed, even the Second Circuit majority conceded that Padilla appeared to be a national security threat.

While it is, moreover, a foreign concept to many federal judges today, it bears noting that the president is a coordinate constitutional actor, of equal status to the judicial branch. He takes an oath to uphold the Constitution just like judges do. Given that prosecution of war is uniquely a presidential prerogative, why should anyone have more faith in the courts than the president to decide who the combatants are and what must be done to neutralize them?

The Second Circuit's decision would do immeasurable damage to the prosecution of the war on terror—undermining those who are fighting it, clothing terrorists actively abetting al Qaeda in the rights of common criminal defendants, and forcing the government to reveal sensitive information to those terrorists in civilian criminal proceedings at the very time that information is most needed to defeat the enemy and protect national security. The government has the option of seeking review from the entire Second Circuit (i.e., all thirteen judges) or proceeding directly to the Supreme Court. It must do so with all appropriate speed.

NO

Lewis Z. Koch

Dirty Bomber? Dirty Justice

On May 8, 2002, 31-year-old Brooklyn-born Jose Padilla was arrested by FBI agents at Chicago's O'Hare International Airport and held as a witness in connection with the September 11, 2001, attacks.

Speaking at a special news conference in Moscow a month later, U.S. Attorney General John Ashcroft accused Padilla of being a new kind of terrorist bomber. Ashcroft professed no doubts and offered no equivocation—just a flat out accusation: "We have captured a known terrorist who was exploring a plan to build and explode a radiological dispersion device, or 'dirty bomb,' in the United States." Ashcroft said the arrest of Padilla "disrupted an unfolding terrorist plot," one that could have caused "mass death and injury." President George W. Bush accused Padilla of "conduct in preparation for acts of international terrorism" and declared him an "enemy combatant." Using the little understood USA Patriot Act, Padilla was denied access to an attorney.

In a matter of minutes, the 40-plus-year history of Miranda rights was swept away. At the time of this writing, Padilla is still sitting in a cell at the Consolidated Naval Brig in Charleston, South Carolina, subject to an unknown number of hours or days or months of questioning, ignorant of his legal rights and the charges against him, and without the advice of an attorney. The government contends Padilla falls under a special exception to the Constitution, but a host of legal scholars feel otherwise.

You Have the Right . . .

Anyone with a television set is familiar with Miranda rights; they've been repeated on thousands of cop shows: "You have the right to remain silent. Anything you say can and will be used against you in a court of law. You have the right to speak to an attorney, and to have an attorney present during any questioning. If you cannot afford a lawyer, one will be provided for you at government expense." The Miranda warning stems from the 1960 case of Clarence Earl Gideon, a two-bit criminal charged and convicted of breaking and entering the Bay Harbor Poolroom in Panama City, Florida, and stealing some coins and wine. The Supreme Court decided that Gideon had been wrongly denied the right to a lawyer in his criminal trial.

From the *Bulletin of the Atomic Scientists*, January/February 2004, pp. 59–60, 65–68. Copyright © 2004 by the Bulletin of the Atomic Scientists. Reprinted with permission.

Six years later, the Supreme Court applied similar principles to Ernesto Miranda, a man arrested and accused of kidnapping and raping a mildly retarded 18-year-old woman. The court ruled Miranda deserved to have an attorney present at his questioning.

Thus, one would surely think that in 2002 a man publicly described by the attorney general of the United States as a "known terrorist," whose arrest disrupted an unfolding plot to attack the United States by exploding a dirty bomb, would be entitled to legal counsel.

As Pulitzer Prize-winning journalist Anthony Lewis asked in an April 20, 2003, *New York Times* magazine article, who but an advocate for Padilla could challenge Ashcroft's statement? Who but Padilla's lawyer could challenge the news media to test the truth of the accusation? By denying Padilla an attorney, Ashcroft's comments amounted to "conviction by government announcement," Lewis wrote.

In light of the threat from Al Qaeda, exactly how far should the government be allowed to go in denying its citizens constitutional guarantees and rights? How far is too far? Should Jose Padilla, an untried, unconvicted, alleged dirty bomber, be denied his constitutional rights and guarantees? As an enemy combatant, is Padilla in the same class as foreign soldiers captured in Afghanistan and now held for questioning and perhaps military tribunals at Guantanamo Bay?

The Sixth Amendment employs clear and precise language: "In all criminal prosecutions, the accused shall enjoy the right to a speedy and public trial, by an impartial jury of the state and district wherein the crime shall have been committed . . . and to be informed of the nature and cause of the accusation; to be confronted with the witnesses against him; to have compulsory process for obtaining witnesses in his favor, and to have the assistance of counsel for his defense."

Padilla has not had a speedy public trial nor is it known if he has been fairly confronted with the nature of the charges against him—nor has he had "the assistance of counsel for his defense." Never before in the history of the Justice Department, or solely through as assertion by the attorney general, has an American citizen been deliberately deprived of these rights. . . .

After being arrested in Chicago, Padilla was taken to the Metropolitan Correctional Center in New York. He appeared before Michael B. Mukasey, U.S. district judge of the Southern District of New York. Mukasey, regarded as a no-nonsense jurist, insisted that legal charges be leveled against Padilla. But Justice Department attorneys claimed Padilla was a witness who needed to give testimony before a federal grand jury and that they couldn't foresee how long that requirement would last, so there was no end in sight to Padilla's detention.

In response to objections from Mukasey, the FBI reluctantly managed to cough up a paper affidavit created by Special Agent Joseph Ennis that claimed (without proof or cross examination) that Padilla "appeared to have knowledge of facts relevant to a grand jury investigation into the September 11 attacks. That investigation includes an ongoing inquiry into the activities of Al Qaeda, an organization believed to be responsible for the September 11 attacks, among others, and to be committed to and involved in planning further attacks."

Neither Ashcroft nor Ennis appeared in court to support those claims.

Just as the Supreme Court reasoned in 1962 that Clarence Earl Gideon deserved to have his own attorney, Mukasey reasoned in 2002 that Padilla, charged with being a terrorist and dirty-bomber for Al Qaeda, certainly deserved an attorney, maybe even a gaggle of them. So Mukasey appointed Donna Newman to represent Padilla. Newman met with Padilla on at least two occasions, then asked the judge to vacate the warrant for Padilla because he had not been charged with a crime. . . .

The government insisted on an ex parte (private) meeting with Mukasey. The Justice attorneys told the judge something to the effect of, "Oops, sorry about that, Judge, but the witness subpoena for Padilla is being withdrawn." Mukasey promptly signed papers vacating the warrant. Then the Justice attorneys announced that President Bush had designated Padilla an "enemy combatant," and before you could say *Mr. Mxyztplk*, Padilla was whisked off to the Consolidated Naval Brig, 769 miles away from his attorney. Outraged, Newman conferred with government attorneys—she wanted to see and speak with her client. She was told that she would not be permitted to speak with Padilla. She could write to him, but he might not receive the correspondence.

The government argued that Padilla should not be allowed to see a lawyer because he might pass messages to his fellow terrorists through his attorney. Mukasey didn't buy it. The idea that Padilla would pass on secrets for Al Qaeda through his attorney was, in Mukasey's words, "gossamer speculation." Padilla had already met with Newman, so whatever damage might have been done by those conversations was already done. And finally, "there was no reason that military personnel cannot monitor [within limits] Padilla's contacts," Mukasey said.

When pressed in open court by the angry Mukasey, on August 27, 2002, three and a half months after Padilla's arrest and incarceration, the government finally produced its first "evidence" against Padilla. This was a finding or "declaration" by Michael Mobbs, an obscure Pentagon bureaucrat with the title "Special Adviser to the Under Secretary of Defense for Policy," who claimed that "Padilla and his associate conducted research in the construction of a 'uranium-enhanced' explosive device . . . in particular, they engaged in research on this topic at one of the Al Qaeda safe houses in Lahore, Pakistan . . . [a plan in which] Padilla and his associate [would] build and then detonate a 'radiological dispersal device' (also known as a dirty bomb) within the United States, possibly in Washington, D.C."

There are problems with this declaration. In a footnote, Mobbs reveals that the information about Padilla came from two confidential sources. "It is believed," the footnote reads, "that these confidential sources have not been completely candid about their associations with Al Qaeda and their terrorist activities." It then goes on to explain: "Much of the information from these sources has, however, been corroborated and proven accurate and reliable." On the other hand, it went on, "some information by the sources remains uncorroborated and may even be part of an effort to mislead or confuse U.S. officials." But not to worry, or as *Mad Magazine's* Alfred E. Neuman puts it, "What, me worry?" The Mobbs footnote concludes, "One of the sources, for example, in a subsequent interview with a U.S. law enforcement official recanted some of the information he provided, but most of this information has been independently corroborated by other sources. In addition, at the time of being interviewed by U.S. officials, one of the sources was being treated with various types of drugs to treat medical conditions."

Padilla's attorneys as well as the judge were unable to cross-examine Mobbs. The government offered a written statement, unaccompanied by Mobbs himself, on the witness stand. June 2003 reports suggest that some of the translations of captured sources may have been deliberately mistranslated by American translators working as Syrian spies.

The government, in what many believe is a highly unusual legal move, also appealed Mukasey's decision to grant Padilla the right to an attorney, sending it on to the court of appeals. A group of 14 legal scholars, world-class attorneys, and former federal court appellate judges, many of whom served in high positions with the federal government, filed *amici curiae* briefs with the court of appeals, demanding Padilla be accorded constitutional protections. They noted that Padilla is an American citizen, arrested on American territory. Even John Walker Lindh, who was arrested in Afghanistan, armed and attempting to kill U.S. forces, had an attorney throughout his legal negotiations and public trial. . . .

The government's case rests on an unusual argument. The spokesman for the Justice Department's Criminal Division, Bryan Sierra, contends that U.S. Code 18, section 4001(a), which reads, "No citizen shall be imprisoned or otherwise detained by the United States except pursuant to an Act of Congress," provides no check on the president's powers as commander in chief. Instead, Sierra cites section 4001(b)(1), which reads, "The control and management of federal penal and correctional institutions, except military or naval institutions, shall be vested in the attorney general." And to whom does the attorney general report? The president. In other words, in the Justice Department's tortured logic, as commander in chief, the president is not bound by Congress's rules on imprisonment and detention.

But it gets even more tenuous. According to Sierra, "It is our [Justice's] position that Congress drafted the law not to restrict the president's power, and according to the record, that point was even noted by then-Rep. Abner Mikva during the debate."

But Mikva, an eminent jurist and now a visiting professor at the University of Chicago Law School, says the law was not about giving the president more power, but rather, taking it away. The "debate," Mikva told me, had to do with delegitimizing American internment camps, such as those authorized by the president and built at the outset of World War II to house American citizens of Japanese ancestry. It was passed during the heyday of Sen. Joseph McCarthy and the House Un-American Activities committee, when rumors were rampant that the government was building camps to house Americans suspected of leftist leanings. Mikva's position then and now (as a signatory to the *amicus* brief in Padilla) was to restrict the president (or his chain of command) from exercising extralegal powers to detain or imprison without fulfilling the letter of the law.

Ashcroft's argument is based on a single Civil War case: In 1864, one man, Lambdin P. Milligan, a U.S. citizen from Indiana, was tried on charges of conspiracy before a military commission and sentenced to be hanged. The Supreme Court rejected the verdict, holding that "military courts could not function in states where federal courts were open and operating," as Louis Fisher writes in his book *Nazi Saboteurs on Trial: A Military Tribunal and American Law.*

Congress was not pleased with the Supreme Court decision, Fisher says, and "passed legislation to limit the court's jurisdiction to hear cases involving martial law and military trials." The statute reads: "No civil court of the United States, or of any state, or of the District of Columbia, shall have or take jurisdiction of, or in any manner reverse any of the proceedings had or acts done as aforesaid." But this was in 1867, and it's a slim legal reed for Ashcroft to rest his case against Padilla on.

Ron Sievert, a University of Texas at Austin law school professor and U.S. assistant attorney, in his comprehensive book *Cases and Materials on U.S. Laws and National Security,* questions the powers of so-called military commissions, especially when a military commander, including the president acting as commander in chief, substitutes "military force for and to the exclusion of the laws and punish[es] all persons, as he thinks right and proper, without fixed and certain rules."

If unchecked, such power would mean that republican government, and liberty regulated by law, would come to an end. With such powers, martial law could be used to destroy every guarantee of the Constitution, and effectually render the military independent of and superior to civil power. The idea was deemed such an offense by this country's founders that they cited it as one of the main reasons for declaring independence from England. "Civil liberty and this kind of martial law cannot endure together; the antagonism is irreconcilable; and, in the conflict, one or the other must perish," Sievert writes.

During the turbulent Civil War years, Abraham Lincoln declared an emergency, suspended the writ of habeas corpus, and declared martial law both in 1861 and 1862. Chief Justice of the Supreme Court Roger B. Taney ruled that Lincoln did not have the right. In 1866, after the end of the Civil War, the Supreme Court reinstated habeas corpus. Despite the reinstatement, the government now contends it can hold Padilla incommunicado and subject him to constant and endless questioning without allowing him an attorney, or presenting him in court.

Illegal, say other former federal appellate court judges and legal scholars, whose *amicus curiae* brief states, "The right to habeas corpus—that is, to have a *court* determine the legality of detention—was one of the few individual rights enshrined in the Constitution itself, even before the Bill of Rights." The brief notes that President Bush's declaration of Padilla as an enemy combatant "would also strip away the most basic due process rights of notice and an opportunity to be heard by forbidding Padilla from even learning about this case or communicating in any manner with his counsel—*or even with the court.*". . .

The most important precedent for denying Padilla legal representation comes from a World War II example where the prisoners were in fact accorded legal representation, some of it outstanding. Eight ill-equipped "spies" were sent by Germany to work against the United States in 1942. They were far from rocket scientists. Most had previously worked in the United States for a short while as fry cooks, chauffeurs, or tool and die makers; one worked in the meatpacking industry. After four months of spy and saboteur training, they were put aboard submarines and shipped to the United States.

When four of the eight landed on Long Island, the first person they encountered on the beach was an unarmed U.S. Coast Guardsman, Frank Collins, whom they tried to bribe. When Collins returned to base that night, he told his superiors, who then hurried to the beach, where they found Nazi paraphernalia and explosive devices. Five days later, when the four spies were in New York City, one of them, George Dasch, phoned the FBI in an effort to turn himself and his co-spies in. The FBI didn't believe him. Dasch then phoned government information and was told to call the Adjunct General's Office, but the secretary said her boss wasn't in.

In desperation, Dasch called the FBI again, and while the agent really didn't believe him, he was nevertheless told to go to a specific office in the Justice Department. The FBI agents still thought they were wasting their time until Dasch opened a suitcase with $82,550 in cash.

A few days later, four other German spies landed in Florida, but by now the FBI was hot on the case, and they were all rounded up.

President Franklin D. Roosevelt did not want the eight spies tried in a civilian court; the most prison time they might serve would be two years. Roosevelt wanted them dead, period. He wanted a trial by a military commission, something akin to a military tribunal. Roosevelt issued Proclamation 2561, creating a military tribunal referencing what he called the "law of war"—not all that different from President Bush calling an American citizen arrested on American territory an "enemy combatant." If Roosevelt had cited the Articles of War, he would have had to conform to the laws established by Congress for court-martial. But this way, "acts of war" could mean whatever Roosevelt and Attorney General Francis Biddle meant them to be, and the trial could be run by their rules, including allowing a two-thirds vote of the commission/tribunal to approve the death penalty and closing all proceedings to the public, except for 15 minutes when a few photographers snapped pictures and a few reporters took notes. Roosevelt got his way, and six of the eight were sentenced to death.

What makes the Padilla case different from the Nazi spy case is that even with the formation of Roosevelt's ad hoc, make-the-rules-up-as-you-go-along plan, no one argued that the Nazi spies did not deserve to have defense attorneys. In fact, one defense attorney, Col. Kenneth Royall, acknowledged that he worked under the military chain of command and would cease his efforts if so ordered. But his orders were for him to do what he thought was right, and Royall was rigorous in his defense, contending that his commander in chief, Roosevelt, had acted illegally in forming the commission. Once the verdict was rendered, Royall pressed for the case to be heard by the Supreme Court. The public, too, began to tire of all the secrecy and demanded more openness. The hearings before the Supreme Court were open to all, though it would take almost three months before a full-blown decision could be handed down.

The Supreme Court found in favor of the commission—months after six of the spies were executed. Later, Justice Felix Frankfurter said the finding "was not a happy precedent. The American legal system would do well not to see its like again."

A year after the spies were caught, Hans Haupt, the father of one of the men, was arrested and sentenced to death because he had hidden some of his son's cash. In reversing that conviction, the appellate court in the Seventh Circuit unanimously denounced the Supreme Court's decision in the Nazi spy case for its failure to protect the fundamental right of a jury trial:

"Of the many rights guaranteed to the people of this Republic, there is none more sacred than that of trial by jury. Such right comprehends a fair determination, free from passion or prejudice, of the issues involved. The right is all-inclusive; it embraces every class and type of person. Those for whom we have contempt or even hatred are equally entitled to its benefits. It will be a sad day for our system of government if the time should come when any person, whoever he may be, is deprived of this fundamental safeguard. No more important responsibility rests upon courts than its preservation unimpaired. How wasted is American blood now being spilled in all parts of the world if we at home are unwilling or unable to accord every person charged with a crime a trial in conformity with this constitutional requirement."

Ashcroft would have it otherwise. In remarks before the Senate Judiciary Committee on December 7, 2001, Ashcroft denounced those who had voiced opposition to the extrajudicial, extralegal steps the Bush administration was taking: "Your tactics only aid terrorists, for they erode our national unity and diminish our resolve. They give ammunition to America's enemies and pause to America's friends."

A day after the Judiciary Committee hearing, the Justice Department announced that Ashcroft had not intended to discourage public debate; what he found unhelpful to the country were "misstatements and the spread of misinformation about the actions of the Justice Department."

But, according to Fisher, "Ashcroft appeared to claim that tribunals are created under the exclusive authority of the president and that according to judicial precedents Congress may not limit that authority. The legal and historical record of military tribunals presents quite a different picture: The creation of tribunals is typically decided jointly by Congress and the president; Congress has not recognized a unilateral presidential authority to create those tribunals; and the Supreme Court has repeatedly held that Congress has the constitutional authority to create tribunals, decide their authorities and jurisdiction, and limit the president if he acts unilaterally by military order or proclamation to create those tribunals."

In the Padilla case and other "terrorist" cases, American justice is sailing into uncharted territory. . . .

POSTSCRIPT

Should the President Be Allowed to Detain Citizens Indefinitely in Wartime?

The conviction with which Andrew McCarthy defends the power of internment and other measures to protect national security is equaled by the conviction with which Lewis Koch opposes indeterminate detention and the denial of habeas corpus as violations of the most basic constitutional rights. Writing before America became involved in the present struggle against terrorism, Chief Justice William Rehnquist sought to strike a balance between these opposing views when he warned that "it is all too easy to slide from a case of genuine military necessity . . . to one where the threat is not critical and the power either dubious or nonexistent."

The congressional resolution of October, 23, 2002 authorizes the use of force against Iraq and allows him to use "all necessary and appropriate force" to protect the national security. Doesn't "all" include everything? On the other hand, some years earlier, in reacting to what by then were regarded as excesses committed against American citizens of Japanese descent during World War II, Congress declared: "No person shall be imprisoned or otherwise detained by the United States except pursuant to an Act of Congress." This seems to go the other way, canceling out the "all" and restricting the president. Lawyers must somehow reconcile these two declarations of Congress.

Other questions that must be pondered in trying to balance the competing values of liberty and security: What rights does an American citizen retain who has been declared by presidential authority to be an enemy combatant? Does it make any difference whether he has been detained at home or abroad? If prisoners taken during the "war on terror" are not actual prisoners of war but "unlawful combatants," does this mean that such persons do not have the human rights protection that common criminals receive? What if "the other side"—terrorists or enemy nations—use the same rationale in their treatment of captured Americans? These are not meant to be rhetorical questions; they may indeed be answerable. But they do have to be addressed.

The most extensive example of American detention of American citizens is recounted in Peter Irons, *Justice Delayed: The Record of the Japanese American Internment Cases* (Wesleyan University Press, 1989). Both Japanese citizens and American citizens of Japanese descent were relocated from the West Coast to government internment camps for the duration of the Second World War. Many young men volunteered to serve in the American armed forces. No one of Japanese descent was indicted, let alone convicted, of subversion or any other crime against the United States. The legal arguments will find resolution in the decisions in *Rumsfeld v. Padilla* and *Hamdi v. Rumsfeld*, both of which were argued before the U.S. Supreme Court in April 2004. Rich Lowry, "Throw Away the Key," *National Review Online* (June 20, 2002) presents the case for the detainment of Jose Padilla as long as necessary, without suspending the writ of habeas corpus. Lowry states: "Intelligence is crucial to our fight, and interrogation is the way to get it." David Cole, *Enemy Aliens: Double Standards and Constitutional Freedoms in the War on Terrorism* (The New Press, 2003), argues that interning citizens without charges or legal defense is both constitutionally and morally wrong, and will endanger national security by increasing anti-American hostility. Terrorism is examined in a different context in Caleb Carr, *The Lessons of Terror: A History of Warfare Against Civilians: Why It Has Always Failed and Why It Will Fail Again* (Random House, 2002). Carr bolsters his case with the example of Great Britain in World War II, which actually stiffened its spine during the terror bombing by the Nazis.

Few thoughtful Americans are untroubled by the idea of assigning the power of indefinite detention to the President during wartime. Yet Americans are also united in their horror of what happened on September 11, 2001, and determined to strain every nerve to prevent it from happening again. Can Americans follow the logic of that imperative without sacrificing the freedom that essentially defines this country? It is an unsettling question, but perhaps it will be settled in the years ahead.

ISSUE 11

Is "Middle Eastern" Profiling Ever Justified?

YES: Daniel Pipes, from "Fighting Militant Islam, Without Bias," *City Journal* (November 2001)

NO: David A. Harris, from "'Flying While Arab,' Immigration Issues, and Lessons from the Racial Profiling Controversy," *Testimony before the U.S. Commission on Civil Rights* (October 12, 2001)

ISSUE SUMMARY

YES: Daniel Pipes, director of the Middle East Forum, argues that "heightened scrutiny" of Muslims and Middle Eastern–looking people is justified because, while not all Muslims are Islamic extremists, all Islamic extremists are Muslims.

NO: Law professor David A. Harris opposes profiling people of Middle Eastern appearance because, like racial profiling, it compromises civil liberties and actually damages our intelligence efforts.

The word "stereotype" was introduced into political and social discourse by journalist-philosopher Walter Lippmann in *Public Opinion,* a book he published in 1922. Lippmann called stereotypes the "pictures in our heads," images of reality that we have in our minds even before sense data arrive there. Often these *a priori* definitions produce hasty, distorted generalizations of what is "out there" in the real world. He gives as an example, news reports describing the appearance of "radical" gatherings:

> There is, of course, some connection between the scene outside and the mind through which we watch it, just as there are some long-haired men and short-haired women in radical gatherings. But to the hurried observer a slight connection is enough. If there are two bobbed heads and four beards in the audience, it will be a bobbed and bearded audience to the reporter who knows beforehand that such gatherings are composed of people with these tastes in the management of their hair.

A reporter who consistently brings these stereotypes into news coverage is doing the readers a disservice, but at least they are free to check the reports for accuracy by comparing them to those in another news source. The case is different, though, if the stereotyping is being done by a government official. Government has a monopoly of coercive powers, so when an official engages in stereotyping, a perfectly innocent man or woman may be forced to submit to heightened scrutiny, or humiliating searches, or long interrogations, simply because of the person's appearance. This raises serious issues about civil liberties and civil rights.

Yet the issues are not easy to resolve. We tend to think of stereotyping as invariably wrong, but that was not Lippmann's view. First of all, he insisted, stereotyping cannot be avoided. We do not innocently perceive all the "facts" around us—we decide *which* facts are relevant and then combine them in our own ways. "A report is the joint product of the knower and known, in which the role of the observer is always selective and usually creative." Secondly, he contended, stereotypes are essential if we are to make sense of our world. A stereotype, then, is not unlike a road map, providing a simplified, schematic picture of what is otherwise an impossibly complicated set of facts.

How might Lippmann's observations, made in 1922, apply to the case of Middle Eastern profiling in the twenty-first century? If Lippmann were right to say that stereotyping is inevitable and even necessary to make sense of the world, then perhaps a case can be made for such profiling. Should we require an 82-year-old grandmother to remove her shoes at the airline gate, simply because we just asked a 25-year-old single man from Yemen to do the same? Our stereotype tells us that she is far less likely to have a bomb in her shoe; our common sense tells us that we can more efficiently use resources by concentrating our attention on people like him.

Notice, however, that our stereotype is more complicated than it may seem at first. The Middle Easterner in this hypothetical case is also male, unmarried, and in his twenties. This invites us to complicate the picture a little more. Remembering that Timothy McVeigh, the Oklahoma City bomber, and John Walker Linde, who consorted with the Taliban in Afghanistan, were Caucasian Americans, suppose we compare an 82-year-old Middle Eastern grandmother to a young white American man who has just bought a one-way ticket and looks nervous and shifty-eyed. Which of the two passengers deserves closer scrutiny? If we agree that in this case it would be the American, then there would seem to be qualitative differences among stereotypes; some are better than others. That was Lippmann's view. We need to put "more inclusive patterns" in our stereotypes, and, realizing that they *are* only stereotypes, "to hold them lightly, to modify them gladly."

In these dangerous times, we must somehow strike a balance between liberty and security.

In the following selections, Daniel Pipes, director of the Middle East Forum, argues that in the post–9/11 world, "heightened scrutiny" of Muslims and Middle Eastern–looking people is justified because, while not all Muslims are Islamic extremists, all Islamic extremists are Muslims. Law professor David A. Harris opposes profiling people of Middle Eastern appearance because, like racial profiling, it compromises civil liberties and actually damages our intelligence efforts.

Daniel Pipes  **YES**

Fighting Militant Islam, Without Bias

The whole country, and New York especially, has to face an urgent question in the wake of the September 11 attacks, organized by a militant Islamic network and carried out by Arabic-speaking Muslims resident in North America: how should Americans now view and treat the Muslim populations living in their midst?

Initial reactions have differed widely. Elite opinion, as voiced by President Bush, rushed to deny any connection between the acts of war and the resident Muslim population. "Islam is peace," Bush assured Americans, adding, "we should not hold one who is a Muslim responsible for an act of terror." Attorney General Ashcroft, Governor Pataki, and Mayor Giuliani closely echoed these comments. Secretary of State Powell went further still, declaring that the attacks "should not be seen as something done by Arabs or Islamics; it is something that was done by terrorists"—as though Arabs and Muslims by definition can't be terrorists.

This approach may have made sense as a way to calm the public and prevent attacks against Muslims, but it clearly failed to convince everyone. Rep. John Cooksey (R-La.) told a radio interviewer that anyone wearing "a diaper on his head and a fan belt wrapped around the diaper" should be "pulled over" for extra questioning at airports. And survey research shows that Americans overwhelmingly tie Islam and Muslims to the horrifying events of September. One poll found that 68 percent of respondents approved of "randomly stopping people who may fit the profile of suspected terrorists." Another found that 83 percent of Americans favor stricter controls on Muslim entry into the country and 58 percent want tighter controls on Muslims traveling on planes or trains. Remarkably, 35 percent of New Yorkers favor establishing internment camps for "individuals who authorities identify as being sympathetic to terrorist causes." Nationally, 31 percent of Americans favor detention camps for Arab-Americans, "as a way to prevent terrorist attacks in the United States."

What in fact are the connections between the atrocities and the Muslim minority resident in the United States and Canada? And what policies can protect the country from attack while protecting the civil rights of Muslims?

The problem at hand is not the religion of Islam but the totalitarian ideology of Islamism. As a faith, Islam has meant very different things over 14 centuries and several continents. What we can call "traditional Islam," forged in the medieval period, has inspired Muslims to be bellicose and quiescent, noble and not: one can't generalize over such a large canvas. But one can note two common points: Islam is, more than any other major religion, deeply political, in the sense that it pushes its adherents to hold power; and once Muslims do gain power, they feel a strong impetus to apply the laws of Islam, the shari`a. So Islam does, in fact, contain elements that can justify conquest, theocracy, and intolerance.

In the course of the twentieth century, a new form of Islam arose, one that now has great appeal and power. Militant Islam (or Islamism—same thing) goes back to Egypt in the 1920s, when an organization called the Muslim Brethren first emerged, though there are other strains as well, including an Iranian one, largely formulated by Ayatollah Khomeini, and a Saudi one, to which the [formerly] ruling Taliban in Afghanistan and Usama bin Ladin both belong. Islamism differs in many ways from traditional Islam. It is faith turned into ideology, and radical ideology at that. When asked, "Do you consider yourself a revolutionary?" Sudanese Islamist politician Hasan al-Turabi replied, "Completely." Whereas traditional Islam places the responsibility on each believer to live according to God's will, Islamism makes this duty something for which the state is responsible. Islam is a personal belief system that focuses on the individual; Islamism is a state ideology that looks to the society. Islamists constitute a small but significant minority of Muslims in the U.S. and worldwide, perhaps 10 to 15 percent.

Apologists would tell us that Islamism is a distortion of Islam, or even that it has nothing to do with Islam, but that is not true; it emerges out of the religion, while taking features of it to a conclusion so extreme, so radical, and so megalomaniacal as to constitute something new. It adapts an age-old faith to the political requirements of our day, sharing some key premises of the earlier totalitarianisms, fascism and Marxism-Leninism. It is an Islamic-flavored version of radical utopianism. Individual Islamists may appear law-abiding and reasonable, but they are part of a totalitarian movement, and as such, all must be considered potential killers.

Traditional Muslims, generally the first victims of Islamism, understand this ideology for what it is and respond with fear and loathing, as some examples from northern Africa suggest. Naguib Mahfouz, Egypt's Nobel Prize—winning novelist, said to his country's prime minister and interior minister as they were suppressing Islamism: "You are fighting a battle for the sake of Islam." Other traditional Egyptian Muslims concur with Mahfouz, with one condemning Islamism as "the barbaric hand of terrorism" and another calling for all extremists to be "hanged in public squares." In Tunisia, Minister of Religion Ali Chebbi says that Islamists belong in the "garbage can." Algeria's interior minister, Abderrahmane Meziane-Cherif, likewise concludes: "You cannot talk to people who adopt violence as their credo; people who slit women's throats, rape them, and mutilate their breasts; people who kill innocent foreign guests." If Muslims feel this way, non-Muslims may join them without embarrassment: being against Islamism in no way implies being against Islam.

Islamists of all stripes have a virulent attitude toward non-Muslims and have a decades-long history of fighting with British and French colonial rulers, as well as with such non-Muslim governments as those of India, Israel, and the Philippines. They also have had long and bloody battles against Muslim governments that reject the Islamist program: in Egypt, Pakistan, Syria, Tunisia, and Turkey, for instance—and, most spectacularly, in Algeria, where 100,000 persons so far are estimated to have lost their lives in a decade of fighting.

Islamist violence is a global phenomenon. During the first week of April, [2001], for example, I counted up the following incidents, relying only on news agency stories, which are hardly exhaustive: deaths due to violent Islamist action occurred in Algeria (42 victims), Kashmir (17), the southern Philippines (3), Bangladesh (2), and the West Bank (1); assorted violence broke out in many other countries, including Afghanistan, Indonesia, Nigeria, and Sudan; courts handed down judgments against radical Muslims in France, Germany, Italy, Jordan, Turkey, the United States, and Yemen. Islamists are well organized: fully 11 of the 29 groups that the State Department calls "foreign terrorist organizations" are Islamist, as are 14 out of 21 groups outlawed by Britain's Home Office.

Starting in 1979, Islamists have felt confident enough to extend their fight against the West. The new militant Islamic government of Iran assaulted the U.S. embassy in Tehran at the end of that year and held nearly 60 Americans captive for 444 days. Eight American soldiers (the first casualties in this war) died in the failed U.S. rescue attempt in 1980. Violence against Americans began in earnest in 1983 with an attack on the U.S. embassy in Lebanon, killing 63. Then followed a long sequence of assaults on Americans in embassies, ships, planes, barracks, schools, and elsewhere.

Islamists have also committed at least eight lethal attacks on the soil of the United States prior to September 11, 2001: the July 1980 murder of an Iranian dissident in the Washington area; the January 1990 murder of an Egyptian Islamic freethinker in Tucson; the November 1990 assassination of Rabbi Meir Kahane in New York; the January 1993 assault on CIA personnel, killing two, outside the agency's Langley, Virginia, headquarters; the February 1993 World Trade Center bombing, killing six; the March 1994 shooting attack on a van full of Orthodox Jewish boys driving over the Brooklyn Bridge, killing one; the February 1997 murder of a Danish tourist at the top of the Empire State Building; and the deliberate October 1999 crash of an EgyptAir flight by the Egyptian pilot into the Atlantic near New York City, killing 217. All but one of these murders took place near or in New York City or Washington, D.C. This partial list doesn't include a number of fearsome near misses, including the "day of terror" planned for June 1993 that would have culminated with the simultaneous bombing of the United Nations and the Lincoln and Holland Tunnels, and a thwarted plot to disrupt Seattle's millennial celebrations.

In short, the massacre of upward of 6,000 Americans in September 2001 was not the start of something new but the intensification of an Islamist campaign of violence against the U.S. that has been raging for more than two decades.

No one knows exactly how many Muslims live in the United States—the estimates, prone to exaggeration, range widely—but their numbers clearly range in the several millions. The faithful divide into two main groups, immigrants and converts, with immigrants two to three times more numerous than converts. The immigrants come from all over the world, but especially from South Asia, Iran, and the Arabic-speaking countries; converts tend overwhelmingly to be African-American.

This community now faces a profound choice: either it can integrate within the United States or it can be Islamist and remain apart. It's a choice with major implications for both the U.S. and the Muslim world.

Integrationist Muslims—some pious, others not—can live simultaneously as patriotic Americans and as committed Muslims. Such Muslims have no problem giving their allegiance to a non-Muslim government. Integrationists believe that what American culture calls for—hard work, honesty, tolerance—is compatible with Islamic beliefs, and they even see Islam as reaffirming such classic American values. They accept that the United States is not a Muslim country, and they seek ways to live successfully within its Constitutional framework. Symbolic of this positive outlook, the Islamic Supreme Council of America proudly displays an American flag on its Internet home page.

American Muslims who go the Islamist route, however, reject American civilization, based as it is on a mix of Christian and Enlightenment values that they find anathema. Islamists believe that their ways are superior to America's, and they want to impose these on the entire country. In the short term, they promote Islam as the solution to the nation's social and moral ills. Over time, however, and much more radically, they want to transform the United States into a Muslim country run along strict Islamist lines. Giving expression to this radical view, Zaid Shakir, a former Muslim chaplain at Yale University, argues that Muslims cannot accept the legitimacy of the existing American order, since it "is against the orders and ordainments of Allah." "[T]he orientation of the Quran," he adds, "pushes us in the exact opposite direction." However outlandish a political goal this might seem, it is widely discussed in Islamist circles, and the events of September 11 should make clear just how seriously U.S. authorities must take this ambition.

The great debate among Islamists is, in fact, not over the desirability or plausibility of transforming the U.S. into a Muslim nation but whether to work toward this goal in a legal but slow way, through conversion, or by taking a riskier but swifter illegal path that would require violence. Shamim A. Siddiqi, a Pakistani immigrant, expects that vast numbers of Americans will peacefully convert to Islam in what he calls a "Rush-to-Islam." Omar Abdel Rahman, the blind sheikh behind the 1993 World Trade Center bombing, wants Muslims to "conquer the land of the infidels." These two approaches can and do overlap, with some pinstripe-suited lobbyists in

Washington doing things that help terrorists, such as closing down the practice of profiling Middle Eastern–looking airline passengers.

Integrationists tend to be thankful to live in the United States, with its rule of law, democracy, and personal freedoms. Islamists despise these achievements and long to bring the ways of Iran or Afghanistan to America. Integrationists seek to create an American Islam and can take part in American life. Islamists, who want an Islamic America, cannot.

The good news is that integrationists far outnumber Islamists. The bad news—and this poses a real and still largely unacknowledged problem for the United States—is that Islamists are much more active in Muslim affairs than integrationists and control nearly all of the nation's Muslim institutions: mosques, schools, community centers, publications, websites, and national organizations. It is the Islamists who receive invitations to the White House and the State Department. It was primarily Islamists with whom President Bush, in gestures intended to reassure American Muslims, met with twice after September 11.

What must Americans do to protect themselves from Islamists while safeguarding the civil rights of law-abiding Muslims? The first and most straightforward thing is not to allow any more Islamists into the country. Each Islamist who enters the United States, whether as a visitor or an immigrant, is one more enemy on the home front. Officials need to scrutinize the speech, associations, and activities of potential visitors or immigrants for any signs of Islamist allegiances and keep out anyone they suspect of such ties. Some civil libertarian purists will howl, as they once did over similar legislation designed to keep out Marxist-Leninists. But this is simply a matter of national self-protection.

Laws already on the books allow for such a policy, though excercising them these days is extremely difficult, requiring the direct involvement of the secretary of state. . . . Though written decades before Islamism appeared on the U.S. scene, for example, the 1952 McCarren-Walter Act permits the exclusion of anyone seeking to overthrow the U.S. government. Other regulations would keep out people suspected of terrorism or of committing other acts with "potentially serious adverse foreign policy consequences." U.S. officials need greater leeway to enforce these laws.

Keeping Islamists out of the country is an obvious first step, but it will be equally important to watch closely Islamists already living here as citizens or residents. Unfortunately, this means all Muslims must face heightened scrutiny. For the inescapable and painful fact is that, while anyone might become a fascist or communist, only Muslims find Islamism tempting. And if it is true that most Muslims aren't Islamists, it is no less true that all Islamists are Muslims. Muslims can expect that police searching for suspects after any new terrorist attack will not spend much time checking out churches, synagogues, or Hindu temples but will concentrate on mosques. Guards at government buildings will more likely question pedestrians who appear Middle Eastern or wear headscarves.

Because such measures have an admittedly prejudicial quality, authorities in the past have shown great reluctance to take them, an attitude Islamists and their apologists have reinforced, seeking to stifle any attempt to single out Muslims for scrutiny. When Muslims have committed crimes, officials have even bent over backward to disassociate their motives from militant Islam. For example, the Lebanese cabdriver who fired at a van full of Orthodox Jewish boys on the Brooklyn Bridge in 1994, leaving one child dead, had a well-documented fury at Israel and Jews—but the FBI ascribed his motive to "road rage." Only after a persistent campaign by the murdered boy's mother did the FBI finally classify the attack as "the crimes of a terrorist," almost seven years after the killing. Reluctance to come to terms with militant Islam might have been understandable before September 11—but no longer.

Heightened scrutiny of Muslims has become de rigueur at the nation's airports and must remain so. Airline security personnel used to look hard at Arabs and Muslims, but that was before the relevant lobbies raised so much fuss about "airline profiling" as a form of discrimination that the airlines effectively abandoned the practice. The absence of such a commonsense policy meant that 19 Muslim Arab hijackers could board four separate flights on September 11 with ease.

Greater scrutiny of Muslims also means watching out for Islamist "sleepers"—individuals who go quietly about their business until, one day, they receive the call from their controllers and spring into action as part of a terrorist operation. The four teams of September 11 hijackers show how deep deception can go. As one investigator, noting the length of time the 19 terrorists spent in the United States, explained, "These weren't people coming over the border just to attack quickly. . . . They cultivated friends, and blended into American society to further their ability to strike." Stopping sleepers before they are activated and strike will require greater vigilance at the nation's borders, good intelligence, and citizen watchfulness.

Resident Muslim aliens who reveal themselves to be Islamist should be immediately expelled from the country before they have a chance to act. Citizen Islamists will have to be watched very closely and without cease.

Even as the nation monitors the Muslim world within its borders more closely for signs of Islamism, it must continue, of course, to protect the civil rights of law-abiding American Muslims. Political leaders should regularly and publicly distinguish between Islam, the religion of Muslims, and Islamism, the totalitarian ideology. In addition, they should do everything in their power to make sure that individual Muslims, mosques, and other legal institutions continue to enjoy the full protection of the law. A time of crisis doesn't change the presumption of innocence at the core of our legal system. Police should provide extra protection for Muslims to prevent acts of vandalism against their property or their persons.

Thankfully, some American Muslims (and Arab-Americans, most of whom actually are Christian) understand that by accepting some personal inconvenience—and even, let's be honest, some degree of humiliation—they are helping to protect both the country and themselves. Tarek E. Masoud, a Yale graduate student, shows a good sense that many of his elders seem to lack: "How many thousands of lives would have been saved if people like me had been inconvenienced with having our bags searched and being made to answer questions?" he asks. "People say profiling makes them feel like criminals. It does—I know this firsthand. But would that I had been made to feel like a criminal a thousand times over than to live to see the grisly handiwork of real criminals in New York and Washington."

A third key task will be to combat the totalitarian ideology of militant Islam. That means isolating such noisy and vicious Islamist institutions as the American Muslim Council, the Council on American-Islamic Relations, and the Muslim Public Affairs Council. Politicians, the press, corporations, voluntary organizations, and society as a whole—all must shun these groups and grant them not a shred of legitimacy. Tax authorities and law enforcement should watch them like hawks, much as they watch the Teamsters.

Fighting Islamist ideology will also require shutting down Internet sites that promote Islamist violence, recruit new members to the terrorist campaign against the West, and raise money for militant Islamic causes ("Donate money for the military Jihad," exhorts one such website). The federal government began to take action even before September 11, closing InfoCom, a Dallas-based host for many Islamist organizations, some of them funneling money to militant Islamic groups abroad.

Essential, too, in the struggle against Islamist ideology will be reaching out to moderate non-Islamist Muslims for help. These are the people unfairly tarred by Islamist excesses, after all, and so are eager to stop this extremist movement. Bringing them on board has several advantages: they can provide valuable advice, they can penetrate clandestine Islamist organizations, and their involvement in the effort against Islamism blunts the inevitable charges of "Islamophobia."

Further, experts on Islam and Muslims—academics, journalists, religious figures, and government officials—must be held to account for their views. For too long now, they have apologized for Islamism rather than interpreted it honestly. As such, they bear some responsibility for the unpreparedness that led to September's horror. The press and other media need to show greater objectivity in covering Islam. In the past, they have shamefully covered up for it. The recent PBS documentary *Islam: Empire of Faith* is a case in point, offering, as the *Wall Street Journal* sharply put it, an "uncritical adoration of Islam, more appropriate to a tract for true believers than a documentary purporting to give the American public a balanced account." Islamists in New York City celebrated the destruction on September 11 at their mosques, but journalists refused to report the story for fear of offending Muslims, effectively concealing this important information from the U.S. public.

Taking these three steps—keeping Islamists out, watching them within the nation's borders without violating the civil liberties of American Muslims, and delegitimating extremists—permits Americans to be fair toward the moderate majority of Muslims while fighting militant Islam. It will be a difficult balancing act, demanding sensitivity without succumbing to political correctness. But it is both essential and achievable.

NO

David A. Harris

"Flying while Arab," Immigration Issues, and Lessons from the Racial Profiling Controversy

What changes in the law might we see? We know that we are a nation of immigrants—that, in many ways, immigrants built our great nation. We know that the immigrant experience has, in many ways, been at the core of the American experience, and that the diversity that these people have brought to our country has been, and continues to be, our greatest strength. But we also know that we have sometimes dealt harshly and unfairly with them, especially in times of national emergency and crisis. Thus the Commission does exactly the right thing by inquiring into these issues now, even as new legislative proposals continue to unfold in the Congress. In short, we seek to understand what the implications will be of the changes that will surely come because of the events of September 11—changes in the very idea of what America is, and what it will be in the future.

History

I said earlier that our history gives us reason to feel concern at such a critical juncture. Any serious appraisal of American history during the some of the key periods of the twentieth century would counsel an abundance of caution; when we have faced other national security crises, we have sometimes overreacted—or at the very least acted more out of emotion than was wise. In the wake of World War I, the infamous Palmer Raids resulted in the rounding up of a considerable number of immigrants. These people were deported, often without so much as a scintilla of evidence. During the Second World War, tens of thousands of Japanese—immigrants and native born, citizens and legal residents—were interned in camps, their property confiscated and sold off at fire-sale prices. To its everlasting shame, the U.S. Supreme Court gave the internment of the Japanese its constitutional blessing in the infamous Korematsu case. It took the United States government decades, but eventually it apologized and paid reparations to the Japanese. And during the 1950s, the Red Scare resulted in the ruining of lives and careers and the

From Testimony before U.S. Commission on Civil Rights, October 12, 2001.

jailing of citizens, because they had had the temerity to exercise their constitutionally protected rights to free association by becoming members of the Communist Party years before.

Categorical Thinking

We must hope that we have learned the lessons of this history—that the emotions of the moment, when we feel threatened, can cause us to damage our civil liberties and our fellow citizens, and that this is particularly true for our immigrant populations. And it is this legacy that should make us think now, even as we engage in a long and detailed investigation of the September 11 terror attacks. As we listen to accounts of that investigation, reports indicate that the investigation has been strongly focused on Arab Americans and Muslims. What's more, private citizens have made Middle Eastern appearance an important criterion in deciding how to react to those who look different around them. Many of these reports have involved treatment of persons of Middle Eastern descent in airports.

In itself, this is not really surprising. We face a situation in which there has been a catastrophic terrorist attack by a small group of suicidal hijackers, and as far as we know, all of those involved were Arabs and Muslims and had Arabic surnames. Some or all had entered the country recently. Given the incredibly high stakes, some Americans have reacted to Middle Easterners as a group, based on their appearance. In a way, this is understandable. We seldom have much information on any of the strangers around us, so we tend to think in broad categories. It is a natural human reaction to fear to make judgments concerning our safety based on these broad categories, and to avoid those who arouse fear in us. This may translate easily into a type of racial and ethnic profiling, in which—as has been reported in the last few weeks—passengers on airliners refuse to fly with other passengers who have a Middle Eastern appearance.

Use of Race and Ethnic Appearance in Law Enforcement

The far more worrying development, however, is the possibility that profiling of Arabs and Muslims will become standard procedure in law enforcement. Again, it is not hard to understand the impulse; we want to catch and stop these suicidal hijackers, every one of whom fits the description of Arab or Muslim. So we stop, question, and search more of these people because we believe it's a way to play the odds. If all the September 11 terrorists were Middle Easterners, then we get the biggest bang for the enforcement buck by questioning, searching, and screening as many Middle Easterners as possible. This should give us the best chance of finding those who helped the terrorists or those bent on creating further havoc.

But as we embark in this new world, a world changed so drastically by the events of September 11, we need to be conscious of some of the things that we have learned over the last few years in the ongoing racial profiling controversy. Using race or ethnic appearance as part of a *description* of particular suspects may indeed help an investigation; using race or ethnic appearance as a broad *predictor* of who is involved in crime or terrorism will likely hurt our investigative efforts. All the evidence indicates that profiling Arab Americans or Muslims would be an ineffective waste of law enforcement resources that would damage our intelligence efforts while it compromises basic civil liberties. If we want to do everything we can to secure our country, we have to be smart about the steps we take.

As we think about the possible profiling of Arabs and Muslims, recall that much the same argument has been made for years about domestic efforts against drugs and crime. African Americans and Latinos are disproportionately involved in drug crime, the reasoning goes; therefore concentrate on them. Many state and local police agencies, led by the federal Drug Enforcement Administration, did exactly that from the late 1980s on. We now know that police departments in many jurisdictions used racial profiling, especially in efforts to get drugs and guns off the highways and out of the cities. But as we look back, what really stands out is how ineffective this profile-based law enforcement was. In departments that focused on African Americans, Latinos, and other minorities, the "hit rates"—the rates of successful searches—were actually *lower* for minorities than they were for whites, who were not apprehended by using a racial or ethnic profile. That's right: when these agencies used race or ethnic appearance as a factor—not as *the only* factor but *one factor among many*—they did not get the higher returns on their enforcement efforts that they were expecting.

This is because race and ethnic appearance are very poor predictors of behavior. Race and ethnicity describe people well, and there is absolutely nothing wrong with using skin color or other features to describe known suspects. But since only a very small percentage of African Americans and Latinos participate in the drug trade, race and ethnic appearance do a bad job identifying the *particular* African Americans and Latinos in whom police should be interested. Racial and ethnic profiling caused police to spread their enforcement net far too widely and indiscriminately.

The results of this misguided effort have been disastrous for law enforcement: constant efforts to stop, question, and search people who "look like" suspects, the vast majority of whom are hard working, tax paying citizens. This treatment has alienated African Americans, Latinos, and other minorities from the police—a critical strategic loss in the fight against crime, since police can only win this fight if they have the full cooperation and support of those they serve. And it is precisely this lesson we ought to think about now, as the cry goes up to use profiling and intensive searches against people who look Middle Eastern or Muslim.

Even if the hijackers share a particular ethnic appearance or background, subjecting *all* Middle Easterners to intrusive questioning, stops, or searches will have a perverse and unexpected effect: it will spread our enforcement and detection efforts over a huge pool of people who we would not otherwise think worthy of any police attention. Profiling will drain enforcement efforts and resources away from more worthy investigative efforts and tactics that focus on the close observation of behavior—like the buying of expensive one-way tickets with cash just a short time before take-off, as some of the World Trade Center hijackers did. Focusing on race and ethnicity keeps police attention on a set of surface details that tell us very little, and draw officers' attention away from what is much more important and concrete: conduct.

At least as important, one of the most crucial tools we can use against terrorism is intelligence. And if we are concerned about terrorists of Middle Eastern origin, among the most fertile places from which to gather intelligence will the Arab American and Muslim communities. If we adopt a security policy that stigmatizes every member of these groups in airports and other public places with intrusive stops, questioning, and searches, we will alienate them from the enforcement efforts at precisely the time we need them most. And the larger the population we subject to this treatment, the greater the total amount of damage we inflict on law-abiding persons.

And of course the profiling of Arabs and Muslims assumes that we need worry about only one type of terrorist. We must not forget that, prior to the attacks on September 11, the most deadly terrorist attack on American soil was carried out not by Middle Easterners with Arabic names and accents, but by two very average American white men: Timothy McVeigh, a U.S. Army veteran from upstate New York, and Terry Nichols, a farmer from Michigan. Yet we were smart enough in the wake of McVeigh and Nichols' crime not to call for a profile emphasizing the fact that the perpetrators were white males. The unhappy truth is that we just don't know what the next group of terrorists might look like.

Treatment of Immigrants

The numbers from the 2000 census of our country's population tell us that the 1990s were a time of considerable immigration to the United States. Some of this immigration came from Asia and the Middle East. These immigrants helped many of our older cities make population gains not seen in some time, and helped the American economy to achieve unprecedented growth and prosperity. This was especially true in the high technology sector, which has become a crucial mainstay of growth over the last ten years despite a shortage of American workers to fill computer-oriented positions. Immigrants stepped into the breach for us, bolstering our high-tech labor force just when we needed it.

Yet under the antiterrorism proposal now circulating in the U.S. Senate, immigrants could suffer treatment that smacks strongly of racial profiling and associated practices. Popularly referred to as the USA Act, S. 1510 allows the unlimited detention of noncitizens whom the Attorney General moves to deport or charge criminally, when the Attorney General "reasonably believes" these noncitizens to be engaged in certain terrorist activities. If none of the specifically mentioned activities applies, the Attorney General can still detain the noncitizens based on his or her own determination that the noncitizen "is engaged in any other activity that endangers the national security of the United States." . . .

The Attorney General is empowered to hold these noncitizens even in the face of a court's determination that they are not terrorists. And if the government attempts to deport them and no nation will take them, the legislation appears to allow the Attorney General to detain them indefinitely. The slippery slope here is obvious; the dangers of abuse are easy to see. The basic structure of Section 412 allows the Attorney General to make the decision of who is a terrorist suspect, and to continue to detain these people even in the face of contrary judicial review. The checks and balances built into our basic system of government vanish under this scheme—a worrisome development under any circumstances.

Conclusion

The terrorist attacks in New York and Washington present us with many difficult choices that will test our resolve and our abilities. We must find effective ways to secure ourselves without giving up what is best about our country; the proper balance will often be difficult to discern. But we should not simply repeat the mistakes of the past as we take on this new challenge. Nobody would gain from that—except those who would destroy us.

POSTSCRIPT

Is "Middle Eastern" Profiling Ever Justified?

Both David Harris and Daniel Pipes tend to use "Muslim" and Middle Eastern" interchangeably. This is understandable, since the Middle East is predominantly Muslim, but it conflates terms that are quite distinct. Muslim refers to a religion, that of Islam. In this case, the religion is relevant, since Al Qaeda and other terrorist groups claim to be acting in the name of it. But a person's religion (absent some religious insignia) is invisible to the eye, so the tendency is to shift one's attention into something connected with appearance, such as skin color or facial features. The result can be confusing—and unfair. There are tan-complexioned Catholics from the Middle East and blond Chechnyan Muslims. Who are more likely to be scrutinized at the airport?

In his testimony, Harris makes reference to his earlier book, *Profiles in Injustice: Why Racial Profiling Cannot Work* (New Press, 2003), an analysis of racial profiling, its uses, and, he believes, its ultimate failure in crime prevention. In Daniel Pipes' *Militant Islam Reaches America* (Norton, 2003), one of the dozen or so he has published on the Middle East and what he calls "Islamism," he portrays it as the greatest threat to the United States since the end of the Cold War. While not directly addressing the issue of profiling, Samuel P. Huntington's seminal *The Clash of Civilizations and the Remaking of the World Order* (Touchstone Books, 1998) still remains as a powerful challenge to those who hope that "modernization" will bring Western-style democracy to the Middle East. Bernard Lewis's *What Went Wrong: The Clash Between Islam and Modernity in the Middle East* (Perennial, 2003) and his more recent *From Babel to Dragomans; Interpreting the Middle East* (Oxford, 2004) reach back far into the history of the Middle East and attempt to demonstrate his long-held contention that Islam presents a formidable obstacle to modernization. Michael Wolfe, ed., *Taking Back Islam: American Muslims Reclaim Their Faith* (Rodale Press, 2002) is a collection of writings from several American Muslims, including Yusuf Islam (Cat Stevens) and newer voices such as Aasma Khan, all of whom claim to represent a silent majority of "progressive" Muslims determined to divest their religion of its associations with terrorism and sexism.

The arguments for and against profiling are likely to continue as long as the threat of terror remains, which would appear to be indefinitely. But perhaps some sort of compromise is possible between the contending points of view. The case of Richard Reid, the would-be "shoe bomber," is instructive. Reid's attempt to ignite the explosive charge in his shoe was first detected by a flight attendant, who smelled the sulfur from his burning match, and he was wrestled to the ground by quick-thinking passengers. The lesson is that suspicious *actions* may be a better indication of the potential for terrorism than anything having to do with appearance—though, judging from the menacing photos of Reid, it is possible to speculate that the flight attendant was already keeping an eye on him.

ISSUE 12

Should Hate Speech Be Punished?

YES: Charles R. Lawrence III, from "Crossburning and the Sound of Silence: Antisubordination Theory and the First Amendment," *Villanova Law Review* (vol. 37, no. 4, 1992)

NO: Jonathan Rauch, from "In Defense of Prejudice: Why Incendiary Speech Must Be Protected," *Harper's Magazine* (May 1995)

ISSUE SUMMARY

YES: Law professor Charles R. Lawrence III asserts that speech should be impermissible when, going beyond insult, it inflicts injury on its victims.

NO: Author Jonathan Rauch maintains that there can be no genuine freedom of expression unless it includes the freedom to offend those who oppose the expressed opinion.

In 1942, on a busy public street in Rochester, New Hampshire, a man named Walter Chaplinsky was passing out literature promoting the Jehovah's Witnesses, which would have been all right except that the literature denounced all other religions as "rackets." As might be expected, Chaplinsky's activities caused a stir. The city marshal warned Chaplinsky that he was on the verge of creating a riot and told him that he ought to leave, whereupon Chaplinsky answered him in these words: "You are a Goddamned racketeer . . . a damned Fascist, and the whole government of Rochester are Fascists or agents of Fascists." Chaplinsky was arrested for disturbing the peace, and he appealed on the grounds that his First Amendment right to free speech had been violated. The Supreme Court of the United States ruled unanimously against him. In *Chaplinsky v. New Hampshire* (1942) the Court said that his words were "fighting words," not deserving of First Amendment protection because they were "likely to provoke the average person to retaliation."

In 1984 a Texan named Gregory Lee Johnson stood in front of Dallas City Hall, doused an American flag in kerosene, and set it on fire while chanting, "Red, white, and blue, we spit on you." When he was arrested for flag desecration, he appealed to the Supreme Court on grounds of free speech—and won. In *Texas v. Johnson* (1989) the Court ruled that flag burning was a form of "symbolic speech" protected by the First Amendment.

So Chaplinsky used his mouth and was punished for it, and Johnson burned a flag and was not. How do we square these decisions, or should we? If a state can punish a person for calling someone a "Goddamned racketeer," can it also punish someone for shouting racial epithets?

Some municipalities have enacted laws that punish "hate speech" directed at women and minorities. The intention of these codes and laws is to ensure at least a minimum of civility in places where people of very diverse backgrounds must live and work together. But do they infringe upon essential freedoms?

In 1992 the Supreme Court confronted this issue in a case testing the constitutionality of a St. Paul, Minnesota, statute punishing anyone who displays symbols attacking people because of their "race, color, creed, religion, or gender." A group of St. Paul teenagers had burned a cross in the yard of a black family. Prosecutors used this newly enacted law, which raised the essential issues in the case: Did the statute violate freedoms guaranteed by the First Amendment? If so, why? In its decision of *R. A. V. v. St. Paul* (1992), the Court gave a unanimous answer to the first question. All nine justices agreed that the statute was indeed a violation of the First Amendment. But on the second question—*why* was it a violation?—the Court was deeply divided. Four members thought that it was unconstitutional because it was "overbroad," that is, worded in such general language that it would reach beyond the narrow bounds of speech activities that the Court has deemed punishable. But the majority, in an opinion by Justice Antonin Scalia, struck down the statute for a very different reason: because it contained "content discrimination." By punishing speech that attacks people because of their "race, color, creed, religion, or gender," it was prohibiting speech "solely on the basis of the subjects the speech addresses." A statute punishing speech may not single out specific categories like race or creed for protection, for to do so is to involve the state in deciding which sorts of people deserve protection against "hate speech."

In response to increasing incidents of highly derogatory racial, religious, and sexual remarks and writing on college campuses, a number of colleges adopted speech codes that went beyond what the Supreme Court had characterized as "fighting words" in *Chaplinsky*. These restrictions prompted outcries that "political correctness" was stifling the expression of unpopular ideas. Lower federal courts voided antidiscrimination codes at the Universities of Michigan and Wisconsin as overbroad and vague, calling into question similar codes at other public and private institutions.

However, the Supreme Court in *Wisconsin v. Mitchell* (1993) unanimously upheld a hate crimes law. This case was distinguished from hate speech cases in that the speech per se was not punished, but the determination that hatred inspired the commission of a crime could be the basis for increasing the penalty for that crime.

In the following selections, Charles R. Lawrence III argues that speech has the power to inflict injury and curtail the freedom of the victims of hate. Jonathan Rauch defends incendiary speech on the ground that the rights of all are better protected by pluralism than purism.

Charles R. Lawrence III  **YES**

Crossburning and the Sound of Silence: Antisubordination Theory and the First Amendment

In the early morning hours of June 21, 1990, long after they had put their five children to bed, Russ and Laura Jones were awakened by voices outside their house. Russ got up, went to his bedroom window and peered into the dark. "I saw a glow," he recalled. There, in the middle of his yard, was a burning cross. The Joneses are black. In the spring of 1990 they had moved into their four-bedroom, three-bathroom dream house on 290 Earl Street in St. Paul, Minnesota. They were the only black family on the block. Two weeks after they had settled into their predominantly white neighborhood, the tires on both their cars were slashed. A few weeks later, one of their cars' windows was shattered, and a group of teenagers had walked past their house and shouted "nigger" at their nine-year-old son. And now this burning cross. Russ Jones did not have to guess at the meaning of this symbol of racial hatred. There is not a black person in America who has not been taught the significance of this instrument of persecution and intimidation, who has not had emblazoned on his mind the image of black men's scorched bodies hanging from trees, and who does not know the story of Emmett Till.[1] One can only imagine the terror which Russell Jones must have felt as he watched the flames and thought of the vulnerability of his family and of the hateful, cowardly viciousness of those who would attack him and those he loved under cover of darkness.

This assault on Russ Jones and his family begins the story of *R.A.V. v. City of St. Paul,* the "hate speech" case recently decided by the United States Supreme Court. The Joneses, however, are not the subject of the Court's opinion. The constitutional injury addressed in *R.A.V.* was not this black family's right to live where they pleased, or their right to associate with their neighbors. The Court was not concerned with how this attack might impede the exercise of the Joneses' constitutional right to be full and valued participants in the political community, for it did not view *R.A.V.* as a case about the Joneses' injury. Instead, the Court was concerned primarily with the alleged constitutional injury to those who assaulted the Joneses, that is, the First Amendment rights of the crossburners.

From Charles R. Lawrence III, "Crossburning and the Sound of Silence: Antisubordination Theory and the First Amendment," *Villanova Law Review,* vol. 37, no. 4 (1992), pp. 787–804. Copyright © 1992 by Villanova University. Reprinted by permission. Some notes omitted.

There is much that is deeply troubling about Justice Scalia's majority opinion in *R.A.V.* But it is the utter disregard for the silenced voice of the victims that is most frightening. Nowhere in the opinion is any mention made of the Jones family or of their constitutional rights. Nowhere are we told of the history of the Ku Klux Klan or of its use of the burning cross as a tool for the suppression of speech. Justice Scalia turns the First Amendment on its head, transforming an act intended to silence through terror and intimidation into an invitation to join a public discussion. In so doing, he clothes the crossburner's terroristic act in the legitimacy of protected political speech and invites him to burn again.

"Let there be no mistake about our belief that burning a cross in someone's front yard is reprehensible," writes Justice Scalia at the close of his opinion. I am skeptical about his concern for the victims. These words seem little more than an obligatory genuflection to decency. For even in this attempt to assure the reader of his good intentions, Justice Scalia's words betray his inability to see the Joneses or hear their voices. "Burning a cross in *someone's* front yard is *reprehensible,*" he says. It is reprehensible but not injurious, or immoral, or violative of the Joneses' rights. For Justice Scalia, the identity of the "someone" is irrelevant. As is the fact that it is a *cross* that is burned.

When I first read Justice Scalia's opinion it felt as if another cross had just been set ablaze. This cross was burning on the pages of U.S. Reports. It was a cross like the cross that Justice Taney had burned in 1857,[2] and that which Justice Brown had burned in 1896.[3] Its message: "You have no rights which a white man is bound to respect (or protect).[4] If you are injured by this assaultive act, the injury is a figment of your imagination that is not constitutionally cognizable."[5]

For the past couple of years I have been struggling to find a way to talk to my friends in the civil liberties community about the injures which are ignored in the *R.A.V.* case. I have tried to articulate the ways in which hate speech harms its victims and the ways in which it harms us all by undermining core values in our Constitution.

The first of these values is full and equal citizenship expressed in the Fourteenth Amendment's Equal Protection Clause. When hate speech is employed with the purpose and effect of maintaining established systems of caste and subordination, it violates that core value. Hate speech often prevents its victims from exercising legal rights guaranteed by the Constitution and civil rights statutes. The second constitutional value threatened by hate speech is the value of free expression itself. Hate speech frequently silences its victims, who, more often than not, are those who are already heard from least. An understanding of both of these injuries is aided by the methodologies of feminism and critical race theory that give special attention to the structures of subordination and the voices of the subordinated.

My own understanding of the need to inform the First Amendment discourse with the insights of an antisubordination theory began in the context of the debate over the regulation of hate speech on campus. As I lectured at universities throughout the United States, I learned of serious racist and anti-Semitic hate incidents. Students who had been victimized told me of swastikas appearing on Jewish holy days. Stories of cross burnings, racist slurs and vicious verbal assaults made me cringe even as I heard them secondhand. Universities, long the home of institutional and euphemistic racism, were witnessing the worst forms of gutter racism. In 1990, the Chronicle of Higher Education reported that approximately 250 colleges and universities had experienced serious racist incidents since 1986, and the National Institute Against Prejudice and Violence estimated that 25% of all minority students are victimized at least once during an academic year.

I urged my colleagues to hear these students' voices and argued that *Brown v. Board of Education* and its antidiscrimination principle identified an injury of constitutional dimension done to these students that must be recognized and remedied. We do not normally think of *Brown* as being a case about speech. Most narrowly read, it is a case about the rights of black children to equal educational opportunity. But *Brown* teaches us another very important lesson: that the harm of segregation is achieved by the meaning of the message it conveys. The Court's opinion in *Brown* stated that racial segregation is unconstitutional not because the "physical separation of black and white children is bad or because resources were distributed unequally among black and white schools. *Brown* held that segregated schools were unconstitutional primarily because of the message segregation conveys—the message that black children are an untouchable caste, unfit to be educated with white children." Segregation stamps a badge of inferiority upon blacks. This badge communicates a message to others that signals their exclusion from the community of citizens.

The "Whites Only" signs on the lunch counter, swimming pool and drinking fountain convey the same message. The antidiscrimination principle articulated in *Brown* presumptively entitles every individual to be treated by the organized society as a respected, responsible and participating member. This is the principle upon which all our civil rights laws rest. It is the guiding principle of the Equal Protection Clause's requirement of nondiscriminatory government action. In addition, it has been applied in regulating private discrimination.

The words "Women Need Not Apply" in a job announcement, the racially exclusionary clause in a restrictive covenant and the racial epithet scrawled on the locker of the new black employee at a previously all-white job site all convey a political message. But we treat these messages as "discriminatory practices" and outlaw them under federal and state civil rights legislation because they are more than speech. In the context of social inequality, these verbal and symbolic acts form integral links in historically ingrained systems of social discrimination. They work to keep traditionally victimized groups in socially isolated, stigmatized and disadvantaged positions through the promotion of fear, intolerance, degradation and violence. The Equal Protection Clause of the Fourteenth Amendment requires the disestablishment of these practices and systems. Likewise, the First Amendment does *not* prohibit our accomplishment of this compelling constitutional interest simply because those discriminatory practices are achieved through the use of words and symbols.

The primary intent of the cross burner in *R.A.V.* was not to enter into a dialogue with the Joneses, or even with the larger community, as it arguably was in *Brandenburg v. Ohio*. His purpose was to intimidate—to cast fear in the hearts of his victims, to drive them out of the community, to enforce the practice of residential segregation, and to encourage others to join him in the enforcement of that practice. The discriminatory impact of this speech is of even more importance than the speaker's intent. In protecting victims of discrimination, it is the presence of this discriminatory impact, which is a compelling government interest unrelated to the suppression of the speaker's political message, that requires a balancing of interests rather than a presumption against constitutionality. This is especially true when the interests that compete with speech are also interests of constitutional dimension.

One such interest is in enforcing the antidiscrimination principle. Those opposed to the regulation of hate speech often view the interest involved as the maintenance of civility, the protection of sensibilities from offense, or the prohibition of group defamation. But this analysis misconstrues the nature of the injury. "Defamation—injury to group reputation— is not the same as discrimination—injury to group status and treatment." The former "is more ideational and less material" than the latter, "which recognizes the harm of second-class citizenship and inferior social standing with the attendant deprivation of access to resources, voice, and power."

The Title VII paradigm of "hostile environment" discrimination best describes the injury to which victims of racist, sexist and homophobic hate speech are subjected. When plaintiffs in employment discrimination suits have been subjected to racist or sexist verbal harassment in the workplace, courts have recognized that such assaultive speech denies the targeted individual equal access to employment. These verbal assaults most often occur in settings where the relatively recent and token integration of the workplace makes the victim particularly vulnerable and where the privately voiced message of denigration and exclusion echoes the whites-only and males-only practices that were all-too-recently official policy.

Robinson v. Jacksonville Shipyards, Inc., a Title VII case that appears to be headed for review in the Supreme Court, presents a clear example of the tension between the law's commitment to free speech and its commitment to equality. Lois Robinson, a welder, was one of a very small number of female skilled craft-workers employed by Jacksonville Shipyards. She brought suit under Title VII of the Civil Rights Act of 1964, alleging that her employer had created and encouraged a sexually hostile, intimidating work environment. A U.S. District Court rules in her favor, finding that the presence in the workplace of pictures of women in various stages of undress and in sexually suggestive or submissive poses, as well as remarks made by male employees and supervisors which demeaned women, constituted a violation of Title VII "through the maintenance of a sexually hostile work environment." Much of District Court Judge Howell Melton's opinion is a recounting of the indignities that Ms. Robinson and five other women experienced almost daily while working with 850 men over the course of ten years. In addition to the omnipresent display of sexually explicit drawings, graffiti, calendars, centerfold-style pictures, magazines and cartoons, the trial record contains a number of incidents in which sexually suggestive pictures and comments were directed at Robinson. Male employees admitted that the shipyard was "a boys' club" and "more or less a man's world."

The local chapter of the American Civil Liberties Union (ACLU) appealed the District Court's decision, arguing that "even sexists have a right to free speech." However, anyone who has read the trial record cannot help but wonder about these civil libertarians' lack of concern for Lois Robinson's right to do her work without being subjected to assault.

The trial record makes clear that Lois Robinson's male colleagues had little concern for advancing the cause of erotic speech when they made her the target of pornographic comments and graffiti. They wanted to put the usurper of their previously all-male domain in her place, to remind her of her sexual vulnerability and to send her back home where she belonged. This speech, like the burning cross in *R.A.V.*, does more than communicate an idea. It interferes with the victim's right to work at a job where she is free from degradation because of her gender.

But it is not sufficient to describe the injury occasioned by hate speech only in terms of the countervailing value of equality. There is also an injury to the First Amendment. When Russ Jones looked out his window and saw that burning cross, he heard a message that said, *"Shut up, black man, or risk harm to you and your family."* It may be that Russ Jones is especially brave, or especially foolhardy, and that he may speak even more loudly in the face of this threat. But it is more likely that he will be silenced, and that *we* will lose the benefit of his voice.

Professor Laurence H. Tribe has identified two values protected by the First Amendment. The first is the intrinsic value of speech, which is the value of individual self expression. Speech is intrinsically valuable as a manifestation of our humanity and our individuality. The second is the instrumental value of speech. The First Amendment protects dissent to maximize public discourse, and to achieve the great flowering of debate and ideas that we need to make our democracy work. Both of these values are implicated in the silencing of Russ Jones by his nocturnal attacker.

For African-Americans, the intrinstic value of speech as self-expression and self-definition has been particularly important. The absence of a "black voice" was central to the ideology of European-American racism, an ideology that denied Africans their humanity and thereby justified their enslavement. African-American slaves were prevented from learning to read and write, and they were prohibited from engaging in forms of self-expression that might instill in them a sense of self-worth and pride. Their silence and submission was then interpreted as evidence of their subhuman status. The use of the burning cross as a method of disempowerment originates, in part, in the perpetrators' understanding of how, in the context of their ideology, their victims are rendered subhuman when they are silenced. When, in the face of threat and intimidation, the oppressors' victims are afraid to give full expression to their individuality, the oppressors achieve their purpose of denying the victims the liberty guaranteed to them by the Constitution.

When the Joneses moved to Earl Street in St. Paul, they were expressing their individuality. When they chose their house and their neighbors, they were saying, "This is who we are. We are a proud black family and we want to live here." This self-expression and self-definition is the intrinsic value of speech. The instrumental value of speech is likewise threatened by this terrorist attack on the Joneses. Russ and Laura Jones also brought new voices to the political discourse in this St. Paul community. Ideally, they will vote and talk politics with their neighbors. They will bring new experiences and new perspectives to their neighborhood. A burning cross not only silences people like the Joneses, it impoverishes the democratic process and renders our collective conversation less informed.

First Amendment doctrine and theory have no words for the injuries of silence imposed by private actors. There is no language for the damage that is done to the First Amendment when the hateful speech of the cross-burner or the sexual harasser silences its victims. In antidiscrimination law, we recognize the necessity of regulating private behavior that threatens the values of equal citizenship. Fair housing laws, public accommodations provisions and employment discrimination laws all regulate the behavior of private actors. We recognize that much of the discrimination in our society occurs without the active participation of the state. We know that we could not hope to realize the constitutional ideal of equal citizenship if we pretended that the government was the only discriminator.

But there is no recognition in First Amendment law of the systematic private suppression of speech. Courts and scholars have worried about the heckler's veto, and, where there is limited access to speech fora, we have given attention to questions of equal time and the right to reply. But for the most part, we act as if the government is the only regulator of speech, the only censor. We treat the marketplace of ideas as if all voices are equal, as if there are no silencing voices or voices that are silenced. In the discourse of the First Amendment, there is no way to talk about how those who are silenced are always less powerful than those who do the silencing. First Amendment law ignores the ways in which patriarchy silences women, and racism silences people of color. When a woman's husband threatens to beat her the next time she contradicts him, a First Amendment injury has occurred. "Gay-bashing" keeps gays and lesbians "in the closet." It silences them. They are denied the humanizing experience of self-expression. We *all* are denied the insight and beauty of their voices.

Professor Mari Matsuda has spoken compellingly of this problem in a telling personal story about the publication of her own thoughtful and controversial *Michigan Law Review* article on hate speech, "Public Response to Racist Speech: Considering the Victim's Story." When she began working on the article, a mentor at Harvard Law School warned her not to use this topic for her tenure piece. "It's a lightning rod," he told her. She followed his advice, publishing the article years later, only after receiving her university tenure and when visiting offers from prestigious schools were in hand.

"What is the sound of a paper unpublished?" writes Professor Matsuda. "What don't we hear when some young scholar chooses tenure over controversial speech? Every fall, students return from summer jobs and tell me of the times they didn't speak out against racist or anti-Semitic comments, in protest over unfairness or ethical dilemmas. They tell of the times they were invited to discriminatory clubs and went along in silence. What is the sound of all those silenced because they need a job? These silences, these things that go unsaid, aren't seen as First Amendment issues. The absences are characterized as private and voluntary, beyond collective cure."

In the rush to protect the "speech" of crossburners, would-be champions of the First Amendment must not forget the voices of their victims. If First Amendment doctrine and theory is to truly serve First Amendment ideals, it must recognize the injury done by the private suppression of speech; it must take into account the historical reality that some members of our community are less powerful than others and that those persons continue to be systematically silenced by those who are more powerful. If we are truly committed to free speech, First Amendment doctrine and theory must be guided by the principle of antisubordination. There can be no free speech where there are still masters and slaves.

Notes

1. Emmett Till, a 14-year-old boy from Chicago, was killed while visiting relatives in Mississippi in 1955. His alleged "wolf whistle" at a white woman provoked his murderer. CONRAD LYNN, THERE IS A FOUNTAIN: THE AUTOBIOGRAPHY OF A CIVIL RIGHTS LAWYER 155 (1979); *see also* STEPHEN J. WHITFIELD, A DEATH IN THE DELTA: THE STORY OF EMMETT TILL (1988) (recounting story of black teenager murdered for allegedly whistling at white woman).

2. Dred Scott v. Sanford, 60 U.S. (19 How.) 393 (1856).

3. Plessy v. Ferguson, 163 U.S. 537 (1896).

4. Justice Taney, in holding that African Americans were not included and were not intended to be included under the word "citizen" in the Constitution, and could therefore claim none of the rights and privileges which that instrument provides for and secures opined, "[the colored race] had for more than a century before been regarded as being of an inferior order, and altogether unfit to associate with the white race, either in social or political relations; and so far inferior, that they had no rights which the white man was bound to respect." *Dred Scott*, 60 U.S. at 407.

5. In rejecting plaintiff's argument in *Plessy v. Ferguson* that enforced separation of the races constituted a badge of inferiority Judge Brown stated, "[i]f this be so, it is not by reason of anything found in the act, but solely because the colored race chooses to put that construction upon it." *Plessy*, 163 U.S. at 551. . . .

NO

Jonathan Rauch

In Defense of Prejudice: Why Incendiary Speech Must Be Protected

The war on prejudice is now, in all likelihood, the most uncontroversial social movement in America. Opposition to "hate speech," formerly identified with the liberal left, has become a bipartisan piety. In the past year, groups and factions that agree on nothing else have agreed that the public expression of any and all prejudices must be forbidden. On the left, protesters and editorialists have insisted that Francis L. Lawrence resign as president of Rutgers University for describing blacks as "a disadvantaged population that doesn't have that genetic, hereditary background to have a higher average." On the other side of the ideological divide, Ralph Reed, the executive director of the Christian Coalition, responded to criticism of the religious right by calling a press conference to denounce a supposed outbreak of "name-calling, scapegoating, and religious bigotry." Craig Rogers, an evangelical Christian student at California State University, recently filed a $2.5 million sexual-harassment suit against a lesbian professor of psychology, claiming that anti-male bias in one of her lectures violated campus rules and left him feeling "raped and trapped."

In universities and on Capitol Hill, in workplaces and newsrooms, authorities are declaring that there is no place for racism, sexism, homophobia, Christian-bashing, and other forms of prejudice in public debate or even in private thought. "Only when racism and other forms of prejudice are expunged," say the crusaders for sweetness and light, "can minorities be safe and society be fair." So sweet, this dream of a world without prejudice. But the very last thing society should do is seek to utterly eradicate racism and other forms of prejudice. . . .

Indeed, "eradicating prejudice" is so vague a proposition as to be meaningless. Distinguishing prejudice reliably and nonpolitically from nonprejudice, or even defining it crisply, is quite hopeless. We all feel we know prejudice when we see it. But do we? At the University of Michigan, a student said in a classroom discussion that he considered homosexuality a disease treatable with therapy. He was summoned to a formal disciplinary hearing for violating the school's policy against speech that "victimizes" people based on "sexual orientation." Now, the evidence is abundant that this particular hypothesis is wrong, and any American homosexual can attest to the harm that the student's hypothesis has inflicted on many real people. But was it a statement of prejudice or of misguided belief? Hate speech or hypothesis? Many Americans who do not regard themselves as bigots or haters believe that homosexuality is a treatable disease. They may be wrong, but are they all bigots? I am unwilling to say so, and if you are willing, beware. The line between a prejudiced belief and a merely controversial one is elusive, and the harder you look the more elusive it becomes. "God hates homosexuals" is a statement of fact, not of bias, to those who believe it; "American criminals are disproportionately black" is a statement of bias, not of fact, to those who disbelieve it. . . .

Pluralism is the principle that protects and makes a place in human company for that loneliest and most vulnerable of all minorities, the minority who is hounded and despised among blacks and whites, gays and straights, who is suspect or criminal among every tribe and in every nation of the world, and yet on whom progress depends: the dissident. I am not saying that dissent is always or even usually enlightened. Most of the time it is foolish and self-serving. No dissident has the right to be taken seriously, and the fact that Aryan Nation racists or Nation of Islam anti-Semites are unorthodox does not entitle them to respect. But what goes around comes around. As a supporter of gay marriage, for example, I reject the majority's view of family, and as a Jew I reject its view of God. I try to be civil, but the fact is that most Americans regard my views on marriage as a reckless assault on the most fundamental of all institutions, and many people are more than a little discomfited by the statement "Jesus Christ was no more divine than anybody else" (which is why so few people ever say it). Trap the racists and anti-Semites, and you lay a trap for me too. Hunt for them with eradication in your mind, and you have brought dissent itself within your sights.

The new crusade against prejudice waves aside such warnings. Like earlier crusades against antisocial ideas, the mission is fueled by good (if cocksure) intentions and a genuine sense of urgency. Some kinds of error are held to be intolerable, like pollutants that even in small traces poison the water for a whole town. Some errors are so pernicious as to damage real people's lives, so wrong-headed that no person of right mind or goodwill could support them. Like their forebears of other stripe—the Church in its campaigns against heretics, the McCarthyites in their campaigns against Communists—the modern anti-racist and anti-sexist and anti-homophobic campaigners are totalists, demanding not that misguided ideas and ugly expressions be corrected or criticized but that they be eradicated. They make war not on errors but on error, and like other totalists they act in the name of public safety—the safety, especially, of minorities.

‹•◦•›

The sweeping implications of this challenge to pluralism are not, I think, well enough understood by the public at large. Indeed, the new brand of totalism has yet even to be properly named. "Multiculturalism," for instance, is much too broad. "Political correctness" comes closer but is too trendy and snide. For lack of anything else, I will call the new anti-pluralism "purism," since its major tenet is that society cannot be just until the last traces of invidious prejudice have been scrubbed away. Whatever you call it, the purists' way of seeing things has spread through American intellectual life with remarkable speed, so much so that many people will blink at you uncomprehendingly or even call you a racist (or sexist or homophobe, etc.) if you suggest that expressions of racism should be tolerated or that prejudice has its part to play. . . .

⋅❦⋅

What is especially dismaying is that the purists pursue prejudice in the name of protecting minorities. In order to protect people like me (homosexual), they must pursue people like me (dissident). In order to bolster minority self-esteem, they suppress minority opinion. There are, of course, all kinds of practical and legal problems with the purists' campaign: the incursions against the First Amendment; the inevitable abuses by prosecutors and activists who define as "hateful" or "violent" whatever speech they dislike or can score points off of; the lack of any evidence that repressing prejudice eliminates rather than inflames it. But minorities, of all people, ought to remember that by definition we cannot prevail by numbers, and we generally cannot prevail by force. Against the power of ignorant mass opinion and group prejudice and superstition, we have only our voices. If you doubt that minorities' voices are powerful weapons, think of the lengths to which Southern officials went to silence the Reverend Martin Luther King Jr. (recall that the city commissioner of Montgomery, Alabama, won a $500,000 libel suit, later overturned in *New York Times v. Sullivan* [1964], regarding an advertisement in the *Times* placed by civil-rights leaders who denounced the Montgomery police). Think of how much gay people have improved their lot over twenty-five years simply by refusing to remain silent. Recall the Michigan student who was prosecuted for saying that homosexuality is a treatable disease, and notice that he was black. Under that Michigan speech code, more than twenty blacks were charged with racist speech, while no instance of racist speech by whites was punished. In Florida, the hate-speech law was invoked against a black man who called a policeman a "white cracker"; not so surprisingly, in the first hate-crimes case to reach the Supreme Court, the victim was white and the defendant black.

In the escalating war against "prejudice," the right is already learning to play by the rules that were pioneered by the purist activists of the left. Last year leading Democrats, including the President, criticized the Republican Party for being increasingly in the thrall of the Christian right. Some of the rhetoric was harsh ("fire-breathing Christian radical right"), but it wasn't vicious or even clearly wrong. Never mind: when Democratic Representative Vic Fazio said Republicans were "being forced to the fringes by the aggressive political tactics of the religious right," the chairman of the Republican National Committee, Haley Barbour, said, "Christian-bashing" was the "left's preferred form of religious bigotry." Bigotry! Prejudice! "Christians active in politics are now on the receiving end of an extraordinary campaign of bias and prejudice," said the conservative leader William J. Bennett. One discerns, here, where the new purism leads. Eventually, any criticism of any group will be "prejudice."

Here is the ultimate irony of the new purism: words, which pluralists hope can be substituted for violence, are redefined by purists *as* violence. "The experience of being called 'nigger,' 'spic,' 'Jap,' or 'kike' is like receiving a slap in the face," Charles Lawrence wrote in 1990. "Psychic injury is no less an injury than being struck in the face, and it often is far more severe." This kind of talk is commonplace today. Epithets, insults, often even polite expressions of what's taken to be prejudice are called by purists "assaultive speech," "words that wound," "verbal violence." "To me, racial epithets are not speech," one University of Michigan law professor said. "They are bullets." In her speech accepting the 1993 Nobel Prize for Literature in Stockholm, Sweden, the author Toni Morrison said this: "Oppressive language does more than represent violence; it is violence."

It is not violence. I am thinking back to a moment on the subway in Washington, a little thing. I was riding home late one night and a squad of noisy kids, maybe seventeen or eighteen years old, noisily piled into the car. They yelled across the car and a girl said, "Where do we get off?"

A boy said, "Farragut North."

The girl: "*Faggot* North!"

The boy: "Yeah! Faggot North!"

General hilarity.

First, before the intellect resumes control, there is a moment of fear, an animal moment. Who are they? How many of them? How dangerous? Where is the way out? All of these things are noted preverbally and assessed by the gut. Then the brain begins an assessment: they are sober, this is probably too public a place for them to do it, there are more girls than boys, they were just talking, it is probably nothing.

They didn't notice me and there was no incident. The teenage babble flowed on, leaving me to think. I became interested in my own reaction: the jump of fear out of nowhere like an alert animal, the sense for a brief time that one is naked and alone and should hide or run away. For a time, one ceases to be a human being and becomes instead a faggot.

꿈

The fear engendered by these words is real. The remedy is as clear and as imperfect as ever: protect citizens against violence. This, I grant, is something that American society has never done very well and now does quite poorly. It is no solution to define words as violence or prejudice as oppression, and then by cracking down on words or thoughts pretend that we are doing something about violence and oppression. No doubt it is easier to pass a speech code or hate-crimes law and proclaim the streets safer than actually to make the streets safer, but the one must never be confused with the other. Every cop or prosecutor chasing words is one fewer chasing criminals. In a world rife with real violence and oppression, full of Rwandas and Bosnias and eleven-year-olds spraying bullets at children in Chicago and in turn being executed by gang lords, it is odious of Toni Morrison to say that words are violence.

Indeed, equating "verbal violence" with physical violence is a treacherous, mischievous business. Not long ago a writer was charged with viciously and gratuitously wounding the feelings and dignity of millions of people. He was charged, in effect, with exhibiting flagrant prejudice against Muslims and outrageously slandering their beliefs. "What is freedom of expression?" mused Salman Rushdie a year after the ayatollahs sentenced him to death and put a price on his head. "Without the freedom to offend, it ceases to exist." I can think of nothing sadder than that minority activists, in their haste to make the world better, should be the ones to forget the lesson of Rushdie's plight: for minorities, pluralism, not purism, is the answer. The campaigns to eradicate prejudice—all of them, the speech codes and workplace restrictions and mandatory therapy for accused bigots and all the rest—should stop, now. The whole objective of eradicating prejudice, as opposed to correcting and criticizing it, should be repudiated as a fool's errand. Salman Rushdie is right, Toni Morrison wrong, and minorities belong at his side, not hers.

POSTSCRIPT

Should Hate Speech Be Punished?

Many forms of hate speech are punished in countries other than the United States, but other democracies do not have the American tradition of freedom of opinion and expression. At the same time, the United States has more races, religions, and nationalities than other countries, giving rise to suspicion, prejudice, and hostility.

On one hand, this diversity has given rise to sharp political disagreement on issues relating to race, religion, women, homosexuals, and others. On the other hand, this diversity has stimulated greater sensitivity to the claims of these groups for equal treatment and social justice. Free speech on controversial issues risks giving offense. At what point, if any, does giving offense curtail the liberty of the offended group? Should such speech be punished?

Nowhere have these questions provoked greater controversy than on college campuses. Do college codes inhibiting or punishing racist, sexist, or other biased speech protect the liberty of the victims of these insults or injuries? Or do they prevent the examination of disapproved beliefs and threaten the suppression of other unpopular ideas?

Steven H. Shiffrin, in *Dissent, Injustice, and the Meanings of America* (Princeton University Press, 1999), argues that Americans should not just tolerate controversial speech, they should encourage it. Timothy C. Shiell, in *Campus Hate Speech on Trial* (University Press of Kansas, 1998), provides background for some of the recent court cases involving hate speech. Edward J. Cleary's *Beyond the Burning Cross: The First Amendment and the Landmark R. A. V. Case* (Random House, 1994) is an account of the attorney who represented the accused youth in *R. A. V. v. St. Paul*. Robert J. Kelly, ed., *Bias Crime: American Law Enforcement and Legal Responses,* rev. ed. (Office of International Criminal Justice, 1993) includes essays on a variety of issues, including religious and gay bias, bias on college campuses, and the Rodney King case, in which four white Los Angeles police officers were filmed beating a black suspect.

Arguing for absolute freedom of expression is Nat Hentoff, *Free Speech for Me—But Not for Thee: How the American Left and Right Relentlessly Censor Each Other* (HarperCollins, 1992). Less absolutist in defending all speech is Cass R. Sunstein, in *Democracy and the Problem of Free Speech* (Free Press, 1993), who attempts to define a distinction between protected and unprotected speech. A case for suppressing speech based on what the authors call "critical race theory" can be found in the essays in Mari J. Matsuda et al., *Words That Wound: Critical Race Theory, Assaultive Speech, and the First Amendment* (Westview Press, 1993).

A somewhat similar arguments is developed by Richard Delgado and Jean Stefancic in *Must We Defend Nazis? Hate Speech, Pornography, and the First Amendment* (New York University Press, 1996). The authors insist that free speech must always be weighed against the sometimes-competing values of human dignity and equality. Judith Butler, in *Excitable Speech: A Politics of the Performance* (Routledge, 1997), examines the linguistics of hate and reflects on the implications of speech as a form of conduct. Milton Heumann et al., eds., *Hate Speech on Campus: Cases, Case Studies, and Commentary* (Northeastern University Press, 1997) reprints some classic Supreme Court opinions on free speech as well as excerpts from essays by John Stuart Mill, Herbert Marcuse, and others who have struggled with the question of whether or not freedom should be allowed for "words that wound." Finally, in *Destructive Messages: How Hate Speech Paves the Way for Harmful Social Movements* (New York University Press, 2002), Alexander Tsesis argues that hate speech should not be measured only by its immediate threat but also for its long-term effects—making hatred of minorities an acceptable part of civic debate.

ISSUE 13

Should There Be a Constitutional Amendment Banning Gay Marriage?

YES: Katherine Shaw Spaht, from Testimony Before Committee on the Judiciary, U.S. Senate, March 23, 2004

NO: Cass Sunstein, from Testimony Before Committee on the Judiciary, U.S. Senate, March 23, 2004

ISSUE SUMMARY

YES: Louisiana State University law professor Katherine Shaw Spaht argues that if a constitutional amendment banning same-sex marriage is not passed, the courts will take the issue away from the American people and abolish traditional marriage.

NO: University of Chicago law professor Cass Sunstein, recalling that amendments have almost always been reserved to ones expanding individual rights and correcting structural problems of the government, and observing the marriage amendment fit neither category, concludes that such an amendment is neither desirable nor necessary.

T he definition of "marry" in any dictionary published before 2005 will likely show some version of the first two definitions found in *Webster's New Universal Unabridged Dictionary* (1979):

> mar'ry, *v.t.* . . . from L. *maritare,* to wed, marry, from *maritus,* husband.
> 1. to unite in wedlock; to join as husband and wife
> 2. to join (a man) to a woman as her husband, or (a woman) to a man as his wife.

By 2004, however, a number of dictionary publishers were scrambling to revise their definitions, removing any references to gender. The immediate cause of these revisions was a 4–3 decision by Massachusetts' highest court in 2003 legalizing gay marriage within the state.

The Massachusetts case began when seven gay and lesbian couples sought and were denied marriage licenses by the clerks of various cities and towns in the state. The couples went to court, arguing, on a number of grounds, that the denial of licenses was improper. One argument was that, since the word "marriage" in the state's licensing statute did not specifically limit marriage to heterosexual couples, they should have been given licenses. In reply, the state's attorney pointed out that since "marriage" in the state's licensing statute was based on a definition of marriage (involving a man and woman) that was not only in every dictionary but derived from traditional English common law, the clerks acted properly in denying the licenses. The state won in the lower court, and the plaintiffs then appealed to the state Supreme Court.

Interestingly, the state Supreme Court agreed with the lower court that, under the existing licensing statute the clerks were right to deny the licenses. Even though the statute did not specifically deny gay couples the right to marry, the word "marriage" in it was implicitly based on a centuries-old common law definition of marriage as between a man and a woman. Nevertheless, the court held that definition to be contrary to the rights of equal protection and due process of law in the state constitution, at least as interpreted through the prism of "evolving constitutional standards." Accordingly, it ordered the legislature to go back and rewrite the common-law meaning of marriage in language that would include gay couples.

The decision touched a raw nerve in America. Public opinion polls showed large majorities opposed to it, and, more surprisingly, a shrinkage in public support for other gay-rights measures. The reason for the backlash is not hard to discern: the decision abruptly ended an understanding of marriage that was not just centuries old, as the Massachusetts court conceded, but as old as humanity itself. Nowhere in the historical records is there any case of a regime sanctioning homosexual marriage. Not even the ancient Greeks, who tolerated homosexual behavior, went that far.

Still, it is well to be wary of invoking tradition to discredit innovation. Slavery also has a long tradition in the world, and not long ago there were laws against interracial marriage. Of course, whether it is valid to compare racial prohibitions, which are based on physical attributes, to prohibitions in the area of sexual behavior, is debatable. But that is a debate in moral philosophy. Politically, the more relevant question is why a court decision in a single state should have caused such a national ruckus. As Massachusetts goes, so must the nation? Some fear that the answer is yes.

The fears have generated support for a new Constitutional amendment defining marriage as between a man and a woman and preventing courts from requiring states or the federal government to legalize gay marriage. This proposed amendment has been introduced in both the U.S. House of Representatives and the Senate. In the following selections, Professor Katherine Shaw Spaht argues that the amendment is necessary; otherwise, the courts will take the issue away from the American people and abolish traditional marriage. Opposing this view is Professor Cass Sunstein, who argues that such an amendment is neither desirable nor necessary.

Testimony

I can honestly tell this committee that, when I entered the area of family law over thirty years ago, I never imagined that I would be here in the United States Senate, endorsing a constitutional amendment defining and defending the traditional institution of marriage. With all my years working at the state legislative level, I am well aware of the prominent role that the states play in the area of family law. So it is fair to ask: Why do I support the federal marriage amendment?

Law professors are fond of giving long-winded answers, and in my written testimony, I try to provide a more extensive response. But the answer is really quite simple: If this body does not approve a federal constitutional amendment defending marriage, the courts will take this issue away from the American people, and they will abolish traditional marriage. It is really that simple. It is, with regret, my considered legal opinion that the courts have left us with no middle ground for this body and for the American people. I see that over three-fourths of this body—including the distinguished Ranking Minority Member, Senator Leahy—voted for the federal Defense of Marriage, which defined marriage as the union of one man and one woman for purposes of federal law. If those votes sincerely expressed the views of members of Congress, then the only choice you have is to support a federal constitutional amendment.

Until the last few months, every citizen in this country shared a common understanding of what marriage is, a social institution, consisting of a union of a man and a woman. Every dictionary defines marriage in those well understood, millennia-old terms. As a public institution, marriage serves society's most basic function—the acculuration of children, which is a time-intensive, exceedingly expensive proposition—marriage serves that societal purpose efficiently, and we have all understood it to be a union of a man and a woman. A union that biologically is the only one that can create the children that must be acculurated if we as a society are to survive. In my thirty years of experience in family law, I can attest that the traditional institution of marriage is important in every American community—across different races, cultures, and religions.

Testimony before the U.S. Senate Judiciary Committee, March 23, 2004.

I was moved by the testimony of Reverend Richard Richardson and Pastor Daniel de Leon at the last hearing. They explained that, as far as their communities are concerned, marriage is not about discrimination—it's about children. And of course they are right. But there are law professors, lawyers, and judges who clearly view things differently. Those who say that the federal marriage amendment "writes discrimination into the Constitution" clearly believe that traditional marriage must be abolished by courts. For the rest of us—the vast majority of Americans who respect and love all people, as well as the institution of marriage—we are left with no middle ground, no other option than to either acknowledge defeat and give up traditional marriage, or support a constitutional amendment defending it.

Despite these false charges of discrimination, there seems to be bipartisan consensus that the traditional definition of marriage is worth defending— and worth defending at the federal level and at the constitutional level. The federal Defense of Marriage Act was signed by President Clinton with the support of over three-fourths of the Senate. The federal marriage amendment was first introduced by a Democrat in the House. And I notice that, in previous hearings, Democratic witnesses have agreed with Republican witnesses in supporting at least some version of a constitutional amendment defending (if not defining) marriage—including Rev. Richard Richardson, Professor Dale Carpenter, and Chuck Muth.

There also seems to be bipartisan consensus that, without a constitutional amendment, traditional marriage laws across the country—including the federal DOMA [(Defense of Marriage Act)]—will likely be invalidated by activist judges around the country. Indeed, that is already happening. And the reason is simple. I have carefully examined the Supreme Court's recent decision in Lawrence v. Texas. That decision gives activist courts and local officials all the excuse they need to abolish traditional marriage laws nationwide. In Lawrence, the Court stated that "our laws and tradition afford constitutional protection to personal decisions relating to marriage, procreation, contraception, family relationships, child rearing, and education. . . . Persons in a homosexual relationship may seek autonomy for these purposes, just as heterosexual persons do." The Court specifically identified "marriage" as a federal constitutional issue, and analyzed it, if not explicitly in terms of equal protection, nonetheless in terms of discrimination. Not once did the Court indicate that marriage is about children—and not about adult love, or discrimination. Indeed, at least one Supreme Court justice has already taken the position that traditional marriage laws may infringe upon the right of privacy and thus must be abolished by courts. In 1974, Justice Ruth Bader Ginsburg wrote that any polygamy law or by inference any other traditional marriage law "is of questionable constitutionality since it appears to encroach impermissibly upon private relationships."

Because activist lawyers and judges see marriage as about discrimination, rather than about children, courts have begun to abolish traditional marriage laws under Lawrence. Just look at the Massachusetts court. Rather than affirm traditional marriage, it characterized it as a "stain" on our laws that must be "eradicated" by judges. It recognized that "[m]any people hold deep-seated religious, moral, and ethical convictions that marriage should be limited to the union of one man and one woman," language virtually identical to that in the Lawrence decision. Not surprisingly, just as the Supreme Court in the Lawrence decision rejected those convictions as a consideration in deciding what constitutes the protected "liberty" interest, the Goodridge court[1] found "no rational reason" for such laws, and said that traditional marriage is "rooted in persistent prejudices" and based on "invidious discrimination." It even suggested that "[i]f . . . the Legislature were to jettison the term 'marriage' altogether, it might well be rational and permissible." And throughout its analysis, the court in the Goodridge case repeatedly and consistently relied on federal constitutional law and the Lawrence decision.

The nation's top constitutional law scholars don't often agree, but in this area, there appears to be a rare consensus. Harvard Law School Professor Laurence Tribe has said that "You'd have to be tone deaf not to get the message from Lawrence" that traditional marriage laws are now "constitutionally suspect." Tribe has said that under Lawrence marriage is now "a federal constitutional issue," and predicts that the U.S. Supreme Court will follow the Massachusetts court. Another constitutional law expert, Yale Law School's William Eskridge, has said that "Justice Scalia is right" that Lawrence signals the end of traditional marriage laws. Eskridge has repeatedly stated that, under the Court's rulings, "DOMA is unconstitutional." Erwin Chemerinsky has similarly written that "Justice Scalia likely is correct in his dissent in saying that laws that prohibit same-sex marriage cannot, in the long term, survive the reasoning of the majority in Lawrence."

And of course, my fellow panelist, Professor Cass Sunstein, has expressed the view that "the ban on same-sex marriages is unconstitutional." Prof. Sunstein testified as early as 1996—even before Lawrence—that courts would strike down the federal Defense of Marriage Act. He testified that "there is a big problem under the equal protection component of the due process clause, as construed just a few weeks ago by the U.S. Supreme Court in Romer v. Evans." Prof. Sunstein has argued that "the prohibition on same-sex marriages, as part of the social and legal insistence on 'two kinds,' is . . . deeply connected with male supremacy," and "has everything to do with constitutionally unacceptable stereotypes about the appropriate roles of men and women." He has said that "Massachusetts [got] it right." Notably, he has said that "the [Massachusetts] court drew some support from federal precedents."

There is, of course, no way to prevent what has been predicted by these professors other than a federal constitutional amendment. As Senator Cornyn has correctly noted, throughout history we have approved a number of constitutional amendments to reverse judicial decisions with which the American people disagree. The reason why the defense of marriage is a federal issue, and not a state issue, is simple: Because the courts have made it a federal issue. My written testimony goes even further, by explaining why in any event, family law has largely been federalized for some time now. I will not belabor the point here, but simply ask that that written testimony be submitted for the record. . . .

Why Not Permit States to Define Marriage in State Law?

Even though the subject matter of marriage and family law has historically been left to the states, the differences among states' laws (other than divorce laws, which narrowed after Williams v. North Carolina in 1942 and now are very similar) have varied at the edges of the common understanding of marriage—can first cousins marry? is a blood test required? who can perform the ceremony? But the core common understanding of marriage—that marriage bridges the differences in the sexes, a bridge that is essential to procreation—has never been touched, until now.

State experimentation as fifty individual laboratories has not been permitted when the question is as fundamental as what is marriage. Consider the examples in the Wall St. Journal opinion editorial by Ed Meese. We don't permit a state to experiment with socialism or printing its own currency. Denying such experimentation is especially prevalent if there is concern for the welfare of children—such as Congress' response to the aftermath of the divorce revolution in the 1980's and low, inconsistent child support awards. Congress enacted laws essentially requiring the states to adopt child support guidelines and more recently efficient uniform child support collection mechanisms. Children's welfare is central and at stake in a common understanding of marriage.

Furthermore, it is not as if marriage law has not been increasingly a concern of a branch of the federal government. U.S. v. Reynolds concerned Congress' regulation of marriage in the territory of Utah and whether polygamy as a religious practice was protected by the constitutional provision respecting the free exercise of religion. Marriage as a union of one man and one woman unaffected by religious practice was affirmed—a common, and most (but surely not all) would argue, fundamental understanding about the meaning of marriage. But, NOT as fundamental, or at the heart or core of marriage, as the understanding that marriage is a union of a man and a woman. Marriage is a societal method for managing heterosexual bonding. Or as we now even more clearly understand and uniformly acknowledge, the need a child has for his mother and his father.

The Reynolds case is surely not the only example of the federal judiciary's concern with and affecting of a state's (territory's) law of marriage. In a series of more recent cases the court as a federal instrumentality affected marriage with Loving v. Virginia declaring unconstitutional a Virginia statute prohibiting interracial marriages; Zablocki v. Redhail striking down a Wisconsin statute regulating entry into marriage by a person owing child support; and subsequently, Turner v. Safley declaring a Nevada prison regulation of the marriage of inmates unconstitutional.

Why a state definition of marriage in a statute or state constitutional provision may not survive even if state experimentation was desirable[.] With the "right to marry" as a fundamental right guaranteed by the Fourteenth Amendment's "liberty" clause, the definition of what is marriage within that context is ultimately within the purview of the United States Supreme Court. A state statutory definition, even a state constitutional definition of marriage, may not survive even if state experimentation were desirable. In Turner v. Safley, the description of the aspects of marriage inmates in prison continue to enjoy, contains no mention of children whatsoever in the description. Nonetheless, until the Supreme Court's decision in Lawrence v. Texas less than a year ago, I relied on Bowers v. Hardwick to anchor the "liberty" interest, the fundamental right to marry, in the history and traditions of our country (reaffirmed to an extent in footnote 6 in Michael H. v. Gerald D.)—thus the right to marry could only be defined as the right of one woman to marry one man. After the Lawrence decision explicitly overruled Bowers, the court unmoored the "liberty" interests. "Liberty" defined in Lawrence is a radical right of individual autonomy without the tempering language of "the common good." This radical right of autonomy has been substituted for the anchor of earlier interpretations of "liberty," our country's history and traditions. I can no longer predict what the definition of marriage will be. My state's statutory definition of marriage is at risk as would be my state's constitutional definition. The federal statutory definition of marriage in DOMA is at risk. In fact Lawrence v. Texas poses a potential and serious threat to virtually the entire body of state statutory family law, law which regulates marriage and the family and often elevates the "best interest of the family" over that of any individual member. . . .

Ultimately, what the proponents of the FMA are asking is simply, let the American people decide if marriage should be remain defined as a union of a man and a woman. The issue of what should be the definition of marriage is not a difficult, hyper technical, or legally complicated one. The American people can easily understand what it is that they are asked to consider. The process of amendment is purposefully difficult, potentially tedious and lengthy. If the American people are not permitted to decide the meaning of the word "marriage," the judiciary, state judges and ultimately the United States Supreme Court, will decide for us. And, among the judiciary, many individual judges at the state and federal level, are openly hostile to traditional marriage and the deeply held convictions of the majority of the American public. They are ready to redefine marriage, if not immediately in the near future. Even though, as the Supreme Court in Lawrence opines, it is unwilling to consider the deeply held moral and religious convictions of American citizens, in interpreting our Constitution, the Court may instead consult the laws of other countries—such as the Western European countries who have adopted laws redefining traditional marriage—or international declarations crafted and released by international bodies, including the United Nations.

Furthermore, those same judges often are highly disdainful of the People's decision making ability. Although the simple act of a majority of judges of a single court ordering the legislature to enact particular legislation is astounding in light of the separation of powers recognized in both state and federal systems, how much more astounding is it to find in those same opinions (Baker v. Vermont and Goodridge v. Massachusetts) sincere reluctance to permit the legislature, who represent the People, ANY limited prerogative afforded it by the court. You need only look at the dissenting opinion in Baker v. Vermont decided in 1999 to find an example in which a dissenting judge urged the majority not to offer the citizens of Vermont the option in the legislative arena to consider another legal relationship with the rights of traditional marriage.

The only safety that can be afforded traditional marriage is the safe harbor of the United States Constitution, but only if the People of this country decide to create it. Why not ask the People themselves, directly? We do not have to rely on a court's unscientific determination of whether the opinion of the People has evolved to the point of relinquishing the common understanding of traditional marriage. After all, should we leave the issue to the courts, the moment in time is chosen by the litigants. Let the People decide; they will do so in a localized venue where both proponents and opponents have realistic options by which to exert influence and to persuade those making the decision. Only those issues about which there is a substantial and sustained consensus are ultimately resolved by a constitutional amendment. Is marriage worthy of that national focus and resulting debate? Yes—never more so than at this point in our nation's history. We, the citizens, need to know if we live in and can rely on a strong marriage culture focused on the welfare of children free from the risk of experimentation.

Let them vote. That is all we ask—let the People vote.

Note

1. Spaht refers to the Massachusetts Supreme Court's decision in *Goodridge v. Department of Public Health* (2003) striking down the practice in Massachusetts of limiting marriage to heterosexual couples.

Testimony

My basic conclusion is that from the standpoint of the constitutional structure, the proposed amendment is an unfortunate idea. Our constitutional traditions demonstrate that change in the founding document is appropriate only on the most rare occasions—most notably, to correct problems in governmental structure or to expand the category of individual rights. The proposed amendment does not fall in either of these categories. Those who endorse the amendment fear that if one state recognizes same-sex marriages, others will be compelled to do so as well. But the fear is unrealistic; the federal system permits states to refuse to recognize marriages that violate their own policies. In short, the existing situation creates no problem for which constitutional change is the appropriate solution.

My testimony comes in two parts. The first explores constitutional amendments in general. The second responds to the suggestion that an amendment is necessary to eliminate the possibility that activist judges, at the federal or state level, will impose same-sex marriages on states that do not wish to recognize them.

I. The American Tradition of Constitutional Amendment

A. Stability and Passion: The View from the Founding

By intentional design, the Constitution is exceedingly difficult to amend. James Madison outlined the basic reasons. In the Federalist No. 43, he noted that amending the Constitution must not be made so difficult as to "perpetuate its discovered faults." But he warned "against that extreme facility" of constitutional amendment "which would render the Constitution too mutable." In the Federalist No. 49, he elaborating the point, stressing that amendment should be reserved for "certain great and extraordinary occasions."

Madison's thinking on this count had two principal strands. First, the national Constitution should be stable; a well-functioning republic

Testimony before the U.S. Senate Judiciary Committee, March 23, 2004.

works best if the text of the underlying framework remains essentially fixed. Thus Madison wrote that "the greatest objection of all" is that constitutional amendment would threaten "the constitutional equilibrium of the government." Second, and more subtly, constitutional change creates the serious "danger of disturbing the public tranquility by interesting too strongly the public passions" in the issues proposed for constitutional change. Madison emphasized that the founding document had been adopted in a truly extraordinary period, "which repressed the passions most unfriendly to order and concord," and "which stifled the ordinary diversity of opinions on great national questions." The result was to ensure that "no spirit of party, connected with the changes to be made, or the abuses to be reformed," could distort the process. Madison thought that no "equivalent security" could be found in "future situations"—that in ordinary political life, "passions" that were "unfriendly to order and concord" could break out in constitutional debates. In Madison's view, constitutional change should be reserved for "great and extraordinary occasions" to keep our founding document stable and to reduce the level of national polarization and conflict.

B. Amendment Traditions: Rights and Structure

Since its ratification in 1789, the Constitution has been amended only twenty-seven times. Nearly every amendment falls into one of two categories. Most of them expand individual rights. The rest attempt to remedy problems in the structure of the government itself. Thus the nation has developed, over time, a firm tradition governing constitutional amendment, a tradition that elaborates Madison's concerns by restricting fundamental change to two categories of cases.

The first ten amendments, ratified in 1791, make up the Bill of Rights, which guarantees liberties ranging from freedom of speech, assembly and religion to protection of private property and freedom from cruel and unusual punishment. In the aftermath of the Civil War, three new amendments were ratified: to prohibit slavery, to guarantee African-Americans the right to vote, and to assure everyone a panoply of rights against state governments, including the "equal protection of the laws." During the twentieth century, a number of constitutional amendments have expanded the right to vote, which has become a centerpiece of the amendment process. Thus for example, the franchise was granted to women (1920) and to 18-year-olds (1971); poll taxes were forbidden in federal elections (1964); and the District of Columbia was granted representation in the Electoral College (1961).

Many other amendments fix problems in the structure of the government, sometimes by filling gaps in the original document, sometimes by increasing the democratic character of our basic charter. An early amendment, ratified in 1804, specifies the rules for the operation of the Electoral College. In 1913, the Constitution was changed to require popular election of senators; in the same year, an amendment authorized Congress to impose an income tax (and thus solved what the nation believed to be an important defect in the original document). A 1951 amendment, responding to Franklin Roosevelt's four terms as president, bans the president from serving more than two terms. A related amendment from 1967 specifies what happens in the event that the president dies or becomes disabled while in office. This amendment, like those just discussed, makes a clarification or correction to structural defects in the Constitution as originally designed.

Only two amendments fall unambiguously outside of the defining categories of expanding individual rights and responding to structural problems. Ratified in 1919, the 18th Amendment prohibits the sale of "intoxicating liquors." Ratified in 1933, the 21st Amendment repeals the 18th.

C. Theory and Practice: Stability, Polarization, and Clarity

What accounts for our remarkable unwillingness to amend the Constitution except to expand rights and to fix structural problems? The simple answer borrows from Madison. From the founding period, Americans have prized constitutional stability. The nation has agreed that the document should not be amended merely to incorporate the majority's position on the great issues of the day. For those issues, we rely on the federal system and on democracy. More than that, Americans have feared that large-scale constitutional debates could lead not only to ill-considered change but could also split and polarize the country. When our citizens differ, we use the other institutions that we have, not constitutional reform. And when the nation's citizens and leaders object to trends within the Supreme Court, or within other institutions of the federal or state government, they have almost always avoided constitutional amendment, even on concrete issues on which they feel deeply.

In the 1930s, for example, President Franklin Delano Roosevelt was repeatedly rebuffed by an aggressively conservative Supreme Court, which endangered the legislation of his New Deal. Change was made not through constitutional amendment, but through the democratic process, which eventually helped lead to dramatic alterations in constitutional understandings. In the 1960s, President Richard Nixon sharply challenged an aggressively liberal Supreme Court; change was made not via constitutional amendment, but through political processes, which led the Court to shift its direction. The examples could easily be multiplied. More recently, the Constitution has not been amended in the face of many controversial Supreme Court decisions—protecting the right to choose abortion and striking down campaign finance regulation, the Violence Against Women Act, the Religious Freedom Restoration Act, and many more. (Indeed the Rehnquist Court has struck down more than two dozen Acts of Congress in recent years, and none of these invalidations has spurred serious calls for constitutional amendment.)

In short, the nation has built firmly on Madison's judgment about the need for caution in altering the founding document. The result was been to create a kind of common law tradition of constitutional change, reserving alterations to expansions in fundamental rights or to remedying important problems in governmental structure.

There is an equally general point in the background. Many constitutional amendments raise novel and complex questions of interpretation, in a way that produces grave uncertainty and a potentially significant increase in federal judicial power. Many American citizens, though committed to equal rights for women, opposed the proposed Equal Rights Amendment on the ground that it would create interpretive difficulties, amount to a bonanza for the legal profession, and produce unanticipated and unintended outcomes from the federal bench. The same arguments were made, plausibly, by critics of the proposed Balanced Budget Amendment. Any amendment dealing with family law is likely to create serious difficulties in this vein. . . .

II. Same-Sex Marriage: A Problem Requiring Amendment?

None of these points shows that the Constitution should never be amended for reasons that fall outside of the two basic categories that define our amendment tradition. We could certainly imagine situations in which the citizenry believed that formal amendment was necessary (for example) to overrule a damaging and egregiously wrong Supreme Court decision or to correct serious and otherwise irremediable blunders at the state level.

In this light, the impetus for the proposed amendment is easy to understand. The Full Faith and Credit Clause states: "Full Faith and Credit shall be given in each State to the public Acts, Records, and judicial Proceedings of every other State. And the Congress may by general Laws prescribe the Manner in which such Acts, Records and Proceedings shall be proved, and the Effect thereof." U.S. Const., art, IV, section 1. Suppose that one state—Massachusetts, for example—recognizes same-sex marriages. Is there not a danger that other states, whatever their views, will be forced to accept same-sex marriages as well? Perhaps people will travel to Massachusetts, marry there, and effectively "bind" the rest of the union to one state's rules, forcing all states to recognize marriages that violate their policies and judgments. A national solution might seem necessary if one state's unusual judgments threaten to unsettle the practices of forty-nine other states. This is the hypothetical scenario that motivates some people to favor constitutional change.

A. Marriage and Public Policy

The response to the underlying fear here is simple. The hypothetical scenario is unlikely in the extreme. The central reason is that the full faith and credit clause has never been understood to bind the states in this way. For over two hundred years, states have worked out issues of this kind on their own. It is entirely to be expected that in a union of fifty diverse states, different states will have different rules governing marriage. American law has established practical strategies for ensuring sensible results in these circumstances, as each state consults its own "public policy," and its own connection to the people involved, in deciding what to do with a marriage entered into elsewhere. In short: States have not been bound to recognize marriages if (a) they have a significant relation with the relevant people and (b) the marriage at issue violates a strongly held local policy. In the particular context of marriages (involving licenses rather than formal judicial judgments), states have had room to pursue policies of their own. . . .

In Corpus Juris, Vol. 38, § 3, p. 1276, the rule as what law governs in determining the validity of marriage is thus stated: "The general rule is that validity of a marriage is determined by the law of the place where it was contracted; if valid there it will be held valid everywhere, and conversely if invalid by the lex loci contractus, it will be held invalid wherever the question may arise. An exception to the general rule, however, is ordinarily made in the case of marriages repugnant to the public policy of the domicile of the parties, in respect of polygamy, incest, or miscegenation, or otherwise contrary to its positive laws." . . .

Under the same principle, states may refuse to recognize marriages by a person who has recently divorced, if such marriages violate their public policy.

All this demonstrates that the proposed amendment would respond to an old and familiar problem that has heretofore been settled through long-settled principles at the state level and without federal intervention. If some states do recognize same-sex marriage, the problem would be handled in the same way that countless similar problems have been handled, via "public policy" judgments by states having significant relationships with the parties. Different "public policies" will produce different results. This is consistent with longstanding practices and with the essential constitutional logic of the federal system. In the area of marriage, states have always been authorized to adopt diverse practices, consistent with the norms and values of their citizens. What one state has not been allowed to do is to bind other states to its preferred norms and values. Hence the hypothetical scenario rests on a misunderstanding of the applicable legal principles.

Might federal courts invalidate, on either grounds of equal protection or privacy, state court refusals to recognize same-sex marriages? Under existing law, it would not be frivolous to argue that such refusals are a form of discrimination, raising serious problems under the equal protection clause (a question discussed below). But there is a large distance between "not frivolous" and "likely to be convincing to current federal judges." If federal courts accepted this argument, and ruled that the Constitution prohibits states from discriminating against same-sex marriages in this way, they would be essentially ruling that the Constitution requires states to recognize same-sex marriages. No such ruling should be anticipated.

B. The Defense of Marriage Act

The Defense of Marriage Act (DOMA) . . . attempts to anticipate and to prevent the hypothetical scenario, expressly freeing states from whatever obligation they might have to recognize same-sex marriages: I have suggested that DOMA is unnecessary to produce this result; but if DOMA is taken in accordance with its terms, the scenario will not transpire. Some people urge that federal judges will strike down DOMA, and they are right to speculate that constitutional objections might be mounted. Notably, however, no such challenge has been made, and even if it were successful, the preceding discussion suggests that the hypothetical scenario would be most unlikely to occur. . . .

Even if DOMA were invalidated, the longstanding tradition, outlined above, would be unaffected: States would be permitted to decline to recognize same-sex marriages that are inconsistent with their own policies.

C. Judicial Activism

Many proponents of the proposed amendment have voiced concerns about "activist judges," and especially about activist judges at the federal level, reading the federal Constitution to require states to permit same-sex marriages. I share this general concern. In the domain of family law, as elsewhere, judges should tread cautiously. This point is especially important for federal judges interpreting the national Constitution. At least if issued by the Supreme Court, such interpretations are final and binding until they are overruled, either by the Court itself or by constitutional amendment. Even those who favor same-sex marriages, or who do not object to them, should be skeptical about the idea that federal courts should require states to recognize them.

But here too the underlying concern is hypothetical in the extreme. No federal judge has said—not once—that the existing Constitution requires states to recognize same-sex marriages. No member of the Supreme Court has indicated that the equal protection clause imposes such a requirement. In both Romer and Lawrence, the Court has issued narrow, cautious rulings. To be sure, the picture is different in a very few state courts. Most important, the Supreme Judicial Court of Massachusetts has ruled that the state constitution forbids Massachusetts to refuse to give marriage licenses to same-sex couples. See Goodridge v. Department of Public Health, 798 N.E.2d 941 (2003). But even in Massachusetts, well-established processes are now underway for amending the state constitution, if the citizens wish, to overturn the court's decision. In fact constitutional amendments are far more common at the state than the federal level. (The Alabama Constitution, for example, has been amended over 700 times; the California Constitution, over 500 times; the Texas Constitution, over 300 times; and the New York Constitution, over 200 times.)

In the overwhelming majority of states, there is no effort to redefine marriage to include same-sex couples, and indeed about three-quarters of the states have defined marriage to preclude such marriages on their own.

I have urged that constitutional amendments are inconsistent with our traditions if they fall outside of the two categories that have defined American practices. But even if those categories do not exhaust the proper grounds for changing our charter, there is no good argument for doing so here, simply because the current situation creates no problem that an amendment is necessary to solve.

Conclusion

By tradition, amendments to the constitution are limited to "great and extraordinary occasions." By tradition, amendments are almost always reserved to the expansion of individual rights and to the correction of serious problems in governmental structure. Whatever one thinks of same-sex marriage, the existing situation cannot plausibly be placed in either category. Issues of family law are best handled at the state and local level, as different norms and values give rise to differences in state and local law. This is an area in which federal judges have been treading exceedingly cautiously, as they should. The system of federalism is perfectly capable of resolving the issues that might arise if states seek, on grounds of public policy, to deny recognition to marriages that are valid where performed.

The proposed amendment responds to a situation that is best handled through existing institutions. It would violate the founders' commitments to constitutional stability and to eliminating unnecessary divisions among American citizens. And it would violate our tradition, based on over two centuries of practice, of resolving almost all of our disputes through the federal system and through democratic processes. For these reasons, the proposed amendment should be rejected.

POSTSCRIPT

Should There Be a Constitutional Amendment Banning Gay Marriage?

In both of the above arguments we find an interesting interplay of radicalism and traditionalism. To protect the traditional meaning of marriage, Katherine Shaw Spaht is prepared to take radical, or at least extraordinary, route of amending the U.S. Constitution. Cass Sunstein, for his part, supports gay marriage and regards opposition to it as a manifestation of "male supremacy," yet for all his social radicalism he opposes the Marriage Amendment because it is "inconsistent with our traditions."

Andrew Sullivan, in *Virtually Normal: An Argument about Homosexuality* (Alfred A. Knopf, 1995), contends that legalizing gay marriage would be a humanizing step because such marriages would promote social stability and teach valuable lessons even to "straights." Criticizing this view is James Q. Wilson ("Against Homosexual Marriage," *Commentary*, March 1996.) Despite its rather hyperbolic title, Jonathan Rauch's *Gay Marriage: Why It Is Good for Gays, Good for Straights, and Good for America* (Times Books, 2004), takes a more cautious approach, convinced as he is that "same sex marriage will work best when people accept and understand it, whereas a sudden national enactment, were it suddenly to happen, might spark a culture war on the order of the abortion battle." The legal aspects of same-sex marriage are examined by Mark Strasser in *The Challenge of Same-Sex Marriages: Federalist Principles and Constitutional Protections* (Praeger, 1999). Essays arguing opposing positions can be found in Andrew Sullivan, et al., eds., *Same-Sex Marriage, Pro and Con: A Reader* (Vintage Books, 1997).

Though perhaps not impossible, it is highly unlikely that a Federal Marriage Amendment will ever be added to the U.S. Constitution. American constitutional history is strewn with the bones of once-popular proposals, such as the Equal Rights Amendment and the Balanced Budget Amendment, which were killed either by the failure to obtain the necessary two-thirds vote in both houses of Congress, or by the failure to be ratified by at least three-fourths of the states. For the foreseeable future, Congress, especially the Senate, will be narrowly divided by party, with most Democrats and even some Republicans opposed to the Marriage Amendment. Why, then, introduce such an amendment? First, to win applause and perhaps valuable support from social conservatives, with little risk of alienating numerically larger groups in the electorate; second, to keep the issue alive and in the news—thus, perhaps, to signal the Supreme Court that a large portion of the nation would be most unhappy with a ruling similar to that of the Massachusetts court.

ISSUE 14

Should Abortion Be Restricted?

YES: Robert P. George, from *The Clash of Orthodoxies: Law, Religion, and Morality in Crisis* (ISI Books, 2001)

NO: Mary Gordon, from "A Moral Choice," *The Atlantic Monthly* (March 1990)

ISSUE SUMMARY

YES: Legal philosopher Robert P. George asserts that, since each of us was a human being from conception, abortion is a form of homicide and should be banned.

NO: Writer Mary Gordon maintains that having an abortion is a moral choice that women are capable of making for themselves, that aborting a fetus is not killing a person, and that antiabortionists fail to understand female sexuality.

U ntil 1973 the laws governing abortion were set by the states, most of which barred legal abortion except where pregnancy imperiled the life of the pregnant woman. In that year, the U.S. Supreme Court decided the controversial case *Roe v. Wade.* The *Roe* decision acknowledged both a woman's "fundamental right" to terminate a pregnancy before fetal viability and the state's legitimate interest in protecting both the woman's health and the "potential life" of the fetus. It prohibited states from banning abortion to protect the fetus before the third trimester of a pregnancy, and it ruled that even during that final trimester, a woman could obtain an abortion if she could prove that her life or health would be endangered by carrying to term. (In a companion case to *Roe,* decided on the same day, the Court defined *health* broadly enough to include "all factors—physical, emotional, psychological, familial, and the woman's age—relevant to the well-being of the patient.") These holdings, together with the requirement that state regulation of abortion had to survive "strict scrutiny" and demonstrate a "compelling state interest," resulting in later decisions striking down mandatory 24-hour waiting periods, requirements that abortions be performed in hospitals, and so-called informed consent laws.

The Supreme Court did uphold state laws requiring parental notification and consent for minors (though it provided that minors could seek permission from a judge if they feared notifying their parents). And federal courts have affirmed the right of Congress not to pay for abortions. Proabortion groups, proclaiming the "right to choose," have charged that this and similar action at the state level discriminates against poor women because it does not inhibit the ability of women who are able to pay for abortions to obtain them. Efforts to adopt a constitutional amendment or federal law barring abortion have failed, but antiabortion forces have influenced legislation in many states.

Can legislatures and courts establish the existence of a scientific fact? Opponents of abortion believe that it is a fact that life begins at conception and that the law must therefore uphold and enforce this concept. They argue that the human fetus is a live human being, and they note all the familiar signs of life displayed by the fetus: a beating heart, brain waves, thumb sucking, and so on. Those who defend abortion maintain that human life does not begin before the development of specifically human characteristics and possibly not until the birth of a child. As Justice Harry A. Blackmun put it in 1973, "There has always been strong support for the view that life does not begin until live birth."

Antiabortion forces sought a court case that might lead to the overturning of *Roe v. Wade*. Proabortion forces rallied to oppose new state laws limiting or prohibiting abortion. In *Webster v. Reproductive Health Services* (1989), with four new justices, the Supreme Court pulled back from its proabortion stance. In a 5–4 decision, the Court upheld a Missouri law that banned abortions in public hospitals and abortions that were performed by public employees (except to save a woman's life). The law also required that tests be performed on any fetus more than 20 weeks old to determine its viability—that is, its ability to survive outside the womb.

In the later decision of *Planned Parenthood v. Casey* (1992), however, the Court affirmed what it called the "essence" of the constitutional right to abortion while permitting some state restrictions, such as a 24-hour waiting period and parental notification in the case of minors.

During the Clinton presidency, opponents of abortion focused on what they identified as "partial-birth" abortions; that is, where a fetus is destroyed during the process of birth. President Clinton twice vetoed partial-birth bans that allowed such abortions to save a woman's life but not her health. By early 1998, 22 states adopted such bans, but in 11 of these states challenges to the law's constitutionality were upheld in federal or state courts. In 1998, in the first of these cases to reach the U.S. Supreme Court, the Court let stand without a written opinion (but with three dissenters) a federal court of appeals decision declaring Ohio's law unconstitutional. The Supreme Court did not confront the question of how it would decide a law that narrowly defined the procedure and provided a maternal health exception.

In the following selections, Robert P. George contends that, since each of us was a human being from conception, abortion is a form of homicide and should be banned. Mary Gordon asserts that the fetus removed in most abortions may not be considered a person and that women must retain the right to make decisions regarding their sexual lives.

Robert P. George  **YES**

God's Reasons

In his contributions to the February 1996 issue of *First Things* magazine—contributions in which what he has to say (particularly in his critique of liberalism) is far more often right than wrong—Stanley Fish of Duke University cites the dispute over abortion as an example of a case in which "incompatible first assumptions [or] articles of opposing faiths"—make the resolution of the dispute (other than by sheer political power) impossible. Here is how Fish presented the pro-life and pro-choice positions and the shape of the dispute between their respective defenders:

> A pro-life advocate sees abortion as a sin against God who infuses life at the moment of conception; a pro-choice advocate sees abortion as a decision to be made in accordance with the best scientific opinion as to when the beginning of life, as we know it, occurs. No conversation between them can ever get started because each of them starts from a different place and they could never agree as to what they were conversing *about*. A pro-lifer starts from a belief in the direct agency of a personal God, and this belief, this religious conviction, is not incidental to his position; it is his position, and determines its features in all their detail. The "content of a belief" is a *function* of its source, and the critiques of one will always be the critique of the other.

It is certainly true that the overwhelming majority of pro-life Americans are religious believers and that a great many pro-choice Americans are either unbelievers or less observant or less traditional in their beliefs and practice than their fellow citizens. Indeed, although most Americans believe in God, polling data consistently show that Protestants, Catholics, and Jews who do not regularly attend church or synagogue are less likely than their more observant co-religionists to oppose abortion. And religion is plainly salient politically when it comes to the issue of abortion. The more secularized a community, the more likely that community is to elect pro-choice politicians to legislative and executive offices.

Still, I don't think that Fish's presentation of the pro-life and pro-choice positions, or of the shape of the dispute over abortion, is accurate. True, inasmuch as most pro-life advocates are traditional religious believers who, as such, see gravely unjust or otherwise immoral acts as sins—and understand sins precisely as offenses against God—"a pro-life advocate sees abortion as a sin against God." But most pro-life advocates see abortion as a sin against God *precisely because it is the unjust taking of innocent human life.* That is their reason for opposing abortion; and that is God's reason, as they see it, for opposing abortion and requiring that human communities protect their unborn members against it. And, they believe, as I do, that this reason can be identified and acted on even independently of God's revealing it. Indeed, they typically believe, as I do, that the precise content of what God reveals on the subject ("in they mother's womb I formed thee") cannot be known without the application of human intelligence, by way of philosophical and scientific inquiry, to the question.

Fish is mistaken, then, in *contrasting* the pro-life advocate with the pro-choice advocate by depicting (only) the latter as viewing abortion as "a decision to be made in accordance with the best scientific opinion as to when the beginning of life . . . occurs." First of all, supporters of the pro-choice position are increasingly willing to sanction the practice of abortion even where they concede that it constitutes the taking of innocent human life. Pro-choice writers from Naomi Wolfe to Judith Jarvis Thomson have advanced theories of abortion as "justifiable homicide." But, more to the point, people on the pro-life side *insist* that the central issue in the debate is the question "as to when the beginning of life occurs." And they insist with equal vigor that this question is not a "religious" or even "metaphysical" one: it is rather, as Fish says, "scientific." In response to this insistence, it is pro-choice advocates who typically want to transform the question into a "metaphysical" or "religious" one. It was Justice Harry Blackmun who claimed in his opinion for the Court legalizing abortion in *Roe v. Wade* (1973) that "at this point in man's knowledge" the scientific evidence was inconclusive and therefore could not determine the outcome of the case. And twenty years later, the influential pro-choice writer Ronald Dworkin went on record claiming that the question of abortion is inherently "religious." It is pro-choice advocates, such as Dworkin, who want to distinguish between when a human being comes into existence "in the biological sense and when a human being comes into existence" in the moral sense. It is they who want to distinguish a class of human beings "with rights" from pre- (or post-) conscious human beings who "don't have rights." And the reason for this, I submit, is that, short of defending abortion as "justifiable homicide," the pro-choice position collapses if the issue is to be settled purely on the basis of scientific inquiry into the question of when a new member of Homo sapiens comes into existence as a self-integrating organism whose unity, distinctiveness, and identity remain intact as it develops without substantial change from the point of its beginning through the various stages of its development and into adulthood.

All this was, I believe, made wonderfully clear at a debate at the 1997 meeting of the American Political Science Association between Jeffrey Reiman of American University, defending the pro-choice position, and John Finnis of Oxford and Notre Dame, defending the pro-life view. That debate was remarkable for the skill, intellectual honesty, and candor of the interlocutors.

What is most relevant to our deliberations, however, is the fact that it truly was a debate Reiman and Finnis did not talk past each other. They did not proceed from "incompatible first assumptions." They *did* manage to agree as to what they were talking *about*—and it was not about whether or when life was infused by God. It was precisely about the *rational* (i.e., scientific and philosophical) grounds, if any, available for distinguishing a class of human beings "in the moral sense" (with rights) from a class of human beings "in the (merely) biological sense" (without rights). Finnis did not claim any special revelation to the effect that no such grounds existed. Nor did Reiman claim that Finnis's arguments against his view appealed implicitly (and illicitly) to some such putative revelation. Although Finnis is a Christian and, as such, believes that the new human life that begins at conception is in each and every case created by God in His image and likeness, his argument never invoked, much less did it "start from a belief in the direct agency of a personal God." It proceeded, rather, by way of point-by-point philosophical challenge to Reiman's philosophical arguments. Finnis marshaled the scientific facts of embryogenesis and intrauterine human development and defied Reiman to identify grounds, compatible with those facts, for denying a right to life to human beings in the embryonic and fetal stages of development.

Interestingly, Reiman began his remarks with a statement that would seem to support what Fish said in *First Things*. While allowing that debates over abortion were useful in clarifying people's thinking about the issue, Reiman remarked that they "never actually cause people to change their minds." It is true, I suppose, that people who are deeply committed emotionally to one side or the other are unlikely to have a road-to-Damascus type conversion after listening to a formal philosophical debate. Still, any open-minded person who sincerely wishes to settle his mind on the question of abortion—and there continue to be many such people, I believe—would find debates such as the one between Reiman and Finnis to be extremely helpful toward that end. Anyone willing to consider the *reasons* for and against abortion and its legal prohibition or permission would benefit from reading or hearing the accounts of these reasons proposed by capable and honest thinkers on both sides. Of course, when it comes to an issue like abortion, people can have powerful motives for clinging to a particular position even if they are presented with conclusive reasons for changing their minds. But that doesn't mean that such reasons do not exist.

I believe that the pro-life position is superior to the pro-choice position precisely because the scientific evidence, considered honestly and dispassionately, fully supports it. A human being is conceived when a human sperm containing twenty-three chromosomes fuses with a human egg also containing twenty-three chromosomes (albeit of a different kind) producing a single-cell human zygote containing, in the normal case, forty-six chromosomes that are mixed differently from the forty-six chromosomes as found in the mother or father. Unlike the gametes (that is, the sperm and egg), the zygote is genetically unique and distinct from its parents. Biologically, it is a separate organism. It produces, as the gametes do not, specifically human enzymes and proteins.

It possesses, as they do not, the active capacity or potency to develop itself into a human embryo, fetus, infant, child, adolescent, and adult. Assuming that it is not conceived *in vitro*, the zygote is, of course, in a state of dependence on its mother. But independence should not be confused with distinctness. From the beginning, the newly conceived human being, not its mother, directs its integral organic functioning. It takes in nourishment and converts it to energy. Given a hospitable environment, it will, as Dianne Nutwell Irving says, "develop continuously without any biological interruptions, or gaps, throughout the embryonic, fetal, neo-natal, childhood and adulthood stages—until the death of the organism."

۔۔

Some claim to find the logical implication of these facts—that is, that life begins at conception—to be "virtually unintelligible." A leading exponent of that point of view in the legal academy is Jed Rubenfeld of Yale Law School, author of an influential article entitled "On the Legal Status of the Proposition that 'Life Begins at Conception.'" Rubenfeld argues that, like the zygote, *every* cell in the human body is "genetically complete"; yet nobody supposes that every human cell is a distinct human being with a right to life. However, Rubenfeld misses the point that there comes into being at conception, not a mere clump of human cells, but a distinct, unified, self-integrating organism, which develops itself, truly himself or herself, in accord with its own genetic "blueprint." The significance of genetic completeness for the status of newly conceived human beings is that no outside genetic material is required to enable the zygote to mature into an embryo, the embryo into a fetus, the fetus into an infant, the infant into a child, the child into an adolescent, the adolescent into an adult. What the zygote needs to function as a distinct self-integrating human organism, a human being, it already possesses.

At no point in embryogenesis, therefore, does the distinct organism that came into being when it was conceived undergo what is technically called "substantial change" (or a change of natures). It is human and will remain human. This is the point of Justice Byron White's remark in his dissenting opinion in *Thornburgh v. American College of Obstetricians & Gynecologists* that "there is no non-arbitrary line separating a fetus from a child." Rubenfeld attacks White's point, which he calls "[t]he argument based on the gradualness of gestation," by pointing out that, "[n]o non-arbitrary line separates the hues of green and red. Shall we conclude that green is red?"

White's point, however, was *not* that fetal development is "gradual," but that it is *continuous* and is the (continuous) development of a single lasting (fully human) being. The human zygote that actively develops itself is, as I have pointed out, a genetically complete organism directing its own integral organic functioning. As it matures, *in utero* and *ex utero*, it does not "become" a human being, for it is a human being *already*, albeit an immature human being, just as a newborn infant is an immature human being who will undergo quite dramatic growth and development over time.

These considerations undermine the familiar argument, recited by Rubenfeld, that "the potential" of an *unfertilized* ovum to develop into a whole human being does not make it into "a person." The fact is, though, that an ovum is not a whole human being. It is, rather, a part of another human being (the woman whose ovum it is) with merely the potential to give rise to, in interaction with a part of yet another human being (a man's sperm cell), a new and whole human being. Unlike the zygote, it lacks both genetic distinctness and completeness, as well as the active capacity to develop itself into an adult member of the human species. It is living human cellular material, but, left to itself, it will never become a human being, however hospitable its environment may be. It will "die" as a human ovum, just as countless skin cells "die" daily as nothing more than skin cells. If successfully fertilized by a human sperm, which, like the ovum (but dramatically unlike the zygote), lacks the active potential to develop into an adult member of the human species, then *substantial* change (that is, a change of *natures*) will occur. There will no longer be merely an egg, which was part of the mother, sharing her genetic composition, and a sperm, which was part of the father, sharing his genetic composition; instead, there will be a genetically complete, distinct, unified, self-integrating human organism, whose nature differs from that of the gametes—not mere human material, but a human being.

These considerations also make clear that it is incorrect to argue (as some pro-choice advocates have argued) that, just as "I" was never a week-old sperm or ovum, "I" was likewise never a week-old embryo. It truly makes no sense to say that "I" was once a sperm (or an unfertilized egg) that matured into an adult. Conception was the occasion of substantial change (that is, change from one complete individual entity to another) that brought into being a distinct self-integrating organism with a specifically human nature. By contrast, it makes every bit as much sense to say that I was once a week-old embryo as to say that I was once a week-old infant or a ten-year-old child. It was the new organism created at conception that, without itself undergoing any change of substance, matured into a week-old embryo, a fetus, an infant, a child, an adolescent, and, finally, an adult.

But Rubenfeld has another argument: "Cloning processes give to non-zygotic cells the potential for development into distinct, self-integrating human beings; thus to recognize the zygote as a human being is to recognize all human cells as human beings, which is absurd."

It is true that a distinct, self-integrating human organism that came into being by a process of cloning would be, like a human organism that comes into being as a monozygotic twin, a human being. That being, no less than human beings conceived by the union of sperm and egg, would possess a human nature and the active potential to mature as a human being. However, even assuming the possibility of cloning human beings from non-zygotic human cells, the non-zygotic cell must be activated by a process that effects substantial change and not mere development or maturation. Left to itself, apart from an activation process capable of effecting a change of substance or natures, the cell will mature and die as a human cell, not as a human being.

The scientific evidence establishes the fact that each of us was, from conception, a human being. Science, not religion, vindicates this crucial premise of the pro-life claim. From it, there is no avoiding the conclusion that deliberate feticide is a form of homicide. The only real questions remaining are moral and political, not scientific: Although I will not go into the matter here, I do not see how direct abortion can even be considered a matter of "justified homicide." It is important to recognize, however, as traditional moralists always have recognized, that not all procedures that foreseeably result in fetal death are, properly speaking, abortions. Although any procedure whose precise objective is the destruction of fetal life is certainly an abortion, and cannot be justified, some procedures result in fetal death as an unintended, albeit foreseen and accepted, side effect. Where procedures of the latter sort are done for very grave reasons, they may be justifiable. For example, traditional morality recognizes that a surgical operation to remove a life-threateningly cancerous uterus, even in a woman whose pregnancy is not far enough along to enable the child to be removed from her womb and sustained by a life support system, is ordinarily morally permissible. Of course, there are in this area of moral reflection, as in others, "borderline" cases that are difficult to classify and evaluate. Mercifully, modern medical technology has made such cases exceptionally rare in real life. Only in the most extraordinary circumstances today do women and their families and physicians find it necessary to consider a procedure that will result in fetal death as the only way of preserving maternal life. In any event, the political debate about abortion is not, in reality, about cases of this sort; it is about "elective" or "social indication" abortions, viz., the deliberate destruction of unborn human life for non-therapeutic reasons.

A final point: In my own experience, conversion from the pro-choice to the pro-life cause is often (though certainly not always) a partial cause of religious conversion rather than an effect. Frequently, people who are not religious, or who are only weakly so, begin to have doubts about the moral defensibility of deliberate feticide. Although most of their friends are pro-choice, they find that position increasingly difficult to defend or live with. They perceive practical inconsistencies in their, and their friends', attitudes toward the unborn depending on whether the child is "wanted" or not. Perhaps they find themselves arrested by sonographic (or other even more sophisticated) images of the child's life in the womb. So the doubts begin creeping in. For the first time, they are really prepared to listen to the pro-life argument (often despite their negative attitude toward people—or "the kind of people"—who are pro-life); and somehow, it sounds more compelling than it did before. Gradually, as they become firmly pro-life, they find themselves questioning the whole philosophy of life—in a word, secularism—associated with their former view. They begin to understand the reasons that led them out of the pro-choice and into the pro-life camp as God's reasons, too.

Mary Gordon  **NO**

A Moral Choice

I am having lunch with six women. What is unusual is that four of them are in their seventies, two of them widowed, the other two living with husbands beside whom they've lived for decades. All of them have had children. Had they been men, they would have published books and hung their paintings on the walls of important galleries. But they are women of a certain generation, and their lives were shaped around their families and personal relations. They are women you go to for help and support. We begin talking about the latest legislative act that makes abortion more difficult for poor women to obtain. An extraordinary thing happens. Each of them talks about the illegal abortions she had during her young womanhood. Not one of them was spared the experience. Any of them could have died on the table of whatever person (not a doctor in any case) she was forced to approach, in secrecy and in terror, to end a pregnancy that she felt would blight her life.

I mention this incident for two reasons: first as a reminder that all kinds of women have always had abortions; second because it is essential that we remember that an abortion is performed on a living woman who has a life in which a terminated pregnancy is only a small part. Morally speaking, the decision to have an abortion doesn't take place in a vacuum. It is connected to other choices that a woman makes in the course of an adult life.

Anti-choice propagandists paint pictures of women who choose to have abortions as types of moral callousness, selfishness, or irresponsibility. The woman choosing to abort is the dressed-for-success yuppie who gets rid of her baby so that she won't miss her Caribbean vacation or her chance for promotion. Or she is the feckless, promiscuous ghetto teenager who couldn't bring herself to just say no to sex. A third, purportedly kinder, gentler picture has recently begun to be drawn. The woman in the abortion clinic is there because she is misinformed about the nature of the world. She is having an abortion because society does not provide for mothers and their children, and she mistakenly thinks that another mouth to feed will be the ruin of her family, not understanding that the temporary truth of family unhappiness doesn't stack up beside the eternal verity that abortion is murder. Or she is the dupe of her husband or boyfriend, who talks her into having an abortion because a child will be a drag on his life-style. None of these pictures created by the anti-choice movement assumes that the decision to have an abortion is made responsibly, in the context of a morally lived life, by a free and responsible moral agent.

The Ontology of the Fetus

How would a woman who habitually makes choices in moral terms come to the decision to have an abortion? The moral discussion of abortion centers on the issue of whether or not abortion is an act of murder. At first glance it would seem that the answer should follow directly upon two questions: Is the fetus human? and Is it alive? It would be absurd to deny that a fetus is alive or that it is human. What would our other options be—to say that it is inanimate or belongs to another species? But we habitually use the terms "human" and "live" to refer to parts of our body—"human hair," for example, or "live red-blood cells"—and we are clear in our understanding that the nature of these objects does not rank equally with an entire personal exist-ence. It then seems important to consider whether the fetus, this alive human thing, is a *person,* to whom the term "murder" could sensibly be applied. How would anyone come to a decision about something so impalpable as person-hood? Philosophers have struggled with the issue of personhood, but in language that is so abstract that it is unhelpful to ordinary people making decisions in the course of their lives. It might be more productive to begin thinking about the status of the fetus by examining the language and customs that surround it. This approach will encourage us to focus on the choosing, acting woman, rather than the act of abortion—as if the act were performed by abstract forces without bodies, histories, attachments.

This focus on the acting woman is useful because a pregnant woman has an identifiable, consistent ontology, and a fetus takes on different ontological identities over time. But common sense, experience, and linguistic usage point clearly to the fact that we habitually consider, for example, a seven-week-old fetus to be different from a seven-month-old one. We can tell this by the way we respond to the involuntary loss of one as against the other. We have different language for the experience of the involuntary expulsion of the fetus from the womb depending upon the point of gestation at which the experience occurs. If it occurs early in the pregnancy, we call it a miscarriage; if late, we call it a stillbirth.

We would have an extreme reaction to the reversal of those terms. If a woman referred to a miscarriage at seven weeks as a stillbirth, we would be alarmed. It would shock our sense of propriety; it would make us uneasy; we would find it disturbing, misplaced—as we do when a bag lady sits down in a restaurant and starts shouting, or an octogenarian arrives at our door in a sailor suit. In short, we would suspect that the speaker was mad. Similarly, if a doctor or a nurse referred to the loss of a seven-month-old fetus as a mis-carriage, we would be shocked by that person's insensitivity: could she or he not understand that a fetus that age is not what it was months before?

Our ritual and religious practices underscore the fact that we make distinc-tions among fetuses. If a woman took the bloody matter—indistinguishable from a heavy period—of an early miscarriage and insisted upon putting it in a tiny coffin and marking its grave, we would have serious concerns about her mental health. By the same token, we would feel squeamish about flushing a seven-month-old fetus down the toilet—something we would quite normally do with an early miscarriage. There are no prayers for the matter of a miscarriage, nor do we feel there should be. Even a Catholic priest would not baptize the issue of an early miscarriage.

The difficulties stem, of course, from the odd situation of a fetus's ontology: a complicated, differentiated, and nuanced response is required when we are dealing with an entity that changes over time. Yet we are in the habit of making distinctions like this. At one point we know that a child is no longer a child but an adult. That this question is vexed and problematic is clear from our difficulty in determining who is a juvenile offender and who is an adult criminal and at what age sexual intercourse ceases to be known as statutory rape. So at what point, if any, do we on the pro-choice side say that the developing fetus is a person, with rights equal to its mother's?

The anti-choice people have one advantage over us; their monolithic position gives them unity on this question. For myself, I am made uneasy by third-trimester abortions, which take place when the fetus could live outside the mother's body, but I also know that these are extremely rare and often performed on very young girls who have had difficulty comprehending the realities of pregnancy. It seems to me that the question of late abortions should be decided case by case, and that fixation on this issue is a deflection from what is most important: keeping early abortions, which are in the majority by far, safe and legal. I am also politically realistic enough to suspect that bills restricting late abortions are not good-faith attempts to make distinctions about the nature of fetal life. They are, rather, the cynical embodiments of the hope among anti-choice partisans that technology will be on their side and that medical science's ability to create situations in which younger fetuses are viable outside their mothers' bodies will increase dramatically in the next few years. Ironically, medical science will probably make the issue of abortion a minor one in the near future. The RU-486 pill, which can induce abortion early on, exists, and whether or not it is legally available (it is not on the market here, because of pressure from anti-choice groups), women will begin to obtain it. If abortion can occur through chemical rather than physical means, in the privacy of one's home, most people not directly involved will lose interest in it. As abortion is transformed from a public into a private issue, it will cease to be perceived as political; it will be called personal instead.

An Equivocal Good

But because abortion will always deal with what it is to create and sustain life, it will always be a moral issue. And whether we like it or not, our moral thinking about abortion is rooted in the shifting soil of perception. In an age in which much of our perception is manipulated by media that specialize in the sound bite and the photo op, the anti-choice partisans have a twofold advantage over us on the pro-choice side. The pro-choice moral position is more complex, and the experience we defend is physically repellent to contemplate. None of us in the pro-choice movement would suggest that abortion is not a regrettable occurrence. Anti-choice proponents can offer pastel photographs of babies in buntings, their eyes peaceful in the camera's gaze. In answer, we can't offer the material of an early abortion, bloody, amorphous in a paper cup, to prove that what has just been removed from the woman's body is not a child, not in the same category of being as the adorable bundle in an adoptive mother's arms. It is not a pleasure to look at the physical evidence of abortion, and most of us don't get the opportunity to do so.

The theologian Daniel Maguire, uncomfortable with the fact that most theological arguments about the nature of abortion are made by men who have never been anywhere near an actual abortion, decided to visit a clinic and observe abortions being performed. He didn't find the experience easy, but he knew that before he could in good conscience make a moral judgment on abortion, he needed to experience through his senses what an aborted fetus is like: he needed to look at and touch the controversial entity. He held in his hand the bloody fetal stuff; the eight-week-old fetus fit in the palm of his hand, and it certainly bore no resemblance to either of his two children when he had held them moments after their birth. He knew at that point what women who have experienced early abortions and miscarriages know: that some event occurred, possibly even a dramatic one, but it was not the death of a child.

Because issues of pregnancy and birth are both physical and metaphorical, we must constantly step back and forth between ways of perceiving the world. When we speak of gestation, we are often talking in terms of potential, about events and objects to which we attach our hopes, fears, dreams, and ideals. A mother can speak to the fetus in her uterus and name it; she and her mate may decorate a nursery according to their vision of the good life; they may choose for an embryo a college, a profession, a dwelling. But those of us who are trying to think morally about pregnancy and birth must remember that these feelings are our own projections onto what is in reality an inappropriate object. However charmed we may be by an expectant father's buying a little football for something inside his wife's belly, we shouldn't make public policy based on such actions, nor should we force others to live their lives conforming to our fantasies.

As a society, we are making decisions that pit the complicated future of a complex adult against the fate of a mass of cells lacking cortical development. The moral pressure should be on distinguishing the true from the false, the real suffering of living persons from our individual and often idiosyncratic dreams and fears. We must make decisions on abortion based on an understanding of how people really do live. We must be able to say that poverty is worse than not being poor, that having dignified and meaningful work is better than working in conditions of degradation, that raising a child one loves and has desired is better than raising a child in resentment and rage, that it is better for a twelve-year-old not to endure the trauma of having a child when she is herself a child.

When we put these ideas against the ideas of "child" or "baby," we seem to be making a horrifying choice of life-style over life. But in fact we are telling the truth of what it means to bear a child, and what the experience of abortion really is. This is extremely difficult, for the object of the discussion is hidden, changing, potential. We make our decisions on the basis of approximate and inadequate language, often on the basis of fantasies and fears. It will always be crucial to try to separate genuine moral concern from phobia, punitiveness, superstition, anxiety, a desperate search for certainty in an uncertain world.

One of the certainties that is removed if we accept the consequences of the pro-choice position is the belief that the birth of a child is an unequivocal good. In real life we act knowing that the birth of a child is not always a good thing: people are sometimes depressed, angry, rejecting, at the birth of a child. But this is a difficult truth to tell; we don't like to say it, and one of the fears preyed on by anti-choice proponents is that if we cannot look at the birth of a child as an unequivocal good, then there is nothing to look toward. The desire for security of the imagination, for typological fixity, particularly in the area of "the good," is an understandable desire. It must seem to some anti-choice people that we on the pro-choice side are not only murdering innocent children but also murdering hope. Those of us who have experienced the birth of a desired child and felt the joy of that moment can be tempted into believing that it was the physical experience of the birth itself that was the joy. But it is crucial to remember that the birth of a child itself is a neutral occurrence emotionally: the charge it takes on is invested in it by the people experiencing or observing it.

The Fear of Sexual Autonomy

These uncertainties can lead to another set of fears, not only about abortion but about its implications. Many anti-choice people fear that to support abortion is to cast one's lot with the cold and technological rather than with the warm and natural, to head down the slippery slope toward a brave new world where handicapped children are left on mountains to starve and the old are put out in the snow. But if we look at the history of abortion, we don't see the embodiment of what the anti-choice proponents fear. On the contrary, excepting the grotesque counterexample of the People's Republic of China (which practices forced abortion), there seems to be a real link between repressive anti-abortion stances and repressive governments. Abortion was banned in Fascist Italy and Nazi Germany; it is illegal in South Africa and in Chile. It is paid for by the governments of Denmark, England, and the Netherlands, which have national health and welfare systems that foster the health and well-being of mothers, children, the old, and the handicapped.

Advocates of outlawing abortion often refer to women seeking abortion as self-indulgent and materialistic. In fact these accusations mask a discomfort with female sexuality, sexual pleasure, and sexual autonomy.

It is possible for a woman to have a sexual life unriddled by fear only if she can be confident that she need not pay for a failure of technology or judgment (and who among us has never once been swept away in the heat of a sexual moment?) by taking upon herself the crushing burden of unchosen motherhood.

It is no accident, therefore, that the increased appeal of measures to restrict maternal conduct during pregnancy—and a new focus on the physical autonomy of the pregnant woman—have come into public discourse at precisely the time when women are achieving unprecedented levels of economic and political autonomy. What has surprised me is that some of this new anti-autonomy talk comes to us from the left. An example of this new discourse is an article by Christopher Hitchens that appeared in *The Nation* last April, in which the author asserts his discomfort with abortion. Hitchens's tone is impeccably British: arch, light, we're men of the left.

> Anyone who has ever seen a sonogram or has spent even an hour with a textbook on embryology knows that the emotions are not the deciding factor. In order to terminate a pregnancy, you have to still a heartbeat, switch off a developing brain, and whatever the method, break some bones and rupture some organs. As to whether this involves pain on the "Silent Scream" scale, I have no idea. The "right to life" leadership, again, has cheapened everything it touches. ["Silent Scream" refers to Dr. Bernard Nathanson's widely debated antiabortion film *The Silent Scream*, in which an abortion on a 12-week-old fetus is shown from inside the uterus.—Eds.]

"It is a pity," Hitchens goes on to say, "that . . . the majority of feminists and their allies have stuck to the dead ground of 'Me Decade' possessive individualism, an ideology that has more in common than it admits with the prehistoric right, which it claims to oppose but has in fact encouraged." Hitchens proposes, as an alternative, a program of social reform that would make contraception free and support a national adoption service. In his opinion, it would seem, women have abortions for only two reasons: because they are selfish or because they are poor. If the state will take care of the economic problems and the bureaucratic messiness around adoption, it remains only for the possessive individualists to get their act together and walk with their babies into the communal utopia of the future. Hitchens would allow victims of rape or incest to have free abortions, on the grounds that since they didn't choose to have sex, the women should not be forced to have the babies. This would seem to put the issue of volition in a wrong and telling place. To Hitchens's mind, it would appear, if a woman chooses to have sex, she can't choose whether or not to have a baby. The implications of this are clear. If a woman is consciously and volitionally sexual, she should be prepared to take her medicine. And what medicine must the consciously sexual male take? Does Hitchens really believe, or want us to believe, that every male who has unintentionally impregnated a woman will be involved in the lifelong responsibility for the upbringing of the engendered child? Can he honestly say that he has observed this behavior—or, indeed, would want to see it observed—in the world in which he lives?

Real Choices

It is essential for a moral decision about abortion to be made in an atmosphere of open, critical thinking. We on the pro-choice side must accept that there are indeed anti-choice activists who take their position in good faith. I believe, however, that they are people for whom childbirth is an emotionally overladen topic, people who are susceptible to unclear thinking because of their unrealistic hopes and fears. It is important for us in the pro-choice movement to be open in discussing those areas involving abortion which are nebulous and unclear. But we must not forget that there are some things that we know to be undeniably true. There are some undeniable bad consequences of a woman's being forced to bear a child against her will. First is the trauma of going through a pregnancy and giving birth to a child who is not desired, a trauma more long-lasting than that experienced by some (only some) women who experience an early abortion. The grief of giving up a child at its birth—and at nine months it is a child whom one has felt move inside one's body—is underestimated both by anti-choice partisans and by those for whom access to adoptable children is important. This grief should not be forced on any woman—or, indeed, encouraged by public policy.

We must be realistic about the impact on society of millions of unwanted children in an overpopulated world. Most of the time, human beings have sex not because they want to make babies. Yet throughout history sex has resulted in unwanted pregnancies. And women have always aborted. One thing that is not hidden, mysterious, or debatable is that making abortion illegal will result in the deaths of women, as it has always done. Is our historical memory so short that none of us remember aunts, sisters, friends, or mothers who were killed or rendered sterile by septic abortions? Does no one in the anti-choice movement remember stories or actual experiences of midnight drives to filthy rooms from which aborted women were sent out, bleeding, to their fate? Can anyone genuinely say that it would be a moral good for us as a society to return to those conditions?

Thinking about abortion, then, forces us to take moral positions as adults who understand the complexities of the world and the realities of human suffering, to make decisions based on how people actually live and choose, and not on our fears, prejudices, and anxieties about sex and society, life and death.

POSTSCRIPT

Should Abortion Be Restricted?

The real issue dividing George and Gordon is whether or not the fetus is fully human, in the sense of being entitled to the treatment that civilized society gives to human beings. Their respective arguments use different methods of proof. George reasons from the biological premise that sperm and egg, each with 23 chromosomes, produce a fertilized human organism with the human's full 46 chromosomes; what occurs after that is simply human growth, which no one has the right to interrupt. Gordon reasons from the appearance of the fetus and how people normally react to it. Since even pro-lifers do not conduct funeral services and memorials for the "bloody matter" resulting from an early miscarriage, Gordon reasons, the Supreme Court was right to exclude early fetuses from legal protection. Such reactions, in George's view, proceed from emotion rather than reason.

Dozens of books have dealt with these questions since the Supreme Court's decision in *Roe v. Wade* in 1973. A comprehensive selection can be found in J. Douglas Butler and David F. Walbert, eds., *Abortion, Medicine, and the Law*, 3rd ed. (Facts on File, 1986). More briefly, most of the legal, ethical, and medical issues are considered in Hyman Rodman, Betty Sarvis, and Joy Walker Bonar, *The Abortion Question* (Columbia University Press, 1987). In *Real Choices* (Multnomah Press, 1994), Frederica Mathewes-Green argues the case against abortion from the standpoint of the harm (physical and psychological) that it inflicts on women. A similar approach is taken by David C. Reardon in *Making Abortion Rare* (Acorn Books, 1996) and in *Victims and Victors* (Acorn Books, 2000), coauthored with Julie Makimaa and Amy Sobie.

Robert M. Baird and Stuart E. Rosenbaum, eds., *The Ethics of Abortion: Pro-Life vs. Pro-Choice*, rev. ed. (Prometheus Books, 1993), contains a wide variety of views. An unbiased history of abortion as an American political issue can be found in Barbara Hinkson Craig and David M. O'Brien, *Abortion and American Politics* (Chatham House, 1993). In the world arena, Andrzej Kulczycki's *The Abortion Debate in the World Arena* (Routledge, 1999) examines how cultural history, feminist movements, the Catholic Church, and international influences have shaped abortion policies in Kenya, Mexico, and Poland.

If, as Gordon argues, the best way to determine the humanity of the fetus is by its appearance, what of late-term abortions? By the sixth month of pregnancy, the fetus begins to look very much like a baby. Should it then be protected by law? Although she confesses to be "uneasy" about third-trimester abortions, Gordon suspects that those who advocate bans on late-term abortions are not doing so in good faith. The suspicion between the warring parties to the abortion debate will likely continue.

ISSUE 15

Are Tax Cuts Good for America?

YES: Amity Shlaes, from *The Greedy Hand: How Taxes Drive Americans Crazy and What to Do About It* (Random House, 1999)

NO: Paul Krugman, from "The Tax-Cut Con," *The New York Times Magazine* (September 14, 2003)

ISSUE SUMMARY

YES: *Wall Street Journal* editorial writer Amity Shlaes maintains that the federal income tax is too high, too complex, and biased against high-income earners who invest in economic growth.

NO: Economist Paul Krugman believes that the Bush tax cuts increase economic inequality, contribute to a huge budget deficit, and endanger the future of Medicare and Social Security.

Benjamin Franklin is credited with having first said, "In this world nothing is certain but death and taxes." That does not mean that we have to look forward to either one. When the colonists confronted the collection of taxes by Great Britain, they proclaimed "No taxation without representation" and moved toward revolution and the creation of the United States.

In 1912 the Sixteenth Amendment to the Constitution was adopted, enabling the federal government to levy taxes directly on income. The following year Congress adopted a graduated income tax, ranging from a 1 percent tax on individuals and businesses earning over $4,000 (most Americans did not earn that much) up to 6 percent on incomes over $500,000. Since then, tax rates have gone up and down, but some measure of progressivity—higher rates for higher incomes—has been retained. However, every change in the tax code has produced new deductions, concessions, and loopholes that benefit some groups to the disadvantage of others, lengthen and complicate the law, and stimulate a major tax-filing occupation for accountants and tax lawyers.

No one likes taxes, but upon reflection most Americans are likely to agree with Supreme Court Justice Oliver Wendell Holmes, Jr., that "taxes are what we pay for civilized society." No other way has been devised to pay for such essential services as public education, police and fire protection, roads and public transport, and the military defense of the nation. So the question is not whether or not Americans should be taxed but how and how much.

By the standards of other nations, American taxes are low. In fact, every other industrial nation has higher rates of taxation, except Japan, whose tax rate is about the same as that of the United States. Nevertheless, Americans appear to respond more favorably than citizens of other countries to proposals to lower taxes. When presidential candidate George Bush in 1988 said, "Read my lips: No new taxes," he enhanced his prospects for election. But when then–president Bush ran for reelection in 1992, his broken promise contributed to his defeat.

President George W. Bush secured the enactment of substantial tax cuts in 2001, 2002, and 2003. Bush argued that these would result in new investments that would revive a declining economy after the end of the Internet boom of the 1990s. His critics maintained that the tax cuts were of significant benefit only for the wealthiest Americans and blamed them, in part, for the nation's half-trillion dollar deficit.

President Bush sought the elimination, and achieved the reduction, of the estate tax. The estate tax is imposed on the inheritances left by the wealthiest Americans. Opponents of this tax characterized it as a death tax that taxes for a second time money that had been taxed when it was initially earned. Defenders of the tax argued that only a small number of the wealthiest Americans are subject to the tax, which would raise hundreds of billions of dollars within two decades. Warren Buffett, the second wealthiest person in America (Bill Gates, founder of Microsoft, is the first) commented: "All those people who think that food stamps are debilitating and lead to a cycle of poverty are the same ones who want to leave a ton of money to their kids."

Almost all critics of federal taxation, apart from anarchists who oppose all government and extreme libertarians who oppose almost all government, acknowledge that government has an essential role in protecting national security, creating trade policy, preserving the environment, and continuing specific social welfare policies, such as Social Security and Medicare. Disagreement arises over how much government should do, how much it should tax, and how the tax burden should be shared.

In the following selections, Amity Shlaes argues that the American tax rate is too high, too complex, unfair in withholding income from wage earners, and biased against high-income earners. Paul Krugman believes that cutting taxes doesn't benefit the middle class, doesn't create jobs or growth, and will create a severe fiscal crisis that will lower the quality of education and health care for Americans of modest means.

 **YES**

The Greedy Hand

The father of the modern American state was a pipe-puffing executive at R. H. Macy & Co. named Beardsley Ruml. Ruml, the department store's treasurer, also served as chairman of the board of directors of the Federal Reserve Bank of New York and advisor to President Franklin Roosevelt during World War II. In those years Washington was busy marshaling the forces of the American economy to halt Japan and Germany. In 1942, not long after Pearl Harbor, lawmakers raised income taxes radically, with rates that aimed to capture twice as much revenue as in the previous year. They also imposed the income tax on tens of millions of Americans who had never been acquainted with the levy before. The change was so dramatic that the chroniclers of that period have coined a phrase to describe it. They say that the "class tax" became a "mass tax."

The new rates were law. But Americans were ill-prepared to face a new and giant tax bill. A Gallup poll from the period showed that only some 5 million of the 34 million people who were subject to the tax for the first time were saving to make their payment. In those days, March 15, not April 15, was the nation's annual tax deadline.

The Treasury nervously launched a huge public relations campaign to remind Americans of their new duties. A Treasury Department poster exhorted citizens: "You are one of 50,000,000 Americans who must fill out an income tax form by March 15. DO IT NOW!" For wartime theatergoers, Disney had prepared an animated short film featuring citizen Donald Duck laboring over his tax return beside a bottle of aspirin. Donald claimed exemptions and dependent credits for Huey, Dewey, and Louie.

As March 15, 1943 neared, though, it became clear that many citizens still were not filing returns. Henry Morgenthau, the Treasury secretary, confronted colleagues about the nightmarish prospect of mass tax evasion: "Suppose we have to go out and try to arrest five million people?"

The Macy's Model

Enter Ruml, man of ideas. At Macy's, he had observed that customers didn't like big bills. They preferred making payments bit by bit, in the installment plan, even if they had to pay for the pleasure with interest. So Ruml devised a plan, which he unfolded to his colleagues at the Federal Reserve and to anyone in Washington who would listen. The government would get business to do its work, collecting taxes for it. Employers would retain a percentage of taxes from workers every week—say, 20 percent—and forward it directly to Washington's war chest. This would hide the size of the new taxes from the worker. No longer would the worker ever have to look his tax bill square in the eye. Workers need never even see the money they were forgoing. Withholding as we know it today was born.

This was more than change, it was transformation. Government would put its hand into the taxpayer's pocket and grab its share of tax—without asking.

Ruml hadn't invented withholding. His genius was to make its introduction palatable by adding a powerful sweetener: the federal government would offer a tax amnesty for the previous year, allowing confused and indebted citizens to start on new footing. It was the most ambitious bait-and-switch plan in America's history.

Ruml advertised his project as a humane effort to smooth life in the disruption of the war. He noted it was a way to help taxpayers out of the habit of carrying income tax debt, debt that he characterized as "a pernicious fungus permeating the structure of things." The move was also patriotic. At Macy's, executives had found that a "young man in the comptroller's office who was making $75 or $100 [a week was] called into the navy at a salary of $2,600 and we had to get together and take care of his income tax for him." The young man, Ruml saw, would face a tax bill for a higher income at a time when he was earning less money in the service of his country. This Ruml deemed "an impossible situation."

Ruml had several reasons for wagering that his project would work. One was that Americans, smarting from the Japanese assault, were now willing to sacrifice more than at any other point in memory. The second was that the federal government would be able to administer withholding—six successful years of Social Security showed that the government, for the first time ever, was able to handle such a mass program of revenue collection. The third was packaging. He called his program not "collection at source" or "withholding," two technical terms for what he was doing. Instead he chose a zippier name: "pay as you go." And most important of all, there was the lure of the tax amnesty.

The policy thinkers of the day embraced the Ruml arrangement. This was an era in which John Maynard Keynes dominated the world of economics. The Keynesians placed enormous faith in government. The only thing they liked about the war was that it demonstrated to the world all the miracles that Big Government could work. The Ruml plan would give them the wherewithal to have their projects even, they sensed, after the war ended. Keynesianism also said high taxes were crucial to controlling inflation. The Keynesians saw withholding as the right tool for getting those necessary high taxes.

Conservatives played their part in the drama. Among withholding's backers was the man who was later to become the world's leading free-market economist, Milton Friedman. Decades after the war, Friedman called for the abolition of the withholding system. In his memoirs he wrote that "we concentrated single-mindedly on promoting the war effort. We gave next to no consideration to any longer-run consequences. It never occurred to me at the time that I was helping to develop machinery that would make possible a government that I would come to criticize severely as too large, too intrusive, too destructive of freedom. Yet, that was precisely what I was doing." With an almost audible sigh, Friedman added: "There is an important lesson here. It is far easier to introduce a government program than to get rid of it."

Such questions, though, had no place in the mind of a nation under attack. At the moment what seemed most important was that voters accepted the Ruml plan. Randolph Paul, a Treasury Department official and Ruml critic, wrote resignedly that "his plan had political appeal. Though he conceived the plan as getting people out of debt to the government, the public thought that Ruml had found a very white rabbit"—a magic trick—"which would somehow lighten their tax load."

❦

. . . Adam Smith described the "invisible hand," the hand of free commerce that brings magic order and harmony to our lives. Thomas Paine wrote of another hand, all too visible and intrusive: "the greedy hand of government, thrusting itself into every corner and crevice of industry." Today the invisible hand is a very busy one. Markets are wider and freer than ever, and we profit from that by living better than before. But the "greedy hand of government" is also at work. Indeed, in relative terms, the greedy hand has grown faster than the invisible hand. In the late 1990s, economists noted with astonishment that federal taxes made up one-fifth of the economy, a rate higher than at any time in American history outside of war. We cannot assign the blame for changes of such magnitude to Beardsley Ruml, who was, after all, not much more than a New Deal package man. The real force here is not even withholding, whatever its power. Behind Ruml's withholding lurks Paine's greedy hand.

. . . Today, more than half of the budget goes to social transfers mandated by expensive programs whose value many Americans question. Working citizens sense that someone is getting something, but that someone is often not they.

The avid tax haters who pop up occasionally in the news are the expression of this national unease. Their froth-mouthed manifestos strike us as extreme—how many of us truly want to "kill the IRS"?—but they reflect something that all Americans feel to some degree. Even the most moderate of us often feel a tick of sympathy when we hear the shouts of the tax haters. We think of our forefathers who felt compelled to rebel against the Crown for "imposing Taxes on us without our consent." We know we live in a democracy, and so must have chosen this arrangement. Yet nowadays we too find ourselves feeling that taxes are imposed on us "without our consent."

Washington doesn't necessarily recognize the totality of this tax frustration. The purview of the House Ways and Means Committee is limited to federal taxes, and so the committee writes tax law as if the federal income tax were the only tax in the country. The commissions that monitor Social Security concern themselves only with the solvency of Social Security, and so ignore the consequences of raising payroll taxes, or taxing pensions, at a time when income taxes are already high. Old programs with outdated aims stay in place. Newer ones, added piecemeal, often conflict with the old.

"Rube Goldberg machine," "unstoppable contraption"—none of the stock phrases adequately captures the complication that is our tax structure. As William E. Simon, a former Treasury secretary, once said, "The nation should have a tax system which looks like someone designed it on purpose." . . .

◦◦◦

Americans today are more prosperous than we have ever been. As a nation, we have come very far, so far that even our past is beginning to look different. In the 1960s, 1970s, and even the 1980s, we took Big Government America, the America of the postwar period, to be the only America, an America that permanently supplanted something antiquated. This conviction strengthened when we considered the enormous troubles that plagued us in those decades. Who else but government could end the underclass, right the wrongs of Vietnam, combat inflation?

We can see now that in those years we had a foreshortened view of history. From the heights of our new achievement, we recognize that the Great Society, for all its ideals, was something of an aberration. It is clear now that the self-doubt and gray misgivings of the Vietnam period were, in their way, just a momentary interruption. The inflation of the 1970s was an acute and terrible problem but a short-lived one. Our famous deficit agony— which so many commentators and foreigners alleged would bring us down—has, at least for the moment, receded. Today we are in many ways more like the America of Andrew Jackson or even Thomas Jefferson than we are like the America of Jimmy Carter.

This change was the result of enormous and serious work. We developed microchips and computers that secured our global economic dominance. We started the welfare state and then, when we saw it wasn't working, successfully ended it. We grew a stock market that will provide pensions for the baby boom and beyond. Serious challenges loom ahead. Unpredictable rogue states threaten our national security; the economy will not always live up to its 1990s boom. But we understand now that the key to sustaining our prosperity is recognizing that we are our own best providers. Thinkers from left, center, and right agree: we don't need a nanny state.

This American confidence is not new. It is simply a homecoming to older ideals, ideals that we held through most of our history. Self-reliance is the ultimate American tradition. Even through a good part of the Depression "no handouts" was Americans' self-imposed rule. We are coming to a new appreciation of what Tocqueville admiringly called "self-interest, rightly understood."

Yet we are still saddled with our tax structure, the unwieldy artifact of an irrelevant era.

Unburdening ourselves is not easy, but it is something we have in our power to do. Our impasse, in fact, contains the outline of its own solution, if only we allow ourselves to look at it clearly. What, exactly, does our long struggle with Paine's greedy hand tell us?

Taxes have to be visible. Beardsley Ruml's trap worked because it made taxes invisible. No one today willingly gives a third or a half of his income into a strange hand; we only pay our taxes now because the trap locked shut long ago. We never see our tax bill in its entirety except during the madness of filing season.

When we rewrite our arrangement with government, we need to write into it a tax structure that is clear and comprehensible, whose outlines we can see and consider whenever we choose.

Taxes have to be simple. The tax code is a monster of complexity, but it doesn't have to be. When rules are added to rules, the change may benefit certain classes, but they hurt the rest of us. The best thing is to settle on one system, even if someone shouts that it's not "fair" to everyone.

Taxes are for revenue. For fifty years we have used taxes to steer behavior. Indeed, politicians often used the argument that they were promoting social good through the tax code as window dressing for their real aim: getting at the revenue. None of us likes the result. We are responsible for our own fate; let government take what we choose to give it and then retreat.

Taxes have to be lower. We have managed to achieve prosperity notwithstanding high taxes. But that prosperity would have been greater without those taxes. The microchip, in its way, has allowed us to postpone our date with tax reform.

But epochal transformations like the computer revolution, or the Industrial Revolution for that matter, cannot be counted on to come every decade. Taxes will slow our economy if we don't bring them down to rates that allow us to sustain desirable growth.

We don't have to load extra taxes on the rich. We've learned that a tax system that punishes the rich also punishes the rest of us. Those who have money should pay taxes like everyone else. In fact the rich already carry more of the tax burden than any other income group. Yet history—the history of the 1980s in particular—has shown an amazing thing—that lower rates on the rich produce more revenue from them.

Progressivity has had its day. Let us move on to a tax system that is more worthy of us, one that makes sense for the country.

It's time to privatize Social Security. Many of the core tax problems we face today are in reality Social Security problems. Markets have taught us that they can do a better job than government in providing public pensions. We should privatize a portion of Social Security—at least three of the percentage points that individuals carry.

The only thing to guard against is a privatization that is not a true privatization. When government enters the stock market on behalf of citizens, as many advocates of Social Security privatization would like, that is not privatization. That is expanding the public sector at the cost of the private sector. An office in government that invests on behalf of citizens, as many are proposing, is an office open to enormous moral hazard. To understand this you need only to consider what would happen if the chairman of the Securities and Exchange Commission directly controlled a few hundred million shares of blue-chip stocks.

Individuals need to control their own accounts, just as they control the rest of their money. Government guarantees of returns are also guarantees of disaster. One need only look to our recent history with savings and loans to see that. Raising the ceiling on federal insurance of S & L accounts led to that disaster by giving S & L directors license without accountability. The cost ran into the hundreds of billions, but it was far lower than the cost a government guarantee on privatized Social Security would be.

Local is good. The enduring lesson of our schools crisis is that centralizing school finance to the state and federal level has not given us the equity or the academic performance we hoped for. These results have ramifications far beyond schools. The federal government cannot solve everything. Many problems—from school to health care to welfare—are better handled lower down. A wise tax reform is a tax reform that leaves much of the nation's work to the people and the officials they know. Trying to write a federal tax law that addresses all our national problems is a recipe for a repeat of the current trouble.

We must lock in change. In the 1980s, through tremendous political and social exertion, the nation joined together to lower tax rates and prune out many of the code's absurdities. Within a few years, Washington had destroyed its own child. This time we must fix our change so the fiddlers can't get at it. . . .

Most Americans are not fire-breathing radicals or Ruby Ridge survivalists. They don't want to "kill the IRS." They just want a common-sense change in the system. And that is what they are telling lawmakers. When Steve LaTourette, a Republican congressman from Ohio, surveyed his constituents, he found that just about half wanted the IRS abolished. But a full three quarters wanted to see the tax code itself abolished. They saw that the code, not the bureaucrats, was the problem.

The second part of the program is to make the change truly permanent through a constitutional amendment. Our nation's last experience of trying to pass a significant-seeming constitutional amendment—the Equal Rights Amendment—was a bitter one. It soured Washington on amendments in general. Hesitation over amendments goes a long way toward explaining the current Republican foundering.

A constitutional amendment that calls for limiting federal taxes, including Social Security, to 25 percent of our income, or even a lower share, would be an important first step out of the logjam. For one thing, states would have to ratify the change, and that would allow us to have a much needed national discussion about taxes. Citizens would have to consider what lawmakers were proposing. This would give voters a chance to get around the lobbies and politicians who have kept the tax debate to themselves. It would get us all back into the discussion.

The third step is to realize that as a people we want to pay taxes. Roosevelt called taxes "the dues we pay for organized society." We still feel that way.

But people want a tax system that doesn't intrude on our private lives while it collects those dues; and we want those dues to be spent in a reasonable, limited way. We want a tax code that, to quote former Treasury secretary William Simon again, looks as if somebody designed it on purpose. Not a giant machine that collects our money merely to feed the monster.

NO

Paul Krugman

The Tax-Cut Con

1. The Cartoon and the Reality

Bruce Tinsley's comic strip, "Mallard Fillmore," is, he says, "for the average person out there: the forgotten American taxpayer who's sick of the liberal media." In June, that forgotten taxpayer made an appearance in the strip, attacking his TV set with a baseball bat and yelling: "I can't afford to send my kids to college, or even take 'em out of their substandard public school, because the federal, state and local governments take more than 50 percent of my income in taxes. And then the guy on the news asks with a straight face whether or not we can 'afford' tax cuts."

But that's just a cartoon. Meanwhile, Bob Riley has to face the reality.

Riley knows all about substandard public schools. He's the governor of Alabama, which ranks near the bottom of the nation in both spending per pupil and educational achievement. The state has also neglected other public services—for example, 28,000 inmates are held in a prison system built for 12,000. And thanks in part to a lack of health care, it has the second-highest infant mortality in the nation.

When he was a member of Congress, Riley, a Republican, was a staunch supporter of tax cuts. Faced with a fiscal crisis in his state, however, he seems to have had an epiphany. He decided that it was impossible to balance Alabama's budget without a significant tax increase. And that, apparently, led him to reconsider everything. "The largest tax increase in state history just to maintain the status quo?" he asked. "I don't think so." Instead, Riley proposed a wholesale restructuring of the state's tax system: reducing taxes on the poor and middle class while raising them on corporations and the rich and increasing overall tax receipts enough to pay for a big increase in education spending. You might call it a New Deal for Alabama.

Nobody likes paying taxes, and no doubt some Americans are as angry about their taxes as Tinsley's imaginary character. But most Americans also care a lot about the things taxes pay for. All politicians say they're for public education; almost all of them also say they support a strong national defense, maintaining Social Security and, if anything, expanding the coverage of Medicare. When the "guy on the news" asks whether we can afford a tax cut, he's asking whether, after yet another tax cut goes through, there will be enough money to pay for those things. And the answer is no.

But it's very difficult to get that answer across in modern American politics, which has been dominated for 25 years by a crusade against taxes.

I don't use the word "crusade" lightly. The advocates of tax cuts are relentless, even fanatical. An indication of the movement's fervor—and of its political power—came during the Iraq war. War is expensive and is almost always accompanied by tax increases. But not in 2003. "Nothing is more important in the face of a war," declared Tom DeLay, the House majority leader, "than cutting taxes." And sure enough, taxes were cut, not just in a time of war but also in the face of record budget deficits. Nor will it be easy to reverse those tax cuts: the tax-cut movement has convinced many Americans—like Tinsley—that everybody still pays far too much in taxes.

A result of the tax-cut crusade is that there is now a fundamental mismatch between the benefits Americans expect to receive from the government and the revenues government collect. This mismatch is already having profound effects at the state and local levels: teachers and policemen are being laid off and children are being denied health insurance. The federal government can mask its problems for a while, by running huge budget deficits, but it, too, will eventually have to decide whether to cut services or raise taxes. And we are not talking about minor policy adjustments. If taxes stay as low as they are now, government as we know it cannot be maintained. In particular, Social Security will have to become far less generous; Medicare will no longer be able to guarantee comprehensive medical care to older Americans; Medicaid will no longer provide basic medical care to the poor.

How did we reach this point? What are the origins of the antitax crusade? And where is it taking us? To answer these questions, we will have to look both at who the antitax crusaders are and at the evidence on what tax cuts do to the budget and the economy. But first, let's set the stage by taking a look at the current state of taxation in America.

2. How High Are Our Taxes?

The reason Tinsley's comic strip about the angry taxpayer caught my eye was, of course, that the numbers were all wrong. Very few Americans pay as much as 50 percent of their income in taxes; on average, families near the middle of the income distribution pay only about half that percentage in federal, state and local taxes combined.

In fact, though most Americans feel that they pay too much in taxes, they get off quite lightly compared with the citizens of other advanced countries. Furthermore, for most Americans tax rates probably haven't risen for a generation. And a few Americans—namely those with high incomes— face much lower taxes than they did a generation ago.

To assess trends in the overall level of taxes and to compare taxation across countries, economists usually look first at the ratio of taxes to gross domestic product, the total value of output produced in the country. In the United States, all taxes—federal, state and local—reached a peak of 29.6 percent of G.D.P. in 2000. That number was, however, swollen by taxes on capital gains during the stock-market bubble.

By 2002, the tax take was down to 26.3 percent of G.D.P., and all indications are that it will be lower still this year and next.

This is a low number compared with almost every other advanced country. In 1999, Canada collected 38.2 percent of G.D.P. in taxes, France collected 45.8 percent and Sweden, 52.2 percent.

Still, aren't taxes much higher than they used to be? Not if we're looking back over the past 30 years. As a share of G.D.P., federal taxes are currently at their lowest point since the Eisenhower administration. State and local taxes rose substantially between 1960 and the early 1970's, but have been roughly stable since then. Aside from the capital gains taxes paid during the bubble years, the share of income Americans pay in taxes has been flat since Richard Nixon was president.

Of course, overall levels of taxation don't necessarily tell you how heavily particular individuals and families are taxed. As it turns out, however, middle-income Americans, like the country as a whole, haven't seen much change in their overall taxes over the past 30 years. On average, families in the middle of the income distribution find themselves paying about 26 percent of their income in taxes today. This number hasn't changed significantly since 1989, and though hard data are lacking, it probably hasn't changed much since 1970.

Meanwhile, wealthy Americans have seen a sharp drop in their tax burden. The top tax rate—the income-tax rate on the highest bracket—is now 35 percent, half what it was in the 1970's. With the exception of a brief period between 1988 and 1993, that's the lowest rate since 1932. Other taxes that, directly or indirectly, bear mainly on the very affluent have also been cut sharply. The effective tax rate on corporate profits has been cut in half since the 1960's. The 2001 tax cut phases out the inheritance tax, which is overwhelmingly a tax on the very wealthy: in 1999, only 2 percent of estates paid any tax, and half the tax was paid by only 3,300 estates worth more than $5 million. The 2003 tax act sharply cuts taxes on dividend income, another boon to the very well off. By the time the Bush tax cuts have taken full effect, people with really high incomes will face their lowest average tax rate since the Hoover administration.

So here's the picture: Americans pay low taxes by international standards. Most people's taxes haven't gone up in the past generation; the wealthy have had their taxes cut to levels not seen since before the New Deal. Even before the latest round of tax cuts, when compared with citizens of other advanced nations or compared with Americans a generation ago, we had nothing to complain about—and those with high incomes now have a lot to celebrate. Yet a significant number of Americans rage against taxes, and the party that controls all three branches of the federal government has made tax cuts its supreme priority. Why?

3. Supply-Siders, Starve-the-Beasters and Lucky Duckies

It is often hard to pin down what antitax crusaders are trying to achieve. The reason is not, or not only, that they are disingenuous about their motives—though as we will see, disingenuity has become a hallmark of the movement in recent years. Rather, the fuzziness comes from the fact that today's antitax movement moves back and forth between two doctrines. Both doctrines favor the same thing: big tax cuts for people with high incomes. But they favor it for different reasons.

One of those doctrines has become famous under the name "supply-side economics." It's the view that the government can cut taxes without severe cuts in public spending. The other doctrine is often referred to as "starving the beast," a phrase coined by David Stockman, Ronald Reagan's budget director. It's the view that taxes should be cut precisely in order to force severe cuts in public spending. Supply-side economics is the friendly, attractive face of the tax-cut movement. But starve-the-beast is where the power lies.

The starting point of supply-side economics is an assertion that no economist would dispute: taxes reduce the incentive to work, save and invest. A businessman who knows that 70 cents of every extra dollar he makes will go to the I.R.S. is less willing to make the effort to earn that extra dollar than if he knows that the I.R.S. will take only 35 cents. So reducing tax rates will, other things being the same, spur the economy.

This much isn't controversial. But the government must pay its bills. So the standard view of economists is that if you want to reduce the burden of taxes, you must explain what government programs you want to cut as part of the deal. There's no free lunch.

What the supply-siders argued, however, was that there was a free lunch. Cutting marginal rates, they insisted, would lead to such a large increase in gross domestic product that it wouldn't be necessary to come up with offsetting spending cuts. What supply-side economists say, in other words, is, "Don't worry, be happy and cut taxes." And when they say cut taxes, they mean taxes on the affluent: reducing the top marginal rate means that the biggest tax cuts go to people in the highest tax brackets.

The other camp in the tax-cut crusade actually welcomes the revenue losses from tax cuts. Its most visible spokesman today is Grover Norquist, president of Americans for Tax Reform, who once told National Public Radio: "I don't want to abolish government. I simply want to reduce it to the size where I can drag it into the bathroom and drown it in the bathtub." And the way to get it down to that size is to starve it of revenue. "The goal is reducing the size and scope of government by draining its lifeblood," Norquist told U.S. News & World Report.

What does "reducing the size and scope of government" mean? Tax-cut proponents are usually vague about the details. But the Heritage Foundation, ideological headquarters for the movement, has made it pretty clear. Edwin Feulner, the foundation's president, uses "New Deal" and "Great Society" as terms of abuse, implying that he and his organization want to do away with the institutions Franklin Roosevelt and Lyndon Johnson created. That means Social Security, Medicare, Medicaid—most of what gives citizens of the United States a safety net against economic misfortune.

The starve-the-beast doctrine is now firmly within the conservative mainstream. George W. Bush himself seemed to endorse the doctrine as the budget surplus evaporated: in August 2001 he called the disappearing surplus "incredibly positive news" because it would put Congress in a "fiscal straitjacket."

Like supply-siders, starve-the-beasters favor tax cuts mainly for people with high incomes. That is partly because, like supply-siders, they emphasize the incentive effects of cutting the top marginal rate; they just don't believe that those incentive effects are big enough that tax cuts pay for themselves. But they have another reason for cutting taxes mainly on the rich, which has become known as the "lucky ducky" argument.

Here's how the argument runs: to starve the beast, you must not only deny funds to the government; you must make voters hate the government. There's a danger that working-class families might see government as their friend: because their incomes are low, they don't pay much in taxes, while they benefit from public spending. So in starving the beast, you must take care not to cut taxes on these "lucky duckies." (Yes, that's what The Wall Street Journal called them in a famous editorial.) In fact, if possible, you must *raise* taxes on working-class Americans in order, as The Journal said, to get their "blood boiling with tax rage."

So the tax-cut crusade has two faces. Smiling supply-siders say that tax cuts are all gain, no pain; scowling starve-the-beasters believe that inflicting pain is not just necessary but also desirable. Is the alliance between these two groups a marriage of convenience? Not exactly. It would be more accurate to say that the starve-the-beasters hired the supply-siders—indeed, created them—because they found their naive optimism useful.

A look at who the supply-siders are and how they came to prominence tells the story.

The supply-side movement likes to present itself as a school of economic thought like Keynesianism or monetarism—that is, as a set of scholarly ideas that made their way, as such ideas do, into political discussion. But the reality is quite different. Supply-side economics was a political doctrine from Day 1; it emerged in the pages of political magazines, not professional economics journals.

That is not to deny that many professional economists favor tax cuts. But they almost always turn out to be starve-the-beasters, not supply-siders. And they often secretly—or sometimes not so secretly—hold supply-siders in contempt. N. Gregory Mankiw, now chairman of George W. Bush's Council of Economic Advisers, is definitely a friend to tax cuts; but in the first edition of his economic-principles textbook, he described Ronald Reagan's supply-side advisers as "charlatans and cranks."

It is not that the professionals refuse to consider supply-side ideas; rather, they have looked at them and found them wanting. A conspicuous example came earlier this year when the Congressional Budget Office tried to evaluate the growth effects of the Bush administration's proposed tax cuts. The budget office's new head, Douglas Holtz-Eakin, is a conservative economist who was handpicked for his job by the administration. But his conclusion was that unless the revenue losses from the proposed tax cuts were offset by spending cuts, the resulting deficits would be a drag on growth, quite likely to outweigh any supply-side effects.

But if the professionals regard the supply-siders with disdain, who employs these people? The answer is that since the 1970's almost all of the prominent supply-siders have been aides to conservative politicians, writers at conservative publications like National Review, fellows at conservative policy centers like Heritage or economists at private companies with strong Republican connections. Loosely speaking, that is, supply-siders work for the vast right-wing conspiracy. What gives supply-side economics influence is its connection with a powerful network of institutions that want to shrink the government and see tax cuts as a way to achieve that goal. Supply-side economics is a feel-good cover story for a political movement with a much harder-nosed agenda.

This isn't just speculation. Irving Kristol, in his role as co-editor of The Public Interest, was arguably the single most important proponent of supply-side economics. But years later, he suggested that he himself wasn't all that persuaded by the doctrine: "I was not certain of its economic merits but quickly saw its political possibilities." Writing in 1995, he explained that his real aim was to shrink the government and that tax cuts were a means to that end: "The task, as I saw it, was to create a new majority, which evidently would mean a conservative majority, which came to mean, in turn, a Republican majority—so political effectiveness was the priority, not the accounting deficiencies of government."

In effect, what Kristol said in 1995 was that he and his associates set out to deceive the American public. They sold tax cuts on the pretense that they would be painless, when they themselves believed that it would be necessary to slash public spending in order to make room for those cuts.

But one supposes that the response would be that the end justified the means—that the tax cuts did benefit all Americans because they led to faster economic growth. Did they?

4. From Reaganomics to Clintonomics

Ronald Reagan put supply-side theory into practice with his 1981 tax cut. The tax cuts were modest for middle-class families but very large for the well-off. Between 1979 and 1983, according to Congressional Budget Office estimates, the average federal tax rate on the top 1 percent of families fell from 37 to 27.7 percent.

So did the tax cuts promote economic growth? You might think that all we have to do is look at how the economy performed. But it's not that simple, because different observers read different things from Reagan's economic record.

Here's how tax-cut advocates look at it: after a deep slump between 1979 and 1982, the U.S. economy began growing rapidly. Between 1982 and 1989 (the first year of the first George Bush's presidency), the economy grew at an average annual rate of 4.2 percent. That's a lot better than the growth rate of the economy in the late 1970's, and supply-siders claim that these "Seven Fat Years" (the title of a book by Robert L. Bartley, the long-time editor of The Wall Street Journal's editorial page) prove the success of Reagan's 1981 tax cut.

But skeptics say that rapid growth after 1982 proves nothing: a severe recession is usually followed by a period of fast growth, as unemployed workers and factories are brought back on line. The test of tax cuts as a spur to economic growth is whether they produced more than an ordinary business cycle recovery. Once the economy was back to full employment, was it bigger than you would otherwise have expected? And there Reagan fails the test: between 1979, when the big slump began, and 1989, when the economy finally achieved more or less full employment again, the growth rate was 3 percent, the same as the growth rate between the two previous business cycle peaks in 1973 and 1979. Or to put it another way, by the late 1980's the U.S. economy was about where you would have expected it to be, given the trend in the 1970's. Nothing in the data suggests a supply-side revolution.

Does this mean that the Reagan tax cuts had no effect? Of course not. Those tax cuts, combined with increased military spending, provided a good old-fashioned Keynesian boost to demand. And this boost was one factor in the rapid recovery from recession that developed at the end of 1982, though probably not as important as the rapid expansion of the money supply that began in the summer of that year. But the supposed supply-side effects are invisible in the data.

While the Reagan tax cuts didn't produce any visible supply-side gains, they did lead to large budget deficits. From the point of view of most economists, this was a bad thing. But for starve-the-beast tax-cutters, deficits are potentially a good thing, because they force the government to shrink. So did Reagan's deficits shrink the beast?

A casual glance at the data might suggest not: federal spending as a share of gross domestic product was actually slightly higher at the end of the 1980's than it was at the end of the 1970's. But that number includes both defense spending and "entitlements," mainly Social Security and Medicare, whose growth is automatic unless Congress votes to cut benefits. What's left is a grab bag known as domestic discretionary spending, including everything from courts and national parks to environmental cleanups and education. And domestic discretionary spending fell from 4.5 percent of G.D.P. in 1981 to 3.2 percent in 1988.

But that's probably about as far as any president can shrink domestic discretionary spending. And because Reagan couldn't shrink the belly of the beast, entitlements, he couldn't find enough domestic spending cuts to offset his military spending increases and tax cuts. The federal budget went into persistent, alarming, deficit. In response to these deficits, George Bush the elder went back on his "read my lips" pledge and raised taxes. Bill Clinton raised them further. And thereby hangs a tale.

For Clinton did exactly the opposite of what supply-side economics said you should do: he raised the marginal rate on high-income taxpayers. In 1989, the top 1 percent of families paid, on average, only 28.9 percent of their income in federal taxes; by 1995, that share was up to 36.1 percent.

Conservatives confidently awaited a disaster—but it failed to materialize. In fact, the economy grew at a reasonable pace through Clinton's first term, while the deficit and the unemployment rate went steadily down. And then the news got even better: unemployment fell to its lowest level in decades without causing inflation, while productivity growth accelerated to rates not seen since the 1960's. And the budget deficit turned into an impressive surplus.

Tax-cut advocates had claimed the Reagan years as proof of their doctrine's correctness; as we have seen, those claims wilt under close examination. But the Clinton years posed a much greater challenge: here was a president who sharply raised the marginal tax rate on high-income taxpayers, the very rate that the tax-cut movement cares most about. And instead of presiding over an economic disaster, he presided over an economic miracle.

Let's be clear: very few economists think that Clinton's policies were primarily responsible for that miracle. For the most part, the Clinton-era surge probably reflected the maturing of information technology: businesses finally figured out how to make effective use of computers, and the resulting surge in productivity drove the economy forward. But the fact that America's best growth in a generation took place after the government did exactly the opposite of what tax-cutters advocate was a body blow to their doctrine.

They tried to make the best of the situation. The good economy of the late 1990's, ardent tax-cutters insisted, was caused by the 1981 tax cut. Early in 2000, Lawrence Kudlow and Stephen Moore, prominent supply-siders, published an article titled "It's the Reagan Economy, Stupid."

But anyone who thought about the lags involved found this implausible—indeed, hilarious. If the tax-cut movement attributed the booming economy of 1999 to a tax cut Reagan pushed through 18 years earlier, why didn't they attribute the economic boom of 1983 and 1984—Reagan's "morning in America"—to whatever Lyndon Johnson was doing in 1965 and 1966?

By the end of the 1990's, in other words, supply-side economics had become something of a laughingstock, and the whole case for tax cuts as a route to economic growth was looking pretty shaky. But the tax-cut crusade was nonetheless, it turned out, poised for its biggest political victories yet. How did that happen?

5. Second Wind: The Bush Tax Cuts

As the economic success of the United States under Bill Clinton became impossible to deny, there was a gradual shift in the sales strategy for tax cuts. The supposed economic benefits of tax cuts received less emphasis; the populist rationale—you, personally, pay too much in taxes—was played up.

I began this article with an example of this campaign's success: the creator of Mallard Fillmore apparently believes that typical families pay twice as much in taxes as they in fact do. But the most striking example of what skillful marketing can accomplish is the campaign for repeal of the estate tax.

As demonstrated, the estate tax is a tax on the very, very well off. Yet advocates of repeal began portraying it as a terrible burden on the little guy. They renamed it the "death tax" and put out reports decrying its impact on struggling farmers and businessmen—reports that never provided real-world examples because actual cases of family farms or small businesses broken up to pay estate taxes are almost impossible to find. This campaign succeeded in creating a public perception that the estate tax falls broadly on the population. Earlier this year, a poll found that 49 percent of Americans believed that most families had to pay the estate tax, while only 33 percent gave the right answer that only a few families had to pay.

Still, while an insistent marketing campaign has convinced many Americans that they are overtaxed, it hasn't succeeded in making the issue a top priority with the public. Polls consistently show that voters regard safeguarding Social Security and Medicare as much more important than tax cuts.

Nonetheless, George W. Bush has pushed through tax cuts in each year of his presidency. Why did he push for these tax cuts, and how did he get them through?

You might think that you could turn to the administration's own pro-nouncements to learn why it has been so determined to cut taxes. But even if you try to take the administration at its word, there's a problem: the public rationale for tax cuts has shifted repeatedly over the past three years.

During the 2000 campaign and the initial selling of the 2001 tax cut, the Bush team insisted that the federal government was running an excessive budget surplus, which should be returned to taxpayers. By the summer of 2001, as it became clear that the projected budget surpluses would not materialize, the administration shifted to touting the tax cuts as a form of demand-side economic stimulus: by putting more money in consumers' pockets, the tax cuts would stimulate spending and help pull the economy out of recession. By 2003, the rationale had changed again: the administration argued that reducing taxes on dividend income, the core of its plan, would improve incentives and hence long-run growth—that is, it had turned to a supply-side argument.

These shifting rationales had one thing in common: none of them were credible. It was obvious to independent observers even in 2001 that the budget projections used to justify that year's tax cut exaggerated future revenues and understated future costs. It was similarly obvious that the 2001 tax cut was poorly designed as a demand stimulus. And we have already seen that the supply-side rationale for the 2003 tax cut was tested and found wanting by the Congressional Budget Office.

So what were the Bush tax cuts really about? The best answer seems to be that they were about securing a key part of the Republican base. Wealthy campaign contributors have a lot to gain from lower taxes, and since they aren't very likely to depend on Medicare, Social Security or Medicaid, they won't suffer if the beast gets starved. Equally important was the support of the party's intelligentsia, nurtured by policy centers like Heritage and professionally committed to the tax-cut crusade. The original Bush tax-cut proposal was devised in late 1999 not to win votes in the national election but to fend off a primary challenge from the supply-sider Steve Forbes, the presumptive favorite of that part of the base.

This brings us to the next question: how have these cuts been sold?

At this point, one must be blunt: the selling of the tax cuts has depended heavily on chicanery. The administration has used accounting trickery to hide the true budget impact of its proposals, and it has used misleading presentations to conceal the extent to which its tax cuts are tilted toward families with very high income.

The most important tool of accounting trickery, though not the only one, is the use of "sunset clauses" to understate the long-term budget impact of tax cuts. To keep the official 10-year cost of the 2001 tax cut down, the administration's Congressional allies wrote the law so that tax rates revert to their 2000 levels in 2011. But, of course, nobody expects the sunset to occur: when 2011 rolls around, Congress will be under immense pressure to extend the tax cuts.

The same strategy was used to hide the cost of the 2003 tax cut. Thanks to sunset clauses, its headline cost over the next decade was only $350 billion, but if the sunsets are canceled—as the president proposed in a speech early this month—the cost will be at least $800 billion.

Meanwhile, the administration has carried out a very successful campaign to portray these tax cuts as mainly aimed at middle-class families. This campaign is similar in spirit to the selling of estate-tax repeal as a populist measure, but considerably more sophisticated.

The reality is that the core measures of both the 2001 and 2003 tax cuts mainly benefit the very affluent. The centerpieces of the 2001 act were a reduction in the top income-tax rate and elimination of the estate tax—the first, by definition, benefiting only people with high incomes; the second benefiting only heirs to large estates. The core of the 2003 tax cut was a reduction in the tax rate on dividend income. This benefit, too, is concentrated on very high-income families.

According to estimates by the Tax Policy Center—a liberal-oriented institution, but one with a reputation for scrupulous accuracy—the 2001 tax cut, once fully phased in, will deliver 42 percent of its benefits to the top 1 percent of the income distribution. (Roughly speaking, that means families earning more than $330,000 per year.) The 2003 tax cut delivers a somewhat smaller share to the top 1 percent, 29.1 percent, but within that concentrates its benefits on the really, really rich. Families with incomes over $1 million a year—a mere 0.13 percent of the population—will receive 17.3 percent of this year's tax cut, more than the total received by the bottom 70 percent of American families. Indeed, the 2003 tax cut has already proved a major boon to some of America's wealthiest people: corporations in which executives or a single family hold a large fraction of stocks are suddenly paying much bigger dividends, which are now taxed at only 15 percent no matter how high the income of their recipient.

It might seem impossible to put a populist gloss on tax cuts this skewed toward the rich, but the administration has been remarkably successful in doing just that.

One technique involves exploiting the public's lack of statistical sophistication. In the selling of the 2003 tax cut, the catch phrase used by administration spokesmen was "92 million Americans will receive an average tax cut of $1,083." That sounded, and was intended to sound, as if every American family would get $1,083. Needless to say, that wasn't true.

Yet the catch phrase wasn't technically a lie: the Tax Policy Center estimates that 89 million people will receive tax cuts this year and that the total tax cut will be $99 billion, or about $1,100 for each of those 89 million people. But this calculation carefully leaves out the 50 million taxpayers who received no tax cut at all. And even among those who did get a tax cut, most got a lot less than $1,000, a number inflated by the very big tax cuts received by a few wealthy people. About half of American families received a tax cut of less than $100; the great majority, a tax cut of less than $500.

But the most original, you might say brilliant, aspect of the Bush administration's approach to tax cuts has involved the way the tax cuts themselves are structured.

David Stockman famously admitted that Reagan's middle-class tax cuts were a "Trojan horse" that allowed him to smuggle in what he really wanted, a cut in the top marginal rate. The Bush administration similarly follows a Trojan horse strategy, but an even cleverer one. The core measures in Bush's tax cuts benefit only the wealthy, but there are additional features that provide significant benefits to some—but only some—middle-class families. For example, the 2001 tax cut included a $400 child credit and also created a new 10 percent tax bracket, the so-called cutout. These measures had the effect of creating a "sweet spot" that could be exploited for political purposes. If a couple had multiple children, if the children were all still under 18 and if the couple's income was just high enough to allow it to take full advantage of the child credit, it could get a tax cut of as much as 4 percent of pretax income. Hence the couple with two children and an income of $40,000, receiving a tax cut of $1,600, who played such a large role in the administration's rhetoric. But while most couples have children, at any given time only a small minority of families contains two or more children under 18—and many of these families have income too low to take full advantage of the child tax credit. So that "typical" family wasn't typical at all. Last year, the actual tax break for families in the middle of the income distribution averaged $469, not $1,600.

So that's the story of the tax-cut offensive under the Bush administration: through a combination of hardball politics, deceptive budget arithmetic and systematic misrepresentation of who benefits, Bush's team has achieved a major reduction of taxes, especially for people with very high incomes. But where does that leave the country?

6. A Planned Crisis

Right now, much of the public discussion of the Bush tax cuts focuses on their short-run impact. Critics say that the 2.7 million jobs lost since March 2001 prove that the administration's policies have failed, while the administration says that things would have been even worse without the tax cuts and that a solid recovery is just around the corner.

But this is the wrong debate. Even in the short run, the right question to ask isn't whether the tax cuts were better than nothing; they probably were. The right question is whether some other economic-stimulus plan could have achieved better results at a lower budget cost. And it is hard to deny that, on a jobs-per-dollar basis, the Bush tax cuts have been extremely ineffective. According to the Congressional Budget Office, half of this year's $400 billion budget deficit is due to Bush tax cuts. Now $200 billion is a lot of money; it is equivalent to the salaries of four million average workers. Even the administration doesn't claim its policies have created four million jobs. Surely some other policy—aid to state and local governments, tax breaks for the poor and middle class rather than the rich, maybe even W.P.A.-style public works—would have been more successful at getting the country back to work.

Meanwhile, the tax cuts are designed to remain in place even after the economy has recovered. Where will they leave us?

Here's the basic fact: partly, though not entirely, as a result of the tax cuts of the last three years, the government of the United States faces a fundamental fiscal shortfall. That is, the revenue it collects falls well short of the sums it needs to pay for existing programs. Even the U.S. government must, eventually, pay its bills, so something will have to give.

The numbers tell the tale. This year and next, the federal government will run budget deficits of more than $400 billion. Deficits may fall a bit, at least as a share of gross domestic product, when the economy recovers. But the relief will be modest and temporary. As Peter Fisher, under secretary of the treasury for domestic finance, puts it, the federal government is "a gigantic insurance company with a sideline business in defense and homeland security." And about a decade from now, this insurance company's policyholders will begin making a lot of claims. As the baby boomers retire, spending on Social Security benefits and Medicare will steadily rise, as will spending on Medicaid (because of rising medical costs). Eventually, unless there are sharp cuts in benefits, these three programs alone will consume a larger share of G.D.P. than the federal government currently collects in taxes.

Alan Auerbach, William Gale and Peter Orszag, fiscal experts at the Brookings Institution, have estimated the size of the "fiscal gap"—the increase in revenues or reduction in spending that would be needed to make the nation's finances sustainable in the long run. If you define the long run as 75 years, this gap turns out to be 4.5 percent of G.D.P. Or to put it another way, the gap is equal to 30 percent of what the federal government spends on all domestic programs. Of that gap, about 60 percent is the result of the Bush tax cuts. We would have faced a serious fiscal problem even if those tax cuts had never happened. But we face a much nastier problem now that they are in place. And more broadly, the tax-cut crusade will make it very hard for any future politicians to raise taxes.

So how will this gap be closed? The crucial point is that it cannot be closed without either fundamentally redefining the role of government or sharply raising taxes.

Politicians will, of course, promise to eliminate wasteful spending. But take out Social Security, Medicare, defense, Medicaid, government pensions, homeland security, interest on the public debt and veterans' benefits—none of them what people who complain about waste usually have in mind— and you are left with spending equal to about 3 percent of gross domestic product. And most of that goes for courts, highways, education and other useful things. Any savings from elimination of waste and fraud will amount to little more than a rounding-off error.

So let's put a few things back on the table. Let's assume that interest on the public debt will be paid, that spending on defense and homeland security will not be compromised and that the regular operations of government will continue to be financed. What we are left with, then, are the New Deal and Great Society programs: Social Security, Medicare, Medicaid and unemployment insurance. And to close the fiscal gap, spending on these programs would have to be cut by around 40 percent.

It's impossible to know how such spending cuts might unfold, but cuts of that magnitude would require drastic changes in the system. It goes almost without saying that the age at which Americans become eligible for retirement benefits would rise, that Social Security payments would fall sharply compared with average incomes, that Medicare patients would be forced to pay much more of their expenses out of pocket—or do without. And that would be only a start.

All this sounds politically impossible. In fact, politicians of both parties have been scrambling to expand, not reduce, Medicare benefits by adding prescription drug coverage. It's hard to imagine a situation under which the entitlement programs would be rolled back sufficiently to close the fiscal gap.

Yet closing the fiscal gap by raising taxes would mean rolling back all of the Bush tax cuts, and then some. And that also sounds politically impossible.

For the time being, there is a third alternative: borrow the difference between what we insist on spending and what we're willing to collect in taxes. That works as long as lenders believe that someday, somehow, we're going to get our fiscal act together. But this can't go on indefinitely. Eventually—I think within a decade, though not everyone agrees—the bond market will tell us that we have to make a choice.

In short, everything is going according to plan.

For the looming fiscal crisis doesn't represent a defeat for the leaders of the tax-cut crusade or a miscalculation on their part. Some supporters of President Bush may have really believed that his tax cuts were consistent with his promises to protect Social Security and expand Medicare; some people may still believe that the wondrous supply-side effects of tax cuts will make the budget deficit disappear. But for starve-the-beast tax-cutters, the coming crunch is exactly what they had in mind.

7. What Kind of Country?

The astonishing political success of the antitax crusade has, more or less deliberately, set the United States up for a fiscal crisis. How we respond to that crisis will determine what kind of country we become.

If Grover Norquist is right—and he has been right about a lot—the coming crisis will allow conservatives to move the nation a long way back toward the kind of limited government we had before Franklin Roosevelt. Lack of revenue, he says, will make it possible for conservative politicians— in the name of fiscal necessity—to dismantle immensely popular government programs that would otherwise have been untouchable.

In Norquist's vision, America a couple of decades from now will be a place in which elderly people make up a disproportionate share of the poor, as they did before Social Security. It will also be a country in which even middle-class elderly Americans are, in many cases, unable to afford expensive medical procedures or prescription drugs and in which poor Americans generally go without even basic health care. And it may well be a place in which only those who can afford expensive private schools can give their children a decent education.

But as Governor Riley of Alabama reminds us, that's a choice, not a necessity. The tax-cut crusade has created a situation in which something must give. But what gives—whether we decide that the New Deal and the Great Society must go or that taxes aren't such a bad thing after all—is up to us. The American people must decide what kind of a country we want to be.

POSTSCRIPT

Are Tax Cuts Good for America?

There is an obvious conflict between wanting to keep (and perhaps extend) most of the services and benefits that government provides and simultaneously wanting to lower taxes. Americans are increasingly skeptical about the uses to which their tax money is put. They do not understand how taxes are imposed, and they suspect that somebody else is getting a tax cut at their expense.

The consequences will likely be debated for many years. Do these tax cuts increase incentives for investment and spending, thus bolstering the economy and increasing tax revenues in the long run? Or do they unfairly reward upper-income earners, re-create federal deficits, and make it more difficult for Congress to adopt costly reforms that would benefit lower- and middle-income citizens?

The significant tax reductions that were adopted in 2001, 2002, and 2003 have contributed to the replacement of an anticipated federal surplus by a huge deficit in federal income.

John Podhoretz, *Bush Country: How Dubya Became a Great President While Driving Liberals Insane* (St. Martin's Press, 2004) defends the tax cuts and other fiscal policies as essential elements of the strategic policies of the Bush administration in reversing economic slowdown, encouraging business investment, and supporting the new expenditures for the war in Iraq and the war on terrorism. Current articles in *The Weekly Standard* and *National Review* make the case for eliminating dividend and estate taxes and reducing the cost of non-essential government services.

The title of David Cay Johnston's book criticizing tax policies of the second Bush administration clearly indicates its point of view: *Perfectly Legal: The Covert Campaign to Rig Our Tax System to Benefit the Super Rich— and Cheat Everybody Else* (Portfolio, 2003). Johnston believes that the tax code perpetuates a widening gulf between the super-rich and everyone else. Charles Lewis and Bill Allison, in *The Cheating of America: How Tax Avoidance and Evasion by the Super Rich Are Costing the Country Billions and What You Can Do About It* (William Morrow, 2001), are persuaded that the problem is not that Americans are taxed too much but that too many get away with paying too little.

John O. Fox, *If Americans Really Understood the Income Tax: Uncovering Our Most Expensive Ignorance* (Westview Press, 2001), cannot be characterized as favoring more or less taxation, but urges tax reform by eliminating special tax benefits and instituting lower taxes rate across the board.

ISSUE 16

Is America Becoming More Unequal?

YES: Jeff Madrick, from "Inequality and Democracy," in George Packer, *The Fight Is for Democracy* (Perennial, 2003)

NO: Christopher C. DeMuth, from "The New Wealth of Nations," Commentary, October 1997

ISSUE SUMMARY

YES: Editor and author Jeff Madrick maintains that the striking recent increase in income and wealth inequality reflects increasing inequality of opportunity and threatens the civil and political rights of less wealthy Americans.

NO: American Enterprise Institute president Christopher C. DeMuth asserts that Americans have achieved an impressive level of wealth and equality and that a changing economy ensures even more opportunities.

There has always been a wide range in real income in the United States. In the first three decades after the end of World War II, family incomes doubled, income inequality narrowed slightly, and poverty rates declined. Prosperity declined in the mid-1970s, when back-to-back recessions produced falling average incomes, greater inequality, and higher poverty levels. Between the mid-1980s and the late 1990s, sustained economic recovery resulted in a modest average growth in income, but high poverty rates continued.

Defenders of the social system maintain that, over the long run, poverty has declined. Many improvements in social conditions benefit virtually all people and, thus, make us more equal. The increase in longevity (attributable in large measure to advances in medicine, nutrition, and sanitation) affects all social classes. In a significant sense, the U.S. economy is far fairer now than at any time in the past. In the preindustrial era, when land was the primary measure of wealth, those without land had no way to improve their circumstances. In the industrial era, when people of modest means needed physical strength and stamina to engage in difficult and hazardous labor in mines, mills, and factories, those who were too weak, handicapped, or too old stood little chance of gaining or keeping reasonable jobs.

In the postindustrial era, many of the manufactured goods that were once "Made in U.S.A.," ranging from clothing to electronics, are now made by cheaper foreign labor. Despite this loss, America achieved virtually full employment in the 1990s, largely because of the enormous growth of the information and service industries. Intelligence, ambition, and hard work—qualities that cut across social classes—are likely to be the determinants of success.

In the view of the defenders of the American economic system, the sharp increase in the nation's gross domestic product has resulted in greater prosperity for most Americans. Although the number of superrich has grown, so has the number of prosperous small business owners, middle-level executives, engineers, computer programmers, lawyers, doctors, entertainers, sports stars, and others who have gained greatly from the longest sustained economic growth in American history. For example, successful young pioneers in the new technology and the entrepreneurs whose capital supported their ventures have prospered, and so have the technicians and other workers whom they hired. Any change that mandated more nearly equal income would greatly diminish the incentives for invention, discovery, and risk-taking enterprises. As a result, the standard of living would be much lower and rise much more slowly, and individual freedom would be curtailed by the degree of state interference in people's private lives.

None of these objections satisfies those who deplore what they characterize as an increasing disparity in the distribution of income and wealth. In 2002 the U.S. Census Bureau concluded that the relative prosperity of the 1990s left poverty virtually unchanged, with 8 percent of American families earning less than $17,600, the income level below which a family of four is considered to be living in poverty. One in five households was broke, with nothing to tide them over when confronted with unemployment or a health crisis—not to mention being unable to save for college or retirement. Contrary to the popular cliché, a rising tide does not lift all boats; it does not lift the leaky boats or those who have no boat. *Business Week* reported that the pay gap between top executives and production workers in the 362 largest U.S. companies soared from a ratio of 42 to 1 to 475 to 1 in 1989. The financial wealth of the top 1 percent of households now exceeds the combined household financial wealth of the bottom 98 percent.

Advocates of more nearly equal income argue that a reduced pay gap would lead to less social conflict, less crime, more economic security, and better and more universal social services. Also, more nearly egalitarian societies (Scandinavia and Western Europe, for example) offer more nearly equal access to education, medical treatment, and legal defense. What happens to democracy, some ask, when more money means better access to those who write and administer the laws and to the very offices of political power themselves?

In the following selections, Jeff Madrick examines the causes and consequences of income and wealth inequality, while Christopher C. DeMuth outlines a number of forces that have reduced inequality.

Jeff Madrick  **YES**

Inequality and Democracy

W hen I was a boy in the 1950s, "equality" was central to the public discourse. The word was seemingly everywhere. Equality before the law was widely thought of as an unquestioned good, charged with positive associations. Equality was an unquestioned component of American greatness, and of its democracy. We experienced it directly. Almost all of us went to public schools, drove on free and quite extraordinary public highways, and got our federally subsidized polio shots. Our GI parents went to college on the government dole and our teachers got federal subsidies for their education after Russia launched Sputnik.

Not all was ideal. Inequality of health care was never adequately or objectively discussed. That millions of African Americans were originally, and for a long time thereafter, excluded from this equality was still the nation's stunning hypocrisy. But in the 1950s, America was at least beginning to address this central tragedy more directly. "Separate but equal," the prevailing idea that justified legalizing school segregation, was disturbing because it clearly meant separate but unequal to a nation committed in its traditions to equality as a principle. Without that tradition, legal racism would have had an even more extended life.

But if equal rights before the law was an accepted principle of democracy, what can we say about economic equality and democracy? In this period, political and economic equality unmistakably went hand in hand. In fact, the association between political and economic equality made the very idea of equality fine and noble for us. In the 1950s, for example, civil rights clearly implied equality of economic opportunity, and equal economic opportunity implied a middle class life. It was a glorious time for the economy. Incomes grew for all levels of workers on average in America in these years, and the income distribution, which narrowed significantly during World War II, remained that way and even improved slightly for the next twenty-five years. The benefits of this most rapid period of growth in American history—at the least, on a par with the more uneven growth of the late 1800s—accrued to a new middle class.

Naïveté still abounded about how widespread prosperity was. In 1962 Michael Harrington's landmark book, *The Other America*, awakened the nation to convincing evidence that a large proportion of the population was still poor. Much of the nation was in truth appalled precisely because equality was a central American value. With the rise of a counter-culture and eventual antagonism toward the prosecution of the Vietnam War, America was no longer thought blemish-free, and the fight for equality, or at least rough fairness, became imperative in many spheres. Relatively few disputed that poverty implied unequal opportunity. The majority increasingly favored programs that were outright grants to the poor, which went against the grain of much of American history. In the past, we typically (with a few exceptions) only gave money to those who already worked or sacrificed for their country—Social Security, unemployment insurance, and war veterans. Now, there were new programs, such as expanded welfare and Medicaid, that simply handed out money with relatively few qualifications. The commitment to equality in these years extended to the new feminists, marked by a threshold book, *The Feminine Mystique,* and it was again not confined to matters of civil rights for women. The wide gap in pay for the same work became a key issue in the struggle for equality.

Times are entirely different today, and regrettably so. Political discussion about economic equality has essentially become a taboo. Social Security is no longer the third rail of politics; equality is. Congressmen and senators are cautioned against discussing it because it sounds like class warfare to the public. A wide range of people believe they are put at an unfair disadvantage by affirmative action, welfare, a minimum wage, and other social programs designed to level the playing field. Ironically, the aversion to discussing equality intensified as inequality of incomes and wealth increased over twenty years to levels not seen since the 1920s.

Where does income and wealth inequality start to impinge on civil and political rights, and on America's long commitment to equality of economic opportunity? Where does it both reflect a failure of democracy and contribute to its weakening? There is a good argument to be made that we are already there.

The past few decades are not the first period in which the nation devalued equality. In the second half of the 1800s and in the 1920s, economic inequality rose rapidly. It was accompanied by a contraction of American ideology that limited the nation's focus to the individualistic components and excluded the egalitarian aspects of the national character. Social Darwinism was the simplistic individualistic philosophy of the day in the late 1800s. Survival of the fittest was a natural law with which government should not interfere, its advocates argued. In the 1920s, there was again a momentary return to rough individualism. Rates for the relatively new income tax were slashed, for example.

In the national mythology, if Americans are left to their own devices, to fall and rise according to their talents, the simple values of early America will reassert themselves and all will be well. If there is more inequality as a result, that merely reflects the abilities and tenacity of individuals, not a failure of the nation. The dominant ideological tenet of the time held that, left to their own devices, most Americans would do well.

Was this ever true? There was plenty of poverty in early America, a strong landed plutocracy, and by any modern standards, times were difficult for most. But compared to conditions in the Old World, the romantic notions about opportunity in early America were based in a large measure of fact. Equal rights did mean in the 1700s and early 1800s, to a greater extent than ever before, equal economic opportunity, even if mere self-sufficiency for most. And self-sufficiency meant political independence that was entirely new for most whites. Many people today fail to realize that equality was a reigning principle of the early 1800s and even the colonial years. . . .

Today, . . . America accepts its growing inequality equably. Yet the increase in income and wealth inequality since the late 1970s is striking. In 1979 the top 5 percent of earners made eleven times more than those in the bottom 20 percent. Now they earn nineteen times what the bottom quintile earns. The top 10 percent earn 40 percent of total income in America: They earned only about 30 percent from the 1940s to the late 1970s. We are now back to the income-distribution levels of the 1920s. In terms of wealth—homes and financial assets such as stocks and bonds (less debt)—the top 1 percent have 40 percent of all assets, again about the same as in the 1920s.

Some of the skewing toward the wealthy has been the result of capital gains on stocks during the extraordinary bull market of the late 1990s, which are temporary. If we include only wages, salaries, government payments, rent, dividends, and interest, however, we find that income became highly unequal, anyway. Families in the top 20 percent earned ten and a half times what families in the bottom quintile earned in the 1970s.

Forbes magazine's four hundred richest Americans were almost ten times richer in 2002, on average, even after the market crash, than the four hundred richest were in 1982. The economy grew by only three times over this period, and typical family incomes only doubled. In 1982, when the list was started, it required only $50 million to make it; in 2002, it required $550 million. The average net worth was almost $2.2 billion. Kevin Phillips, author most recently of *Wealth and Democracy,* figures that ten thousand families in 2000, at the height of the market, were worth $65 million. A quarter of a million may have been worth $10 million or more.

The CEOs, of course, ate their cake and had it, too. In the late 1970s, the average CEO made twenty-five times what the average worker made each year. By 1988, that ratio had soared with the stock market and the enormous Reagan tax cuts. The CEO now made nearly one hundred times what the typical worker made. By 2000, with stock options and a bull market like no other, the CEO made five hundred times on average what the typical worker made.

Phillips and others point out that the last twenty years or so are a period much like the late 1800s, the era of the robber barons. But, in fact, there is a disturbing difference. When such fabulous wealth accrued in the past, such as in the late 1880s and the 1920s, the economy grew rapidly. Wages on average rose handsomely, even if unevenly, over these years for most levels of workers. So did the typical family's net worth. Rising revenues enabled the nation to afford a federal government that ultimately minimized worker abuses and established new regulations for trade and markets. A case could at least be made that rising inequality was a price worth paying for rapid economic growth—a case I nevertheless think is wrong. Had incomes been more equal and abuse less prevalent, I believe that the economy would have grown still faster.

Since the rise of inequality in the recent era, however, the economy grew unusually slowly with the exception of the late 1990s. Even including the rise in wages in the late 1990s, average wages in 2002 were still only slightly higher than they were in 1973. Male workers bore the brunt of this decline. As they grew older and more experienced, nearly half of them lost ground over twenty years and another 10 percent made almost no gain—an extraordinary failure unprecedented in American history over so long a period of time. Women, by contrast, experienced fairly rapid wage increases, but they were still earning less than men, often when they were doing the same job. Businesses clearly substituted lower-wage women for men in these years. But this did not explain the decline in the average wage for all workers. And, even with so many spouses working, family income rose at an unusually slow rate. It could no longer be argued that rising inequality was worth the price, as it could have been argued in the late 1800s and the 1920s, because the economy raised the standard of living for all others. In the last quarter century, this was not true.

Arguably, the accrual of individual wealth in this period was as extreme as in the Gilded Age, although comparisons are difficult to draw. By the late 1990s, the great fortunes were surely much larger than they were, comparatively speaking, in the 1920s or 1960s when the American economy as a whole did far better. When we analyze the data further, we find more disheartening news. Average retirement wealth rose over this period, but highly unequally. The economist Edward Wolff calculates that retirement wealth actually fell between 1983 and 1998 for well more than half of America's families. Childhood poverty rates are simply alarming. Every way they can be calculated, whether in absolute terms or by comparison to median or high incomes, a higher proportion of children live in poverty in America than in any other developed nation. Nearly one out of five children grow up in poverty in America, compared to one in twelve in much of Europe. Moreover, the gap between better off and poor children, according to economist Timothy Smeeding, was significantly wider in America than almost everywhere else in comparably advanced nations. Only British children were almost as disadvantaged.

The pressures of inequality are by now quite severe. The strain on working people and on family life, as spouses have gone to work in dramatic numbers, has become significant. VCRs and television sets are cheap, but higher education, health care, public transportation, drugs, housing, and cars have risen faster in price than typical family incomes and in many cases, such as higher education, health care, and drugs, much faster. Life has grown neither calm nor secure for most Americans, by any means. Only in the late 1990s did all levels of workers do well, but they still had not compensated for falling behind in the prior twenty-odd years.

Some argue that Americans did better all along than the data indicated. For a while, some even argued that inequality did not rise, a claim now totally discredited. But the data are clear and, furthermore, anecdotal evidence vastly supports the stagnating economic indicators.

Yet most Americans have accepted slow-growing or stagnating wages and widening inequality with little complaint about the economy, business, or the traditional guarantees of equal opportunity before the law. A key question is: *Why?*

There are a few possible explanations. By the 1970s, America was exhausted by the modern liberal social policies of Presidents Kennedy and Johnson, even though they worked better than was recognized. Welfare programs created dependencies, but poverty was dramatically reduced, racism was seriously circumscribed, good education was made widely available, Medicare was created, and under President Nixon, Social Security was seriously enhanced. Incomes had become much more equal over these early post–World War II decades.

The bigger source of moral exhaustion was probably the Vietnam War, a mostly liberal venture. By the time it ended, the nation seemed tired of government. And the prosecution of the war was not equal. As noted, it fell largely on young working-class men to fight. The educated easily escaped the draft.

But set against this moral political exhaustion, I think it was mostly slow economic growth, high inflation and interest rates, and lost jobs that turned the nation against its long-standing progressive attitudes. The nation had to apportion a pie that was growing much more slowly—that was simply much smaller than Americans had come to expect it would be, based on their history and traditions. Government was now easily portrayed as the cause of, not the solution to, economically tightened conditions. To many, equality now meant taking from those who worked to give to those who didn't, taking from the working class who were not disposed to higher education to give to those advantaged young people who were, helping people of color at the expense of people who were white. In the past, equality meant that most people's opportunities were expanded. But working people were now suffering, and they needed a scapegoat or two. Business escaped blame partly because government had dominated the previous period. We were tired of government. It did indeed wage an unpopular war and develop expensive new social programs. Moreover, businesspeople were not making fortunes in the 1970s. Profits in general were poor. The stock market stagnated at 1960s levels. There was less obvious cause to direct anger at them.

Ultimately, financially straitened workers did not want to pay more taxes; to the contrary, they wanted to pay less. Beginning in the difficult 1970s, victimized by both high inflation and deep recession, and before Ronald Reagan's large tax cut of 1981, the electorate rewarded politicians who promised tax cuts. . . .

A fundamental question for Americans is whether the inequality in outcomes since the 1980s reflected an inequality in opportunity in these decades. In other words, did it amount to a direct challenge to one of our basic ideals? I think it did. What stands out most is childhood poverty. When one out of five children is so disadvantaged, and another one in five is nearly poor, one simply cannot argue that opportunity is equal in America. The parents of these children are typically at work, they do not get decent childcare, and early education is out of the question. Their standard primary schools are almost always below average. Measures of education quality across America are not as bad as they are often reported to be. But there are huge pockets of inadequate education in poorer and working-class neighborhoods. Some other economies also produce large numbers of poor children. In France, for example, as high a proportion of children are poor as in America. But their significant government social programs raise the lower levels to acceptable standards. Because schools are financed locally in America, poverty and poor education have become a vicious circle. Money matters. As the Nobel Prize–winning economist George Akerlof points out, the evidence is considerable that money spent in these schools has productive results.

Further, as economies become more complex and change in other ways, burdens on people change as well, and they fall on them unequally. Not only the poor, but those in the middle now bear these burdens, and slow-growing incomes for the wide middle of America make opportunity unequal. In recent times, the so-called New Economy of the 1990s placed even more emphasis on education. This economy has created greater need for public childcare because spouses have to go to work. Its demand for worker flexibility means that as workers lose jobs, they also lose pension and health-care benefits. These are all "dis-equalizing" circumstances to which the government should respond but has not.

To the contrary, it has gone energetically in the other direction, creating inequalities rather than ameliorating them. Consider the litany. The rise of defined-contribution pension plans, which supplanted old-style defined-benefits plans, helped corporations reduce their contributions but, it turns out, only the better-off were better off with them. The middle- and lower-income workers did worse. If Social Security is privatized, elderly incomes will become significantly more unequal. The march toward deregulation and privatization—partly, but only partly, necessary—often favored the well-off at the expense of middle- and lower-income workers. The nation in these years steadfastly refused to raise the minimum wage until relatively recently. America did not seriously enforce worker-safety regulations. It did not support laws to enable labor unions to organize. It found no way to provide health insurance for the nearly 20 percent of people who were not covered. It did not strengthen accounting regulations, even when the Securities and Exchange Commission tried to, beaten back by angry legislators who were lectured to by their investment-banking and accounting-industry campaign supporters. CEOs took tens of millions of dollars, workers lost their savings. The government did not adopt new protective regulations, even after the debacle of Long-Term Capital Management. It wholeheartedly supported regulation-free capital flows around the world, even when they were a primary cause of the Asian financial crisis. It reduced the coverage of unemployment insurance significantly. It reduced tax rates dramatically for upper-income workers. In general, as noted, it allowed a financial movement on Wall Street to emphasize job cuts as the best path to profitability; taking on debt was not discouraged. Many economists exalted the restraint on wages but said nothing about overinvestment in high technology and telecommunications and absurdly romantic securities speculation. The Federal Reserve under Alan Greenspan was far more concerned about wage increases than about a stock-market bubble.

Let me be clear that some of these changes were necessary. Profits were probably too low in the 1960s and '70s, wages too high. Some federal programs were poorly thought out. Private business had become more sophisticated and government direction and sometimes even oversight were often no longer necessary. Some social programs will inevitably get more expensive, especially as the population ages, and therefore the nation has to deal with how to pay for them. International competition had toughened, and required leaner and more flexible companies. In general, tax revenues no longer grow as rapidly because the economy grows more slowly, so ultimately we can afford less. But the movement was carried too far, and government's role as a protector of equal opportunity and equal rights was often abandoned. The results showed up in falling wages, slow-growing family incomes, and rising inequality. It is not just the bottom 10 percent who have fared poorly. The lower 50 percent have, and in some ways, even the lower three-quarters are more strained than at any time in the post–World War II era. International competition from low-wage nations, a more sophisticated workplace, and slow growth all contributed to inequality. But government did not perform its traditional role of a counterforce to balance these other factors, and often exacerbated inequality in the name of self-reliance and limiting regulation in general.

What, then, is the case for equality in a democracy? Equal political rights may remain the most important issue. They are an end in themselves. But in practice, fairly equal economic outcomes have helped guarantee equal political rights. Nowhere has this been more true than in the American experience. The original source of political equality was not a simple social contract arrived at through agreement or revolution. Of course, John Locke's ideas mattered, and the European Enlightenment emboldened the Western world and valued the individual and his or her rights. But in America, the primary source of political equality was access to land. It was not an accident that Jefferson promised land to the thousandth generation when he purchased the Louisiana Territory. Land was not an issue of wealth to him but an issue of spreading political power.

Our current acceptance of inequality is dangerous for at least four reasons. First, it is unjust socially and may eventually generate spreading, if unarticulated, discontent, which will seek further scapegoats. Second, contrary to much conventional wisdom, inequality undermines economic growth because it limits the strength of demand, the optimism of a nation, and the capacity for people to educate themselves. Even now, only 60 percent of families own a PC; in contrast, by 1955, 90 percent of families had a television set, which was relatively much more expensive then. Wages were not sufficient to support booming demand in the late 1990s; consumers borrowed at record levels. Contrary to conventional wisdom of the moment, high levels of inequality imply generally low wages, and low-wage economies are generally inimical to growth. They do not create an internal market for goods and services on a sufficient scale to make production efficient. In *Why Economies Grow,* I argue that, historically, growing internal markets are a major source of economic growth, and perhaps the most important source. In fact, almost all economies that have taken off historically, such as those of the Netherlands in the 1600s or Britain in the 1700s, have been more egalitarian than those of their competitors. These domestic markets are themselves often the most important stimulants to capital investment and technological innovation. As British economic historian J.H. Habakkuk argued long ago, low wages do not provide incentives for business to invest in modern equipment or to train and provide private services for their workers. America's South, as economist Gavin Wright has shown time and again, beginning with his book *Old South, New South,* is still dominated by low-wage industries. Slow growth, in turn, invariably hurts lower-level workers more than the rest.

Third, unequal incomes can in themselves mean unequal opportunity. Poor families and even median-income families often cannot afford to live in neighborhoods that will provide their children with a decent education; they cannot get quality childcare when they have to work, and they cannot get adequate health care for the family. Costs of being middle class today— the costs of health care, education, transportation, and housing—have far outrun the incomes of the typical family, not merely those of the poor. Serious inequality of incomes and wealth already reflect unequal opportunity. Today, more than ever before, opportunity means a competitive education, and typically a decent higher education. But America probably has the most unequal education system in the developed world, supported by local tax revenues that reflect the incomes of the community. Vouchers are typical of the current response: They will save a few and discourage many, and on balance, will lead to more inequality. Those in the bottom half of America also cannot afford the best health care. They have jobs that do not provide health benefits. Poor health undermines equality of opportunity as well.

Fourth, inequality can lead to a skewing of political power toward elite interests. The congressional turn toward deregulation and lower taxes, many observers argue, is a function of the growing importance of money in politics. New well-financed think tanks supported by conservatives spread an ideology about the unimportance of equality and the dangers of government. Reforms, even of accounting principles, are beaten back by aggressive lobbyists with millions of dollars of campaign funds. Rightist foundations spend tens of millions of dollars to fight ideological battles. Most distressing, the growing numbers of those who do not vote in America are dominated by the least well off.

In my view, inequality means exclusion, and the nation needs something like a new social contract that emphasizes both inclusiveness and change. New programs should include a higher minimum wage, a still more expansive earned income tax credit, and serious savings subsidies for college. Efforts to universalize health care are critical, yet hardly addressed. Serious public investment must be directed toward equalizing education locally. Ideally, open discussion of how a high-wage economy can promote rather than impede growth will begin to change social norms about the expendability of workers. Campaign-finance reform should be enacted to minimize the growing political power of rich people and corporations.

The nation must also recognize that times change. Americans used to look forward, not backward. We built canals, railroads, primary and then high schools, public universities, vast public health systems to sanitize cities; we regulated business and put down a vast highway system. In retrospect, we think all this was inevitable, that the decisions made were obvious. But they were all reactions to change by an open and optimistic society. Now we scorn government responses to change. We look back, unwilling to risk. If we confronted change, we would emphasize new ideas. This means family-friendly policies like flexible hours and high quality day care. In a changing economy, with an increasingly expendable labor force, corporate benefits should be made portable.

A new New Deal? Of sorts, yes. Can we afford it? There are limits. But such programs can enhance economic growth, while reinforcing our long-held beliefs in equality. After a period of soaring income for the wealthy, higher progressive rates on very high incomes are entirely in order to pay for part of what we need. The preponderance of economic research suggests high marginal rates do not impede economic growth by undermining incentives for the wealthy.

But none of this is politically possible without a reinvigoration of fundamental principles. Our democracy is no longer working as it should. The influence of moneyed corporations has never been higher. But the most vigorous democracies are essentially about equality—in the case of America, about equality of civil rights and equality of economic opportunity in a complex and changing environment. Democracy is not about making economic outcomes equal. Americans want everyone and anyone to be able to make a fortune. But when outcomes are as skewed as they have been, it is clear that something in the process is badly wrong. Sustaining democracy may now depend on maintaining a vibrant spirit of national equality. If equality—let's call it inclusion, because that is what it is—were again the passion of the people, as it was two centuries ago, we might accomplish what is necessary. I doubt there is any true democracy without such a passion.

NO

Christopher C. DeMuth

The New Wealth of Nations

The Nations of North America, Western Europe, Australia, and Japan are wealthier today than they have ever been, wealthier than any others on the planet, wealthier by far than any societies in human history. Yet their governments appear to be impoverished—saddled with large accumulated debts and facing annual deficits that will grow explosively over the coming decades. As a result, government spending programs, especially the big social-insurance programs like Social Security and Medicare in the United States, are facing drastic cuts in order to avert looming insolvency (and, in France and some other European nations, in order to meet the Maastricht treaty's criteria of fiscal rectitude). American politics has been dominated for several years now by contentious negotiations over deficit reduction between the Clinton administration and the Republican Congress. This past June, first at the European Community summit in Amsterdam and then at the Group of Eight meeting in Denver, most of the talk was of hardship and constraint and the need for governmental austerity ("Economic Unease Looms Over Talks at Denver Summit," read the *New York Times* headline).

These bloodless problems of governmental accounting are said, moreover, to reflect real social ills: growing economic inequality in the United States; high unemployment in Europe; an aging, burdensome, and medically needy population everywhere; and the globalization of commerce, which is destroying jobs and national autonomy and forcing bitter measures to keep up with the bruising demands of international competitiveness.

How can it be that societies so surpassingly wealthy have governments whose core domestic-welfare programs are on the verge of bankruptcy? The answer is as paradoxical as the question. We have become not only the richest but also the freest and most egalitarian societies that have ever existed, and it is our very wealth, freedom, and equality that are causing the welfare state to unravel.

◦◐◦

That we have become very rich is clear enough in the aggregate. That we have become very equal in the enjoyment of our riches is an idea strongly resisted by many. Certainly there has been a profusion of reports in the

From Christopher C. DeMuth, "The New Wealth of Nations," *Commentary* (October 1997). Copyright © 1997 by The American Jewish Committee. Reprinted by permission. Notes omitted.

media and political speeches about increasing income inequality: the rich, it is said, are getting richer, the poor are getting poorer, and the middle and working classes are under the relentless pressure of disappearing jobs in manufacturing and middle management.

Although these claims have been greatly exaggerated, and some have been disproved by events, it is true that, by some measures, there has been a recent increase in income inequality in the United States. But it is a very small tick in the massive and unprecedented leveling of material circumstances that has been proceeding now for almost three centuries and in this century has accelerated dramatically. In fact, the much-noticed increase in measured-income inequality is in part a result of the increase in real social equality. Here are a few pieces of this important but neglected story.

• First, progress in agriculture, construction, manufacturing, and other key sectors of economic production has made the material necessities of life—food, shelter, and clothing—available to essentially everyone. To be sure, many people, including the seriously handicapped and the mentally incompetent, remain dependent on the public purse for their necessities. And many people continue to live in terrible squalor. But the problem of poverty, defined as material scarcity, has been solved. If poverty today remains a serious problem, it is a problem of individual behavior, social organization, and public policy. This was not so 50 years ago, or ever before.

• Second, progress in public health, in nutrition, and in the biological sciences and medical arts has produced dramatic improvements in longevity, health, and physical well-being. Many of these improvements—resulting, for example, from better public sanitation and water supplies, the conquest of dread diseases, and the abundance of nutritious food—have affected entire populations, producing an equalization of real personal welfare more powerful than any government redistribution of income.

The Nobel prize-winning economist Robert Fogel has focused on our improved mastery of the biological environment—leading over the past 300 years to a doubling of the average human life span and to large gains in physical stature, strength, and energy—as the key to what he calls "the egalitarian revolution of the 20th century." He considers this so profound an advance as to constitute a distinct new level of human evolution. Gains in stature, health, and longevity are continuing today and even accelerating. Their outward effects may be observed, in evolutionary fast-forward, in the booming nations of Asia (where, for example, the physical difference between older and younger South Koreans is strikingly evident on the streets of Seoul).

• Third, the critical *source* of social wealth has shifted over the last few hundred years from land (at the end of the 18th century) to physical capital (at the end of the 19th) to, today, human capital—education and cognitive ability. This development is not an unmixed gain from the standpoint of economic equality. The ability to acquire and deploy human capital is a function of intelligence, and intelligence is not only unequally distributed but also, to a significant degree, heritable. As Charles Murray and the late Richard J. Herrnstein argue in *The Bell Curve*, an economy that rewards sheer brainpower replaces one old source of inequality, socioeconomic advantage with a new one, cognitive advantage.

✦❀✦

But an economy that rewards human capital also tears down far more artificial barriers than it erects. For most people who inhabit the vast middle range of the bell curve, intelligence is much more equally distributed than land or physical capital ever was. Most people, that is, possess ample intelligence to pursue all but a handful of specialized callings. If in the past many were held back by lack of education and closed social institutions, the opportunities to use one's human capital have blossomed with the advent of universal education and the erosion of social barriers.

Furthermore, the material benefits of the knowledge-based economy are by no means limited to those whom Murray and Herrnstein call the cognitive elite. Many of the newest industries, from fast food to finance to communications, have succeeded in part by opening up employment opportunities for those of modest ability and training—occupations much less arduous and physically much less risky than those they have replaced. And these new industries have created enormous, widely shared economic benefits in consumption; I will return to this subject below.

• Fourth, recent decades have seen a dramatic reduction in one of the greatest historical sources of inequality: the social and economic inequality of the sexes. Today, younger cohorts of working men and women with comparable education and job tenure earn essentially the same incomes. The popular view would have it that the entry of women into the workforce has been driven by falling male earnings and the need "to make ends meet" in middle-class families. But the popular view is largely mistaken. Among married women (as the economist Chinhui Juhn has demonstrated), it is wives of men with high incomes who have been responsible for most of the recent growth in employment.

• Fifth, in the wealthy Western democracies, material needs and desires have been so thoroughly fulfilled for so many people that, for the first time in history, we are seeing large-scale voluntary reductions in the amount of time spent at paid employment. This development manifests itself in different forms: longer periods of education and training for the young; earlier retirement despite longer life spans; and, in between, many more hours devoted to leisure, recreation, entertainment, family, community and religious activities, charitable and other nonremunerative pursuits, and so forth. The dramatic growth of the sports, entertainment, and travel industries captures only a small slice of what has happened. In Fogel's estimation, the time devoted to nonwork activities by the average male head of household has grown from 10.5 hours per week in 1880 to 40 hours today, while time per week at work has fallen from 61.6 hours to 33.6 hours. Among women, the reduction in work (including not only outside employment but also household work, food preparation, childbearing and attendant health problems, and child rearing) and the growth in nonwork have been still greater.

There is a tendency to overlook these momentous developments because of the often frenetic pace of modern life. But our busy-ness actually demonstrates the point: time, and not material things, has become the scarce and valued commodity in modern society.

᠊ᡂᠺᡧᠣ᠊

One implication of these trends is that in very wealthy societies, income has become a less useful gauge of economic welfare and hence of economic equality. When income becomes to some degree discretionary, and when many peoples' incomes change from year to year for reasons unrelated to their life circumstances, *consumption* becomes a better measure of material welfare. And by this measure, welfare appears much more evenly distributed: people of higher income spend progressively smaller shares on consumption, while in the bottom ranges, annual consumption often exceeds income. (In fact, government statistics suggest that in the bottom 20 percent of the income scale, average annual consumption is about twice annual income—probably a reflection of a substantial underreporting of earnings in this group.) According to the economist Daniel Slesnick, the distribution of consumption, unlike the distribution of reported income, has become measurably *more* equal in recent decades.

If we include leisure-time pursuits as a form of consumption, the distribution of material welfare appears flatter still. Many such activities, being informal by definition, are difficult to track, but Dora Costa of MIT has recently studied one measurable aspect—expenditures on recreation—and found that these have become strikingly more equal as people of lower income have increased the amount of time and money they devote to entertainment, reading, sports, and related enjoyments.

Television, videocassettes, CD's, and home computers have brought musical, theatrical, and other entertainments (both high and low) to everyone, and have enormously narrowed the differences in cultural opportunities between wealthy urban centers and everywhere else. Formerly upper-crust sports like golf, tennis, skiing, and boating have become mass pursuits (boosted by increased public spending on parks and other recreational facilities as well as on environmental quality), and health clubs and full-line book stores have become as plentiful as gas stations. As some of the best things in life become free or nearly so, the price of pursuing them becomes, to that extent, the "opportunity cost" of time itself.

The substitution of leisure activities for income-producing work even appears to have become significant enough to be contributing to the recently much-lamented increase in inequality in measured income. In a new AEI study, Robert Haveman finds that most of the increase in earnings inequality among U.S. males since the mid-1970's can be attributed not to changing labor-market opportunities but to voluntary choice—to the free pursuit of nonwork activities at the expense of income-producing work.

Most of us can see this trend in our own families and communities. A major factor in income inequality in a wealthy knowledge economy is age—many people whose earnings put them at the top of the income curve in their late fifties were well down the curve in their twenties, when they were just getting out of school and beginning their working careers. Fogel again: today the average household in the top 10 percent might consist of a professor or accountant married to a nurse or secretary, both in their peak years of earning. As for the stratospheric top 1 percent, it includes not only very rich people like Bill Cosby but also people like Cosby's fictional Huxtable family: an obstetrician married to a corporate lawyer. All these individuals would have appeared well down the income distribution as young singles, and that is where their young counterparts appear today.

That more young people are spending more time in college or graduate school, taking time off for travel and "finding themselves," and pursuing interesting but low- or non-paying jobs or apprenticeships before knuckling down to lifelong careers is a significant factor in "income inequality" measured in the aggregate. But this form of economic inequality is in fact the social equality of the modern age. It is progress, not regress, to be cherished and celebrated, not feared and fretted over.

⁂

Which brings me back to my contention that it is our very wealth and equality that are the undoing of the welfare state. Western government today largely consists of two functions. One is income transfers from the wages of those who are working to those who are not working: mainly social-security payments to older people who have chosen to retire rather than go on working and education subsidies for younger people who have chosen to extend their schooling before beginning work. The other is direct and indirect expenditures on medical care, also financed by levies on the wages of those who are working. It is precisely these aspects of life—nonwork and expenditures on medical care and physical well-being—that are the booming sectors of modern, wealthy, technologically advanced society.

When the Social Security program began in America in the 1930's, retirement was still a novel idea: most men worked until they dropped, and they dropped much earlier than they do today. Even in the face of our approaching demographic crunch, produced by the baby boom followed by the baby bust, we could solve the financial problems of the Social Security program in a flash by returning to the days when people worked longer and died younger. Similarly, a world without elaborate diagnostic techniques, replaceable body parts, and potent pharmaceutical and other means of curing or ameliorating disease—a world where medical care consisted largely of bed rest and hand-holding—would present scant fiscal challenge to government as a provider of health insurance.

Our big government-entitlement programs truly are, as conservatives like to call them, obsolete. They are obsolete not because they were terrible ideas to begin with, though some of them were, but because of the astounding growth in social wealth and equality and because of the technological and economic developments which have propelled that growth. When Social Security was introduced, not only was retirement a tiny part of most people's lives but people of modest means had limited ability to save and invest for the future. Today, anyone can mail off a few hundred dollars to a good mutual fund and hire the best investment management American finance has to offer.

In these circumstances it is preposterous to argue, as President Clinton has done, that privatizing Social Security (replacing the current system of income transfers from workers to retirees with one of individually invested retirement savings) would be good for Warren Buffett but bad for the little guy. Private savings—through pension plans, mutual funds, and personal investments in housing and other durables—are *already* a larger source of retirement income than Social Security transfers. Moreover, although there is much talk nowadays about the riskiness of tying retirement income to the performance of financial markets, the social developments I have described suggest that the greater risk lies in the opposite direction. The current Social Security program ties retirement income to the growth of wage earners' payrolls; that growth is bound to be less than the growth of the economy as a whole, as reflected in the financial markets.

Similarly, Medicare is today a backwater of old-fashioned fee-for-service medicine, hopelessly distorted by a profusion of inefficient and self-defeating price-and-service controls. Over the past dozen years, a revolution has been carried out in the private financing and organization of medical care. The changes have not been unmixed blessings; nor could they be, so long as the tax code encourages people to overinsure for routine medical care. Yet substantial improvements in cost control and quality of service are now evident throughout the health-care sector—except under Medicare. These innovations have not been greeted by riots or strikes at the thousands of private organizations that have introduced them. Nor will there be riots in the streets if, in place of the lame-brained proposals for Medicare "spending cuts" and still more ineffective price controls currently in fashion in Washington, similar market-based innovations are introduced to Medicare.

◦❀◦

In sum, George Bush's famous statement in his inaugural address that "we have more will than wallet" was exactly backward. Our wallets are bulging; the problems we face are increasingly problems not of necessity, but of will. The political class in Washington is still marching to the tune of economic redistribution and, to a degree, "class warfare." But Washington is a lagging indicator of social change. In time, the progress of technology and the growth of private markets and private wealth will generate the political will to transform radically the redistributive welfare state we have inherited from an earlier and more socially balkanized age.

There are signs, indeed, that the Progressive-era and New Deal programs of social insurance, economic regulation, and subsidies and protections for farming, banking, labor organization, and other activities are already crumbling, with salutary effects along every point of the economic spectrum. Anyone who has been a business traveler since the late 1970's, for example, has seen firsthand how deregulation has democratized air travel. Low fares and mass marketing have brought such luxuries as foreign travel, weekend getaways to remote locales, and reunions of far-flung families—just twenty years ago, pursuits of the wealthy—to people of relatively modest means. Coming reforms, including the privatization of Social Security and, most of all, the dismantling of the public-school monopoly in elementary and secondary education, will similarly benefit the less well-off disproportionately, providing them with opportunities enjoyed today primarily by those with high incomes.

I venture a prediction: just as airline deregulation was championed by Edward Kennedy and Jimmy Carter before Ronald Reagan finished the job, so the coming reforms will be a bipartisan enterprise. When the political class catches on (as Prime Minister Tony Blair has already done in England), the Left will compete vigorously and often successfully with the Right for the allegiance of the vast new privileged middle class. This may sound implausible at a moment when the Clinton administration has become an energetic agent of traditional unionism and has secured the enactment of several new redistributive tax provisions and spending programs. But the watershed event of the Clinton years will almost certainly be seen to be not any of these things but rather the defeat of the President's national health-insurance plan in the face of widespread popular opposition.

The lesson of that episode is that Americans no longer wish to have the things they care about socialized. What has traditionally attracted voters to government as a provider of insurance and other services is not that government does the job better or more efficiently or at a lower cost than private markets; it is the prospect of securing those services through taxes paid by others. That is why today's advocates of expanding the welfare state are still trying to convince voters to think of themselves as members of distinct groups that are net beneficiaries of government: students, teachers, women, racial minorities, union members, struggling young families, retirees, and so forth. But as the material circumstances of the majority become more equal, and as the proficiency and social reach of private markets increasingly outstrip what government can provide, the possibilities for effective redistribution diminish. The members of an egalitarian, middle-class electorate cannot improve their lot by subsidizing one another, and they know it.

With the prospects dimming for further, broad-based socialization along the lines of the Clinton health-care plan, the private supply of important social services will continue to exist and, in general, to flourish alongside government programs. Defenders of the welfare state will thus likely be reduced to asserting that private markets and personal choice may be fine for the well-off, but government services are more appropriate for those of modest means. This is the essence of President Clinton's objection to privatizing Social Security and of the arguments against school choice for parents of students in public elementary and high schools. But "capitalism for the rich, socialism for the poor" is a highly unpromising banner for liberals to be marching under in an era in which capitalism has itself become a profound egalitarian force.

Where, then, will the battlegrounds be for the political allegiance of the new middle class? Increasingly, that allegiance will turn on policies involving little or no redistributive cachet but rather society-wide benefits in the form of personal amenity, autonomy, and safety: environmental quality and parks, medical and other scientific research, transportation and communications infrastructure, defense against terrorism, and the like. The old welfare-state debates between Left and Right will be transformed into debates over piecemeal incursions into private markets that compete with or replace government services. Should private insurers be required to cover annual mammograms for women in their forties? Should retirement accounts be permitted to invest in tobacco companies? Should parents be permitted to use vouchers to send their children to religious schools? Thus transformed, these debates, too, will tend to turn on considerations of general social advantage rather than on the considerations of social justice and economic desert that animated the growth of the welfare state.

Political allegiance will also turn increasingly on issues that are entirely nonmaterial. I recently bumped into a colleague, a noted political analyst, just after I had read the morning papers, and asked him to confirm my impression that at least half the major political stories of the past few years had something to do with sex. He smiled and replied, "Peace and prosperity."

What my colleague may have had in mind is that grave crises make all other issues secondary: President Roosevelt's private life received less scrutiny than has President Clinton's, and General Eisenhower's private life received less scrutiny than did that of General Ralston (whose nomination to become chairman of the Joint Chiefs of Staff was torpedoed by allegations of an extramarital affair). There is, however, another, deeper truth in his observation. The stupendous wealth, technological mastery, and autonomy of modern life have freed man not just for worthy, admirable, and self-improving pursuits but also for idleness and unworthy and self-destructive pursuits that are no less a part of his nature.

And so we live in an age of astounding rates of divorce and family breakup, of illegitimacy, of single teenage motherhood, of drug use and crime, of violent and degrading popular entertainments, and of the "culture of narcissism"—and also in an age of vibrant religiosity, of elite universities where madrigal singing and ballroom dancing are all the rage and rampant student careerism is a major faculty concern, and of the Promise Keepers, over a million men of all incomes and races who have packed sports stadiums around the United States to declare their determination to be better husbands, fathers, citizens, and Christians. Ours is an age in which obesity has become a serious public-health problem—and in which dieting, fitness, environmentalism, and self-improvement have become major industries.

It is true, of course, that the heartening developments are in part responses to the disheartening ones. But it is also true that *both* are the results of the economic trends I have described here. In a society as rich and therefore as free as ours has become, the big question, in our personal lives and also in our politics, is: what is our freedom for?

POSTSCRIPT

Is America Becoming More Unequal?

Almost from the day of its publication, *The Bell Curve: Intelligence and Class Structure in American Life* by Richard J. Herrnstein and Charles Murray (Free Press, 1994) became the basic text against equality in America. Murray insists that the book is about intelligence; his critics say that it is about race. It is about both, but above all it is about equality, why it does not exist (people are very unequal intellectually), why it cannot exist (intelligence is largely a product of inheritance), and why we should reconcile ourselves to its absence (because income differences and intermarriage among intelligent people will widen the gap).

The enormous publicity and sales generated by *The Bell Curve* led to the publication of books and essays rejecting its thesis. A large number of critical essays (by biologist Stephen Jay Gould, philosopher Alan Ryan, educator Howard Gardner, psychologist Leon J. Kamin, and others) purporting to refute what the authors call the unwarranted premises, shaky statistics, and pseudo-science of *The Bell Curve* have been gathered together in Russell Jacoby and Naomi Glauberman, eds., *The Bell Curve Debate: History, Documents, Opinions* (Times Books, 1995).

The issue of inherited intelligence and other capacities is not new. It is relevant to any consideration of whether or not America can or should be more egalitarian. What kind of equality—education, right to vote, before the law, economic opportunity, income—and what degree of equality is necessary for democracy to exist and thrive?

Scholarly studies tend to support the conclusion that the distance between the wealthiest Americans and the rest is increasing. Lisa Keister, in *Wealth in America: Trends in Wealth Inequality* (Cambridge University Press, 2000), provides an account of how wealth is acquired (she does not find a high correlation between income and wealth) and how it declines and increases over decades. In *Wealth and Democracy: How Great Fortunes and Government Created America's Aristocracy* (Broadway Books, 2002), Kevin Phillips argues that "laissez-faire is a pretense" because the rich consciously and successfully use government to increase their wealth and political power.

The differences in income, wealth, and social circumstances between whites and blacks are explored in Dalton Conley, *Being Black, Living in the Red: Race, Wealth, and Social Policy in America* (University of California Press, 1999). Conley concludes that the inheritance of property and net worth results in better schools, preferable residences, higher wages, and more opportunities for whites, further increasing the gap. Conley suggests an affirmative action policy based on social class as defined by family wealth rather than on race.

ISSUE 17

Does the Patriot Act Abridge Essential Freedom?

YES: Nat Hentoff, from *The War on the Bill of Rights and the Gathering Resistance* (Seven Stories Press, 2003)

NO: Heather Mac Donald, from "Straight Talk on Homeland Security," *City Journal* (Summer 2003)

ISSUE SUMMARY

YES: *Village Voice* columnist Nat Hentoff opposes the Patriot Act as an unjustified invasion of private belief and behavior, in the conviction that the sacrifice of liberty for security will result in the loss of both.

NO: Manhattan Institute fellow Heather Mac Donald believes that, since the new terrorism poses an unprecedented threat to America's survival, the Patriot Act is an appropriate response and contains adequate protection of fundamental liberties.

Ten days before the Declaration of Independence was adopted, the Continental Congress recommended that all colonies adopt laws punishing as treasonous persons those who levy war on the colonies or adhere to the king of Great Britain and other enemies. When independence was won, treason was the only crime against the nation mentioned in the Constitution, and it was defined as providing "aid and comfort" to an enemy.

Eleven years later, the threat of war with France led Congress to adopt and President John Adams to support the Sedition Act, which punished "whoever shall by word or act support or favor the cause of any country with which the United States is at war or by word or act oppose the cause of the United States therein." In 1918, when the United States was engaged in the First World War, another Sedition Act punished anyone who would "willfully utter, print, write or publish any disloyal, profane, scurrilous, or abusive language" about our form of government. The Second World War and the Cold War waged against the Soviet Union led to the passage of the Internal Security Act and Communist Control Act, which reacted in similar ways to perceived threats to national security. All of these measures were accompanied by efforts to punish, intern, or expel suspected aliens.

Wars inspire a response to strengthen internal security, and the declaration of a war against terrorism is no different. The most far-reaching reaction to the 9/11 attack on the United States was the quick passage of the USA Patriot Act. (The official title is The Uniting and Strengthening America by Providing Appropriate Tools Required to Intercept and Obstruct Terrorism Act.) The USA Patriot Act permits tracking Web sites and e-mails if the law enforcement agency certifies that it relates to an ongoing investigation; searching a business or residence with a warrant but without notifying the owner that the search has been conducted until some later time; installing wiretaps to be granted against individuals, instead of a particular phone, allowing government wiretaps of public phones used by suspected persons; seizing voice-mail messages under a warrant; detaining non-citizens without a hearing; denying entry to non-citizens based on their speech or deportation based on support of a terrorist group, even if that support is unrelated to terrorist activity, and a variety of other measures.

Less controversially, the Act encourages the exchange of information among the FBI, the CIA, and other law enforcement groups. Many critics had blamed the poor communications between the FBI and CIA for America's failure to put together pieces of information that might have alerted the nation to the terrorist threat before 9/11.

To its critics, the very title of the USA Patriot Act implicitly suggests that those who oppose it are less than patriotic, or at least are dangerously foolish. As proof, they cite this statement of Attorney General John Ashcroft: "To those who pit Americans against immigrants, citizens against non-citizens, to those who scare peace-loving people with phantoms of lost liberty, my message is this: Your tactics only aid terrorists for they erode our national unity and diminish our resolve. They give ammunition to America's enemies and pause to America's friends. They encourage people of good will to remain silent in the face of evil." They oppose the law's increase in the surveillance and investigative powers of law enforcement because they believe that it sacrifices the checks and balances vital to safeguarding civil liberties.

To its defenders, the Patriot Act is essential to the nation's security. The 9/11 acts were part of a war against the United States unlike any fought before. The enemy, bent upon the mass slaughter of civilians, is hidden on American soil and must be ferreted out—for which the techniques used for catching bank robbers and other traditional criminals are totally inadequate. From the perspective of its defenders, then, the Patriot Act is a modest step toward dealing with the new reality of massive terrorist strikes within this country. But what of the dangers the Patriot Act poses to civil liberties? Its defenders charge that the critics ignore the many safeguards for civil liberties built into the law, such as the fact that before FBI agents can demand records of any citizen they must first obtain judicial approval.

In the following selections, Nat Hentoff deplores the fact that, under this law, there is no need to show probable cause that a crime has been or is about to be committed, and that there is no effective check upon the executive power. Heather Mac Donald believes that civil liberties have been safeguarded, but that terrorist "acts of war" require new weapons in dealing with unidentified combatants within the United States.

Nat Hentoff  **YES**

How We Began to Lose
Our Liberties

Two nights after the September 11 attack, the Senate swiftly, by voice vote after thirty minutes of debate, attached to a previously written appropriations bill an amendment making it much easier for the government to wiretap computers of terrorism suspects without having to go to various courts to get multiple search warrants. The bipartisan bill was introduced by Senators Orrin Hatch, Republican of Utah, and Dianne Feinstein, Democrat of California. "Terrorism" was not defined.

That was the beginning of the steamroller. Attorney General John Ashcroft then got his way with his originally titled Anti-Terrorism Act of 2001, which coolly contradicted the earnest assertions of the president and the secretary of defense that necessary security measures would not violate our fundamental liberties because our freedom is what we are fighting for. The final legislation passed the Senate on October 25 by a vote of 98 to 1, with only Russ Feingold, Democrat of Wisconsin, dissenting. In the House, the bill passed 356 to 66.

The law permits government agents to search a suspect's home without immediately notifying the object of the search. In J. Edgar Hoover's day, this was known as a "black bag job." The FBI then never bothered to get a search warrant for such operations. Now, a warrant would be required, but very few judges would turn a government investigator down in this time of fear. Ashcroft's "secret searches" provision can now extend to *all* criminal cases and can include taking photographs, the contents of your hard drive, and other property. This is now a permanent part of the law, not subject to any "sunset" review by Congress.

Ashcroft also asked for roving wiretaps—a single warrant for a suspect's telephone must include any and all types of phones he or she uses in any and all locations, including pay phones. If a suspect uses a relative's phone or your phone, that owner becomes part of the investigative database. So does anyone using the same pay phone or any pay phone in the area.

Ashcroft neglected to tell us, however, that roving wiretaps already became law under the Clinton Administration in 1998. At that time, only

From THE WAR ON THE BILL OF RIGHTS AND THE GATHERING RESISTANCE, September 1, 2003, pp. 19–25, 134–141. Copyright © 2003 by Seven Stories Press. Reprinted with permission.

Congressman Bob Barr, Republican of Georgia, spoke against it in Congress, while the media paid little attention to this revision of the Fourth Amendment.

But Ashcroft demanded and received a radical extension of these roving wiretaps: a one-stop *national* warrant for wiretapping these peripatetic phones. Until now, a wiretap warrant was valid only in the jurisdiction in which it was issued. But now, the government won't have to waste time by having to keep going to court to provide a basis for each warrant in each locale.

The expansion of wiretapping to computers, and thereby the Internet, makes a mockery of Internet champion John Perry Barlow's 1996 "Declaration of the Independence of Cyberspace":

> Governments of the industrial world, on behalf of the future, I ask you of the past to leave us alone. . . . You have no sovereignty where we gather . . . nor do you possess any methods of enforcement we have true reason to fear. Cyberspace does not lie within your borders.

This government invasion of cyberspace fulfills the prophecy of Justice Louis Brandeis, who warned, in his dissent in the first wiretapping case before the Supreme Court, *Olmstead v. United States* (1928), "Ways may some day be developed by which the Government, without removing papers from secret drawers, can reproduce them in court, and by which it will be enabled to expose to a jury the most intimate occurrences of the home."

This has come to pass. The government now has access to bank records, credit card purchases, what has been searched for on the Internet, and a great deal more data from those who have "supported," or are suspected of, terrorism.

Moreover, as Brandon Koerner, a fellow at the New America Foundation, has pointed out in the *Village Voice*, the bill that Congress passed so hastily on the night of September 13—and that is now part of the law— "lowers the legal standards necessary for the FBI to deploy its infamous Carnivore surveillance system." Without showing—as the Fourth Amendment requires—probable cause that a crime has been committed or is about to be committed, the government invades your privacy through Carnivore.

The fearful name "Carnivore" disturbed some folks, and so it has been renamed DCS1000. Carnivore, Koerner notes, is "a computer that the Feds attach to an Internet service provider. Once in place, it scans e-mail traffic for 'suspicious' subjects which, in the current climate, could be something as innocent as a message with the word 'Allah' in the header." Or maybe: "SAVE THE FOURTH AMENDMENT FROM TYRANTS!" Carnivore also records other electronic communications.

There was resistance to the assault on the Bill of Rights. In Congress, such previously unlikely alliances between Maxine Waters and Bob Barr, Barney Frank and Dick Armey, helped hold back Ashcroft's rush to enact his antiterrorism weapons within a week, as he had demanded. In the Senate, Patrick Leahy, chairman of the Judiciary Committee, also tried to allow some deliberation, but Majority Leader Tom Daschle usurped and undermined Leahy's authority. Leahy ultimately caved and declared the law signed by Bush on October 26 "a good bill that protects our liberties."

The House Judiciary Committee did pass by a 36-to-0 vote a bipartisan bill that restored some mention of the Bill of Rights to Ashcroft's proposals. But, late at night, that bill was scuttled behind closed doors by Speaker of the House Dennis Hastert and other Republican leaders, along with emissaries from the White House.

As a result, on October 12, the House, 337 to 39, approved a harsh bill that most of its members had not had time even to read. David Dreier, chairman of the Committee on Rules, often seen being smoothly disingenuous on television, said casually that it was hardly the first time bills had been passed that House members had not read.

Democrat David Obey of Wisconsin accurately described the maneuver as "a back-room quick fix."

And Barney Frank made the grim point that this subversion of representative government was "the least democratic process for debating questions fundamental to democracy I have ever seen. A bill drafted by a handful of people in secret, subject to no committee process, comes before us immune from amendment."

Among those voting against the final bill were Barney Frank, John Conyers, David Bonior, Barbara Lee, Cynthia McKinney, John Dingell, Jesse Jackson Jr., Jerrold Nadler, Melvin Watt, and Maxine Waters. Unaccountably, Bob Barr voted for the bill.

But House Judiciary Committee Chairman James Sensenbrenner, as reported on National Public Radio, assured us all that this steamrollered bill did not diminish the freedom of "innocent citizens."

Providing, of course, that the presumption of innocence holds. (Sensenbrenner was later to change his mind.)

Also late at night, on October 11, the Senate, in a closed-door session attended only by Senate leaders and members of the Administration, created a similar, expansive antiterrorism bill that the Senate went on to pass by a vote of ninety-six to one. Only Russ Feingold, a Wisconsin Democrat, had the truly patriotic courage to vote against this attack on the Bill of Rights that the president and the secretaries of state and defense have said we are fighting for.

As Feingold had said while the Senate was allegedly deliberating the bill, "It is crucial that civil liberties in this country be preserved. Otherwise I'm afraid terror will win this battle without firing a shot."

In essence, the new law will, as the *Wall Street Journal* noted, "make it easier for government agents to track e-mail sent and Web sites visited by someone involved in an investigation; to collect call records for phones such a person might use; and to share information between the Federal Bureau of Investigation and the Central Intelligence Agency."

Until now, the CIA was not legally allowed to spy on Americans. Also, previously secret grand jury proceedings will now be shared among law enforcement and intelligence agencies.

In addition, the new law subverts the Fourth Amendment's standards of reasonable searches and seizures by allowing antiterrorism investigations to obtain a warrant not on the basis of previously defined "probable cause," as has been required in domestic criminal probes, but on the much looser basis that the information is "relevant to an ongoing criminal investigation" somehow linked to alleged terrorism.

The new law has a "sunset clause," requiring it to be reviewed in December 2005, to determine if these stringent measures are still needed. But before this collusion in reducing our liberties was effected, George W. Bush had assured us that the war on worldwide terrorism will be of indeterminate length. A Congress that so overwhelmingly passed this antiterrorism bill is hardly likely to expunge parts of it unless there is rising citizen resistance. And even if it did, evidence gathered in the first four years could be used in prosecutions after that. Moreover, not every part of the PATRIOT ACT is subject to the sunset clause. There are sections that are now part of our permanent laws.

In self-defense, all of us should be interested in how terrorism is defined in this historic legislation. As summarized by the ACLU, the language in the final bill said: A person "commits the crime of domestic terrorism if within the U.S., activity is engaged in that involves acts dangerous to human life that violate the laws of the United States or any State, and appear to be intended to: (1) intimidate or coerce a civilian population; (2) influence the policy of a government by intimidation or coercion; or (3) affect the conduct of the government by mass destruction, assassination, or kidnapping." (Note the words: "appear to be intended to" and "intimidate.")

Considering the loose language of the first two provisions, the ACLU points out that "this over-broad terrorism definition would sweep in people who engage in acts of political protest if those acts were dangerous to human life. People associated with organizations such as Operation Rescue and the Environmental Liberation Front, and the World Trade Organization protesters, have engaged in activities that should subject them to prosecution as terrorists."

Furthermore, "once the government decides that conduct is 'domestic terrorism,' law enforcement agents have the authority to charge anyone who provides assistance to that person, even if the assistance is an act as minor as providing lodging. They would have the authority to wiretap the home of anyone who is providing assistance."

"Assistance" includes "support." So, contributions to any group later charged with domestic terrorism—even if the donor was unaware of its range of activities—could lead to an investigation of those giving "support."

As Judge Learned Hand once said, " Liberty lies in the hearts of men and women; when it dies there, no constitution, no law, no court can even do much to help it. While it lies there, it needs no constitution, no law, no court to save it."

We and the Constitution have survived the contempt for the Bill of Rights in the Alien and Sedition Acts of 1798; Abraham Lincoln's suspension of *habeas corpus*, and the jailing of editors and other dissenters during the Civil War; Woodrow Wilson's near annihilation of the First Amendment in the First World War; and the Red Scares of 1919 and the early 1920s when Attorney General A. Mitchell Palmer and his enthusiastic aide, J. Edgar Hoover, rounded up hundreds of "radicals," "subversives," and "Bolsheviks" in thirty-three cities and summarily deported many of them. And we also survived Joe McCarthy. But will liberty still survive "in the hearts" of Americans?

This will be one of our severest tests yet to rescue the Constitution from our government. Benjamin Franklin has been quoted a lot since the USA PATRIOT Act and its progeny. "They that can give up essential liberty to obtain a little temporary safety deserve neither liberty nor safety."

On October 11, 2001, Senator Russ Feingold, dissenting to the PATRIOT Act, said on the floor of the Senate:

> There is no doubt that if we lived in a police state, it would be easier to catch terrorists. If we lived in a country where the police were allowed to search your home at any time for any reason; if we lived in a country where the government is entitled to open your mail, eavesdrop on your phone conversations, or intercept our e-mail communications; if we lived in a country where people could be held in jail indefinitely based on what they write or think, or based on mere suspicion that they are up to no good, the government would probably, discover and arrest more terrorists or would-be terrorists, just as it would find more lawbreakers generally.
>
> But that wouldn't be a country in which we would want to live, and it wouldn't be a country for which we could, in good conscience, ask our young people to fight and die. In short, that country wouldn't be America.
>
> I think it is important to remember that the Constitution was written in 1789 by men who had recently won the Revolutionary War... They wrote the Constitution and the Bill of Rights to protect individual liberties in times of war as well as in times of peace.
>
> There have been periods in our nation's history when civil liberties have taken a back seat to what appeared at the time to be legitimate exigencies of war. Our national consciousness still bears the stain and the scars of those events.
>
> We must not allow this piece of our past to become prologue. Preserving our freedom is the reason we are now engaged in this new war on terrorism. We will lose that war without a shot being fired if we sacrifice the liberties of the American people in the belief that by doing so we will stop the terrorists.

Russ Feingold predicted much of what was to come.

◦⟨◉⟩◦

During the fierce debates in the new America on whether the Constitution, written in 1787, should be ratified, there was fear among the dissenters that a national federal government would be too powerful. During that debate, the proposed Constitution, which did not yet have a Bill of Rights, was attacked by Robert Yates, writing under the pseudonym "Brutus."

In Bernard Bailyn's *To Begin the World Anew* (Knopf, 2003), Brutus, much concerned with the new government's power to tax, predicted that this federal government "will introduce itself into every corner of the city and country. It [the national government] will wait upon the ladies at their toilett, and will not leave them in any of their domestic concerns; it will accompany them to the ball, the play, the assembly . . . it will enter the house of every gentlemen . . . it will take cognizance of the professional man in his office, or his study . . . it will follow the mechanic to his shop, and in his work, and will haunt him in his family, in his bed . . . it will penetrate into the most obscure cottage; and finally, it will light upon the head of every person in the United States."

It was as if "Brutus" could have foreseen beyond the power to tax, Admiral John Poindexter's Terrorism Information Awareness System in the Pentagon, or the ever increasing electronic surveillance of the citizenry by John Ashcroft. Soon after the hasty passage of the USA PATRIOT Act in the immediate wake of 9/11, Mindy Tucker, then the spokesperson for the Justice Department, promised: "This is just the first step. There will be additional items to come." . . .

In the April 11, 2003, issue of *The Chronicle of Higher Education*, the authoritative source of news and analysis concerning college and university affairs, Judith Grant, an associate professor of political science and women's studies at the University of Southern California, wrote in an article titled "Uncle Sam Over My Shoulder":

> I am now experiencing what American legal scholars call 'a chilling effect,' and I was indeed aware of it as a sort of chill running up my spine—a half-second of anxiety, almost subconscious, the moment I heard that the [USA PATRIOT] Act had been passed.
>
> I feel that chill again when I realize that I now pause a moment before I write almost anything. I think about how a government official might read my writing if he or she were trying to build a (completely unjustified) case against me. I worried even while I wrote that last sentence, then I worried about my worry. Might someone in the Justice Department ask: "Why would she be worried if she were doing nothing wrong?"

In the April 20, 2003, Letters section of the *New York Times*, Tina Rosan of Cambridge, Massachusetts, comments on a previous *Times* story, "Muslims Hesitating on Gifts as U.S. Scrutinizes Charities":

> Of course Muslims in the United States are "hesitating" to give money to charities because they are afraid . . . Many have been detained without trial. Given this environment, Muslims are trying to stay under the radar. They don't want a contribution to a charity to put them on a suspect list or cause them to end up in jail. Unfortunately the news media have not been paying attention to the severe violation of civil liberties at home. The real truth is much deeper and darker.

In the April 21, 2003, *Newsday,* columnist Sheryl McCarthy told of a twenty-six-year-old mechanical engineer, Daniel Ueda, and twenty-eight-year-old Carey Larsen, who were arrested in a demonstration "outside the offices of The Carlyle Group, a private investment house with holdings in the defense industry":

> At police headquarters both Ueda and Larsen were asked questions that seemed strange, considering the minor offenses with which they were charged. Questions like: how man protests had they participated in, what groups were they affiliated with, how they heard about the demonstrations . . . how they felt about the war with Iraq and whether they thought the United States should have entered World War II. Yes, really.
>
> When they balked at answering the political questions, they were warned they'd be held longer if they didn't cooperate.

When *New York Times* columnist Joyce Purnick (April 21) asked the New York City Police Department if the information obtained from such questioning could be used to infiltrate political groups, the Police Department's chief spokesman, Michael O'Looney, said: "I'm going to leave it with that." He refused to answer the question that brought back my memories of the days of J. Edgar Hoover's COINTELPRO, when the FBI, at will, infiltrated and disrupted entirely lawful groups.

Donna Lieberman, executive director of the New York Civil Liberties Union, is aware of the history of COINTELPRO, and she told Joyce Purnick: "When people are asked about their political affiliations, it's intimidation. It's discouraging people from exercising their fundamental right to criticize government."

So when Judith Grant feels "a chilling effect" when she writes for *The Chronicle of Higher Education,* she may not be entirely without reason to be somewhat intimidated by the environment that John Ashcroft has created.

Sam Adams, the eighteenth-century patriot, once said of this new sweet land of liberty: "Driven from every other corner of the earth, freedom of thought and the right of private judgement in matters of conscience, direct their course to this happy country as their last asylum."

Like "Brutus," Sam Adams did not foresee the Bush-Ashcroft omnivorous surveillance of the residents of this "last asylum."

Sam Adams was overly sanguine about the future of freedom of conscience here. In 1858, Abraham Lincoln, speaking in Edwardsville, Illinois—before assuming the powers of the presidency—spoke to a truth that George W. Bush would do well to keep in mind:

> What constitutes the bulwark of our own liberty and independence? It is not our frowning battlements, our bristling seacoasts, our army and navy. These are not our reliance against tyranny . . . Our reliance is the love of liberty . . . Destroy this spirit and you have planted the seeds of despotism at your door.

This was the same Abraham Lincoln who suspended *habeas corpus,* imprisoned many Americans who dissented from his policies, and set up military tribunals to dispose of citizens of contrary views—even though the civilian courts were still open.

Then there was Franklin Delano Roosevelt, who earnestly told the nation:

> We must scrupulously guard the civil liberties of all citizens, whatever their background. We must remember that any oppression, any injustice, any hatred, is a wedge designed to attack our civilization.

It was the same Franklin Delano Roosevelt who signed Executive Order No. 9066 that sent Japanese-Americans into detention camps, which they rightly regarded as concentration camps.

When, in August 2002, Federal Judge Damon J. Keith, writing for the Sixth Circuit Court of Appeals, ruled against the Bush administration's closing of all deportation hearings to the press and the public, though the Third Circuit voted the other way, he emphasized:

> Democracies die behind closed doors. The only safeguard on this extraordinary government power is in the public, deputizing the press as the guardians of their liberty. An informed public is the most potent of all restraints on government . . . the First Amendment, through a free press, protects the people's right to know that their government acts fairly, lawfully, and accurately.

But veteran journalist Jack Nelson, retired Washington bureau chief of the *Los Angeles Times,* told a First Amendment Center conference on March 12, 2003:

> President Bush has gone beyond just being extremely secretive about the conduct of the government's business. In the name of fighting terrorism, he has amassed powers and wrapped them in a cloak of resilience to normal oversight by Congress and the judiciary. *No president since I've been a reporter has so tried to change the very structure of government to foster secrecy.* (Emphasis added.)

Even the Fourth Circuit Court of Appeals—the most conservative Federal appellate court in the country—rebuked the Bush administration in the case of Zacarias Moussaoui, accused of involvement in a terrorist conspiracy. Reported the April 2, 2003, *Washington Post:*

> The court chided the government for "simultaneously prosecuting the defendant and attempting to restrict his ability to use information [in court] that he feels is necessary to defend himself against the prosecution . . .
>
> Courts must not be remiss in protecting a defendant's right to a full and meaningful presentation of his claim to innocence."

Concerning this case, Donald Rehkopf, chairman of the Military Law Committee of the National Association of Criminal Defense Lawyers, accused the government of "inventing the law as they go along. The Constitution," he reminded the administration—echoing the Supreme Court in the 1866 *Milligan* case—"is not suspended, even during time of war."

And when the government proposed, in "Patriot Act II," to strip Americans of their citizenship if they give "support" to an organization cited by the administration as implicated in terrorism—even if the accused American is unaware of that part of the group's activities—human rights attorney Joanne Mariner noted in an article on www.findlaw.com ("Patriot II's Attack on Citizenship", March 3, 2003) how Ashcroft and Bush also invent the law in proposing to take away the most essential of all American rights, our citizenship. Professor Mariner wrote:

> If you help fund an orphanage administered by one of the three Chechen separatist groups that the government has labeled as terrorist, or if you give pharmaceutical supplies to a medical outpost run by the East Turkestan Islamic Movement, or if you are on the wrong side of any of a number of other political conflicts in the world, you are vulnerable to the loss of your citizenship.

Although you "would be able to challenge this determination in court," she continued, you would "not necessarily succeed." Particularly, if during the limitless war on terrorism, our courts keep deferring to the government, bypassing the separation of powers in the Constitution.

Through the years, I have often quoted a warning by Supreme Court Justice Louis Brandeis that resonates throughout a study of American history. It is especially relevant now:

> Experience should teach us to be most on our guard to protect liberty when the government's purposes are beneficent. Men born to freedom are naturally alert to repel invasion of their liberty by evil-minded rulers. The greatest dangers to liberty lurk in insidious encroachment by men of zeal, well-meaning but without understanding.

Brandeis's warning was part of his dissent in the first wiretapping case, *Olmstead v. the United States* (1928). The year before, in a less often quoted but even more profound definition of the spirit that has enabled this country to remain the freest in the world—despite severe misunderstandings of the Constitution by past administrations—Justice Brandeis again spoke to us now.

The case, *Whitney v. California*, concerned the prosecution of Charlotte Anita Whitney for violating the Criminal Syndication Act of California. That law, as constitutional scholar Louis Fisher noted, penalized "efforts of trade union and industrial workers to gain control of production through general strikes, sabotage, violence, or other criminal means."

Whitney "was found guilty of having organized and participated in a group assembled to advocate, teach, aid, and abet criminal syndicalism." In

1919, at a convention in Oakland, California, held to organize a California branch of the Communist Labor Party, Charlotte Whitney, as a member of the Resolutions Committee, signed this statement: "The Communist Labor Party proclaims and insists that the capture of political power, locally or nationally by the revolutionary working class, can be of tremendous assistance to the workers in their struggle for emancipation."

The Supreme Court upheld California's Criminal Syndication Act. But, in a concurring opinion, which was really a dissent, Brandeis wrote:

> A State is ordinarily denied the power to prohibit the dissemination of social, economic, and political doctrine [even though] a vast majority of its citizens believes [it] to be false and fraught with evil consequence . . . It is . . . always open to Americans to challenge a law abridging free speech and assembly by showing that there was no emergency justifying [its abridgement.]

That is precisely what the continually growing number of Bill of Rights Defense Committees around the nation are doing in challenging the USA PATRIOT Act and the other violations of the Bill of Rights by Ashcroft and Bush. However, what Brandeis also said in *Whitney v. California* underlines this book's celebration of the gathering resistance to the war on the Bill of Rights:

> Those who won our independence . . . believed that the greatest menace to freedom is an inert people . . . They knew that order cannot be secured merely through fear of punishment for its infraction . . . that fear breeds repression; that repression breeds hate; that hate menaces stable government . . .
>
> Believing in the power of reason as applied through public discussion, they eschewed silence coerced by law—the argument of force in its worst form . . .
>
> Fear of serious injury cannot alone justify suppression of free speech and assembly. Men feared witches and burnt women [as in the Salem witchcraft trials] . . .
>
> *Those who won our independence by revolution were not cowards . . . They did not exalt order at the cost of liberty.* (Emphasis added.)

The challenge to Americans now is to act with the determination of those who won our independence because what we do now to recover the Bill of Rights will decide for years to come—as Justice William Brennan used to say—whether those words "will come off the page and into the very lives of the American people."

Heather Mac Donald  **NO**

Straight Talk on Homeland Security

The backlash against the Bush administration's War on Terror began on 9/11 and has not let up since. Left- and right-wing advocacy groups likened the Bush administration to fascists, murderers, apartheid ideologues, and usurpers of basic liberties. Over 120 cities and towns have declared themselves "civil liberties safe zones"; and the press has amplified at top volume a recent report by the Justice Department's inspector general denouncing the government's handling of suspects after 9/11. Even the nation's librarians are shredding documents to safeguard their patrons' privacy and foil government investigations.

The advocates' rhetoric is both false and dangerous. Lost in the blizzard of propaganda is any consciousness that 9/11 was an act of war against the U.S. by foreign enemies concealed within the nation's borders. If the media and political elites keep telling the public that the campaign against those terrorist enemies is just a racist power grab, the most essential weapon against terror cells—intelligence from ordinary civilians—will be jeopardized. A drumbeat of ACLU propaganda could discourage a tip that might be vital in exposing an al-Qaida plot.

It is crucial, therefore, to demolish the extravagant lies about the anti-terror initiatives. Close scrutiny of the charges and the reality that they misrepresent shows that civil liberties are fully intact. The majority of legal changes after September 11 simply brought the law into the twenty-first century. In those cases where the government has its powers—as is inevitable during a war—important judicial and statutory safeguards protect the rights of law-abiding citizens. And in the one hard case where a citizen's rights appear to have been curtailed—the detention of a suspected American al-Qaida operative without access to an attorney—that detention is fully justified under the laws of war.

The anti–War on Terror worldview found full expression only hours after the World Trade Center fell, in a remarkable e-mail that spread like wildfire over the Internet that very day. Sent out by Harvard Law School research fellow John Perry Barlow, founder of the cyber-libertarian Electronic Freedom Foundation, the message read: "Control freaks will dine on

From *City Journal*, Summer 2003. Copyright © 2003 by City Journal—Manhattan Institute, Inc. Reprinted with permission.

this day for the rest of our lives. Within a few hours, we will see beginning the most vigorous efforts to end what remains of freedom in America. . . . I beg you to begin NOW to do whatever you can . . . to prevent the spasm of control mania from destroying the dreams that far more have died for over the last two hundred twenty-five years than died this morning. Don't let the terrorists or (their natural allies) the fascists win. Remember that the goal of terrorism is to create increasingly paralytic totalitarianism in the government it attacks. Don't give them the satisfaction. . . . And, please, let us try to forgive those who have committed these appalling crimes. If we hate them, we will become them."

Barlow, a former lyricist for the Grateful Dead, epitomizes the rise of the sixties counterculture into today's opinion elite, for whom no foreign enemy could ever pose as great a threat to freedom as the U.S. For Barlow, the problem isn't the obvious evil of Islamic terrorism but the imputed evil of the American government—an inversion that would characterize the next two years of anti-administration jeremiads. In this spirit, critics would measure each legal change not against the threat it responded to, but in a vacuum. Their verdict: "increasingly paralytic totalitarianism."

Right-wing libertarians soon joined forces with the Left. A few months after the Twin Towers fell, the Rutherford Institute, a Christian think tank concerned with religious liberty, added the final piece to the anti-administration argument: the 9/11 attacks were not war but, at most, a crime. Rutherford president John Whitehead denounced the Bush administration's characterization of the terror strikes as "acts of war by foreign aggressors," without however offering a single argument to support his view. Since that characterization has produced, in Whitehead's view, growing "police statism" that is destroying Americans' freedom, the characterization must be false.

In fact, of course, the 9/11 bombings were classic decapitation strikes, designed to take out America's political and financial leadership. Had a state carried them out, no one could possibly deny that they were acts of war, as John Yoo and James Ho point out in a forthcoming *Virginia Journal of International Law* article. The aim of the 19 foreign terrorists and their backers was not criminal but ideological: to revenge U.S. policies in the Middle East with mass destruction.

Recognizing that the World Trade Center and Pentagon attacks were acts of war entails certain consequences. First, the campaign against al-Qaida and other Islamic terror organizations is really war, not a metaphor, like the "war on drugs." Second, it is a war unlike any the U.S. has ever fought. The enemy, mostly but not exclusively foreign, is hidden on American soil in the civilian population, with the intention of slaughtering as many innocent noncombatants as possible. The use of military force abroad, while necessary, is by no means sufficient: domestic counterterrorism efforts by the FBI and other domestic law enforcement agencies are at least as essential to defeating the enemy.

When these agencies are operating against Islamic terrorists, they are operating in an unprecedented war mode—but most of the rules that govern them were designed for crime fighting. The tension between the Justice Department's and FBI's traditional roles as law enforcement agencies and their new roles as terror warriors lies at the heart of the battle over the Bush administration's post-9/11 homeland-security policies: critics refuse to recognize the reality of the war and thus won't accept the need for expanded powers to prosecute it.

Most of the changes in the law that the Justice Department sought after 9/11 concern the department's ability to gather intelligence on terror strikes before they happen—its key responsibility in the terror war. Yet the libertarian lobby will not allow the department to budge from the crime paradigm, refusing to admit that surveillance and evidence-gathering rules designed to protect the rights of suspected car thieves and bank robbers may need modification when the goal is preventing a suitcase bomb from taking out JFK. But of course the libertarians rarely acknowledge that suitcase bombs and the like are central to this debate.

Ironically, none of the changes instituted by Attorney General Ashcroft comes anywhere near what the government *could* ask for in wartime, such as the suspension of *habeas corpus,* as Lincoln ordered during the Civil War. The changes preserve intact the entire criminal procedural framework governing normal FBI and police actions, and merely tinker around the edges. But the left and right civil libertarians are having none of it.

The charges they have brought against the War on Terror have been so numerous, impugning every single administration action since 9/11, that it would take hundreds of pages to refute them all. But the following analysis of only the main charges will amply illustrate the range of duplicitous strategies that the anti-government forces deploy.

Strategy #1: Hide the Judge

Jan O'Rourke, a librarian in Bucks County, Pennsylvania, is preparing for the inevitable post-9/11 assault: She is destroying all records of her patrons' book and Internet use and is advising other Bucks County libraries to do the same. The object of her fear? The U.S. government. O'Rourke is convinced that federal spooks will soon knock on her door to spy on her law-abiding clients' reading habits. So, like thousands of librarians across the country, she is making sure that when that knock comes, she will have nothing to show. "If we don't have the information, then they can't get it," she explains.

O'Rourke is suffering from Patriot Act hysteria, a malady approaching epidemic levels. The USA-PATRIOT Act, which President Bush signed in October 2001, is a complex measure to boost the federal government's ability to detect and prevent terrorism. Its most important provision relaxed a judge-made rule that, especially after Clinton administration strengthening, had prevented intelligence and law enforcement officials from sharing information and collaborating on investigations (see "Why the FBI Didn't Stop 9/11," Autumn 2002). But the act made many other needed changes too: updating surveillance law to take into account new communications technology, for instance, enhancing the Treasury Department's ability to disrupt terrorist financing networks, and modestly increasing the attorney general's power to detain and deport suspected terrorist aliens.

From the moment the administration proposed the legislation, defenders of the status quo started ringing the tyranny alarm. When the law passed, the Electronic Privacy Information Center depicted a tombstone on its website, captioned: "The Fourth Amendment: 1789–2001." The *Washington Post* denounced the bill as "panicky." And the ever touchy American Library Association decided that a particular provision of the Patriot Act—section 215—was a "present danger to the constitutional rights and privacy of library users," though the section says not a word about libraries.

The furor over section 215 is a case study in Patriot Act fear-mongering. Section 215 allows the FBI to seek business records in the hands of third parties—the enrollment application of a Saudi national in an American flight school, say—while investigating terrorism. The section broadens the categories of institutions whose records and other "tangible items" the government may seek in espionage and terror cases, on the post-9/11 recognition that lawmakers cannot anticipate what sorts of organizations terrorists may exploit. In the past, it may have been enough to get hotel bills or storage-locker contracts (two of the four categories of records covered in the narrower law that section 215 replaced) to trace the steps of a Soviet spy; today, however, gumshoes may find they need receipts from scuba-diving schools or farm-supply stores to piece together a plot to blow up the Golden Gate Bridge. Section 215 removed the requirement that the records must concern an "agent of a foreign power" (generally, a spy or terrorist), since, again, the scope of an anti-terror investigation is hard to predict in advance.

From this tiny acorn, Bush administration foes have conjured forth a mighty assault on the First Amendment. The ACLU warns that with section 215, "the FBI could spy on a person because they don't like the books she reads, or because they don't like the websites she visits. They could spy on her because she wrote a letter to the editor that criticized government policy." Stanford Law School dean Kathleen Sullivan calls section 215 "threatening." And librarians, certain that the section is all about them, are scaring library users with signs warning that the government may spy on their reading habits.

These charges are nonsense. Critics of section 215 deliberately ignore the fact that any request for items under the section requires judicial approval. An FBI agent cannot simply walk into a flight school or library and demand records. The bureau must first convince the court that oversees anti-terror investigations (the Foreign Intelligence Surveillance Act, or FISA, court) that the documents are relevant to protecting "against international terrorism on clandestine intelligence activities." The chance that the FISA court will approve a 215 order because the FBI "doesn't like the books [a person] reads . . . or because she wrote a letter to the editor that criticized government policy" is zero. If the bureau can show that someone using the Bucks County library computers to surf the web and send e-mails has traveled to Pakistan and was seen with other terror suspects in Virginia, on the other hand, then the court may well grant an order to get the library's Internet logs.

Moreover, before the FBI can even approach the FISA court with any kind of request, agents must have gone through multiple levels of bureaucratic review just to open an anti-terror investigation. And to investigate a U.S. citizen (rather than an alien) under FISA, the FBI must show that he is knowingly engaged in terrorism or espionage.

Ignoring the Patriot Act's strict judicial review requirements is the most common strategy of the act's critics. Time and again, the Cassandras will hold up a section from the bill as an example of rampaging executive power—without ever mentioning that the power in question is overseen by federal judges who will allow its use only if the FBI can prove its relevance to a bona fide terror (or sometimes criminal) investigation. By contrast, in the few cases where a law enforcement power does not require judicial review, the jackboots-are-coming brigade screams for judges as the only trustworthy check on executive tyranny.

Strategy #2: Invent New Rights

A running theme of the campaign against section 215 and many other Patriot Act provisions is that they violate the Fourth Amendment right to privacy. But there is no Fourth Amendment privacy right in records or other items disclosed to third parties. A credit-card user, for example, reveals his purchases to the seller and to the credit-card company. He therefore has no privacy expectations in the record of those purchases that the Fourth Amendment would protect. As a result, the government, whether in a criminal case or a terror investigation, may seek his credit-card receipts without a traditional Fourth Amendment showing to a court that there is "probable cause" to believe that a crime has been or is about to be committed. Instead, terror investigators must convince the FISA court that the receipts are "relevant."

Despite librarians' fervent belief to the contrary, this analysis applies equally to library patrons' book borrowing or Internet use. The government may obtain those records without violating anyone's Fourth Amendment rights, because the patron has already revealed his borrowing and web browsing to library staff, other readers (in the days of handwritten book checkout cards), and Internet service providers. Tombstones declaring the death of the Fourth Amendment contain no truth whatsoever.

What's different in the section 215 provision is that libraries or other organizations can't challenge the FISA court's order and can't inform the target of the investigation, as they can in ordinary criminal proceedings. But that difference is crucial for the Justice Department's war-making function. The department wants to know if an al-Qaida suspect has consulted maps of the Croton reservoir and researched the toxic capacities of cyanide in the New York Public Library not in order to win a conviction for poisoning

New York's water supply but to preempt the plot before it happens. The battleground is not the courtroom but the world beyond, where speed and secrecy can mean life or death.

Strategy #3: Demand Antiquated Laws

The librarians' crusade against section 215 has drawn wide media attention and triggered an ongoing congressional battle, led by Vermont socialist Bernie Sanders, to pass a law purporting to protect the "Freedom to Read." But the publicity that administration-hostile librarians were able to stir up pales in comparison to the clout of the Internet privacy lobby. The day the Patriot Act became law, the Center for Democracy and Technology sent around a warning that "privacy standards" had been "gutt[ed]." The Electronic Freedom Foundation declared that the "civil liberties of ordinary Americans have taken a tremendous blow." Jeffrey Rosen of *The New Republic* claimed that the law gave the government "essentially unlimited authority" to surveil Americans. The ACLU asserted that the FBI had suddenly gained "wide powers of phone and internet surveillance." And the Washington Post editorialized that the act made it "easier" to wiretap by "lowering the standard of judicial review."

The target of this ire? A section that merely updates existing law to modern technology. The government has long had the power to collect the numbers dialed from, or the incoming numbers to, a person's telephone by showing a court that the information is "relevant to an ongoing criminal investigation." Just as in section 215 of the Patriot Act, this legal standard is lower than traditional Fourth Amendment "probable cause," because the phone user has already forfeited any constitutional privacy rights he may have in his phone number or the number he calls by revealing them to the phone company.

A 1986 federal law tried to extend the procedures for collecting phone-number information to electronic communications, but it was so poorly drafted that its application to e-mail remained unclear. Section 216 of the Patriot Act resolves the ambiguity by making clear that the rules for obtaining phone numbers apply to incoming and outgoing e-mail addresses as well. The government can obtain e-mail headers—but not content—by showing a court that the information is "relevant to an ongoing criminal investigation." Contrary to cyber-libertarian howls, this is not a vast new power to spy but merely the logical extension of an existing power to a new form of communication. Nothing else has changed: the standard for obtaining information about the source or destination of a communication is the same as always.

Section 216 made one other change to communications surveillance law. When a court issues an order allowing the collection of phone numbers or e-mail headers, that order now applies nationally. Before, if a phone call was transmitted by a chain of phone companies headquartered in different states, investigators needed approval from a court in each of those states to track it. This time-consuming procedure could not be more dangerous in the age of terror. As Attorney General John Ashcroft testified in September 2001, the "ability of law enforcement officers to trace communications into different jurisdictions without obtaining an additional court order can be the difference between life and death for American citizens." Yet the ACLU has complained that issuing national warrants for phone and e-mail routing information marginalizes the judiciary and gives law enforcement unchecked power to search citizens.

The furor over this section of the Patriot Act employs the same deceptions as the furor over section 215 (the business records provision). In both cases, Patriot Act bashers ignore the fact that a court must approve the government's access to information. Despite the *Washington Post's* assertion to the contrary, section 216 does not lower any standards of judicial review. Both the anti-216 and anti-215 campaigns fabricate privacy rights where none exists. And neither of these anti-government campaigns lets one iota of the reality of terrorism intrude into its analyses of fictional rights violations—the reality that communications technology is essential to an enemy that has no geographical locus, and whose combatants have mastered the Internet and every form of modern communications, along with methods to defeat surveillance, such as using and discarding multiple cell phones and communicating from Internet cafés. The anti–Patriot Act forces would keep anti-terror law enforcement in the world of Ma Bell and rotary phones, even as America's would-be destroyers use America's most sophisticated technology against it.

Strategy #4: Conceal Legal Precedent

Section 213 of the Patriot Act allows the FBI (with court approval) to delay notifying a property owner that his property will be or has been searched, if notice would have an "adverse result": if he might flee the country, for example, or destroy documents or intimidate witnesses before agents can acquire sufficient evidence to arrest him. In such cases, the court that issues the search warrant may grant a delay of notice for a "reasonable period" of time.

The advocates dubbed Section 213 the "sneak-and-peek" section and have portrayed it as one of the most outrageous new powers seized by Attorney General John Ashcroft. The ACLU's fund-raising pitches warn: "Now, the government can secretly enter your home while you're away . . . rifle through your personal belongings . . . download your computer files . . . and seize any items at will. . . . And, because of the Patriot Act, you may never know what the government has done." Richard Leone, president of the Century Foundation and editor of *The War on Our Freedoms: Civil Liberties in an Age of Terrorism*, cites the fact that the Patriot Act "allows the government to conduct secret searches without notification" to support his hyperbolic claim that the act is "arguably the most far-reaching and invasive legislation passed since the espionage act of 1917 and the sedition act of 1918."

These critics pretend not to know that, long before anyone imagined such a thing as Islamic terrorism, federal judges have been granting "sneak-and-peak" warrants in criminal cases under identical standards those of section 213. The possibility of seeking delayed notice is a long-standing law enforcement prerogative, sanctioned by numerous courts. Section 213 merely codified the case law to make the process uniform across different jurisdictions. Portraying section 213 as a new power is simple falsehood, and portraying it as an excessive and unnecessary power is extraordinarily ignorant. Delayed notice under life-threatening conditions is not just reasonable but absolutely imperative.

Strategy #5: Keep the FBI off the Web

In May 2002, Attorney General Ashcroft announced that FBI agents would for the first time be allowed to surf the web, just like hundreds of millions of people across the globe. Previously, the Internet was strictly off-limits to federal law enforcement, unless agents had already developed evidence that a crime was under way. In other words, although a 12-year-old could sit in on a *jihadi* chat room where members were praising Usama bin Ladin, visit sites teaching bombmaking, or track down the links for the production of anthrax—all information essential to mapping out the world of Islamic terrorists or finding out how much terrorists might know—intelligence officials couldn't inspect those same public sites until they had already discovered a terror plot. But for an FBI agent in Arizona to wait for specific information about a conspiracy before researching his local biochem lab to see if it might have any connection to the Washington anthrax attacks, or might be a target for sabotage, is not the best strategy for fighting terrorism.

But Ashcroft's critics say the bureau *should* wait. According to the Electronic Privacy Information Center, for instance, the new guidelines "threaten Fourth Amendment rights" because they permit the FBI to "engage in prospective searches without possessing any evidence of suspicious behavior." But there are no Fourth Amendment rights in the web. Far from expecting privacy on a website, its designers hope for the greatest possible exposure to all comers. The Internet is more public even than a newspaper, since it is free and unbound by geography; it is the most exhibitionistic communication medium yet designed. To require the FBI to be the one entity on earth that may not do general web searches, as the civil libertarians have demanded, makes no sense.

In fact, the new guidelines are unduly narrow. They prohibit searches by an individual's name—Usama bin Ladin, say—unless agents have cause to suspect him of involvement in a terror plot. But since millions of web users may conduct searches of Usama bin Ladin's name or of any other individual without violating anyone's privacy rights, it is hard to discern a basis for barring the government from also obtaining that information in preliminary criminal or terror investigations. Law enforcement agencies need to survey as much information as possible about Islamic terrorism before, not after, attacks happen, so that they can recognize an early warning sign or pattern in what an uninformed observer may see as an innocuous set of events.

Opening the web to the FBI, common sense for any criminal investigation, is particularly essential in fighting Islamic terrorism, because the web is the most powerful means of spreading jihad. Rohan Gunaratna, an al-Qaida expert at Scotland's Saint Andrews University, argues that unless the authorities shut down jihadist sites, "we will not able to end terrorism." But even if the U.S. can't shut down web pages celebrating mass destruction in the name of holy war, it should at least be able to visit them to learn what's out there.

The May guidelines also permit agents to attend public meetings for the first time since 1976 in order to "detect or prevent terrorist activities." Let's say a Moroccan imam at a Brooklyn mosque regularly preaches vengeance against America for its support of Israel. The imam was banished from Morocco for his agitation against the secular government. Visitors from Saudi Arabia known to associate with radical fundamentalists regularly visit.

Under previous guidelines, the FBI could not attend public worship at the mosque to learn more about the imam's activities unless it had actual evidence that he was planning to release sarin in the subways, say. But most of the preparations leading up to a terror attack—such as casing transportation systems, attending crop-dusting school, or buying fertilizer—are legal. Only intelligence gathering and analysis can link them to terrorist intent. To require evidence before permitting the intelligence gathering that would produce it is a suicidal Catch-22.

Yet the civil libertarian lobby would keep the FBI in the dark about public events until the last minute. The Electronic Privacy Information Center brands the public-meeting rule a "serious threat to the right of individuals to speak and assemble freely without the specter of government monitoring." But the First Amendment guarantees free speech and assembly, not freedom from government attendance at public meetings. Even so, the new guidelines narrow the government's power anyway, by allowing agents to participate in public meetings only for a terror investigation, not for criminal investigations.

Strategy #6: Exploit Hindsight

Early this June, anti–War on Terror advocates and journalists pulled out all the stops to publicize a report by the Justice Department's inspector general criticizing the department's detention of illegal immigrants suspected of terrorist ties. Headlines blared: DETAINEES ABUSED, CIVIL RIGHTS OF POST-SEPT. 11 DETAINEES VIOLATED, REPORT FINDS (*Washington Post*); U.S. FINDS ABUSES OF 9/11 DETAINEES; JUSTICE DEPT. INQUIRY REVEALS MANY VIOLATIONS OF IMMIGRANTS' RIGHTS (*Los Angeles Times*); THE ABUSIVE DETENTIONS OF SEPT. 11 (*New York Times* editorial). Advocacy groups declared full vindication of their crusade against the Bush administration.

These headlines exaggerated the report only modestly. To be sure, Inspector General Glenn Fine did not declare any rights violations in the Justice Department's policies or practices, but he did decry "significant problems in the way the 9/11 detainees were treated." He charged that the investigation and clearance of terror suspects took too long, that the Justice Department did not sufficiently differentiate moderately suspicious detainees from highly suspect ones, and that the conditions in one New York City detention center, where guards were charged with taunting detainees and slamming them against walls, were unduly.

Fine's report, however measured its language, is ultimately as much a misrepresentation of the government's post-9/11 actions as the shrillest press release from Amnesty International. While it pays lip service to the "difficult circumstances confronting the department in responding to the terror attacks," it fails utterly to understand the terrifying actuality of 9/11. Fine's cool and sensible recommendations—"timely clearance process, timely service of immigration charges, careful consideration of where to house detainees . . . ; better training of staff . . . ; and better oversight"— read, frankly, like a joke, in light of the circumstances at the time.

Recall what the Justice Department and FBI were facing on 9/11: an attack by an invisible, previously unsuspected enemy on a scale unprecedented in this country, with weapons never imagined. Utter uncertainty prevailed about what the next hour or day or week might bring: if these 19 men had remained undetected while plotting their assault with such precision, who else was ready to strike next, and with what weapons? In New York, the FBI office, seven blocks from Ground Zero, had to evacuate on 9/11 to a temporary command center set up in a parking garage; the New York INS evacuated its processing center downtown as well. Electricity and other utilities were down, as was delivery and express mail service. One week after the attacks, 96,000 leads had flooded in to FBI offices around the country; tens of thousands more would soon follow, requiring round-the-clock operations at FBI headquarters, with thousands of agents following up the leads. Recriminations over the government's failure to prevent the catastrophe also flooded in: Why hadn't the intelligence community "connected the dots"? Why didn't the CIA and FBI communicate better? How had the State Department and INS let in foreign terrorists bent on destroying America?

Given the magnitude of the carnage and the depth of the uncertainty, the government would have failed in its duty had it not viewed suspects as serious risks. These were, possibly, enemy combatants, not car thieves or muggers. Justice Department officials declared that any suspect picked up in the course of a terror investigation, if an illegal immigrant, would be held in detention until the FBI cleared him of any possible terror connections. Moreover, if agents, following a lead, were looking for a particular individual and discovered half a dozen illegal immigrants at his apartment, all seven would be detained as suspects, since the FBI had no way of knowing who might be an accomplice of the wanted man. In another safeguard against letting a terrorist go, FBI headquarters ruled that it needed to sign off on all clearances, since only bureau brass possessed the full national picture of developing intelligence. Finally, the FBI mandated CIA background checks on all detainees.

These policies are eminently reasonable. That they ended up delaying clearance for an average of 80 days for the 762 illegal aliens detained after 9/11 does not discredit their initial rationale. (That delay is not unlawful, since the government can hold illegal aliens for an undefined period under emergency circumstances.) Justice Department officials expected to release innocent detainees in days, or at most several weeks, and they were concerned as the process stretched out; memos about the need to speed things up flew around the department daily. Officials worried about staying within the law and not violating anyone's rights (which they did not), but they also worried—and for good reason—about releasing even one deadly person. Even in retrospect, this calculus is unimpeachable: the costs of being legally held as an illegal alien and terror suspect for three months without ultimate conviction, while huge for the person held, pale in comparison to the costs of allowing terrorists to go free. (That some prison guards may have abused about 20 detainees is deplorable but does not invalidate the detention policy.)

The inspector general has plenty of good-government suggestions for how to make sure that, after the next terror attack, suspects are efficiently processed, but he is silent on the paramount questions that will face the government should a bomb go off in the nation's capital or a biological weapon in the subway at rush hour: how to find out who did it and who is waiting in the wings, and how to protect the country in the face of grossly inadequate knowledge. Should the country experience another attack on the scale of 9/11, the aftermath undoubtedly will not follow administrative law procedures perfectly. As long as the government does not deliberately or flagrantly abuse suspects' rights, it need have no apology for the slow functioning of bureaucracy through the crisis. . . .

Strategy #7: Treat War as a Continuation of Litigation by Other Means

The Bush bashers are correct that the Padilla case, with its serious liberty issues weighing against serious national peril, has pushed the law where it has never gone before. But that is because the threat the country is facing is without precedent, not because the administration is seizing unjustified power.

When the War on Terror's opponents intone, "We need not trade liberty for security," they are right—but not in the way they think. Contrary to their slogan's assumption, there is no zero-sum relationship between liberty and security. The government may expand its powers to detect terrorism without diminishing civil liberties one iota, as long as those powers remain subject to traditional restraints: statutory prerequisites for investigative action, judicial review, and political accountability. So far, these conditions have been met.

But the larger fallacy at the heart of the elites' liberty-versus-security formula is its blindness to all threats to freedom that do not emanate from the White House. Nothing the Bush administration has done comes close to causing the loss of freedom that Americans experienced after 9/11, when air travel shut down for days, and fear kept hundreds of thousands shut up in their homes. Should al-Qaida strike again, fear will once again paralyze the country far beyond the effects of any possible government restriction on civil rights. And that is what the government is trying to forestall, in the knowledge that preserving security is essential to preserving freedom.

POSTSCRIPT

Does the Patriot Act Abridge Essential Freedoms?

Those who deplore the USA Patriot Act are likely to share Nat Hentoff's conviction, expressed in quotations from Benjamin Franklin and Supreme Court Justice Louis Brandeis, that security cannot be obtained by the sacrifice of essential liberty. Defenders of the law will agree with Heather Mac Donald that liberty can be preserved while adopting new weapons in dealing with a new kind of threat to national security, and liberty will be lost if we do not respond effectively.

With the stakes so high and passions so great, it appears to be difficult for partisans on either side to retain civility in assessing the appropriate balance of civil liberty and national security. If we accept the accusations on both sides, rational discussion is impossible. Americans who favor the USA Patriot Act have been accused of being totalitarians who are enemies of civil liberty and individual privacy. Those who oppose many provisions of the law have been slandered in turn as implicitly unpatriotic and blind to all threats that do not originate with the American government.

Elaine Scarry, in "Resolving to Resist" (*Boston Review,* February–March 2004), sympathetically examines the opposition of more than 200 communities whose local governments have in different ways resolved not to assist the federal government in enforcing this law. A series of essays critical of the government's response to terrorism, largely but not exclusively focused on the USA Patriot Act, appear in the Winter 2002 issue of *Human Rights,* published by the American Bar Association. John Podesta, in "USA Patriot Act: The Good, the Bad, and the Sunset," acknowledges that some provisions are necessary, but others infringe on civil liberties and lack protective mechanisms to prevent abuse by the executive. Kate Martin, in "Intelligence, Terrorism, and Civil Liberties," concludes; "History has repeatedly demonstrated the dangers of allowing governments to secretly collect intelligence on their own people."

"The 2001 Patriot Act," in *The Federalist.com,* points out that defining domestic terrorism too narrow would allow terrorists to slip through loopholes. The Act "is a bold and timely piece of legislation, in keeping with the constitutional values of our nation's history, and essential to our nation's future." Robert H. Bork, in "Civil Liberties After 9/11" (*Commentary,* July–August 2003), points out that lawful prisoners of war are held without the right to a lawyer, and unlawful enemy combatants are entitled to even fewer rights. "A judicial system with rights of due process is crucial to a free society, but it is not designed for the protection of enemies engaged in armed conflict against us." Because some controversial features of the law are due to expire, debate will be vigorously renewed.

ISSUE 18

Should America Restrict Immigration?

YES: Patrick J. Buchanan, from *The Death of the West: How Dying Populations and Immigrant Invasions Imperil Our Country and Civilization* (Thomas Dunne Books, 2002)

NO: Daniel T. Griswold, from "Immigrants Have Enriched American Culture and Enhanced Our Influence in the World," *Insight on the News* (March 11, 2002)

ISSUE SUMMARY

YES: Political commentator Patrick J. Buchanan argues that large-scale, uncontrolled immigration has increased America's social and economic problems and deprived it of the shared values and common language that define a united people.

NO: Daniel T. Griswold, associate director of the Cato Institute's Center for Trade Policy Studies, while acknowledging the need to protect the U.S. against terrorists, contends that immigration gives America an economic edge, does not drain government finances, and is not remarkably high compared with past eras.

In 1949 a delegation of Native Americans went to Washington to tell lawmakers about the plight of America's original occupants. After meeting with Vice President Alben Barkley, one old Sioux chief delivered a parting word to the vice president. "Young fellow," he said, "let me give you a little advice. Be careful with your immigration laws. We were careless with ours."

As America prospered and offered the hope of opportunity and freedom, increasing numbers of immigrants came to the United States. In the last two decades of the nineteenth century, Congress barred further immigration by convicts, paupers, idiots, and Chinese. That, however, did not stem the tide.

Between 1870 and 1920, more than 26 million people came to live in the United States. The National Origins Act was adopted in 1924 to restrict the number of new immigrants, ban east Asian immigration, and establish a European quota based on the population of the United States in 1890, when there had been far fewer new arrivals from eastern and southern Europe. In 1965 the national origins formula was abandoned, but strict limits on the number of immigrants were retained. The end of quotas spurred a dramatic increase of immigrants from Central and South America and Asia. Between 1965 and 1995, nearly one-half of all immigrants came from Mexico, the Caribbean, and the rest of Latin America, and nearly one-third arrived from Asia.

The number of illegal arrivals from Latin America prompted passage of the Immigration Reform and Control Act of 1987, requiring that employers confirm the legal status of their employees. At the same time, undocumented workers who had entered the United States before 1982 were granted amnesty.

Do immigrants endanger or improve the American standard of living? Critics fear that the new immigrants, who are generally willing to work longer hours at lower pay, will take jobs away from American workers. Supporters of immigration believe that the new immigrants fill jobs that most Americans do not want and that they stimulate economic growth.

Do immigrants undermine or enrich American culture? New immigrant groups have enriched the culture with new ideas, new customs, and new artistic expression, but critics argue that the cultural coherence and political unity of the United States are now being threatened. They maintain that the new immigrants are less educated, more isolated, less motivated to join the mainstream, and more likely to become an economic burden to society.

Two-thirds of America's population growth in the 1990s was due to immigration, and two-thirds of those immigrants were Hispanic. Hispanics, defined as both whites and blacks who identify themselves as being of Hispanic origin, are now as numerous in the United States as blacks. Based on present population trends, it is estimated that by 2050, Hispanics will constitute 25 percent of the American population; blacks, 13 percent; Asians, 8 percent; American Indians, less than 1 percent; and whites, slightly more than 50 percent.

Earlier immigrants who came to America speaking a variety of languages quickly assimilated, learned English, and adopted American cultural patterns. Conversely, it is likely that modern Spanish-speaking immigrants, particularly illegal immigrants, find it easier to live within a closed culture that largely excludes adoption of the morals, manners, and language of the larger society. The effects of this change in population and culture can be seen most dramatically in California, the nation's most populous state, which has the greatest influx of illegal immigrants. For example, California's effort to deny welfare and public education to the children of illegal immigrants has been opposed in the courts.

Many of the criticisms of the new immigration are voiced in the following selection by Patrick J. Buchanan, who sees a decline in American traditions and values as a result of immigration. In the second selection, Daniel T. Griswold rejects criticisms of immigration as unfounded, citing the economic and cultural contributions that immigrants make to American society.

La Reconquista

Our old image is of Mexican folks as docile, conservative, friendly, Catholic people of traditional beliefs and values. There are still millions of these hard-working, family-oriented, patriotic Americans of Mexican heritage, who have been among the first to answer America's call to arms. And any man, woman, or child, from any country or continent, can be a good American. We know that from our history.

But the demographic sea change, especially in California, where a fourth of the people are foreign-born and almost a third are Latino, has spawned a new ethnic chauvinism. When the U.S. soccer team played Mexico in the Los Angeles Coliseum a few years back, the "Star-Spangled Banner" was hooted and jeered, an American flag was torn down, and the American team and its few fans were showered with water bombs, beer bottles, and garbage.

Two years ago, the south Texas town of El Cenizo declared Spanish its official language and ordered that all official documents be written in Spanish and all town business conducted in Spanish. Any cooperation with U.S. immigration authorities was made a firing offense. El Cenizo has, de facto, seceded from the United States.

In the New Mexico legislature in 2001, a resolution was introduced to rename the state "Nuevo Mexico," the name it carried before it became a part of the American Union. When the bill was defeated, the sponsor, Rep. Miguel Garcia, suggested to reporters that "covert racism" may have been the cause—the same racism, he said, that was behind naming the state New Mexico in the first place.

A spirit of separatism, nationalism, and irredentism has come alive in the barrio. The Latino student organization MEChA [Movement Estudiantil Chicano de Aztlan] demands return of the Southwest to Mexico. Charles Truxillo, a professor of Chicano Studies at the University of New Mexico, says a new "Aztlan" [the mythical place of origin of the Aztec peoples] with its capital in Los Angeles is inevitable, and Mexicans should seek it by any means necessary.

"We're recolonizing America, so they're afraid of us. It's time to take back what is ours," rants Ricky Sierra of the Chicano National Guard. One demonstration leader in Westwood exulted, "We are here . . . to show white Protestant Los Angeles that we're the majority . . . and we claim this land as ours. It's always been ours and we're still here . . . if anybody is going to be deported it's going to be you."

José Angel Gutierrez, a political science professor at the University of Texas at Arlington and director of the UTA Mexican-American Study Center, told a university crowd: "We have an aging white America. They are not making babies. They are dying. The explosion is in our population. They are shitting in their pants in fear! I love it."

Now, this may be Corona talk in the cantina, but more authoritative voices are sounding the same notes, and they resonate in the barrio. The Mexican consul general José Pescador Osuna remarked in 1998, "Even though I am saying this part serious, part joking, I think we are practicing La Reconquista in California." California legislator Art Torres called Proposition 187, to cut off welfare to illegal aliens, "the last gasp of white America."

"California is going to be a Mexican State. We are going to control all the institutions. If people don't like it, they should leave," exults Mario Obledo, president of the League of United Latin American Citizens and recipient of the Medal of Freedom from President Clinton. Mexican president Ernesto Zedillo told Mexican-Americans in Dallas: "You are Mexicans, Mexicans who live north of the border."

Why should Mexican immigrants not have greater loyalty to their homeland than to a country they broke into simply to find work? Why should nationalistic and patriotic Mexicans not dream of *reconquista?*. . .

⁂

Meanwhile, the invasion rolls on. America's once-sleepy two-thousand-mile Mexican border is now the scene of daily confrontations. Ranches in Arizona have become nightly bivouac areas for thousands of aliens, who cut fences and leave poisoned cattle and trails of debris in the trek north. Even the Mexican army is showing its contempt. The State Department reported fifty-five military incursions in the five years before the incident in 2000, when truckloads of Mexican soldiers barreled through a barbed wire fence, fired shots, and pursued two mounted officers and a U.S. Border Patrol vehicle. Border Patrol agents believe some Mexican army units collaborate with the drug cartels.

America has become a spillway for an exploding population that Mexico is unable to employ. With Mexico's population growing by ten million every decade, there will be no end to the long march north before the American Southwest is fully Hispanicized. Mexican senator Adolfo Zinser conceded that Mexico's "economic policy is dependent on unlimited emigration to the United States." The Yanqui-baiting academic and "onetime Communist supporter" Jorge Casteñada warned in *Atlantic Monthly,* six years ago, that any American effort to cut back immigration "will make social peace in . . . Mexico untenable. . . . Some Americans dislike immigration, but there is very little they can do about it." These opinions take on weight, with Senator Zinser now President Fox's national security adviser and Jorge Casteñada his foreign minister. . . .

America is no longer the biracial society of 1960 that struggled to erase divisions and close gaps in a nation 90 percent white. Today we juggle the rancorous and rival claims of a multiracial, multiethnic, and multicultural country. Vice President Gore captured the new America in his famous howler, when he translated our national slogan, "E Pluribus Unum," backward, as "Out of one, many."

Today there are 28.4 million foreign-born in the United States. Half are from Latin America and the Caribbean, a fourth from Asia. The rest are from Africa, the Middle East, and Europe. One in every five New Yorkers and Floridians is foreign-born, as is one of every four Californians. With 8.4 million foreign-born, and not one new power plant built in a decade, small wonder California faces power shortages and power outages. With endless immigration, America is going to need an endless expansion of its power sources—hydroelectric power, fossil fuels (oil, coal, gas), and nuclear power. The only alternative is blackouts, brownouts, and endless lines at the pump.

In the 1990s, immigrants and their children were responsible for 100 percent of the population growth of California, New York, New Jersey, Illinois, and Massachusetts, and over half the population growth of Florida, Texas, Michigan, and Maryland. As the United States allots most of its immigrant visas to relatives of new arrivals, it is difficult for Europeans to come, while entire villages from El Salvador are now here.

The results of the Third World bias in immigration can be seen in our social statistics. The median age of Euro-Americans is 36; for Hispanics, it is 26. The median age of all foreign-born, 33, is far below that of the older American ethnic groups, such as English, 40, and Scots-Irish, 43. These social statistics raise a question: Is the U.S. government, by deporting scarcely 1 percent of an estimated eleven million illegal aliens each year, failing in its constitutional duty to protect the rights of American citizens? Consider:

- A third of the legal immigrants who come to the United States have not finished high school. Some 22 percent do not even have a ninth-grade education, compared to less than 5 percent of our native born.
- Over 36 percent of all immigrants, and 57 percent of those from Central America, do not earn twenty thousand dollars a year. Of the immigrants who have come since 1980, 60 percent still do not earn twenty thousand dollars a year.
- Of immigrant households in the United States, 29 percent are below the poverty line, twice the 14 percent of native born.
- Immigrant use of food stamps, Supplemental Social Security, and school lunch programs runs from 50 percent to 100 percent higher than use by native born.
- Mr. Clinton's Department of Labor estimated that 50 percent of the real-wage losses sustained by low-income Americans is due to immigration.

- By 1991, foreign nationals accounted for 24 percent of all arrests in Los Angeles and 36 percent of all arrests in Miami.
- In 1980, federal and state prisons housed nine thousand criminal aliens. By 1995, this had soared to fifty-nine thousand criminal aliens, a figure that does not include aliens who became citizens or the criminals sent over by Castro in the Mariel boat lift.
- Between 1988 and 1994, the number of illegal aliens in California's prisons more than tripled from fifty-five hundred to eighteen thousand.

None of the above statistics, however, holds for emigrants from Europe. And some of the statistics, on low education, for example, do not apply to emigrants from Asia.

Nevertheless, mass emigration from poor Third World countries is "good for business," especially businesses that employ large numbers at low wages. In the spring of 2001, the Business Industry Political Action Committee, BIPAC, issued "marching orders for grass roots mobilization." The *Wall Street Journal* said that the 400 blue-chip companies and 150 trade associations "will call for continued normalization of trade with China . . . and easing immigration restrictions to meet labor needs. . . ." But what is good for corporate America is not necessarily good for Middle America. When it comes to open borders, the corporate interest and the national interest do not coincide, they collide. Should America suffer a sustained recession, we will find out if the melting pot is still working.

But mass immigration raises more critical issues than jobs or wages, for immigration is ultimately about America herself.

What Is a Nation?

Most of the people who leave their homelands to come to America, whether from Mexico or Mauritania, are good people, decent people. They seek the same better life our ancestors sought when they came. They come to work; they obey our laws; they cherish our freedoms; they relish the opportunities the greatest nation on earth has to offer; most love America; may wish to become part of the American family. One may encounter these newcomers everywhere. But the record number of foreign-born coming from cultures with little in common with Americans raises a different question: What is a nation?

Some define as one people of common ancestry, language, literature, history, heritage, heroes, traditions, customs, mores, and faith who have lived together over time on the same land under the same rulers. This is the blood-and-soil idea of a nation. Among those who pressed this definition were Secretary of State John Quincy Adams, who laid down these conditions on immigrants: "They must cast off the European skin, never to resume it. They must look forward to their posterity rather than backward to their ancestors." Theodore Roosevelt, who thundered against "hyphenated-Americanism," seemed to share Adam's view. Woodrow Wilson, speaking to newly naturalized Americans in 1915 in Philadelphia, echoed T.R.: "A man who thinks of himself as belonging to a particular national group in America has yet to become an American." This idea, of Americans as a separate and unique people, was first given expression by John Jay in *Federalist 2:*

> Providence has been pleased to give this one connected country to one united people—a people descended from the same ancestors, speaking the same language, professing the same religion, attached to the same principles of government, very similar in their manners and customs, and who, by their joint counsels, arms, and efforts, fighting side by side throughout a long and bloody war, have nobly established their general liberty and independence.

But can anyone say today that we Americans are "one united people"?

We are not descended from the same ancestors. We no longer speak the same language. We do not profess the same religion. We are no longer simply Protestant, Catholic, and Jewish, as sociologist Will Herberg described us in his *Essay in American Religious Sociology* in 1955. We are now Protestant, Catholic, Jewish, Mormon, Muslim, Hindu, Buddhist, Taoist, Shintoist, Santeria, New Age, voodoo, agnostic, atheist, humanist, Rastafarian, and Wiccan. Even the mention of Jesus' name at the Inauguration by the preachers Mr. Bush selected to give the invocations evoked fury and cries of "insensitive," "divisive," and "exclusionary." A *New Republic* editorial lashed out at these "crushing Christological thuds" from the Inaugural stand. We no longer agree on whether God exists, when life begins, and what is moral and immoral. We are not "similar in our manners and customs." We never fought "side by side throughout a long and bloody war." The Greatest Generation did, but it is passing away. If the rest of us recall a "long and bloody war," it was Vietnam, and, no, we were not side by side.

We remain "attached to the same principles of government." But common principles of government are not enough to hold us together. The South was "attached to the same principles of government" as the North. But that did not stop Southerners from fighting four years of bloody war to be free of their Northern brethren.

In his Inaugural, President Bush rejected Jay's vision: "America has never been united by blood or birth or soil. We are bound by ideals that move us beyond our background, lift us above our interests, and teach us what it means to be a citizen." In his *The Disuniting of America*, Arthur Schlesinger subscribes to the Bush idea of a nation, united by shared belief in an American Creed to be found in our history and greatest documents: the Declaration of Independence, the Constitution, and the Gettysburg Address. Writes Schlesinger:

> The American Creed envisages a nation composed of individuals making their own choices and accountable to themselves, not a nation based on inviolable ethnic communities. For our values are not matters or whim and happenstance. History has given them to us. They are

anchored in our national experience, in our great national documents, in our national heroes, in our folkways, our traditions, and standards. [Our values] work for us; and, for that reason, we live and die by them.

But Americans no longer agree on values, history, or heroes. What one-half of America sees as a glorious past the other views as shameful and wicked. Columbus, Washington, Jefferson, Jackson, Lincoln, and Lee—all of them heroes of the old America—are all under attack. Those most American of words, equality and freedom, today hold different meanings for different Americans. As for our "great national documents," the Supreme Court decisions that interpret our Constitution have not united us; for forty years they have divided us, bitterly, over prayer in school, integration, busing, flag burning, abortion, pornography, and the Ten Commandments.

Nor is a belief in democracy sufficient to hold us together. Half of the nation did not even bother to vote in the presidential election of 2000; three out of five do not vote in off-year elections. Millions cannot name their congressman, senators, or the Supreme Court justices. They do not care.

Whether one holds to the blood-and-soil idea of a nation, or to the creedal idea, or both, neither nation is what it was in the 1940s, 1950s, or 1960s. We live in the same country, we are governed by the same leaders, but can we truly say we are still one nation and one people?

It is hard to say yes, harder to believe that over a million immigrants every year, from every country on earth, a third of them breaking in, will reforge the bonds of our disuniting nation. John Stuart Mill warned that "free institutions are next to impossible in a country made up of different nationalities. Among a people without fellow-feeling, especially if they read and speak different languages, the united public opinion necessary to the working of representative government cannot exist."

We are about to find out if Mill was right.

Daniel T. Griswold  **NO**

Immigrants Have Enriched American Culture and Enhanced Our Influence in the World

Immigration always has been controversial in the United States. More than two centuries ago, Benjamin Franklin worried that too many German immigrants would swamp America's predominantly British culture. In the mid-1800s, Irish immigrants were scorned as lazy drunks, not to mention Roman Catholics. At the turn of the century a wave of "new immigrants"— Poles, Italians, Russian Jews—were believed to be too different ever to assimilate into American life. Today the same fears are raised about immigrants from Latin America and Asia, but current critics of immigration are as wrong as their counterparts were in previous eras.

Immigration is not undermining the American experiment; it is an integral part of it. We are a nation of immigrants. Successive waves of immigrants have kept our country demographically young, enriched our culture and added to our productive capacity as a nation, enhancing our influence in the world.

Immigration gives the United States an economic edge in the world economy. Immigrants bring innovative ideas and entrepreneurial spirit to the U.S. economy. They provide business contacts to other markets, enhancing America's ability to trade and invest profitably in the global economy. They keep our economy flexible, allowing U.S. producers to keep prices down and to respond to changing consumer demands. An authoritative 1997 study by the National Academy of Sciences (NAS) concluded that immigration delivered a "significant positive gain" to the U.S. economy. In testimony before Congress [in 2001], Federal Reserve Board Chairman Alan Greenspan said, "I've always argued that this country has benefited immensely from the fact that we draw people from all over the world."

Contrary to popular myth, immigrants do not push Americans out of jobs. Immigrants tend to fill jobs that Americans cannot or will not fill, mostly at the high and low ends of the skill spectrum. Immigrants are disproportionately represented in such high-skilled fields as medicine, physics and computer science, but also in lower-skilled sectors such as hotels and restaurants, domestic service, construction and light manufacturing.

From Daniel T. Griswold, "Immigrants Have Enriched American Culture and Enhanced Our Influence in the World," *Insight on the News* (March 11, 2002). Copyright © 2002 by News World Communications, Inc. Reprinted by permission of *Insight on the News*.

Immigrants also raise demand for goods as well as the supply. During the long boom of the 1990s, and especially in the second half of the decade, the national unemployment rate fell below 4 percent and real wages rose up and down the income scale during a time of relatively high immigration.

Nowhere is the contribution of immigrants more apparent than in the high-technology and other knowledge-based sectors. Silicon Valley and other high-tech sectors would cease to function if we foolishly were to close our borders to skilled and educated immigrants. These immigrants represent human capital that can make our entire economy more productive. Immigrants have developed new products, such as the Java computer language, that have created employment opportunities for millions of Americans.

Immigrants are not a drain on government finances. The NAS study found that the typical immigrant and his or her offspring will pay a net $80,000 more in taxes during their lifetimes than they collect in government services. For immigrants with college degrees, the net fiscal return is $198,000. It is true that low-skilled immigrants and refugees tend to use welfare more than the typical "native" household, but the 1996 Welfare Reform Act made it much more difficult for newcomers to collect welfare. As a result, immigrant use of welfare has declined in recent years along with overall welfare rolls.

Despite the claims of immigration opponents, today's flow is not out of proportion to historical levels. Immigration in the last decade has averaged about 1 million per year, high in absolute numbers, but the rate of 4 immigrants per year per 1,000 U.S. residents is less than half the rate during the Great Migration of 1890–1914. Today, about 10 percent of U.S. residents are foreign-born, an increase from 4.7 percent in 1970, but still far short of the 14.7 percent who were foreign-born in 1910. Nor can immigrants fairly be blamed for causing "overpopulation." America's annual population growth of 1 percent is below our average growth rate of the last century. In fact, without immigration our labor force would begin to shrink within two decades. According to the 2000 Census, 22 percent of U.S. counties lost population between 1990 and 2000. Immigrants could help revitalize demographically declining areas of the country, just as they helped revitalize New York City and other previously declining urban centers.

Drastically reducing the number of foreigners who enter the United States each year only would compound the economic damage of Sept. 11 while doing nothing to enhance our security. The tourist industry, already reeling, would lose millions of foreign visitors, and American universities would lose hundreds of thousands of foreign students if our borders were closed.

Obviously the U.S. government should "control its borders" to keep out anyone who intends to commit terrorist acts. The problem is not that we are letting too many people into the United States but that the government has failed to keep the wrong people out. We can stop terrorists from entering the United States without closing our borders or reducing the number of hardworking, peaceful immigrants who settle here.

We must do whatever is necessary to stop potentially dangerous people at the border. Law-enforcement and intelligence agencies must work closely with the State Department, the Immigration and Naturalization Service (INS) and U.S. Customs to share real-time information about potential terrorists. Computer systems must be upgraded and new technologies adopted to screen out the bad guys without causing intolerable delays at the border. More agents need to be posted at ports of entry to more thoroughly screen for high-risk travelers. We must bolster cooperation with our neighbors, Canada and Mexico, to ensure that terrorists cannot slip across our long land borders.

In the wake of Sept. 11, longtime critics of immigration have tried to exploit legitimate concerns about security to argue for drastic cuts in immigration. But border security and immigration are two separate matters. Immigrants are only a small subset of the total number of foreigners who enter the United States every year. Only about one of every 25 foreign nationals who enter the United States come here to immigrate. The rest are tourists, business travelers, students and Mexican and Canadians who cross the border for a weekend to shop or visit family and then return home with no intention of settling permanently in the United States.

The 19 terrorists who attacked the United States on Sept. 11 did not apply to the INS to immigrate or to become U.S. citizens. Like most aliens who enter the United States, they were here on temporary tourist and student visas. We could reduce the number of immigrants to zero and still not stop terrorists from slipping into the country on nonimmigrant visas.

To defend ourselves better against terrorism, our border-control system requires a reorientation of mission. For the last two decades, U.S. immigration policy has been obsessed with nabbing mostly Mexican-born workers whose only "crime" is their desire to earn an honest day's pay. Those workers pose no threat to national security.

Our land border with Mexico is half as long as our border with Canada, yet before Sept. 11 it was patrolled by 10 times as many border agents. On average we were posting an agent every five miles along our 3,987-mile border with Canada and every quarter-mile on the 2,000-mile border with Mexico. On the Northern border there were 120,000 entries per year per agent compared with 40,000 entries on the Southwestern border. This is out of proportion to any legitimate fears about national security. In fact terrorists seem to prefer the northern border. Let's remember that it was at a border-crossing station in Washington state in December 1999 that a terrorist was apprehended with explosives that were to be used to blow up Los Angeles International Airport during the millennium celebrations.

At a February 2000 hearing, former Sen. Slade Gorton (R-Wash.) warned that "understaffing at our northern border is jeopardizing the security of our nation, not to mention border personnel, while in at least some sections of the southern border, there are so many agents that there is not enough work to keep them all busy."

We should stop wasting scarce resources in a self-destructive quest to hunt down Mexican construction workers and raid restaurants and chicken-processing plants, and redirect those resources to track potential terrorists and smash their cells before they can blow up more buildings and kill more Americans.

For all these reasons, President George W. Bush's initiative to legalize and regularize the movement of workers across the U.S.-Mexican border makes sense in terms of national security as well as economics. It also is politically smart.

In his latest book, *The Death of the West,* Pat Buchanan argues that opposing immigration will be a winning formula for conservative Republicans. His own political decline and fall undermine his claim. Like former liberal Republican Gov. Pete Wilson in California, Buchanan has tried to win votes by blaming immigration for America's problems. But voters wisely rejected Buchanan's thesis. Despite $12 million in taxpayer campaign funds, and an assist from the Florida butterfly ballot [a ballot with candidates' names on both sides of a column of punch holes, which caused some voters to mistakenly vote for Buchanan instead of Gore], Buchanan won less than 0.5 percent of the presidential vote in 2000. In contrast Bush, by affirming immigration, raised the GOP's share of the Hispanic vote to 35 percent from the 21 percent carried by Bob Dole in 1996. If conservatives adopt the anti-immigrant message, they risk following Buchanan and Wilson into political irrelevancy.

It would be a national shame if, in the name of security, we closed the door to immigrants who come here to work, save and build a better life for themselves and their families. Immigrants come here to live the American Dream; terrorists come to destroy it. We should not allow America's tradition of welcoming immigrants to become yet another casualty of Sept. 11.

POSTSCRIPT

Should America Restrict Immigration?

There is no accurate census of illegal immigrants, but the best estimate is that 5 million people have entered the United States illegally within the past 10 years. What are the consequences for American society? The issue of immigration encompasses both legal and illegal immigrants. Immigration policy should begin by examining who comes and the consequences for the nation. Who are they, and what impact do they have? What do they cost, and what do they contribute?

Until the early years of the new republic, immigrants were predominantly white, English-speaking, Protestant Europeans and African slaves who were forcibly brought to the New World. This soon changed, and for a half-century—until the adoption of laws restricting immigration in the 1920s—Catholics and Jews, southern and eastern Europeans, most of them non-English speakers, came to the United States. Since World War II, Asian and Hispanic immigrants have come in ever-increasing numbers.

Few issues arouse such contradictory emotions as does immigration. We are proud of our immigrant past because we are all immigrants or the descendants of immigrants. At the same time, we are concerned about how new immigrants may change what we perceive to be American values and interests. A very useful perspective is provided in Roger Daniels, *Guarding the Golden Door: American Immigration Policy and Immigrants since 1882* (Hill and Wang, 2004). Daniels examines immigration practices and consequences from the Chinese Exclusion Act of 1882 to the Homeland Security response to 9/11.

Georgie Anne Geyer's *Americans No More* (Atlantic Monthly Press, 1996) is a lament on the decline of civic life in America as a result of both legal and illegal immigration. Geyer does not deplore illegal immigration but the recent tendency of legal immigrants to resist assimilation. Peter Brimelow, in *Alien Nation: Common Sense About America's Immigration Disaster* (Random House, 1995), catalogs what he perceives to be the consequences of what he calls America's "immigration disaster." Brimelow argues that no multicultural society has lasted. Otis L. Graham, Jr., *Unguarded Gates: A History of America's Immigration Crisis* (Rowman and Littlefield, 2004) offers a post–9/11 critique of current immigration policy.

In opposition to Brimelow's view, Sanford J. Ungar, in *Fresh Blood: The New American Immigrants* (Simon & Schuster, 1995), argues, "To be American means being part of an ever more heterogeneous people and participating in the constant redefinition of a complex, evolving cultural fabric." Somewhere in between multiculturalists like Ungar and assimilationists like

Brimelow and Geyer is Peter D. Salins. In *Assimilation, American Style* (Basic Books, 1997), Salins argues that the naturalization process is the best means for absorbing the flood of immigrants who arrive in America each year. Often forgotten in these debates are the experiences of the immigrants themselves. Newer immigrants to America have recounted some of these experiences in recent books by and about them. In *Becoming American: Personal Essays by First Generation Immigrant Women* (Hyperion, 2000), Ghanaian American writer Meri Nana-Ama Danquah brings together the personal recollections and reflections by immigrant women from Europe, Latin America, Africa, Asia, and the Caribbean. In *American by Choice: The Remarkable Fulfillment of an Immigrant's Dreams* (Thomas Nelson, 1998), Sam Moore describes his rise in America from a poor Lebanese immigrant to president and CEO of Thomas Nelson Publishers, a major religious publishing house. A more troubling account of the immigrant experience is that of Mary C. Waters, in *Black Identities: West Indian Immigrant Dreams and American Realities* (Harvard University Press, 2000). Waters finds that when West Indian immigrants first arrive, their skills, knowledge of English, and general optimism carry them forward, but later on, a variety of influences, from racial discrimination to low wages and poor working conditions, tend to erode their self-confidence.

Attitudes toward immigration change with time and circumstances. September 11, 2001, was one of those times. The terrorist attacks on the World Trade Center have increased the fear that many Americans have of all foreigners. Tamar Jacoby examines the changing circumstances in "Too Many Immigrants?" *Commentary* (April 2002).

The literature on immigration seems to grow as rapidly as immigration itself. Christopher Jencks has assessed this literature in two long essays entitled "Who Should Get In?" *New York Review of Books* (November 29 and December 20, 2001). Among the controversial issues that he examines is whether or not permanent status can be granted to illegal immigrants who are presently residing in the United States without encouraging the influx of many more and, if so, how. In 2004, President Bush proposed an amnesty program for illegal aliens. Mark Krikorian, in *"Amnesty Again"* (*The National Review,* January 26, 1994), criticizes the plan because it would lead to the permanent importation of thousands of new workers.

Americans confront a choice. On the one hand, there are the ethical and political consequences of restricting immigration into a country whose attraction to poor or persecuted people is as great as its borders are vast. On the other hand, there are the problems of absorbing new, generally non-English-speaking populations into an economy that may have to provide increasing public support and into a society whose traditions and values may clash with those of the newcomers.

On the Internet . . .

In addition to the Internet sites listed below, type in key words, such as "free trade," "Iraq," "Iraqi war," and "American world leadership," to find other listings.

U.S. State Department

View this site for understanding into the workings of a major U.S. executive branch department. Links explain exactly what the department does, what services it provides, and what it says about U.S. interests around the world, as well as provide other information.

http://www.state.gov

Marketplace of Political Ideas/University of Houston Libraries

Here is a valuable collection of links to campaign, conservative/liberal perspectives, and political party sites. There are general political sites, Democratic sites, Republican sites, third-party sites, and much more.

http://info.lib.uh.edu/politics/markind.htm

United States Senate Committee on Foreign Relations

This site is an excellent up-to-date resource for information about the United States' reaction to events regarding foreign policy.

http://www.senate.gov/~foreign/

Voice of the Shuttle: Politics and Government

This site, created and maintained by Alan Liu of the University of California, Santa Barbara, offers numerous links to political resources on the Internet. In addition to general political resources, categories include general International politics, political theory and philosophy, and political commentary.

http://vos.ucsb.edu/browse.asp?id=2726

American Diplomacy

American Diplomacy is an online journal of commentary, analysis, and research on U.S. foreign policy and its results around the world.

http://www.unc.edu/depts/diplomat/

Foreign Affairs

This page of the well-respected foreign policy journal *Foreign Affairs* is a valuable research tool. It allows users to search the journal's archives and provides indexed access to the field's leading publications, documents, online resources, and so on. Link to dozens of other related Web sites from here too.

http://www.foreignaffairs.org

PART 4

America and the World

*T*he *United States long ago could isolate itself from much of the rest of the world, and it did. That possibility disappeared long before the terrorist attack on September 11, 2001. Today America's unsurpassed wealth and military power mean that it cannot escape influencing and being influenced by world events. What are the advantages and risks of free trade for the America economy? To what extent should it engage in aggressive action in foreign countries to protect American security, punish tyranny, or encourage the spread of democracy? In short, what role should America play in world affairs?*

- Is Free Trade Fair Trade?

- Was the Invasion of Iraq Justified?

- Must America Exercise World Leadership?

ISSUE 19

Is Free Trade Fair Trade?

YES: Douglas A. Irwin, from *Free Trade Under Fire* (Princeton University Press, 2002)

NO: David Morris, from "Free Trade: The Great Destroyer," in Jerry Mander and Edward Goldsmith, eds., *The Case Against the Global Economy: And for a Return to the Local* (Sierra Club Books, 1996)

ISSUE SUMMARY

YES: Professor of economics Douglas A. Irwin asserts that all countries benefit from free trade because it promotes efficiency, spurs production, and forces the least productive companies to reduce their output or shut down, resulting in better goods at lower prices.

NO: David Morris, vice president of the Institute for Local Self-Reliance, argues that free trade is unnecessary because gains in efficiency do not require large-scale multinational enterprises and undesirable because it widens the standard-of-living gap between rich and poor nations.

An economic and cultural revolution like none before it has taken place over the past two decades. In centuries marked by Western imperialism, weak nations were ruled by powerful nations, and their raw and natural resources were expropriated for manufacture by the imperial powers. Now the owners are multinational corporations that know no national boundaries (although their principal owners are usually citizens of the industrial nations), and the manufacturing of the most highly sophisticated techno-logical products takes place in the poorer nations, which achieve higher rates of employment, albeit for much lower wages than workers in the richer nations had earned.

This is globalization—a profound change in the ways in which large-scale business is conducted. Globalization is supported by technological breakthroughs, the new markets and profits that powerful corporations now pursue, and governments that subscribe to the changes it brings. For the underdeveloped nations, the advantages include training and employment for poor people and economic development support from international agencies. For the economically advanced nations, the advantages include cheaper manufactured goods and the profits that accrue to stockholders.

Globalization seems inescapable. Perhaps the most important and controversial characteristic of this change has been a movement toward free markets, or the removal of trade barriers and other constraints on doing business. Free trade is advocated because it fosters openness to new ideas and innovation, with a minimum degree of regulation, and, in the view of its supporters, it encourages the spread of democracy in societies that have not enjoyed political freedom.

Globalization and free trade are opposed by those who believe that the principal and perhaps only beneficiaries are the multinational corporations that sharply reduce their labor costs and even more sharply increase their profits. Opponents acknowledge that investors gain added value, but they maintain that highly skilled and well-paid workers in America and other advanced nations lose good jobs and that poorly paid workers in the under-developed countries are exploited. Furthermore, because the owners and most of the customers of industry do not live in the countries where the electronics, clothing, and other manufactured goods are produced, they have little or no concern for the consequences of their investments for those countries.

Thus, the critics charge, free trade is not fair trade. This protest comes from members of labor unions, who witness declining membership as their jobs are taken by workers in poor countries who will accept a fraction of the pay; environmentalists, who deplore deforestation, the pollution of rivers and the air by toxic chemicals, and other health hazards that accompany unregulated industry; and human rights groups, which oppose low wages that perpetuate poverty and exploitation. These groups organized the demonstrations at the 1999 World Trade Organization (WTO) ministerial meeting in Seattle, Washington, which have been repeated at subsequent meetings of the WTO and the World Bank.

The WTO denies that it advocates free trade at any cost. The organization maintains that countries must decide for themselves when, how, and how much to protect domestic producers from dumped or subsidized imports. However, agreements such as the North American Free Trade Agreement (NAFTA) permit foreign investors to sue a national government if their company's property assets, including the intangible property of expected profits, are damaged by that nation's laws, even if those laws were designed to protect the environment or public safety and health. Some advocates of free trade oppose NAFTA and other regional agreements on the grounds that they are preferential arrangements that compromise true free trade.

In the following selection, Douglas A. Irwin concludes that free trade is beneficial because countries that adopt it, improve their productivity and increase their per capita income. According to trade studies, says Irwin, the complete elimination of global barriers to trade brings gains to all nations. In the second selection, David Morris discusses the environmental harm and devastating effects in local communities that result from free trade.

Douglas A. Irwin  **YES**

The Case for Free Trade: Old Theories, New Evidence

For more than two centuries, economists have pointed out the benefits of free trade and the costs of trade restrictions. As Adam Smith argued more than two centuries ago, "All commerce that is carried on betwixt any two countries must necessarily be advantageous to both," and therefore "all duties, customs, and excise [on imports] should be abolished, and free commerce and liberty of exchange should be allowed with all nations." The economic case for free trade, however, is not based on outdated theories in musty old books. The classic insights into the nature of economic exchange between countries have been refined and updated over the years to retain their relevance to today's circumstances. More importantly, over the past decade economists have gathered extensive empirical evidence that contributes appreciably to our understanding of the free trade. This [selection] reviews the classic theories and examines the new evidence, noting as well the qualifications to the case for free trade.

Specialization and Trade

The traditional case for free trade is based on the gains from specialization and exchange. These gains are easily understood at the level of the individual. Most people do not produce for themselves even a fraction of the goods they consume. Rather, we earn an income by specializing in certain activities and then using our earnings to purchase various goods and services—food, clothing, shelter, health care—produced by others. In essence, we "export" the goods and services that we produce with our own labor and "import" the goods and services produced by others that we wish to consume. This division of labor enables us to increase our consumption beyond that which would be possible if we tried to be self-sufficient and produce everything for ourselves. Specialization allows us access to a greater variety and better quality of goods and services.

Trade between nations is simply the international extension of this division of labor. For example, the United States has specialized in the

From Douglas A. Irwin, *Free Trade Under Fire* (Princeton University Press, 2002). Copyright © 2002 by Princeton University Press. Reprinted by permission of Princeton University Press. Notes omitted.

production of aircraft, industrial machinery, and agricultural commodities (particularly corn, soybeans, and wheat). In exchange for exports of these products, the United States purchases, among other things, imports of crude oil, clothing, and iron and steel mill products. Like individuals, countries benefit immensely from this division of labor and enjoy a higher real income than countries that forgo such trade. Just as there seems no obvious reason to limit the free exchange of goods within a country without a specific justification, there is no obvious reason why trade between countries should be limited in the absence of a compelling reason for doing so. . . .

Adam Smith, whose magnificent work *The Wealth of Nations* was first published in 1776, set out [the] case for free trade with a persuasive flair that still resonates today. Smith advocated the "obvious and simple system of natural liberty" in which individuals would be free to pursue their own interests, while the government provided the legal framework within which commerce would take place. With the government enforcing a system of justice and providing certain public goods (such as roads, in Smith's view), the private interests of individuals could be turned toward productive activities, namely, meeting the demands of the public as expressed in the marketplace. Smith envisioned a system that would give people the incentive to better themselves through economic activities, where they would create wealth by serving others through market exchange, rather than through political activities, where they might seek to redistribute existing wealth through, for example, legal restraints on competition. Under such a system, the powerful motivating force of self-interest could be channeled toward socially beneficial activities that would serve the general interest rather than socially unproductive activities that might advance the interests of a select few but would come at the expense of society as a whole.

Free trade is an important component of this system of economic liberty. Under a system of natural liberty in which domestic commerce is largely free from restraints on competition, though not necessarily free from government regulation, commerce would also be permitted to operate freely between countries. According to Smith, free trade would increase competition in the home market and curtail the power of domestic firms by checking their ability to exploit consumers through high prices and poor service. Moreover, the country would gain by exchanging exports of goods that are dear on the world market for imports of goods that are cheap on the world market. . . .

Comparative Advantage

In 1799, a successful London stockbroker named David Ricardo came across a copy of *The Wealth of Nations* while on vacation and quickly became engrossed in the book. Ricardo admired Smith's great achievement, but thought that many of the topics deserved further investigation. For example, Smith believed that a country would export goods that it produces most efficiently and import goods that other countries produce most efficiently. In this way, trade is a mutually beneficial way of increasing total world output and thus the consumption of every country. But, Ricardo asked, what if one country was the most efficient at producing everything? Would that country still benefit from trade? Would disadvantaged countries find themselves unable to export anything?

To overcome this problem, Ricardo arrived at a brilliant deduction that became known as the theory of comparative advantage. Comparative advantage implies that a country could find it advantageous to import some goods even if it could produce those same goods more efficiently than other countries. Conversely, a country would be able to export some goods even if other countries could produce them more efficiently. In either case, countries would be able to benefit from trade. Ricardo's conclusions about the benefits of trade were similar to Smith's, but his approach contains a deeper insight.

At first, the principle of comparative advantage seems counterintuitive. Why would a country ever import a good that it could produce more efficiently than another country? Yet comparative advantage is the key to understanding the pattern of international trade. For example, imagine a consulting firm hired to examine the factors explaining international trade in textiles. The consultants would probably start by examining the efficiency of textile production in various countries. If one country was found to be more efficient than another in producing textiles, the firm might conclude that this country would export textiles and other countries would import them. Yet because this single comparison is insufficient for determining the pattern of trade, this conclusion might well be wrong.

According to Ricardo and the other classical economists of the early nineteenth century, international trade is not driven by the *absolute* costs of production, but by the *opportunity* costs of production. The country most efficient at producing textiles might be even more efficient than other countries at producing other goods, such as shoes. In that case, the country would be best served by directing its labor to producing shoes, in which its margin of productive advantage is even greater than in textiles. As a result, despite its productivity advantage in textiles, the country would export shoes in exchange for imports of textiles. In the absence of other information, the absolute efficiency of one country's textile producers in comparison to another country's is insufficient to determine whether the country produces all of the textiles it consumes or imports some of them. . . .

The Gains From Trade

While the idea that all countries can benefit from international trade goes back to Smith and Ricardo, subsequent research has described the gains from trade in much greater detail. In the *Principles of Political Economy* (1848), John Stuart Mill, one of the leading economists of the nineteenth century, pointed to three principal gains from trade. First, there are what Mill called the "direct economical advantages of foreign trade." Second, there are "indirect effects" of trade, "which must be counted as benefits of a high order." Finally, Mill argued that the economical benefits of commerce are surpassed in importance by those of its effects which are intellectual and moral." What, specifically, are these three advantages of trade?

The "direct economical advantages" of trade are the standard gains that arise from specialization, as described by Smith and Ricardo. By exporting some of its domestically produced goods in exchange for imports, a country engages in mutually advantageous trade that enables it to use its limited productive resources (such as land, labor, and capital) more efficiently and therefore achieve a higher real national income than it could in the absence of trade. A higher real income translates into an ability to afford more of all goods and services than would be possible without trade.

These static gains from specialization are sizable. The classic illustration of the direct gains from trade comes from Japan's opening to the world economy. In 1858, as a result of American pressure, Japan opened its ports to international trade after decades of autarky (economic isolation). The gains from trade can be summarized by examining the prices of goods in Japan before and after the opening of trade. For example, the price of silk and tea was much higher on world markets than in Japan prior to the opening of trade, while the price of cotton and woolen goods was much lower on world markets. Japan therefore exported silk and tea in exchange for imports of clothing and other goods. With the introduction of trade, prices of those goods in Japan converged to the prices on the world market. Japan's terms of trade—the prices of the goods it exported relative to the prices of the goods it imported—improved by a factor of more than three and increased Japan's real income by as much as 65 percent.

Unlike nineteenth-century Japan, most countries have been open to some international trade for centuries, making it difficult to measure the overall gain from free trade. However, economists can estimate the gains from increased trade as a result of the reduction in trade barriers. Computable general equilibrium models, which are complex computational models used to simulate the impact of various trade policies on specific industries and the overall economy, calculate the gains that arise from shifting resources between various sectors of the economy. Specifically, these models examine the shift of labor and capital away from industries that compete against imports toward those in which the country has a comparative advantage as a result of changes in trade policy.

For example, one study showed that the agreements to reduce trade barriers reached under the Uruguay Round of multilateral trade negotiations in 1994 would result in an annual gain of $13 billion for the United States, about 0.2 percent of its GDP [gross domestic product], and about $96 billion in gains for the world, roughly 0.4 percent of world GDP. Another recent study suggests that the gains from further global liberalization are even larger. If a new trade round reduced the world's tariffs on agricultural and industrial goods and barriers on services trade by one third, the welfare gain for the United States would by $177 billion, or 1.95 percent of GDP. Most of this gain comes from liberalizing trade in services.

The gain for the world amounts to $613 billion, or about 2 percent of world GDP.

As these examples indicate, the calculated welfare gains that emerge from these simulations are sometimes small as a percentage of GDP. Even some economists have interpreted these calculations to mean that trade liberalization is not especially valuable. But the small numbers arise partly because these agreements usually lead to modest policy changes for the United States. For example, what the United States undertook in signing the Uruguay Round or the North American Free Trade Agreement [NAFTA], essentially making already low import tariffs somewhat lower, cannot be compared to Japan's move from autarky to free trade. The numbers do not reflect the entire gains from trade, just the marginal gains from an additional increase in trade as a consequence of a partial reduction in trade barriers. A complete elimination of global barriers to trade in goods and services would bring much larger gains. According to the last study mentioned in the previous paragraph, removing all such barriers would generate $537 billion in gains for the United States (5.9 percent of GDP) and $1,857 billion in gains for the world (6.2 percent of world GDP).

More importantly, the reallocation of resources across industries as calculated in the simulation models does not take into account the other channels by which trade can improve economic performance. What are these other channels? One view is that greater openness to trade allows firms to sell in a potential larger market, and that firms are able to reduce their average costs of production by expanding the size of their output. The lower production costs resulting from these economies of scale are passed on to consumers and thereby generate additional gains from trade. In evaluating the impact of NAFTA through general equilibrium simulations, for example, moving from the assumption of constant returns to scale to increasing returns to scale boosted the calculated U.S. welfare gain from 1.67 percent of 2.55 percent of its GDP, Canadian welfare gain from 4.87 percent to 6.75 percent of its GDP, and Mexican welfare gain from 2.28 percent to 3.29 of its GDP, according to one study.

These numbers are more impressive, but there are also reasons to be skeptical. Evidence from both developed and developing economies suggests that economies of scale at the plant level for most manufacturing firms tend to be small relative to the size of the market. As a result, most plants have attained their minimum efficient scale. Average costs seem to be relatively unaffected by changes in output, so that a big increase in a firm's output does not lead to lower costs, and a big reduction in output does not lead to higher costs. For example, many firms are forced to reduce output as a result of competition from imports, but these firms' production costs rarely rise significantly. This suggests that the importance of scale economies may be overstated, and yet the simulation models sometimes include them.

There is much better, indeed overwhelming, evidence that free trade improves economic performance by increasing competition in the domestic market. This competition diminishes the market power of domestic firms and leads to a more efficient economic outcome. This benefit does not arise because foreign competition changes a domestic firm's costs through changes in the scale of output, as just noted. Rather, it comes through a change in the pricing behavior of imperfectly competitive domestic firms. Firms with market power tend to restrict output and raise prices, thereby harming consumers while increasing their own profits. With international competition, firms cannot get away with such conduct and are forced to behave more competitively. After Turkey's trade liberalization in the mid-1980s, for example, price-cost margins fell for most industries, consistent with a more competitive outcome. Numerous studies confirm this finding in other countries, providing powerful evidence that trade disciplines domestic firms with market power. Yet the beneficial effects of increasing competition are not always taken into account in simulation models because they frequently assume that perfect competition already exists. . . .

Productivity Gains

Trade improves economic performance not only by allocating a country's resources to their most efficient use, but by making those resources more productive in what they are doing. This is the second of John Stuart Mill's three gains from trade, the one he called "indirect effects." These indirect effects include "the tendency of every extension of the market to improve the processes of production. A country which produces for a larger market than its own can introduce a more extended division of labour, can make greater use of machinery, and is more likely to make inventions and improvements in the processes of production."

In other words, trade promotes productivity growth. The higher is an economy's productivity level, the higher is that country's standard of living. International trade contributes to productivity growth in at least two ways: it serves as a conduit for the transfer of foreign technologies that enhance productivity, and it increases competition in a way that stimulates industries to become more efficient and improve their productivity, often by forcing less productive firms out of business and allowing more productive firms to expand. After neglecting them for many decades, economists are finally beginning to study these productivity gains from trade more systematically.

The first channel, trade as a conduit for the transfer of foreign technologies, operates in several ways. One is through the importation of capital goods. Imported capital goods that embody technological advances can greatly enhance an economy's productivity. For example, the South Carolina textile magnate Roger Milliken (an active financier of anti-free-trade political groups) has bought textile machinery from Switzerland and Germany because domestically produced equipment is more costly and less sophisticated. This imported machinery has enabled his firms to increase productivity significantly. Between a quarter and half of growth in U.S. total factor productivity may be attributed to new technology embodied in capital equipment. To the extent that trade barriers raise the price of imported capital goods, countries are hindering their ability to benefit from technologies that could raise productivity. In fact, one study finds that about a quarter of the differences in productivity across countries can be attributed to differences in the price of capital equipment.

Advances in productivity are usually the result of investment in research and development, and the importation of foreign ideas can be a spur to productivity. Sometimes foreign research can be imported directly. For example, China has long been struggling against a devastating disease known as rice blast, which in the past destroyed millions of tons of rice a year, costing farmers billions of dollars. Recently, under the direction of an international team of scientists, farmers in China's Yunnan province started planting a mixture of two different types of rice in the same paddy. By this simple technique of biodiversity, farmers nearly eliminated rice blast and doubled their yield. Foreign R&D [research and development] enabled the Chinese farmers to increase yields of a staple commodity and to abandon the chemical fungicides they had previously used to fight the disease.

At other times, the benefits of foreign R&D are secured by importing goods that embody it. Countries more open to trade gain more from foreign R&D expenditures because trade in goods serves as a conduit for the spillovers of productive knowledge generated by that R&D. Several studies have found that a country's total factor productivity depends not only on its own R&D, but also on how much R&D is conducted in the countries that it trades with. Imports of specialized intermediate goods that embody new technologies, as well as reverse-engineering of such goods, are sources of R&D spillovers. Thus, developing countries, which do not conduct much R&D themselves, can benefit from R&D done elsewhere because trade makes the acquisition of new technology less costly. These examples illustrate Mill's observation that "whatever causes a greater quantity of anything to be produced in the same place, tends to the general increase of the productive powers of the world."

The second channel by which trade contributes to productivity is by forcing domestic industries to become more efficient. We have already seen that trade increases competition in the domestic market, diminishing the market power of any firm and forcing them to behave more competitively. Competition also stimulates firms to improve their efficiency; otherwise they risk going out of business. Over the past decade, study after study has documented this phenomenon. After the Côte d'Ivoire reformed its trade policies in 1985, overall productivity growth tripled, growing four times more rapidly in industries that became less sheltered from foreign competition. Industry productivity in Mexico increased significantly after its trade liberalization in 1985, especially in traded-goods sectors. Detailed studies of India's trade liberalization in 1991 and Korea's in the 1980s reached essentially the same conclusion: trade not only disciplines domestic firms and forces them to behave more like a competitive industry, but helps increase their productivity.

Competition can force individual firms to adopt more efficient production techniques. But international competition also affects the entry and exit decisions of firms in a way that helps raise the aggregate productivity of an industry. In any given industry, productivity is quite heterogeneous among firms: not all firms are equally efficient. Trade acts to promote high-productivity firms and demote low-productivity firms. On the export side, exposure to trade allows more productive firms to become experts and thereby expand their output. In the United States, plants with higher labor productivity within an industry tend to be the plants that export; in other words, more efficient firms are the ones that become exporters. The opportunity to trade, therefore, allows more efficient firms to grow.

On the import side, competition forces the least productive firms to reduce their output or shut down. For example, when Chile began opening up its economy to the world market in the 1970s, exiting plants were, on average, 8 percent less productive than plants that continued to produce. The productivity of plants in industries competing against imports grew 3 to 10 percent more than in non-traded-goods sectors. Protection had insulated less productive firms from foreign competition and allowed them to drag down overall productivity within an industry, whereas open trade weeded out inefficient firms and allowed more efficient firms to expand. Thus, trade brings about certain firm-level adjustments that increase average industry productivity in both export-oriented and import-competing industries.

The impact of the U.S.-Canada Free Trade Agreement on Canadian manufacturing is also suggestive. Tariff reductions helped boost labor productivity by a compounded rate of 0.6 percent per year in manufacturing as a whole and by 2.1 percent per year in the most affected (i.e., high tariff) industries. These are astoundingly large effects. This amounts to a 17 percent increase in productivity in the post-FTA period in the highly affected sectors, and a 5 percent increase for manufacturing overall. These productivity effects were not achieved through scale effects or capital investment, but rather due to a mix of plant turnover and rising technical efficiency within plants. By raising productivity, the FTA also helped increase the annual earnings of production workers, particularly in the most protected industries.

To sum up, traditional calculations of the gains from trade stress the benefits of shifting resources from protected industries to those with an international comparative advantage. But new evidence shows that, because large productivity differences exist between plants within any given industry, shifting resources between firms within an industry may be even more important. Trade may affect the allocation of resources among firms within an industry as much as, if not more than, it affects the allocation of resources among different industries. In doing so, trade helps improve productivity.

While difficult to quantify, these productivity effects of trade may be an order of magnitude more important than the standard gains. Countries that have embarked upon the course of trade liberalization over the past few decades, such as Chile, New Zealand, and Spain, have experienced more rapid grown in productivity than previously. Free trade contributes to a process by which a country can adopt better technology and exposes domestic industries to new competition that forces them to improve their productivity. As a consequence, trade helps raise per capita income and economic well-being more generally.

Free Trade: The Great Destroyer

$\mathbf{F}$ree trade is the religion of our age. With its heaven as the global economy, free trade comes complete with comprehensive analytical and philosophical underpinnings. Higher mathematics are used in stating its theorems. But in the final analysis, free trade is less an economic strategy than a moral doctrine. Although it pretends to be value-free, it is fundamentally value-driven. It assumes that the highest good is to shop. It assumes that mobility and change are synonymous with progress. The transport of capital, materials, goods, and people takes precedence over the autonomy, the sovereignty, and, indeed, the culture of local communities. Rather than promoting and sustaining the social relationships that create a vibrant community, the free trade theology relies on a narrow definition of efficiency to guide our conduct.

The Postulates of Free Trade

For most of us, after a generation of brain washing about its supposed benefits, the tenets of free trade appear almost self-evident:

- Competition spurs innovation, raises productivity, and lowers prices.
- The division of labor allows specialization, which raises productivity and lowers prices.
- The larger the production unit, the greater the division of labor and specialization, and thus the greater the benefits.

The adoration of bigness permeates all political persuasions. The Treasury Department proposes creating five to ten giant U.S. banks. "If we are going to be competitive in a globalized financial services world, we are going to have to change our views on the size of American institutions," it declares. The vice chair of Citicorp warns us against "preserving the heartwarming idea that 14,000 banks are wonderful for our country." The liberal *Harper's* magazine agrees: "True, farms have gotten bigger, as has nearly every other type of economic enterprise. They have done so in order to take advantage of the economies of scale offered by modern production

From David Morris, "Free Trade: The Great Destroyer," in Jerry Mander and Edward Goldsmith, eds., *The Case Against the Global Economy: And for a Return to the Local* (Sierra Club Books, 1996). Copyright © 1996 by Jerry Mander and Edward Goldsmith. Reprinted by permission of Sierra Club Books.

techniques." Democratic presidential adviser Lester Thurow criticizes anti-trust laws as an "old Democratic conception [that] is simply out of date." He argues that even IBM, with $50 billion in sales, is not big enough for the global marketplace. "Big companies do sometimes crush small companies," Thurow concedes, "but far better that small American companies be crushed by big American companies than that they be crushed by foreign companies." The magazine *In These Times,* which once called itself an independent socialist weekly, concluded, "Japanese steel companies have been able to outcompete American steel companies partly by building larger plants."

The infatuation with large-scale systems leads logically to the next postulate of free trade: the need for global markets. Anything that sets up barriers to ever-wider markets reduces the possibility of specialization and thus raises costs, making us less competitive.

The last pillar of free trade is the law of comparative advantage, which comes in two forms: absolute and relative. Absolute comparative advantage is easier to understand: Differences in climate and natural resources suggest that Guatemala should raise bananas and Minnesota should raise walleyed pike. Thus, by specializing in what they grow best, each region enjoys comparative advantage in that particular crop. Relative comparative advantage is a less intuitive, but ultimately more powerful concept. As the nineteenth-century British economist David Ricardo, the architect of free trade economics, explained: "Two men can both make shoes and hats and one is superior to the other in both employments; but in making hats he can only exceed his competitor by one-fifth or 20 percent, and in making shoes he can exceed him by one-third or 33 percent. Will it not be for the interest of both that the superior man should employ himself exclusively in making shoes and the inferior man in making hats?"

Thus, even if one community can make every product more efficiently than another, it should specialize only in those items it produces most efficiently, in relative terms, and trade for others. Each community, and ultimately each nation, should specialize in what it does best.

What are the implications of these tenets of free trade? That communities and nations abandon self-reliance and embrace dependence. That we abandon our capacity to produce many items and concentrate only on a few. That we import what we need and export what we produce.

Bigger is better. Competition is superior to cooperation. Material self-interest drives humanity. Dependence is better than independence. These are the pillars of free trade. In sum, we make a trade. We give up sovereignty over our affairs in return for a promise of more jobs, more goods, and a higher standard of living.

❧

The economic arguments in favor of free trade are powerful. Yet for most of us it is not the soundness of its theory but the widely promoted idea that free trade is an inevitable development of our market system that makes us believers. We believe that economies, like natural organisms, evolve from the simple to the complex.

From the Dark Ages, to city-states, to nation-states, to the planetary economy, and, soon, to space manufacturing, history has systematically unfolded. Free trade supporters believe that trying to hold back economic evolution is like trying to hold back natural evolution. The suggestion that we choose another developmental path is viewed, at best, as an attempt to reverse history and, at worst, as an unnatural and even sinful act.

This kind of historical determinism has corollaries. We not only move from simple to complex economies. We move from integrated economies to segregated ones, separating the producer from the consumer, the farmer from the kitchen, the power plant from the appliance, the dump site from the garbage can, the banker from the depositor, and, inevitably, the government from the citizenry. In the process of development we separate authority and responsibility—those who make the decisions are not those who are affected by the decisions.

Just as *Homo sapiens* is nature's highest achievement, so the multinational and supranational corporation becomes our most highly evolved economic animal. The planetary economy demands planetary institutions. The nation-state itself begins to disappear, both as an object of our affection and identification and as a major actor in world affairs.

The planetary economy merges and submerges nations. Yoshitaka Sajima, vice president of Mitsui and Company, USA, asserts, "The U.S. and Japan are not just trading with each other anymore—they've become a part of each other." Lamar Alexander, former Republican Governor of Tennessee, agreed with Sajima's statement when he declared that the goal of his economic development strategy was "to get the Tennessee economy integrated with the Japanese economy."

In Europe, the Common Market has grown from six countries in the 1950s to ten in the 1970s to sixteen today, and barriers between these nations are rapidly being abolished. Increasingly, there are neither Italian nor French nor German companies, only European supracorporations. The U.S., Canadian, and Mexican governments formed NAFTA [North American Free Trade Agreement] to merge the countries of the North American continent economically.

Promotion of exports is now widely accepted as the foundation for a successful economic development program. Whether for a tiny country such as Singapore or a huge country such as the United States, exports are seen as essential to a nation's economic health.

Globalism commands our attention and our resources. Our principal task, we are told, is to nurture, extend, and manage emerging global systems. Trade talks are on the top of everybody's agenda, from Yeltsin to Clinton. Political leaders strive to devise stable systems for global financial markets and exchange rates. The best and the brightest of this generation use their ingenuity to establish the global financial and regulatory rules that will enable the greatest possible uninterrupted flow of resources among nations.

This emphasis on globalism rearranges our loyalties and loosens our neighborly ties. "The new order eschews loyalty to workers, products, corporate structure, businesses, factories, communities, even the nation," the *New York Times* announces. Martin S. Davis, chair of Gulf and Western, declares, "All such allegiances are viewed as expendable under the new rules. You cannot be emotionally bound to any particular asset."

We are now all assets.

Jettisoning loyalties isn't easy, but that is the price we believe we must pay to receive the benefits of the global village. Every community must achieve the lowest possible production cost, even when that means breaking whatever remains of its social contract and long-standing traditions.

The revised version of the American Dream is articulated by Stanley J. Mihelick, executive vice president for production at Goodyear: "Until we get real wage levels down much closer to those of the Brazils and Koreas, we cannot pass along productivity gains to wages and still be competitive."

Wage raises, environmental protection, national health insurance, and liability lawsuits—anything that raises the cost of production and makes a corporation less competitive—threatens our economy. We must abandon the good life to sustain the economy. We are in a global struggle for survival. We are hooked on free trade.

The Doctrine Falters

At this very moment in history, when the doctrines of free trade and globalism are so dominant, the absurdities of globalism are becoming more evident. Consider the case of the toothpick and the chopstick.

A few years ago I was eating at a Saint Paul, Minnesota, restaurant. After lunch, I picked up a toothpick wrapped in plastic. On the plastic was printed the word *Japan*. Japan has little wood and no oil; nevertheless, it has become efficient enough in our global economy to bring little pieces of wood and barrels of oil to Japan, wrap the one in the other and send the manufactured product to Minnesota. This toothpick may have traveled 50,000 miles. But never fear, we are now retaliating in kind. A Hibbing, Minnesota, factory now produces one billion disposable chopsticks a year for sale in Japan. In my mind's eye, I see two ships passing one another in the northern Pacific. One carries little pieces of Minnesota wood bound for Japan; the other carries little pieces of Japanese wood bound for Minnesota. Such is the logic of free trade.

Nowhere is the absurdity of free trade more evident than in the grim plight of the Third World. Developing nations were encouraged to borrow money to build an economic infrastructure in order to specialize in what they do best, (comparative advantage, once again) and thereby expand their export capacity. To repay the debts, Third World countries must increase their exports.

One result of these arrangements has been a dramatic shift in food production from internal consumption to export. Take the case of Brazil. Brazilian per capita production of basic foodstuffs (rice, black beans, manioc, and potatoes) fell 13 percent from 1977 to 1984. Per capita output of exportable food-stuffs (soybeans, oranges, cotton, peanuts, and tobacco) jumped 15 percent. Today, although some 50 percent of Brazil suffers malnutrition, one leading Brazilian agronomist still calls export promotion "a matter of national survival." In the global village, a nation survives by starving its people.

cᴑᴑ

What about the purported benefits of free trade, such as higher standards of living?

It depends on whose standards of living are being considered. Inequality between and, in most cases, within countries has increased. Two centuries of trade has exacerbated disparaties in world living standards. According to economist Paul Bairoch, per capita GNP in 1750 was approximately the same in the developed countries as in the underdeveloped ones. In 1930, the ratio was about 4 to 1 in favor of the developed nations. Today it is 8 to 1.

Inequality is both a cause and an effect of globalism. Inequality within one country exacerbates globalism because it reduces the number of people with sufficient purchasing power; consequently, a producer must sell to wealthy people in many countries to achieve the scale of production necessary to produce goods at a relatively low cost. Inequality is an effect of globalism because export industries employ few workers, who earn disproportionately higher wages than their compatriots, and because developed countries tend to take out more capital from Third World countries than they invest in them.

Free trade was supposed to improve our standard of living. Yet even in the United States, the most developed of all nations, we find that living standards have been declining since 1980. More dramatically, according to several surveys, in 1988 U.S. workers worked almost half a day longer for lower real wages than they did in 1970. We who work in the United States have less leisure time in the 1990s than we had in the 1970s.

A New Way of Thinking

It is time to re-examine the validity of the doctrine of free trade and its creation, the planetary economy. To do so, we must begin by speaking of values. Human beings may be acquisitive and competitive, but we are also loving and cooperative. Several studies have found that the voluntary, unpaid economy may be as large and as productive as the paid economy. There is no question that we have converted more and more human relationships into commercial transactions, but there is a great deal of question as to whether this was a necessary or beneficial development.

We should not confuse change with progress. Bertrand Russell once described change as inevitable and progress as problematic. Change is scientific. Progress is ethical. We must decide which values we hold most dear and then design an economic system that reinforces those values.

Reassessing Free Trade's Assumptions

If price is to guide our buying, selling, and investing, then price should tell us something about efficiency. We might measure efficiency in terms of natural resources used in making products and the lack of waste produced in converting raw material into a consumer or industrial product. Traditionally, we have measured efficiency in human terms; that is, by measuring the amount of labor-hours spent in making a product.

But price is actually no measure of real efficiency. In fact, price is no reliable measure of anything. In the planetary economy, the prices of raw materials, labor, capital, transportation, and waste disposal are all heavily subsidized. For example, wage-rate inequities among comparably skilled workforces can be as disparate as 30 to 1. This disparity overwhelms even the most productive worker. An American worker might produce twice as much per hour as a Mexican worker but is paid ten times as much.

In Taiwan, for example, strikes are illegal. In South Korea, unions cannot be organized without government permission. Many developing nations have no minimum wage, maximum hours, or environmental legislation. As economist Howard Wachtel notes, "Differences in product cost that are due to totalitarian political institutions or restrictions on economic rights reflect no natural or entrepreneurial advantage. Free trade has nothing to do with incomparable political economic institutions that protect individual rights in one country and deny them in another."

The price of goods in developed countries is also highly dependent on subsidies. For example, we in the United States decided early on that government should build the transportation systems of the country. The public, directly or indirectly, built our railroads, canals, ports, highways and airports.

Heavy trucks do not pay taxes sufficient to cover the damage they do to roads. California farmers buy water at as little as 5 percent of the going market rate; the other 95 percent is funded by huge direct subsidies to corporate farmers. In the United States, society as a whole picks up the costs of agricultural pollution. Having intervened in the production process in all these ways, we then discover it is cheaper to raise produce near the point of sale.

Prices don't provide accurate signals within nations; they are not the same as cost. *Price* is what an individual pays; cost is what the community as a whole pays. Most economic programs in the industrial world result in an enormous disparity between the price of a product or service to an individual and the cost of that same product or service to the society as a whole.

When a U.S. utility company wanted to send electricity across someone's property, and that individual declined the honor, the private utility received governmental authority to seize the land needed. This is exactly what happened in western Minnesota in the late 1970s. Since larger power plants produced electricity more cheaply than smaller ones, it was therefore in the "public interest" to erect these power lines. If landowners' refusal to sell had been respected, the price of electricity would be higher today, but it would reflect the cost of that power more accurately.

Because the benefit of unrestricted air transportation takes precedence over any damage to public health and sanity, communities no longer have the authority to regulate flights and noise. As a consequence, airplanes awaken us or our children in the middle of the night. By one survey, some four million people in the United States suffer physical damage due to airport noise. If communities were given the authority to control noise levels by planes, as they already control noise levels from radios and motorcycles, the price of a plane ticket would increase significantly. Its price would be more aligned with its actual cost to society.

It is often hard to quantify social costs, but this doesn't mean they are insignificant. Remember urban renewal? In the 1950s and 1960s inner-city neighborhoods were leveled to assemble sufficient land area to rebuild our downtowns. Skyscrapers and shopping malls arose; the property tax base expanded; and we considered it a job well done. Later, sociologists, economists, and planners discovered that the seedy areas we destroyed were not fragmented, violence-prone slums but more often cohesive ethnic communities where generations had grown up and worked and where children went to school and played. If we were to put a dollar figure on the destruction of homes, the pain of broken lives, and the expense of relocation and re-creation of community life, we might find that the city as a whole actually lost money in the urban renewal process. If we had used a full-cost accounting system, we might never have undertaken urban renewal.

Our refusal to understand and count the social costs of certain kinds of development has caused suffering in rural and urban areas alike. In 1944, Walter Goldschmidt, working under contract with the Department of Agriculture [USDA], compared the economic and social characteristics of two rural California communities that were alike in all respects, except one. Dinuba was surrounded by family farms; Arvin by corporate farms. Goldschmidt found that Dinuba was more stable, had a higher standard of living, more small businesses, higher retail sales, better schools and other community facilities, and a higher degree of citizen participation in local affairs. The USDA invoked a clause in Goldschmidt's contract forbidding him to discuss his finding. The study was not made public for almost thirty years. Meanwhile, the USDA continued to promote research that rapidly transformed the Dinubas of our country into Arvins. The farm crisis we now suffer is a consequence of this process.

How should we deal with the price-versus-cost dilemma as a society? Ways do exist by which we can protect our life-style from encroachment by the global economy, achieve important social and economic goals, and pay about the same price for our goods and services. In some cases we might have to pay more, but we should remember that higher prices may be offset by the decline in overall costs. Consider the proposed Save the Family Farm legislation drafted by farmers and introduced in Congress several years ago by Iowa Senator Tom Harkin. It proposed that farmers limit production of farm goods nationwide at the same time as the nation establishes a minimum price for farm goods that is sufficient to cover operating and capital costs and provides farm families with an adequate living. The law's sponsors estimate that such a program would increase the retail cost of agricultural products by 3 to 5 percent, but the increase would be more than offset by dramatically reduced public tax expenditures spent on farm subsidies. And this doesn't take into consideration the cost benefits of a stable rural America: fewer people leaving farms that have been in their families for generations; less influx of jobless rural immigrants into already economically depressed urban areas; and fewer expenditures for medical bills, food stamps, and welfare.

Economists like to talk about externalities. The costs of job dislocation, rising family violence, community breakdown, environmental damage, and cultural collapse are all considered "external." External to what, one might ask?

The theory of comparative advantage itself is fast losing its credibility. Time was when technology spread slowly. Three hundred years ago in northern Italy, stealing or disclosing the secrets of silk-spinning machinery was a crime punishable by death. At the beginning of the Industrial Revolution, Britain protected its supremacy in textile manufacturing by banning both the export of machines and the emigration of men who knew how to build and run them. A young British apprentice, Samuel Slater, brought the Industrial Revolution to the United States by memorizing the design of the spinning frame and migrating here in 1789.

Today, technology transfer is simple. According to Dataquest, a market research firm, it takes only three weeks after a new U.S.-made product is introduced before it is copied, manufactured, and shipped back to the U.S. from Asia. So much for comparative advantage.

The Efficiencies of Small Scale

This brings us to the issue of scale. There is no question that when I move production out of my basement and into a factory, the cost per item produced declines dramatically. But when the factory increases its output a hundredfold, production costs no longer decline proportionately. The vast majority of the cost decreases are captured at fairly modest production levels.

In agriculture, for example, the USDA studied the efficiency of farms and concluded, "Above about $40–50,000 in gross sales—the size that is at the bottom of the end of medium sized sales category—there are no greater efficiencies of scale." Another USDA report agreed: "Medium sized family farms are as efficient as the large farms."

Harvard Professor Joseph Bain's pioneering investigations in the 1950s found that plants far smaller than originally believed can be economically competitive. Further, it was found that the factory could be significantly reduced in size without requiring major price increases for its products. In other words, we might be able to produce shoes for a region rather than for a nation at about the same price per shoe. If we withdrew government subsidies to the transportation system, then locally produced and marketed shoes might actually be less expensive than those brought in from abroad.

Modern technology makes smaller production plants possible. For instance, traditional float glass plants produce 550 to 600 tons of glass daily, at an annual cost of $100 million. With only a $40 to 50 million investment, new miniplants can produce about 250 tons per day for a regional market at the same cost per ton as the large plants.

The advent of programmable machine tools may accelerate this tendency. In 1980, industrial engineers developed machine tools that could be programmed to reproduce a variety of shapes so that now a typical Japanese machine tool can make almost one hundred different parts from an individual block of material. What does this mean? Erich Bloch, director of the National Science Foundation, believes manufacturing "will be so flexible that it will be able to make the first copy of a product for little more than the cost of the thousandth." "So the ideal location for the factory of the future," says Patrick A. Toole, vice president for manufacturing at IBM, "is in the market where the products are consumed."

Conclusion

When we abandon our ability to produce for ourselves, when we separate authority from responsibility, when those affected by our decisions are not those who make the decisions, when the cost and the benefit of production or development processes are not part of the same equation, when price and cost are no longer in harmony, we jeopardize our security and our future.

You may argue that free trade is not the sole cause of all our ills. Agreed. But free trade as it is preached today nurtures and reinforces many of our worst problems. It is an ideological package that promotes ruinous policies. And, most tragically, as we move further down the road to giantism, globalism, and dependence, we make it harder and harder to back up and take another path. If we lose our skills, our productive base, our culture, our traditions, our natural resources; if we erode the bonds of personal and familial responsibility, it becomes ever more difficult to re-create community. It is very, very hard to put Humpty Dumpty back together again.

Which means we must act now. The unimpeded mobility of capital, labor, goods, and raw materials is not the highest social good. We need to challenge the postulates of free trade head on, to propose a different philosophy, to embrace a different strategy. There is another way. To make it the dominant way, we must change the rules; indeed, we must challenge our own behavior. And to do that requires not only that we challenge the emptiness of free trade but that we promote a new idea: economics as if community matters.

POSTSCRIPT

Is Free Trade Fair Trade?

In 2002, in order to overcome congressional objections based on the possible negative economic impact of foreign goods on particular districts, President George W. Bush imposed tariff barriers on steel imports to protect domestic manufacturers against cheaper or better imported steel. This is old-fashioned protectionism, the economic opposite of free trade. The president calculated that he could not get the trade power he sought without disarming some anti–free trade sentiment, so he made his concession to business owners, workers, and communities in which the steel industry is located. Underdeveloped nations, calling such concessions hypocritical, contend that they have more reasons to protect their weaker businesses but, unlike the United States, they are subject to the pressures of the international agencies that lend them investment capital as well as of the multinational enterprises whose investment they want to get, keep, and enlarge.

Laissez-faire economics holds that if Asian countries can produce electronic products better and less expensively than other nations, then those products will be sold throughout the world. Similarly, if the United States can produce movies that are more entertaining than those made elsewhere, then they will be seen throughout the world. According to Brink Lindsay, in *Against the Dead Hand: The Uncertain Struggle for Global Capitalism* (John Wiley, 2002), if these results have not yet followed in every economic area, it is because the economy has not yet gotten rid of state ownership, price controls, trade barriers, and other remnants of an earlier age. Protectionism has been discredited but it has not yet been banished, says Jagdish N. Bhagwati in *Free Trade Today* (Princeton University Press, 2002). Critics of free trade maintain that the agencies providing economic support to the poorer countries sponsor a kind of capitalism that may not be congenial to other cultures. In *Open Society: Reforming Global Capitalism* (Public Affairs, 2000), George Soros, one of the foremost capitalist investors, advocates for spending more money on global public goods and foreign aid.

Edward S. Herman, in "Free Trade: The Sophistry of Imperialism," *Z Magazine* (March 2002), argues that free trade diminishes the ability of less developed countries to shape their economic policies, provide public services, and protect the environment. In addition, he contends that free trade agreements protect investor rights against taxes, business rules, labor practices, and other policies by which a sovereign state can protect its interests. This and other anti–free trade views are amplified in the essays in Jerry Mander and Edward Goldsmith, eds., *The Case Against the Global Economy: And for a Return to the Local* (Sierra Club Books, 1996).

ISSUE 20

Was the Invasion of Iraq Justified?

YES: Robert Kagan and William Kristol, from "The Right War for the Right Reasons," *The Weekly Standard* (February 23, 2004)

NO: Michael Ignatieff, from "Why Are We in Iraq?" *The New York Times Magazine* (September 7, 2003)

ISSUE SUMMARY

YES: *The Weekly Standard* editors Robert Kagan and William Kristol argue that the Iraq war is justified because it has put an end to three decades of tyranny, and will encourage liberalization throughout the region.

NO: Michael Ignatieff, director of the Carr Center at the Kennedy School of Government, views the Iraq war as a unilateral act of territorial conquest, with costs far higher than anyone bargained for.

It may be decades before historians will be able to reach even a challenge-able consensus about what happened in Iraq between 2003 and 2005. During those years, reported events not only moved with dizzying speed but almost immediately became ammunition in an increasingly bitter polemical war here at home.

Perhaps the best way of setting up the introduction to the Iraq debate is not to avoid controversy but to wade right into it—on both sides. Each side, it is clear, has its own narrative.

Narrative A

Despite seventeen resolutions over several years by the U.N. Security Council, including Resolution 1414 in November 2002, which threatened "serious consequences" if he failed to comply, Iraqi dictator Saddam Hussein refused to submit an honest accounting of his weapons of mass destruction (WMD) that he had used on his own people and neighboring peoples. The United States then called on the Security Council to back up its resolutions by authorizing the use of force. When the U.S. proposal was vetoed by France and Russia (both of which, it was later discovered, were secretly doing business with Saddam), the United States and a coalition of more than thirty other nations entered Iraq and swiftly liberated it. The Coalition forces soon began to uncover the horrors visited on the people of Iraq by Saddam's regime. The coalition forces also searched for the WMD, and, while failing to find weapons stockpiles, found extensive evidence of chemical and biological weapons programs, and other blatant violations of Resolution 1441. Overall, the liberation of Iraq was moving forward as planned, despite the inevitable setbacks and bumps in the road that accompany an enterprise of this scale—fierce resistance from hard-line Baathists, foreign terrorists, and local thugs, together with the damage suffered from the prison-abuse scandal in May 2004. The larger picture showed continual progress being made toward the building of a prosperous, free, and democratic Iraq. Iraq's damaged and obsolete infrastructure was rapidly being rebuilt, as were schools, hospitals, and other public institutions. Together with a special envoy from the United Nations, the Occupation Authority laid the groundwork for writing a new constitution and preparing for the nation's first democratic elections in 2005. On June 28, 2004 sovereignty was officially transferred from the Coalition Authority to a provisional government of the Iraqi people.

Narrative B

The roots of the Iraq war go back to September 2000, when Project for the New American Century, a neoconservative think tank, wrote a report advocating strong military action against the regime of Saddam Hussein. Upon the election of George W. Bush, some of the authors of that report assumed positions in the inner circle of presidential advisors. After 9/11, there was even consideration of going into Afghanistan and Iraq simultaneously, despite the absence of any evidence linking Saddam to the 9/11 attacks. Shortly afterwards, the Bush administration announced a "war on terrorism," accompanied by the doctrine of preemptive military action. A year later, Bush asked Congress for authorization to use force against Iraq on grounds that Saddam possessed WMD. Relying heavily on that rationale, Bush invaded Iraq in March 2003, despite the failure to receive U.N. authorization. The regime fell quickly, and on May 1, 2003, President Bush landed on an aircraft carrier in a fighter plane and, with a banner in background saying "Mission Accomplished," announced the end of major combat operations. Fierce resistance followed from a variety of sources. American casualties mounted rapidly, and by the first anniversary of invasion, over 500 American military personnel had been killed, the majority of them since Bush announced the end of major combat. By early summer of 2004, the resistance was growing, becoming more coordinated, and using increasingly sophisticated tactics. American deaths in combat reached 800, and the new American-trained Iraqi policemen who were supposed to keep order when Americans left quickly, capitulated whenever they were challenged by armed insurgents. In addition to these military setbacks, America's reputation in the Arab world plunged to a new low when photos of American soldiers physically and sexually abusing Iraqi prisoners appeared in the media. Finally, despite an intense, year-long search by a special team, the WMD—the weapons used to justify the invasion—were not found.

Robert Kagan and
William Kristol

 **YES**

The Right War for
the Right Reasons

With all the turmoil surrounding David Kay's comments on the failure
to find stockpiles of biological and chemical weapons in Iraq, it is time to
return to first principles, and to ask the question: Was it right to go to war?

Critics of the war, and of the Bush administration, have seized on the
failure to find stockpiles of weapons of mass destruction in Iraq. But while
his weapons were a key part of the case for removing Saddam, that case was
always broader. Saddam's pursuit of weapons of mass destruction was inextricably intertwined with the nature of his tyrannical rule, his serial aggression, his defiance of international obligations, and his undeniable ties to a
variety of terrorists, from Abu Nidal to al Qaeda. . . . Together, this pattern
of behavior made the removal of Saddam desirable and necessary, in the
judgment of both the Clinton and Bush administrations. That judgment
was and remains correct.

It is fashionable to sneer at the moral case for liberating an Iraqi people
long brutalized by Saddam's rule. Critics insist mere oppression was not sufficient reason for war, and in any case that it was not Bush's reason. In fact,
of course, it was one of Bush's reasons, and the moral and humanitarian
purpose provided a compelling reason for a war to remove Saddam. It
should certainly have been compelling to those (like us) who supported
the war on Slobodan Milosevic a few years ago. In our view—and here we
disagree with what Paul Wolfowitz said to *Vanity Fair* a few months ago—
liberating the Iraqi people from Saddam's brutal, totalitarian dictatorship
would by itself have been sufficient reason to remove Saddam.

Such a rationale is not "merely" moral. As is so often the case in international affairs, there was no separating the nature of Saddam's rule at
home from the kinds of policies he conducted abroad. Saddam's regime ter-
rorized his own people, but it also posed a threat to the region, and to us.
The moral case for war was linked to strategic considerations related to the
peace and security of the Middle East. . . .

From *The Weekly Standard,* February 23, 2004, pp. 20–28. Copyright © 2004 by Weekly Standard.
Reprinted with permission.

The last time we restated the case for war in Iraq (in October 2003), we quoted extensively from a speech delivered by President Clinton in February 1998. This time we quote extensively from another speech, delivered ten months later, in December 1998, by President Clinton's national security adviser, Sandy Berger. Like President Clinton, Berger did a masterful job of laying out the case for removing Saddam Hussein. And Berger's argument extended beyond the issue of weapons.

Yes, Berger acknowledged, America's "most vital national interest in dealing with Iraq" was to "prevent Saddam from rebuilding his military capability, including weapons of mass destruction, and from using that arsenal to move against his neighbors or his own people." But the threat Saddam posed, by his "continued reign of terror inside Iraq and intimidation outside Iraq," was broader than that. The future course of the Middle East and the Arab world were at stake in Iraq.

"The future of Iraq," Berger argued, "will affect the way in which the Middle East and the Arab world in particular evolve in the next decade and beyond." Those peoples were engaged in a "struggle between two broad visions of the future." One vision was of "political pluralism" and "economic openness." The other vision fed on discontent and fear; it stood for "violent opposition to liberalizing forces." So long as Saddam remained "in power and in confrontation with the world," Berger argued, Iraq would remain "a source of potential conflict in the region," and perhaps more important, "a source of inspiration for those who equate violence with power and compromise with surrender."

In the end, Berger explained, containment of Saddam would not be enough. The "immediate military threat" might be held at bay for the moment. "But even a contained Saddam" was "harmful to stability and to positive change in the region." And in fact, containment was probably not "sustainable over the long run." It was "a costly policy, in economic and strategic terms." The pattern of the previous years—"Iraqi defiance, followed by force mobilization on our part, followed by Iraqi capitulation"— had left "the international community vulnerable to manipulation by Saddam." The longer the standoff continued, Berger warned, "the harder it will be to maintain" international support. Nor was there any question what Saddam would do if and when containment collapsed. "Saddam's history of aggression, and his recent record of deception and defiance, leave no doubt that he would resume his drive for regional domination if he had the chance. Year after year, in conflict after conflict, Saddam has proven that he seeks weapons, including weapons of mass destruction, in order to use them."

For this reason, Berger continued, the Clinton administration had concluded it would be necessary at some point to move beyond containment to regime change. At stake was "our ability to fight terror, avert regional conflict, promote peace, and protect the security of our friends and allies." Quoting President Clinton, Berger suggested "the best way to address the challenge Iraq poses is 'through a government in Baghdad—a new government—that is committed to represent and respect its people, not repress them; that is committed to peace in the region.'" . . .

◆

So the threat of Saddam's weapons of mass destruction was related to the overall political and strategic threat his regime posed to the Middle East. Still, there is no question that Saddam's history with and interest in weapons of mass destruction made his threat distinctive. The danger was not, however, that Iraq would present a direct threat to the physical security of the United States or, in the current popular phrase, pose an "imminent" threat to the American homeland. Our chief concern in 1998, like Berger's, was the threat Saddam posed to regional security and stability, the maintenance of which was in large part the responsibility of the United States. If Saddam "does acquire the capability to deliver weapons of mass destruction," we argued, which eventually he was "almost certain to do if we continue along the present course," American troops in the region, American allies, the stability of the Middle East, and the world's supply of oil would all be put at risk. The threat to the United States was that we would be compelled to defend our allies and our interests in circumstances made much more difficult and dangerous by Saddam's increasingly lethal arsenal.

That was why Saddam's weapons of mass destruction programs, both what we knew about them and what we did not know about them, gave the situation a special urgency. It was urgent in 1998, and it was urgent four years later. There was no doubt in 1998—and there is no doubt today, based on David Kay's findings—that Saddam was seeking both to pursue WMD programs and to conceal his efforts from U.N. weapons inspectors. After 1995, when the defection of Saddam Hussein's son-in-law and chief organizer of the weapons programs, Hussein Kamal, produced a wealth of new information about Iraqi weapons programs and stockpiles—information the Iraqis were forced to acknowledge was accurate—the U.N. weapons inspections process had become an elaborate cat-and-mouse game. As President Clinton recalled in his speech three years later, Kamal had "revealed that Iraq was continuing to conceal weapons and missiles and the capacity to build many more." The inspectors intensified their search. And they must have been having some success, for as they drew closer to uncovering what the Iraqis were hiding, Saddam grew less and less cooperative and began to block their access to certain facilities.

Finally, there was the famous confrontation over the so-called "presidential palaces"—actually vast complexes of buildings and warehouses that Saddam simply declared off-limits to inspectors. Clinton intelligence officials observed the Iraqis moving equipment that could be used to manufacture weapons out of the range of video cameras that had been installed by U.N. inspectors. By the end of 1997, the *New York Times* reported, the U.N. inspection team could "no longer verify that Iraq is not making weapons of mass destruction" and specifically could not monitor "equipment that could grow seed stocks of biological agents in a matter of hours."

President Clinton declared in early 1998 that Saddam was clearly attempting "to protect whatever remains of his capacity to produce weapons of mass destruction, the missiles to deliver them, and the feed stocks necessary to produce them." The U.N. inspectors believed, Clinton continued, that "Iraq still has stockpiles of chemical and biological munitions . . . and the capacity to restart quickly its production program and build many, many more weapons." Meanwhile, a February 13, 1998, U.S. government White Paper on Iraq's weapons of mass destruction stated that "in the absence of UNSCOM inspectors, Iraq could restart limited mustard agent production within a few weeks, full-production of sarin within a few months, and pre–Gulf War production levels—including VX—within two or three years."

It was President Clinton who, in February 1998, posed the critical question: "What if [Saddam] fails to comply and we fail to act, or we take some ambiguous third route, which gives him yet more opportunities to develop this program of weapons of mass destruction. . . . Well, he will conclude that the international community has lost its will. He will then conclude that he can go right on and do more to rebuild an arsenal of devastating destruction. And some day, some way, I guarantee you he'll use this arsenal." "In the next century," Clinton predicted, "the community of nations may see more and more of the very kind of threat Iraq poses now—a rogue state with weapons of mass destruction, ready to use them or provide them to terrorists . . . who travel the world among us unnoticed." . . .

The situation as it stood at the beginning of 1999 was troubling to all concerned, and not just to American officials. A report to the U.N. Security Council in January 1999 by Richard Butler, head of the U.N. weapons inspections team, warned that much was not known about the Iraqi program but that there was ample reason to believe a significant weapons of mass destruction program still existed in Iraq. Butler recounted a seven-year history of Iraqi deception and concealment of proscribed weapons and activities. During the first four years of inspections, Butler noted, the inspectors "had been very substantially misled by Iraq both in terms of its understanding of Iraq's proscribed weapons programs and the continuation of prohibited activities, even under the [U.N.'s] monitoring." Only the defection of Hussein Kamal had revealed that the inspectors had been wrong in their "positive conclusions on Iraq's compliance." But even after Kamal's defection, the Iraqis had continued to conceal programs and mislead the inspectors. The Iraqis were caught lying about whether they had ever put VX nerve agent in so-called "special warheads." Scientific examinations proved that they had.

The Iraqis were also caught lying about their biological weapons program. First they denied having one; then, when that falsehood was exposed, they denied weaponizing their biological weapons agents. Eventually they were forced to admit that they "had weaponized BW agents and deployed biological weapons for combat use." The U.N. inspectors reported that hundreds of shells filled with mustard agent had been declared "lost" by Iraq and remained unaccounted for. There were some 6,000 aerial bombs filled with chemical agent that were unaccounted for. There were also some "special warheads" with biological weapons agent unaccounted for. Butler's report concluded that, in addition, "it needs to be recognized that Iraq possesses an industrial capacity and knowledge base, through which biological warfare agents could be produced quickly and in volume, if the Government of Iraq decided to do so."

The inspectors left, and for the next four years, Saddam's activities were shrouded in darkness. After all, many prohibited Iraqi activities had escaped detection even while the inspectors were trying to monitor them. Without the inspectors, the task of keeping track of Saddam's programs was well-nigh impossible.

                              ◆

When the Bush administration came to office, therefore, it had no less reason to worry about Saddam's potential capabilities than the Clinton administration. And it had no more reason to believe that containment would be sustainable. In the early months of the administration, Bush officials began to contemplate some increased support for Iraqi opposition forces, pursuant to legislation passed overwhelmingly in 1998, which was supported by the Clinton administration. (The Iraq Liberation Act chronicled Saddam's use of chemical weapons and declared that Iraq "has persisted in a pattern of deception and concealment regarding the history of its weapons of mass destruction programs." It continued; "It should be the policy of the United States to support efforts to remove the regime headed by Saddam Hussein from power in Iraq and to promote the emergence of a democratic government to replace that regime.") Meanwhile, Secretary of State Colin Powell was trying to prevent the collapse of the international sanctions regime and to staunch the hemorrhaging of consensus at the U.N. Security Council by instituting a more streamlined effort, the so-called "smart sanctions."

Then came the terrorist attacks of September 11, 2001. September 11 shocked the nation, and it shocked the president. Its effect was to make many both inside and outside the administration take a closer look at international threats, because it was clear that all of us had been too sanguine about such threats prior to September 11. Nor was it in the least surprising that the issue of Iraq arose immediately. True, neither candidate in the 2000 election had talked much about Iraq. But that was not because anyone believed it had ceased to be an urgent and growing problem. The Clinton administration didn't want to talk about it because it felt it had run out of options. The Bush campaign didn't talk about it because Bush was running a campaign, ironic in retrospect, which promised a less active, more restrained American role in the world. But that did not mean the Iraq issue had gone away, and after September 11, it returned to the fore. After all, we had a decade-long history of confrontation with Iraq, we were flying military missions in Iraqi air space, President Clinton had declared Saddam the greatest threat to our security in the 21st century, Clinton officials like Sandy Berger and Madeleine Albright had concluded that Saddam must eventually be removed, and U.N. weapons inspectors had written one alarming report after another about Saddam's current and potential weapons capabilities.

So the Bush administration concluded that it had to remove the Saddam Hussein regime once and for all, just as Clinton and Berger had suggested might someday be necessary. For all the reasons that Berger had outlined, Saddam's regime itself was the problem, above and beyond his weapons capabilities. It was an obstacle to progress in the Middle East and the Arab world. It was a threat to the Iraqi people and to Iraq's neighbors. But a big part of the threat involved Saddam's absolute determination to arm himself with both conventional and unconventional weapons.

September 11 had added new dimensions to the danger. For as Bush and many others argued, what if Saddam allowed his weapons capabilities to be shared with terrorists? What if, someday in the future, terrorists like those who crashed airplanes into the World Trade Center and the Pentagon had nuclear, chemical, or biological weapons? Would they hesitate to use them? The possible nexus between terrorism and Iraq's weapons program made Iraq an even more urgent issue. Was this concern far-fetched? If so, it was exactly the same far-fetched concern that had preoccupied President Clinton in 1998, when he warned, in his speech on Iraq, about a "rogue state with weapons of mass destruction, ready to use them or provide them to terrorists," and when he had spoken of an "unholy axis" of international terrorists and outlaw states as one of the greatest threats Americans faced.

Nor was it surprising that as President Bush began to move toward war with Iraq in the fall and winter of 2002, he mustered substantial support among Democrats as well as Republicans. A majority of Democratic senators—including, of course, John Kerry and John Edwards—voted for the resolution authorizing the president to use force against Iraq. And why not? The Bush administration's approach to Iraq was fundamentally in keeping with that of the Clinton administration, except that after September 11, inaction seemed even less acceptable. The majority of the Democratic party foreign policy establishment supported the war, and not because they were misled by the Bush administration's rhetorical hype leading up to the war. (Its hype was appreciably less than that of Clinton secretary of defense William Cohen, who appeared on national television in late 1997 holding a bag of sugar and noting that the same amount of anthrax "would destroy at least half the population" of Washington, D.C. At a Pentagon press briefing on Iraq's WMD, Cohen also noted that if Saddam had "as much VX in storage as the U.N. suspects," he would "be able to kill every human being on the face of the planet.") Nor did they support the war because they were fundamentally misled by American intelligence about the nature and extent of Saddam's weapons programs. Most of what they and everyone else knew about those programs we had learned from the U.N. inspectors, not from U.S. intelligence.

Some of that intelligence has now turned out to be wrong. Some of it has turned out to be right. And it is simply too soon to tell about the rest. The press has focused attention almost entirely on David Kay's assertion that there were no stockpiles of chemical and biological weapons when the United States and its allies invaded Iraq last March. We'll address that assertion in a moment. But what about the rest of Kay's testimony?

The key question for more than a decade, for both the Clinton and the Bush administrations, was not only what weapons Saddam had but what weapons he was trying to obtain, and how long it might be before containment failed and he was able to obtain them. The goal of American policy, and indeed of the U.N. Security Council over the course of the dozen years after the end of the Gulf War in 1991, was not primarily to find Saddam's existing stockpiles. That was subsidiary to the larger goal, which was to achieve Iraq's disarmament, including the elimination not only of existing prohibited weapons but of all such weapons programs, to ensure that Iraq would not possess weapons of mass destruction now or in the future. As Richard Butler and other weapons inspectors have argued, this task proved all but impossible once it became clear that Saddam was determined to acquire such weapons at some point. As Butler repeated time and again in his reports to the Security Council, the whole inspections regime was premised on Saddam's cooperation. But Saddam never cooperated, not in the 1990s and not in 2003.

It is important to recall that the primary purpose of Security Council Resolution 1441, passed on November 8, 2002, was not to discover whether Saddam had weapons and programs. There was little doubt that Saddam had them. The real question was whether he was ready to make a clean breast of everything and give up not only his forbidden weapons but also his efforts to acquire them once and for all. The purpose was to give Saddam "one final chance" to change his stripes, to offer full cooperation by revealing and dismantling all his programs and to forswear all such efforts in the future.

After all, what would be accomplished if Saddam turned over stockpiles and dismantled programs, only to restart them the minute the international community turned its back? Saddam might be slowed, but he would not be stopped. This was the logic that had led the Clinton administration to conclude that someday, somehow, the only answer to the problem would be Saddam's removal from power. Not surprisingly, the Bush administration was even more convinced that Saddam's removal was the only answer. That the administration went along with the inspections process embodied in Resolution 1441 was a concession to international and domestic pressure. No senior official, including Secretary Powell, believed there was any but the smallest chance Saddam would comply with the terms of Resolution 1441.

Resolution 1441 demanded that, within 30 days, Iraq provide "a currently accurate, full, and complete declaration of all aspects of its programs to develop chemical, biological, and nuclear weapons, ballistic missiles, and other delivery systems such as unmanned aerial vehicles and dispersal systems designed for use on aircraft, including any holdings and precise locations of such weapons, components, sub-components, stocks of agents, and related material and equipment, the locations and work of its research, development and production facilities, as well as all other chemical, biological, and nuclear programs, including any which it claims are for purposes not related to weapon production or material." Administration officials doubted Saddam would do this. They hoped only that, once Saddam's noncompliance became clear, they would win unanimous support for war at the U.N. Security Council.

And it was pretty clear at the time that Saddam was not complying. In his May 30, 2003, report to the Security Council, Hans Blix reported that the declared stocks of anthrax and VX remained unaccounted for. And he elaborated: "Little progress was made in the solution of outstanding issues. . . . The long list of proscribed items unaccounted for and as such resulting in unresolved disarmament issues was not shortened either by the inspections or by Iraqi declarations and documentation."

Now, of course, we know more definitively that Saddam did not comply with Resolution 1441. That is a part of Kay's testimony that has been widely ignored. What Kay discovered in the course of his eight-month-long investigation was that Iraq had failed to answer outstanding questions about its arsenal and programs. Indeed, it had continued to engage in an elaborate campaign of deception and concealment of weapons activities throughout the time when Hans Blix and the UNMOVIC inspectors were in the country, and right up until the day of the invasion, and beyond.

As Kay told the Senate Armed Services Committee . . ., the Iraq Survey Group "discovered hundreds of cases, based on both documents, physical evidence and the testimony of Iraqis, of activities that were prohibited under the initial U.N. Resolution 687 and that should have been reported under 1441, with Iraqi testimony that not only did they not tell the U.N. about this, they were instructed not to do it and they hid material." Kay reported, "We have had a number of Iraqis who have come forward and said, 'We did not tell the U.N. about what we were hiding, nor would we have told the U.N.,'" because the risks were too great. And what were the Iraqis hiding? As Kay reports, "They maintained programs and activities, and they certainly had the intentions at a point to resume their programs. So there was a lot they wanted to hide because it showed what they were doing was illegal." As Kay reported last October, his survey team uncovered "dozens of WMD-related program activities and significant amounts of equipment that Iraq concealed from the U.N. during the inspections that began in late 2002." . . .

As Kay has testified repeatedly, Iraq was "in clear material violation of 1441." So if the world had known in February 2003 what Kay says we know now—that there were no large stockpiles of weapons, but that Iraq continued to pursue weapons of mass destruction programs and to deceive and conceal these efforts from the U.N. inspectors led by Blix during the time allocated by Resolution 1441—wouldn't there have been at least as much, and probably more, support for the war? For Saddam would have been in flagrant violation of yet another set of commitments to disarm. He would have demonstrated once again that he was unwilling to abandon these programs, that he was unwilling to avail himself of this "last chance" and disarm once and for all. Had the world discovered unambiguously in February 2003 that Saddam was cheating on its commitments in Resolution 1441, surely even the French would have found it difficult to block a U.N. resolution authorizing war. As Dominique de Villepin acknowledged in the contentious months before the war, "We all realize that success in the inspections presupposes that we get full and complete cooperation from Iraq." What if it were as clear then as it is now that Saddam was engaged in another round of deceit and concealment? . . .

There was an argument against going to war [in 2003]. But let's remember what that argument was. It had nothing to do with whether or not Saddam had weapons of mass destruction and WMD programs. Everyone from Howard Dean to the *New York Times* editorial board to Dominique de Villepin and Jacques Chirac assumed that he had both. Most of the arguments against the war concerned timing. The most frequent complaint was that Bush was rushing to war. Why not give Blix and his inspectors another three months or six months?

We now know, however, that giving Blix a few more months would not have made a difference. [In January of 2004] Kay was asked what would have happened if Blix and his team had been allowed to continue their mission. Kay responded, "All I can say is that among an extensive body of Iraqi scientists who are talking to us, they have said: The U.N. interviewed us; we did not tell them the truth, we did not show them this equipment, we did not talk about these programs; we couldn't do it as long as Saddam was in power. I suspect regardless of how long they had stayed, that attitude would have been the same." Given the "terror regime of Saddam," Kay concluded, he and his team learned things after the war "that no U.N. inspector would have ever learned" while Saddam was still in power.

So it is very unlikely that, given another three months or six months, the Blix team would have come to any definitive conclusion one way or another. Nor, therefore, would there have been a much greater probability of winning a unanimous vote at the Security Council for war once those additional six months had passed. Whether the United States could have kept 200,000 troops on a permanent war footing in the Persian Gulf for another six months is even more doubtful.

༺◉༻

Did the administration claim the Iraqi threat was imminent, in the sense that Iraq possessed weapons that were about to be used against the United States? That is the big charge leveled by the Bush administration's critics these days. It is rather surprising, given the certainty with which this charge is thrown around, how little the critics have in the way of quotations from administration officials to back it up. Saying that action is urgent is not the same thing as saying the threat is imminent. In fact, the president said the threat was not imminent, and that we had to act (urgently) before the threat became imminent. This was well understood. As Senate Democratic leader Tom Daschle said on October 10, 2002, explaining his support for the legislation authorizing the president to go to war, "The threat posed by Saddam Hussein may not be imminent, but it is real, it is growing and it cannot be ignored." ...

❧

On *Meet the Press* on February 8, Tim Russert asked the president whether the war in Iraq was "a war of choice or a war of necessity." The president paused before responding, asking Russert to elaborate, as if unwilling to accept the dichotomy. He was right.

After all, fighting a "war of choice" sounds problematic. But how many of our wars have been, strictly speaking, wars of necessity? How often did the country face immediate peril and destruction unless war was launched? Was World War I a war of necessity? Was World War II before the attack on Pearl Harbor, or afterwards with respect to fighting Germany in Europe? Was the Spanish-American War a war of necessity? Was the Korean War? Never mind Vietnam, the Dominican Republic, Grenada, Panama, Somalia, Haiti, Bosnia, and Kosovo. And what about the first Gulf War? Many argued that Saddam could be (indeed, was) contained in Kuwait, and that he could eventually have been forced to retreat by economic sanctions.

In some sense all of these wars were wars of choice. But when viewed in the context of history and international circumstances, they were all based on judgments about the costs of inaction, the benefits of action, and on strategic calculations that action then would be far preferable to action later in less favorable circumstances. In other words, war was necessary to our national interest, if not absolutely necessary to the immediate protection of the homeland. ...

❧

So what about those stockpiles? The failure to find them, and now David Kay's claim that they did not exist at the time of the invasion last year (a claim reported by an astonishing number of journalists as meaning they never existed at all), has led many to maintain that the entire war was fought on false pretenses. We have addressed that claim. But we also want to address Kay's assertion.

We are prepared to believe that the large stockpiles of anthrax, ricin, VX, and other biological and chemical weapons that once existed were at some point destroyed by the Iraqis. But we do not understand why Kay is so confident he knows what happened to those stockpiles, or to other parts of Saddam's weapons programs that have not been found.

According to Kay's testimony before the Senate (and since he has provided no written report and no documentation to support his recent claims, this is all anyone has to go on), Kay and his team "went after this not in the way of trying to find where the weapons are hidden." When the Survey Group did not find the weapons in "the obvious places," presumably meaning the places that had been identified by intelligence and other sources, Kay explains, he tried other means of discovering the truth. His principal method appears to have been interviews with scientists who would have known what was produced and where it might be stored, as well as a search through a portion of the documents uncovered after the war. Kay acknowledges that stockpiles may, in fact, still be hidden somewhere. But he does not believe they are.

Under questioning from the senators, however, Kay admitted a few areas of uncertainty. The first concerns his interviews with Iraqi scientists. On some occasions Kay has claimed that, with Saddam out of power, it could be assumed that scientists once fearful of telling the truth would now be willing to speak. Therefore, their testimony that no weapons stockpiles exist could be trusted. But when asked whether people involved in Iraqi weapons programs might now fear prosecution for war crimes, Kay said, "Absolutely. And a number of those in custody are worried about that greatly," which is "one reason they're not talking." So it turns out there are scientists who are not talking. This produces, Kay suggests, "a level of unresolvable ambiguity" about Saddam's weapons programs. But is the ambiguity truly "unresolvable," or was it just unresolvable within the limited time of Kay's investigation? Is it possible that when all the scientists feel safe enough to talk, we may learn more? . . .

Finally there is the question of Iraqi documents. We understand that thousands of pages of documents seized at the end of the war have still not been read. During the 1990s, U.N. inspectors frequently opened treasure troves of information simply with the discovery of a single document in a mountain of paper. Is it possible that some of the unread documents contain useful information? In addition, according to Kay's October report and his most recent testimony, Iraqi officials undertook a massive effort to destroy evidence, burning documents and destroying computer harddrives. The result, Kay acknowledged, is that "we're really not going to be able to prove . . . some of the positive conclusions that we're going to come to." Yet another level of ambiguity. . . .

Whatever the results of that search, it will continue to be the case that the war was worth fighting, and that it was necessary. For the people of Iraq, the war put an end to three decades of terror and suffering. The mass graves uncovered since the end of the war are alone sufficient justification for it. Assuming the United States remains committed to helping establish a democratic government in Iraq, that will be a blessing both to the Iraqi people and to their neighbors. As for those neighbors, the threat of Saddam's aggression, which hung over the region for more than two decades, has finally been eliminated. The prospects for war in the region have been substantially diminished by our action.

It is also becoming clear that the battle of Iraq has been an important victory in the broader war in which we are engaged, a war against terror, against weapons proliferation, and for a new Middle East. Already, other terror-implicated regimes in the region that were developing weapons of mass destruction are feeling pressure, and some are beginning to move in the right direction. Libya has given up its weapons of mass destruction program. Iran has at least gestured toward opening its nuclear program to inspection. The clandestine international network organized by Pakistan's A.Q. Khan that has been so central to nuclear proliferation to rogue states has been exposed. From Iran to Saudi Arabia, liberal forces seem to have been encouraged. We are paying a real price in blood and treasure in Iraq. But we believe that it is already clear—as clear as such things get in the real world—that the price of the liberation of Iraq has been worth it.

Michael Ignatieff  **NO**

Why Are We in Iraq? (And Liberia? And Afghanistan?)

In the back alleys of Iraq, the soldiers from the 101st Airborne and First Armored Divisions are hot, dirty and scared. They want to go home, but instead they're pinned down, fighting off hit-and-run attacks and trying to stop sabotage on pipelines, water mains and electric grids. They were told they would be greeted as liberators, but now, many months later, they are an army of occupation, trying to save the reputation of a president who never told them—did he know himself?—what they were getting into. The Muslim fighters rushing to join the remnants of Saddam Hussein's loyalists in a guerrilla war to reclaim Iraq have understood all along what the war has been about—that it was never simply a matter of preventing the use of weapons of mass destruction; rather, it was about consolidating American power in the Arab world. Some in the administration no doubt understood this, too, though no one took the trouble to explain all their reasons for going to war to the American people or, for that matter, the rest of the world.

But now we know, Iraq may become for America what Afghanistan became for the Soviet empire: the place where its fight against Islamic jihad will be won or lost. Nor is the United States the only target. The suicide bomb that killed Sergio Vieira de Mello and decimated his team has drawn the United Nations into the vortex. The United Nations came to Baghdad to give American nation-building a patina of legitimacy. Now the world body has been targeted as an accomplice of occupation. If the United States fails in Iraq, so will the United Nations.

To see what is really unfolding in Iraq, we need to place it in the long history of American overseas interventions. It is worth remembering, for example, that when American soldiers have occupied countries before, for example Japan and Germany, the story started out much the same: not enough food, not enough electricity, not enough law and order (and, in Germany, ragtag Nazi fighters). And if this history is part of what drove us into Iraq, what doctrine, if any, has determined when and where Americans are sent to fight? Before the United States sends troops to any future front— Syria? North Korea? Iran?—it is crucial to ask: What does the history of American intervention teach us to hope and to fear? And how might the

From the *New York Times Magazine*, September 7, 2003, pp. 38, 40–43, 71–72, 85. Copyright © 2003 by Eliza Griswold. Distributed by The New York Times Special Features. Reprinted by permission.

United States devise a coherent strategy of engagement suited for the perils—and possibilities—of the 21st century?

❧

From the very beginning, the American republic has never shrunk from foreign wars. A recent Congressional study shows that there has scarcely been a year since its founding that American soldiers haven't been overseas "from the halls of Montezuma to the shores of Tripoli," chasing pirates, punishing bandits, pulling American citizens out of harm's way, intervening in civil wars, stopping massacres, overturning regimes deemed (fairly or not) unfriendly and exporting democracy. American foreign policy largely consists of doctrines about when and where to intervene in other people's countries. In 1823, James Monroe committed the United States—militarily, if it came to that—to keeping foreign colonial powers out of the entire Western Hemisphere. In 1906, Theodore Roosevelt added a corollary giving the United States the right to send in troops when any of its Latin American neighbors engaged in "flagrant wrong-doing." Most Latin Americans, then and now, took that to mean that the United States would topple any government in the hemisphere that acted against American interests. Early in the last century, American troops went ashore to set up governments in Haiti and the Dominican Republic and chased Pancho Villa around Mexico. And this kind of intervention wasn't just confined to pushing around Latin Americans. Twelve thousand troops were sent to support the White armies fighting the Communists in the Russian Civil War that began in 1918. In the 1920's, during the civil war in China, there were 6,000 American soldiers ashore and a further 44 naval vessels in the China Sea protecting American interests. (Neither venture was much of a success. Both Russia and China eventually went Communist.)

Despite George Washington's call to avoid foreign entanglements and John Quincy Adams's plea that America should abjure slaying monsters abroad, splendid isolation has never proved to be a convincing foreign policy for Americans, First in 1917 and then again in 1941, American presidents thought they could keep America out of Europe's wars only to discover that isolation was not an option for a country wanting to be taken seriously as a world power—which, from the beginning, is precisely what America desired. Intervention required huge sacrifice—the haunting American graveyards in France are proof of this—but American soldiers helped save Europe from dictatorship, and their hard fighting turned America into the most powerful nation on earth. . . .

❧

Never pick on someone your own size, which in our time means someone with nuclear weapons: this has been Rule No. 1 of intervention since the end of the Second World War. Minor rogues, would-be tough guys like Saddam Hussein, perhaps, but never someone who can actually deliver a nuclear bomb. (We are about to see whether this rule holds with regard to North

Korea.) Even the enormous American intervention in Vietnam took great care to avoid a direct clash with Russia and China.

When Lyndon Johnson sent half a million troops to Vietnam, he thought he was containing Communism in Asia (without threatening either the Chinese or Russian regimes that were financing North Vietnam's campaign). Johnson never realized his ultimate enemy was Vietnamese nationalism. The 58,000 names carved into the black granite of the Vietnam Memorial in Washington are the measure of Johnson's mistake. Rule No. 2 of American intervention evolved out of Vietnam: Never fight someone who is more willing to die than you are. (This is the rule now being tested by the hit-and-run attackers and suicide bombers in Iraq.) The Vietnam veterans who came to command the American military—led by Colin Powell—also settled on Rule No. 3, which remains much debated: Never intervene except with overwhelming force in defense of a vital national interest. (Thus [the] gingerly approach to Liberia.)

But what has been the national interest once the cold war ended and the threat of a growing Communist empire evaporated? No clear national interest has emerged. No clear *conversation* about the national interest has emerged. Policy—if one can even speak of policy—has seemed to be mostly the prisoner of interventionist lobbies with access to the indignation machine of the modern media. America in the 1990's intervened to oust an invader (the first gulf war), to stop civil war (Bosnia), to stop ethnic cleansing (Kosovo), to feed the starving (Somalia) and to prevent a country from falling apart (Macedonia). America also dithered on the sidelines and watched 800,000 people die in three awful months in Rwanda, when airstrikes against the government sponsors of the genocide, coupled with reinforcement of the United Nations troops on the ground, might have stopped the horror. Rule No. 4: Never use force except as a last resort (sometimes turned into an alibi for doing nothing).

During the Clinton years, there were presidential directives that sought to define exactly what the Clinton doctrine on intervention might be. But no doctrine was ever arrived at. There was a guiding principle: reluctance to shed American blood. Thus, Rule No. 5 in American interventions: When force is used as a last resort, avoid American casualties. Since the Clinton administration's interventions were not of necessity to protect the national interest—whatever that was at the time—but matters of choice, this made a certain amount of sense, at least in terms of domestic politics.

The problem with Rule No. 5 is that it made force protection as important as mission accomplishment and may have sent the wrong signal to the enemy. But cutting and running after the botched intervention in Somalia in 1993, for instance, Clinton might have led Osama bin Laden to believe that Americans lacked the stomach for a fight. Ten years later, we may still be paying the price for that mistake.

By the end of the 1990's, conservative commentators were complaining that Clinton's intervention doctrine, such as it was, had lost touch with national interest and had degenerated into social work. The Bush campaign vowed that the 101st Airborne wouldn't be wasted escorting foreign children to school and promised to bring the boys home from Bosnia. (They remain.) As far as the Bush administration was concerned, too much intervention, where too little was at stake, was blunting the purpose of the military, which was to "fight and win the nation's wars." Of course, at the time he became president, the nation had no wars, and none loomed on the horizon.

Then came Sept. 11—and then came first Afghanistan and then Iraq. These two reversed Rule No. 4. (Only use force as a last resort.) Now the Bush administration was committing itself to use force as a first resort. But the Bush doctrine on intervention is no clearer than Clinton's. The Bush administration is committed to absolute military pre-eminence, but does anyone think that Clinton's military was less determined to remain the single—and overwhelming—superpower? The Bush doctrine is also burdened with contradiction. The president took office ruling out humanitarian interventions, yet marines did (finally) go ashore in war-torn Liberia. During the 2000 campaign, George Bush ruled out intervention in the cause of nation-building, only to find himself staking his presidency on the outcome of nation-building in Afghanistan and Iraq. Having called for a focused intervention strategy, he has proclaimed a war on terror that never clearly defines terrorism; never differentiates among terrorist organizations as to which explicitly threaten American interests and which do not; and never has settled on which states supporting or harboring terrorists are targets of American intervention. An administration whose supposed watchword is self-discipline regularly leaks to the press, for example, that its intervention list might include Syria or Iran—or might not, depending on the day of the week you ask. The administration, purposefully or not, routinely conflates terrorism and the nuclear threat from rogue nations. These are threats of a profoundly different order and magnitude. Finally, the administration promises swift and decisive interventions that will lead to victory. But as Afghanistan shows (and Iraq is beginning to show), this expectation is deluded. Taking down the state that sheltered Osama bin Laden was easy; shutting down Al Qaeda has proved frustratingly difficult. Interventions don't end when the last big battle is won. In a war on terror, containing rather than defeating the enemy is the most you can hope for. Where is the doctrine acknowledging that truth?

The Bush administration, as no administration before it, has embraced "pre-emption." It's a strategy of sorts, but hardly a doctrine. Where is the definition of when pre-emption might actually be justified? The angry postwar debate about whether the American public (and the British public, too) were duped into the Iraq war is about much more than whether intelligence estimates were "sexed up" to make the threat from Hussein seem more compelling. It is about what level of threat warrants pre-emptive use of force. Almost 20 years ago, George P. Shultz, as Reagan's secretary of state, gave a speech warning that America would have to make pre-emptive intervention against terrorist threats on the basis of evidence that would be less than clear. Since Shultz, no one has clarified how intervention decisions are to be made when intelligence is, as it is bound to be, uncertain. As Paul Wolfowitz, the Bush administration's deputy secretary of defense, has candidly acknowledged, the intelligence evidence used to justify force in Iraq was "murky." If so, the American people should have been told just that. Instead, they were told that intervention was necessary to meet a real and imminent threat. Now the line seems to be that the war wasn't much of an act of pre-emption at all, but rather a crusade to get rid of an odious regime. But this then makes it a war of choice—and the Bush administration came to power vowing not to fight those. At the moment, the United States is fighting wars in two countries with no clear policy of intervention, no clear end in sight and no clear understanding among Americans of what their nation has gotten itself into.

꒰◉꒱

There has always been an anti-intervention party in American politics, one that believes that the Republic should resist the temptations of empire and that democracy at home is menaced when force is used to export democracy abroad. During the war to annex the Philippines in 1898, the fine flower of the American intellectual and moral elite was dead set against the war: the humorist Mark Twain, the union leader Samuel Gompers, the multi-millionaire Andrew Carnegie, the social critic and activist Jane Addams. From these luminaries of yesteryear to the luminaries of today—Norman Mailer, Noam Chomsky, the Dixie Chicks—intervention has been excoriated as an imperial misadventure, justified in the language of freedom and democracy but actually prosecuted for venal motive: oil, power, revenge, political advantage at home and nefarious designs abroad.

The anti-intervention party in American politics often captures the high moral ground but usually loses the war for public opinion. With the single exception of Vietnam—where the sheer cost in blood made the exercise seem futile both to moralists and realists alike—the American public has never been convinced that the country would lose its soul in overseas wars. On the contrary, Americans have tended to get caught up in the adventure. They have also believed at times that intervention can serve their interests. When anti-interventionists in the months before the invasion of Iraq thundered, "No blood for oil!" many Americans no doubt thought, "If you won't fight to defend the oil supply, what will you fight for?" . . .

Yet oil is not the whole story, as capitalist interest has never been. From Teddy Roosevelt to George W. Bush, moral feeling has made a real difference to the timing and scope of interventions. Just compare Bush the father with Bush the son. The father is a cold-eyed realist. In 1991, he did not think the oppression of the Kurds and Shiites justified going all the way to Baghdad. His son is more a hotblooded moralist. Bringing freedom to the Iraqis seems to matter to him, which is why, perhaps, he rushed to Baghdad not caring whether he had a coalition behind him or not. This is not to say that this president's moralism is unproblematic or that it has gone unchallenged. When he went to the United Nations in September 2002 to make his case for action against Hussein, Amnesty International released a statement objecting to his citation of Hussein's abject human rights record as a ground for the use of force. Nothing makes human rights activists angrier than watching political leaders conscript human rights into a justification for aggression. Human Rights Watch and Amnesty International, both of which had denounced Hussein's tyranny for some 20 years with little or no support from successive American administrations, had good reason to be suspicious of the motives of a presidential Johnny-come-lately to the human rights cause. Nonetheless, this put human rights advocates in the curious position of denouncing Hussein but objecting when someone finally proposed to do something about him. To oppose an intervention that was bound to improve the human rights of Iraqis because the man leading that intervention was late to the cause would seem to value good intentions more than good consequences.

Some of the immediate consequences of the Iraq intervention have been good indeed: a totalitarian regime is no longer terrorizing Iraqis; Shiites marching in their hundreds of thousands to celebrate at their shrine at Karbala, along with professors, policemen and office workers demonstrating in the streets of Baghdad, are tasting freedom for the first time; Iraqis as a whole are discovering the truth about the torture chambers, mass graves and other squalid secrets of more than two decades of tyranny. . . .

Human rights could well be improved in Iraqi as a result of the intervention. But the Bush administration did not invade Iraq just to establish human rights. Nor, ultimately, was this intervention about establishing a democracy or saving lives as such. And here we come to the heart of the matter—to where the Bush administration's interventions fit into America's long history of intervention. All such interventions have occurred because a president has believed going in that it would increase both his and his country's power and influence. To use Joseph S. Nye Jr.'s definition, "power is the ability to obtain the outcomes one wants." Presidents intervene because successful interventions enhance America's ability to obtain the outcomes it wants.

The Iraq intervention was the work of conservative radicals, who believed that the status quo in the Middle East was untenable—for strategic reasons, security reasons and economic reasons. They wanted intervention to bring about a revolution in American power in the entire region. What made a president take the gamble was Sept. 11 and the realization, with 15 of the hijackers originating in Saudi Arabia, that American interests based since 1945 on a presumed Saudi pillar were actually built on sand. The new pillar was to be a democratic Iraq, at peace with Israel, Turkey and Iran, harboring no terrorists, pumping oil for the world economy at the right price and abjuring any nasty designs on its neighbors. . . .

The manipulation of popular consent over Iraq—together with and tangled up with the lack of an intervention policy—is why the anti-war party is unresigned to its defeat and the pro-war party feels so little of the warm rush of vindication. Even those who supported intervention have to concede that in justifying his actions to the American people, the president was, at the least, economical with the truth. Because the casus belli over Iraq was never accurately set out for Americans, the chances of Americans hanging on for the long haul—and it will be a long haul—have been under-cut. Also damaged has been the trust that a president will need from his people when he seeks their support for intervention in the future.

❧

Critics view Iraq as a perilous new step in the history of American inter-vention: unilateral, opposed by most of the world, an act of territorial conquest. The truth is we have been here before. The Iraq operation most resembles the conquest of the Philippines between 1898 and 1902. Both were wars of conquest, both were urged by an ideological elite on a divided country and both cost much more than anyone had bargained for. Just as in Iraq, winning the war was the easy part. The Spanish fell to Commodore Dewey even more quickly than Hussein's forces fell to Tommy Franks. But it was afterward that the going got rough. More than 120,000 American troops were sent to the Philippines to put down the guerrilla resistance, and 4,000 never came home. It remains to be seen whether Iraq will cost thousands of American lives—and whether the American public will accept such a heavy toll as the price of success in Iraq. The Philippines also provides a humbling perspective on nation-building in Iraq. A hundred years on, American troops are back in the Philippines, hunting down guerrillas, this time tied to Al Qaeda, and the democracy that Teddy Roosevelt sought to bring to that nation remains chronically insecure. . . .

❧

If we take stock and ask what will curb the American appetite for interven-tion, the answer is, not much. Interventions are popular, and they remain popular even if American soldiers die. Even failure and defeat aren't much of a restraint: 30 years after Vietnam, America is intervening as robustly as ever. What Thomas Jefferson called "decent respect to the opinions of mankind" doesn't seem to exert much influence, either. About Iraq, the opinions of mankind told the Bush White House that the use of force was a dangerous and destabilizing adventure, but the intervention went ahead because the president believes that the ultimate authority over American decisions to intervene is not the United Nations or the world's opinion, but his constitutional mandate as commander in chief to "preserve, protect and defend" the United States. The unilateral doctrine alarms America's allies, but there is not a lot they can do about it. When Bush went to war, he set the timetable, and not even Tony Blair, who desperately needed more time to bring his domestic opinion with him, was able to stretch it out.

To date, the only factor that keeps the United States from intervening is if the country in question has nuclear weapons. One of the factors driv-ing pre-emptive action in Iraq was the belief that were Hussein to acquire a nuclear or mass-casualty chemical or biological weapon, it would then be too late to use force. No wonder a Pakistani general is supposed to have remarked in 1999 that the chief lesson he drew from the display of American precision air power in Kosovo was for his country to acquire nuclear weapons as quickly as possible. . . .

◆

For all its risks, Americans, by and large, still think of intervening as a noble act in which the new world comes to the rescue of the old. They remember the newsreels of G.I.'s riding into Rome in 1943 or driving through the lanes of northern Europe in 1944, kissing the girls and grabbing the bouquets and wine bottles held out to them by people weeping with gratitude at their liberation. All this has changed. There were few tearful embraces when the marines rode into Nasiriya, no bouquets and prayers of thanks when the Army rode into Baghdad. True, Iraq is not the first time an American intervention has been unpopular. Iranians were not happy that the C.I.A. engineered the overthrow of Mossadegh in 1953, Chilean democrats didn't like what was done to Allende and students the world over protested against Vietnam. But these occasions apart, and right through the Kosovo intervention in 1999, our allies kept faith with American good intentions. Now all that moral capital has been spent. Some Europeans actually think, to judge from a few polls, that George Bush is more of a threat to world peace than Osama bin Laden. This may be grotesque, but it makes it much harder for American interventions to find favor in world opinion.

Its allies wept with America after Sept. 11 and then swiftly concluded that only America was under attack. The idea that Western civilization had been the target was not convincing. While America and its allies stood shoulder to shoulder when they faced a common Soviet foe, Islamic terrorism seemed to have America alone in its sights. Why cozy up to a primary target, America's allies asked themselves, when it will only make you a secondary one? Indeed, after Sept. 11 an astonishing number of the United States' friends went further. They whispered, America had it coming. Aggrieved Americans were entitled to ask, For what? For guaranteeing the security of their oil supplies for 60 years? For rebuilding the European economy from the ruins of 1945? For protecting innumerable countries from Communist takeover? No matter, after Sept. 11, memories of American generosity were short, and the list of grievances against it was long.

As the Iraq debate at the United Nations showed so starkly, the international consensus that once provided America with coalitions of the willing when it used force has disappeared. There is no Soviet ogre to scare doubters into line. European allies are now serious economic rivals, and they are happy to conceal their absolute military dependence with obstreperously independent foreign policies. Throughout the third world, states fear Islamic political opposition even more than American disapproval and are disposed to appease their Islamic constituencies with anti-American poses whenever they can get away with it.

There are those who think that the damage done by the Iraq debate at the United Nations can be repaired and that a coalition of the willing, at least one with more active players, might have been possible if the United

States hadn't been so backhanded with its diplomacy. Yet the days when the United States intervenes as the servant of the international community may be well and truly over. When it intervenes in the future, it will very likely go it alone and will do so essentially for itself.

If this is the new world order, it will have costs that the rest of the world will have to accept: fewer humanitarian interventions on behalf of starving or massacred people in the rest of the world, fewer guarantees of other people's security against threat and invasion. Why bother with rescue and protection if you have to do everythings one? Why bother maintaining a multilateral order—of free trade, open markets and common defense—if your allies only use it to tie Gulliver down with leading strings? . . .

·⁂·

There is a way out of this mess of interventionist policy, but it is also a route out of American unilateralism. It entails allowing other countries to have a say on when and how the United States can intervene. It would mean returning to the United Nations and proposing new rules to guide the use of force. This is the path that Franklin Roosevelt took in 1944, when he put his backing behind the creation of a new world organization with a mandate to use force to defend "international peace and security." What America needs, then, is not simply its own doctrine for intervention but also an international doctrine that promotes and protects its interests *and* those of the rest of the international community.

The problem is that the United Nations that F.D.R. helped create never worked as he intended. What passes for an "international community" is run by a Security Council that is a museum piece of 1945 vintage. Everybody knows that the Security Council needs reform, and everybody also knows that this is nearly impossible. But if so, then the United Nations has no future. The time for reform is now or never. If there ever was a reason to give Great Britain and France a permanent veto while denying permanent membership to Germany, India, Brazil or Japan, that day is over. The United States should propose enlarging the number of permanent members of the council so that it truly represents the world's population. In order to convince the world that it is serious about reform, it ought to propose giving up its own veto so that all other permanent members follow suit and the Security Council makes decisions to use force with a simple majority vote. As a further guarantee of its seriousness, the United States would commit to use force only with approval of the council, except where its national security was directly threatened. . . .

Putting the United States at the head of a revitalized United Nations is a huge task. For the United States is as disillusioned with the United Nations as the world is disillusioned with the United States. Yet it needs to be understood that the alternative is empire: a muddled, lurching America policing an ever more resistant world alone, with former allies sabotaging it at every turn. Roosevelt understood that Americans can best secure their own defense and pursue their own interests when they unite with other states and, where necessary, sacrifice unilateral freedom of action for a common good. The signal failure of American foreign policy since the end of the cold war has not been a lack of will to lead and to intervene; it has been a failure to imagine the possibility of a United States once again cooperating with others to create rules for the international community. Pax Americana must be multilateral, as Franklin Roosevelt realized, or it will not survive. Without clear principles for intervention, without friends, without dreams to serve, the soldiers sweating in their body armor in Iraq are defending nothing more than power. And power without legitimacy, without support, without the world's respect and attachment, cannot endure.

POSTSCRIPT

Was the Invasion of Iraq Justified?

The temptation to call Robert Kagan and William Kristol "hawks" and Michael Ignatieff a "dove"—labels left over from the Vietnam era—must be resisted. As we can see from his selection, Ignatieff would have supported the use of force in Rwanda in 1994 to stop the genocide. And concerning Somalia in 1993, though he considers the original intervention "botched," he is criticial of President Clinton's decision to "cut and run" once the war-lords began inflicting causalities on U.S. forces. As for Kagan and Kristol, though they do not mention it here, remarks they have made elsewhere suggest that these two "hawks" are likely to become doves once anyone proposes U.S. intervention in Haiti or Liberia.

In *Disarming Iraq* (Pantheon, 2004) former U.N. weapons inspector Hans Blix provides an insider's account of his efforts to find Saddam's weapons of mass destruction and argues that the invasion was unnecessary and counterproductive. On the other hand, Kenneth Pollack, a former CIA analyst and national Security Council staffer, calls the invasion the "least bad option" in *The Threatening Storm: The Case for Invading Iraq* (Random House, 2002). Micah L. Sifry and Christopher Cerf, eds., *The Iraq War: History, Documents, Opinions* (Touchstone Books, 2003) is a substantial anthology of opinions on the war, from those of Barbara Ehrenreich on the left to Ann Coulter on the right. Norman Solomon and Reese Erlich, *Target Iraq: What the News Media Didn't Tell You* (Context Books, 2003), written before the war began, suggests that the media can't be trusted to present all sides of the debate, either because of their own self-interest or because of pressure from the administration and its corporate allies. (Howard Zinn writes the introduction, and it has an afterward by Sean Penn.) Sandra MacKey, *The Reckoning: Iraq and the Legacy of Saddam Hussein* (Norton, 2002), also written before the war, traces the forty-year history of Saddam's rule in Iraq and predicts the future disintegration of the country into warring cantons if Bush goes ahead with the invasion. Toby Dodge, *Inventing Iraq: the Failure of Nation-Building and a History Denied* (Colmbia University Press, 2003) studies Britain's previous occupation of Iraq and shows why it failed. *Los Angeles Times* correspondent David Zucchino, in *Thunder Run: The Armored Strike to Capture Baghdad* (Atlantic Monthly Press, 2004), reconstructs the "lightning armored strike" that brought U.S. troops quickly into Baghdad in 2003.

Both defenders and critics of the Iraq war use the example of previous wars to try to foretell its outcome. Vietnam is the critics' favorite: Iraq, they say, will become a similar "quagmire." Defenders like to compare it to World War II, where the U.S. defeated brutal regimes, occupied their countries, and brought democracy to peoples thought to be incapable of it. This, of course, does not exhaust all the possibilities. Another war that might be considered for comparison is the American Civil War, which was full of tragic reverses for the Union forces—they often seemed to be on the verge of losing it all, or at least being locked into an indefinite stalemate—until the capture of Atlanta on September 2, 1864, two months before an election that Lincoln had resigned himself to losing.

Michael Ignatieff, director of the Carr Center at the Kennedy School. He regards the war as a unilateral act of territorial conquest that has brought unacceptable human and material costs and has damaged America's respect in the world.

ISSUE 21

Must America Exercise World Leadership?

YES: Charles Krauthammer, from "The Unipolar Moment Revisited," *The National Interest* (Winter 2002/2003)

NO: Niall Ferguson, from "An Empire in Denial," *Harvard International Review* (Fall 2003)

ISSUE SUMMARY

YES: Political writer Charles Krauthammer believes that America's mission as the sole superpower to keep the peace and extend democracy takes priority over the considerations of its allies or the international community.

NO: Author Niall Ferguson maintains that despite America's military and economic dominance, it lacks both the long-term will and the capital and human investment that would be necessary to sustain its dominance.

For centuries, great empires conquered and exploited distant colonies. All this changed with the World War II, from which the United States emerged as the greatest military and economic power the world had ever known, without creating a network of colonies.

How was that power to be employed, if it was to be used at all? Before 1940, the United States avoided involvement in international relations beyond the Americas. This sentiment went back to the warning in President Washington's farewell address to avoid "entangling alliances." As long as the United States felt separated from most of the rest of the world by two great oceans, it thought it was impregnable and remained out of the League of Nations. Isolation no longer seemed possible after the World War II, and an international role became inescapable as a consequence of instant communications, rapid transportation, increasing dependence on international trade, and the development of weapons of mass destruction (WMD).

For forty-five years after the World War II, the supremacy of the United States was challenged by the military expansionism of the Soviet

Union. Confronted by this threat, liberal internationalism took the place of isolationism as the world seemed to divide between two superpowers, both capable of building and employing nuclear and other WMD's. Only the prospect of what seemed the certainty of what was dubbed Mutual Assured Destruction (MAD) kept both nations from using these weapons. The United States relied on the doctrine of containment to confine communist power. This policy called for the participation of allies in multinational treaties, United Nations resolutions, the North Atlantic Treaty Organization (NATO), and other political and military alliances.

This liberal internationalism was identified with the advocacy of self-determination, democracy, and human rights. The United States sometimes fell short of such ideals when it embraced anti-communist regimes that were not democratic or overlooked gross abuses of human rights, but it never discarded its moral posture in opposition to what President Reagan called "the evil empire" of the Soviet Union. The disintegration of the Soviet empire as a threat to Western democracy left the United States as the sole superpower.

Since the 9/11 attack, the United States has assumed a mantle of world leadership. If America is a new empire (as both authors in the following selections agree), it is different from empires of the past, without vast colonies, but with unparalleled military and economic strength, as well as unprecedented cultural and technological impact. The clearest official statement of the Bush foreign policy is found in "The National Security Strategy of the United States of America," issued by the National Security Council in 2002 (available on the Internet), which proclaims America's world leadership in fighting terrorism, preempting threats, and spreading democracy, development, free markets, and free trade throughout the world.

Where this differs most significantly from that of previous administrations is in its unilateralism. The U.S. government proclaimed a commitment to act on behalf of America's best interests irrespective of the objections or reservations of its allies or the United Nations. Contrast the unwillingness of President George H. W. Bush in 1991 to have the American army enter Baghdad and overthrow the regime of Saddam Hussein, because it would alienate some of America's allies, with the determination of President George W. Bush in 2003 to engage in the second war against Iraq despite the failure of the United Nations or many nominal allies to support that action.

An unwillingness to compromise the American government's perception of its best interests led the second President Bush to reject treaties on land mines, nuclear proliferation, biological and chemical warfare, the International Criminal Court, and other international agreements, and to justify preemptive strikes in the absence of an attack upon the United States or a treaty ally.

Charles Krauthammer  **YES**

The Unipolar Moment Revisited

In late 1990, shortly before the collapse of the Soviet Union, it was clear that the world we had known for half a century was disappearing. The question was what would succeed it. I suggested then that we had already entered the "unipolar moment." The gap in power between the leading nation and all the others was so unprecedented as to yield an international structure unique to modern history: unipolarity.

At the time, this thesis was generally seen as either wild optimism or simple American arrogance. The conventional wisdom was that with the demise of the Soviet empire the bipolarity of the second half of the 20th century would yield to multipolarity. The declinist school, led by Paul Kennedy, held that America, suffering from "imperial overstretch", was already in relative decline. The Asian enthusiasm, popularized by (among others) James Fallows, saw the second coming of the Rising Sun. The conventional wisdom was best captured by Senator Paul Tsongas: "The Cold War is over; Japan won."

They were wrong, and no one has put it more forcefully than Paul Kennedy himself in a classic recantation published earlier this year. "Nothing has ever existed like this disparity of power; nothing", he said of America's position today. "Charlemagne's empire was merely western European in its reach. The Roman empire stretched farther afield, but there was another great empire in Persia, and a larger one in China. There is, therefore, no comparison." Not everyone is convinced. Samuel Huntington argued in 1999 that we had entered not a unipolar world but a "uni-multipolar world." Tony Judt writes mockingly of the "loud boasts of unipolarity and hegemony" heard in Washington today. But as Stephen Brooks and William Wohlforth argue in a recent review of the subject, those denying unipolarity can do so only by applying a ridiculous standard: that America be able to achieve all its goals everywhere all by itself. This is a standard not for unipolarity but for divinity. Among mortals, and in the context of the last half millennium of history, the current structure of the international system is clear: "If today's American primacy does not constitute unipolarity, then nothing ever will."

A second feature of this new post-Cold War world, I ventured, would be a resurgent American isolationism. I was wrong. It turns out that the

From *The National Interest*, Winter 2002/2003, pp. 5–17. Copyright © 2002 by Charles Krauthammer. Reprinted by permission of the author.

new norm for America is not post-World War I withdrawal but post-World War II engagement. In the 1990s, Pat Buchanan gave 1930s isolationism a run. He ended up carrying Palm Beach.

Finally, I suggested that a third feature of this new unipolar world would be an increase rather than a decrease in the threat of war, and that it would come from a new source: weapons of mass destruction wielded by rogue states. This would constitute a revolution in international relations, given that in the past it was great powers who presented the principal threats to world peace.

Where are we twelve years later? The two defining features of the new post-Cold War world remain: unipolarity and rogue states with weapons of mass destruction. Indeed, these characteristics have grown even more pronounced. Contrary to expectation, the United States has not regressed to the mean; rather, its dominance has dramatically increased. And during our holiday from history in the 1990s, the rogue state/WMD problem grew more acute. Indeed, we are now on the eve of history's first war over weapons of mass destruction.

Unipolarity After September 11, 2001

There is little need to rehearse the acceleration of unipolarity in the 1990s. Japan, whose claim to power rested exclusively on economics, went into economic decline. Germany stagnated. The Soviet Union ceased to exist, contracting into a smaller, radically weakened Russia. The European Union turned inward toward the great project of integration and built a strong social infrastructure at the expense of military capacity. Only China grew in strength, but coming from so far behind it will be decades before it can challenge American primacy—and that assumes that its current growth continues unabated.

The result is the dominance of a single power unlike anything ever seen. Even at its height Britain could always be seriously challenged by the next greatest powers. Britain had a smaller army than the land powers of Europe and its navy was equaled by the next two navies combined. Today, American military spending exceeds that of the next *twenty* countries combined. Its navy, air force and space power are unrivaled. Its technology is irresistible. It is dominant by every measure: military, economic, technological, diplomatic, cultural, even linguistic, with a myriad of countries trying to fend off the inexorable march of Internet-fueled MTV English.

American dominance has not gone unnoticed. During the 1990s, it was mainly China and Russia that denounced unipolarity in their occasional joint communiqués. As the new century dawned it was on everyone's lips. A French foreign minister dubbed the United States not a superpower but a hyperpower. The dominant concern of foreign policy establishments everywhere became understanding and living with the 800-pound American gorilla.

And then September 11 *heightened* the asymmetry. It did so in three ways. First, and most obviously, it led to a demonstration of heretofore latent American military power. Kosovo, the first war ever fought and won exclusively from the air, had given a hint of America's quantum leap in military power (and the enormous gap that had developed between American and European military capabilities). But it took September 11 for the United States to unleash with concentrated fury a fuller display of its power in Afghanistan. Being a relatively pacific, commercial republic, the United States does not go around looking for demonstration wars. This one was thrust upon it. In response, America showed that at a range of 7,000 miles and with but a handful of losses, it could destroy within weeks a hardened, fanatical regime favored by geography and climate in the "graveyard of empires."

Such power might have been demonstrated earlier, but it was not. "I talked with the previous U.S. administration", said Vladimir Putin shortly after September 11,

> and pointed out the bin Laden issue to them. They wrung their hands so helplessly and said, 'the Taliban are not turning him over, what can one do?' I remember I was surprised: If they are not turning him over, one has to think and do something.

Nothing was done. President Clinton and others in his administration have protested that nothing could have been done, that even the 1998 African embassy bombings were not enough to mobilize the American people to strike back seriously against terrorism. The new Bush Administration, too, did not give the prospect of mass-casualty terrorism (and the recommendations of the Hart-Rudman Commission) the priority it deserved. Without September 11, the giant would surely have slept longer. The world would have been aware of America's size and potential, but not its ferocity or its full capacities. (Paul Kennedy's homage to American power, for example, was offered in the wake of the Afghan campaign.)

Second, September 11 demonstrated a new form of American strength. The center of its economy was struck, its aviation shut down, Congress brought to a halt, the government sent underground, the country paralyzed and fearful. Yet within days the markets reopened, the economy began its recovery, the president mobilized the nation, and a united Congress immediately underwrote a huge new worldwide campaign against terror. The Pentagon started planning the U.S. military response even as its demolished western façade still smoldered.

America had long been perceived as invulnerable. That illusion was shattered on September 11, 2001. But with a demonstration of its recuperative powers—an economy and political system so deeply rooted and fundamentally sound that it could spring back to life within days—that sense of invulnerability assumed a new character. It was transmuted from impermeability to resilience, the product of unrivaled human, technological and political reserves.

The third effect of September 11 was to accelerate the realignment of the current great powers, such as they are, behind the United States. In

1990, America's principal ally was NATO. A decade later, its alliance base had grown to include former members of the Warsaw Pact. Some of the major powers, however, remained uncommitted. Russia and China flirted with the idea of an "anti-hegemonic alliance." Russian leaders made ostentatious visits to pieces of the old Soviet empire such as Cuba and North Korea. India and Pakistan, frozen out by the United States because of their nuclear testing, remained focused mainly on one another. But after September 11, the bystanders came calling. Pakistan made an immediate strategic decision to join the American camp. India enlisted with equal alacrity, offering the United States basing, overflight rights and a level of cooperation unheard of during its half century of Nehruist genuflection to anti-American non-alignment. Russia's Putin, seeing both a coincidence of interests in the fight against Islamic radicalism and an opportunity to gain acceptance in the Western camp, dramatically realigned Russian foreign policy toward the United States. (Russia has already been rewarded with a larger role in NATO and tacit American recognition of Russia's interests in its "near abroad.") China remains more distant but, also having a coincidence of interests with the United States in fighting Islamic radicalism, it has cooperated with the war on terror and muted its competition with America in the Pacific.

The realignment of the fence-sitters simply accentuates the historical anomaly of American unipolarity. Our experience with hegemony historically is that it inevitably creates a counterbalancing coalition of weaker powers, most recently against Napoleonic France and Germany (twice) in the 20th century. Nature abhors a vacuum; history abhors hegemony. Yet during the first decade of American unipolarity no such counterbalancing occurred. On the contrary, the great powers lined up behind the United States, all the more so after September 11.

The American hegemon has no great power enemies, an historical oddity of the first order. Yet it does face a serious threat to its dominance, indeed to its essential security. It comes from a source even more historically odd: an archipelago of rogue states (some connected with transnational terrorists) wielding weapons of mass destruction.

The threat is not trivial. It is the single greatest danger to the United States because, for all of America's dominance, and for all of its recently demonstrated resilience, there is one thing it might not survive: decapitation. The detonation of a dozen nuclear weapons in major American cities, or the spreading of smallpox or anthrax throughout the general population, is an existential threat. It is perhaps the only realistic threat to America as a functioning hegemon, perhaps even to America as a functioning modern society.

Like unipolarity, this is historically unique. WMD are not new, nor are rogue states. Their conjunction is. We have had fifty years of experience with nuclear weapons—but in the context of bipolarity, which gave the system a predictable, if perilous, stability. We have just now entered an era in which the capacity for inflicting mass death, and thus posing a threat both to world peace and to the dominant power, resides in small, peripheral states.

What does this conjunction of unique circumstances—unipolarity and the proliferation of terrible weapons—mean for American foreign policy? That the first and most urgent task is protection from these weapons. The catalyst for this realization was again September 11. Throughout the 1990s, it had been assumed that WMD posed no emergency because traditional concepts of deterrence would hold. September 11 revealed the possibility of future WMD-armed enemies both undeterrable and potentially undetectable. The 9/11 suicide bombers were undeterrable; the author of the subsequent anthrax attacks has proven undetectable. The possible alliance of rogue states with such undeterrables and undetectables—and the possible transfer to them of weapons of mass destruction—presents a new strategic situation that demands a new strategic doctrine.

The Crisis of Unipolarity

Accordingly, not one but a host of new doctrines have come tumbling out since September 11. First came the with-us-or-against-us ultimatum to any state aiding, abetting or harboring terrorists. Then, pre-emptive attack on any enemy state developing weapons of mass destruction. And now, regime change in any such state.

The boldness of these policies—or, as much of the world contends, their arrogance—is breathtaking. The American anti-terrorism ultimatum, it is said, is high-handed and permits the arbitrary application of American power everywhere. Pre-emption is said to violate traditional doctrines of just war. And regime change, as Henry Kissinger has argued, threatens 350 years of post-Westphalian international practice. Taken together, they amount to an unprecedented assertion of American freedom of action and a definitive statement of a new American unilateralism.

To be sure, these are not the first instances of American unilateralism. Before September 11, the Bush Administration had acted unilaterally, but on more minor matters, such as the Kyoto Protocol and the Biological Weapons Convention, and with less bluntness, as in its protracted negotiations with Russia over the ABM treaty. The "axis of evil" speech of January 29, however, took unilateralism to a new level. Latent resentments about American willfulness are latent no more. American dominance, which had been tolerated if not welcomed, is now producing such irritation and hostility in once friendly quarters, such as Europe, that some suggest we have arrived at the end of the opposition-free grace period that America had enjoyed during the unipolar moment.

In short, post-9/11 U.S. unilateralism has produced the first crisis of unipolarity. It revolves around the central question of the unipolar age: Who will define the hegemon's ends?

The issue is not one of style but of purpose. Secretary of Defense Donald Rumsfeld gave the classic formulation of unilateralism when he said (regarding the Afghan war and the war on terrorism, but the principle is universal), "the mission determines the coalition." We take our friends where we find them, but only in order to help us in accomplishing the mission. The mission comes first, and we decide it.

Contrast this with the classic case study of multilateralism at work: the U.S. decision in February 1991 to conclude the Gulf War. As the Iraqi army was fleeing, the first Bush Administration had to decide its final goal: the liberation of Kuwait or regime change in Iraq. It stopped at Kuwait. Why? Because, as Brent Scowcroft has explained, going further would have fractured the coalition, gone against our promises to allies and violated the UN resolutions under which we were acting. "Had we added occupation of Iraq and removal of Saddam Hussein to those objectives", wrote Scowcroft in the *Washington Post* on October 16, 2001, ". . . our Arab allies, refusing to countenance an invasion of an Arab colleague, would have deserted us." The coalition defined the mission.

Who should define American ends today? This is a question of agency but it leads directly to a fundamental question of policy. If the coalition— whether NATO, the wider Western alliance, *ad hoc* outfits such as the Gulf War alliance, the UN, or the "international community"—defines America's mission, we have one vision of America's role in the world. If, on the other hand, the mission defines the coalition, we have an entirely different vision.

Liberal Internationalism

For many Americans, multilateralism is no pretense. On the contrary: It has become the very core of the liberal internationalist school of American foreign policy. In the October 2002 debate authorizing the use of force in Iraq, the Democratic chairman of the Senate Armed Services Committee, Carl Levin, proposed authorizing the president to act only with prior approval from the UN Security Council. Senator Edward Kennedy put it succinctly while addressing the Johns Hopkins School of Advanced International Studies on September 27: "I'm waiting for the final recommendation of the Security Council before I'm going to say how I'm going to vote."

This logic is deeply puzzling. How exactly does the Security Council confer moral authority on American action? The Security Council is a committee of great powers, heirs to the victors in the Second World War. They manage the world in their own interest. The Security Council is, on the very rare occasions when it actually works, realpolitik by committee. But by what logic is it a repository of international morality? How does the approval of France and Russia, acting clearly and rationally in pursuit of their own interests in Iraq (largely oil and investment), confer legitimacy on an invasion?

That question was beyond me twelve years ago. It remains beyond me now. Yet this kind of logic utterly dominated the intervening Clinton years. The 1990s were marked by an obsession with "international legality" as expressed by this or that Security Council resolution. To take one long forgotten example: After an Iraqi provocation in February 1998, President Clinton gave a speech at the Pentagon laying the foundation for an attack on Iraq (one of many that never came). He cited as justification for the use of force the need to enforce Iraqi promises made under post-Gulf War ceasefire conditions that "the United Nations demanded—not the United States—the United Nations." Note the formulation. Here is the president of the most powerful nation on earth stopping in mid-sentence to stress the primacy of commitments made to the UN over those made to the United States.

This was not surprising from a president whose first inaugural address pledged American action when "the will and conscience of the international community is defied." Early in the Clinton years, Madeleine Albright formulated the vision of the liberal internationalist school then in power as "assertive multilateralism." Its principal diplomatic activity was the pursuit of a dizzying array of universal treaties on chemical weapons, biological weapons, nuclear testing, global environment, land mines and the like. Its trademark was consultation: Clinton was famous for sending Secretary of State Warren Christopher on long trips (for example, through Europe on Balkan policy) or endless shuttles (uncountable pilgrimages to Damascus) to consult; he invariably returned home empty-handed and diminished. And its principal objective was good international citizenship: It was argued on myriad foreign policy issues that we could not do X because it would leave us "isolated." Thus in 1997 the Senate passed a chemical weapons convention that even some of its proponents admitted was unenforceable, largely because of the argument that everyone else had signed it and that failure to ratify would leave us isolated. Isolation, in and of itself, was seen as a diminished and even morally suspect condition.

A lesson in isolation occurred during the 1997 negotiations in Oslo over the land mine treaty. One of the rare holdouts, interestingly enough, was Finland. Finding himself scolded by his neighbors for opposing the land mine ban, the Finnish prime minister noted tartly that this was a "very convenient" pose for the "other Nordic countries" who "want Finland to be their land mine."

In many parts of the world, a thin line of American GIs is the land mine. The main reason we oppose the land mine treaty is that we need them in the DMZ in Korea. We man the lines there. Sweden and France and Canada do not have to worry about a North Korean invasion killing thousands of their soldiers. As the unipolar power and thus guarantor of peace in places where Swedes do not tread, we need weapons that others do not. Being uniquely situated in the world, we cannot afford the empty platitudes of allies not quite candid enough to admit that they live under the umbrella of American power. That often leaves us "isolated."

Multilateralism is the liberal internationalist's means of saving us from this shameful condition. But the point of the multilateralist imperative is not merely psychological. It has a clear and coherent geopolitical objective. It is a means that defines the ends. Its means—internationalism (the moral, legal and strategic primacy of international institutions over national interests) and legalism (the belief that the sinews of stability are laws, treaties and binding international contracts)—are in service to a larger vision: remaking the international system in the image of domestic civil society. The multilateralist imperative seeks to establish an international order based not on sovereignty and power but on interdependence—a new order that, as Secretary of State Cordell Hull said upon returning from the Moscow Conference of 1943, abolishes the "need for spheres of influence, for alliances, for balance of power."

Liberal internationalism seeks through multilateralism to transcend power politics, narrow national interest and, ultimately, the nation-state itself. The nation-state is seen as some kind of archaic residue of an anarchic past, an affront to the vision of a domesticated international arena. This is why liberal thinkers embrace the erosion of sovereignty promised by the new information technologies and the easy movement of capital across borders. They welcome the decline of sovereignty as the road to the new globalism of a norm-driven, legally-bound international system broken to the mold of domestic society.

The greatest sovereign, of course, is the American superpower, which is why liberal internationalists feel such acute discomfort with American dominance. To achieve their vision, America too—America especially—must be domesticated. Their project is thus to restrain America by building an entangling web of interdependence, tying down Gulliver with myriad strings that diminish his overweening power. Who, after all, was the ABM treaty or a land mine treaty going to restrain? North Korea?

This liberal internationalist vision—the multilateral handcuffing of American power—is, as Robert Kagan has pointed out, the dominant view in Europe. That is to be expected, given Europe's weakness and America's power. But it is a mistake to see this as only a European view. The idea of a new international community with self-governing institutions and self-enforcing norms—the vision that requires the domestication of American power—is the view of the Democratic Party in the United States and of a large part of the American foreign policy establishment. They spent the last decade in power fashioning precisely those multilateral ties to restrain the American Gulliver and remake him into a tame international citizen. The multilateralist project is to use—indeed, to use up—current American dominance to create a new international system in which new norms of legalism and interdependence rule in America's place—in short, a system that is no longer unipolar.

Realism and the New Unilateralism

The basic division between the two major foreign policy schools in America centers on the question of what is, and what should be, the fundamental basis of international relations: paper or power. Liberal internationalism envisions a world order that, like domestic society, is governed by laws and not men. Realists see this vision as hopelessly utopian. The history of paper treaties—from the prewar Kellogg-Briand Pact and Munich to the post-Cold War Oslo accords and the 1994 Agreed Framework with North Korea—is a history of naiveté and cynicism, a combination both toxic and volatile that invariably ends badly. Trade agreements with Canada are one thing. Pieces of parchment to which existential enemies affix a signature are quite another. They are worse than worthless because they give a false sense of security and breed complacency. For the realist, the ultimate determinant of the most basic elements of international life—security, stability and peace—is power.

Which is why a realist would hardly forfeit the current unipolarity for the vain promise of goo-goo one-worldism. Nor, however, should a realist want to forfeit unipolarity for the familiarity of traditional multipolarity. Multipolarity is inherently fluid and unpredictable. Europe practiced multipolarity for centuries and found it so unstable and bloody, culminating in 1914 in the catastrophic collapse of delicately balanced alliance systems, that Europe sought its permanent abolition in political and economic union. Having abjured multipolarity for the region, it is odd in the extreme to then prefer multipolarity for the world.

Less can be said about the destiny of unipolarity. It is too new. Yet we do have the history of the last decade, our only modern experience with unipolarity, and it was a decade of unusual stability among all major powers. It would be foolish to project from just a ten-year experience, but that experience does call into question the basis for the claims that unipolarity is intrinsically unstable or impossible to sustain in a mass democracy.

I would argue that unipolarity, managed benignly, is far more likely to keep the peace. Benignity is, of course, in the eye of the beholder. But the American claim to benignity is not mere self-congratulation. We have a track record. Consider one of history's rare controlled experiments. In the 1940s, lines were drawn through three peoples—Germans, Koreans and Chinese—one side closely bound to the United States, the other to its adversary. It turned into a controlled experiment because both states in the divided lands shared a common culture. Fifty years later the results are in. Does anyone doubt the superiority, both moral and material, of West Germany vs. East Germany, South Korea vs. North Korea and Taiwan vs. China?

Benignity is also manifest in the way others welcome our power. It is the reason, for example, that the Pacific Rim countries are loath to see our military presence diminished: They know that the United States is not an imperial power with a desire to rule other countries—which is why they so readily accept it as a balancer. It is the reason, too, why Europe, so seized with complaints about American high-handedness, nonetheless reacts with alarm to the occasional suggestion that America might withdraw its military presence. America came, but it did not come to rule. Unlike other hegemons and would-be hegemons, it does not entertain a grand vision of a new world. No Thousand Year Reich. No New Soviet Man. It has no great desire to remake human nature, to conquer for the extraction of natural resources, or to rule for the simple pleasure of dominion. Indeed, America is the first hegemonic power in history to be obsessed with "exit strategies." It could not wait to get out of Haiti and Somalia; it would get out of Kosovo and Bosnia today if it could. Its principal aim is to maintain the stability and relative tranquility of the current international system by enforcing, maintaining and extending the current peace.

The form of realism that I am arguing for—call it the new unilateralism—is clear in its determination to self-consciously and confidently deploy American power in pursuit of those global ends. Note: global ends. There is a form of unilateralism that is devoted only to narrow American self-interest and it has a name, too: It is called isolationism. Critics of the new unilateralism often confuse it with isolationism because both are prepared to unashamedly exercise American power. But isolationists *oppose* America acting as a unipolar power not because they disagree with the unilateral means, but because they deem the ends far too broad. Isolationists would abandon the larger world and use American power exclusively for the narrowest of American interests: manning Fortress America by defending the American homeland and putting up barriers to trade and immigration.

The new unilateralism defines American interests far beyond narrow self-defense. In particular, it identifies two other major interests, both global: extending the peace by advancing democracy and preserving the peace by acting as balancer of last resort. Britain was the balancer in Europe, joining the weaker coalition against the stronger to create equilibrium. America's unique global power allows it to be the balancer in every region. We balanced Iraq by supporting its weaker neighbors in the Gulf War. We balance China by supporting the ring of smaller states at its periphery (from South Korea to Taiwan, even to Vietnam). Our role in the Balkans was essentially to create a microbalance: to support the weaker Bosnian Muslims against their more dominant neighbors, and subsequently to support the weaker Albanian Kosovars against the Serbs.

Of course, both of these tasks often advance American national interests as well. The promotion of democracy multiplies the number of nations likely to be friendly to the United States, and regional equilibria produce stability that benefits a commercial republic like the United States. America's (intended) exertions on behalf of pre-emptive non-proliferation, too, are clearly in the interest of both the United States and the international system as a whole.

Critics find this paradoxical: acting unilaterally but for global ends. Why paradoxical? One can hardly argue that depriving Saddam (and potentially, terrorists) of WMD is not a global end. Unilateralism may be required to pursue this end. We may be left isolated in so doing, but we would be acting nevertheless in the name of global interests—larger than narrow American self-interest and larger, too, than the narrowly perceived self-interest of smaller, weaker powers (even great powers) that dare not confront the rising danger.

What is the essence of that larger interest? Most broadly defined, it is maintaining a stable, open and functioning unipolar system. Liberal internationalists disdain that goal as too selfish, as it makes paramount the preservation of both American power and independence. Isolationists reject the goal as too selfless, for defining American interests too globally and thus too generously.

A third critique comes from what might be called pragmatic realists, who see the new unilateralism I have outlined as hubristic, and whose objections are practical. They are prepared to engage in a pragmatic multilateralism. They value great power concert. They seek Security Council support not because it confers any moral authority, but because it spreads risk. In their view, a single hegemon risks far more violent resentment than would a power that consistently acts as *primus inter pares*, sharing rule-making functions with others.

I have my doubts. The United States made an extraordinary effort in the Gulf War to get UN support, share decision-making, assemble a coalition and, as we have seen, deny itself the fruits of victory in order to honor coalition goals. Did that diminish the anti-American feeling in the region? Did it garner support for subsequent Iraq policy dictated by the original acquiescence to the coalition?

The attacks of September 11 were planned during the Clinton Administration, an administration that made a fetish of consultation and did its utmost to subordinate American hegemony and smother unipolarity. The resentments were hardly assuaged. Why? Because the extremist rage against the United States is engendered by the very structure of the international system, not by the details of our management of it.

Pragmatic realists also value international support in the interest of sharing burdens, on the theory that sharing decision-making enlists others in our own hegemonic enterprise and makes things less costly. If you are too vigorous in asserting yourself in the short-term, they argue, you are likely to injure yourself in the long-term when you encounter problems that require the full cooperation of other partners, such as counter-terrorism. As Brooks and Wohlforth put it, "Straining relationships now will lead only to a more challenging policy environment later on."

If the concern about the new unilateralism is that American assertiveness be judiciously rationed, and that one needs to think long-term, it is hard to disagree. One does not go it alone or dictate terms on every issue. On some issues such as membership in and support of the WTO, where the long-term benefit both to the American national interest and global interests is demonstrable, one willingly constricts sovereignty. Trade agreements are easy calls, however, free trade being perhaps the only mathematically provable political good. Others require great skepticism. The Kyoto Protocol, for example, would have harmed the American economy while doing nothing for the global environment. (Increased emissions from China, India and Third World countries exempt from its provisions would have more than made up for American cuts.) Kyoto failed on its merits, but was nonetheless pushed because the rest of the world supported it. The same case was made for the chemical and biological weapons treaties—sure, they are useless or worse, but why not give in there in order to build good will for future needs? But appeasing multilateralism does not assuage it; appeasement merely legitimizes it. Repeated acquiescence to provisions that America deems injurious reinforces the notion that legitimacy derives from international consensus, thus undermining

America's future freedom of action—and thus contradicting the pragmatic realists' own goals.

America must be guided by its independent judgment, both about its own interest and about the global interest. Especially on matters of national security, war-making and the deployment of power, America should neither defer nor contract out decision-making, particularly when the concessions involve permanent structural constrictions such as those imposed by an International Criminal Court. Prudence, yes. No need to act the superpower in East Timor or Bosnia. But there is a need to do so in Afghanistan and in Iraq. No need to act the superpower on steel tariffs. But there is a need to do so on missile defense.

The prudent exercise of power allows, indeed calls for, occasional concessions on non-vital issues if only to maintain psychological good will. Arrogance and gratuitous high-handedness are counterproductive. But we should not delude ourselves as to what psychological good will buys. Countries will cooperate with us, first, out of their own self-interest and, second, out of the need and desire to cultivate good relations with the world's superpower. Warm and fuzzy feelings are a distant third. Take counterterrorism. After the attack on the U.S.S. *Cole*, Yemen did everything it could to stymie the American investigation. It lifted not a finger to suppress terrorism. This was under an American administration that was obsessively accommodating and multilateralist. Today, under the most unilateralist of administrations, Yemen has decided to assist in the war on terrorism. This was not a result of a sudden attack of good will toward America. It was a result of the war in Afghanistan, which concentrated the mind of heretofore recalcitrant states like Yemen on the costs of non-cooperation with the United States. Coalitions are not made by superpowers going begging hat in hand. They are made by asserting a position and inviting others to join. What "pragmatic" realists often fail to realize is that unilateralism is the high road to multilateralism. When George Bush senior said of the Iraqi invasion of Kuwait, "this will not stand", and made it clear that he was prepared to act alone if necessary, that declaration— and the credibility of American determination to act unilaterally—in and of itself created a coalition. Hafez al-Asad did not join out of feelings of good will. He joined because no one wants to be left at the dock when the hegemon is sailing.

Unilateralism does not mean *seeking* to act alone. One acts in concert with others if possible. Unilateralism simply means that one does not allow oneself to be hostage to others. No unilateralist would, say, reject Security Council support for an attack on Iraq. The nontrivial question that separates unilateralism from multilateralism—and that tests the "pragmatic realists"—is this: What do you do if, at the end of the day, the Security Council refuses to back you? Do you allow yourself to be dictated to on issues of vital national—and international—security?

When I first proposed the unipolar model in 1990, I suggested that we should accept both its burdens and opportunities and that, if America did not wreck its economy, unipolarity could last thirty or forty years.

That seemed bold at the time. Today, it seems rather modest. The unipolar moment has become the unipolar era. It remains true, however, that its durability will be decided at home. It will depend largely on whether it is welcomed by Americans or seen as a burden to be shed—either because we are too good for the world (the isolationist critique) or because we are not worthy of it (the liberal internationalist critique).

The new unilateralism argues explicitly and unashamedly for maintaining unipolarity, for sustaining America's unrivaled dominance for the foreseeable future. It could be a long future, assuming we successfully manage the single greatest threat, namely, weapons of mass destruction in the hands of rogue states. This in itself will require the aggressive and confident application of unipolar power rather than falling back, as we did in the 1990s, on paralyzing multilateralism. The future of the unipolar era hinges on whether America is governed by those who wish to retain, augment and use unipolarity to advance not just American but global ends, or whether America is governed by those who wish to give it up—either by allowing unipolarity to decay as they retreat to Fortress America, or by passing on the burden by gradually transferring power to multilateral institutions as heirs to American hegemony. The challenge to unipolarity is not from the outside but from the inside. The choice is ours. To impiously paraphrase Benjamin Franklin: History has given you an empire, if you will keep it.

NO

Niall Ferguson

An Empire in Denial: The Limits of U.S. Imperialism

It used to be only foreigners and those on the fringes of US politics who referred to the "American Empire." Invariably, they did so in order to criticize the United States. Since the attack on the World Trade Center in September 2001, however, there has been a growing volume of more serious writing on the subject of an American empire. The phrase is now heard both in polite academic company and in mainstream public debate. The striking thing is that not all those who now openly use the term "empire" do so pejoratively. A number of commentators—notably Max Boot, Thomas Donnelly, Robert Kaplan, and Charles Krauthammer—seem to relish the idea of a US imperium. "Today there is only one empire." James Kurth of Swarthmore College declared in a recent article in the *National Interest,* "the global empire of the United States."

Officially, however, the United States remains an empire in denial. In the words of US President George Bush during his presidential election campaign in 2000: "America has never been an empire. We may be the only great power in history that had the chance, and refused—preferring greatness to power, and justice to glory." Freud defined denial as a primitive psychological defense mechanism against trauma. Perhaps it was therefore inevitable that, in the aftermath of the September 11 attacks, US citizens would deny their country's imperial character more vehemently than ever. It may nevertheless be therapeutic to determine the precise nature of this American Empire—since empire it is, in all but name.

Imperial denial may simply be a matter of semantics. Many post-war writers about US power have used words like "hegemon" to convey the idea that US overseas influence is great but not imperial. There are other useful alternatives to the term "empire," including "unipolarity," global "leadership," and "the only superpower." Define the term "empire" narrowly enough, and the United States can easily be excluded from the category. Suppose empire is taken to mean "the forcible military occupation and governance of territory whose citizens remain permanently excluded from political representation." By that definition, the American Empire is laughably small. The United States accounts for around 6.5 percent of the world's surface, but its 14 formal dependencies add up to a mere

0.007 percent. In demographic terms, the United States and its dependencies account for barely five percent of the world's population, whereas the British ruled between one-fifth and one-quarter of the world's population at the zenith of their empire.

Yet this narrow definition of empire is as simplistic as it is convenient. To begin with, the expansion of the original 13 US states westwards and southwards in the course of the 19th century was itself a quintessentially imperialist undertaking. In both the US and British empires, indigenous populations were vanquished, expropriated and marginalized. The people living in the newer states were all ultimately enfranchised, but so were the settler populations of large tracts of the British Empire: "responsible government" was, after all, granted to Canada, Australia, New Zealand, and South Africa. The only substantial difference between the two processes of white settlement was that the United States absorbed most of its new territories—even Alaska and Hawaii—into its federal system, whereas the British never did more than toy with the idea of imperial federation.

In any case, the US empire is—and can afford to be—much less concerned with the acquisition of large areas of overseas territory than Britain's was. The United States has few formal colonies, but it possesses a great many small areas of territory within notionally sovereign states that serve as bases for its armed services. Before the deployment of troops for the invasion of Iraq, the US military had around 752 military installations located in more than 130 countries. New wars have meant new bases, like Camp Bondsteel in Kosovo, acquired during the 1999 war against Yugoslavia, and the Bishkek airbase in Kyrgyzstan, an "asset" picked up during the war against the Taliban regime in Afghanistan.

When the full extent of US military presence overseas is made plain, then the claim that the United States is not an empire rings hollow indeed. Nor should it be forgotten what formidable military technology can be unleashed from these bases. Commentators like to point out that the Pentagon's budget equals the combined military expenditures of the next 12 to 15 states. Such fiscal measures nevertheless understate the quantitative and qualitative lead currently enjoyed by US armed forces. In military terms, the British Empire did not dominate the full spectrum of military capabilities, as the United States does today; it was never so far ahead of its imperial rivals. If military power is the *sine qua non* of an empire, then it is hard to deny the imperial character of the United States today. The US sphere of military influence is now quite literally global.

It is, of course, conventional wisdom that large-scale overseas military commitments can have deleterious economic effects. Yet the United States seems a very long way from the kind of "overstretch" Paul Kennedy warned against in the late 1980s. According to one estimate, "America's 31 percent share of world product (at market prices) is equal to the next four countries (Japan, Germany, Britain, and France) combined," which exceeds the highest share of global output ever achieved by Great Britain by a factor of three. In terms of raw resources, then, the United States is already a vastly more powerful empire than Britain ever was. The rapid growth of the US economy since the late 1980s partly explains how the United States has managed to achieve a unique revolution in military affairs while at the same time substantially reducing the share of defense expenditures as a proportion of gross domestic product (GDP). The Defense Department Green Paper published in March 2003 forecast total expenditure on national defense to remain at 3.5 percent of GDP for at least three years, compared with an average figure during the Cold War of seven percent. Bearing in mind Paul Kennedy's "formula" that "if a particular nation is allocating *over the long term* more than 10 percent of gross national product (GNP) to armaments, that is likely to limit its growth rate," there seems little danger of imminent "overstretch."

In short, in terms of military capability and economic resources the United States not only resembles the last great Anglophone empire but exceeds it. Nor are its goals so very different. In September 2002, the Office of the President produced a document on "National Security Strategy" that explicitly states that it is a goal of US foreign policy "to extend the benefits of freedom . . . to every corner of the world." There are those who argue that such altruism is quite different from the more self-serving aims of British imperialism, but this betrays an ignorance of the comparably liberal ethos of the Victorian Empire. In any case, the National Security Strategy also asserts that the United States reserves the right, if the President should deem it necessary, to take pre-emptive military action against any state perceived as a threat to US security. If the US population still refuses to acknowledge that they have become an empire, the doctrine of pre-emption suggests—by way of a compromise—a possible neologism. Perhaps the United States today should be characterized as a pre-empire.

City on a Hill

One argument sometimes advanced to distinguish US "hegemony" from British Empire is qualitative. US power, it is argued, consists not just of military and economic power but also of "soft" power. According to Joseph Nye, "A country may obtain the outcomes it wants in world politics because other countries want to follow it, admiring its values, emulating its example, aspiring to its level of prosperity and openness." Soft power, in other words, is getting what you want without sticks or carrots. In the case of the United States, "it comes from being a shining 'city upon a hill' "—an enticing New Jerusalem of economic and political liberty. Nye is not so naïve as to assume that the US way is inherently attractive to everyone, everywhere. But he does believe that making it attractive matters more than ever before because of the global spread of information technology. To put it simply, soft power can reach the parts of the world that hard power cannot.

But does this really make US power so very different from imperial power? On the contrary. If anything, it illustrates how very like the last Anglophone empire the United States has become. The British Empire, too, sought to make its values attractive to others, though initially the job had to be done by "men on the spot." British missionaries, businessmen, administrators, and schoolmasters fanned out across the globe to "entice and attract" people toward British values.

These foot-slogging efforts were eventually reinforced by technology. It was the advent of wireless radio—and specifically the creation of the British Broadcasting Corporation (BBC)—which really ushered in the age of soft power in Nye's sense of the term. Within six years, the BBC had launched its first foreign language service—in Arabic, significantly—and, by the end of 1938, it was broadcasting around the world in all the major languages of continental Europe.

In some ways, the soft power that Britain could exert in the 1930s was greater than the soft power of the United States today. In a world of newspapers, radio receivers, and cinemas—where the number of content-supplying corporations (often national monopolies) was relatively small—the overseas broadcasts of the BBC could hope to reach a relatively large number of foreign ears. Yet whatever soft power Britain thereby wielded did nothing to halt the precipitous decline of British power after the 1930s.

This raises the question of how much US soft power really matters today. If the term is to denote anything more than cultural background music to more traditional forms of dominance, it surely needs to be demonstrated that the United States can secure what it wants from other countries without coercing or suborning them, but purely because its cultural exports are seductive. One reason for skepticism about the extent of US soft power today is the very nature of the channels of communication for US culture, the various electronic media through which US culture is currently transmitted tend to run from the United States to Western Europe, Japan, and in the case of television, Latin America. It would be too much to conclude that US soft power is abundant where it is least needed, for it may well be that a high level of exposure to US cinema and television is one of the reasons why Western Europe, Japan, and Latin America are on the whole less hostile to the United States than countries in the Middle East and Asia. But the fact remains that the *range* of US soft power in Nye's sense is more limited than is generally assumed.

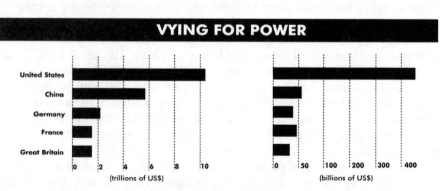

VYING FOR POWER

(trillions of US$)   (billions of US$)

The graph on the left shows five selected countries with large gross domestic products (GDPs), derived from purchasing power parity calculations. The graph on the right depicts the military spending budgets of those countries. The graphs suggest that the United States is clearly the dominant economic and military power today, much like the British Empire at its height.

One important qualification applies. Whatever the critics of the United States may say, the United States is indeed a very attractive place—and its attraction extends for beyond of range of AOL-Time Warner and CNN. It is so attractive that millions of foreigners want either to visit the country or to move here permanently. In 2000, for example, more than 50 million people visited the United States, making it the world's second most popular holiday destination (after France). That figure is more than double the approximately 20 million US citizens who traveled abroad on vacation. The United States also remains a popular destination for immigrants, with an annual net influx of around three people per thousand of population. Between 1974 and 1998, around 16.7 million foreigners came to live in the United States. About 26 million current US residents were born abroad, a number that vastly exceeds the four million US-born residents abroad. This is, of course, in marked contrast to the experience of Great Britain, which was a remarkable exporter of people throughout its imperial heyday. Between 1850 and 1950, nearly 18 million people left the British Isles.

But does this make the United States more or less powerful? Proponents of the "soft power" thesis argue that the very large numbers of foreign students who come to US universities act–unwittingly–as the agents of US empire when they return to their native lands, imbued with the distinctive value systems of the Harvard Business School or the Stanford Political Science Department. "The ability of the American empire to govern its domains," argues James Kurth, "will depend upon its success in producing this distinct kind of immigrant/emigrant to serve as its distinct kind of imperial civil official." There are two reasons why this seems over-optimistic. First, a substantial proportion of the foreign students simply never return home to spread the good news about US principles and practice. The second is that a very substantial number of the leading nationalists who opposed and ultimately supplanted British rule in both Asia and Africa were themselves the beneficiaries of British university education.

The United States, then, is an empire—but a peculiar kind of empire. It is militarily and economically peerless. It has great, though not unbounded, cultural reach. Yet it has distinctive limitations. It is an empire based not on colonization, but on net immigration. There are also important limits to the way in which its wealth can be deployed. First, there is good reason to fear that, in the foreseeable future, the costs of the US welfare system—specifically, the systems of Medicare and Social Security—will begin to outstrip tax revenues. According to one recent estimate, the difference between the present value of all the federal government's future liabilities and the present value of all its future tax receipts amounts to a staggering US$44 trillion. Only steep cuts in public expenditure or increases in taxation will enable the government to avoid a grave fiscal crisis.

Secondly, the prosperity of the United States has become heavily reliant on very large inflows of foreign capital. With the current account deficit rising above five percent of GDP last year, much (not least the exchange rate of the dollar) depends on the continued willingness of foreign investors to put their savings into dollar-denominated assets. Once again, the contrast between Britain in her imperial prime is pronounced. In the British case, net foreign investment was consistently positive between the mid 1870s and World War I, rising to a peak of nine percent of GDP in 1913. Moreover, the destinations of British overseas investment were very diverse: substantial shares flowed to those relatively poor countries in which Britain had a disproportionate strategic interest. By comparison, US citizens who invest abroad favor Europe (especially Britain) and the Pacific (especially Japan, Australia, and Hong Kong). Barely one percent of US Foreign Direct Investment goes to the Middle East, and even less (0.8 percent) goes to China. This is a far cry from the "dollar diplomacy" of the 1920s, when US loans to strategically important countries in Europe and Latin America played an important role in underpinning US foreign policy. Today, foreign investors are theoretically the ones who have leverage over the United States, since fully 40 percent of the federal debt in public hands is held by foreigners.

This is not to say that those pessimists are right who predict imminent relative decline for the United States. What it does mean is that the United States is not quite the *hyperpuissance* of French nightmares. And what it also means is that, in dealing with transnational threats such as terrorism, international crime, nuclear proliferation, and infectious diseases like AIDS or SARS—to say nothing of global warming—the United States can achieve relatively little by acting unilaterally. As surely as the continuation of international free trade depends on multilateral institutions, so too does the successful prosecution of the war against terrorism.

Does this mean that the United States is not, after all, an empire? On the contrary. As that great imperial statesman Lord Salisbury well understood, there was nothing more dangerous to a great empire than what he called, with heavy irony, "splendid isolation." Then as now, the great Anglophone empire needs perforce to work in concert with the lesser—but not negligible—great powers in order to achieve its objectives.

Consider just one example. It is becoming abundantly clear following the invasions of Afghanistan and Iraq that the United States is not capable of effective peacekeeping—that is to say, policing—without some foreign assistance. Peacekeeping is not what US soldiers are trained to do, nor do they have much appetite for it. It also seems reasonable to assume that the US electorate will not tolerate US soldiers' prolonged exposure to the unglamorous hazards of "low-intensity conflict," with suicide bombers at checkpoints, snipers down alleys, and missile grenade attacks on convoys. The obvious solution is to continue the now well established practice of delegating peacekeeping to the United Nations and, under its auspices, to the US European allies. According to figures published in *Foreign Policy* magazine, the EU states contributed more than twice as much on UN peacekeeping operations as the United States in the years 2000 and 2001.

It is also noteworthy the EU states also contributed three times as much in effective aid to poor countries. Those, like Robert Kagan, who dismiss the Europeans as Kant-reading Venusians—as opposed to America's macho Martians—overlook the crucial significance of Pluto in the process of "nation building." Without hefty investment in creating the rule of law and priming the pump of economic recovery, countries like Afghanistan and Iraq will stagnate, if not disintegrate altogether. Unless the United States radically alters its attitudes toward peacekeeping and aid, it will have little option but to cooperate with the more generous Europeans. Unilaterialism, like isolation, is not so splendid after all. Indeed, it is seldom a realistic option for an empire.

Dangers of Denial

The Victorian historian J.R. Seeley famously joked that the British had "conquered and peopled half the world in a fit of absence of mind." In acquiring their empire, the United States has followed this example. Few Europeans today doubt the existence of a US empire. But as the German theologian Reinhold Niebuhr noted in 1960, Americans persist in "frantically avoiding recognition of the imperialism [they] in fact exercise."

Does it matter? The answer is yes. The problem with an empire that is in denial about its own imperial nature is that it tends to make two mistakes when it chooses to intervene in the affairs of lesser states. The first is to attempt economic and political transformation in an unrealistically short timeframe. The second is to allocate insufficient resources to the project. As I write, both of these mistakes are being made in Iraq and Afghanistan. By insisting that US forces will remain in Iraq until a democratic government can be established "and not a day longer," US spokesmen unintentionally create a powerful disincentive for local people to cooperate with them. Who in Iraq today can feel confident that, if he lends support to US initiatives, he will not simply lay himself open to the charge of collaboration when the US troops depart?

Moreover, who would wish to cooperate with an occupying force that spent all its resources on itself and devoted next to nothing to aid or reconstruction? A successful empire is seldom solely based on coercion; there must be some economic dividends for the ruled as well as the rulers, if only to buy the loyalty of indigenous elites. Yet in Iraq and Afghanistan the amounts of money the United States has made available to potential local partners have been paltry.

To put it bluntly, the United States is acting like a colossus with an attention deficit disorder engaged in cut-price colonization. And that is perhaps the reason why this vastly powerful economy, with its extraordinary military capability, has had such a very disappointing record when it has sought to bring about changes of regime abroad. According to one recent study, just four out of 16 US military interventions in foreign countries have been successful in establishing US-style institutions over the past century. The worst failures—in Haiti, Vietnam, Cuba, and Cambodia— might well be attributed to this fatal combination of a truncated time horizon and inadequate resources for non-military purposes.

There is no question, as we have seen, that the United States has the raw economic resources to take on the old British role as underwriter of a globalized, liberalized economic system. Nor is there any doubt that it has the military capability to do the job. On both scores, the United States is already a far more powerful empire than Britain's ever was. Perhaps—though I am less persuaded about this—its "soft power" is also greater. Yet the unspoken American Empire suffers from serious structural weaknesses. It imports rather than exports high quality human capital. It also imports more capital than it exports—and exports virtually none to pivotal regions like the Middle East. It underestimates the need to act in partnership with allied great powers. And its efforts at nation-building are both short-term and under-funded.

Some US neo-imperialists like to quote Kipling's "White Man's Burden," written in 1899 to encourage US President William McKinley's empire-building efforts in the Philippines. But Kipling wrote another poem, two years earlier, which they would also do well to remember. Entitled "Recessional," it was a somber intimation of mortality, perfectly crafted to temper late Victorian delusions of grandeur:

> Far-called our navies melt away—
> On dune and headland sinks the fire—
> Lo, all our pomp of yesterday
> Is one with Nineveh and Tyre!
> Judge of the Nations, spare us yet,
> Lest we forget—lest we forget!

POSTSCRIPT

Must America Exercise World Leadership?

The conflict between the views of Charles Krauthammer and Niall Ferguson mirrors the conflict between the architects of America's unilateral post–9/11 foreign policy and those who favor the multilateralism of the post–Second World War era. Both approaches lead critics to raise probing questions. Does Ferguson underestimate the commitment of the United States to eradicate terrorism and spread democracy? Does he fail to take into account the influence of American culture—movies, television, fiction, and music—in shaping the attitudes and preferences of young people throughout the world? Does the rejection of preemptive war mean that the United States must wait for its enemies to strike and inflict human and psychological damage comparable to the 9/11 attacks? The choice seems to come down to the liberal internationalism that characterized American foreign policy during the Cold War waged by America and its allies against Soviet communism and its satellites or the unilateral approach undertaken by the administration of President George W. Bush after the terrorist attack on American soil on September 11, 2001.

The evolution of American international relations is related in Walter Russell Mead, *Special Providence: American Foreign Policy and How It Changed the World* (Alfred A. Knopf, 2001). Preemption is supported by John Lewis Gaddis, "A Grand Strategy of Transformation" (*Foreign Policy*, November–December 2002) who rhetorically asks: "Who would not have preempted Hitler or Milosevic [the Serbian leader who precipitated war in the former Yugoslavia] or Mohammed Atta [leader of the 9/11 terrorists], if given the chance?" Note Robert Kagan and William Kristol's essay in Issue 20, in which they defend America's "role as guarantor of peace and security in the Middle East." America as the world leader is rejected by Clyde Prestowitz, *Rogue Nation: American Unilateralism and the Failure of Good Intentions* (Basic Books, 2003), and George Soros, "The Bubble of American Supremacy" (*The Atlantic Monthly*, December 2003). Ivo H. Daalder and James M. Lindsay, *America Unbound: The Bush Revolution in Foreign Policy* (Brookings Institution, 2003) conclude that "the fundamental premise of the Bush revolution—that America's security rested on an America unbound—was mistaken." Robert Jervis, "Understanding the Bush Doctrine" (*Political Science Quarterly*, 118:3, 2003), speculates that other nations may "see themselves better off with the United States as an assertive hegemon, allowing them to gain the benefits of world order while being spared the costs."

The question remains whether, when and to what extent, the United States can expect other major nations to bear the human and economic costs of world leadership. Will recalcitrant nations join because, as Krauthammer puts it, "no one wants to be left at the dock when the hegemon is sailing"? Do Americans have the will and are they prepared to pay the cost in money and lives to stay the course? As usual, the future is unpredictable, however confidently the advocates—on both sides—make their projections.

Contributors to This Volume

EDITORS

GEORGE McKENNA is a professor of political science and chair of the Department of Political Science at City College, City University of New York, where he has been teaching since 1963. He received a B.A. from the University of Chicago in 1959, an M.A. from the University of Massachusetts in 1962, and a Ph.D. from Fordham University in 1967. He has written numerous articles in the fields of American government and political theory, and his publications include *American Populism* (Putnam, 1974) and *American Politics: Ideals and Realities* (McGraw-Hill, 1976). He is the author of the textbook *The Drama of Democracy: American Government and Politics,* 3rd ed. (Dushkin/McGraw-Hill, 1998).

STANLEY FEINGOLD, recently retired, held the Carl and Lily Pforzheimer Foundation Distinguished Chair for Business and Public Policy at Westchester Community College of the State University of New York. He received his bachelor's degree from the City College of New York, where he taught courses in American politics and political theory for 30 years, after completing his graduate education at Columbia University. He spent four years as Visiting Professor of Politics at the University of Leeds in Great Britain, and he has also taught American politics at Columbia University in New York and the University of California, Los Angeles. He is a frequent contributor to the *National Law Journal* and *Congress Monthly,* among other publications.

STAFF

Larry Loeppke	Managing Editor
Jill Peter	Senior Developmental Editor
Nichole Altman	Developmental Editor
Beth Kundert	Production Manager
Jane Mohr	Project Manager
Tara McDermott	Design Coordinator
Bonnie Coakley	Editorial Assistant

AUTHORS

AMITY SHLAES is an editorialist on tax policy at the *Wall Street Journal*. Her writing has also been published in *Commentary* and *The New Yorker*, and she is the author of *Germany: The Empire Within* (Farrar, Straus & Giroux, 1991).

ANDREW C. McCARTHY is a former chief United States attorney who led the 1995 terrorism prosecution that resulted in the conviction of a dozen Islamic militants for conducting urban terrorism against the United States, including the 1993 World Trade Center bombing. His essays have been published in the *Weekly Standard, Commentary*, the *Middle East Quarterly*, and other publications.

ANTHONY KING is a professor of political science at the University of Essex and the author of *Running Scared: Why America's Politicians Campaign Too Much and Govern Too Little* (Martin Kessler Books, 1997).

BERNARD GOLDBERG is an Emmy Award-winning broadcast journalist who has worked for three decades as a reporter and producer at CBS.

CARL T. BOGUS is an associate professor at Roger Williams University School of Law in Bristol, Rhode Island. He is also a contributor to *The American Prospect*.

CASS R. SUNSTEIN is the Distinguished Service Professor of Jurisprudence in the Law School and the Department of Political Science at the University of Chicago. Among his recent publications is *Designing Democracy: What Constitutions Do* (Oxford, 2001).

CHARLES KRAUTHAMMER, winner of the 1987 Pulitzer Prize for distinguished commentary and the 1984 National Magazine Award for essays, has written a nationally syndicated editorial page column in *The Washington Post* since 1985. His column now appears in more than 100 newspapers. He has written for *Time*, the *Weekly Standard*, and other magazines, and has been a frequent political commentator on television.

CHARLES R. LAWRENCE III is a professor in the School of Law at Georgetown University in Washington, D.C. He is coauthor, with Mari J. Matsuda, of *We Won't Go Back: Making the Case for Affirmative Action* (Houghton Mifflin, 1997) and *Affirmative Action* (Houghton Mifflin, 1997).

CHRISTOPHER C. DeMUTH is president of the American Enterprise Institute for Public Policy Research.

DANIEL CASSE is a senior director of the White House Writers Group, a Washington-based public policy communications firm. Mr. Casse served in the White House as a special assistant to President George Bush in the Office of Cabinet Affairs. A former managing editor of *The Public Interest* magazine in New York, his writing on politics and policy has appeared frequently in *The Wall Street Journal, Commentary, The Weekly Standard, National Review*, and other national publications. He has authored longer studies on American philanthropy, the cost of higher education, and the role of economics in presidential elections.

DANIEL PIPES is director of the Middle East Forum, a member of the presidentially-appointed U.S. Institute for Peace, and a columnist for the *New York Sun* and the *Jerusalem Post*. His most recent book is *Miniatures: View of Islamic and Middle Eastern Politics* (Transaction Publishers, 2003).

DANIEL T. GRISWOLD, associate director of the Cato Institute's Center for Trade Policy Studies, focuses on the movement of goods, services, capital, and people across international borders. He earned a master's degree in the politics of the world economy from the London School of Economics.

DAVID A. HARRIS is Balk Professor of Law and Values at University of Toledo College of Law and Soros Senior Justice Fellow. He is the author of *Profiles in Injustice: Why Racial Profiling Cannot Work* (New Press, 2002).

DAVID MORRIS is cofounder and vice president of the Institute for Local Self-Reliance. He is also the editor of the institute's publications, including *The New Rules* and *The Carbohydrate Economy*.

DOUGLAS A. IRWIN is a professor of economics at Dartmouth College and a research associate of the National Bureau of Economic Research. He is the author of *Against the Tide: An Intellectual History of Free Trade* (Princeton University Press, 1996) and *Managed Trade: The Case Against Import Targets* (AEI Press, 1994).

ERIC ALTERMAN is the media columnist for The Nation, the "Altercation" weblogger for MSNBC.com, and a fellow at the Center for American Progress, where he writes and edits the "Think Again" column. His most recent book is *The Book on Bush: How George W. (Mis)leads America* (with Mark Green, 2004).

ERIC M. FREEDMAN is a professor of law in the School of Law at Hofstra University. He chairs the Committee on Civil Rights of the Association of the Bar of the City of New York and is a member of the association's Special Committee on Representation in Capital Cases. Freedman earned his M.A. at Victoria University of Wellington in New Zealand and his J.D. at Yale University. He is coauthor, with Monroe H. Freedman, of *Group Defamation and Freedom of Speech: The Relationship Between Language and Violence* (Greenwood, 1995).

FAREED ZAKARIA is editor of *Newsweek International* and a columnist in the national edition of *Newsweek, Newsweek International* and, often, the *Washington Post*. He also serves as commentator for ABC's "This Week" and an analyst on several ABC News programs.

HEATHER MacDONALD is contributing editor of *City Journal* and a Fellow at the Manhattan Institute. She is the author of *The Burden of Bad Ideas: How Modern Intellectuals Misshape Our Society* and *Are Cops Racist?: How the War Against the Police Harms Black Americans*. She contributes frequently to the New York *Daily News*, the *New York Post*, and the *Weekly Standard*.

JEFF MADRICK, editor of *Challenge,* a bimonthly magazine devoted to economic issues, also writes a monthly column on economics for *The New York Times*. He is the author of several books, including *Taking America*, a history of hostile corporate takeovers, and *The End of Affluence*.

He is a frequent contributor to *The American Prospect* and other magazines and has frequently appeared on television.

JOHN B. JUDIS, a senior editor for The New Republic, has been a contributor since 1982. His articles have also appeared in *The American Prospect, The New York Times Magazine, The Washington Post, Foreign Affairs, The Washington Monthly, American Enterprise, Mother Jones,* and *Dissent.* His books include *The Paradox of American Democracy: Elites, Special Interests, and the Betrayal of Public Trust.*

JOHN C. EASTMAN is a professor of law at Chapman University School of Law and director of the Claremont Institute Center for Constitutional Jurisprudence. His testimony is based on an article in *NeXus: A Journal of Opinion,* which he co-authored with Timothy Sandefur.

JOHN R. LOTT, JR., earned his Ph.D. in economics from the University of California, Los Angeles, in 1984. He served as a senior research scholar at the Yale University Law School (1999–2001) and taught at the University of Chicago Law School as the John M. Olin Visiting Law and Economics Fellow (1995–1999).

JONATHAN RAUCH is a writer for *The Economist* in London and the author of *Kindly Inquisitors: The New Attacks on Free Thought* (University of Chicago Press, 1993).

KATHERINE SHAW SPAHT is the Jules F. and Frances L. Landry Professor of Law at Louisiana State Law Institute (LSLI). She serves as the reporter for the Revision of the Law of Marriage for the LSLI and helped draft Louisiana's covenant marriage legislation.

LEWIS Z. KOCH has won awards for investigative journalism at NBC television news and as a syndicated columnist. He is the author of an online column, *CyberSense.* He was one of the founding editors of the *Chicago Journalism Review* and has been a contributing editor of *Chicago* magazine, for which he has written on a variety of legal and education issues.

LINDA CHAVEZ is president of the Center for Equal Opportunity, a non-profit public policy research organization in Washington, D.C. She also writes a weekly syndicated column that appears in newspapers across the country, and she is a political analyst for FOX News Channel.

MARCIA GREENBERGER is the founder and co-president of the National Women's Law Center. She has served as counsel or co-counsel in a number of landmark Supreme Court cases involving women's rights in educational institutions.

MARY FRANCES BERRY, author of seven books, is a prominent social scholar and historian and is currently the Geraldine R. Segal Professor of Social Thought at the University of Pennsylvania, where she teaches history and law. Berry has served as the Civil Rights Commission chairwoman under a number of different administrations.

MARY GORDON is a novelist and short-story writer. She is the author of *Penal Discipline: Female Prisoners* (Gordon Press, 1992), *The Rest of Life: Three Novellas* (Viking Penguin, 1993), and *The Other Side* (Wheeler, 1994).

MICHAEL IGNATIEFF is Carr Professor of Human Right Practice and Director of the Carr Center at the John F. Kennedy School of Government, Harvard University. Among his recent books is *The Lesser Evil: Political Ethics in an Age of Terror* (Princeton, 2004).

NAT HENTOFF writes a weekly column for *The Village Voice*, the leading New York alternative weekly. He has written novels, biographies, and books on civil liberties, including *Free Speech for Me and Not for Thee: How the American Left and Right Relentlessly Censor Each Other*. Among other publications, he was written for *The New Yorker*, the *Atlantic*, *New Republic*, *Commonweal*, and on jazz for *The Wall Street Journal*.

NIALL FERGUSON has been a professor of modern European history at Oxford University and financial history at New York University. He is the author of *The Pity of War*, a history of the first World War, and *The Cash Nexus: Money and Power in the Modern World*. His book, *Empire: How Britain Made the Modern World*, was adapted for a television series. His most recent work is *Colossus: The Price of America's Empire*.

PATRICK J. BUCHANAN is founder of the American Cause, an educational foundation dedicated to the principles of freedom, federalism, limited government, traditional values, and a foreign policy that puts America first. He was a senior adviser to three American presidents before he challenged President George Bush for the 1992 Republican presidential nomination. He has been a nationally syndicated newspaper columnist, cohost of CNN's *Crossfire*, and host of Mutual Radio's *Buchanan & Co.*

PAUL KRUGMAN an Op-Ed columnist for *The New York Times* and a professor of economics and international affairs at Princeton University. He is the author or editor of twenty books and more than 200 papers in professional journals and edited volumes. *The Great Unraveling* is a collection of recent newspaper columns as well as new material on economic and political issues.

ROBERT KAGAN is a senior associate of the Carnegie Endowment for International Peace as well as a cofounder of the Project for a New American Century. He is also a contributing editor to *The Weekly Standard*, a member of the Council on Foreign Relations, and the author of *A Twilight Struggle: American Power and Nicaragua, 1977–1990* (Free Press, 1996).

ROBERT P. GEORGE is the McCormick Professor of Jurisprudence and director of the James Madison Program in American Ideals and Institutions at Princeton University. Recently, he was appointed by President George W. Bush to the President's Council on Bioethics. He previously served on the U.S. Commission on Civil Rights and as a judicial fellow at the Supreme Court of the United States.

ROBERT W. LEE is a contributing editor to *The New American* and the author of *The United Nations Conspiracy* (Western Islands, 1981).

RUY TEIXEIRA is a Senior Fellow at *The Century Foundation* and the *Center for American Progress*, and co-author of *The Emerging Democratic Majority* (Scribner, 2002).

SAMUEL L. POPKIN is a professor of political science at the University of California, San Diego. He has been an active participant in and an academic analyst of presidential elections for over 20 years, and he served as a consultant to the Clinton campaign in 1992, for which he worked on polling and strategy.

STEPHEN G. BREYER is an associate justice of the U.S. Supreme Court. He received his A.B. from Stanford University in 1959, his B.A. from Oxford University in 1961, and his LL.B. from Harvard University in 1964. A former U.S. Circuit Court of Appeals judge, he was nominated to the Supreme Court by President Bill Clinton in 1994.

WILLIAM H. REHNQUIST became the 16th chief justice of the U.S. Supreme Court in 1986. He engaged in a general practice of law with primary emphasis on civil litigation for 16 years before being appointed assistant attorney general, Office of Legal Counsel, by President Richard Nixon in 1969. He was nominated by Nixon to the Supreme Court in 1972.

WILLIAM KRISTOL is the editor of *The Weekly Standard* and a regular contributor to Fox News Sunday and the Fox News Channel. He is the co-author of *The War Over Iraq: America's Mission and Saddam's Tyranny.*

Index